Pistoleros and Popular Movements

THE MEXICAN EXPERIENCE

William H. Beezley, series editor

Pistoleros and Popular Movements

The Politics of State
Formation in
Postrevolutionary
Oaxaca

BENJAMIN T. SMITH

University of Nebraska Press
Lincoln & London

∞

A part of chapter 4 originally appeared as "Defending 'Our
Beautiful Freedom': State Formation and Local Autonomy in
Oaxaca, 1930–1940," *Mexican Studies/Estudios Mexicanos*
37, no. 1 (February 2007): 125–53. Copyright © 2007 by the
University of California Institute for Mexico and the United
States, and the Universidad Nacional Autónoma de México.
Reprinted with permission.

A part of chapter 5 originally appeared as "Inventing Tradition at Gunpoint: Culture, Caciquismo and State Formation
in the Region Mixe, Oaxaca (1930–1959)," *Bulletin of Latin
American Research* 27, no. 2 (April 2008): 215–34. Published
by Wiley-Blackwell. Reprinted with permission.

Library of Congress Cataloging-in-Publication Data

Smith, Benjamin T.
Pistoleros and popular movements : the politics of state
formation in postrevolutionary Oaxaca / Benjamin T. Smith.
p. cm. — (The Mexican experience)
Includes bibliographical references and index.
ISBN 978-0-8032-2280-9 (pbk. : alk. paper)
1. Oaxaca (Mexico : State)—Politics and government—
20th century. 2. Oaxaca (Mexico : State)—History—20th
century. 3. Social movements—Mexico—Oaxaca (State)—
History—20th century. 4. Central-local government relations—Mexico—History—20th century. 5. Federal government—Mexico—History—20th century. 6. Government,
Resistance to—Mexico—Oaxaca (State)—History—20th
century. I. Title.
F1321.S64 2009
972'.74082—dc22
2008055277

For my wife, Noemi

Contents

Illustrations

Figures

Maps

Tables

Acknowledgments

This book would not have been possible without the financial support of the University of Cambridge and Michigan State University. I would particularly like to thank Chris Bayly, who organized a Domestic Research Scholarship from the University of Cambridge to study Mexico. At Michigan State University, this book would not have been possible without the administrative skills and moral support of my head of department, Mark Kornbluh, who organized a sabbatical for me in my third year and has been the architect of a truly wonderful history department.

The work is based on the array of sources in Mexico City and Oaxaca's archives. As a result, I would particularly like to thank the staff at the Archivo General de la Nación, Archivo General del Poder Ejecutivo de Oaxaca, Hemeroteca Pública de Oaxaca, and Hemeroteca Nacional as well as the host of smaller archives I perused. A special mention must go to the staff of the Biblioteca Bustamante Vasconcelos, the municipal authorities of Tlahuitoltepec, and the diocesan authorities of Huajuapam de León, who were all generous with their precious documents and their time.

A project like this can only be completed with the intellectual and moral support of a host of academic colleagues and friends. In Cambridge I was inspired and guided by Keith Brewster and then David Brading, whose knowledge of Mexico over the past five centuries seemed to be infinite. I would also like to thank William O'Reilly, David Lehman, Clare Hariri, Julie Coimbra, and Celia Wu for gentle encouragement and an occasional meal or pint. Julie and Clare were the heart of the Centre of Latin American Studies and were extremely kind to me and my wife.

In Michigan I have been fortunate to join an extremely vibrant and exciting department. There are few colleagues in the history department who have not been kind enough to offer a few words of advice to a lost ex-patriate. I would particularly like to thank David Bailey, John Waller, Peter Alegi, Peter Beattie, Walter Hawthorne, Erica Windler, Jerry Garcia, Morgan Sweeney, Laurent Dubois, Emine Evered, Lisa Fine, Peter Knupfer, Lewis Siegelbaum, Pero Dagbovie, and Leslie Moch. In Mexico I was assisted by Carlos Sánchez Silva from the local university, the Universidad Autónoma "Benito Juárez" de Oaxaca. Outside the various institutions to which I have been attached I have been fortunate to be involved with a large number of superb scholars of Mexico at various conferences and roundtables, who have all helped discuss and develop my work. They include Alan Knight, Paul Gillingham, Edward Wright Rios, Thom Rath, Andrew Paxman, Ben Fallaw, Roberto Blancarte, Robert Curley, Adrian Bantjes, Mary Kay Vaughan, Bill Beezley, and Bill French. A special mention must go to Matthew Butler, without whose friendship and intellectual help this book would have been far poorer.

Outside academia I have been fortunate enough to have been aided by the companionship and support of various friends in the United Kingdom and Mexico who have been kind enough to put me up, offer a good meal, or listen to my stories of Oaxaca's history. They include Joe, Ian, Todd, James, Will, Nick, Tom, Ted, Ed, Susana, John, Abby, Miguel "El Diablo," José Alfonso, Guillermo, Montserrat, Alma, and Claudia. I must also thank both my family in Britain, especially Granny, Grandpa, Grandma, Mum, Dad, and Claire, and my family in Mexico, who have welcomed me with open arms. A special mention must go to *mis suegros*, my parents-in-law Don Eloy Davíd Morales Jiménez and Doña Catalina

Sánchez Ruiz; *mis cuñados*, my siblings-in-law Efrain, Michael, Elvia, Edith, and Avi; and other family members, Serafin, Melissa, Ceilmor, and Troy. This project would have been both more difficult and less enjoyable without the love, friendship, and support of my wife, Noemi Morales Sánchez, who not only tolerated the time when her often bad-tempered, confused, and dispirited husband lived in the past rather than the present but also helped me delve into that past by spending two months interviewing *locatarias*, market women, for this book. A last mention must go to my daughter, Emilia Francesca, whose recent birth has made me understand why in what Eric Hobsbawm has termed this "ahistorical era" it is so important to put down our knowledge of the past for future generations.

Abbreviations

AACM	Archivo de Acción Católica Mexicana
AAO	Archivo de la Arquidiócesis de Oaxaca
ACLD	Archivo de la Camera Local de Diputados
ACM	Acción Católica Mexicana
AGN	Archivo General de la Nación
AGPEO	Archivo General del Poder Ejecutivo de Oaxaca
AHSDN	Archivo Histórico de la Secretaría de la Defensa Nacional
AHSEP	Archivo Histórico de la Secretaría de Educación Pública
AJA	Archivo Joaquín Amaro
AMOJ	Archivo Municipal de Oaxaca de Juárez
AMT	Archivo del Municipio de Tlahuitoltepec
APEC	Archivo de Plutarco Elías Calles y Fernando Torreblanca
AR	Fondo Presidentes, Ramo Abelardo Rodríguez
ARPP	Archivo del Registro Público de Propiedades
BTS	Benjamin Thomas Smith, interviewer
CCM	Confederación Campesina Mexicana
CCO	Comité Civico Oaxaqueño
CDEM	Comité de la Defensa de Expendedores de Mercados
CLSO	Confederación de Ligas Socialistas de Oaxaca
CNC	Confederación Nacional Campesina
CNOP	Confederación Nacional de Organizaciones Populares
COC	Confederación Oaxaqueña de Campesinos
CPSO	Confederación de Partidos Socialistas de Oaxaca

CROM	Confederación Regional de Obreros Mexicanos
CTM	Confederación de Trabajadores de México
CUT	Confederatión Unica de Trabajadores
DAAI	Departamento Autónomo de Asuntos Indigenas
FOA	Foreign Office Archive
FPLP	Frente Popular Libertador Pochutleco
FPPM	Federación de los Partidos del Pueblo Mexicano
FROC	Federación Regional de Obreros y Campesinos
FRTEO	Federación Regional de Trabajadores del Estado de Oaxaca
FTOC	Federación Tuxtepecana de Obreros y Campesinos
GCLSO	Genuina Confederación de Ligas Socialistas de Oaxaca
IACA	Instituto Autónomo de Ciencias y Artes
ICA	Instituto de Ciencias y Artes
INI	Instituto Nacional Indigenista
IPS	Investigaciones Políticas y Sociales
LNCUG	Liga Nacional Campesina "Ursulo Galván"
LRUAO	Liga de Resistencia de los Usuarios de Agua de Oaxaca
MAC	Fondo Presidentes, Ramo Manuel Avila Camacho
MAV	Fondo Presidentes, Ramo Miguel Alemán Valdés
NAA	National Anthropological Archive
NMS	Noemi Morales Sánchez, interviewer
PAN	Partido Acción Nacional
PCM	Partido Comunista Mexicano
PNR	Partido Nacional Revolucionario
PRI	Partido Revolucionario Institucional
PRM	Partido de la Revolución Mexicana
SEP	Secretaría de la Educación Pública
UEM	Unión de Expendedores de Mercados

Pistoleros and Popular Movements

Introduction

On 24 January 1947, a week after Edmundo Sánchez Cano was deposed as governor of Oaxaca, a pressure group called the Alianza-Revolucionaria-Oaxaqueña published an open letter to President Miguel Alemán Valdés. The dispatch stated that since the Revolution, the state had failed to assert any measure of control over Oaxaca. The national party was nonexistent. Worker and peasant organizations remained autonomous. Successive state governments had eschewed national ideological programs and instead based their meager power on combinations of nepotism, *caciquismo* (bossism), and a handful of state employees.[1] Five years later, during another successful popular movement to remove the incumbent governor, the Oaxaca academic Enrique Othon Díaz wrote a series of articles in the national press titled "The Enigma of Oaxaca." The articles claimed that Oaxaca was "not a state, like the other states of the republic." Its sheer ethnic, political, and geographic diversity had prevented "traditional ties and common bonds." Instead, various regions operated entirely independent of the state capital. Commercial routes and ethnic links connected the Mixteca to the neighboring state of Puebla, the Costa Chica to Guerrero, the Isthmus to Chiapas, and Tuxtepec to Veracruz (map 1). He concluded that Oaxaca was "a dislocated and anemic political entity, more apparent than real, more in form than in deed."[2]

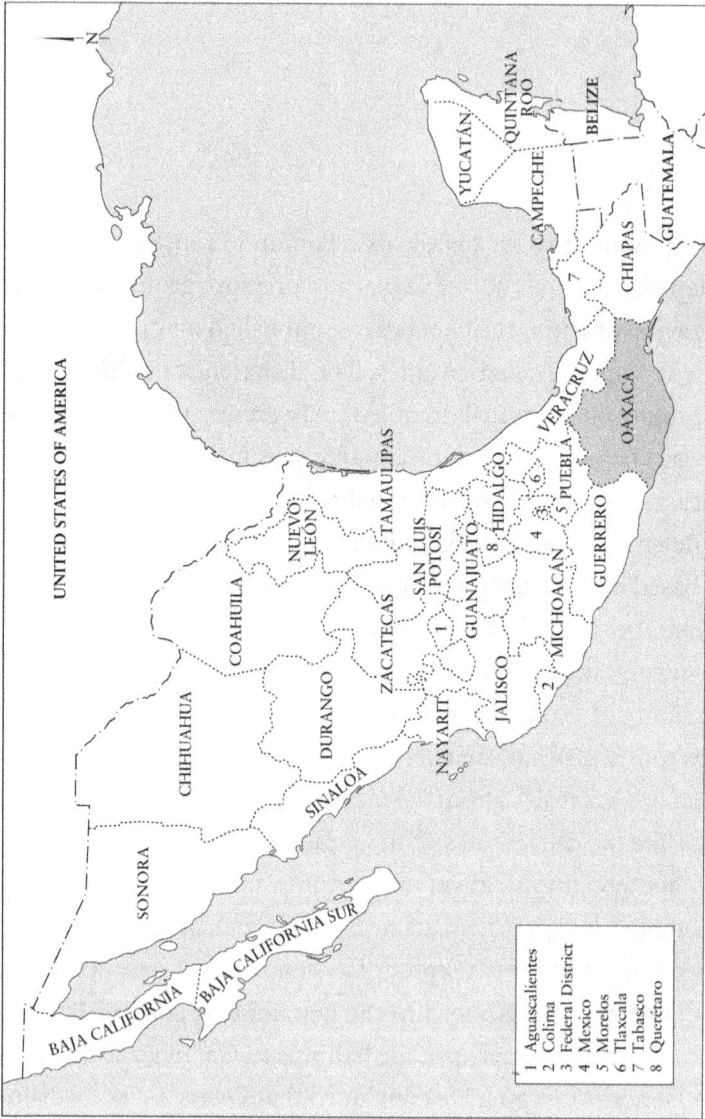

MAP 1. Mexico

These two pessimistic estimations of the state's role in Oaxaca are borne out by the rapid marshaling of some quantitative data relating to what Alan Knight has termed "the weight of the state."[3] At the most prosaic level, the number of federal administrators in Oaxaca was low, even by Mexican standards. The 1940 census indicates that the state had less than 1 bureaucrat per 329 citizens compared to a national average of around 1 for every 176.[4] These bureaucrats faced the most ethnically diverse state in Mexico, with sixteen indigenous groups and more than a hundred mutually unintelligible indigenous dialects.[5] The state's communications network, which might have favored political and economic integration, was notoriously poor. The economist Moises de la Peña claimed it was "the worst in Mexico."[6] Despite the persistence of a few unreliable railway lines and the construction of the Pan-American Highway, travel was still predominantly by mule, horse, or foot. As a result, tax collection was also notoriously difficult. In 1950 in Oaxaca, state taxes per head of population were around seven pesos per year or the lowest per capita rate in Mexico. In 1947 Oaxaca produced only 2.2 percent of the country's tax revenue. Furthermore, tax collection was completely uneven. Nine of Oaxaca's thirty fiscal districts contributed over 90 percent of the state's taxes.[7] Although grinding poverty obviously kept duties low, the general hostility of both rural and urban inhabitants to federal, state, or even municipal taxation compounded the problem for the handful of fiscal agents. In Aldous Huxley's account of his travels in Oaxaca during the early 1930s he described the goring of a local tax collector at the annual bull fight. On seeing the administrator drunk, bloody and prostrate, the crowd let out a "great shout of excitement." According to Huxley "the crowd had got what it wanted. This was good, this was very good indeed."[8] In fact, the state's complete inability to penetrate many regions of Oaxaca is borne out by the deficiency of the census data. De la Peña stated that the 1930 census had covered only 49.5 percent of the surface area of the state, and the 1940 census had covered only 36.7 percent.[9] Census takers repeatedly complained that indigenous communities failed to fill out forms, completed questionnaires incorrectly, or ran the administrators out of town. In 1940 one census taker working in the Costa Chica grumbled that during his stay in the region, he had been robbed twice and forcibly removed from three communities.[10]

However, despite the state's political, ethnic, linguistic, and cultural diversity and the general hostility of many to state interference, there is no doubt that the state did start to penetrate many regions of Oaxaca during the postrevolutionary period. Although Oaxaca often appeared to be a geographical and political anomaly, it was gradually subsumed into the national project of state formation. As in the rest of Mexico, successive politicians undertook the reconstruction of the state's governmental apparatus and attempted to assert a measure of control over the Revolution's bellicose caciques, obstreperous peasants, and radical workers. Despite Oaxaca's relative isolation, between 1920 and 1952 national leaders and local elites enacted a series of political deals, mass mobilizations, military repressions, and institutional changes, which brought about an end to periodic outbreaks of revolutionary conflict and the beginning of the "miracle" of political stability and economic growth. Nevertheless, these actions were not applied in an integrated, homogeneous, or rigorous manner. At every level, political intermediaries negotiated, resisted, appropriated, or ignored the dictates of the central government.

As a result, national policy reverberated through Oaxaca's local political networks in countless different ways and resulted in "the simultaneous forging of a multitude of regional arrangements."[11] It is this process of diffusion, politicking, and conflict that forms the basis of this book. By understanding the multivalent contradictions, fragmentations, and crises of the state formation at the regional level, it is possible to reconstruct a more realistic appreciation of the national project.

Over the past century, three successive generations of historians, sociologists, and political scientists have attempted to construct models of state formation according to their visions of the contemporary Mexican political system. In broad terms, they can be described as pluralist, revisionist, and neo-Gramscian. I argue that although these models work at particular times, in particular regions, or at particular levels, each fails to describe the sheer panoply of regional arrangements enacted by the Mexican state. Starting with the panegyrics and hagiographies of U.S. journalists, there was a wave of favorable reaction to the postrevolutionary regime.[12] Above all, these saw the period 1934 to 1940 as the apotheosis of the Mexican Revolution. Their opinions were predicated on President Cárdenas's support for labor, land reform, and a "socialist" education program and on his general character, "his simplicity, his complete devotion to and identification with the common people of the country, especially the Indians, the peons, and the little farmers."[13] Political theorists of the 1950s and 1960s, working within the paradigm of the state as a neutral arena, developed this idea of a pluralist and representative state, moored on the popular reforms of the Cárdenas period.[14] Mexico could "be regarded as a developing democracy because of its representative government structure and its recent progress in the direction of the responsibility of the people."[15]

After the massacre of students at Tlatelolco in 1968, revisionist scholars began to modify their appreciation of the Mexican political regime.[16] Historians now viewed the mass mobilizations and concomitant reforms of Cárdenas's presidency as base palliatives, designed to weaken, co-opt, and utilize the popular forces of the Revolution. This program came to a head with the creation of the Party of the Mexican Revolution (Partido de la Revolución Mexicana, PRM), "a corporatist instrument that centralised and solidified the control of the state over the workers."[17] Instead of praising the ill-defined socialism of the period, they censured the project for its capitalist intent or at least its capitalist outcome.[18] By 1940 there was a "powerful economic machine at the service of the capitalist development of Mexico, with private business as a base of that development and with the State leading the way and intervening opportunely to correct its deviations."[19] Political scientists challenged the paradigm of the state as a neutral arena and instead argued that the growth of the state was the central explanatory factor behind the country's postrevolutionary history.[20] Building on seminal works on authoritarianism and corporatism, these scholars argued that government control had been imposed through the legalization and institutionalization of peasant and labor movements, which were now sanctioned and regulated by the state.[21] There was "a multi-class, integrative, hegemonic, one party-dominant system." The centerpiece of the system, the Institutional Revolutionary Party (Partido Revolucionario Institucional, PRI), "ha[d] become so efficient, and all-encompassing in its incorporation of interest groups that it embrace[d] not only those unions which support it politically but even those which d[id] not."[22]

Over the past decade, historians and political scientists have started to reevaluate the formation and structure of the Mexican political system. Many scholars have turned to Antonio Gramsci's concept of hegemony. Although previous literature had employed the theory to describe how elites prevented class conflict by inflicting a kind of false consciousness on the masses, recent works of neo-Gramscian scholarship have emphasized the role of hegemony in framing the boundaries of debate between different social groups.[23] According to William Roseberry, hegemony constructs "a meaningful framework for living through, talking about and acting upon social orders characterised by domination."[24] Although resistance is possible, domination channels any opposition to the social or political status quo in directions that make the overthrow of the regime extremely difficult. It is perhaps unsurprising that this new interpretation has witnessed its most coherent implementation in examining the construction of the seemingly interminable reign of the PRI. In particular, by reformulating hegemony as a negotiated process rather than an imposed and static outcome, scholars have started to reimagine state formation in the years immediately following the Revolution. Mary Kay Vaughan has challenged revisionist conceptions of socialist education by employing the theory to describe how popular groups accepted, resisted, co-opted, and reappropriated the state discourse during the 1930s. As long as the state that emerged from this process of intense political interaction remained capable of "meet[ing] social demands and satisfactorily process[ing] grievances," it was able to maintain a degree of stability.[25]

Although thinking about hegemony has undoubtedly helped scholars move away from previous static interpretations of the relationship between domination and resistance in the process of state building, there are certain dangers inherent in this effort. First, in the case of hegemony, however broadly defined, there is the risk of according hegemonic structures a coherency and strength that they lack. In doing so, the historian may overlook spaces, improvisations, and contradictions within the hegemonic project.[26] Second, when dealing with postrevolutionary Mexico, there is an almost prescriptive urge to find the "end point" of hegemony, that instant at which national domination became irreversible. For example, Marjorie Becker asserts that the brief period of dialogue between Cárdenas and Michoacán's P'urhépecha Indians in the early 1930s resulted in ample state hegemony by 1940.[27] As will become clear, caciques, ethnic strategies of resistance, devout Catholicism, and popular urban movements often delayed the moment at which groups started to speak the state's "language of contention." Third, by stressing the various manifestations of popular consent, scholars have often overlooked the utilization of coercion and violence as vital political tools even during the 1940s and 1950s. Although many groups undeniably "negotiated" a working relationship with the state based on a common cultural framework, others refused all forms of compliance and were in turn targeted for military or paramilitary repression.[28] Fourth by "plac[ing] state building at the core of the revolutionary process," there is a tendency to overestimate the nature, function, and intrusiveness of the post-revolutionary state.[29] Alan Knight has argued that despite this process of state building, even the more muscular state of the 1940s and 1950s was relatively powerless, riven by faction, and plagued by the demands of various social movements; it "appeared full of holes like Swiss Cheese."[30] Jeffrey Rubin's work on the town of Juchitán, Oaxaca, has offered a local example of the broad political practice, and he argues that the weak Mexican state often failed to penetrate the country's provinces but instead relied on autonomous, decentralized, and distinct "domains of sovereignty."[31] The weakness of the state obviously does not preclude hegemony. However, in Mexico where the state was sometimes cripplingly feeble and internal colonial relationships and strategies of resistance endured, it is important to remember Raymond Williams's broad assertion that hegemony is not only "resisted, limited, altered and challenged by pressures not at all its own" but also that "the concepts of counter-hegemony and alternative hegemony . . . are real and persistent elements of practice."[32]

All three models of state formation in Mexico are useful but also problematic. As will become clear, in postrevolutionary Oaxaca, the prevalence and persistence of counter-hegemonies, alternative hegemonies, and political violence undermine the historian's ability even to employ the looser framework of the neo-Gramscians with any degree of efficacy. Instead, I suggest a move away from these overarching models of state formation and toward an analysis of distinct, contained moments of interaction between regional elites, popular groups, and the state. Over the past two decades, scholars of other geographically and ethnically diverse administrative units have increasingly employed this flexible, locally specific vision in describing the process of state formation.[33] In his work on early twentieth-century China, Prasenjit Duara has argued that although social theories offer the scholar certain insights, "their universalistic scope makes them too abstract for the social historian who has to deal with the details of a particular culture." Instead, he proposes framing the process of state formation by viewing it as in constant interaction with a complex, regional "cultural nexus of power," including hierarchical institutions of kinship, religion, and mercantile control and patron-client networks.[34] In so doing, Duara manages to explain an ambivalent process of state formation that exchanged greater tax extraction and apparent centralization with slippage in local control. Karen Barkey has also moved away from overarching, nominally Western models of state formation and toward a local framing of state intervention. In the seventeenth century Ottoman Empire, the central state combined a patrimonial system of rule with a brokerage style of centralization. As a result, the optical illusion of centralization belied regional arrangements based on a series of deals with local bandits as state control was "developed by a series of fits and starts and using a combination of rational-legal and traditional aspects of rule."[35]

In describing the process of state formation in an ethnically and geographically disjointed state like Oaxaca, moving away from static, comprehensive social science models toward these dynamic, supple, localized antimodels holds certain advantages. First, on a methodological level, they permit a constant dialogue between the diachronic and the synchronic, the persuasive, unilinear narrative of state formation and the necessary analysis of local institutions and cultures. Second, they allow for the sheer diversity of local responses to federal interaction. In Oaxaca, national projects of *agrarismo*, socialist education, and centralized rule reached into the miasma of local politics and developed along distinct, often contradictory paths. Third, they offer space for the paradoxes and dualities within the process of state formation. The same institutions in different regions and at different times promoted competition and cooperation, generated consensus and dissent, engendered stability and ended in civil war. In fact, the postrevolutionary state in its entirety was deeply incongruous. Although various levels of the national government sought to subordinate, co-opt, or destroy the relatively autonomous authority of local communities and organizations, the effects were mixed. As Ben Fallaw and Adrian Bantjes have argued, local power structures— developed according to a series of historical, political, cultural, and social contexts—modified, contradicted, and paralyzed the state's projects.[36] In many regions, individual local political narratives failed to entwine themselves around the national account of state formation. The historical cord that attached the Revolution to the postrevolutionary PRI state was inchoate and frayed as individual strands wrapped themselves around locally formulated alternate narratives.

Methodologies

Despite building on these alternative investigative frameworks for state formation, exact comparison with either early twentieth-century China or the late seventeenth-century Ottoman Empire is, of course, absurd. Although both suggest strong parallels— including the prevalence of informal armed factions, the system of centralization and decentralization, and the importance of local interest groups—in Mexico the state was forced to reach into differing local power relationships based on the country's colonial, postcolonial, and revolutionary past. By looking beyond conventional chronologies and geographies of Mexican state formation, the historian is able to observe these interconnected associations, which include urban social movements, *cabecera*-village relations (i.e., dealings with district centers), ethnic interaction, caciques, and camarillas.

Alan Knight has identified a "chronological and conceptual gulf" in the study of postrevolutionary state formation. On the one hand, almost all historical appreciations of the regime have remained in a vortex, repeating the same cycle of arguments over

popular movements and authoritarianism bound by a chronological constraint that portrays the Revolution (and hence historical inquiry), as ending in 1940.[37] On the other hand, political scientists and sociologists of the later period have tended to jump
from ill-defined appreciations of the reforms of the Cárdenas period to structural analyses of the present day.[38] As a result, despite
sparse and inconclusive study of the presidencies of Manuel Avila
Camacho and Miguel Alemán Valdés, most scholarship, and especially that of the revisionists, has tended to portray the period
as one of increasing, uncontested right-wing politics, centralization, and authoritarianism.[39] In contrast, I look at the politics of
the 1930s, 1940s, and early 1950s and ask how the radical socioeconomic and political reforms of the Cárdenas era translated into
the *sexenios* (six-year terms) of his two successors. When, where,
and how did the creation of the PRM in 1938 lead to the eradication of regionalism, traditional cacique politics, popular peasant
militancy, and chronic instability? Or, from another perspective,
to what extent did the rise of an organized opposition to the postrevolutionary regime persist during the 1940s and 1950s?

However, study of the period 1940 to 1952 not only offers
the scholar a long-term vision of the political ramifications of
Cardenismo; it also opens up other avenues of inquiry. In particular, this book builds on the works of Christina Jiménez, Andrew
Grant Wood, Ariel Rodíguez Kuri, and John Lear on late nine-
teenth- and early twentieth-century Mexican urban political cultures to investigate the series of popular social movements, promoted and populated by the city's market women, that plagued
Oaxaca during the postwar years.[40] Traditional accounts of the
period have tended to ignore these mass mobilizations or, following the PRI, to paint them as right-wing attempts to gain political

ground. However, as Alan Knight argues, between 1940 and 1965 "there was an almost constant undercurrent of local and regional mobilization, both multiclass in its social makeup and electoral in its political strategy."[41] I argue that these movements were central to the creation of the modern Mexican state. Lower-class involvement in the movements has often been lost beneath heavily skewed official descriptions. Consequently, it is often necessary to uncover "hidden transcripts" of popular mobilizations and motivations.[42] In order to do this, my work also employs some of the tools laid out by social movement theorists such as Charles Tilly, Sidney Tarrow, and Doug McAdam.[43] By investigating in detail the political actors, mobilization structures, and movements' trajectories, many of the popular elements of the cross-class coalitions emerge. These "hidden transcripts" reveal a dynamic process of interaction between federal, state, and local bureaucrats, rural caciques, academic and commercial elites, and most important, a differentiated mass of urban poor, including artisans, market vendors, and workers. These examples of popular "public, collective interaction" took advantage of formal and informal mobilization structures, a growing literate public sphere, opening access to power and cleavages within the local elites to push for better urban infrastructure, tax reforms, and greater electoral participation. As a result, there emerged a changing "repertoire of collective action." Protest became general rather than specific, flexible rather than rigid, and indirect rather than direct. Bread rioting, archive burning, and functionary beating now took a back seat to organized marches, mass petitions, and the publication of protest newspapers. As Peter Guardino argues, investigation of these multiform and changing repertoires allows the historian to develop and weld innovation and improvisation in forms of resistance to the general narrative of state formation. These movements not only had important short-term effects, including the dismissal of two governors, the abolition of two unpopular tax laws, and the reform of urban water services; they also affected the creation of the Mexican state. First, once used and understood, this new repertoire of collective action was diffused elsewhere and employed on behalf of the broader claims of wider social coalitions in later movements in Oaxaca and in other Mexican towns and cities. Second, the state became increasingly aware of the need to placate not only the country's striking workers and land-hungry peasants but also the mass of small merchants, artisans, and female market vendors who populated Mexico's growing urban centers.

I also seek to examine a region little studied by scholars of postrevolutionary Mexico. Although recently it has become commonplace to acknowledge the "Many Mexicos" that constitute Mexico, in the stampede to pursue these local patterns, students of the postrevolutionary Mexican regime have (perhaps wisely) followed two things: the action and the sources. While the action has taken them to areas of Catholic (Cristero) insurrection and large land expropriations, the sources have led them to concentrate on states where scholars have already worked.[44] This has created a sort of hierarchy of regional relevance, which, for the most part, has ignored the predominantly indigenous southern areas of Mexico. By examining the state of Oaxaca, this study attempts to expand the geography of political inquiry and, by taking a "view from the south," to modify some of the conclusions gleaned from an overemphasis on the center and north of the country.[45] Most important, revisionist historians have often searched for the roots of the authoritarian, corporatist regime in regions where the government asserted control over large land expropriations or mass labor movements.

However, by observing the political map of a deeply disjointed state like Oaxaca, other power relationships and narratives of state formation emerge. In particular, the historian can observe the centrality of ethnic relationships to the process of nation building in Mexico. Florencia Mallon has argued that during the twentieth century, Mexico developed "a post-revolutionary mestizo national hegemony." In many ways, the "Indian problem" was "relegated to the frontier and peripheral regions."[46] Study of one of the peripheral regions thus allows the scholar not only to examine the intersection of national ideals and local responses at the borders of internal colonialism, where discourses of *indigenismo* and incorporation confronted a mosaic of interlinking ethnic groups, but also to question the extent of the state's hegemonic effort. The state of Oaxaca contains sixteen of the fifty-six pre-Columbian ethnic groups in Mexico.[47] These divergent ethnicities are not spread equally over the state. Mixtec and Zapotec-speaking Indians form the majority of Oaxaca's indigenous peoples. While Mixtecs dominate the west of the state, Zapotecs constitute the greater part of the inhabitants of the Central Valleys, the Sierra Juárez, the Isthmus, and the south. The fourteen other ethnic groups dot the state's tropical plains and sheer ravines. Some groups, such as the Mixes, who inhabit the east of the Sierra Juárez, are numerous and constitute hundreds of communities. Others, such as the Triquis, who live in the Mixteca, comprise only a handful of small villages. In addition to the indigenous people of Oaxaca, Hispanic immigrants form important minorities in the state's capital and its principal commercial towns. Finally, over the past five centuries, mestizos have come to comprise an important stratum of Oaxaca society. In Oaxaca, state formation has always depended on this complex tapestry of interethnic and interracial relationships.[48] As will become clear, local responses to government intervention were molded by an array of intertwining geographical, historical, and cultural factors, including the size of ethnic group, the penetration of Hispanic and mestizo immigrants, the distance from major commercial centers, the development of nineteenth-century capitalism, and perhaps most important, the "ethnic strategies of resistance"—the culturally bound, historically formed approaches to dealing with the outside world. Furthermore, as the Zapatista rebellion in 1994 made clear, these relationships at the periphery have been and still are central to the development of the Mexican state. Although Oaxaca often appears as a historical outlier, strategies developed within the state's complex montage have been replicated throughout Mexico's heterogeneous ethnic cartography. Despite the seemingly featureless carapace of mestizo national identity, postrevolutionary Mexico abounded with the kinds of fractures and boundaries that are concentrated in Oaxaca.

In Oaxaca, the relationship between the state and the diverse ethnic groups was negotiated at the level of the ex-district, an administrative unit that lay between the state governor and the municipality (see map 3). Although the Constitution of 1917 had posited an end to the structure of the *jefe político* and the administrative district and a return to unimpeded free municipalities, Oaxaca's elites ignored the thrust of the new prescriptions and simply adjusted the nomenclature of the administrative units. Thus, although districts were renamed "ex-districts," they remained the organizational loci of postrevolutionary governance. As Moises de la Peña remarked in 1950, "it is improper to call them ex-districts, as although politically they don't have that category, they continue to have it in reality."⁴⁹ The agent of public ministry, tax collector, judge, school inspector, and often the *defensa social* or local military force were still arranged according to ex-districts and were based in their district centers, the *cabeceras*.⁵⁰ As a result, although the government had terminated the office of the *jefe político*, the political strongmen, agrarian administrators, and commercial conglomerates were still able to dominate local village politics through control of the *cabeceras* of the ex-districts.⁵¹ Moreover, as this book demonstrates, this was the key level at which the revolutionary practice and process was debated, appropriated, or dismissed. The agrarian functionaries, union leaders, local caciques, regional businessmen, and their self-interested camarillas, who together dominated Oaxaca's thirty ex-districts, were the pivots upon which national policy hinged. Furthermore, the federal government was well aware of the nature of Mexico's provincial administration and, as a result, constructed its governance of Oaxaca's regions through manipulation of the relations between state governor, district leaders, local bureaucrats, and village councils.

Investigation of midlevel politics involves an understanding of two key organizing concepts, the cacique and the camarilla. Caciques dominated the governance of individual ex-districts. Paul Friedrich defined the Mexican cacique as "a strong and autocratic leader in local and regional politics whose characteristically informal, personalistic, and often arbitrary rule" was buttressed by a core of relatives, pistoleros (gunmen), and dependents and was "marked by the diagnostic threat and practise of violence."⁵² Eric Wolf added the idea of the cacique as a political middleman, the link between central government doctrine and local village practice.[53] Revisionist scholars welded a chronological conception of *caciquismo* to their image of the overarching postrevolutionary state. Many historians held that after the "Golden Age" of the "traditional" revolutionary *cacicazgo* in the 1920s, the state "came to lose its dependence on the strong military caciques of the interior."[54] Martial strongmen were replaced by less bellicose bureaucrats or forced to adapt to the more restrictive rules of the "modern" *cacicazgo*.[55] However, recently scholars have started to add a certain fluidity to this rather stark chronological dichotomy, refuting the idea of the "modern" cacique shepherding his recalcitrant herd on behalf of the overbearing party and examining continuities between local political rule in the immediate and later postrevolutionary periods.[56] Building on these arguments, I contend that this insistence on the arrival of a new "modern" political middleman not only ignores the reality of the Oaxacan countryside; it also prevents the historian from examining the multifarious and contradictory political faces of the postrevolutionary cacique.

At the same time, investigation of the relationship between the state and the localities also depends on comprehension of the camarilla. As Paul Friedrich argues, friendship was key to the pursuit of Mexican politics.[57] Camarillas were (and still are) the informal networks of elite friends who controlled regional political and economic resources.[58] As caciques could rarely extend control over a whole region or penetrate every office of the state and federal government, politics relied on the alliances caciques made with these other powerholders. As Roderic Camp argues, these camarillas were rarely groups of likeminded individuals, but rather "crosscut ideological, social, and sectoral barriers" and were "welded together by personal loyalties." As their formation was "permeable and pragmatic" to the untrained eye, Mexican politics can often appear remarkably fluid and adaptable.[59] During the period in question, the state of Oaxaca had three permanent camarillas of major political import: the rich elite of the Central Valleys (often called the *vallistocracia*); the hacendados of Jamiltepec, and the *finqueros* (commercial farmers) of Tuxtepec. However, multiple other groups rose and fell, unified and divided, allied and split, including the coffee *finqueros* of Pochutla, the market traders of Oaxaca de Juárez, the "fanatical" Catholics of the Mixteca Baja, the red and green factions of the Isthmus, the railway workers of Matias Romero, and, of course, the groups surrounding individual caciques and the state's various peasant and worker organizations. Once attention is paid to the bewildering and oft-changing array of personal, familial, and economic alliances, the historian can begin to understand the motion and direction of midlevel political interaction.

In this book I aim to broaden investigation of the political formation of the Mexican state by examining the intricacies of popular social movements, ethnic relations, and cacique and camarilla politics in Oaxaca. I argue that the overarching process of state formation emerged not only from the process of unionization, co-option, and repression but also through dynamic, diverse, and complex relationships between federal and state bureaucrats, semiautonomous caciques, diverse ethnic groups, and contentious independent social movements. This process delineated a broad and extremely divergent chronology and geography of state formation. In rural districts the state interacted with complex local histories of *caciquismo*, factionalism, ethnic relations, and strategies of resistance. In some regions, the state drew peasant organizations into the party apparatus through offers of land, credit, and political representation. In others, recent capitalization forced indigenous groups into a state of almost permanent revolt. In others, caciques or acephalous ethnic groups molded state policy to local circumstances and resisted direct co-option into the national party. In contrast, in Oaxaca City, the process of revolutionary state formation arrived later and was predicated upon a series of negotiations over modernization, taxation, popular political participation, and social mobilization.

The book begins with a brief historiographical introduction to Porfirian, revolutionary, and early postrevolutionary Oaxaca, covering the years 1876 to 1928. During the late nineteenth century the state underwent a radical but uneven process of economic and political modernization. This, in turn, affected the trajectory and geography of Oaxaca's complex revolutionary movements. After the end of armed conflict in 1920, successive governors struggled to bring together the Revolution's diverse rival factions. Only with the succession of Governor Genaro V. Vásquez in 1925 was there any systematic attempt to draw regional caciques and camarillas within the ambit of the state administration.

The rest of the book is divided into three narrative sections addressing the periods 1928 to the mid-1930s, 1936–40, and 1940–52. Chapters 2 and 3 concern the first concerted effort to regiment the state's regions through an incipient corporatist system, examining the establishment, contradictions, and demise of regional labor and peasant unions and a state party under the tutelage of the strongman Francisco López Cortés. Although the caudillo enacted a smattering of social reforms, he was eventually deposed by an alliance of out-of-favor caciques, opportunistic politicians, and militant peasants under the broad umbrella of Cardenismo. The second section involves the stuttering formation of a broad-

based political system under the new president, Lázaro Cárdenas. Although Cárdenas sought to impose a compliant governor
on Oaxaca, outside the state capital the attempts at state formation led to multiple local arrangements. Chapters 4–6 delineate
these various *pactos* by looking at how *caciquismo, agrarismo,*
and socialist education affected Oaxaca's assorted ethnic groups.
The final chapters explore the effects of the presidencies of Manuel Avila Camacho and Miguel Alemán Valdés in Oaxaca. On
the one hand, the developing tensions between central, state, and
local government during the 1940s are examined. On the other
hand, I look at the rise of the urban social movement as an integral part of Oaxaca's postrevolutionary political formation. Entering the 1950s, political relationships began to merge the interests of the Oaxacan elite and the central government into an
alignment that has altered but never quite settled the interplay of
acquiescence and resistance.

ONE

Revolution and Stasis in Oaxaca, 1876–1928

The regional process of state formation in twentieth-century Oaxaca has depended on its rugged and uneven geography. Most of the state's terrain is extremely mountainous. Over 60 percent of the state is located at heights of more than five hundred meters. The most important mountain ranges are the Mixteca Alta to the northwest of Oaxaca City, the Sierra Juárez to the northeast, and the Sierra Madre del Sur to the south (map 2). The mountains serve to encircle the rich Central Valleys of Oaxaca. These comprise three extremely fertile interlinking troughs that converge on the site of the state capital, Oaxaca City. Outside Oaxaca's mountainous core, the state is composed of three peripheral lowland areas. These are the Costa Chica, a narrow coastal strip by the Pacific; the Isthmus of Tehuantepec, a windswept, craggy landscape to the east of Oaxaca City; and the Papaloapan basin around Tuxtepec. Within these geographical zones there are multiple differences in vegetation, temperature, and rainfall, which have served to develop myriad local economies within the same region. The state contains tropical jungle in regions such as Tuxtepec and parts of Pochutla, rugged mountainous scrublands in the Mixteca Alta, and pine woodlands and even mist forest in the Sierra Juárez. In fact, the sheer complexity and importance of Oaxaca's topography has inspired a cavalcade of attempted geographical codifications. Most have followed Jorge

Tamayo's division of the state into eight regions: the Central Valleys, Mixteca Alta, Mixteca Baja, Cañada, Sierra, Isthmus, Pacific Coast, and Papaloapan basin. Many authors have pointed out that this system ignores the Costa Chica and the Sierra Madre del Sur, which both have their own intimate geographies and divergent local histories. As will become clear, regional geography, however defined, delineated ethnic strategies of resistance, mestizo incursion, capitalist development, and by extension state formation, throughout the state. The enormous importance of geography to Oaxaca's regional histories can be observed in this brief overview of the substantial work done by Mexican, European, and U.S. historians on Porfirian, revolutionary, and early postrevolutionary Oaxaca.

The Porfiriato, 1876–1910

Until recently, historians had depicted nineteenth-century Oaxaca as "an island in the middle of the convulsions of the Porfirian sea," "a backward, provincial society, resistant to change."[1] However, recent works have attempted to reconfigure this vision of the state's economic development and stress the importance of the construction of infrastructure, European immigration, industrialization, commercialization, and agricultural capitalization, especially in low-lying tropical regions of the state. As Paul Garner argues, Oaxaca was "at the vanguard of the regional development in the Porfiriato."[2] After an array of ill-thought-out schemes, hopeful speculations, and foreign ambivalence, investors began to erect a network of railways in the state in the late 1880s.[3] In late 1892 the Mexican Southern Railway linked Puebla to Oaxaca City, and in the following decades, arterial lines were constructed to link various mining communities to the state capital.[4] Between 1899 and

23

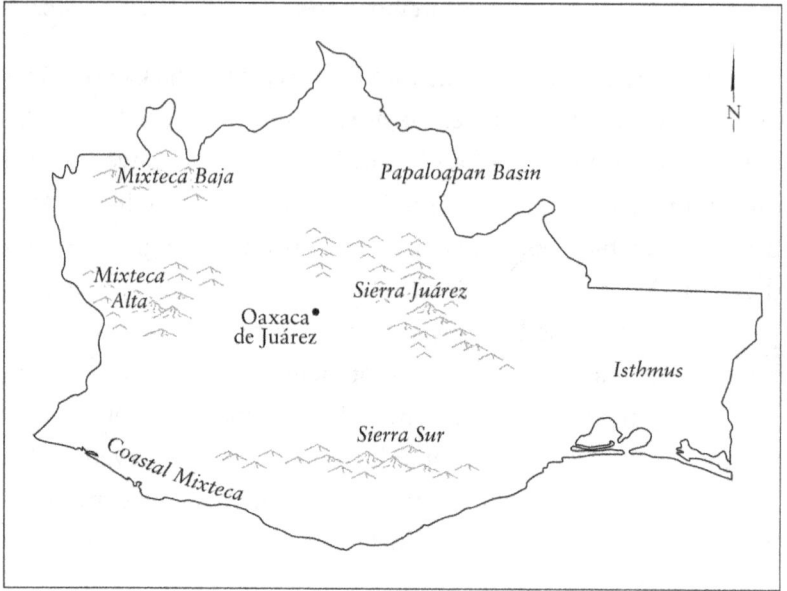

MAP 2. Geography of Oaxaca

1907 a British investment company constructed the Tehuantepec Railway, which crossed the Isthmus between Minatitlán and Salina Cruz.[5] At the same time, various smaller lines were built in the districts of Juchitán to the east and Tuxtepec to the north (map 3). By 1910 the state had 1,829 kilometers of new track. Railways also anticipated other advances in infrastructure. Telegraph and telephone lines, roads, bridges, postal services, and electrical facilities now dotted and crisscrossed Oaxaca's terrain.[6] Enlarged communications allowed the expansion of industrial concerns. Between 1902 and 1907 U.S. investors sank $10 million into iron, carbon, and silver mining in the state. Only Guanajuato received more. By 1911, and despite the deprivations caused by the slump of 1907, the Official Mining Directory of Mexico listed 111 mining companies in Oaxaca.[7]

New railroads, roads, and ports also facilitated the capitalization and commercialization of agriculture. During the Porfiriato, frontier farmers and commercial agriculture usurped indigenous lands and cut back the jungles to plant a variety of labor-intensive cash crops. In the tropical districts of Pochutla, Cuicatlán, Tuxtepec and Choapam (map 3), Mexican and foreign landowners harvested coffee for export to expanding U.S. and European markets.[8] In the municipality of San Juan Bautista Valle Nacional, Tuxtepec, a multinational cabal enforced a regime of near slavery to take advantage of the high global price of tobacco. According to U.S. journalist John Kenneth Turner, contractors shanghaied minor delinquents, petty thieves, pickpockets and "unruly" factory workers from Mexico's urban centers and sent them to the brutal tropical plantations of "Death Valley," where "they often dropped down dead and were ploughed back into the earth."[9] Outside San Juan Bautista Valle Nacional, the landscape of Tuxtepec changed with the arrival of other export crops, such as cotton, sugarcane, cocoa beans, rubber, and, after 1909, bananas. In 1883 amateur historian Manuel Martínez Gracida had listed only one hacienda in the region. Thirty years later there were 123, or 23 percent of the large agricultural properties in the state.[10] Finally, the production of livestock became more widespread as hacendados and ranchers moved into the districts of Jamiltepec and Juquila and joined the annual cattle run from the Costa Chica up the Mixteca to Puebla.[11]

The dramatic increase in agricultural and industrial capitalization necessitated rapid changes in the state's economic relations. Land, which had been concentrated in the hands of indigenous villages and a few Central Valley hacendados, became an increasingly valuable commodity as central and state governments demanded the privatization of communal properties.[12] In 1878 the governor of the state, Francisco Meixueiro, grumbled that the disentailment of lands, first announced in a circular of 1856, had "not been conducted in many populations."[13] According to Manuel Esparza this was the "start of a renewed fight against the communal lands," which continued until the end of the Porfiriato and was enforced by a series of ever more shrill decrees.[14] He notes more than a thousand sales in the period, with the 1890s as the decade of highest turnover, and posits that the number and size of haciendas in Oaxaca expanded greatly.[15] In particular, the quantity of capitalized haciendas, or what Francie R. Chassen-López has termed "fincas," rose dramatically, "especially [in] the tropical districts of Tuxtepec, Cuicatlán, Choapam, Jamiltepec and Pochutla."[16] In the governor's report of 1879, there had been 98 large landholdings in the state. By 1912 the *jefes políticos* of the state claimed that there were 450.[17] However, new liberal laws and

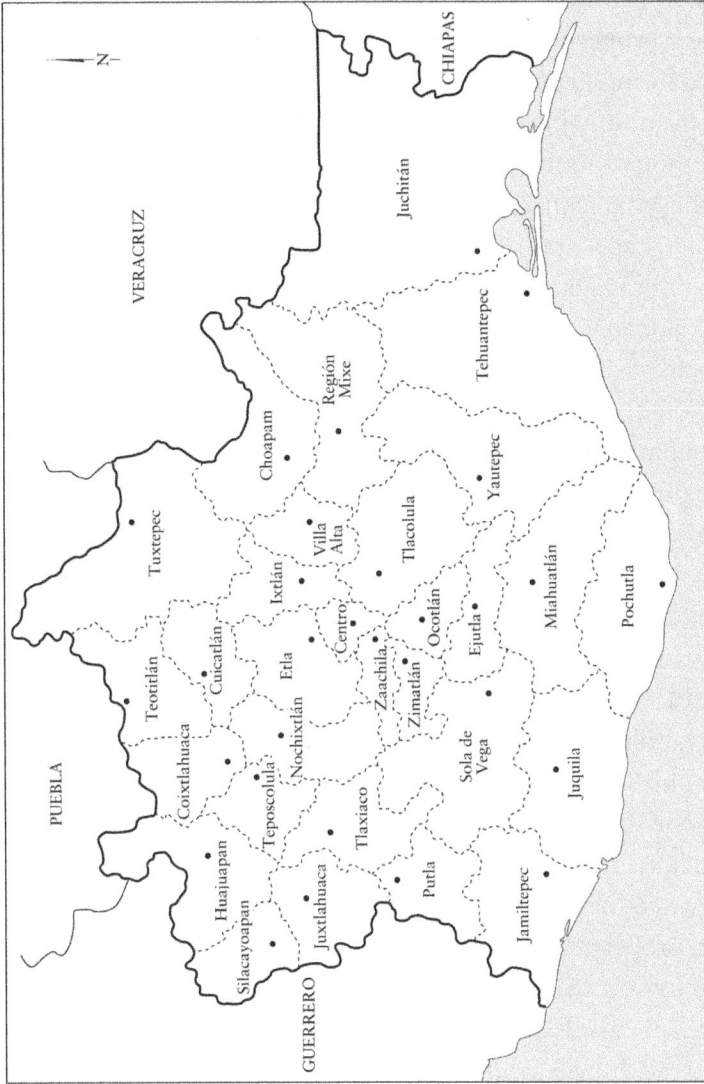

MAP 3. Administrative Districts of Oaxaca

an increasingly muscular central state did not lead to the whole-sale disappearance of indigenous forms of land tenure. Although the new properties were frequently "situated on land originally owned by indigenous communities," they were also often carved from the uninhabited areas of jungle.[18] Moreover, in many of the more mountainous areas of the state, such as the Sierra Juárez and the Mixteca, indigenous villages survived the attentions of rapacious speculators not only because of their less profitable lands but also through complex legal maneuvering and the po-litical patronage of Porfirio Díaz and other liberal leaders, who had acted as military commanders in both areas during the Lib-eral-Conservative and French Intervention wars.[19]

Economic changes also inevitably transformed social relations. In the provinces the defense of "communal possession of land . . . community customs and . . . forms of indigenous government" led to patterns of political resistance and, at times, rebellion. In the Isthmus, Leticia Reina has discerned what she terms an "ac-celerated rhythm" of rebellions against the Porfirian project in the area, as if the Revolution had arrived early.[20] Armed revolt against political impositions and the privatization of communal lands and salt flats broke out in 1872, 1876, 1879, and 1880–82.[21] The unrest spread to the Zapotecs of Pochutla in 1881.[22] These uprisings were often expressed in ethnic terms. On 5 Feb-ruary 1896 the governor, General Martín Gonzalez, introduced a tax on properties valued at under one hundred pesos. The Chati-nos of Juquila had recently divided up their communal lands into individual parcels and balked at the new levy. On 6 April they at-tacked the district capital of Juquila, shouting "death to all those who wear pants." They beheaded twenty-two whites and mesti-zos dressed in European garb and placed the town telegrapher's head on a pike. Although the army's Fourth Battalion effectively and brutally suppressed the revolt, there were echoes of the unrest in pueblos in the Central Valleys.[23]

The process of modernization also affected the higher echelons of society. Oaxaca City's elite, the *vallistocracia*, was supplemented by an influx of foreign capitalists from Germany, Italy, the United Kingdom, the United States, Spain, and France. The traditional upper class and the nouveaux riches combined to dominate the city and the state's new economic concerns. The investors of La Natividad mine in the Sierra Juárez included members from a multinational array of families. Intermarriage cemented these financial and political links. At the same time the ruling elite reinforced its economic control by developing and participating in a number of social, cultural, and recreational aspects of life in the state capital. Tennis clubs, bowling alleys, country clubs, and theatres were opened. In addition, the archbishop, Eulogio Gillow, encouraged a degree of urban Social Catholicism and extended the ambit of the cult of Our Lady of Solitude to appeal to the state capital's status-conscious elite and its popular classes.[24] Finally, the Oaxaca City elite through its connections to Porfirio Díaz dominated the city, state, and even the nation's politics. The upper class managed and controlled the city's municipal elections and influenced the appointment of *jefes políticos* almost throughout the state.[25] As Peter Smith reveals, this power extended beyond the state's borders, and Díaz "drew a disproportionate share of top-level leaders from his home state."[26]

The Revolution, 1910–1920

By 1910 Oaxaca had undergone a series of socioeconomic transformations. Roads, railways, and export capitalism had exposed huge areas of the state to the demands of the Porfirian liberal program. Yet despite the emergence of a thin tier of middle-class professionals, politics was still dominated by the economic elite of the state, supplemented and strengthened by a culturally and socially adaptable faction of foreign capitalists. As a result, although historians have often portrayed Oaxaca as essentially "passive" or a bastion of conservatism, the indigenous peasants, agricultural workers, literate bourgeoisie, and ostracized members of the elite all militated against the persistence of the Porfirian status quo. As Alan Knight has argued, "the extent of popular rebellion in Oaxaca has been underestimated and its character somewhat misconceived."[27] At one level, the excluded mestizo middle class—for example, the anarchist Flores Magón brothers; Camilo Arriaga, publisher of the rabble-rousing "Invitation to the Liberal Party"; Rafael Odriozola, head of the Regional "Benito Juárez" Club; Heliodoro Díaz Quintas, interim governor of the state in 1912, and a whole host of anarchist conspirators rounded up in a 1907 government crackdown—protested against the government for much of the early 1900s and during the decade of the Revolution.[28] But the Revolution in Oaxaca comprised not only the disgruntled provincial petit-bourgeoisie.

At another level, outside the state and district capitals there were a series of popular revolutions. Some were what Alan Knight has termed "*serrano* revolts," that is, multiclass agglomerations, often led by middle-class mestizos, fighting against the centralizing attempts of the Porfirian or later the Carrancista state. Angel Barrios in Cuicatlán, Che Gómez and Heliodoro Charis in Juchitán, and the villagers of Santa Catarina Ixtepeji in the Sierra Juárez all resisted the political, military, and economic incursions of the national and state governments.[29] Paul Garner has even redrawn the Soberanista (Sovereignty) movement as a more flexible, popular, and radical rebellion by people who longed for a return to economic and political independence established during the early Porfiriato. The rebellion, which spread throughout the Sierra Juárez, Sierra Madre del Sur, and Mixteca, fought the Oaxaca City–based Carrancista government from 1915 to 1920. This rebellion has long been tarnished as an anachronistic association of docile peasants and Porfirian caciques. Garner admits that the movement was led by Guillermo Meixueiro, a Porfirian functionary, and that its coup against Governor Emilio Bolaños Cacho in 1915 was motivated at least in part by his persecution of the supporters of Felix Díaz, Porfirio's nephew.[30] Nevertheless, the Soberanistas' leaders were also constantly forced to acknowledge the demands of their obstreperous and independent followers for food and political autonomy. Elite leaders, such as Meixueiro and José Iñes Dávila, who possessed little of the subtlety and suppleness required of a revolutionary martial cacique, quickly lost support, and more plebeian chiefs, such as Isaac M. Ibarra and Onofre Jiménez, came to the fore. In fact, Ibarra's alliance with Obregonismo in May 1920 "appeared to confirm his membership of the generation of revolutionary caudillos who were to assume political control over Mexico after 1920."[31]

Other rebellions were agrarian and demanded the division of haciendas and the return of communal indigenous lands. Many were imposed or at least inspired from outside as Zapatistas joined up with local rebels in the Mixteca.[32] Others tied into *serrano* revolts. Some of Barrios's followers returned to their villages, "their heads full of new ideas." One group arrived in San Juan Bautista Atatlauca, Etla, "full of the intention of dividing up the Hacienda of Concepción."[33] During the Porfiriato the mestizo hacendados, cattlemen, and ranchers of Jamiltepec had expanded their holdings at the expense of their Mixtec neighbors, thus incurring hostility and armed opposition. During the Revolution, this had its epicenter in the indigenous village of Poza Verde. A local rancher, Juan José Baños, who announced that he was Madero's representative in the region, put down the initial revolt but was soon faced with another. In summer 1914 the Mixtecs mounted a successful coup against the *cabecera*, sacking some properties and getting the support of the new state authorities under Guillermo Meixueiro. Baños reacted as revolutionary logic dictated: he repudiated the Oaxaca authorities, recognized the Carranza regime and the Plan of Guadalupe, and organized four companies of "Constitutionalists of the South" to drive out the Poza Verde rebels.[34]

Oaxaca did not react to the Revolution with passivity and indifference, nor through recourse to a return to the Porfirian order. Rather it reacted according to a series of confused and complex local situations. Given the disparate and fragmented population of Oaxaca and the perverse power of revolutionary logic, it is perhaps not surprising that the easy dichotomies of revolutionary categorization broke down. However, entering the 1920s, the popular classes and many of the politicians were neither relics of the days of Don Porfirio nor Luis González's "revolucionizados."[35] In fact, many were truly radicalized by the Revolution.[36] Similarly, the relationship between center and periphery—federal, state, and municipal governments—could not be the same again.[37] But it must be stressed that the Revolution did not precipitate a complete collapse of the state's socioeconomic and political system. Some regions of Oaxaca, including Pochutla and Choapam, had barely been touched by the decade of revolutionary strife. Elites adapted and persisted. The *vallistocracia* may have been trimmed of its exotic foreign imports, its mining and commercial agriculture enterprises left to the malicious militant masses, and its national power delimited, but the Oaxaca City elite maintained extensive commercial, industrial, real estate, and agricultural interests, especially around the state capital. Other elites also adapted to the rhetoric and praxis of the Mexican Revolution.[38] On the Costa Chica the ranchers and hacendados led by the Baños clan claimed revolutionary heritage while continuing to exploit Mixtec peasants and divest them of their lands.

The First Postrevolutionary Governors, 1920–1928

The immediate postrevolutionary period in Oaxaca was marked by political instability. First, the state governors were continually beset by the regional revolts of powerful camarillas. In particular, Oaxaca suffered the incessant rivalry of traditionally influential interest groups from the Central Valleys, Sierra Juárez, and Isthmus. From 1920 to 1928 five governors ruled the state. Second, outside Oaxaca City smaller factional conflicts continued to affect the rural periphery of the state. Former Porfirian strongmen, revolutionary caciques, and independent villages struggled for regional control. At the same time, the badly funded state governments failed to assert any measure of control over these areas. The revolutionary quartet of changes—land reform, workers' rights, rural education, and municipal independence—was at best unevenly implemented. Governors concentrated on appeasing the politically vital peasants of the Central Valleys, who surrounded the state capital and offered a potential source of quick support. Only under Governor Genaro V. Vásquez did the central government start to make a concerted effort to bring the state under control with the creation of the Confederación de Partidos Socialistas de Oaxaca (CPSO).

For five years the Revolution had pitted Carrancistas based in Oaxaca City against a coalition of Soberanistas, who controlled the state's mountainous hinterlands. In April 1920, Alvaro Obregón published the Plan of Agua Prieta, which announced his rebellion against Venustiano Carranza. In Oaxaca he offered the Soberanistas amnesty in return for regional support. On 3 May Soberanistas and Obregonistas signed a pact of allegiance. The following day, the Soberanistas under Isaac M. Ibarra descended on the state capital, overturned the Carrancista government, and had the rich lawyer José Acevedo elected interim governor.[39]

However, over the next six months it became clear that Obregón favored the appointment of Manuel García Vigil as governor. García Vigil had impeccable revolutionary credentials. He was an early Maderista convert, a decorated artillery commander, an activist journalist, and a close associate of Obregón during the recent struggle against Carrancismo.[40] Despite the opposition of members of the *vallistocracia*, he was elected governor in late 1920.[41] During his brief tenure, García Vigil encountered problems that would continue to beset his successors. As the president's imposed candidate, García Vigil had little support within the state, and as a result he had to placate Oaxaca's traditional and revolutionary elites. But the chaotic state of rural Oaxaca also revealed the need for swift and efficient social reform. The ensuing balancing act inevitably failed to improve the situation in the countryside or the city. Elites sniped at the governor's policies from the state capital. Local caciques, peasants, and agrarian workers continued to operate outside the ambit of state control.

During his brief tenure García Vigil attempted to implement limited agrarian and labor reform and to improve Oaxaca's educational facilities. Between 1920 and 1923 the governor signed land grants totaling 10,411 hectares. Most of these ejidos were located in districts of Zimatlán, Ocotlán, Etla, and Ejutla, around the state capital.[42] This reflected both the political importance of peasants in the Central Valleys and their greater familiarity with the mechanics of the land reform movement. At the same time, García Vigil supported workers in a few distinct regions. In the Soberanista stronghold of Ixtlán, the labor court decided in favor of the miners of La Natividad. In the textile factory in Vistahermosa, Etla, García Vigil also supported workers' demands for better pay and reduced working hours. The governor stressed the importance of free public education, but inadequate finances and limited reach precluded the expansion of a functioning school system outside the district capitals. Although official figures indicate that between 1921 and 1922, the number of schools increased from forty-two to more than seven hundred, most new establishments were "rudimentary" schools and depended on faltering municipal contributions.[43] Despite the governor's intentions, his policies were also circumscribed by the power of the industrialists and merchants of Oaxaca City. García Vigil avoided open conflict with the *vallistocracia* over social reform. Most ejidos were formed of abandoned or foreign-owned haciendas. The governor peppered his annual reports with promises to "respect private property" and "protect industry and commerce."[44] At the same time, he struggled to overcome the poverty of the state treasury and the resistance of the capital's elite to necessary tax increases. The state's major capitalists continued to evade set duties, and when García Vigil attempted to reform public finances in July 1922, the chamber of commerce balked at his proposals.[45] Furthermore, outside the state capital, García Vigil faced the open resistance of multiple armed groups. In 1921 there were rebellions in Huajua-pam, Ejutla, Zaachila, and the Sierra Juárez. The following year saw uprisings in Cuicatlán, Teotitlán, and Sola de Vega.[46]

Although García Vigil faced severe internal problems to state rule, it was the ramifications of national factionalism that eventually led to his downfall and death. On 15 February 1923, the governor was victim of an attempted assassination. Over the following year he began to suspect that Plutarco Elías Calles was behind the unsuccessful effort. As a result, in December 1923 García Vigil launched a manifesto in support of the rebellion of Adolfo de la Huerta against Calles's presidential candidacy. Despite some initial backing from various political groups, on 12 January 1924 the Soberanistas under Isaac M. Ibarra took the state capital. García Vigil and fewer than eight hundred troops fled toward the Isthmus, where they were defeated on 5 April by a coalition of local revolutionary generals. Two weeks later, Callista forces executed the governor in the district of Juchitán.[47] On 28 April Senator Ibarra was appointed interim governor of the state. Over the next six months, conflict centered on the elections for the permanent gubernatorial position. The former head of national education, José Vasconcelos, was supported by an alliance of Oaxaca City's railway workers, students, professionals, and a handful of the *vallistocracia*. The Soberanista general, Onofre Jiménez, was backed by a coalition of regional revolutionary forces. Despite Vasconcelos's ostensibly popular electoral campaign, Ibarra succeeded in levering his fellow Soberanista into office.[48] However, Jiménez barely survived a year. In order to reassure the traditionally hostile Oaxaca City elite, he made a series of concessions to the state's conservatives. He appointed a former Porfirista, Francisco Canseco, as his chief of staff and a prominent

Catholic activist, Gustavo E. Rodríguez, as his private secretary. He protected the lands of the *vallistocracia* by denying a series of petitions for agrarian reform. Consequently relations with the national government deteriorated, as President Calles sought to remove recalcitrant local caudillos from state governorships. On 8 November 1925, the local legislature enacted *el camarazo*, an internal coup d'état, which sacked Jiménez and appointed the noted Callista Genaro V. Vásquez in his place.[49]

With Vásquez's appointment as interim governor, the state administration attempted to assert greater control over Oaxaca's rural periphery. For five years, a series of military governors had sought in vain to suppress the state's numerous political strongmen and their armed groups. In contrast, Vásquez was the first civilian head of postrevolutionary Oaxaca. He was born in Oaxaca City in 1892 to relatively poor indigenous parents. Despite the death of his father in 1902, Vásquez managed to gain a degree from the local teaching college and a law degree from the Instituto de Ciencias y Artes (ICA). During the Revolution, he loitered on the outskirts of Carrancista politics and was elected federal deputy in 1918.[50] During the 1920s he became increasingly close to Calles. When he became interim governor his first report announced his "absolute faith and full confidence in the President of the Republic" and promised to "help with all means possible to strengthen the situation of the National Government."[51] During his tenure, Vásquez eschewed the tentative steps of the previous governors and developed a series of strategies designed to unify the state. Although he was hamstrung by a lack of local support, these tactics would be fully developed by his successor, Francisco López Cortés. First, Vásquez created a centralized regional party out of the myriad local caucuses thrown up by the Revolution.

Second, he started to implement a cultural program that stressed the links among Oaxaca's indigenous groups. Third, he started to set down the rules of the game for the state's local caciques.

The CPSO was founded in May 1926 as a union of twenty-six smaller regional parties, most of which were based in the district capitals.[52] The confederation was designed to act as the governor's political broker for different local factions. Vásquez appointed the leaders of the confederation, and its constituents were not allowed to communicate with outside groups without express permission. All electoral disputes were to be decided within the party, and the directorate of the party was to have the final say.[53] These autocratic pronouncements notwithstanding, it is difficult to judge the efficacy of the CPSO's political control during its first two years. As Jean Meyer argues, Vásquez was not confident enough to pursue the virulent anticlericalism of his political godfather and, as a result, managed to avoid the depredations of a full-scale Cristero revolt.[54] Furthermore, as we shall see, the resolution of political disputes still involved direct contact between the governor and the regional strongmen. Yet despite the organization's political weakness, Vásquez did use the CPSO to push forward his particular vision of state unity based on ill-defined socialism, *indigenismo*, and Oaxaqueñismo, or a celebration of Oaxaca's cultural distinctiveness. Under the auspices of the CPSO, Vásquez published a blizzard of pamphlets to express this vision. They mixed workers' aphorisms such as "the victory of socialism is inevitable" with pious devotions to communist heroes such as Vladimir Lenin.[55] However, despite Vásquez's rhetorical radicalism, his attitude to the state's Indians was mired in the paternalism of the past. Although the governor blamed the problems of Oaxaca's indigenous population on "a lack of water, a lack of good lands, a lack of seeds, excessive payment to the state, social inequality, and endemic illness," he also announced that it was "necessary to give reason to the Indian as he does not have it."[56] Vásquez also sought to unify the various regions of the state. In his pamphlet *El camino de la reconstrucción*, the governor expressed his frustration at Oaxaca's geographical and cultural diversity. He asked why the Juchitecos went to educate themselves in the universities of Mexico City and Huajuapeños sought instruction in the seminaries of Puebla. He complained that the people of Tuxtepec saw themselves as Tuxtepecanos rather than Oaxacan. He suggested that in order to overcome this intense localism, the CPSO, state administration, and teachers had to "saturate the state with Oaxaqueñismo, to teach [the people] what is theirs, their industries, their dances, their music, their languages and their race." Teachers were encouraged to start the day with a rendition of the "Himno socialista regional." Various local artists, musicians, and writers developed "Red Saturdays," cultural programs in Oaxaca City designed to teach the urban citizens the full variety of rural indigenous culture.[57] The poet Gabriel López Chiñas described his memories of Vásquez's arrival in Juchitán during the late 1920s. The governor taught the assembled children regional songs such as "El sarape oaxaqueño," "Tortolita cantadora," "Mañanitas oaxaqueñas," and "Huipilito istmeño." In the evening there were cultural sessions outside the public market where educators lectured the crowds on education, hygiene, health, and regional music.[58]

Vásquez's creation of the CPSO laid the groundwork for the establishment of his successor's corporatist political system in the following years. At the same time, the first civilian governor of Oaxaca also implemented new strategies to deal with the state's multiple armed caciques. Whereas previous governors had responded to political rivalries with policies of exclusion and force, Vásquez attempted to divide opponents with assurances of regional independence and then draw them into his governing camarilla. For example, in October 1927 former governor Onofre Jiménez arrived at the station of El Hule, Tuxtepec, and started to gather forces together in support of the national rebellion of Francisco Serrano and Arnulfo Gómez.[59] Vásquez immediately sent telegrams to other Soberanista leaders such as Otilio Jiménez Madrigal and Absalon Santiago to secure their loyalty and demand that they track down the seditious group. He appealed to the revolutionary generals' sense of regional pride and asked that they stop Jiménez's attempts to "besmirch the reputation of the Sierra Juárez."[60] Vásquez also ordered the chief of the military zone, Matias Ramos, into the Sierra in order to calm the speculation and rumors concerning possible government repression. He warned Ramos that it was imprudent to try to disarm the Soberanistas.[61] On 12 October the zone commander met the assembled authorities of the Sierra and their military commanders at the village of Santa Catarina Lachatao. They agreed to support the governor against Jiménez's incipient rebellion in return for guarantees of regional autonomy and the right to keep their arms.[62] A week later Jiménez retreated from open confrontation, repudiated his links to the Serrano rebellion, and announced that he would do "what the Sierra wanted."[63] In another incident, on 2 June 1928 the entire council of Huautla de Jiménez and four of its supporters were murdered. According to government reports former Soberanista leaders Guadalupe García and José García Parra were behind the attack, together with the head of the *defensa social*, Tiburcio Cuellar.[64] The lurid case made the national press, and Vásquez was forced to act.[65] Employing Solomonic justice, he ordered the two major caciques, García and García Parra, to leave the town but allowed Cuellar to remain to "guard against further violence."[66]

Conclusion

During the Porfiriato, Oaxaca underwent a process of rapid but uneven development. Huge haciendas and highly capitalized fincas were established in low-lying regions such as Tuxtepec, Pochutla, Jamiltepec, Juchitán, and Choapam, while mountainous zones with high concentrations of indigenous inhabitants, such as the Sierra Juárez and Mixteca, prevented the incursion of outside entrepreneurs. The state's divergent economic cartography delineated a bewildering array of regional revolutionary movements. While the Mixtecs of Jamiltepec sought the return of communal properties, the Soberanista movement fought against state interference and tried to carve out a degree of local autonomy. In the postrevolutionary period, consecutive governors failed to unite the state's factions. However, Vásquez's governorship ushered in a new relationship among the national, regional, and local powers. State authority now rested on the governor's close rapport with President Calles, an incipient corporatist system, and a series of negotiated pacts with Oaxaca's local caciques. This arrangement reached its full expression with rule of Vásquez's successor, Francisco López Cortés.

TWO

The Caudillo and the State, 1928–34

Between 1928 and 1934, Mexico was dominated by Plutarco Elías Calles, the Jefe Máximo de la Revolución. Despite his attempts at what Jürgen Buchenau has described as "authoritarian populism," the country was "far from being a monolithic block." In fact it remained "a conjunction of many different forces [including] . . . the unions, the army, the bureaucracy, the government and local regional forces."[1] On the one hand, Calles managed to extinguish the Cristero revolt, eliminate a series of military threats, impose compliant successors on the presidential throne, and establish a unifying national party, the Partido Nacional Revolucionario (PNR).[2] On the other hand, many state administrations remained in the hands of regional caudillos. These figures have been well documented in regional histories of the past three decades. In fact, some have come to personify the radical policies of the period, whether it be the anticlericalism of Tomás Garrido Canabal, the *agrarismo* of Adalberto Tejeda, or the political independence of Saturnino Cedillo. Historians have created a typology of these leaders, describing them as "traditional" or "modern," the former destined to die in a hail of bullets, their support crushed by the onset of political modernization, the latter retiring into wealthy irrelevance, their political system subsumed into the national party.[3] However, it would be wrong to overstate the predominance of these attractive and charismatic figures, a tendency implicit in some revisionist accounts of the period, which view Cardenismo as the curtain call for these free-wheeling revolutionaries.[4]

By examining state formation through the lens of one of these regional strongmen, I argue in this chapter that in reality, Maximato Mexico was as much the preserve of Callista conservatives, men such as Francisco López Cortés, who ruled Oaxaca as governor between 1928 and 1932 and then as the power behind the throne of his successor, Anastasio García Toledo, for the next three years. Building on the initial steps toward greater administrative centralization and control enacted by Governor Vásquez, López Cortés viewed the maintenance of his political power in unquestioning loyalty to Calles, links with local economic and political elites, a faux-radicalism, and corporatist bodies imposed from the top down. This does not mean that the historian should dismiss notions of decentralization and regional independence in favor of state hegemony and federal control. In fact all four co-existed in Oaxaca during the Maximato. As much as the López Cortés administration (known as the Chicolopista regime) relied on the central government, without the deep populist roots of the powerful regional caudillos, it was also forced to mediate control through an array of caciques, their client networks, and armed gangs. With only unsteady agreements with López Cortés himself and without any formal ties to the Callista administration, these local strongmen, rather than the state governor, presented a series of barriers to the penetration of state control.

Francisco López Cortés's Rise to Power

Francisco López Cortés was born in San Jerónimo Ixtepec, Juchitán, in 1899. Like many of the richer Istmeños of the epoch he was sent to study law at the local university, the ICA in Oaxaca City.[5] During the Revolution he showed no signs of the radical rhetoric that would adorn his later career. He did however display his aptitude for political opportunism and a knack for choosing the wrong side. Since the late nineteenth century, politics in the Isthmus had been broadly divided between an indigenous, green party based in Juchitán and a more mestizo, red party centered in Tehuantepec. As a wealthier resident of one of the region's more mestizo towns, López Cortés joined the reds during the Revolution, just as they started to lose power to the greens under Che Gómez.[6] As a result, he spoke in celebration of the Huerta coup in 1913.[7] After finishing his law degree he took a series of jobs throughout the republic, culminating in his position as government minister under Esteban Cantu, Carrancista governor of Baja California. This did not last long; he was forced to flee Mexico after his political godfather backed Carranza during the Agua Prieta revolt.[8] Returning to Oaxaca and his hometown of San Jeronimo Ixtepec he was again caught on the wrong side, leading an ill-conceived rebellion of the red faction in 1922.[9] However, after García Vigil's fall from power during the De la Huerta revolt, he was allowed to return and started to construct a power base in San Jerónimo Ixtepec and the Isthmus. Building on his connections to powerful figures among the Juchitán reds, such as Generals Francisco Luis Castillo and Laureano Pineda, he became a federal deputy in 1925.[10] These links to the Isthmus were to remain central to the Chicolopista regime, and he would choose Anastasio García Toledo, a fellow politician from the Isthmus, to succeed him in 1932.

In 1925 he backed *el camarazo*, the coup against Onofre Jiménez led by Genaro V. Vásquez.[11] According to a government agent, López Cortés was "an unconditional" of Vásquez from this point on.[12] His friendship with the new governor, which was cemented by his marriage into the extended Vásquez clan, was integral to his rise to the governorship over the next three years.[13] Vásquez appointed López Cortés president of the CPSO in late 1926.[14] A year later, at its second annual congress, it voted in its president as official candidate for governorship of the state.[15] Although López Cortés was one of six candidates for the post, his control over the CPSO and his support in the Isthmus eventually led him to be declared sole candidate and then victor in August 1928.[16] Like that of his predecessor, López Cortés's ascendancy depended heavily on his relationship with the Jefe Máximo, and he would remain unfailingly loyal throughout his six-year tenure as effective state leader. Key to this constancy was the Oaxaca governor's pursuit of Callista political policy. Throughout the late 1920s and early 1930s, due to his links to Carlos Riva Palacio, he formed part of the national camarilla of what Alicia Hernández Chavez has termed "ultracallistas."[17] During the period he supported Calles against the supporters of Alvaro Obregón, José Vasconcelos, and Joaquín Amaro.[18]

The narrative of López Cortés's rise to power at first contains many of the characteristics of the "modern" postrevolutionary caudillo. Like Emilio Portes Gil, he was a trained lawyer and professional bureaucrat of middle-class origins who established close links with national and local groups in the early 1920s.[19] However, he showed little interest in social or economic reform or its political paycheck, at least until his appointment as president of the CPSO, where it became a rhetorical necessity. In fact his local power base lay in a suspiciously reactionary Porfirian faction of the Oaxaca government and in friendship with the previous governor. This aligns him with the caudillos of Chihuahua and Mexico, who linked the old and new elites of each state.[20]

The Corporatist Framework

López Cortés could not have survived simply as a Callista stooge supported by a coterie of conservative Istmeños. Although Genaro V. Vásquez had started to construct a corporatist system, it was his successor who strengthened the state party and created its peasant and worker confederations.

Politics, Culture, and the CPSO

From 1926 onward López Cortés dominated the CPSO. After molding its initial structure, as governor he continued to impose control, appointing close political allies among the bureaucratic and economic elite to the executive committee.[21] This allowed him political control of the institutional framework of the state. As one Chicolopista wrote in 1934, from its creation the "the institution . . . controlled all the political-electoral activities of the state of Oaxaca."[22] These included elections for governors and for federal and local deputies. As already noted, López Cortés chose the CPSO head from the Isthmus, Anastasio García Toledo, to succeed him as governor, and the CPSO backed the election campaign of the caudillo's choice.[23] A government agent in Oaxaca in August 1932 noted that although "most look[ed] on García Toledo with marked indifference," the CPSO paid the state capital's police to prevent indigenous market goers leaving the town and to force them to turn up for the gubernatorial elections.[24] Local caciques were allowed a degree of freedom in their choice of municipal authorities, but all decisions were made under the umbrella of the CPSO. At the local level, as Alvarado Mendoza found in

Tamaulipas during the dominance of Emilio Portes Gil, regional interparty rivalry was mediated by the intervention of the central organization.[25] In November 1931, the CPSO called on the warring parties of Tlacolula, Ocotlán, Tuxtepec, and Jamiltepec to assemble in Oaxaca City and form the Alianza de Partidos Revolucionarios. A leading Chicolopista, Germán Gay Baños, headed the alliance.[26] Because of this carefully managed comprehensiveness, the confederation could boast to the PNR at the end of 1931 that "in all the state there does not exist a party independent of the Confederation, so that it can be affirmed that the Confederation of Parties politically controls all the state."[27] The relationship between the PNR and CPSO seems to have been one of mutual interdependence. López Cortés and the CPSO were allowed to organize local elections and were volunteered tacit PNR approval with the understanding that this would produce peace and stability in the state. Any disagreements at the level of high state politics tended to be resolved in the center, with dissatisfied regional politicians offered lucrative federal posts outside the state.[28] This political symbiosis was affirmed with the absorption of the CPSO into the PNR in April 1934. The state executive committee of the local party then became the officers of the national party.[29]

The CPSO was also the mouthpiece of the Chicolopista regime. As such it built on the model established during Vásquez's gubernatorial tenure. As one contemporary commentator wrote, the "CPSO is not only a political institution, but also a center of social activities for the elevating of intellectual and moral planes, not only of its associates but also of the people in general."[30] It utilized many means to impose its cultural program: building night schools and libraries; printing newspapers, pamphlets, and song sheets; and organizing competitions and weekly cultural

FIG. 1. A rally by the Confederación de los Partidos Socialistas de Oaxaca, Oaxaca City. (Courtesy of the Archivo de la Fototeca de la Casa de la Cultura Oaxaqueña)

performances called Red Saturdays.[31] Although these were at first limited to the literate and the inhabitants of Oaxaca City, they began to be pushed into the provinces from the early 1930s onward with the enactment of Red Saturdays demanded of all municipal authorities.[32] Poets such as Juan Vasconcelos and Gabriel López Chinas, writers such as Ricardo Vera Castro and José Muñoz Cota, and musicians such as Guillermo Rosas Solaegui and Samuel Mondragón brought forth a plethora of elite and popular works during the period that were often performed at the Red Saturdays.[33] At the same time Alfonso Caso began work on the excavation of Monte Albán, and the Oaxaca government organized one-off spectacles of political-cultural theatre, such as the fourth centenary of Oaxaca City's establishment, the first Mexican Congress of History, and the Guelaguetza, a celebration of Oaxaca's indigenous culture.[34]

Together these offered the regional and national public a vision of what one historian has described as "romantic socialism," a confused ideological framework that overlay the Chicolopista regime, like a garish quilt formed from myriad ill-fitting pieces.[35] At the center of the experience were the notions of revolutionary socialism, *indigenismo*, and Oaxaqueñismo established during Vásquez's tenure. The rhetoric of the Red Saturdays, May Day celebrations, and CPSO-sponsored newspapers rejoiced in explications of the "new ideology of socialism" that was encapsulated by the achievements of the Mexican Revolution. There were speeches on "What is socialism and why we ought to be socialists," and articles on Marx, Engels and Zapata.[36] However, this radicalism rubbed shoulders with an ambiguous vision of the past and an uneasy appreciation of the ultimate conclusions of socialist cant. Thus the commemorative album of the fourth centenary of Oaxaca City's establishment forsook all mention of the Revolution and instead concentrated on the accomplishments of the Porfiriato.[37]

The deliberately vague definition of socialism and its historical antecedents was paralleled by an equally confused vision of *indigenismo*.[38] Central to Oaxacan *indigenismo* was Caso's excavations of Monte Albán, the gradual expansion of the state's archaeological museum, and the works inspired by the historical congress of 1933, which offered frozen visions of "the wonderful legacy of great Zapotecs and Mixtecs" as artists, builders, and warriors. In contrast, perceptions of contemporary Indians were less adulatory and more variegated. On the one hand they were treated as children or degenerates, their propensity for adult behavior reliant on exposure to modern education.[39] On the other hand, the Indian was lauded as the vessel of important and often sophisticated folk traditions. The 1932 fourth centenary celebrations saw the presentation of a "Racial Homage" and demonstrations of the dance, music, song, and dress of Mixes, Zapotecs, Mixtecs, and Mazatecs. However, as Deborah Poole argues, even overt celebrations of indigenous culture could often descend into homogenization through the establishment of ethnic "types."[40] Furthermore it seems that López Cortés was loath to pursue this more positive *indigenismo* too far, especially in front of the *vallistocracia*. Thus, performances of Isthmus Zapotecs were mixed in with polkas performed by the sallow daughters of wealthy Oaxacans dressed as Dutch maids.[41] Finally, the entire *indigenista* project was overlaid by an economic determinism. Many saw the whole ideological morass as little more than an opportunity to expand Oaxaca's tourism trade. Under López Cortés, the cultural, economic, and political elites endlessly expounded the value of the incipient industry, arguing that it would become "the main source of wealth of the state," and setting up the Local Pro-tourism Commission and the Committee of Tourist Information. All argued that the key attraction of Oaxaca was its ready-packaged indigenous culture.[42]

The CPSO project also consecrated the cultural particularism of Oaxaca, or Oaxaqueñismo. Building on the vision of his predecessor, López Cortés strengthened the internal aspects of this state patriotism. He continued to stress the need to unite people "separated by race, divided by languages, by customs and by regions" into a integrated whole by delineating the common mores of the state in celebrations such as the Guelaguetza and Red Saturdays, songs such as "El alma oaxaqueña," publications such as the *Album literario de Oajaca*, and the creation of a common history institutionalized in the ICA's Oaxaca history course.[43] However, as Claudio Lomnitz argues, the formation of local cultures gave towns potential leverage at the national level.[44] This external aspect of Oaxaqueñismo was often expressed in assertions of Oaxaca's cultural superiority. Thus one commentator argued: "Unlike the rest of Mexico, in Oaxaca we have tried to create and maintain popular song immune from outside influences."[45] The tension between regionalism and the nationalist project could evolve into bitter legal disputes. In 1932 the state congress passed the Law of Dominion and Jurisdiction of Archaeological Monuments, which claimed state control over all pre-Hispanic ruins and their contents. When the Supreme Court declared the law unconstitutional, López Cortés rushed out a series of editorials and pamphlets arguing that the nullification not only infringed the sovereignty of the state but also imperiled the "care and conservation of the monuments, historical relics and objects of archaeological interest in the state."[46]

The motley and often contradictory contents of the state-sponsored Oaxacan cultural revival reflected the CPSO's attempt to include all factions of the local political circuit. The confederation itself was an amalgam of the various parties of Oaxaca and as such contained groups of socialists and liberals, *indigenistas*, believers in the cosmic race and Hispanic supremacists, genuine former revolutionaries, and poorly disguised Porfirian functionaries. López Cortés was at pains to unify these disparate groups or, at the very least, not to alienate any of them from his multiclass, multiregional political project. Consequently coherence took a back seat as he sponsored a local catch-all corporatist culture.

Labor, Industry, and the Confederación
de Ligas Socialistas de Oaxaca

As López Cortés expanded the political and cultural ambit of the CPSO he also added labor organizations to the state corporatist apparatus. Oaxaca was no Tamaulipas or Nuevo León, and its industrial base was limited to a handful of mines, power plants, sugar refineries, and textile businesses.[47] In 1930 only 2.83 percent of the state's population were engaged in industrial activities, most in small artisanal concerns.[48] But during the 1920s Oaxaca saw rapid growth in commercial agriculture in the ex-district of Tuxtepec. Although commercial banana production was initiated in the area in 1909, it was not until 1923 that the big American tropical fruit companies arrived.[49] They were Frutera Transcontinental, Cuyamel, and the Mexican American Fruit and Steamship Company (a conglomeration of the Standard Fruit and Steamship and the Di Giorgio Fruit companies).[50] First, they took advantage of the relatively low price of land in the area, buying up a series of fincas in Tuxtepec and Veracruz.[51] Next they offered landholders in the region loans of between five hundred and fifty thousand pesos to begin growing bananas.[52] The companies then signed contracts with these private producers, exporting the fruit through the "noisy banana center" of El Hule (later renamed Papaloapan), situated where the Veracruz-Isthmus railway crossed the Papaloapan River.[53] The results of the campaign were impressive, tying in much of the land and many of the economic elite of the region as well as attracting investors from the United States, Cuba, Spain, and the United Kingdom. For example, in 1926 revolutionary generals Juan Andrew Almazán, Rodolfo Torreblanco, and Isaac M. Ibarra formed the company Fomento de Tuxtepec with a capital of fifty-one thousand pesos. They used the money to buy the 19,350-hectare Hacienda Santa Rosa. Also in 1926 the representative of Standard Fruit argued that through national and foreign investment the area had been transformed into an "agricultural center of enormous importance," second in Mexico only to La Laguna.[54] By 1929 there were forty fincas devoted to banana production in the ex-district of Tuxtepec.[55] The agricultural census of 1930 estimated that there were 6,330 hectares in Oaxaca devoted to banana production. These produced 2,398,215 pesos per year. Only Tabasco and Veracruz produced more.[56]

Given the relatively small scale of industry in the state, there was little union activity during the mid-1920s, and for the most part it was restricted to the Confederación Regional de Obreros Mexicanos (CROM). The Department of Work registered twelve unions in Oaxaca in 1926, all of them CROM, seven located in Tuxtepec, four in Salina Cruz, and one in Oaxaca City.[57] Relations soured over the next four years as the CROM backed a series of strikes against local capitalists.[58] In particular, Enrique Martínez, the regional leader of the CROM, encouraged strikes throughout the Tuxtepec region by peasants and transport workers.[59] At the end of 1926, Pedro J. Parachini, the representative of the American banana companies in Mexico, complained that Martínez's unionization project was starting to cause serious problems. Workers had slandered supervisors, refused to turn up to work, and were charging the companies high tariffs. Parachini ended his letter with the question: "What could be the end if the unions continue to impose their wishes?" In case the Oaxaca governor was in any doubt, Parachini proceeded to answer, threatening that "it is indubitable that my bosses will not look upon this with favorable eyes and perhaps will close their businesses." He reminded Vásquez that such an outcome would cause the country and the tax coffers of Oaxaca to lose "millions of dollars."[60] The threat of the loss of tax revenue was particularly pertinent given that the state's economy was in "permanent crisis."[61] Over the next eight years, and especially after the devastating earthquake of 1931, all public policy, especially that directed at campesinos and workers, would be influenced by the parlous condition of state finances.[62] The maintenance of a stable tax income from principal sources such as Tuxtepec banana growers, Pochutla coffee *finqueros*, and limited industrial concerns influenced the breadth and depth of state radicalism.[63] In this case, the Oaxaca government responded by regularly placing pressure on the CROM, allowing hacendados and local authorities to attack their members and backing "free workers" linked to the CPSO, but at the same time taking care not to meet Calles's pet labor organization in open hostility.[64]

By 1929 the favorable central government attitudes to the CROM had changed because of the suspicions raised by Obregón's assassination.[65] The CROM organizations were met by a more aggressive attitude on the part of López Cortés's government.[66] The Oaxaca government was also keen to stamp out the influence of increasing Veracruz radicalism, which by 1929 had infiltrated Oaxaca.[67] Central to this new stance was the creation of a statewide labor organization, the Confederación de Ligas Socialistas de Oaxaca (CLSO). With the neighboring states of Puebla in the hands of the CROM and Veracruz under the sway of the agrarian leagues of Governor Adalberto Tejeda, Calles was probably grateful for a worker confederation with no national agenda.[68] The CLSO was founded on 29 June 1929 and was headed by the Jesús Gonthier, a labor organizer from Salina Cruz.[69] Over the next six months the confederation gradually absorbed the CROM unions. In Tuxtepec, the inspector of work, Jorge López, drew groups into the CLSO-linked Federación Tuxtepecana de Obreros y Campesinos (FTOC). The Tuxtepec chamber of commerce drew up an exclusive contract with the FTOC, and all strikes by CROM unions were declared illegal.[70] By the end of 1929, in an interview with Calles, López Cortés asserted that "the banana industry should start to produce enormous crops next year as the state is enjoying absolute calm."[71] By January 1930 the FTOC included twenty-three unions.[72] Over the next four years, the CLSO set up regional branches throughout the state. For the most part they consisted of rural workers involved in commercial agriculture in the Isthmus, La Cañada, and the Central Valleys.[73] By 1934 the CLSO claimed control over 112 unions and 8,901 members in four separate federations.[74]

For the duration of Chicolopista rule, the CLSO acted to diffuse labor problems and create a clientele of rural workers. The birth of the CLSO allowed the regime to enact some overt displays of radicalism. According to Jesús Gonthier, owing to the efforts of López Cortés and his supporters, Oaxaca was "not now a sterile area for unions as many claimed." Later that month at the celebration of the creation of the Unión de Oficios Varios in Oa-xaca City, the governor "sw[ore] an oath to the organized worker for the cause of the Revolution and the proletariat."[75] Both López Cortés and his chosen successor, García Toledo, were present at CLSO-organized May Day celebrations and conferences on workers in the palm industry.[76] However, López Cortés was mindful of the differing audiences for demonstrations and published pronouncements. As a result, he was careful not to drive away the few investors in Oaxaca by overtly radical printed assertions. Like Calles, he often tended to emphasize a balance between the

interests of labor and capital. In his report of 1931, López Cortés averred that his government was "not full of intemperance in
its natural relations with capital, nor is it a party of demagogical
and violent agitation."[77]

Yet the Potemkin village of measured rhetorical radicalism could
not hem in agricultural workers of its own accord. First, the CLSO
employed local caciques as heads of its member leagues to settle potential conflicts. Most notably, the confederation employed
Manuel Martínez Ramírez as head of the FTOC. Martínez Ramírez
had been both judge and tax collector in the region, and by 1930
he was also municipal president of Tuxtepec and head of the *defensa social*.[78] In La Cañada the local strongman and head of the
defensa social, Tiburcio Cuellar, was also appointed to manage
the local labor unions.[79] Second, the CLSO also mediated in the
creation of a series of collective contracts between hacendados
and workers during the period. At least on paper these seemed to
aid Oaxaca's agricultural workers. The contracts that the CLSO
drew up offered workers fixed minimum salaries, a day of rest
per week, indemnification in case of accidents, and eight-hour
days.[80] They seem to have been greeted with enthusiasm by most
workers and enforced intermittently, at least in the sugar mills
of La Cañada, the banana plantations of Tuxtepec, and the haciendas of the Central Valleys, where labor agitation had been at
its most virulent.[81] In fact, by 1933 some fincas were paying harvest workers up to nineteen pesos per week.[82] However the in-
spiration for these contracts was stability and economic growth
rather than social reform.[83] If capital was threatened, the contracts
would be negotiated or ignored altogether. In 1933 the FTOC allowed the owners of the Arroyo Culebra finca to pay workers
1.25 pesos a day rather than the required 1.50 because of the destruction wrought by strong winds.[84] Incoming investors in the

banana boom were allowed to forsake the contracts during the initial years.[85] Furthermore, since the contracts were conceived as political instruments of appeasement rather than as ideologically necessary weapons of class warfare, they were not extended to the state's less agitated areas of commercial agriculture, such as Jamiltepec, Pochutla, and Choapam. Marjorie Clark recounts the response of an American landowner from one of these regions of Oaxaca. When asked how it was possible to work his "people" such long hours and pay them less than fifty centavos a day, he replied, "Oh, they haven't yet learned that there is a labor law, and I hope they don't hear of it soon."[86]

López Cortés formed the CLSO in order to wrest control of the industrial and agrarian workers of the Central Valleys, La Cañada, the Isthmus, and above all Tuxtepec from the CROM, to prevent them from falling under the influence of the increasingly radical Tejedista leagues of Veracruz, and to secure the support of the state's economic elite. Taking advantage of the growing distance between Calles and the CROM after 1928, his regime brought its former members under CLSO control and expanded the confederation's control into other areas of commercial agricultural production. Continuing CLSO hegemony depended on López Cortés's monopoly of rhetorical radicalism, alliances with local caciques, and the offer of favorable if intermittently enforced collective contracts.

Landowners, Agrarian Reform, and the Confederación Oaxaqueña de Campesinos

Oaxaca did not have a unified tradition of land reform during the Revolution, although there were isolated calls for redistribution in areas of the Mixteca, the coast, and the Central Valleys. The

1930 agricultural census confirms that the extensive small hold-ings and communal lands of the Mixteca and the Sierra Juárez coexisted with large landholdings in the Central Valleys, Tuxte-pec, the Isthmus, and the coastal region. It was estimated that over 30 percent of the state's lands were held in 423 properties of between one thousand and ten thousand hectares. A further 91 properties occupied another 40 percent of Oaxaca's territory.[87] Governors Manuel García Vigil, Onofre Jiménez, and Genaro V. Vásquez had done little to change the situation. They had pre-sided over resolutions that offered 36,947 hectares to 12,352 *ejidatarios*.[88] Yet the same administrations actually denied 59 of the 123 requests for land, claiming either that there was no avail-able land or that the pueblos already had enough.[89] The location of the land grants revealed the overtly political impetus of Oa-xaca's *agrarismo*, as they were mapped upon areas of past or po-tential conflict. Nearly 90 percent of the ejidos were in the dis-tricts of the Central Valleys.[90] They reflected the momentum given to *agrarismo* in the area by the constitutionalist governments, the legacy of Angel Barrios's revolutionary movement, and the rel-atively low productivity of the region's haciendas.[91] The district outside the Central Valleys that received the most ejidos in the period, Huajuapam, had been the scene of Zapatista incursions during the Revolution and by 1926 was on the verge of joining the Cristero revolt.[92] Moreover, the lands donated were hardly ec-onomically or politically significant, coming from an abandoned hacienda and a society of small property owners.[93] Last, the geog-raphy of land redistribution reflected the state government's need for taxes from areas of commercial agriculture such as Tuxtepec and Pochutla and for armed support from the campesinos near-est to the administrative seat of Oaxaca City.

As López Cortés was reliant on the collaboration and taxation of the elite, he also maintained a similar policy of tacit support for hacendados and of expedient, poor quality land grants directed at loyal supporters. Like many Callistas, López Cortés himself was no stranger to the attractions of large landholding. According to his accusers, he acquired the Hacienda de Dolores in the ex-district of the Centro through threats of expropriation.[94] Although occasionally carried away on the gusts of avant-garde grandiloquence and promising that there was "no justifiable reason for the disequilibrium in land distribution," he was usually more conservative in his public statements.[95] Before the first local peasant conference in 1932 he reassured landowners that "its function is not to pit campesino against landowner but to produce mutual understanding of each other's duties."[96]

In order to limit the redistribution of land, the governor appointed a series of former Porfirian functionaries and members of the *vallistocracia* to the local agrarian commission, such as Demetrio Bolaños Cacho and Guillermo Rosas Solaegui, "a very popular violinist and composer . . . but a very bad employee of the agrarian bureaucracy."[97] He appears to have allowed hacendados to continue to intimidate, beat, and kill prospective *ejidatarios*, even permitting army officers to rent and guard large landholdings in the Central Valleys.[98] Finally, as governor and later as the power behind the throne, López Cortés maintained an unforgiving tax regime, which harshly penalized *ejidatarios*. From the start, the combination of state property taxes and federal taxes enforced by the Law of Ejidal Patrimony could cripple the funds of *ejidal* committees, especially after the revaluation of prospective ejidos in 1925.[99] Huge debts caused San Jacinto Chilateca and Santa Cruz Xoxocotlán in the Central Valleys to give up their ejidos.[100] Conflict was rampant, and within a few years so many ejido committees were behind in their tax payments and liable to the confiscation of their crops that the state government recognized the impossibility of executing the embargoes. As Buve argues for Tlaxcala, tax arrears were then used by the state government to "enforce loyalty at the village level" and create a peasant clientele.[101] By October 1926 the treasury of the state was demanding debts of 25,600 pesos from the ejido of Villa Díaz Ordaz, Ocotlán. Over the next three years the campesinos paid off some debts, but others mounted. Eventually, in 1929, the government made clear that it was doing the ejido a great favor and reduced the arrears to 12,600 pesos.[102]

Although López Cortés's attitude to land reform was for the most part expressed in negative terms, he never turned off the tap of *agrarismo* completely, like many of his ultracallista colleagues.[103] Depending on which figures one believes, presidential resolutions granting land from 1928 to 1934 totaled somewhere between 112,717 and 142,059 hectares. This was a 300 percent increase on the land distributed in the previous eight years.[104] The land was still poor quality, and 68 percent of it was uncultivable.[105] Nevertheless, the actual land grants reflected a governmental program that amplified the political potential of *agrarismo* into the provincial hinterlands. Between 1928 and 1934 the local agrarian commission made fifty-six provisional decisions.[106] Nine were negative and protected the lands of powerful members of the international economic elite in the state.[107] Six affirmative provisional resolutions in the Central Valleys disclose a continuation of previous state government strategy. However, the twenty-seven resolutions from Miahuatlán, the Mixteca, and Juchitán reveal a more expansive policy of land distribution. As will become clear, many districts of Oaxaca were run by local caciques, and López Cortés was forced either to come to some arrangement with them or to attempt to dislodge them. *Agrarismo* became an element of this policy. Thus the men of the four ejidos created in Miahuatlán formed the *defensa social* of Chicolopista cacique, Genaro Ramos. The nine ejidos created in Juchitán in 1930 were a response to a recent rebellion in the name of local cacique, Heliodoro Charis, and added to the clientele of the leader of the loyal red party, Francisco López Cortés's brother, Artemio.[108]

By 1932 national and local circumstances forced López Cortés into an agrarian policy that went beyond targeted land grants. At the national level the creation of the Confederación Oaxaqueña de Campesinos (COC) was part of a broad ultracallista effort to avoid the extremes of the Tejedista Liga Nacional Campesina "Ursulo Galván" (LNCUG) or the growing ambit of the break-off LNCUG of Enrique Flores Magón and Graciano Sánchez.[109] On the local level the porous border between Veracruz and Oaxaca, which allowed the intrusion of both LNCUGs and a broader socialism, had led to increasing agitation for land among the campesinos of Tuxtepec.[110] By January 1932 the local agrarian commission had ninety-four requests for ejidos in the district and had resolved only one of these. Finally, López Cortés was evidently keen to unite the disparate campesino clients he had created during his governorship before the handover of power in 1932. The COC was founded at the first *ejidal* congress held between 6 and 11 January 1932. Reports from the peasant congresses flaunted the COC's twin ideals of control and increased economic production. López Cortés, in his invitation to the first meeting, stressed the "pressing public need" for "the destiny of agrarian reform in the state of Oaxaca [to be] delineated by sure and well-defined norms." Rather than leaving agrarian reform "to the mercy of the more or less occasional interests of militant politics," it was necessary for the state to "impress on the aborigines a full, sincere and firm vision of the authentic ideal." The constitution of the new organization made the permanent executive committee responsible for policy, membership, and all dialogue with outside organizations.[111] The delegates and the elections to executive posts in the confederation reflected its paternalistic nature. Although the first congress saw many genuine campesino delegates, predominantly representing loyal ejidos from the Central Valleys, by the second congress López Cortés had initiated a more comprehensive but less democratic system of representation. Jesús Ramírez Vásquez was delegate for seven separate coastal pueblos, and Alejandro Ceja C. represented four Tuxtepec agrarian committees. As a result, by 1934 the organization claimed control of 43,954 campesinos in 457 separate groups.[112]

In many ways the Chicolopista agrarian policy followed that of his predecessors. There were minimal land grants, and support, tacit or otherwise, was offered to large landowners, especially in the most productive agricultural zones. At the same time some ejidos were formed in order to offer a peasant clientele to loyal caciques. But by 1932 the pressure on land in Tuxtepec, both from the bottom up and from the top down in the form of the two LNCUGs, had become critical. López Cortés was forced into forming another corporatist organization, which, like the CLSO, attempted to control its members through radicalized political oratory and theatre, the absorption of relevant groups, and their regimentation under bureaucratic or local cacique representatives.

The Chicolopista Caciques

The members of the upper echelons of Oaxaca's corporatist machinery were directly linked to López Cortés. Some were members of the *vallistocracia* and former classmates from the ICA.[113] Some were close associates from the red party of the Isthmus.[114] Others came from outside the state, and others still were provincial academics who had vacated Oaxaca during the Revolution.[115] When they arrived in Oaxaca, all lacked a genuine popular base or support in the federal bureaucracy and rather relied for their position on the backing of the state caudillo. However, outside the Central Valleys, the Isthmus, and the plantations of Tuxtepec and La Cañada, the centralizing corporatist arrangement of the Chicolopista government did not hold. Only 11 percent of the CLSO and 30 percent of the COC came from outside these zones.[116] Thus, instead of attempting to assert corporatist control and its attendant personnel in remaining areas of the state, López Cortés, like his predecessor, left dominance of the economic periphery to an assortment of local caciques. As one opposition pamphlet decried, the public administration really "defends its policies and makes its dictatorship felt by means of the caciques and the *defensas sociales* that are loyal instruments of official Machiavellianism."[117] This section introduces and explains the Chicolopista caciques, their origins, backgrounds, and means of control and starts to sketch a typology of postrevolutionary rural *caciquismo*.

As table 1 demonstrates, control of the *cabeceras* of the ex-districts was crucial for the smooth running of the Chicolopista government, and most caciques were located in or around these administrative centers. However, there were exceptions. The power of Daniel Martínez, cacique of the Mixe-speaking area of the ex-districts of Villa Alta, Yautepec, Tehuantepec, and Choapam, was

63

Table 1. Strongmen of Oaxaca, 1920s

Area of influence	Caciques
Pochutla	Francisco Ramos Ortiz
Miahuatlán	Genaro Ramos
Ixtlán	Onofre Jiménez, Isaac M. Ibarra
Jamiltepec	Juan José Baños
Juxtlahuaca	Librado and Celestino Guzmán, Josefino Feria
Juchitán (from San Jerónimo Ixtepec)	Artemio López Cortés
Huajuapam	Rodolfo Solana Carrion, José Peral Martínez
Ejutla	Andrés Elorza
Tuxtepec	Francisco Moreno Z.
Putla	Isidro Montesinos López
Teotitlán del Camino	Tiburcio Cuellar
Ocotlán	Angel Trapaga
Villa Alta (from Villa Hidalgo Yalalag)	Ezequiel Santillán, Enrique Valle
Mixe Region (from Ayutla)	Daniel Martínez
Nochixtlán	Luis M. Avendano
Yautepec	Celestino Ruíz

Note: This is not a complete list of the caciques in Oaxaca. On the one hand, as Gilbert Joseph makes clear, the discovery, naming, and shaming of caciques is a difficult business. It is undeniable that some caciques (in Tlaxiaco, Juquila, or Choapam, for example) have been missed, owing to their ability to remain below the radar. On the other hand, the caciques listed were certainly not of equal political or military importance. However, all come up with some frequency in the sources, all are periodically described as caciques, and something at least is known about their means of control.
Source: Joseph, *Revolution from Without.*

THE CAUDILLO AND THE STATE

delimited by ethnic rather than political boundaries. (This would change in 1938 with the creation of the administrative unit of the Región Mixe.) In Juchitán and Villa Alta, the *cabeceras* were controlled by opposition caciques, and the Chicolopistas were forced to base themselves in other towns.

Although the origins and backgrounds of Oaxaca's caciques were extremely diverse, patterns do emerge. As James B. Greenberg has argued, the nature of individual rural *cacicazgos* sprang from the ethnic and socioeconomic geography of the particular area. Although there was considerable variation within this framework (see chapter 5), *cacicazgos* in Oaxaca broadly developed along two lines. On the one hand, there were the Indian or mestizo leaders of predominantly indigenous areas, where communal landholding remained. On the other, there were the Hispanic caciques of regions where sharp ethnic divisions and/or commercial agriculture had been introduced in the Porfiriato and had been maintained in the postrevolutionary period.[118] Emblematic of the first group was Daniel Martínez, the son of a Mixe trader from San Pedro y San Pablo Ayutla, Villa Alta. According to anthropologist Ralph L. Beals, Martínez left the town in the late Porfiriato to follow the same career as his father. When he returned during the Revolution, his ease with Spanish, Mixe, and possibly Zapotec meant he "had a technique for dealing with the problems of the outside world." In 1914, the Soberanista government made him head of the *defensa social* in the region. For the next decade he would use his indigenous fighters in support of the Sovereignty movement and its Ixtlán leaders, Isaac M. Ibarra and Onofre Jiménez. In 1923, he helped the former members of the movement defeat Governor García Vigil, leading three hundred Mixes down from the sierra to the Isthmus.[119]

Not all of Oaxaca's caciques were indigenous or founded their power on the postrevolutionary mix of militarism, charisma, and intermediation. Many were of Hispanic origin and had their roots in ethnic conflict and the landholding regime of the Porfiriato. During the colonial period, Jamiltepec had been a predominantly Mixtec region with a smattering of Afro-Mexican communities. However during the Porfiriato, mestizo and Hispanic landholders started to penetrate the region and establish a network of large livestock farms.[120] Tensions between the recent arrivals and the indigenous majority framed the formation of the local *cacicazgo*. Juan José Baños of Jamiltepec was a mestizo and a Porfirian land-owner, who possessed the cattle hacienda of La Noria near Santiago Pinotepa Nacional. He was appointed Maderista *jefe político* of the district of Jamiltepec in 1911, the same year he crushed the chiliastic and agrarian Mixtec revolt in the region. Over the next decade Afro-Mexicans, forces from his La Noria estate, and the haciendas of the Del Valle, Gómez, and Pérez clans fought against the Mixtec inhabitants of the Costa Chica. In 1920 he joined the Agua Prieta revolt and was rewarded for his services with the position of brigadier general and recognition of his ownership of the coastal haciendas of Tamarindo, Yatacu, and Tuzucua.[121] Prudent alliances established to protect large properties and commercial fincas against indigenous insurgencies also allowed the establishment of the *cacicazgos* of Rodolfo Solana Carrion, José Peral Martínez, Francisco Moreno Z., Angel Trapaga, and Francisco Ramos Ortiz in Huajuapam, Pochutla, Ocotlán, and Tuxtepec, respectively.[122]

While substantial differences existed between the individual caciques, all utilized certain common means of control. With their origins in the violence of the Revolution, it is unsurprising that the key method was armed force. In 1933, the commander of the military zone, Maximino Avila Camacho, claimed that there were 1,227 members of the *defensas sociales* in the state.[123] They were intended to combat Oaxaca's endemic banditry as well as the periodic outbreaks of Cristero violence in the Sierra Madre del Sur.[124] The extent of the defense network in the state is testament to the number of minor caciques in the regions. However, it was clear that some commanders possessed considerably more force than others. On average a village *defensa social* had about five or six members, but Daniel Martínez and Genaro Ramos were each in charge of thirty-one armed men, Francisco Ramos Ortiz twenty-four, Enrique Valle twenty-three, and Angel Trapaga eighteen.[125] Although the *defensas* concentrated on the policing of the *cabeceras*, they were often based on rural properties nearby. Ramos Ortiz's band was based in Chacalapa, twelve kilometers from San Pedro Pochutla, while Ramos's so-called *cuerudos* settled on the ejidos of Hacienda San Nicolas, Rancho Lachidoblas, and Rancho San Bernardo.[126]

The Chicolopista *cacicazgo* system was not merely a network of armed thugs. Many caciques bolstered their armed support through their appointment to important official and unofficial regional offices and their control of local political posts. José Peral Martínez was municipal president of San Juan Bautista Huajuapam de León from 1932 to 1934; Moreno Z. was the state tax collector and then federal deputy in Tuxtepec.[127] Francisco Ramos Ortiz was not only head of the *defensa social* but also school inspector and steward of the roads.[128] Local political dominance was complemented by networks of allies and kinsmen in representative positions in the state and national capitals. In fact, the entire Chicolopista regime was founded on this format. While

Francisco López Cortés controlled the state machinery, his brother Artemio, "el Gobernador Chiquito del Istmo," controlled the red faction in the Isthmus from the family base of San Jerónimo Ixtepec. When Francisco stepped down, the former governor was appointed senator.[129] Other camarillas divided into political and military control. In Villa Alta, Valle's military supremacy was backed by Santillán's position as local deputy for the area. Outside the appointments to state positions and the *cabeceras*, caciques used client networks in the surrounding villages to maintain political power.

The nature and function of their client base depended on the historical formation of the particular region. In the Sierra Juárez, Isaac Ibarra and Onofre Jiménez built their client networks on former Soberanista soldiers. Many young soldiers returned to their pueblos after the Revolution to find political opportunity blocked by the cargo system. This static political arrangement, which reserved high office for elder members of the municipality who had already completed more onerous community tasks, chafed against the social mobility and generational independence of the Sovereignty movement army. At first, the support of the district caciques was fundamental to the young soldiers overturning the system and imposing more "democratic" elections.[130] However in Jamiltepec, Juan José Baños relied on the maintenance of tradition and links with village elders for political hegemony. An alliance with the local clergy, which was traditionally responsible for the appointing of the *mandones* or elders in each village, allowed him to dominate the municipal councils.[131]

As Keith Brewster argues, in many *cacicazgos*, force and political monopoly could not function without the general tacit acceptance of the population. In fact, "the very survival of the *cacicazgo* depended upon striking a balance between cooperation and coercion."[132] Although the use of *defensas* to suppress banditry and the critical intermediation of caciques in political disputes may have persuaded some villagers of the efficacy and stability of the cacique arrangement, this was often not enough.[133] The more populist caciques in the Sierra Juárez, Sierra Sur, and Isthmus were obliged to offer locals some of the fruits of the revolutionary bounty. In Oaxaca, *agrarismo* was not the key for cacique support as it had been for the Princes of Naranja described by Paul Friedrich.[134] It was used sparingly by Ramos and López Cortés to ensure a loyal client base in Miahuatlán and Juchitán respectively. But more commonly, like Barrios in the Sierra Norte of Puebla, caciques promoted the advantages of infrastructure and education. Martínez built a telephone line connecting Oaxaca and San Pedro y San Pablo Ayutla, built sixteen kilometers of road from San Pablo Mitla toward the Sierra, and encouraged the pursuit of education among both young and old.[135] Although these efforts were designed for the public good and in general received the approval of the local population, this was not their only function. As Eric Wolf and Guillermo de la Peña argue, the cacique as a political and cultural intermediary was, by necessity, Janus-faced, "able to operate both in terms of community-oriented and nation-oriented expectations."[136] Thus the pursuit of roads and schools appeased not only the local client network but also the state and federal governments. This instrumentalist pursuit of dual objectives often led to contradictions. *Tequio*, or collective communal labor, was one such controversial issue.[137] The government often praised the use of *tequio* for communally beneficial projects. But Martínez's employment of huge numbers of Mixe residents to carve out the road and carry a Chevrolet van over the mountains to San Pedro y San Pablo Ayutla caused considerable ill-feeling among his constituents.[138]

In exchange for the maintenance of relative military and political stability the caciques were permitted a degree of independence from federal or state interference. As Gilbert Joseph shows in Yucatán, on an individual level, caciques could avoid state tax laws and antimonopoly measures to amass huge fortunes.[139] According to reliable sources as well as the accusations of his political enemies, Francisco Moreno Z. maintained a liquor and cigarette monopoly in Tuxtepec and obtained the Santa Rosa, Las Carolinas, Vista Hermosa, Malzaga, San José del Río, and El Cantón fincas through the judicious employment of tax embargoes.[140] Among those areas of Oaxaca dominated by caciques of a less populist bent, this autonomy also allowed the continuation of more generalized "Porfirian" resource distribution, working practices, and control mechanisms. In fact these inequalities were key to the control exerted by this type of cacique, acting as substitutes for the incentive-based arrangement of the more revolutionary strongmen. Cacique rule, with politics mediated through ties of kinship and corruption, permitted the persistence of huge landholdings in Jamiltepec such as the Río Verde hacienda of Damaso Gómez and the enormous Río Grande hacienda of Alfredo and Eleazar del Valle.[141]

The continued misery of the campesino class may have been a small price to pay for stability for a man of questionable socialist beliefs such as López Cortés. In contrast, displays of autonomy that reflected badly on his governorship in front of the federal government forced him into negotiations with his camarilla of local strongmen. The more flagrant displays of violence or blatant infringements of the federal laws over religion and education were embarrassing and often obliged López Cortés to utilize the type of gentle political persuasion employed by his predecessor, Genaro V. Vásquez.[142] In late 1933 the education inspector of Miahuatlán, Benjamín Ramírez, started a Jacobin campaign of anticlericalism in his school zone. He attempted to create village "defanaticization" groups, lectured on the reactionary nature of the Catholic Church, and instituted federal lay teaching in the local schools. At first the program was a disaster. The clergy and the local cacique, Genaro Ramos, opposed the campaign, and, according to teachers from the Secretaría de la Educación Pública (SEP), municipal authorities were trying either to turn federal schools back into municipal foundations or to abolish them completely. By June 1934 the tension was so great that the state government was forced to broker an agreement between Ramos and the SEP. The local cacique was to break with the clergy in exchange for the guarantee of his economic and political interests. Ramírez promised that the social labor in Miahuatlán "should not hurt the personal interests of Genaro Ramos" as long as Ramos himself "did not interfere in the schools as the people must be freed from the great enemies of collective progress: fanaticism and illiteracy."[143]

Although it is widely acknowledged that caciques and their "linkages of clientelism, friendship, and party loyalty came to form the backbone of the regime's capacity to govern rural Mexico during most of the twentieth century," studies of cacique networks are rare indeed.[144] Those that have been undertaken have concentrated on areas where caciques have become part of social movements or postrevolutionary corporatist, agrarian arrangements, rather than patterns of conservative governance.[145] In fact during the Maximato, in areas where social reform and corporatist control were limited, state government was also forced to decentralize and rely on an array of local caciques. Their style of administration and the state leader's ability to negotiate with them hinged upon the historical formation of socioeconomic and ethnic relations in the respective regions. Some were indigenous or mestizo revolutionary leaders, who built on the loyalty and connections constructed during the Oaxaca Sovereignty movement. They continued to demand the constancy of their districts through armed force, political support, and schemes of modernization. Others were Porfirian landowners and merchants, whose power emerged from ethnic tensions and an alliance of the elite and client laborers. Although they also sought support from military might and political imposition, this relied on the preservation rather than the undermining of the status quo. Because of his dependence on these personalist forms of governance and the support of the Callista regime, López Cortés was forced to maintain the equilibrium between cacique independence and the imposition of state policy. In the zones controlled by the economic elite, this was relatively painless, and administrative autonomy was limited to the preservation of unequal land tenure, mercantile monopoly, and personal enrichment. However, in zones where caciques relied more on democratic and populist support, he was forced to undertake more complex negotiations.

Conclusion

How did this initial stage of postrevolutionary state formation enacted by López Cortes compare to the systems established by his Maximato peers? Two issues are of particular relevance: the relative radicalism of the arrangement and its independence from the central state. Despite the national government's retreat from land and labor reform during the Maximato, there was plenty of room for regional variation.[146] A handful of state leaders, such as Adalberto Tejeda and Lázaro Cárdenas, seem to have been convinced *agraristas*, believers in the economic efficacy and redemptive quality of the ejido.[147] Other state leaders, such as Saturnino Cedillo, Emilio Portes Gil, and Saturnino Osornio, distributed large amounts of land for predominantly political ends, either as a postrevolutionary palliative or in order to create a support network of campesino leagues.[148] Although governors' attitudes to labor reform have been less studied than their positions on *agrarismo*, and the existence of the national labor organizations often limited state involvement in the area, it remained an important aspect of their policies. During the 1920s some governors of the more industrially advanced areas of Mexico, such as José Guadalupe Zuno, at first saw widespread labor reforms as a means to cement the adherence of the urban populations.[149] Although Chicolopista policies did not amount to the radicalism of the more renowned caudillos, they were not as openly anti-*agrarista* as those of Victorio R. Grajales in Chiapas or Vicente Estrada Cajigal in Morelos, or as antilabor as those of Cedillo.[150] In the areas of productive commercial agriculture, they mirrored the practices of state leaders such as Carlos Riva Palacio in Mexico, Luis L. León in Chihuahua, and Raymundo Enríquez in Chiapas.[151] Like López Cortés, these men limited land and labor reform in their regions and tacitly supported most industrialists and hacendados. In return they expected the backing of these local elites. However they also instituted a defensive radicalism. Thus they attempted to monopolize the radical rhetoric of land and labor reform, organizing May Day celebrations and campesino congresses and repeatedly referring to the revolutionary roots of their regime. In so doing they could marginalize all

73

opposition as "reactionary," irrespective of their political agendas.[152] At the same time they utilized some partial reforms. The imposition of collective contracts was designed to "minimize the worker-boss conflict" and maintain the status quo.[153] *Ejidal* grants acted to dispel loci of radicalism and then co-opt peasants and workers into state-sponsored patron-client relationships. Outside the Central Valleys and Tuxtepec, the relative state of reform depended on the historical formation of the local *cacicazgos*. Where indigenous or mestizo caciques held sway, changes were offered in return for military and political loyalty. In areas of persistent ethnic or socioeconomic inequality, all improvements were aggressively discouraged, as the caciques depended on prerevolutionary political structures and working patterns.

Although the Chicolopista regime appeared to follow the Callista political and ideological template, did its corporatist formation offer any degree of independence from the PNR and the central state? According to Voss, "the state level, controlled by the military commanders and governors, quickly became the zone of transition and conflict between two contrary forms of political functioning."[154] The support networks of some caudillos, such as Saturnino Cedillo and Adalberto Tejeda, did offer a degree of autonomy for their leaders.[155] Heather Fowler-Salamini has recently argued that even Portes Gil's local party in Tamaulipas was marked by a decided regionalism.[156] Other state leaders, such as Saturnino Osornio and Lázaro Cárdenas, balanced strong local support with unfailing loyalty to the Jefe Máximo. In contrast, López Cortés's transparent radicalism and lack of popular roots did not offer him a firm enough base to assert any measure of real autonomy, although certain aspects of Oaxaqueñismo offered at least the potential for voicing cultural resistance. Furthermore the actual formation of the corporatist organizations was based on the pursuit of (ultra) Callista aims and means, whether it was the organization of regional parties, the regimentation of elections, estrangement from the CROM, or the alienation of the LNCUG. In fact, as regards the Oaxacan corporatist arrangement, it is worth remembering Salvador Maldonaldo Aranda's assertion that "the centrifugal forces that allow political centralism to consolidate come not only from the principal national elites but also from the ends of regional interests to negotiate spaces at the interior of the political regime."[157]

However, two aspects of the Chicolopista system must be noted. First, although the tax-rich areas of the state were bound to the Chicolopista and Callista machinery, the economic periphery remained under the control of a congeries of independent local caciques. Like the *cacicazgo* of Porfirio Rubio in the Sierra Gorda, these remained on the edge of central and state control in return for the enforcement of relative stability.[158] Only when they offended notions of military or cultural control were they forced to bend toward the federal line. Second, although the corporatist organizations had relatively shallow roots and were linked to central state policy, they did offer the first genuine improvements in labor and agrarian practice. As a result, although the organizations of General Cárdenas would offer greater recompense in the long term, as the next chapter demonstrates, the CLSO and COC proved difficult to dislodge or dismantle.

THREE

The Rise of Cardenismo and the Decline of Chicolopismo, 1932–36

By 1933 Mexico had survived the worst of the world depression and the most serious of the military threats to the Callista government. However, at the political level it was far from stable. Despite the creation of the PNR, the regime was still riven by rivalries among regional and personalist factions.[1] Furthermore, the withdrawal from radical socioeconomic policy during the Maximato of Plutarco Elías Calles had not only opened up fresh fissures in the Mexican countryside but also focused debate over the direction of the Mexican Revolution, most notably during the formation of the Six-Year Plan in December 1933.[2] The decision to nominate Lázaro Cárdenas as presidential candidate for the PNR was an attempt to smooth over the emerging cracks in the regime, appease the Callista loyalists, assuage the demands of the radicals, and placate the wavering allegiances of regional strongmen.[3] However, despite Calles's intentions, over the next year, the new president became increasingly estranged from the Jefe Máximo. As Cárdenas encouraged an increasing rhythm of strikes and land expropriations, the alarmed bourgeoisie, confused foreign ambassadors, and angry ultracallistas demanded that Calles intervene.[4] Finally, on 12 June, Calles issued a "patriotic declaration" to the press, in which he strongly attacked the "marathon of radicalism" that the country had witnessed in recent months, adding, "To disturb the march of economic construction is not only ingratitude but treason." The next day governors, senators, and federal deputies queued up to congratulate the Jefe Máximo on his perspicacious and opportune intervention.[5] In the face of such opposition, Cárdenas looked doomed to follow the same path of conflict, rejection, and irrelevance as former president Pascual Ortiz Rubio.[6] Cárdenas survived in the short term by condemning Calles's interference as illegal, throwing his weight behind the actions of the labor and peasant organizations, and dismissing ultracallistas from his cabinet and the higher echelons of the PNR.[7] Over the next six months Cárdenas sought to build on this initial victory. Loyal generals were promoted at the expense of incumbent Calles supporters. Callistas were also purged from the party and the agrarian organizations.[8] At the same time Cárdenas solicited the support of the labor organizations, which formed the Comité Nacional de Defensa Proletaria, and the peasant leagues, which he asked to unite under the banner of the Confederación Campesina Mexicana (CCM).[9] When Calles declared that Cárdenas intended to "carry the country to Communism" in December 1935, he was met by a more muscular presidential machine. By April 1936, Calles's position had become untenable, and he was forced to leave the country.[10]

During the period 1933–35 the drama of national affairs mapped itself upon local politics in Oaxaca. At first the presidential campaign offered political space to opponents of López Cortés's regime. During the late 1920s and early 1930s López Cortés had been able to repress resistance through a mixture of political maneuvers, sponsored violence, and central government support. However, by 1933 the disparate adversaries were able to solidify around new national political movements. While bureaucrats, campesinos, and small-time agrarian caciques drifted into the local branch of the CCM, out-of-favor caciques and minority groups pressing for socioeconomic reform outside Tuxtepec and the Central Valleys sought protection under the broad umbrella of the Cardenista presidential campaign. By December 1934 Oaxaca was split between Chicolopistas and an unwieldy coalition of ideologues, opportunists, and estranged campesinos, who looked to the new president for political guidance and support. When Cárdenas took power, the CCM's promises of quick land grants overcame the COC and the CLSO strategy of maintaining members' loyalty through clientelism, intimidation, and the imposition of collective contracts. With the eventual split at the national level in June 1935, hostilities continued in the countryside but also moved into the executive and legislative branches of state government as Cárdenas attempted to persuade the Callistas to shift loyalties. This caused a division within the Chicolopista political machinery and the eventual downfall of the Isthmus caudillo. But López Cortés's defeat did not lead to a radical overhaul of the state's governing personnel. As such, Cardenas's reluctance to engender wholesale change foreshadowed the concern for political stability that would mark his *sexenio*.

The Rise of the CCM and the Movement against the Chicopolista Organizations

Complaints over poor pay and government hypocrisy were a regular feature of the state bureaucracy of Oaxaca during the 1920s and 1930s. However, the agitation of government employees was not merely a Pavlovian response to a shortage of ready cash. By the early 1930s the unconcealed disjunction between Chicolopista rhetoric and practice had begun to cause disquiet among younger and more radical members of the administration. Carlos

Belleza, the attorney of pueblos in the state, would often voice his unease over the slow pace and inefficiency of *agrarismo*. In 1931 he inspected the recently donated ejido of Santa Cruz Tacache de Mina in Huajuapam. He reported back that the 587 hectares were "completely unsuitable for cultivation and even for the pasture of livestock." In fact all the good land had been left to the hacienda.[11] Although he was offered the political palliative of the position of secretary-general of the COC, he did not hesitate to criticize the nature of agrarian reform in Oaxaca. At the annual conference in January 1933 he argued that *agrarismo* had failed in the state owing to poor funding and the hypocrisy of certain executive members of the peasant organization.[12] Like members of the federal bureaucracy, teachers were also forced to reconcile the wretched reality of Oaxaca's rural life with their own ideals. Although there was a tendency to blame local caciques, landowners, and even campesinos themselves for the resistance to education, some began to question the state government's commitment to the national project. Professor Marciano Z. Martínez, after a disappointing 1932 visit to Chalcatongo de Hidalgo, Tlaxiaco, complained that "the governments of Oaxaca ha[d] not dedicated any interest to popular education" and so the indigenous people remained "as before the Revolution."[13]

While López Cortés could cope with isolated complaints and formless disquiet, the defection of a trio of his senior bureaucrats was more serious. In February 1931 the LNCUG split into a radical Tejedista group from Veracruz and a more moderate wing headed by *agraristas* affiliated with Lázaro Cárdenas and other regional caudillos. Although scholars have concentrated on the moderate organization's role in the elimination of the Tejedistas, the swing away from the *veteranos* in the capital, and the cooption of reformers in Michoacán, San Luis Potosí and Tamaulipas, it also served as a radical counterpoint to provincial, conservative peasant organizations.[14] In July 1932 the head of the CLSO, Jesús Gonthier, and two others members of the executive committee left the Chicolopista organization and formed the Oaxaca branch of the moderate LNCUG, called the Genuina Confederación de Ligas Socialistas de Oaxaca (GCLSO).[15] In February 1933 the GCLSO received the blessing of its parent organization in Veracruz. In May it joined the CCM, which had been formed from the moderate LNCUG in order to support Cárdenas's presidential candidacy.[16] However, the central government, under the sway of General Calles, still supported the Chicolopista organizations, and conflict between the organizations grew.[17]

At first, during 1933 when external support for the organization was limited, the GCLSO appears to have attracted groups of desperate, radicalized peasants, whose attempts to get land had been directly stifled by the targeted labor reform and *agrarismo* of the Chicolopista regime. Unsurprisingly it was particularly successful in the ex-district of Tuxtepec, where socioeconomic inequity was great, the political regime was repressive, and peasants were relatively aware of the new socialist doctrines.[18] In addition, support came from the moderate LNCUG leagues of Veracruz. For example, Las Carolinas in Tuxtepec had been directly affected by Chicolopista campesino policy. Under its previous owner, Juan Andrew Almazán, the workers had achieved a favorable regime, including a wage of two pesos a day, healthcare, and education. To cut costs, the new proprietors, Mexican businessmen José G. de la Lama and Raúl A. Basurto, offered employment to the workers of another of their fincas, the FTOC-affiliated Santa Rosa in San Lucas Ojitlán, rather than to the original inhabitants. In response, in January 1934 the unemployed Las Carolinas men linked up with the GCLSO.[19] By early 1934 Camelia Roja, Las Carolinas, San Silverio el Cedral, El Mirador, La Soledad, Santa Sofia, Monterrosa, and La Isla had all formed GCLSO-affiliated agrarian committees and sent in requests for land.[20] There were also GCLSO factions in La Laguna, San Lucas Ojitlán, and in Maravillas and La Junta, Acatlán de Pérez Figueroa. The Tuxtepec camarilla of merchants, landowners, and FTOC leaders led by federal deputy Francisco Moreno Z. suppressed the growing movement with a mixture of hired thugs, municipal authorities, police, federal troops, and members of the local federation.[21]

Despite the subjugation, the GCLSO survived into 1934. During this crucial year, it gained valuable support from disenfranchised Chicolopista caciques, agrarian authorities, and the local communist party. One such cacique was Daniel Muñoz Estefan, a merchant and a billiards hall owner from San Lucas Ojitlán and a member of the Tuxtepec chamber of commerce.[22] He displayed an obvious talent for the socialist sophistry of the era, writing an article defending the chamber from charges of conservatism. As unions protected workers from exploitation, the chamber was formed to defend the interests of capital "big and small."[23] Although Muñoz Estefan was indicted for wrongful dismissal in 1931, the following year he seems to have concluded that the best route to political advancement was involvement in the nascent Chicolopista mass organizations.[24] He became secretary of San Lucas Ojitlán's local labor court.[25] At the second COC congress in 1933, he represented the agrarian committees of San Lucas Ojitlán, San José Lagunas, and Cafetal Segundo and was voted onto the executive committee.[26] In the same year he was made municipal secretary of San Lucas Ojitlán. But divisions opened up between Muñoz Estefan and the camarilla of banana growers.[27] In particular he appears to have been frustrated by his failure to become federal deputy for the area, a role given to Francisco Moreno Z.[28] In March 1934 Muñoz Estefan swapped allegiances to the CCM and brought his extensive support network, including seven recently formed ejidos, into the new organization.[29] In San Juan Bautista Valle Nacional the local cacique, Mardino D. Sánchez, also saw the CCM as a means to attract support for his political aspirations. Sánchez had been removed from the town's governing group in the early 1930s.[30] Thus in order to "recapture his public posts," the cacique became CCM representative in San Juan Bautista Valle Nacional and the neighboring municipality of San Felipe Usila, promising followers "all the land of the rich landowners" and nonpayment of union quotas and taxes.[31]

Later that year López Cortés lost other key allies, arguably more for ideological than political reasons. In early 1934 the Mexican state created the Agrarian Department and charged its employees with organizing land distribution throughout the country. According to the British author Malcolm Lowry, who befriended one of the engineers of the Oaxaca Agrarian Department, they were committed and underpaid, if intemperate and occasionally overly macho.[32] The department employee Carlos Belleza had long criticized the nature of Oaxaca's land reform from within the COC. With the increasing power of the CCM, he saw a relatively radical, efficient, and national counterpoint to the regional organization. In June 1934 he left the COC and joined the CCM. He was joined by other members of the Agrarian Department, including the organizer of ejidos, Adan Ramírez López; the attorney of pueblos, Ismael Velasco; and Rosendo Reyes and Adalberto Vélez.[33] Finally, Graciano Benitez, head of the Oaxacan branch of the Partido Comunista Mexicano (PCM), ignored the "heavenly certainties" of the national PCM's Stalinist ultra-leftism and turned instead to the "earthly realities" of Mexico's rural situation, allying with the CCM to militate for increased land distribution.[34] These three groups—disenfranchised caciques, employees of the Agrarian Department, and Communist Party members, formed the CCM's leadership during its initial years.

The growing defection from the Chicolopista ranks allowed the CCM to expand into other areas of campesino restlessness. In particular, Agrarian Department members traversed the state promising tangible and rapid rewards in exchange for a switch to the new confederation. In September 1934 Ismael Velasco visited prospective members in the ex-districts of Tlaxiaco, Ejutla, Zimatlán, and the Centro.[35] In January the CCM gained support in Tehuantepec; by June it had a significant presence in Tlacolula.[36] In Tuxtepec the support of Muñoz Estefan saw the organization penetrate deeper into the municipality of Tuxtepec and spread into the municipalities of San Pedro Ixcatlán, San Felipe Usila, San Lucas Ojitlán, San Miguel Soyaltepec, and San Felipe Jalapa de Díaz. By the end of the year he had formed a network of peasant leagues in Tuxtepec.[37] Again the agrarian committees that chose the CCM had been directly affected by the agrarian policy of the governing class. The inhabitants of Santa María Guelace, Tlacolula, had received the lands of the Hacienda de Los Negritos in 1921. But they were prevented from working the lands by the landowner and the neighboring village. The state government nevertheless ordered them to pay taxes on the ejido. In August 1934 they threw their lot in with the Oaxaca branch of the CCM.[38] An increased CCM presence led to an upsurge in requests for ejidos. Many of these were aimed at properties owned by key members of the Chicolopista regime. Confederation apparatchiks helped campesinos from Etla demand possession of López Cortés's Hacienda de Dolores and helped the villagers of Tapanala, Tehuantepec, fight for his finca, Elva.[39]

By the end of 1934 the Oaxacan branch of the CCM had gained considerable force in the state and corresponding support in the national arena. In October 1934 the GCLSO issued a statement of intent. This aimed to juxtapose the "situation of total abandonment and economic misery of our peasants" with the "luxury" enjoyed "by López Cortés and his band," and to attract support for the organization's first congress.[40] The pamphlet blended many of the common allegations of corruption and demagogy with demands for authentic displays of *agrarismo* and *indigenismo* and less reliance on an old guard of Porfirian functionaries. With its stress on the hypocrisy and moral bankruptcy of the old and the radicalism and purity of the new, it was redolent of much literature released in the early 1930s, which saw young, educated but excluded men challenge the sclerotic postrevolutionary order.[41] The so-called Worker-Campesino-Indigenous congress of the GCLSO was finally held from 25 to 27 December 1934. There were frequent accusations regarding the persecution of peasant representatives, but 276 men managed to attend the meeting.[42] The delegates decided on an executive committee consisting of men from the Agrarian Department and original followers of (the now dead) Jesús Gonthier, and they changed the name of their organization from the GCLSO to the CCM "Jesús Gonthier."[43]

By the end of 1934, the CCM had started to make significant inroads into the system of Chicolopista corporatist control. During 1935 it began to assert dominance over the COC and the CLSO as a supportive national government under Lázaro Cárdenas started to funnel funds toward the organization.[44] In January 1935 the CCM supplemented its propaganda effort with the publication of a local newspaper, *El Informador*.[45] The Agrarian Department employees continued to cross the state of Oaxaca, offering the speedy resolution of land grants in return for loyalty to the new organization.[46] During the year, there were twenty presidential resolutions donating 24,657 hectares of land to Oaxacan *ejidatarios*.[47] However, the leaders of the national organization were not simply the myopic ministers of a contemporary campesino creed; they adjusted their policy according to the grievances of local peasants. By July 1935 Belleza had started to rail against the twenty-four-centavo municipal tax on education, in response to hundreds of complaints by individual CCM members.[48] He also demanded justice for the campesinos killed by the authorities.[49] Finally he realized that for the promises of land to become reality, there had to be more agrarian personnel and less endemic corruption.[50] In December 1935 a furious Belleza pointed out to Cárdenas the contradictions in the government program: "On more than one occasion your executive has made public declarations claiming that it will do justice to the working classes and that corrupt functionaries will be punished with all severity. I ask you to make these orders a reality, and then you may deserve the applause of the citizens identified with the program of the Revolution."[51] By July 1935 the COC had been severely weakened by Calles's flight and Cárdenas's request for peasant unification. The following month it was still powerful enough to hold a well-attended demonstration in Oaxaca City in remembrance of two murdered campesino members and invade the offices of *El Informador*. But by September its central organization had all but collapsed, its members defecting to the CCM.[52]

Although at the state level the rift between the CCM and the Chicolopistas was manifested in the conflict between the Agrarian Department and Oaxaca's political and corporatist authorities, divisions at the local level were more complex. As one government representative remarked, there was "a struggle between the peasant organizations in every municipality, in every village."[53] Certain patterns of allegiance started to emerge. In Tuxtepec, where the farming of bananas, cotton, tobacco, and other commercial agricultural products made labor a valuable commodity, the Chicolopista organization, the FTOC, managed to maintain the loyalty of the finca workers through the employment of ever more generous collective contracts extracted from a landholding elite fearful for their extensive properties. During 1935 the FTOC petitioned for new collective contracts or the ratification of existing ones in twenty-five individual fincas.[54] Furthermore, the organization bolstered its support by forcing landowners to take on more workers.[55] The FTOC also attempted to attract a broader range of supporters by offering faithful peasants territory under the Law of Unused Lands. The law, which President Adolfo de la Huerta had passed in 1920, allowed municipal authorities to carve up uncultivated lands for municipal residents.[56] In March 1935 the council of San Lucas Ojitlán co-opted the former CCM *ejidal* committee of El Nanche with the offer of immediate land on the disused Santa Rosa finca.[57]

The FTOC did not work alone. Throughout 1935 it had the backing of municipal authorities and landowners. In January 1935 Governor García Toledo had imposed councils on areas of strong CCM support, such as San Lucas Ojitlán and San Pedro Ixcatlán.[58] These not only offered unused lands to Chicolopista loyalists; they also encouraged the municipal police under their control to intimidate, beat, and often kill CCM supporters.[59] Land-owners supplemented this use of force with their armed bands of pistoleros based on their own fincas.[60] But landowners' support for the FTOC was not unconditional. The organization had to balance the interests of its peasant members with those of its rich backers. There is evidence that by mid-1935 the FTOC was struggling to maintain this equilibrium. Banana *finqueros* formed a cooperative of banana growers and started to complain about the FTOC's increasingly radical actions, especially its use of the Law of Unused Lands.[61] As a result, the FTOC tended to concentrate on extracting concessions from absentee landlords and was prepared to launch a strike against the Mexico City–based landowners José G. de la Lama and Raúl A. Basurto.[62]

When it faced opposition from landowners based in Tuxtepec, however, the FTOC usually backed down from open confrontation. In September 1935 the municipal authorities of San Lucas Ojitlán retreated from the planned invasion of José Casal's finca, La Asunción, when he complained.[63] Still, the FTOC could not retreat too far. Its members were not simply the passive tools of the banana oligarchy. As it became clear that the organization was facing ever-increasing opposition, loyal peasants demanded greater rewards. In May 1935 the men of El Moral, Acatlán de Pérez Figueroa, requested "decisive help" from the governor for their continued adherence to the FTOC "which we have belonged to since the day we first swore allegiance."[64] Similarly, although the men of Aguacate, San Lucas Ojitlán, had been offered seventy-five hectares of the Santa Rosa finca in return for their fidelity, they invaded an extra thirty-five hectares despite FTOC warnings.[65]

In contrast to the FTOC, which had spent almost six years building up a network of peasants and workers and counted on the support of the local elite, the CCM had to rely on a more flexible variety of strategies to attract popular backing. Again certain patterns emerged. As in 1934, the core of its members were disenfranchised peasants, who had often recently lost work. In Paso Domingo, Tembladeras, and in La Palma, Acatlán de Pérez Figueroa, the introduction of livestock farming by the new owners had put large groups of laborers out of work. In response the former workers formed agrarian committees, joined the CCM, invaded the properties, and stole the cattle.[66] The CCM also drew in sharecroppers, whose livelihoods depended on the whims of individual landowners and who often resented the security and relative financial wellbeing of the FTOC workers.[67] The CCM also attracted communities that had received provisional *ejidal* grants and saw support for the national organization as the best means to have the land grants ratified. In the municipality of San Lucas Ojitlán, the villages of Cafetal Segundo and Arroyo Tlacuche invaded their prospective ejidos, backed by the CCM, as they waited the enacting of their land grant by the Agrarian Department.[68]

Although many communities seemed to have joined the CCM with little prompting and in response to what they perceived as the injustices of the existing system, many were also brought into the organization by radical teachers. In 1935 there were schools, established under Article 123 of the Constitution, on the fincas of Santa Flora, La Esperanza, Cafetal Segundo, and Santo Domingo de Hamaca. Despite the persecution of the landowners, all these joined the CCM.[69] According to one enthusiastic school inspector, these peasants linked land reform to the program of socialist education. "The *ejidatarios* of Cafetal Segundo like the *agraristas* of all the region of San Lucas Ojitlán see the school as their only hope for social redemption. At social reunions they dance the dances of Huastecos and Nayaritas without the necessity of alcohol and with great camaraderie."[70] The division between the CCM and FTOC also had a geographical dimension. As the FTOC dominated the municipal *cabeceras* and surrounding lands, the CCM tended to "infiltrate with communist ideas . . . nuclei of campesinos far from the centers of population," often forming a ring of communities on the municipal boundaries.[71]

There is some evidence that the division between the FTOC and CCM also had ethnic characteristics. Over the past three decades, the established Mazatec and Chinantec communities of Tuxtepec had suffered an influx of both temporary and permanent agrarian workers from outside the region. Some were mestizos from central Mexico and Veracruz. Others were Zapotec and Mixtec Indians from Oaxaca.[72] It seems that the competition between the traditional groups and these newcomers mapped themselves onto the union dispute. Thus one CCM document claimed that the FTOC only employed "foreigners" (i.e., workers born outside the region), while the local indigenous population was left to rent and sharecrop lands and look for seasonal work.[73] Of the twenty-seven men of the FTOC union of Vuelta Abajo, only four came from the ex-district, ten were from Veracruz, twelve from other areas of Oaxaca, and one from Michoacán.[74]

In the ex-districts of the Central Valleys, the geography and nature of the conflict between the CCM and the Chicolopista organizations was different from that in Tuxtepec. In general the COC maintained the loyalty of the *ejidatarios* of the ex-districts of Centro and Etla, where forty ejidos had been handed over since 1917.[75] Conflict centered on the ex-districts of Zimatlán, Tlacolula, Ejutla, and Ocotlán, where many peasants had yet to receive *ejidal* lands. As many haciendas did not need the intense labor of the banana plantations, the worker organizations of the Central Valleys were not strong. Lack of productivity also meant that the hacendados were unable to pay remunerative wages to their workers. As a result, although some unions opposed the CCM—such as La Labor, La Asunción, and La Pe—many hacienda workers joined the national organization, notably those of Valdeflores, Santa Gertrudis, and El Vergel.[76] The Chicolopista organizations failed to donate large amounts of land, either in the form of provisional ejidos or under the Law of Unused Lands. As a result, the CCM gained the support of most free villagers and sharecroppers in the region. The CCM also promised more lands to those who had already received ejidos. By the end of 1935 it boasted control of sixteen of the twenty-one *ejidal* commissions in Ocotlán and Ejutla.[77]

Outside Tuxtepec and the Central Valleys, although there was an increase in support for the CCM, there was little conflict between organizations. As we shall see, in Jamiltepec the leader of the COC switched allegiance to the CCM with Cárdenas's plea for peasant unification.[78] In the mountainous hinterland of Oaxaca, the CCM presence was minimal, limited to a few isolated communities and dependent on the influence of radical outsiders or embittered out-of-favor caciques. In Santa Cruz Tayata, Tlaxiaco, the leader of the Oaxaca branch of the Communist Party, Graciano Benitez, formed a peasant league affiliated to the CCM. Despite attacks by the municipal, ex-district, and hacienda authorities, in late 1935 the peasants received 373 hectares of *ejidal* land.[79]

By the end of 1935 the Chicolopista corporatist organizations had all but disappeared, reduced to a few municipalities of the ex-district of Tuxtepec and some of the haciendas of the Central

Valleys. While the worker organizations had been unable to recruit enough members outside the banana fincas, the COC was handicapped by its reluctance to hand out sufficient quantities of land. As a result, the CCM grew in strength. Further, although the Cardenista peasant program was headed by employees of the Agrarian Department and attracted some perspicacious opportunists and ostracized caciques, by 1935 it had started to look genuinely radical (and had even started to infect the lines of the FTOC with an acquisitive progressiveness). First, this was a matter of strategy. The Chicolopista arrangement had the dual purpose of placating the peasantry and maintaining the socioeconomic status quo. Any challenge to this regime had to offer superior benefits for its prospective members by toppling the aristocracy of Valley hacendados and Tuxtepec *finqueros*. Second, it was a tactical necessity. At its apex, the CCM continued to be run by federal bureaucrats, but they were so few that reform could not be imposed from the top down without consultation. Instead, men like Belleza were forced to formulate a broad, generous, and flexible agenda to attract support. In turn the peasantry reformulated this at the local level in order to address their own peculiar grievances, invading haciendas, murdering *peones*, stealing livestock, and refusing to pay municipal taxes. As Alan Knight argues, "rival elites manipulated the masses, but the masses could, to an extent, manipulate the rival elites too."[80]

The Movement against the Chicolopista Caciques

Disaffected bureaucrats and campesinos in the Central Valleys and Tuxtepec were not the sole provenance of opposition to the López Cortés regime. Throughout the six years of Chicolopista dominance, the establishment of a network of cacique supporters had necessarily entailed the estrangement of other local strong-men. Lying on the geographical or social edges of the central cacique's realm, these alternative leaders were often killed, exiled into bureaucratic stasis, or bargained down to positions of minimal political influence. However, by 1933, chance political fractures and the beginning of isolated social movements on the lookout for powerful supporters permitted these caciques to form a contradictory, shifting, and unstable alliance with the Cardenista presidential campaign.

Some of the political divisions that emerged during Cárdenas's political campaign had their origins in the dissolution of the relationship between López Cortés and former governor, Genaro V. Vásquez. When López Cortés became governor in December 1928, his predecessor was made senator and shunted toward political obscurity in the capital, where he would periodically snipe at the Chicolopista regime.[81] Other divisions had their roots in the revolutionary era. In 1919 the Sovereignty movement created a split between the cacique of Villa Alta, Guillermo Meixueiro, and the caciques of Ixtlán, Isaac Ibarra and Onofre Jiménez. Although Guillermo Meixueiro died two years later, the separation was prolonged by his son, Jorge Meixueiro. During the early 1920s local factionalism in the Sierra Juárez intertwined with state politics. Meixueiro supported *el camarazo*, the coup that removed Jiménez as governor. In reply, Ibarra and Jiménez supported López Cortés's gradual exclusion of former governor Vásquez. Both Ixtlán bosses acted as loyal Chicolopista functionaries from 1928 to 1934 and were able to lever in chosen appointees to important positions in the neighboring ex-district of Villa Alta.[82] In September 1931 the Ixtlán caciques ordered the murder of one of Meixueiro's most important clients, Reynaldo Jiménez, in Oaxaca City. In return, Meixueiro announced in the national congress that the murder was "on the orders of López Cortés." He accused López Cortés of being a "bad governor who ignore[d] public matters" and dug up embarrassing details of his less than revolutionary past.[83]

Other divisions had their origins in the provincial politics of the Porfiriato. As earlier noted, during the prerevolutionary period Juchitán was divided between an indigenous, Zapotec green party and a predominantly mestizo red party. The conflict between the two groups continued into the postrevolutionary period. The greens, under the leadership of Heliodoro Charis Castro, maintained control in the *cabecera* and the predominantly Zapotec regions of the ex-district.[84] The reds dominated many of the industrial centers of the region, including Ciudad Ixtepec and Matias Romero. When López Cortés became governor, he started to squeeze Charis's *cacicazgo*. Using a policy of targeted *agrarismo*, he supported the claims of San Blas, Santa María Xadani, and El Espinal to the lands just outside the city of Juchitán. In retaliation, Charis claimed the lands as his own.[85] Hostilities continued over the next two years as López Cortés imposed municipal authorities on Juchitán and reds fought running battles with the *defensa social* of the colony.[86] In April 1931 two Juchitán doctors, Valentin S. Carrasco and Roque Robles, led a rebellion in the name of General Charis, invading Juchitán de Zaragoza and leaving sixteen dead.[87] Although Charis was not directly involved, López Cortés believed he was behind it and publicly condemned Charis in his report of 1931.[88]

Then in 1932, just as the balance of power appeared to settle in López Cortés's favor, there was another radical realignment. In January the governor had imposed a red, Cuauhtémoc Ortiz

Vera, as municipal president of Juchitán de Zaragoza, to the displeasure of the majority of inhabitants. In order to allay his unpopularity, Ortiz Vera changed sides and supported the greens against the financial exactions of the local tax collector. As a result, in September 1932, López Cortés had the local police murder his former political ally.[89] He then shunned the traditional leaders of the red faction, who had allied with Ortiz Vera, and started to operate his own rump of former red leaders.[90] The excluded reds, among them Laureano Pineda, the head of a local *defensa rural*, and Enrique Liekens, a Mexico City bureaucrat, began to search for other collaborators. They turned to four principal groups: teachers, campesinos, railway workers, and former reds. In late 1933 the excluded reds established a school in Juchitán de Zaragoza in the house of a local teacher, Feliciano López Felix. They then formed a local teachers' union.[91] At the same time excluded reds attempted to forge links with the incipient *agrarista* movement in the region, supporting peasants in the villages of Real Sarabia and San Juan Guichicovi.[92] The same group also backed the electoral aspirations of railway workers in the transport hub of Matias Romero.[93] Finally, the excluded reds utilized clients in the region's towns, who acted as cheerleaders for the cause.[94] During late 1932 and 1933 Charis's position regarding the two sides was not clear. But in January 1934 he and López Cortés formed an alliance. National and local newspapers heralded the brokering of a "historic" agreement between greens and reds.[95] But the agreement was a mirage. Throughout 1934 the Isthmus remained divided as Charistas and Chicolopistas put down rising opposition groups that consisted of former reds and incipient teacher, peasant, and worker organizations.

On the coast the bewildering shifts in personal alliances also disrupted Chicolopista control and thrust influential groups into opposition. Juan José Baños had ruled the ex-district of Jamiltepec since the Revolution and resisted all attempts to change the region's political and socioeconomic landscape. However, the arrival of a cultural mission in 1932 had reinvigorated indigenous agrarian hopes along the coast. During its six-month visit, the mission established agrarian committees and organized them in a regional peasant league, under the umbrella of the COC.[96] The municipal secretary of Tepetlapa, Jesús Ramírez Vásquez, took up the mantle of the radical teachers and continued to coordinate *agrarista* efforts. By October 1934 he claimed to have formed fifty-three agrarian committees along the Costa Chica. Many had petitioned for land, while others had "entered into possession of the lands through the Law of Unused Lands in an irregular way, but one which corresponds to the pressing needs of the area."[97] In the events of 1933 the historian can observe vestiges of the 1911 millenarian Mixtec rebellion, not only in the use of land invasions but also in the rare voices of the peasant leaders. At one meeting in Santa Maná Jicaltepec, Santiago Pinotepa Nacional, the president of the agrarian committee, announced: "This movement which arrives makes me feel that this is no less than the epoch of justice and liberation for the lowly campesinos."[98] However, the nascent *agrarismo* movement was soon entwined with the factional disputes of the elites. In early 1934 Juan José Baños died, leaving his followers to squabble over huge landholdings, regional hegemony, and fourteen thousand pesos of government money for a dam project.[99] One faction, led by the Pérez family, saw *agrarismo* as a means to protect their properties while wrestling political control from the Baños family. Campesino demands for lands and the memoranda of the peasant organizations now started to concentrate on acquiring the lands of the opposing faction, composed of Baños's sons and nephews and other large landowners.[100] *Agrarismo* was fluid political material: in late 1934 the Baños clan also organized supporters from their estates into an agrarian league, the Liga de Campesinos y Obreros "Juan José Baños."[101] Violence erupted throughout the region as the ethnic and socioeconomic divide of 1933 was overlaid by elite infighting. Amidst the chaos López Cortés, in an act of some perspicacity, was quick to support the Pérez faction and their peasant supporters. He supported Ramírez Vásquez's appointment to the board of the COC and allowed Claudio M. Pérez to win the key municipal council of Santiago Pinotepa Nacional.[102]

During 1934 these antagonistic groups sought support from national political patrons. The factions that opposed López Cortés or his caciques started to coalesce around the Cardenista campaign. This proved surprisingly easy. Like other ultracallistas, López Cortés backed Manuel Pérez Treviño as PNR candidate for president over Lázaro Cárdenas.[103] Throughout May 1933 he attempted to suppress the first displays of support for Cárdenas in the state. Federal deputy Wilfredo C. Cruz announced on 5 May that "political agitation in the present circumstances is not opportune," and a week later his peasant organization, the COC, warned that "organizations of a political character are surprising the good faith of some agrarista companions." Finally, on 13 May, López Cortés allegedly visited Pérez Treviño to pledge his support.[104] Although he stepped back when Calles announced support for Cárdenas, López Cortés's initial backing of the more conservative candidate allowed space for cross-class alliances to present themselves as the true Cardenistas of the state. In Mexico City dissident bureaucrats such as Genaro V. Vásquez and

Jorge Meixueiro handed out literature on the "Oaxaca problem" and aligned themselves with the growing Cardenista movement in the capital.[105] In Juchitán the excluded reds and their alliance of workers, teachers, and peasants created pro-Cárdenas committees, with which they attempted to infiltrate the Isthmus PNR. In October 1934 they formed a regional alliance of parties and claimed victory in municipal elections under the banner of Cardenismo.[106] On the coast the Baños camarilla also aligned itself with Cardenismo. Key members signed the inflammatory anti-Chicolopista pamphlet *Justicia! Clamor del proletariado de Oaxaca*. They also tried (unsuccessfully) to lever their own peasant organization into the CCM.[107]

Demise of the Chicolopista Regime

By mid-1935 the Chicolopista regime was on the edge of collapse. In the countryside CCM groups and local factions were challenging incumbent corporatist organizations and ruling caciques with national support. In June 1935 a government agent reported that the "political situation in the state [wa]s reduced to the official politicians," but these were harder to dislodge.[108] Francisco López Cortés continued to direct all political appointments by means of the state committee of the PNR. However, with the Calles-Cárdenas split, central support for his regime was removed, and young political entrepreneurs saw Cardenismo as a means to escape the hegemony of the Isthmus caudillo. Although local caciques were reluctant to intervene and attempted to wait out the political clash in expectation of offering their undivided loyalty to the winner, conflicts did arise over the state PNR, municipal elections, the choice of the next governor, and the local legislature. Despite the surprising loyalty of many of his allies

and Cárdenas's effort to compromise rather than confront, López Cortés was destined to lose, and by early 1936 a new interim
camarilla of politicians ruled Oaxaca.

On 12 June 1935 the state government newspaper, *El Oaxaqueño*, released a late supplement containing the controversial interview with General Calles.[109] The following day the paper published Governor García Toledo's message of goodwill to
the Sonoran caudillo, which claimed that Oaxaca "received these
words with the same fondness and interest as always," assuring
him of the state's continued "adhesion and respect." *El Oaxaqueño*
also ran an editorial urging all Oaxacans to obey the diktats of the
Jefe Máximo.[110] On the same day, Francisco López Cortés signed
the letter of the senate congratulating Calles on his auspicious intervention.[111] However, Cárdenas's speed and effrontery discon-
certed the ultracallistas. For three years López Cortés had ruled
Oaxaca through control of the incumbent governor, García Toledo. Now the president cleverly divided the state's governing alliance. On 2 July he invited the governor to Mexico City, where
he demanded García Toledo's loyalty in return for continued federal support.[112] Two days later García Toledo returned to Oaxaca, where peasants and workers held "a spontaneous demonstration of support." Obviously at home in his new role as leader
of the masses, the Cardenista convert gave an extemporaneous
announcement of his faith in the "program of worker actions,"
which he was convinced "would result in the improvement of the
economy of the proletariat."[113]

Although Cárdenas had succeeded in cementing the loyalty of
the Oaxacan governor, he was still far from controlling the political machinery of the state. Conflict centered on the local congress.
Here eight Cardenistas faced nine Chicolopistas in a six-month

administrative stand-off that brought the legislative process to a complete standstill. The division was as much over age as political orientation. The Chicolopistas were of the "generation of the volcano," old allies of López Cortés, such as CPSO founder Germán Gay Baños and the Sierra strongmen Onofre Jiménez and Ezequiel Santillán, whose *cacicazgos* depended on the caudillo. The Cardenistas, who proclaimed themselves the Radical Block of the congress, consisted of younger bureaucrats, whose lack of provincial power lessened their attachment to their former political patron. As one of their number, Roberto Ortiz Gris, proudly announced: "We are young, inexpert politicians, ignorant of politics," but "we know our duties and the needs of the people."[114] On 23 August the Radical Block joined in the debate on local political supremacy and released the pamphlet *Al pueblo del estado de Oaxaca*. This welcomed the national PNR's denigration of the state organization and attacked those who had "given themselves to the ignoble work of political agitation" and thereby "created a state of things bordering on anarchy."[115] In retaliation the Chicolopista deputies sacked five of the provincial judges appointed by García Toledo and then employed a policy of "not doing, discussing or approving any project of law."[116] According to one of Cárdenas's informants, López Cortés wanted to project the impression that "the government of Oaxaca was not in control of public order or administration," that without the firm hand of a regional caudillo, the state was ungovernable.[117] As a result, by September 1935 the division between García Toledo and López Cortés had become critical. Cárdenas was forced to intervene and sent his brother, Dámaso Cárdenas, to forge an accord between the two sides. On 17 September all seventeen local deputies agreed to put their difficulties behind them, back the future administration of the governor, collaborate with the president, and share rule of the permanent commission of the congress between the two groups.[118]

However, despite Cárdenas's attempts at pacification, the conflict continued as both sides fought over local political appointments. By the end of November 1935 attention turned to the next PNR candidate for governor. The nine Chicolopista deputies signed a petition demanding a change to article 68, section VII of the local constitution, which limited the ability of military men to stand for governor. This was designed to open up the PNR's internal election to army officer Edmundo Sánchez Cano, whom López Cortés had now designated García Toledo's successor.[119] Sánchez Caño seemed a good choice. He was ambitious, politically naïve, and an acquaintance of President Cárdenas. Support for Sánchez Cano came not only from traditional followers of López Cortés but also from the wealthy elite of Oaxaca City, who saw his election as a means to curb the excesses of Cardenismo.[120] But without national support, the campaign came to nothing, and supporters of Sánchez Cano were reduced to disrupting the elections for Oaxaca City's municipal authorities.[121]

With Calles's return to Mexico on 13 December tensions in the local congress increased. According to one supporter of García Toledo, local deputy Ezequiel Santillán returned to the Sierra Juárez to prepare former Soberanistas for imminent civil war. On 15 December the nine Chicolopista deputies disobeyed the September agreement and formed the permanent committee of the local congress without members of the Radical Block. They then continued their policy of legislative gridlock, sending away one of their number so that neither group could reach a majority.[122] On 26 December the supporters of García Toledo stormed the congress with the help of the municipal police and started an extraordinary session. They aimed to use article 47 of the local constitution to call the substitutes of the recalcitrant deputies. Once they had control of three-quarters of the congress they could dismiss the Chicolopistas.[123] By 28 December they had recruited four substitutes and needed only one more to achieve a majority vote of thirteen.[124] However, on the same day, Cárdenas sent Juan de la Cruz García, an employee of the Ministry of the Interior, to organize some form of accord. He immediately ordered the supporters of García Toledo to halt their implementation of article 47.[125] Over the next two weeks both groups attempted to gain the support of the federal government, accusing each other of Callismo, the manipulation of elections, corruption, and planned insurrection.[126] Finally the Ministry of the Interior advised Cárdenas that the only solution was the imposition of another substitute. On 23 January five substitutes joined the eight original supporters of García Toledo and removed the other deputies.[127]

With García Toledo's victory over the Chicolopistas in the state congress, López Cortés's power in Oaxaca was close to extinction. The central committee of the PNR removed the state committee of the PNR and imposed a coterie of Cardenistas. Some, such as CCM leader Daniel Muñoz Estefan, had been Cardenista since early 1934. However, the majority were recent coverts to the "broad church" of Cardenismo.[128] Local deputy Efren N. Mata switched sides in June 1935 to become part of the Radical Block, while Adelaido Ojeda and Alejandro Ceja C. were both landowning COC caciques, recently indoctrinated into the CCM. The municipal elections in the disputed towns were decided in favor of the labor unions, even in the Chicolopista stronghold of Ciudad Ixtepec. López Cortés, like his predecessor Genaro V. Vásquez, was forced to renounce effective power and retreat to the senate.

Although Cardenismo had been a political force in Mexico City and the countryside since 1933, it was only with the break from Calles that the new president revealed the shape of his provincial policy. Notwithstanding the division in the revolutionary family, Cárdenas's strategy was designed to ensure unity. In Oaxaca Cárdenas relied on persuasion and negotiation, attempting to goad members of the Callista government into betrayal of the Jefe Máximo. To avoid conflict he used pacts of fraternity, quiet deals in the corridors of his Mexico City residence, and if necessary, chosen federal emissaries to secure fidelity. Furthermore, despite the intransigence of the Chicolopistas, he seemed unwilling to overturn state legislation or elected representatives until all hope of compromise had disappeared. Finally, he was aided by the "wait and see" policy of the majority of Chicolopista caciques, who were unwilling to side openly with either group, in fear of jeopardizing their political futures.

Conclusion

What does the narrative of López Cortés's fall tell us about the early effects of Cardenismo? Populist historians viewed the Cardenista campaign as answering the call of the Mexican masses, as forming what Adolfo Gilly calls "the political expression of the second phase of the Mexican Revolution."[129] However, revisionist interpretations of the mass mobilizations and political conflicts of 1933 and 1934 imagine Cardenismo as operated from the top down, emerging from a twofold process of bargaining and cooption, and designed to "contain and deflect the popular torrent."[130]

According to Heather Fowler-Salamini, "Cárdenas' strategy was Machiavellian, for his goal was simply to consolidate his control over as many regional peasant organizations as possible before the presidential election." He achieved this through the establishment of "political alliances with their leadership."[131] Resistance, according to the revisionists, came from the left, especially the Tejedistas and the PCM.[132] In Oaxaca Cárdenas's candidacy was an important development that caused a fissure through the political landscape of the state. But this was not simply a product of state maneuvering or infighting among the elite. As in Tlaxcala, national politics and cynical attempts at political advancement met with dreams of socioeconomic improvement and together molded themselves around the charismatic michoacano.[133] Caciques from the Porfirian and postrevolutionary eras allied with bureaucratic ideologues and desperate campesinos and formed a "loose, heterogeneous and shifting coalition," a mosaic of "many Cardenismos."[134] All, however, had arisen from the detritus of the Chicopolista regime. By late 1934, although López Cortés nominally supported the PNR candidate, Cardenismo in Oaxaca had become a badge of opposition to his six years of government.[135]

As a result, as the relationship between the Jefe Máximo and the incumbent president deteriorated over the next year, this unwieldy alliance sought to unseat the local caudillo. Historians of Cardenismo have long disputed the significance of the split between Cárdenas and Calles and its national and regional consequences. For some, the defeat of Callismo is the triumph of a new progressive coalition of peasants, workers, and Cardenista politicians over a reactionary cabal of bourgeois Callistas and foreign capitalists.[136] According to Anatol Shulgovski, "only with the support of democratic forces and acting frequently under pressure from the working masses, did the Cardenistas obtain control of the government and defeat the Callistas."[137] For others, the division was little more than an act of political subterfuge, its consequences mapped out by the logic of political expediency rather than by ideological or socioeconomic considerations.[138] In Tlaxcala and Jalisco reactionary Callistas survived the rift, while in Puebla, Sonora, Tabasco, and Querétaro, Cárdenas removed relatively radical governors for both national and local reasons and relied instead on "diverse and conservative group[s] of anti-callistas" or astute political opportunists.[139] Even in states such as Coahuila, Guerrero, and Sinaloa, where the rationale of factionalism allowed the supremacy of a new progressive coalition, Alicia Hernández Chavez contends that Cárdenas was not seeking to "dislodge the base of power of the reigning economic and political groups."[140] Moreover, the division allowed Cárdenas to institute a new form of corporatist presidentialism, as masses and party were now at the service of the executive.[141]

This historical division is, in many ways, a false dichotomy based on an overestimate of the provincial power of both Cárdenas and Calles. As Ben Fallaw argues, the regional manifestations of the national conflict were primarily driven by opportunistic local camarillas. In Yucatán an awkward populist coalition of hacendados and radicals removed one Cardenista governor and then blocked the imposition of the president's projected replacement.[142] In Oaxaca a similar blend of local factionalism and state weakness prevented both bottom-up and top-down forms of Cardenismo from gaining exclusive power. In the countryside the unraveling of the Chicolopista corporatist machinery and the flexibility and isolation of the Cardenista agrarian bureaucracy allowed an increasingly militant peasantry in Tuxtepec, the Central Valleys, and isolated mountain villages to confront the political and economic elite, often bypassing federal law in return for immediate gain. Yet although the CCM formed the backbone of Cardenista support in the state, Oaxaca did not witness the uninterrupted ascendance of a radical coalition. On the one hand, the CCM did not directly interfere at the level of state politics. Its call for Governor García Toledo's replacement by a council of workers and peasants was quickly dismissed.[143] On the other hand, the confederation was interspersed with and connected to opportunistic, out-of-favor caciques. Furthermore, Cárdenas sought to balance his pursuit, or at least his permissiveness, of socioeconomic reform with a political conservatism, which sought unity over divergence and compromise over confrontation. He did not seek to upset the mechanics of state politics through political imposition or military force, as he would do in San Luis Potosí.[144] Nor did he turn to the array of out-of-favor politicians, caciques, and aspirant caudillos to enforce themselves on the state as they did in Puebla, Tabasco, Sonora and Querétaro. Instead Cárdenas sought allies among those on the edges of the regime and was able to persuade the governor and members of the CLSO, COC, PNR, and local congress of the benefits of a switch in allegiances. Despite the obstinacy of many local politicians, Cárdenas failed to start a Callista witch-hunt and at the last minute instituted only a "gentle purge" of loyal Chicolopistas.[145] Thus, although by early 1936 Cardenismo had rid the state of an unpopular Callista caudillo and introduced a powerful strain of socioeconomic radicalism into Oaxaca's countryside, the president's political weakness allowed the persistence of Callista personnel and repressive rural *cacicazgos*. This pattern of regional moderation and local independence, attempted if not entirely successful centralization at the state level, and permitted decentralization in the ex-districts was not simply a short-term policy. Over the next four years, it would form the basis for Cárdenas's political system in Oaxaca.

FOUR

The Politics of Cardenismo, 1936–40

During the period 1936 to 1940 President Cárdenas established his political program, building on the PNR structure and adding a series of modifications based on the socioeconomic reforms enacted by his own administration. Key to the development of Cardenista politics was his recreation of the PNR as a party of mass organizations. From 1936 to 1938 the president stressed the need for peasant and worker unification in the Confederación Nacional Campesina (CNC) and the Confederación de Trabajadores de México (CTM) respectively.[1] At the same time he instigated an "open door" policy of electoral participation, encouraging both groups to contribute to party voting procedures.[2] Finally, in May 1938 he announced the transformation of the PNR into the Partido de la Revolución Mexicana (PRM). The new party was intended to incorporate all four sectors of society, designated as the military, labor, agrarian, and popular. The new party had five times as many members as in 1936, including 2,500,000 campesinos and 1,250,000 workers.[3] At the same time some opposition groups were co-opted into the party structure, while other more disruptive independent elements, such as Saturnino Cedillo, were forced to rebel and were subsequently crushed.[4]

Historians of the Cárdenas era have long debated the significance of the president's political stratagems. For the early biographers of the Michoacán revolutionary, the open door electoral policy of 1936—the unification of peasants and workers and their admittance into the workings of party politics—indicated Cárdenas's reverence for "democratic procedures and respect for the popular will" and that democracy was "instinctive to a man who had never severed his close ties with the common people."[5] However, post-1968 historians and political scientists started to charge Cárdenas with the creation of an authoritarian one-party state. Arnaldo Córdova denied Cárdenas's democratic pretensions, arguing that his interest lay in the strengthening of the revolutionary state, that the open door policy was a "lie" and greater popular participation a "fiction."[6] Not only was the PRM a "corporatist instrument that centralized and solidified the control of the state over the workers," but it also served to concentrate power in the presidency.[7] As a result the executive power came "to dominate local and regional politico-economic forces" as well as the "legislature, judiciary, military, peasantry and workers."[8]

This chapter examines the tensions between centralization and decentralization, political control and local autonomy in Oaxaca during the Cárdenas era by focusing on the elections for state governor and the political arrangement in the ex-district of Ixtlán in the Sierra Juárez. At the state level, Cárdenas limited electoral participation and effectively imposed his own candidate in order to avoid the multiple claims of Oaxaca's regional powerbrokers. However, outside Oaxaca City he was forced to allow a relative degree of political freedom, so long as stability was maintained. In Ixtlán the success of socialist education, the liberal heritage, and the generational divisions within villages compelled the president to allow free elections and wider political participation.

The Competition for Governor

Although in December 1935 Governor García Toledo and his camarilla of Cardenistas had seen off the challenge of the Chicolopista candidate for the office of governor, Edmundo Sánchez Cano,
the competition over the important post continued well into the
following year. With the approval of President Cárdenas, García
Toledo, Oaxaca's Cardenistas, and the CCM had started to rally
around Constantino Chapital as a candidate for the next governor in November 1935.[9] At the time Chapital was a federal deputy, one of only two Oaxacan representatives who had formed
part of the left wing of the congress.[10] Not only was Chapital
one of the first Oaxacans to back Cárdenas in June 1935—he
also had an orthodox, healthy, and, in Oaxaca, rare revolutionary pedigree.[11] During the Revolution Chapital had displayed a
marked loyalty to the government of Venustiano Carranza, forming part of the "Fieles de Oaxaca" battalion in 1914 and holding
a series of military posts throughout the country in the following
years.[12] In the 1920s Chapital continued his military career. Although he fought in few notable engagements, he was rewarded
for his loyalty during the Escobarista revolt in 1929 with entry
into the governor of Oaxaca's inner circle.[13] However, although
he had risen to political power through his military career like
many men, in other respects Chapital did not fit the model of the
buccaneering, imposing, postrevolutionary state governor. He had
little or no power base in the state, owing to his prolonged absence on military duty. He was not related to economically or politically important regional families. Further, the military years
had taken a toll on his mental and physical health. According to
Jorge Tamayo, he possessed "a certain sensitive personal defect

which lamentably meant he could not put into practice his ideas and good will."[14] According to one acquaintance he was racked by guilt over his murder of a fellow officer in Tabasco in 1923.[15] He was also accused of swindling a Mexico City woman out of five thousand pesos in late 1926.[16] In response he had taken to the bottle, and during the 1930s he was moved around series of bureaucratic positions.[17] His drinking seemed to continue, and during his governorship he spent long periods convalescing from a series of chest and stomach complaints.[18] Pamphlets and opposition newspapers ridiculed his appetite for alcohol, accusing him of giving reports to the congress drunk and, most embarrassingly, of failing to join Cárdenas on his trip through the state owing to a crippling hangover.[19]

Oaxaca's historians have pondered Cárdenas's decision to choose such an unknown as the state governor. Jorge F. Iturribarría argues that the governorship was a reward for Chapital's work in the left wing of the federal congress, while Guillermo Rosas Solaegui and J. Guadalupe García claim that Chapital's victory lay in his allegiance to General Juan Andrew Almazán.[20] Héctor Martínez Medina claims these versions are "completely contradictory," as Chapital could not have been supported by both the left and the right, and throws up his hands in incomprehension.[21] While Chapital's loyalty and Almazán's support (which are in no way mutually exclusive) must have influenced Cárdenas's decision, the simplicities of fidelity and reward were not the only matters on the president's mind. Cárdenas cannot have been unaware of Chapital's political inexperience, shallow Oaxaca roots, or dipsomania, but he still supported Chapital for the governorship. In fact it was these very qualities that drove the president into an alliance with this unassuming figure. Cárdenas had worked in Oaxaca as military commander of the Isthmus in the early 1920s. He was aware of the stark political, ethnic, and cultural regionalism of the state and the brutal, factional nature of personal politics.[22] As such he was loath to offer the governorship to another López Cortés, whose roots in a particular district, town, or ethnicity would destabilize the balance between the camarillas and caciques of the different regions and whose ambitions and talents could lead to conflict between the state government and these regional strongmen. Instead he opted for a relatively weak, unknown individual, who was beholden to the center for his position, unencumbered with the hopes and dreams of his home region, and too weak to attempt to assert control over the periphery's jealous, independent, and often heavily armed caciques.

The other candidates for the PNR's nomination also support this theory of Cardenista intent. In March 1936 three other candidates began to canvas for support among local constituents and federal politicians. All possessed regional power bases that might threaten federal control and state stability if they captured the governorship. Ezequiel López Salinas was a Tehuantepec merchant, well respected in the community, according to his supporters, and a puppet of the Juchitán cacique Heliodoro Charis, according to his detractors.[23] Chapital's two major opponents were Alfonso Francisco Ramírez and Benito Zaragoza. Ramírez was a lawyer educated at the local university and a devout Catholic from the Mixteca.[24] As such he counted on the support of three important groups: Catholics, Mixtecs, and the elite of the Central Valleys. Chapital's supporters made constant accusations of Ramírez's affiliation with the *cofradías* of the state and his close relationship with the bishop's representative, Carlos Gracida.[25] Perhaps more important for Cárdenas, who was now moving away from the extremes of Callista anticlericalism, was Ramírez's attachment to the ruling elites of the Mixteca and Oaxaca City. In March 1936 Tlaxiaco merchants formed a regional federation to back Ramírez.[26] During his tour of Oaxaca, Ramírez spent most of his time in the Mixtec districts of Silacayoapam, Tlaxiaco, Huajuapam, and his home district of Teposcolula, where his suspected Catholicism and ethnic affiliation drummed up copious support.[27] Finally, Ramírez's contacts with the local university and his reputed religiosity also drew in members of the Oaxaca City elite.[28]

Benito Zaragoza was the other candidate for the PNR ticket in the elections for governor. He was a former colonel in the Sovereignty movement and was put forward by the camarilla of former generals of the movement, led by Isaac M. Ibarra and Onofre Jiménez.[29] Both now feared that the fall of López Cortés and the appearance in the ranks of the state peasant organization of Jorge Meixueiro, son of Guillermo Meixueiro, spelled the end of their regional hegemony. These fears were realized when the state PNR put forward Artemio Velasco, an old ally of Guillermo Meixueiro, to run for local deputy for Villa Alta.[30] Through links to former comrades-in-arms in the ex-district of Ixtlán, Zaragoza built up a formidable network of support. When support was not forthcoming, he relied on the military strength of loyal captains from his hometown of Santa María Yavesia and the surrounding villages, who were accused of kidnapping, extortion, and forcing people at gunpoint to sign political petitions in support of their commander.[31] He also garnered the backing of many of the leading residents of the district of Tuxtepec, who were fearful of the rise of the CCM and were often drawn in by Zapotec municipal functionaries, who had long played an important intermediary role between the banana growers and the transient Sierra labor force.[32]

Despite the efforts of López Salinas, Zaragoza, and Ramírez and the numerous complaints of electoral fraud, the state's PNR members and all peasants and workers who could prove that they were organized voted in Chapital as the national party's candidate for governor.[33] Although López Salinas and Ramírez dropped out of the race and promised to offer their support to the Chapital, Zaragoza and hardcore former Sovereignty movement members continued to campaign for governor under the banner of the Partido Revolucionario Oaxaqueño.[34] Over the next four months, hostilities between Chapitalistas and Zaragozistas increased. Conflicts were particularly pronounced in the Sierra district of Ixtlán.[35] In June and again in August the governor was forced to send an army detachment to the region to pacify the opposing groups.[36] The conflict soon reached the Oaxaca City, and on 31 July police and Zaragozistas came to blows on the streets of the capital after the authorities attempted to arrest a particularly vocal supporter of the Sierra leader.[37] By the end of July 1936, an inspector from the federal government claimed that Zaragoza had the support of the Zapotec and Mixe Sierras as well as large parts of Oaxaca City and Tuxtepec.[38]

The groups continued to clash up to the day of the election itself. Voting booths were broken, Chapital's canvassers attacked those of Zaragoza, and fights broke out in Oaxaca City and various pueblos of the Sierra.[39] Chapital was acclaimed victor on 4 August 1936, and a month later the local congress declared him governor of the state.[40] Unfortunately, this failed to stop the conflict between the two sides. After complaining to Cárdenas that the election was a "shame on the Revolution," Zaragoza went to

Mexico City in order to plead his case with the president.[41] Receiving Cárdenas's promise to visit the region of the Sierra but no affirmation of his victory, Zaragoza returned to Santa Catarina Lachatao to plan a rebellion against Chapital's imposition.[42] By the end of November rumors were rife that the men of the Sierra would descend on the Oaxaca City, in an echo of their attack on the capital in 1915.[43] The threat reached the pages of the national newspapers and even Mr. Gallop, the British consular emissary, reported that after a "farce" of an election, it was feared that "the people of the Sierra were going to descend on Oaxaca to kill Chapital."[44] The chief of military operations put on a show of strength on the anniversary of the Revolution, parading his forces around the streets of the capital.[45] On 28 November an army plane dropped leaflets over the Sierra declaring that any rebellion would be met by force.[46] Although it appears that the rumors were not without foundation—that weapons were dug up, further arms distributed, and pacts of revolt drawn up—in the end the Sierra did not rebel.[47] Municipal elections, rather than state politics, absorbed the energies of the competing factions. And Cárdenas's promise to visit the Sierra and aid the development of various community projects seemed to placate many of the potential rebels.

The narrative of the 1936 elections for governor reveals an important facet of Cardenista politics. The president could have chosen the prospective governor from an array of possible candidates, including those mentioned but also men who had supported his candidacy in 1933, such as former interim governor Genaro V. Vásquez, Villa Alta cacique and CCM aficionado Jorge Meixueiro, and Isthmus intellectual Enrique Liekens, all of whom were rumored to have aspirations to the gubernatorial palace.[48]

As such the decision to support Chapital was autocratic and centralizing. As Jorge Tamayo argues, Chapital's appointment had been decided from Mexico and "in complete disregard of Oaxacan opinion."[49] However, the choice also had its roots in Cárdenas's desire for unity and the avoidance of conflict. As his relations with the Sierra and local caciques demonstrate, the president was not averse to local autonomy when it served his purpose or when it was forced upon him.

Cárdenas and Local Autonomy in Ixtlán

Although the *serranos* of Ixtlán had failed to descend from the mountains north of Oaxaca City to coincide with Chapital's inauguration on 2 December 1936, tensions between the Zaragozistas and the central and state government remained. Fears for the political stability of the region forced President Cárdenas to act. When he promised to visit the Sierra and "take account of its problems," this was not the idle boast of a metropolitan demagogue but rather an announcement of political intent.[50] His tour of the region and its subsequent politics reveal the president's desire to agree solutions through a sensitive appreciation of a region's cultural, political, and socioeconomic circumstances. However, unlike other *indigenista* attempts to answer specific autochthonous groups' regional demands as pursued among the Yaqui, P'urhépecha, or Chiapas Mayans, in Ixtlán Cárdenas's program was comparatively successful and led neither to abject failure nor to the utter submission of local groups to the state's corporatist apparatus.[51] Unlike in the other regions mentioned, state weakness, the fortuitous absence of now out-of-favor caciques, and most important, the Zapotec Indians' own experience of negotiating outside interference allowed the inhabitants to frame the process of state formation according to their own aspirations and to forge a region of relative political autonomy.

Although Chinantecs dominated the northern tips of Ixtlán and a handful of mestizo merchants plied their trade throughout the region, the district was predominantly populated by Zapotec Indians. Patrick J. McNamara argues that during the second half of the nineteenth century the Zapotecs of Ixtlán, like the inhabitants of the Sierra Norte of Puebla, built a new relationship with the state and federal governments based on their crucial involvement in various national and international conflicts.[52] In 1855 Porfirio Díaz was appointed subprefect of Ixtlán and formed village units of the National Guard. Over the next twenty years he successfully utilized loyal Ixtlán forces to confront conservatives, foreign invaders, and rival liberals. The Zapotec contribution to the liberal cause prompted Ixtlán's inhabitants to employ a carefully constructed strategy of negotiation with the state, which balanced general compliance with the defense of local political and economic structures. On the one hand, Ixtlán's inhabitants accepted and even demanded the establishment of state schools and infrastructure projects. The village leaders remained unfailingly loyal to their former commander and the succession of mestizo caciques he appointed as *jefes políticos*. On the other hand, Díaz's former soldiers also took advantage of the degree of political leverage they felt their combative defense of the liberal state warranted. When Díaz demanded that the National Guard disarm, the Zapotecs returned only the guns that did not work. At the same time, most Zapotecs in Ixtlán retained their lands, dividing fertile areas into individual strips and leaving the large forests as communal property. In 1912 the *jefe político* of Ixtlán announced that "there [wa]s no hacienda nor finca of importance to give work to the workers in a constant manner."[53] Finally, during the late Porfiriato, villagers began a prolonged campaign to defend municipal autonomy, lands, and labor rights against the insensitive application of liberal doctrine. In April 1906 Ixtlán peasants wrote to Díaz to complain about the governor of Oaxaca's new taxes and his growing interference in what they defined as local problems over land and water.[54]

The Revolution strengthened this ambivalent aspect of the Zapotecs' relationship with mestizo outsiders and the state. As described in chapter 1, the Soberanista movement was a *serrano* insurrection against the intervention of Carrancismo. By the late 1910s many Zapotecs had also rejected elite leaders such as Guillermo Meixueiro and turned toward more plebeian local chiefs such as Isaac M. Ibarra and Onofre Jiménez. Furthermore, the successful revolutionary defense of political and economic independence delineated postrevolutionary Ixtlán. Mestizo immigration to the region was still minimal. In the census of 1940, only a few villages around the district's scattered mines possessed a sizable community of exclusively Spanish speakers. Some villages, such as Abejones, San Juan Atepec, San Juan Evangelista Analco, and San Miguel Aloapam, had none. Even in the district capital, Ixtlán de Juárez, less than 2 percent of the population spoke only Spanish. Around 50 percent spoke Zapotec, and the other 48 percent were bilingual.[55] Most Zapotec peasants retained their rights to individual properties and large extensions of communal land. A government report in 1938 stated that there were "no landholdings over 100 hectares."[56] As Rosendo Pérez García argues, the number of small individual private properties closely matched the number of families in the region, while the large properties listed on the census corresponded to communal village lands.[57]

The liberal settlement and the experience of over five years of intermittent Carrancista assaults also prolonged Zapotec attachment to the idea of municipal political autonomy. When the representative of the Departamento Autónomo de Asuntos Indigenas (DAAI) drunkenly shot up the municipal palace of Ixtlán de Juárez in October 1937, the municipal president described how this act "mocked the revolutionary principle of MUNICIPAL AUTONOMY, which cost so many lives."[58]

However, while locals resisted unwanted outside interference in municipal elections or land disputes, as in the Porfirian period they readily accepted state projects that could be molded to their own benefit. In particular, Ixtlán's Zapotec peasants quickly recognized the advantages of socialist education. In many other isolated, indigenous areas of Mexico, entrenched elites, reactionary hacendados, and a reluctant peasantry had combined to resist the steady stream of socialist teachers parachuted into the countryside during the 1930s. In Ixtlán, in contrast, a combination of historical, political, geographical, and cultural factors encouraged the acceptance of the government program. Most important, during the postrevolutionary period many of Oaxaca's teachers came from the Sierra. Inhabitants often saw the state Normal school at the foot of the mountains, which had been refounded in 1923 by a *serrano* teacher, as a means to escape the tedium and regimentation of village life.[59] They were also often inspired by the figure of Benito Juárez, whose cult of liberal anticlericalism had begun to penetrate the environs of his birthplace in the late nineteenth century.[60] After 1930 bilingual teaching, which would be institutionalized only decades later, was introduced in the region, and Zapotec teachers from the Normal were concentrated in the Sierra. "A notable advance was noted" as teachers "translated into their native language."[61] The teachers were also well organized. In late 1930 the state school inspector called together all the teachers from the districts of Ixtlán and Villa Alta and proposed the creation of a teachers' union for the Sierra, which slowly took shape.[62]

These indigenous teachers also tapped into the major political and socioeconomic problems of the area. In particular they were able to form a network of support among progressive village democrats. During the nineteenth century municipal politics had been controlled by village elders at the apex of the cargo system. But revolutionary rhetoric and ten years of fighting had transformed young *serranos'* ideas about the traditional civil-religious hierarchy. As C. M. Young writes, "age was no longer considered an adequate criterion for public office."[63] Returning Sovereignty movement soldiers now attempted to overturn the sclerotic political system of cargos, which had allowed only older villagers to hold high municipal office. Ideas of municipal autonomy were now joined by what these *serrano* soldiers called municipal "democracy." In 1928 the "young men" of Santa Cruz Yagavila complained that "the old men" monopolized political power to the exclusion of "young, revolutionary villagers," who were instead forced to do the bulk of communal labor. They were supported in their demands for "an end to exploitation" and the imposition of "democracy" by their former commander, Onofre Jiménez, who presumably saw the end of the cargo system as a means to cement client loyalty and remove the last vestiges of Meixueiro's supporters.[64] By 1930 these young, progressive "democrats" were also aided by keen rural teachers, who saw the intertwining of civil and religious posts and the accompanying festivities as overtly religious, profligate, and regressive. Throughout the early 1930s teachers in the Sierra campaigned against the persistence of religious and political cargos, attempting to eradicate Catholic trappings of village festivities and at the same time overturn the system of government dominated by the village elders.[65] They did not do away entirely with the communal aspects of religious organizations but rather directed the traditional collection of villagers' excess wealth toward education, forming a series of cooperatives to pay for the needs of the local school.[66]

Teachers also focused on the major causes of inequality and suffering in the region. Although the persistence of communal lands mitigated great disparity in wealth, there were other ways in which the indigenous inhabitants of the Sierra were affected by market capitalism. As in most of Oaxaca, "coffee was the catalyst for capitalist transformation."[67] During the Porifiato, the *jefe político* of the neighboring district of Villa Alta, Fidencio Hernández, had forced many villages to start growing coffee on their individual strips of land. Some peasants in Ixtlán followed suit. The lack of infrastructure and the consequent difficulty in transporting goods into or out of the villages made the population particularly vulnerable to the demands of coffee merchants, who either traversed the Sierra trailing their wares behind them on mule trains or constructed general shops in the pueblos. The problem of commercial monopolies continued after the Revolution. A government report into landholding in 1938 revealed that many villages possessed one or two inhabitants of extreme comparative wealth. While most inhabitants owned goods of around ten to twenty pesos, men such as Absalón Santiago in Santa Catarina Lachatao and Benigno Hernández in San Miguel Amatlán possessed comparative fortunes of five hundred to a thousand pesos. As the report pointed out, their wealth depended on their monopoly of regional commerce in coffee.[68] Similarly, the first regional peasant conference held in Santa Cruz Yagavila at the end of June 1936, organized by the rural teacher Francisco Gómez G., complained that traveling merchants visited the town and the surrounding villages during the fiestas and bought their crops of coffee at well below market price or exchanged them for "cloth, salt and alcohol."[69]

The teachers' solution to the problem of the narrow control of regional commerce, particularly coffee, was fourfold. First they acted to punish particularly rapacious merchants. In July 1935 the visiting cultural mission fined a San Mateo Calpulapam merchant thirty pesos for overpricing his products.[70] Second, teachers began to build alliances between villages and so impede the ability of merchants to threaten villagers with going to another population center if they could not sell their products at the price they desired. The regional peasant meeting in June 1936 argued that to resolve the socioeconomic problems of the area there had to be "good faith between the pueblos." At the end of the congress eight villages signed a pact of solidarity: San Pedro Yaneri, Santa María Zoogochi, Santa Cruz Yagavila, Santa María Jossa, San Juan Yagila, San Miguel Tiltepec, Santo Domingo Cacalotepec, and San Miguel Yotao.[71] Third, the teachers set up agricultural cooperatives in individual villages. Like the intervillage alliances these offered the small farmers greater bargaining power in their dealings with the merchants.[72] Finally, the teachers encouraged the formation of juntas of material improvements to advance the region's infrastructure. In January 1936 Professor Alvaro Pacheco set up one of these organizations in Santa María Yahuiche. Not only did these groups work on projects designed to make the transport of goods easier; they also secularized the traditional practice of *tequio*, drawing it into the ambit of the educators and progressives rather than leaving it to the distribution of village elders.[73] Although coffee distorted the Ixtlán economy, the teachers' efforts mitigated its most destructive effects. Unlike regions such as Juquila, Pochutla, the Región Mixe, or Juxtlahuaca, Ixtlán avoided the spiraling violence of Oaxaca's postrevolutionary coffee boom.

Regional difficulties concerned more than market relations. Health was also a major problem. As a result, in September 1935 the federal school inspector ordered the creation of sanitary brigades. These concentrated on the cure of onchocerciasis, or river blindness, which affected up to 40 percent of elderly Sierra residents.[74] This measure was particularly successful and often managed to paper over the more radical political and socioeconomic changes wrought by the education program. As one teacher exclaimed, "I would like you to see them walking one after another, teachers, municipal authorities, representatives of committees and village inhabitants and at the end the sanitary brigades, animated by the ideal of going to lift up the spirit and health of the pueblos lost in the woods and the deep canyons."[75]

As Zapotec peasants and Zapotec teachers constructed a variant of socialist education that addressed local problems, the project was extremely successful.[76] In early 1937 one teacher, writing in the monthly magazine *Oaxaca en México* under the name Don Observado, claimed that there were only four villages in the Sierra without federal schools. Even small hamlets possessed two or three teachers. Women were educated alongside men, and the inhabitants, in their eager thirst for knowledge, vied among themselves for the employment of federal teachers.[77] Reports to the SEP were equally replete with exclamations of fulfillment and jubilation, compassion and admiration for the *serranos*. One inspector, who in other regions had reached paroxysms of despair and self-doubt, admitted that in the Sierra Juárez, "I had no serious problem with any teacher or any pueblo."[78] Even religious fanaticism was not a great difficulty. In fact it was "fortunate that the indigenous pueblos of this region" were "not fanaticized" but rather "understood the priest as a burden."[79] Of course there were conflicts, especially over municipal and mercantile power. The municipal authorities periodically attacked the cooperative of San Juan Atepec.[80] Priests, municipal authorities, and village elders, often linked through lay groups and church singing organizations, resisted the eradication of the *mayordomias*. One school inspector reported that certain villages still pursued overly expensive "fanatical" fiestas, but he framed this as the exception to the rule.[81] As a result, by late 1936 the majority of inhabitants and teachers had negotiated a constructive agreement over their roles in the political, cultural, and socioeconomic life of the Sierra.

Up to 1936, caciques, state and federal governments, educational authorities, and many of the young progressive *serranos* had for the most part been working in tandem. However, with the break between the state government and the Sierra caciques and their political front man, Zaragoza, conflict became more generalized. Inhabitants were forced to decide between their revolutionary tenets of local political autonomy, which they felt had been infringed by the imposition of Chapital, and the visible benefits of alliance with the federal government. Late 1936 and early 1937 were periods of debate and confusion in the communities of the Sierra as progressives and conservatives, young secular revolutionaries and pious village Methuselahs pondered the divisions of state politics. The municipal elections of December 1936 were marred by a series of violent clashes.[82] Although teachers had increased social and medical work in the Sierra throughout 1936, attempting to draw wavering voters away from the Zaragozista camp, this was not enough to stabilize the region. At the beginning of January 1937 the tax collector relayed rumors to the governor that the men of Santa Catarina Lachatao were going to attack the district capital of Ixtlán.[83] Thus in March 1937 Cárdenas himself descended on the region.

When Cárdenas arrived in the village of San Pablo Guelatao on 15 March 1937, the town was "animated by political rancor and passion." There were "incendiary speeches against Governor Chapital" and "harsh shouts against him" as well as "petitions and praise for the defeated candidate, an individual named Benito Zaragoza."[84] Confronted with such a level of ill-concealed disquiet, Cárdenas attempted to win over the Zapotecs. He announced the creation of an indigenous boarding school in San Pablo Guelatao, the birthplace of Benito Juárez. Then he paid homage to the liberal president at the lake where he had famously lost his sheep and run away in shame to Oaxaca City.[85] According to a local policeman, Cárdenas also displayed his renowned humility, eschewing the lavish dinner offered by Ixtlán's great and good for a meal of tortillas, chilies, and mustard served up by an old peasant couple.[86] But the trip was not merely an exercise in presidential theatre; Cárdenas also offered Sierra villages a wealth of material improvements. In San Pablo Guelatao sanitary new houses were to be constructed for the workers. The Department of Work, now headed by ex-governor Genaro V. Vásquez, was to help with the building of a potable water system and a boarding school for three hundred indigenous children. In Santa Catarina Ixtepeji the president donated a flourmill, two typewriters, and

FIG. 2. The welcoming committee for Lázaro Cárdenas, Oaxaca City, 1937.
(Courtesy of the Biblioteca Bustamante Vasconcelos)

money for the construction of a secondary school and ordered engineers to look at the potential for hydroelectric power. In Santa Ana Yareni Cárdenas ordered the construction of a bridge and another flourmill.[87] He was at pains to impose these improvements in the most sensitive way possible. According to Pérez García, the president suggested working the various mills with cooperatives. But he announced that "if the word cooperative offends you, change it," for "we do not have the right to help you with ideas that annoy you."[88]

However, oratory and the intensification of education and infrastructure were not enough to win over many of the serranos. Over the next three years Cárdenas allowed both increased political autonomy and "democratization" in the form of the breakdown of the traditional cargo system.[89] There were modifications to elections, decision making, and the accountability of federal employees. In late 1936 the elected municipal authorities and municipal agents of the electoral district of Ixtlán in the Sierra Juárez of Oaxaca met to decide on the PRM candidates for the federal and local deputies of the region. Numerous official and nonofficial candidates assured the audience of their plans for the development of the Sierra. When the federal teacher Hermenegildo Luis Pérez Méndez stood up to propose what he would do as local deputy, he announced that he would not promise anything but rather act as the "manager of the aspirations of the people." Such an open display of honesty and political transparency obviously attracted the municipal authorities, and they elected Pérez Méndez as PRM candidate for the federal deputyship rather than the local deputyship he had originally sought. The vote condemned the official candidate, Rosendo Pérez García, to second place. At first Pérez Méndez was reluctant to take up the role, claiming ignorance of national political issues. But a member of the expectant crowd intervened, announcing that his election "was an act of democracy": "Don Hermenegildo, you will see how things happen, but you are going to Mexico." To the surprise of the *serranos*, his candidacy was accepted by the national chamber of deputies despite his defeat of the official entrant, and he arrived in Mexico City to take his place in early 1937.[90]

Not only were the *serranos* allowed to elect their own local representatives free from the influence of the national party; at the same time, the principle of *serrano* unity and self-government was advanced through the creation of the Unión Fraternal de Ayuntamientos Serranos, which was established to promote "friendship, mutual cooperation and peace among the communities." This union of pueblos was permitted to interfere at all levels of regional life. In 1937 the organization worked successfully to press for the dismissal of problematic government employees of the DAAI.[91] They were also permitted to interfere in the running of the SEP. In September 1937 the regional school inspector set up a center consisting of members of the Sierra councils to decide on regional educational issues. This group was allowed to discharge teachers who were felt to have overstepped the boundaries of ethical and moral behavior. At their first meeting two teachers were removed.[92] Interference in the SEP continued into the 1940s. A meeting in November 1941 demonstrates the degree of local autonomy the Sierra Zapotecs achieved. The teachers, the education committees, and the union of councils of the region met in the semiurban school of Ixtlán de Juárez. Two students of the indigenous school at Guelatao complained about the behavior of the school's principal. Although the local representative of the SEP and a host of teachers defended the man, the union of councils and the education committees supported what they described as "good Zapotec students" and voted to have him removed immediately.[93] Finally, the union was allowed to arbitrate in Ixtlán's political problems. Although Cárdenas had announced that decisions over interpueblo land disputes had officially become the preserve of the federal government in December 1937, the organization was allowed to resolve problems between Santa María Jaltianguis and San Juan Evangelista Analco and between Santiago Laxopa and Santa Catarina Yahuio.[94]

In 1939 the Confederación de Pueblos de la Sierra Juárez was installed at a general meeting of three hundred representatives from more than one hundred pueblos. It now comprised the municipalities of the ex-districts of Ixtlán, Villa Alta, Choapam, and the Región Mixe.[95] Although the organization never extended much control over these extra regions, the statutes of the expanded organization demonstrate many of the facets of Ixtlán's novel political system. Major decisions were to be made in biannual general assemblies of all the confederation's members. Here a "free vote" would elect members of the executive committee for the next year. Furthermore, each pueblo or social organization would elect a representative to a "vigilance committee," which would "make sure that the executive committee complie[d] with the desires of the general assembly." The statutes stressed the importance of young men who, rather than acting as lower functionaries within the cargo system, should now be allowed "to participate actively in all aspects of the social order." They also emphasized the role of teachers in the cultural and social formation of the Sierra Juárez. According to statute 3, teachers "have in their hands the most important and decisive role, the dissemination of popular education under a new philosophy." The decrees displayed a strong sense of political, historical, and cultural autonomy. They demanded that the Sierra Juárez form its own electoral district so that all its local and federal deputies were "sons of the region." One of the speakers, Ismael Alvarez, put this into historical context, arguing that the political and martial history of the *serranos* merited the redrawing of the electoral boundaries. He recounted how since the time of Marcos Pérez and Benito Juárez, eight *serranos* had been governors of the state. Moreover during the nineteenth and twentieth centuries, hundreds of *serranos* had "formed themselves into armed groups to defend the country and slowly transformed themselves into professional soldiers." This sense of national importance, regional pride, historical particularity, and political independence was summed up by the anthem of the new organization, "El mosquito," which had been written by what they termed a *maestro rural* on a military operation against Emperor Maximilian in the 1860s. It is worth quoting in full.

> We the Serranos
> Of firm convictions
> Of loyal hearts
> Without doubts or fear
> Having what we have
> By law and by our rights
> We live satisfied
> Without doubts or fear
>
> We love our mountains
> With their high peaks
> So high and hidden
> There in the immensity
> We love our forests
> But with more desire
> With burning passion
> We love our beautiful liberty
>
> It doesn't matter the torrent
> Of bullets the rifle fires at us
> We have our great wall
> Our valor and dignity
> It doesn't matter the thundering
> Of frightening voices
> The formidable voices
> Of the mauser and the cannon
>
> We have our mountains
> Covering our homes

We have the heroism of great Juárez
And our BEAUTIFUL LIBERTY
But if adverse winds blow us
Then crowned
With a red glow
Face forward
Mauser in hand
The last Serrano
Will fall facing the sun.[96]

Despite the declarations and rhetoric of the confederation (which was later renamed the Unión Fraternal de Ayuntamientos de la Sierra Juárez), the contemporary persistence of the cargo system in much of Ixtlán suggests that the eradication of the political branch of the municipal system may have been more a political expedient than a genuine assimilation of government doctrine.[97] As a result, in fact, divisions were probably more political than ideological. Nevertheless, electoral conflicts during the following decade continued to be expressed as a clash between revolutionary, democratic progressives and older reactionaries. For example, in 1940 the teacher of Santa Ana Yareni, Federico S. Vargas, wrote to the confederation to complain that "the traditional leaders of the village" led by Cristobal Cruz had removed the "democratically elected" municipal council by force. The organization sent the federal deputy, Absalón Santiago, to return the original council to the municipal palace.[98] In January 1942 village elders, now supported by the *serrano* cacique Onofre Jiménez, took over the municipal palace of Santiago Comaltepec. The regional union of councils wrote a succession of letters on behalf of the "elected representatives" of the village complaining about the lack of "democracy." They complained that "reaction-aries" imbued with "the ideology of the church" had used force rather than elections to depose the "revolutionary leaders" of Comaltepec.[99] In the report of the Fraternal Union in 1947, the teacher Rosendo Pérez García explained that the union had been established by the "young, revolutionaries of the Sierra Juárez" to "bring democracy" to the region.[100]

In many ways Cárdenas had won. The 1939 meeting of the confederation of Sierra inhabitants endorsed the unknown fig-ure of González Fernández for governor, and the former caciques, who had faced down the power of the federal state in 1936, were forced to retreat from their previous region of influence. The rev-olutionary progressives, who had previously backed them, now swung their support behind the president and the national party. Isaac Ibarra and Onofre Jiménez were left with the support of their previous enemies, the village elders. Benito Zaragoza does not appear again in the historical records in regard to the Sierra Juárez. However, in return, the *serranos* enjoyed a remarkable degree of electoral democracy and political independence. Cárde-nas's promises of reform and the emergence of the union solidified the emergence of the political autonomy and what was described as democracy in the Sierra. The progressives now emerged as the genuine leaders of the region. The political cargo system, which had been gradually disappearing after the Revolution, was rele-gated for the time being to a purely religious role.[101] The power of the village elders diminished, and Sierra peasants now voted on their representatives at the municipal level, who in turn decided on political and educational matters at regular regional meetings. Cardenismo, which in late 1936 had threatened the *serranos'* at-tachment to municipal autonomy and rule, by 1940 had offered the inhabitants a new autonomous modus vivendi, which would last for at least a decade. Only with the changes to electoral practice in the late 1940s and the emergence of a new rapacious timber elite in the late 1950s did the system begin to unravel.[102]

Conclusion

The system of Cardenista politics that emerged in Oaxaca in the 1930s posits a dual policy of state control and local autonomy. Although recently historians have argued that in Puebla, Sonora, and Yucatán the elections of the state governors were forced upon Cárdenas by powerful state camarillas, and that the subsequent administrations of Maximino Avila Camacho, Román Yocupicio Valenzuela, and Florencio Palomo Valencia deviated from Cardenista doctrine and practice, the same cannot be said for Oaxaca.[103] Cárdenas's choice and appointment of Constantino Chapital as governor suggests the type of centralized, authoritarian rule posited by revisionist historians. The state's new governor relied for his position on the favor of the president. Furthermore his policies of *agrarismo*, labor reform, and the federalization of state education followed those of his political godfather. Yet it is not necessarily the case that Cárdenas was motivated by the desire to extend autocratic and centralized control over the state government. Like Querétaro, Tabasco, Chiapas, and Veracruz, Oaxaca was recovering from the hegemony of an influential personal regime.[104] Cárdenas's selection of the anonymous figure of Chapital instead of a representative from one of the local camarillas not only prevented a repeat of the regionalism of the López Cortés regime but also avoided conflict among the camarillas themselves.

The president's acceptance of more autonomous political arrangements is clear in his dealings with the Sierra Juárez. Here the work of rural teachers and the proclivity for municipal and regional political independence forced Cárdenas to permit the expansion of local involvement in the educational and electoral process. Contrary to Arturo Anguiano's judgment that the president's "constant travels" were part of his Machiavellian scheme to "oversee local compliance and control local leaders," his visit to Sierra Juárez was an emergency measure, which ratified existing ideas of democracy and autonomy in the region.[105] As Ben Fallaw argues, Cárdenas freely pursued political egalitarianism, especially when it coincided with the need for unity and security.[106] This was not the mass national democracy of the PRM and the peasant and worker unions, observed by the first generation of Mexican historians and political scientists, but rather a local agreement based on a specific local political context. Although it was a negotiated agreement similar to those studied by Mary Kay Vaughan in the mestizo regions of the Yaqui Valley or the acculturated areas of Puebla, or by Marjorie Becker in indigenous regions of Michoacán, the success of socialist education did not lead to growing power for the federal state. Negotiation did not inevitably precipitate a greater degree of hegemony. Instead, the political system constructed by Cárdenas and the *serranos* appears closer to the establishment of "domains of sovereignty" scrutinized by Jeffrey Rubin in Juchitán during the same period. In the Sierra the Zapotec Indians' strategies of dealing with the outside world—developed during the Porfiriato, honed during the Revolution, and supported by the influx of predominantly indigenous teachers—forced the government into allowing a high level of local autonomy. Socialist education was modified and accepted but other aspects of state control were refused. In fact, local control continued and extended itself over the weak state's federal organizations, such as the SEP, without the interference of the PNR or the PRM. This process, with considerable regional variation, was common throughout the state of Oaxaca during the period. Here, as we shall see in the next chapter, "hybrid" caciques such as Heliodoro Charis in Juchitán and Luis Rodríguez in the Región Mixe maintained control over municipal elections and federal organizations.

But local autonomy did not necessarily involve a politically savvy cacique. In the Sierra Juárez, a series of factors triggered the growing political irrelevance of the region's caciques and the establishment of an autonomous union of democratically elected village councils. As in many other areas of Mexico, the centralizing process of state formation during the 1930s rid the area of its free-wheeling revolutionary strongmen. However, communal ideas of local autonomy, which had originated in the nineteenth century and been reinforced by the Revolution, precluded the establishment of the traditional cacique's customary successor, the "modern" or "corporatist" cacique.[107] Instead, the Sierra's villages founded an autonomous union of village councils, which usurped control of local educational and political disputes. Former *serrano* soldiers utilized the new organization to eradicate the political branch of the cargo system. "Democratic" election and not age now became the prerequisite for municipal office. In many ways the Sierra Juárez was a special case with a peculiar indigenous tradition of popular liberalism. In other areas of Mexico socialist education and the politics of Cardenismo cemented the power of traditional caciques, introduced modern regional leaders, or regimented peasants and workers into the state's new corporatist organizations.

FIVE

Cárdenas's Caciques, 1936–40

From 1934 to 1940 Cárdenas's patronage of mass organizations and the reform of the national party reoriented politics at all levels. Traditional descriptions of this process in the regions have linked the formation of a powerful bureaucratic state to the creation of a network of "modern" caciques with links to the PRM through control of *ejidal* committees and unions.[1] Some traditional caciques adapted to the changing face of national politics. Paul Friedrich describes how Ezequiel "Scarface" Cruz gradually linked his local power base to Michoacán's peasant confederation, eventually becoming head of Michoacán's labor confederation.[2] Others were replaced by a new breed of bureaucratically savvy, politically ambitious young caciques, schooled in the complexities of the state administration. These men fought to obtain the armed, electoral, or organizational power of the campesinos to offer to politicians inside or outside the government in exchange for favors such as grants of land, credit, and social and educational services. In Tlaxcala, Raymond Buve outlines the rapid rise of Emilio Carvajal and Ruben C. Carrizosa, who came to dominate the ejidos of Huamantla.[3] In turn, the emergence of these "new intermediaries" increased state power and centralization as peasant groups were steadily incorporated into mass organizations and, by extension, into the national party.[4] In predominantly indigenous regions, this model of *cacicazgos* has been

particularly strong. In Chiapas, scholars describe how indigenous caciques such as Enrique Uribe utilized programs of *indigenismo* to shanghai Tzotzil Indians to lowland coffee fincas as
part of a new state union.[5]

Over the past decade scholars of *cacicazgos* have started to
modify the sharp temporal bifurcation between traditional and
modern caciques, dissect the cacique's relationship with the state,
and examine in greater detail the modus operandi of Mexico's
myriad local bosses.[6] This chapter attempts to build on that work
by examining how four caciques adapted to the new demands of
Cardenismo and how the resulting *cacicazgos* affected the system
of state control. In general terms, I posit that although Cardenismo
did affect power relations within the Oaxacan countryside, it did
not always develop a pattern of leadership modernization, co-
option, and control. In fact, despite the adoption of some of the
convenient discourses of Cardenismo, many caciques managed
to maintain traditional *cacicazgos* with little or no interference
from the central government and often in opposition to the state's
corporatist organizations. In fact, Cárdenas's concern for stability encouraged the continuation of these practices and, by extension, the prolonged weakness of the Mexican state. In comparing the *cacicazgos* of Heliodoro Charis Castro, Luis Rodríguez,
Francisco Ramos Ortiz, and Celestino Guzmán, this chapter suggests a typology of Oaxaca's caciques based on the dichotomy
suggested by James B. Greenberg. By examining the *cacicazgos*
of Juquila and the Región Mixe, Greenberg has argued that individual systems were dependent on regional histories of capitalist incursion. In late nineteenth-century Juquila, mestizos established huge fincas and exploitative mercantile networks under
the control of a cabal of *cacical* mestizo families. In contrast, in

the Región Mixe, economic control and political power remained in the hands of indigenous leaders such as Luis Rodríguez.[7] The following investigation complicates this dichotomy by also looking at ethnic strategies of resistance and the local composition of the Cardenista state apparatus. The intricate interaction of these three factors delineated not only four different *cacicazgos* but also four different types of continuous resistance to these established boss systems. The ongoing struggle between these divergent factions in the shadow of an ineffective state shaped the regions' future politics.

The Network of Caciques

During the 1920s Francisco López Cortés had relied on a network of strongmen, based in the capitals of the ex-districts. During the next decade little changed. Power still emanated from these centers of legal, fiscal, and educational administration. Local control still depended on the appointment of municipal authorities, school inspectors, tax collectors, judges, agents of the public ministry, and leaders of the *defensas sociales*. The list in table 2 is broadly similar to that posited in table 1 for the Chicolopista period. But there are some differences. As described in chapter 4, democratic progressives in Ixtlán had managed to escape the domination of their revolutionary caciques during the late 1930s. Many state organs were now circumscribed by a union of Ixtlán councils. Further, as discussed in chapter 6, in areas of established agricultural consequence such as Tuxtepec and the Central Valleys, the peasant and worker confederations gradually managed to direct some of these positions. However, in the more isolated regions of the state, traditionally less important strategically and economically, caciques continued to govern by broadly traditional

Table 2. Strongmen of Oaxaca, 1930s

Area of influence	Caciques
Pochutla	Francisco Ramos Ortiz
Miahuatlán	Genaro Ramos
Miahuatlán	Celestino Guzmán
Juchitán	Celestino Guzmán
Huajuapam	Rodolfo Solana Carrion, José Peral Martínez
Putla	Isidro Montesinos López
Región Mixe	Luis Rodríguez
Coixtlahuaca	Agustín Bazán
Teotitlán del Camino	Tiburcio Cuellar
Yautepec	Celestino Ruíz

means. With the emergence of a burgeoning coffee economy, the caciques ruled without or in opposition to the new organizations and even the party itself.

Ethno-Militarist Cacique Heliodoro Charis Castro, Juchitán

In the region of Juchitán the history of struggle between Hispanic and mestizo outsiders and indigenous Zapotec peasants framed the creation of Heliodoro Charis Castro's *cacicazgo*. During the nineteenth century Juchitán had attracted an array of government agents, hacendados, capitalist speculators, and commercial monopolists. They established large landholdings, alienated indigenous lands, attempted to privatize Juchitán's communal salt flats, prohibited the textile trade with Guatemala, and appropriated land for colonization schemes.[8] The opening of the Isthmus railway in 1894 increased the rhythm of Mexican and foreign capitalization. Coffee and rubber plantations now supplemented those devoted to sugar and livestock. According to Karl Kaerger, "the North Americans arrived en masse and planted . . . millions of coffee trees on the lowest slopes of the mountain chain that encircles the Isthmus."[9] By 1901 companies such as the Mexican Land and Coffee Company and the Mexican Tropical Planters Company held enormous landholdings within the district of Juchitán.[10] Commercial agriculture attracted peasants and workers from outside the predominantly Zapotec inhabitants. During the Porfiriato the region's population increased from 70,000 to 130,000.[11]

In response the local Zapotecs forged a dual strategy of resistance. On the one hand, they resorted to occasional armed revolt. In 1848 Che Gorio Melendre led a Juchiteco revolt against salt miners, hacendados, and the state's governing elite. Over the next half century there were multiple revolts against nonnative intervention in the region's politics and economy.[12] During the Revolution José F. Gómez led another Zapotec rebellion against political impositions by Oaxaca City.[13] On the other hand, they also developed strategies of diplomatic negotiation. As Jeffrey Rubin argues, Juchitecos, unlike other indigenous groups, held the "middle ground between isolation and subjugation."[14] As a result, they gradually learned to adapt to the periodic waves of political and economic incursion. In particular, Juchitán's political leaders learned to exploit divisions within the governing elites, often deliberately bypassing the *vallistocracia* and talking directly to the federal government. Che Gorio Melendre announced the independence of the Isthmus with the encouragement of Antonio López de Santa Anna.[15] José F. Gómez attempted to circumvent the Oaxaca City government by going straight to Francisco Madero.[16]

Despite the creation of a resilient Zapotec culture of political resistance during the Porfiriato, and despite the exodus of foreign investors during the Revolution, capitalization and immigration had delineated a geography of ethnic tensions. New towns along the Isthmus railway, such as Matias Romero, Ciudad Ixtepec, and Unión Hidalgo, were predominantly mestizo. In the census of 1940, 93 percent of Ciudad Ixtepec's population and 99 percent in Matias Romero could speak Spanish. Other towns and villages maintained a sizable indigenous population, such as Santa María Xadani, Santa María Petepa, and most important, Juchitán de Zaragoza itself. In the same census 65 percent of the residents of Santa María Xadani and 50 percent of the inhabitants of Juchitán de Zaragoza claimed to speak Zapotec exclusively.[17] Although there was considerable overlap, regional politics followed the contours of ethnic division. The reds were predominantly mestizos from the region's new towns, while the greens dominated in areas where there was a high proportion of Zapotecs. During the postrevolutionary period the reds under Governor López Cortés had dominated the district and almost succeeded in moving the *cabecera* to Ciudad Ixtepec.[18] However, in 1934, the red faction had splintered, and López Cortés had entered into an uneasy association with the leader of the green faction, Heliodoro Charis Castro. In response the excluded reds looked to recapture political ground by allying with the state's expanding corporatist machinery. As a result, despite the alliance, when Cárdenas visited the region in 1934, he was depressed to find that the "endemic division," which he had witnessed as military commander in 1921 and 1922, still "affected the pueblos with political and blood quarrels."[19] Consequently the political demise of the López Cortés faction in late 1936 offered the state an opportunity but also a dilemma. Cárdenas was forced to choose between the indigenous strongman and the corporatist coalition of former reds, workers, teachers, and party organizations. Despite the reds' assumption of this orthodox route to regional power, Cárdenas's emphasis on stability and Charis's assumption of the state policy of socialist education allowed the maintenance of the indigenous *cacicazgo*. But this failed to end the region's ethnic factionalism. The corporatist alliance continued to dispute regional control during the late 1930s and provided a useful alternative for future governors who wished to unseat the regional strongman.

Heliodoro Charis was born in Juchitán de Zaragoza in 1896. During the Revolution he fought for the green faction against the reds and their supporters in Oaxaca City. He first came to prominence in 1919, when he challenged the local coalition of reds and Carrancistas. In May 1920 he took Juchitán and allied with Alvaro Obregón. Over the next decade Charis used the forces he had formed during the Revolution to fight Delahuertistas and Cristeros throughout central Mexico.[20] When he returned to his hometown in 1929 he immediately attracted supporters by opposing Governor Francisco López Cortés's proposal to achieve greater control in Juchitán by distributing the lands of Paso Lagarto among the nearby villages of Santa María Xadani, San Blas, and El Espinal. In order to impede the governor's plans, Charis used his troops and four hundred green colonists to establish the Military Colony Alvaro Obregón.[21]

The military colony would form the cornerstone of Charis's local power. Over the succeeding decades, the colonists not only provided the local boss with the realistic threat of armed force but also a pool of potential pistoleros and a group of willing voters who could be transported to areas of electoral conflict. However, the *cacicazgo* was not simply founded on superior military strength; Charis's regional standing also depended on his appeal to Zapotec ideas of ethnicity. Like most Juchitecos, Charis had no formal schooling, and although he had learned Spanish in adulthood, he spoke Zapotec as his first language. As a result, he eschewed the pretensions of the region's Hispanic or mestizo inhabitants and continued to communicate with the mass of Juchitecos in their own language.[22] Despite his ostensible riches, Charis persisted in dressing, acting, and celebrating as a traditional Juchiteco.[23] By the mid-1930s, despite a few forays regional politics, he had established a distinctly local *cacicazgo* around the town of Juchitán de Zaragoza based on traditional qualities of charisma, local knowledge, friendship, kinship, and force.[24] There is no doubt that Cárdenas's concern for stability influenced his decision to allow Charis's continued rule. The Juchiteco cacique's military muscle and his support in Juchitán suggested that nominating any other source of federal power would involve either prolonged confrontation or shifting the ex-district capital.

Cárdenas's presidency offered Charis not only the confirmation of his local power base but also the opportunity to extend his control over the entire region. Like former Juchiteco leaders, he succeeded in doing this by skirting local political groups and going directly to the federal government. During Cárdenas's visit to Juchitán the future president suggested that the only way to end the perpetual conflict between reds and greens was to establish "a cultural center and sufficient schools" to teach local children to avoid the bitter animosities of their parents.[25] The idea seemed to have gained wider acceptance, and on the advice of

FIG. 3. Heliodoro Charis speaking to the people of Juchitán from the balcony of the municipal palace. (Reprinted from *Mexico South* by Miguel Covarrubias)

General Joaquín Amaro, Charis began to present himself as the region's representative of the state education program.[26] In May 1935, having become municipal president of the town earlier that year, Charis contacted the SEP and proposed the creation of an industrial school in Juchitán de Zaragoza.[27] Over the next two years he supervised the construction of the establishment with the ready support of state and federal authorities. Despite the petitions of members of the local Catholic society, he was able to locate the school in the courtyard of the municipal church.[28] By October 1937 the newspaper *Oaxaca en México* announced that "because of the valiant gestures of the revolutionary general Charis, a school building of great dimensions and beautiful characteristics has been constructed."[29] On 1 August 1938 the "Revolución" industrial school opened its doors to prospective

Isthmus students.[30] At the same time, Charis pushed for other improvements in the town, including the construction of a new federal hospital and an increase in the number of medical personnel sent from Mexico City.

Charis's support for Juchitán de Zaragoza's industrial school clearly impressed the Cardenista authorities, who designated him federal deputy for the region in 1937.[31] As the teacher Feliciano López Felix complained, "With the construction of the school building with which the government has entrusted him, General Charis has been converted into a true Jefe Político, he is now omnipotent in his power over the whole district."[32] The appropriation of the government program of education not only helped Charis gain the support of the national government—his pursuit of educational and healthcare facilities for the local Juchitecos cemented the backing of his traditional supporters and drew former reds into his faction.[33] Many started to see tangible benefits in Charis's rule. The figure of their ill-educated Zapotec representative haranguing the federal government in broken Spanish for local improvements also appealed to a general sense of ethnic identity.[34]

Despite federal government support for Charis's growing hegemony in the region, opposition still remained. By allowing Charis exclusive control of the region, the central and state authorities had ignored the coalition of former reds, workers, and teachers, who had originally supported Cárdenas's presidential candidacy and might have been expected to take power. As a result, this Cardenista *cacicazgo* was disputed throughout the late 1930s by these groups. In May 1936 unionized teachers went on strike in the Isthmus to force the state government to retract the sacking of Juan Carlos Hidalgo and Germán López Trujillo, who were attempting to unionize workers in the port of Salina Cruz.[35] Testament to the teachers' political motives was the demand for the verification of anti-Charista candidates in the recent municipal plebiscites and the support for the strikers by the political leaders of the opposition to Charis.[36] Other teachers who confronted the Juchitán strongman were clearly influenced by Marxist ideology and the hope of socioeconomic reform. According to some teachers, they had "accepted with pleasure to lead the organizations of workers and peasants and reveal the exploitation practiced by Charis in his large landholdings."[37] As the dispute over the employment of teachers dragged on, Charis sided with a rival teachers' union and regional merchants frightened by some of the teachers' more radical rhetoric and attempted to dislodge the obstreperous educators.[38] Feliciano López Felix, the leader of the Juchitán teachers, complained in March 1937 that he and his colleagues lived under a "reign of terror" imposed by General Charis.[39] Finally, in May 1938 Charis persuaded the SEP's director to dismiss the original tutors and impose twenty-one new teachers fresh from the normal schools of Mexico City.[40]

Besides confronting the region's teachers, Charis also came into conflict with Juchitán's nascent union movement. In August 1937 the teacher López Felix called together nine unions from the municipality of Juchitán de Zaragoza to form the CTM-affiliated Sindicato Unico de Trabajadores de Juchitán.[41] By 1938 it claimed representatives from all Juchitán de Zaragoza's barrios and control of over fifteen hundred members.[42] Although Charis attempted to persuade the Junta de Conciliación y Arbitraje not to recognize the new group, persisted in intimidating its members, and formed a white union in league with several salt merchants to exploit the large salt flats, López Felix's union became the center of opposition to Charis in the municipality of Juchitán de Zaragoza.[43] In the elections of 1937 and 1938 it put forward candidates for the municipal presidency and unsuccessfully claimed victory over the candidates imposed by Charis.[44] Outside Juchitán de Zaragoza the CLSO members, who had fought with García Toledo against López Cortés during 1935, now joined the CTM and continued the battle against cacique rule. By 1937 CTM organizations linked to the Federación Regional de Obreros y Campesinos had become the focal points for resistance to Charis's control of the municipal councils. In Unión Hidalgo the Sindicato de Salineros del Istmo was also harassed for its support of an anti-Charista candidate for the municipal presidency.[45] In the municipal agency of Santo Domingo, the same authorities harassed the union of workers of the recently nationalized sugar factory throughout the late 1930s.[46]

The deal struck between Cárdenas and Charis not only disrupted the corporatist organization of teachers and workers; it also undermined the construction of the national party system. During the late 1930s the former politicians from the red party maintained the contacts with teachers and workers forged during the rise of Cardenismo. Together they managed to take control of the emerging party system in the Isthmus. In 1937, perhaps as a means to balance Charis's power, Graciano Pineda, a red politician, was made local deputy. The following year he was appointed to the executive council of the newly formed state PRM.[47] Municipal elections, especially in large mestizo communities, now pitted Charistas against the local representatives of the national party. In December 1937 Charistas led by Francisco Enríquez beat a PNR alliance of CTM workers and teachers for the municipal presidency of Unión Hidalgo.[48] Although the state government, influenced by Pineda, ordered that Enríquez stand down in April 1938, he remained in place for the duration of the year.[49] In late 1939 this pattern of electoral dispute spread throughout the Isthmus as both groups jostled for position before the presidential candidate, Manuel Avila Camacho. In Unión Hidalgo and Reforma, Charista candidates beat the candidates of the local PRM. Attempts to block the impositions were halted by Charis's control of the local judge.[50] In Matias Romero the Charista candidate, Arnulfo Rivas, claimed victory over the PRM-backed Comité Electoral Pro-Avila Camacho. Although Pineda arrived in the town to overturn the election in favor of his own aspirant, the attempt failed. Rivas took the municipal building by force on 1 January 1940 and retained power despite the complaints of the opposition.[51]

The establishment of Charis's *cacicazgo* depended on the historical formation of a distinct Zapotec identity based on prolonged resistance to mestizo incursion. In Juchitán, an indigenous cacique with close connections to the majority of the region's population managed to achieve official recognition from the Cardenista state. Yet the formation of this distinct *cacicazgo* failed to initiate an era of growing federal control. Although Charis appropriated the state policy of socialist education, he failed to construct a network of peasant or worker organizations or a bureaucratic party system. Local control still depended on charisma, ethnic sensitivity, and force. The president's reliance on this Janus-faced figure rather than the shoots of corporatist government displays the premium he placed on local stability and the high degree to which he accepted decentralization as the price the central government had to pay. However, despite Cárdenas's hopes for greater regional stability, support for the cacique outside the city of Juchitán de Zaragoza was demonstrably weak. Divisions, often along ethnic lines, remained. Teachers, workers, and politicians from the red party opposed the regime through the instigation of strikes, the process of unionization, and electoral conflict. Unlike Charis they were quick to see the opportunities offered by the new corporatist party system, which they started to control from 1937. By the end of Cárdenas's presidency, his chosen cacique faced a cross-class alliance of powerful opponents under the banner of the PRM. The federal state's inability to secure cohesive control and the resulting conflict between these two factions would frame the politics of the succeeding decades.

Finquero-Plantocrat Cacique
Francisco Ramos Ortiz, Pochutla

In some areas of Oaxaca, strategies of resistance developed during the nineteenth century permitted the continuation of indigenous leadership despite and, in the case of Juchitán, in opposition to mestizo groups. But the Cárdenas period also witnessed the construction of heavily exploitative mestizo *cacicazgos* in other areas with divergent histories of capitalization, state interference, and ethnic resistance. In regions disrupted by the increasing cultivation of coffee, traditional mestizo caciques were so powerful and the state was so weak that they had little need for the window-dressing of Cardenismo. Many caciques were able to continue previous practices of extortion, imposition, and violence with little or no interference from the state or central governments. In these areas opposition to particular *cacicazgos* was endemic. But for a variety of historical reasons, forms of resistance differed. In regions such as Pochutla, established links with mestizo radicals,

forged over a long period of exploitation, encouraged the formation of numerous agrarian committees and worker unions. Although most petitions and strikes were unsuccessful, the acculturated peasantry gradually learned the rules of the game. In more
isolated regions, such as Juxtlahuaca or the Región Mixe, ethnic
resistance had been historically predicated on general hostility
to state intrusion. Further, the organs of government administration had been almost completely cannibalized by the local cacique. As a result, peasants eschewed the new "language of contention" and instead relied on violent revolt.

The establishment and maintenance of mestizo *cacicazgos* during the Cárdenas era was linked to the increasing importance of
coffee to the regional economy. During the postrevolutionary period, especially as the banana boom drew to a close, coffee was
Oaxaca's chief crop. Although census reports tended to overlook
coffee production on small peasant landholdings, which dominated in some areas of Oaxaca, the figures listed still offered perpetual succor to Oaxaca's frustrated agricultural modernizers. In
1940, 1,004 properties occupying 13,410 hectares harvested an
annual crop of 6.5 million kilograms, which was sold for over 1.7
million pesos. In comparison, other capitalized export crops such
as tobacco, bananas, and sugar produced markedly less annual
revenue. In national terms Oaxaca was the fourth largest coffee
producer in Mexico with only Chiapas, Veracruz, and San Luis
Potosí devoting more lands to the crop and extracting superior
profits.[52] As a result of the political regimes established and encouraged during the Cárdenas era, coffee production expanded
dramatically over the succeeding decade. By 1950 over 34,000
hectares of land produced over 57 million kilograms and an annual income of 85 million pesos. Although other cash crops had

increased their production value, they were now dwarfed by the state's coffee income. The combined value of banana, tobacco, and pineapple income was barely 25 million pesos. Oaxaca now produced around a quarter of Mexico's coffee and was superseded in terms of production only by Veracruz and Chiapas.[53]

As in many regions of Latin America, coffee proved the catalyst for rapid capitalization. But although the establishment of a coffee economy normally forced severe political and socioeconomic change, its exact effects varied greatly, even across a single state. In Pochutla, the introduction of coffee in the 1870s had created an economy of highly capitalized fincas. During the Reform era, cash-strapped cochineal merchants turned their attention to the cultivation of coffee. In 1874 a group of merchants from Miahuatlán formed a company in order to introduce large-scale coffee cultivation to Oaxaca. They established the first coffee plantation, optimistically named La Providencia, in Pochutla. Other mestizo merchants from Miahuatlán followed the speculators and by 1880 the Pochutla coffee region had twenty-six fincas.[54] The government, which was suffering from declining tax revenues from the cochineal trade, encouraged the expansion by offering sizable financial incentives and exemption from military and municipal duties.[55] British, German, and U.S. landowners joined the rush and bought up properties. By 1909 there were 151 fincas in the region worth four million pesos.[56] Between 1883 and 1889 Pochutla's coffee production tripled, and by 1911 the area produced two thirds of Oaxaca's coffee.[57]

The coffee boom brought an influx of new inhabitants. Between 1877 and 1910 the population of the region grew from 11,355 to 27,666.[58] New settlers and Zapotec villagers alike were forced to work the plantations through the provision of cash loans, which they were expected to pay back with seasonal labor. Pochutla never achieved the same degree of productivity as the neighboring plantations of Soconusco. In 1911 Oaxaca grew only a quarter as much coffee as was produced in Chiapas.[59] As many finca owners complained, despite the construction of the port of Puerto Angel in the late nineteenth century, transport from the plantations to the port was still mainly by mule.[60] There was also sustained resistance from the resident Zapotecs to expropriation of village lands. Basilio Rojas, whose grandfather had been instrumental in starting the coffee craze during the early Porfiriato, wrote that the "only obstacle to the development of the project" was "the love that the Indians had for their land, fighting for every piece, even the most miserable, and defending it from strangers."[61]

Some confrontations were violent. In 1894 the inhabitants of San Mateo Piñas attacked the Cafetal Alemania of Leo Von Brandenstein because of his construction work, which "was causing great harm to the population."[62] Zapotec villages became increasingly adept at garnering outside help. The village of Magdalena Piñas spent thousands of pesos on lawyers' fees during more than twenty years of legal disputes over boundaries with the finca El Pilar.[63] Similarly, the village of Santa María Loxicha was involved in more than a decade of legal wrangling over its borders with Marcelino Mendoza's finca in San Baltasar Loxicha.[64] The sustained dialogue between Zapotec peasants and mestizos from outside the region even reached the pages of the Porfiriato's handful of dissident newspapers. Both *Regeneración* and *El Bien Público* wrote damning articles on the local *jefe político*'s corrupt policies.[65]

There is little information on Pochutla during the Revolution. Most accounts claim that the fincas were abandoned for the period, but perhaps surprisingly for an area with connections to metropolitan radicals, there is little evidence of persistent peasant revolt.[66] What is clear is that after the Revolution the planter hegemony returned in force. Cultivation began almost immediately after the end of hostilities. Agustín Dominguez described how he had lost his properties during the Revolution, but with the aid of one Mexican investor and two Americans he had managed to buy back the fincas of Eureka, Margarita, Juárez, Las Nubes, and La Ceiba in Pluma Hidalgo. By the 1930s they were worth 283,115 pesos.[67] The villagers of San Baltasar Loxicha described how their mestizo municipal president had granted another mestizo investor, Manuel Ramírez, rights to plant coffee on their communal lands in 1921.[68] In the same year, an unnamed London company returned to the region and started to supplement its coffee industry with petroleum speculation.[69] The swift return of investors and the subsequent reopening of the coffee economy allowed Rojas to describe San Pedro Pochutla as "a commercial center again" as early as 1922.[70]

The postrevolutionary governments, like the Porfirian government before them, saw the large-scale production of coffee as key to the state's economy and its faltering taxation system. In 1929 Francisco López Cortés had announced that after Tuxtepec's bananas, Pochutla's coffee "was the most important crop in the Oaxacan economy."[71] In 1940 Pochutla produced tax revenue of over 180,000 pesos, or nearly 10 percent of the state's total income. Only the ex-district of Centro produced more.[72] As a result, state incentives were numerous. In 1931 the state's new fiscal law offered valuable financial inducements for potential coffee growers.[73] Perhaps most important, the previous postrevolutionary government had not even attempted to unionize the state's coffee workers. The communist leader Graciano Benitez complained in 1934 that "the government needs the money of Pochutla's hacendados and for this reason they do not allow us to enter the region."[74] By 1938 the number of coffee fincas in the district had reached seventy. Together they covered 82,348 hectares of the ex-district's land. Over a third of the properties were located in the municipality of Pluma Hidalgo. Some were small concerns of 100 hectares divided among family members. Others, such as the 8,925 hectares owned by Santiago Pedro in San Agustín Loxicha or the 8,775 hectares owned by Felipe de Jesús Juárez in San Francisco Loxicha, were huge commercial enterprises.[75] Traveling through Pochutla in the early 1930s, Aldous Huxley described the El Progreso finca of Englishman Roy Fenton as "a small kingdom with its own outlying provinces."[76]

The escalating coffee boom continued to draw the previously isolated Zapotecs into the international division of labor. Although some maintained small holdings in their villages, most now relied on temporary labor on the *cafetales*. During harvest time, from November to February, the CTM estimated that seven to eight thousand Zapotec Indians worked on the fincas.[77] Remuneration was pitiful; even at the height of the coffee season workers were paid from 0.75 to 1.00 peso per day.[78] The long course of commercialization of agriculture and the concomitant influx of outsiders had led to a well-developed process of acculturation in Pochutla's towns and villages. By 1940 only a handful of the most remote villages, such as Candelaria Loxicha and San Mateo Piñas, retained a sizable population of monolingual Zapotecs. In the major coffee town of Pluma Hidalgo 2,410 inhabitants spoke exclusively Spanish, while only 81 were bilingual. Similarly in the commercial center of San Pedro Pochutla itself 5,351 people spoke Spanish, while only 26 were bilingual.[79] Unlike in

Juchitán or Ixtlán, where many of the major towns maintained a powerful and sizable monolingual population, in Pochutla the rapid and violent implementation of a plantation economy forced many Zapotec villagers to forsake certain vestiges of their ethnic identity. As we shall observe, this process of acculturation was a double-edged sword. On the one hand, acculturated peasants from Pochutla initially welcomed mestizo radicals, as they had welcomed mestizo lawyers during the Porfiriato, as part of their continuing strategy of utilizing outside means of resistance to capitalist incursion. On the other hand, as the drive to unionize, demand land, and petition for better collective contracts was directed by outsiders rather than community members, it developed shallow roots. As a result, the regional cacique was able to stop reform by removing the movement's leaders. By 1940 the coffee plantations remained, and although Pochutla's peasants had learned the advantages of linkages with radical groups, official Cardenismo had been all but exterminated.

During the Cárdenas era, the policy of government noninterference established by the early postrevolutionary governments continued. This allowed the local cacique, Francisco Ramos Ortiz, to hold together the system of uneven land tenure and seasonal exploitation of Zapotec workers. Ramos Ortiz was a mestizo merchant originally from Miahuatlán, like many of the region's settlers.[80] His command of the region was military, political, and mercantile. In the immediate postrevolutionary period he had established a *defensa social* just outside the district capital on his own finca of Chacalapa.[81] In 1934 the head of the military zone estimated that it had twenty-three members, which made it the third largest in the state.[82] During the next decade the military force would be used to intimidate strikers, protect merchandise, and enforce the continued practice of debt contracts. Ramos Ortiz also dominated the region's politics through kinship relations to important members of the plantocracy. Although other caciques clearly utilized kinship relations to impose political control, no one was more ostentatiously nepotistic than the Pochutla strongman. In 1937 the local judge, José Manuel Santibanez, was Ramos Ortiz's son-in-law and a prominent coffee *finquero*. The secretary to the judge, Isaias Ramos, was his cousin; the executor of justice, Carlos Ziga Jr., his compadre; and the agent of public ministry, his cousin and employee.[83] When Ramos Ortiz ran out of relatives, he relied on political imposition accompanied by the threat of force. In 1937 he appointed the entire San Pedro Pochutla municipal council without plebiscite or election and invested the council surrounded by armed retainers.[84] In outlying villages he employed the same tactics of imposition. The people of Santa María Huatulco complained in 1933 that Ramos Ortiz simply appointed a handful of mestizos from San Pedro Pochutla as their municipal authorities without consultation.[85] Other potential political appointments were also mediated by the local strongman. As the district school inspector, he appointed compliant municipal educators and, in alliance with the local church, encouraged municipal authorities to refuse entry to federal teachers.[86]

The cacique also managed the two key needs of the recovering coffee industry: commerce and labor. During the late 1920s Ramos Ortiz organized a commercial monopoly in the region. He employed agents in Pluma Hidalgo and other coffee-growing areas to buy coffee from the large fincas and from peasant farmers. The wares were then transported back to Chacalapa, where they were sent off either to Puerto Angel or to the interior of the state.[87] Although other frontier coffee regions in Latin America experienced divisions between mercantile and landholding elites, in Pochutla Ramos Ortiz's monopoly went unopposed.[88] It seems that the *finqueros* were prepared to pay a substantial part of their profit for the safe passage of their goods. In 1938 the council of San Pedro Pochutla defended Ramos Ortiz from accusations of violent misconduct by arguing that he protected the valuable coffee trade and provided "the whole region with security."[89] Ramos Ortiz's mercantile monopoly encompassed not only the export of coffee but also all the import of other merchandise. One visiting teacher admired "his huge general store, fizzy drinks factory, *nixtamal* mill, and great warehouse of coffee that he collected from the fincas of the region, transported to Puerto Angel and sent to other places."[90] A less impressionable member of a visiting cultural mission was less approving and noted that Ramos Ortiz's monopoly on trade into the region and wholesaling to village stores caused important articles to cost four or five times the national average.[91]

The issue of labor was more problematic for the Pochutla cacique. It seems that despite the Revolution, the practice of *enganche* continued. Ramos Ortiz and a coterie of rich planters employed agents in Zapotec villages, who offered cash loans in exchange for contracts promising labor in the coffee fincas during harvest time. Moises de la Peña claimed that the agents were paid two to three pesos per adult contracted.[92] If a contract went unfulfilled, Ramos Ortiz would send members of his *defensa social* to the unwilling worker to exact compliance. In 1935 a handful of residents from Candelaria Loxicha complained that they no longer wanted to work the lowland fincas. But each November they were forced at gunpoint to Pluma Hidalgo to "pay our debts, which we have already returned many times."[93] During the 1920s and early

1930s, resistance to the scheme had been sporadic. The plaintive letters of the Candelaria Loxicha peasants were accompanied by the attempted burning of Ramos Ortiz's house in 1928.[94]

During the late 1930s resistance became endemic as outside radicals descended on the region. Although there are isolated mentions of this organized agitation in 1935 as part of the anti-Calles campaign, Cardenismo arrived later in Pochutla than in the state's other regions of commercial agriculture. In June 1936 an association of *finqueros* warned the local newspaper that "communists" had infiltrated San Pedro Pochutla and were threatening to disrupt the annual coffee harvest.[95] These communists were led by members of the state's branch of the PCM, Graciano Benitez and Jesús Loaeza Cruz. As such they walked the increasingly blurry line between state sanction and official condemnation, testament to the state's reluctance to dismantle Pochutla's valuable coffee plantations. In late 1936 they set up the Frente Popular Libertador Pochutleco (FPLP) and began to press for the dismantling of the plantocracy's hold on local politics and economics.[96] Although Ramos Ortiz had managed to stem the flow of federal teachers to the region, they were helped by a handful of socialist educators who had managed to slip through the local school inspector's net.

This small group employed four distinct tactics to undermine Ramos Ortiz's *cacicazgo*. First, they attempted to unionize the region's workers and obtain a raft of labor demands. During 1937 the FPLP linked up with the radical branch of the regional CTM, the Federación Regional de Trabajadores del Estado de Oaxaca (FRTEO).[97] By August 1937 the organization had created the Liga Socialista de Pochutla and the Grupo de Acción Social Pochutleca.[98] By 1938 the establishment of a handful of badly funded

Article 123 schools on some of the region's coffee fincas allowed the organization to realize a succession of strikes to push improvements in workers rights.[99] On 15 March 1938 the Sindicato "Emiliano Zapata," which consisted of the seasonal workers from the fincas of La Soledad, San Rafael, La Unión, Concordia, and Calvario, went on strike. They demanded an increase in salaries, reduction of working hours, decent living conditions, and the admission of new members to the union.[100] A year later the union of coffee pickers at the Cafetal Unión y Progreso also went on strike, demanding increased pay per bag of coffee picked. At the same time the communists established connections with the various transport workers in Puerto Angel and formed the Sindicato de Trabajadores y Obreros "Benito Juárez."[101] As the coffee harvest arrived in late 1938, the union attempted to squeeze the *finqueros* by threatening a strike if demands over pay, days off, and working conditions were not met.

Second, the mestizo radicals started to push for the return of villages' lands. Some attempts met with concerted indigenous resistance. In Candelaria Loxicha, indigenous ranchers who avoided some of the excesses of the Porfirian land grab denounced the mestizo agitators as "outsiders" and forced their poorer neighbors to dismantle the hastily organized agrarian committee.[102] In other villages, Zapotecs saw the government program as a means to recover lost lands. During the late 1930s, the villages of Santa María Tonameca, San Francisco Cozoaltepec, San Baltasar Loxicha, San Agustín Loxicha, Santa María Loxicha, San Mateo Piñas, and Cafetal San Pablo all petitioned for the restitution of lost lands.[103] In Santa María Tonameca, for example, residents readily accepted the establishment of a federal school in 1936. With the encouragement of the local teacher they formed an antifanaticism league and the Sindicato de Campesinos "Venustiano Carranza." In December 1937 they demanded the return of María Ziga's finca, El Zapotal.[104]

Third, communists, union organizers, and teachers sought to free the Zapotec peasantry from Ramos Ortiz's commercial monopoly. Although Pochutla's economy was dominated by large coffee fincas, many Zapotec villagers, like the Chatinos of the neighboring district of Juquila, had also started to grow coffee plants on their own small strips of land. Unfortunately, these small producers were forced to sell their coffee at risibly cheap rates to Ramos Ortiz's agents.[105] As a result, in 1937 the FPLP started to establish coffee cooperatives designed to sidestep the local cacique's mercantile control. The cooperatives, which were set up in El Bule and Candelaria Loxicha and run by members of the FPLP, offered peasant coffee growers the opportunity to sell their produce at twice the price offered by Ramos Ortiz.[106] Last, the mestizo agitators attempted to wrest political control in the region from the cacique's camarilla. In 1937 the head of the Sindicato de Trabajadores y Obreros "Benito Juárez" established Pochutla's first municipal committee of the PNR and put forward a slate of workers and teachers to run the local council. The state PNR ignored its subcommittee's protests, failed to hold a plebiscite, and allowed Ramos Ortiz to appoint his own council.[107] Three years later a similar raft of unions attempted to hold a popular election again, with similar results.[108]

Despite the attempts of peasants and mestizo radicals to unseat the local plantocracy, by 1940 Ramos Ortiz's *cacicazgo* was still securely in place. None of the requests for land was successful, collective contracts were not signed, the workers' economic and political rights were steadily ignored, and the cooperatives existed in name only. A testament to the failure of this period of radical politics was the report of a visiting government agent in 1942. He was surprised to find a coterie of Nazi-supporting German *finqueros*, who despite the war still owned the *cafetales* of Aurora, San Antonio, Alemania, and La Natividad.[109] The state government, which was seeking to alienate the radical FRTEO, offered no support to its multifarious projects in Pochutla. As Governor Chapital made clear in his report of 1938, federal law forbidding the expropriation of coffee plantations under three hundred hectares would be firmly respected in Oaxaca.[110] In fact state representatives were positively hostile to any efforts that threatened to inhibit the region's valuable tax income. In 1938 the peasants of Santa María Tonameca invaded the neighboring finca of El Zapotal, which comprised 1,500 hectares. In response, the state peasant union encouraged the municipal president to "reprimand or castigate with all energy and severity all anticipated occupation of lands or waters."[111] Two years later the new head of the Confederación Nacional Campesina also warned Santa María Tonameca's president that illegal land invasions would be dealt with "severely and with force."[112]

The state's deliberate myopia to the situation in Pochutla allowed Ramos Ortiz to establish what the FRTEO described as a "reign of terror" in the region.[113] From 1937 onward all union and agrarian committee petitions included demands for Ramos Ortiz's removal from the region and the disarming of his *defensa social*. Violent confrontations between peasants and workers and various representatives of local elites abounded during the Cárdenas period. However, the putative spoils of the coffee trade encouraged Ramos Ortiz to sanction or enact the intimidation, beating, or murder of almost all those connected to the incipient wave of radicalism. At times he struck at the peasant and worker unions. Violence was deliberately public and served as a warning to others.[114] For example, in February 1940 Ramos Ortiz's men imprisoned the head of San Agustín Lochixa's agrarian committee for a week. For four days he was given neither food nor water. Although he was released, the men also arrested his wife and hung her in front of him in the town square.[115] On another occasion soldiers in the cacique's pay had dragged the leader of Santa María Tonameca's agrarian committee, Francisco Gómez, into the plaza. Here he was forced to read his own letter to the municipal president, describing Ramos Ortiz's misconduct and his links to members of the army. Although, in an act of defiance, Gómez threatened to "fuck them up," the soldiers made him eat his letter and gave him a severe beating in front of the whole town.[116] The cacique also persecuted individual peasant coffee growers who sought to evade his commercial monopoly. In November 1937 the FPLP reported that he was using his band of pistoleros to pick off peasant coffee growers who sought to sell through the new cooperatives. These farmers were "endangering his ability to be cacique in the region."[117]

Although Ramos Ortiz organized the murder of countless local peasants, he concentrated violent repression on the mestizo outsiders who had brought Cardenismo to the region. Teachers were constant targets for his gangs. In March 1937 Eufemia Ramírez, the head of San Pedro Pochutla's federal school, was assaulted in her home by Ramos Ortiz and a coterie of armed men. The attackers smashed down her door, chased her through the house, and were about to finish her off when her screams alerted a journalist from Mexico City, who intervened and saved her life.[118] Other members of the FPLP were less fortunate. During the late

1930s Ramos Ortiz had the three major leaders of the organization assassinated. The murders began as soon as the organization was established. In June 1937 the cacique's pistoleros killed one of the first mestizo radicals in the region, Alvaro Martínez Caballero, as he attempted to organize workers in Cafetal Alemania.[119] His *defensa social* attacked FPLP leader Juan Vega in October 1937, as he was introducing the peasant farmers to the new cooperatives in Rancheria Figueroa. The killing was done with "the luxury of cruelty and savagery," and the victim's face was unrecognizable to other members of the organization.[120] The local authorities arrested Jesús Loaeza Cruz in February 1938 for "political agitation." Later that year gunmen mowed him down in San Pedro Pochutla as he went to meet other members of the FPLP.[121] Despite multiple complaints, the elite camarilla around Ramos Ortiz held firm. The local judge, his son-in-law José Manuel Santibanez, discounted the murders as "political squabbles" and refused to take any action.[122] The municipal council of San Pedro Pochutla denounced the dead as agitators and intimated that they had met a deserved fate.[123] The local army commander simply denied that Ramos Ortiz had a *defensa social* and instead claimed that the murders were the result of problems within the FPLP.[124]

Throughout Cárdenas's presidency, established caciques from the revolutionary and Chicolopista eras were permitted to persist in their political, economic, and criminal control of their areas of influence, especially where coffee revenues were high. However, during the late 1930s, mestizo radicals started organize workers and peasants in these regions to push for labor rights and land grants. In Pochutla Ramos Ortiz faced an alliance of communists, teachers, seasonal coffee workers, and Zapotec peasants.

In Teotitlán, Tiburcio Cuellar confronted worker organizations in the region's numerous remaining coffee fincas.[125] In Coixtlahuaca the local cacique Agustín Bazán confronted the emerging *agrarista* enclave of Rio Blanco.[126] But as these new organizations had little outside support, the caciques were nevertheless able to ossify the prevailing socioeconomic order. Although some scholars have claimed that these caciques relied on state organizations to regiment the region's workers, it seems that their means were more traditional.[127] Those I have termed *"finquero-plantocrat"* caciques, such as Ramos Ortiz, continued to utilize kinship, commercial exploitation, and most important, violence. In some ways the local configuration of political and socioeconomic relations that emerged from the Cárdenas period in these areas closely resembled that of the 1920s or even the Porfiriato. Yet peasant tactics had changed. Despite the radical mestizos' failure to enact social reform, the inhabitants of these regions started to incorporate new strategies of resistance into their arsenal. Over the following decades, the areas of Pochutla, Teotitlán, and Río Blanco would become important centers of alliance between the peasantry and (often communist) radical outsiders.

Commercial-Ranchero Cacique Celestino Guzmán, Juxtlahuaca

Francisco Ramos Ortiz ruled a region where over seventy years of the coffee boom had created settlements of peasants and workers, whose strategies of resistance depended on links to outside individuals and organizations. As a result, during the 1930s, a succession of socialist groups from other areas arrived in Pochutla and attempted to break his political and economic stranglehold. However, in the more remote regions of Oaxaca, among smaller ethnic groups, coffee *caciquismo* was not even threatened by the ripples of state socialism. Ethnic strategies of resistance formulated during the nineteenth century and maintained during the twentieth precluded any state intrusion. These were reinforced by blinkered state organizations that portrayed a general refusal to comply with state projects as an irredeemable lack of civilization. In the Triqui region of the ex-district of Juxtlahuaca, a mestizo cacique attempted to assert a vicelike grip on smaller indigenous populations with little or no interference from outside. Although there was widespread resistance, it was not funneled through state social organizations. Instead, peasant groups made vertical alliances with individual mestizos from rival commercial centers, and the region descended into intraethnic factionalism, resembling what Alan Knight has termed "a Hobbesian war against all."[128]

Despite the differences between Pochutla and Juxtlahuaca's political systems, they were united by their dependence on Oaxaca's key export, coffee. The coffee economy had appeared in Oaxaca in two waves. The first wave struck during the Porfiriato and encouraged expropriation of communal properties, opening up of unused lands, and creation of large fincas practicing commercial agriculture in regions such as Pochutla and Teotitlán. The second wave arrived during the 1930s and was driven by growing U.S. demand and a production crisis in Brazil.[129] Between 1938 and 1954 coffee prices rose steadily, and the world market price increased more than twentyfold.[130] But the threat of Cardenista reforms prevented the kind of vast expropriations of the late nineteenth century. Instead, individual coffee entrepreneurs now started to encourage peasants to grow coffee on their lands. In regions where ethnic strategies of resistance had, for the most part, protected communal lands, mestizo merchants used their political, military, and commercial power to enforce the crop on local indigenous groups. In these regions, the attempts to impose a coffee economy on a defensive peasantry had profound political ramifications. As the caciques gradually persuaded or forced certain groups to plant coffee, bitter divisions emerged among the indigenous peasants. In Juxtlahuaca there was sustained violent conflict among the Triquis throughout the 1940s and 1950s.

Juxtlahuaca is an administrative district in the Mixteca of Oaxaca, northwest of Oaxaca City. Although its capital is predominantly mestizo, it also contains both Mixtec and Triqui Indians. The Triquis are a small indigenous group, spread over the highland towns of San Martín Itunyoso, San José Xochixtlán, San Andrés Chicahuaxtla, and Santo Domingo del Estado and the lowland towns of San Miguel Copala and San Juan Copala.[131] During the early nineteenth century the Triquis had sought to forge national alliances with Juan Alvarez and other Guerrero rebels against the centralist state. They were ruthlessly suppressed during the 1830s and 1840s by creoles and mestizos from the provincial capitals of Putla, Juxtlahuaca, and Silacayoapam.[132] Since then, the Triquis had developed a defensive ethnic strategy, redolent of other "regions of refuge" described by Gonzalo Aguirre Beltrán.[133] It appears the Triquis discovered that a reputation for hostility, isolation, and barbarity could be a useful tactic against the kind of outside incursion that had precipitated earlier bloody rebellions.

This form of resistance can be observed by reading between the lines of Frederick Starr's account of his visit to San Andrés Chicahuaxtla in 1896. He reported that the Triquis were "conservative, suspicious and superstitious." They viewed his attempts to take photographs and sculpt busts with alarm. When the local *jefe político* rode in from Juxtlahuaca, he was greeted by a shower of stones from the village's residents. Although one of the *jefe político*'s men died in the attack, he "plainly feared an uprising" and returned without prisoners.[134] This strategy of ethnic resistance continued during the postrevolutionary period. Secular authorities, village priests, and visiting anthropologists all testified to the "absolute isolation" of the Triquis.[135] The priest of Juxtlahuaca, who lauded the qualities of his Mixtec parishioners, confessed that he "never thought" he "was so much in hell" as when he visited San Juan Copala in 1934.[136] Although teachers often disparaged the isolation of Oaxaca's smaller indigenous groups, in no other region were their reports so uniformly condemnatory. Unlike in the Pochutla or Ixtlán regions, where teachers negotiated a functional relationship with indigenous villagers, in the Triqui region of Juxtlahuaca they encountered an ethnic group entirely resistant to outside interference. Some teachers assigned to the village even employed Porfirian racial terminology to word their despairing complaints. Benito Trinidad, the village teacher in 1928, wrote that the "Indians run around like wild animals in the forest while I am dying of hunger."[137] The cultural mission that arrived during the 1930s was equally unsuccessful. The mission complained that it was "not possible to deal with these people. They live unconscious, they are dissimulators and very aggressive." Although it suggested an indigenous boarding school, it warned that the Triquis were addicted to the liquor *aguardiente* and had reached a "very low" and possibly irredeemable "state of degradation."[138]

However, as the mention of *aguardiente* suggests, despite the deliberate isolation of the Triquis, they did not exist in a vacuum. This general defensive strategy combined with increasing interaction between the ethnic group and an acquisitive alliance of mestizo merchants, authorities, and agricultural speculators. The largest Triqui town, San Juan Copala, is situated between Santiago Juxtlahuaca and the other mestizo mercantile center of Putla de Guerrero. During the nineteenth century the Triquis started to feel the pressure of encroachment from these surrounding mestizos, who formed small population centers around San Juan Copola, including Constancia del Rosario, Santa María Pueblo Nuevo, and Hacienda de la Luz.[139] Despite the consecutive policies of armed revolt and studied defensive hostility, mestizo dominance in the region increased. In particular, mestizo ranchers became increasingly interested in the purchase of the fertile lands of the nearby Yosotiche Canyon. At the end of the nineteenth century, two commercial agriculture companies, Hermanos Pacheco and García Veyrán y Compañía, took over lands in the region. The Triquis now started to combine their policy of seclusion and hostility with strategic alliances with surrounding mestizo groups.

As the ethnic group became increasingly involved in local political struggles, divisions within Triqui society increased. Some divisions occurred along village lines. For example, during the war of French Intervention, the villages of Santo Domingo del Estado and San Andrés Chicahuaxtla fought on opposing sides. The most important political split was between the barrios of San Juan Copala. Testament to the lack of Spanish influence in the area, the town of San Juan Copala was formed of a small, sparsely populated center and a series of barrios arranged around familial clans.[140] As the barrios allied with different mestizo groups, divisions increased. In 1915 the town divided in two. Yosoyuxi and La Sabana supported the Carrancistas of the mestizo market town of Putla, while Tilapa, Yerbasanta, Ceniza, Rastrojo, Cruz

Chiquita, and Rancho Señor declared themselves Zapatistas.[141] These divisions and interbarrio alliances under the same nomenclature continued into the postrevolutionary period.

Although the process of what anthropologists León Javier Parra Mora and Jorge Hernandez Díaz have termed "revolutionary acculturation" divided the village during the 1910s, there is evidence that after the end of hostilities the rival Triqui groups reached a rapprochement based on the annual transfer of municipal power from one group to another. This system of alternating the town's ruling council was destroyed during the 1930s by another wave of mestizo intervention fueled by the putative profits of the coffee trade and led by the local cacique, Celestino Guzmán. Guzmán was a mestizo from the district capital of Santiago Juxtlahuaca. During the presidency of Lázaro Cárdenas, he established a *cacicazgo* based on commercial and agricultural wealth. During the early 1930s he received two large loans from the González trading house of Puebla. When he refused to repay, the González family sent their enforcer, Federico Figueroa, to ensure reimbursement. Guzmán murdered Figueroa with a machete and lost his arm in the process.

With the González money he started to buy up urban and agrarian property in Santiago Juxtlahuaca and San Sebastián Tecomaxtlahuaca. He also built an *aguardiente* factory, which produced six barrels of the liquor a day. All the properties were registered under his wife's name for tax purposes.[142] In 1933 he was elected municipal president, and the following year he was appointed propagandist of socialist education. In 1935 he was made agent of the public ministry, and in 1936 he was employed as tax collector and elected as substitute for the local deputy.[143] Guzmán utilized these positions to eliminate local enemies and make contacts with state politicians. In 1933 he ordered the murder of the municipal president of San Sebastián Tecomaxtlahuaca over a land dispute.[144] Three years later he attempted to murder and then imprisoned his main political competitor, the head of the *defensa social*, Josefino Feria.[145] The local deputy, Manuel Díaz Chavez, and the federal deputy, Alfonso Francisco Ramírez, defended the cacique against all charges.[146] Guzmán also used his political positions to persecute, rob, and extort from fellow mestizos in Juxtlahuaca, but during the late 1930s his involvement in the burgeoning coffee trade led him to specialize in the persecution of the Triquis of San Juan Copala.

The village of San Juan Copala possessed a perfect environment for coffee plantations. Multiple sources bear witness to its fertile soils, temperate climate, proximity to the mercantile centers of Juxtlahuaca and Putla, and elevation of around 1,500 meters. Primitivo Pérez claimed that the lands were "great producers of coffee, sugar cane, maize and bananas." Unfortunately, as he went on to write, this awoke the "greed and envy of irresponsible and unprincipled men from Juxtlahuaca and the surrounding region." Foremost among these was Celestino Guzmán. By the mid-1930s Guzmán had become one of the region's leading coffee merchants. According to the reports of teachers and political opponents, he used his *aguardiente* to buy up coffee from Mixtec and mestizo villages. He also gave loans to prospective coffee farmers to plant their first coffee trees. His pistoleros would follow up cash loans with periodic visits to peasant villages to extract repayment.[147] As competition between indigenous groups over valuable coffee-growing lands increased, Guzmán got increasingly involved in local land disputes. At first he supported his clients in the more acculturated Mixtec and mestizo settlements around San Juan Copala in their bids to strip the Triquis of their lands. In 1932 the Mixtec settlement of San Pedro Chayuco was given provisional titles to an ejido, which they claimed was formally owned by foreign hacendado, Lewis Lamm, but which the Triquis from the barrio of Agua Fría believed was theirs. Two years later they received the formal land grant of 681 hectares.[148] According to the Triquis of Agua Fría, Guzmán had lent money for coffee plants to the mestizos of Chayuco and wanted a return on his investments. Guzmán armed the *ejidatarios* of Chayuco and attempted to take the lands by force, attacking San Juan Copala in 1934, burning down houses, killing men, and kidnapping women.[149]

However, in the late 1930s, he became increasingly involved in lending money to the Triqui coffee producers. Although there is some dispute as to when coffee arrived in the region, by the 1930s mestizo merchants from the surrounding areas had started to lend Triquis money for the planting of coffee on their lands. The same merchants then extended credit to the peasants if they agreed to sell their crop at a fixed price well below its value on the international market. The school inspector, Benjamin Ramírez, observed that on market days, mestizo merchants arrived at San Juan Copala from Juxtlahuaca and Putla to buy up the town's coffee. Despite the product's high market value, Ramírez was depressed to see that merchants often paid their planters in *aguardiente* rather than cash. Lamenting the effects of the trade, Ramírez ended his report: "In many ways their wealth is their ruin. Their lands are so rich and produce so many bags of coffee. Yet all they acquire is bottles of liquor which they sit round drinking with their families all day."[150] The coffee economy not only linked San Juan Copala to the vicissitudes of the international market; it also provoked profound internal changes. Previously communal lands were now effectively divided up into de facto strips of private property. By 1940 the census listed 316 Triqui private properties totaling 347 hectares.[151] Gradual economic stratification took place as certain peasants benefited more than others from the coffee economy. On the one hand, Guzmán made commercial alliances with the Triqui community of Santo Domingo Chicahuaxtla and started to support the village in its border disputes with San Juan Copala. In 1938 he imprisoned the municipal authorities of San Juan Copala for ten days and demanded nine hundred pesos and the handing over of their land titles in order to settle their border dispute with the Mixtec village.[152] When the council was eventually released, Guzmán had the president murdered for failing to comply with his demands.[153] On the other hand, Guzmán also started to interfere in the internal politics of San Juan Copala. His first forays into the village seem to have treated the Triquis as an undifferentiated ethnic group. In 1934 he attacked the village council composed of former Carrancistas from the barrio of Yosoyuxi.[154] A year later he extorted taxes and murdered former Zapatistas from Tilapa.[155] In 1938 it appears that Guzmán finally sided with the Zapatista barrios directed by their leader, José de Jesús, against the Carrancistas. The decision seems to have emerged from commercial considerations. Government reports indicate that he was the principal lender to the Zapatista coffee growers, cementing ties with agreements of *compadrazgo*. The Carrancistas had maintained stronger links to the coffee merchants of the rival market town of Putla.[156]

Conflict between the groups centered on election of municipal authorities, customarily organized through the annual alternation of the rival groups. In late 1938 Guzmán broke with that tradition and encouraged the assumption of the municipal authorities by the Zapatista barrio of Tilapa and its leader José de Jesús. On 13 December 1938 Guzmán and Jesús attacked the village and threw out the official council.[157] Unlike the Zapotecs of Pochutla and Juchitán, the Triquis' studied defensiveness precluded alliances with the corporatist state. Instead, the Carrancista barrios followed the nineteenth-century pattern of armed revolt and attempted ethnic autonomy. On 12 January 1939 the leader of the Carrancistas, José Antonio, wrote to the state governor. The hand-written epistle denounced the outside intervention, showed a withering disregard for government policies, and proclaimed Triqui independence. The letter described how the "native and indigenous Triquis of the pueblo of San Juan Copala" were "tired of the persecutions, assassinations and attacks" visited on them by the "authorities, politicians and elements who say they are the representatives of the campesinos." They explained that for ten years Guzmán had attacked their pueblo "without differentiation." However, recently he had become a compadre of José de Jesús. In January 1938 he had sent *aguardiente*, money, pistoleros, and arms to the men of Tilapa in order to turn them against the majority of the village. They began to attack the other barrios of San Juan Copala, killing twenty-four men, kidnapping two women, and stealing fifty head of livestock and a hundred bags of coffee. After denigrating the government's capacity to resolve the problem, they then announced their political independence from the administrative district of Juxtlahuaca and, by extension, from the *cacicazgo* of Celestino Guzmán: "WE DECLARE OURSELVES FREE AND SOVEREIGN WHILE OUR ANNEXATION TO PUTLA HAS NOT BEEN RESOLVED." The letter then declared that they had established an alternative municipal council.[158]

The Carrancista declaration precipitated a complete breakdown in relations between the two groups. Guzmán and Jesús attacked San Juan Copala on 5 and 11 November 1939. The first attack was repelled, but the second was successful and the invaders stole women, children, and livestock from the defenders.[159] The murders blossomed into guerrilla warfare, and inevitably the government gradually became involved. In June 1940, 150 men attacked a military squadron accompanying Guzmán.[160] Six months later the state government sent the agent of the public ministry from the neighboring district of Putla to attempt to resolve the problem and allow "the diverse sections making up the municipality to live in absolute tranquility."[161] The plan failed. Guzmán sent multiple warnings to the government of the partiality of the Putla representatives and in December 1940 invaded the town and removed the Carrancista authorities whom the Putla representatives had put in place.[162] The two groups were now armed, supported by two separate mestizo groups, and would continue fighting until the 1960s.

In the most remote areas of Oaxaca Cardenismo failed to overcome the matrix of ethnic relations. Mestizo "commercial-ranchero" caciques such as Celestino Guzmán continued to exploit indigenous peasants without recourse to state support. In these areas political power was still traditional, decentralized, and destabilizing. The federal state barely touched the lives of Oaxaca's Triquis. Occasional teachers and agrarian engineers merely ignored or compounded the problems of smaller indigenous groups whom they failed to understand. Unlike in Pochutla, where both teachers and mestizo radicals had harnessed indigenous discontent to challenge the local *cacicazgo*, in Juxtlahuaca, resistance took the form of increasingly violent blood feuds. The introduction of

coffee led to the growing privatization of communal landholdings, which in turn caused increasing splits among Juxtlahuaca's
ethnic groups. In response, peasants made vertical alliances with
the region's mestizo merchants, who in turn brought their pistoleros and political power to bear on the divided countryside. In particular, Guzmán's alliances with Mixtec and mestizo communities
and then the Zapatista barrios of San Juan Copala exacerbated
the region's rifts. Indigenous means of controlling dissent and divisions were disrupted, and the Triquis descended into a particularly bloody internecine conflict. James B. Greenberg describes
the emergence of a similar cycle in Juquila. In the same way, alliances between mestizo coffee merchants and Chatino peasants
formed during the 1930s and 1940s instigated increasing intraethnic violence over the following decades.[163]

Authoritarian-Indigenista Cacique Luis Rodríguez, Región Mixe

So far this typology of Oaxaca's caciques has differentiated between districts such as Juchitán, where indigenous bosses defended ethnic groups from mestizo control, and districts such as
Pochutla and Juxtlahuaca, where mestizo strongmen continued to
exploit indigenous villages. The *cacicazgo* of Luis Rodríguez in the
Región Mixe complicates this clear bifurcation. On the one hand,
Rodríguez, like Heliodoro Charis, appropriated state discourses
of socialist education and *indigenismo* to forge an independent
power base. However, in the Región Mixe the failure of both organized Cardenismo and mestizo entrepreneurs to penetrate the
area shaped both Rodríguez's modus operandi and opposition to
the cacique's regime. Although Rodríguez established a degree of
control by presenting himself as the indigenous representative of
Mixe culture and offering a handful of material reforms, in general

pan took a back seat to *palo*. As a result, opposition from other indigenous Mixes was endemic. But Rodríguez's indigenous opponents eschewed the state's corporatist organizations and instead opposed the local boss through armed conflict.

In the postrevolutionary period the Mixes consisted of more than two hundred communities occupying 5,700 square kilometers in the districts of Choapam, Villa Alta, Yautepec, and Tehuantepec.[164] Nineteenth-century mestizo migration and capitalist speculation had, in general, failed to penetrate the Mixe settlements. The Mixes, like the Zapotecs in the Sierra Juárez, had established a system of periodic weekly markets scattered throughout the region, which allowed a degree of self-sufficiency.[165] At the same time, Porfirio Díaz's employment of Mixe troops in his Tehuantepec division may have allowed for a degree of official leniency.[166] As a result, although there were some mestizo settlers, only 2 percent of the inhabitants came from outside the region in 1940.[167] According to Ralph L. Beals, who visited the region in 1933, there were many communities where only one or two people spoke Spanish.[168] Yet the Región Mixe was not completely isolated. During the late nineteenth and early twentieth century, the coffee economy started to encroach upon Mixe territories in three ways.

First, a handful of capitalist entrepreneurs from the surrounding regions started to buy up tracts of communal lands from indigenous villages. In 1899 Guillermo Meixueiro bought a staggering 27,416 hectares of land from the Mixe village of Santa María Puxmetacan for the planting of coffee.[169] Although Meixueiro lost the lands during the Revolution, the 1938 land survey reports that there were still twenty-nine private properties in the village of more than one hundred hectares. More surprisingly they

were all allegedly owned by U.S. citizens.[170] Second, to the east of
the Mixe region, the neighboring district of Choapam resembled
a frontier coffee region such as Pochutla. In 1938 the tax collector estimated that there were still twenty-two properties over one
hundred hectares in Choapam. Some of these coffee plantations
were enormous. Carlos María Gil owned 10,683 hectares in the
village of San Pedro Ocotepec.[171] Most of the properties had been
carved out of the jungle in the previous half century, and the region remained underpopulated.[172] As a result, there was a constant need for seasonal coffee pickers during the annual harvest.
Third, just outside the network of Mixe villages, Zapotec and mestizo coffee merchants in San Pablo Mitla, Yalalag, and Villa Alta
provided tempting sources of capital investment to prospective
coffee growers in the region.[173] The combination of geographical isolation and growing connections to the international coffee
market created a peculiar hybrid of *caciquismo*, mixing a determined hostility to state interference with a distinctive brand of
economic and political exploitation.

During the 1920s and early 1930s the region had been controlled by Daniel Martínez, a cacique from the westerly village of
San Pedro y San Pablo Ayutla. He had relied on the support of the
other Soberanista strongmen, use of a *defensa social*, and a series
of moderate educational and infrastructural reforms. Throughout the period he had faced opposition from villages, caciques,
and merchants on the edges of his *cacicazgo*. With the realization
that the removal of López Cortés could disrupt the support he received from Ixtlán, complaints against the "reactionary" and "exploitative" behavior of Martínez increased.[174] In October 1935
El Oaxaqueño published a series of articles attacking the San Pedro y San Pablo Ayutla boss. Men from the Mixe village of San

Miguel Metepec alleged that he had "converted himself into the cacique of the region" through a mixture of imprisonment, exploitation, and threats. At the same time opposition to Martínez coalesced around the figure of Luis Rodríguez Jacob, the mestizo cacique of Santiago Zacatepec, Choapam.[175]

Luis Rodríguez was the son of coffee *finquero* and former village cacique Manuel Rodríguez. Manuel had purchased the plantation of Las Palmeras, near Santiago Zacatepec, in 1918. He founded a new settlement of around twenty families, who helped to defend the municipality against incursions by the neighboring village of San Pedro Ayacaxtepec. According to oral history, his son Luis left the area to become a priest in Oaxaca. Upon Manuel's death, Luis Rodríguez returned and became effective leader of Santiago Zacatepec. He was elected municipal president in 1930. Rodríguez's heritage suggests that he was the son of one of the few mestizos in the region. As such he formed a bridge between the Mixe inhabitants and the outside world. However, his mixed heritage also suggests that unlike Heliodoro Charis, he perhaps took his assumed role as defender of the Mixes less seriously than did the Juchitán strongman.

From the beginning of the 1930s Rodríguez was aware that power depended on the support of the central government. As the only representatives of the central government in the region were federal teachers and inspectors, he made enormous efforts to appease the visiting and permanent SEP staff. Consequently government reports on the Mixe region of Oaxaca were replete with praise for the educational projects of the Santiago Zacatepec strongman.[176] In October 1935 school inspector Ramón Robles described how all the 318 children in the village census went to school, how Rodríguez had constructed a cooperative store using his own money, and how, confronted with the decreasing crops of maize, beans, and chili, the "*hombre máximo*" had kindly formed an agricultural school for young boys to open up more land for the cultivation of coffee. The Mixe philanthropist had even kept twenty penniless indigenous children in primary school out of his own money and bought a Pony brand plough for the coffee entrepreneurs.[177]

Rodríguez's project of educational redemption and relentless self-publicity continued into 1936. Teachers from the surrounding regions were invited to give courses in bread making, carpentry, and leather work; a road was opened into Villa Alta; and a reservoir was built to provide potable water for the people.[178] At the same time, Rodríguez started a policy of cultural and ethnic promotion that firmly cemented his claim to Martínez's throne. When Governor García Toledo arrived in Santiago Zacatepec in February 1936, Rodríguez eschewed traditional demonstrations of *mestizaje* and modernity and instead offered the state functionaries a history lesson. Students, teachers, and Santiago Zacatepec residents put on a series of plays, skits, and musical pieces describing how the Mixe "race" had "never been conquered by the Spaniards" but rather had maintained the cultural opulence of the pre-Hispanics. Not only did Rodríguez toy with ideas on the Indianist extremes of official *indigenismo*—he also played to the government's obsession with unity, pointing to the "spirit of solidarity and organization" of the Mixes and their consequent avoidance of the kind of bloody interpueblo land disputes that rocked the Zapotec and Mixtec areas of the state.[179]

The demonstration obviously had a considerable effect on the governor. When García Toledo returned from his trip to the Región Mixe, he made the first mention of the possible creation of a judicial and administrative zone encompassing all the Mixe-speaking villages of Oaxaca. Throughout 1936 the idea gained momentum among the followers of Rodríguez and also Martínez, who both now saw the potential in centering official control of the Mixe region in their respective hometowns. Martínez attempted to impress his own revolutionary credentials on the state and central governments through use of the indigenous boarding school based in San Pedro y San Pablo Ayutla. In October the members of the school came down to Oaxaca to present the plays *Historia de un agrarista* and *Eco revolucionario* to assembled dignitaries. In August 1936 he got fifteen Mixe pueblos to sign a petition demanding the creation of the Región Mixe, to prevent mistreatment of the "race" by the mestizo-run ex-district centers. Echoing the rhetoric of Rodríguez's grand performance, the letter reminded the governor that the Mixe "had never been conquered by the Spanish."[180] The protestations of ethnic solidarity were undermined in the months following presentation of the petition by letters claiming no knowledge of the planned administrative change and complaining that Martínez had ordered representatives of the pueblos to San Pedro y San Pablo Ayutla to affix their municipal seals to the official letter without consultation.[181]

In response to Martínez's rather ham-fisted exploitation of ethnicity, Rodríguez focused on strengthening his relationship with most important government representatives in the region, the teachers. Key to his success was his support, as regional director of federal education, of the teachers' demands to abolish some of the more exploitative traditions of municipal rule.[182] In the agencies of the municipality of San Sebastián Totontepec, municipal agents had to hand over 4.50 pesos to the municipal president each January in return for possession of the agency's ceremonial baton, the archive, and the official seal. Together with the assembled teachers, Rodríguez managed to halt the custom.[183] Bolstered by the help and support of SEP representatives, he also presented a petition to the local congress demanding administrative change. Unlike Martínez's petition, which seemed to have been dictated to an illiterate by an overbearing pontiff, Rodríguez's epistle was a model of postrevolutionary punctilio and penmanship. According to the letter, the Mixe-speaking villages had met in Santiago Zacatepec on 3 October 1936 to discuss a pact of unification designed to "liberate themselves from the exploitation to which they have been subject," a general plan of development, and the complaints of the assembled representatives. Luis Rodríguez addressed the meeting on how the Mixes had remained in a state of "perpetual backwardness" because of Martínez, "who in a vile manner had sacrificed the local economy." He suggested the creation of the Consejo Regional Mixe Pro-Cultura y Defensa and unification under a plan of socioeconomic, cultural, and administrative reform, the centerpiece of which was creation of the district of Región Mixe with its seat in Santiago Zacatepec. After his speech was greeted with "applause and unanimous approval," all the villages swore to "use all their effort to remain united as one man, united by the sole ideal of collective improvement and well-being so as to obtain the redemption of the Mixe family."[184] To support his proposal Rodríguez also sent a letter to Cárdenas, explaining that the "Mixe race fighting for the defense of its regional interests" had formed a regional council and assured the president that the "great Mixe family" was "fully unified."[185]

Rodríguez's links to the SEP and his well-judged assumptions of racial unity and educational and *indigenista* rhetoric started to incline state and central governments toward the establishment of the Región Mixe in Santiago Zacatepec.[186] Finally, in June 1938 the local congress passed decree 203, constituting the new judicial and tax-collecting district of the Región Mixe, with its center in the village of Santiago Zacatepec. In Chapital's speech to the congress he linked the themes of *indigenismo* and stability, arguing that the former districts including the Mixe pueblos were unable to execute justice, collect taxes, or "control the Mixe people." Instead he proposed that the area, which "formed one racial and geographic nucleus," should handle its own administrative affairs.[187] On 28 June the state government dispatched a judge and an agent of the public ministry to Santiago Zacatepec. On 1 July the offices were installed.[188] Rodríguez and Benjamin Gómez, representative of the Departamento Autónomo de Asuntos Indigenas (DAAI), which had recently been moved from San Pedro y San Pablo Ayutla to Santiago Zacatepec, presided over mass celebrations. Schools brought pupils and parents to the new district capital to involve them in festivities for this "great conquest for the Mixe race."[189]

During the remaining years of the Cardenista presidency Rodríguez continued his policy of utilizing links with SEP and DAAI staff and parading the merits of Mixe culture and a unified Mixe race. Teachers led pro-Rodríguez parties in the geographically peripheral pueblos. In San Juan Mazatlán, at the southeastern corner of the district, rural teacher Manuel G. Luna led a minority group of villages against the elected municipal president, who wanted to return to administration by Tehuantepec.[190] In August 1939 Rodríguez also used teachers to bring Mixes to the First Grand Convention of Unification of the Pueblos of the Mixe Race. The meeting, which was run by federal teachers Oscar M. Ibarra and Heriberto Jiménez, claimed to be for the "unification and improvement of the Mixe race." They founded a regional peasant confederation (headed by Rodríguez and staffed almost entirely by teachers), discussed the problems of the zone, and ratified plans for the intensification of campaigns for health and popular education and against alcohol.[191] At the same time, Rodríguez started to hone his *indigenista* publicity machine, using the remarkable municipal bands of the area, particularly that of Santiago Zacatepec, to lend credibility to claims of Mixe racial preeminence. In December 1938 the local newspaper ran a special piece on Mixe musical groups, "who always occupy the first places among the bands of the state because of their constant cooperation."[192]

Rodríguez's assumptions of *indigenismo* were not accompanied by swift, visible improvements or the growth of state control. Rather, his professions of ethnic unity acted as a smokescreen for traditional forms of repression connected to the emergence of the coffee industry. First, he maintained the practice of forced labor on his coffee plantations in Santiago Zacatepec. Children from the local school and local peasants were dragooned by his pistoleros to work the extensive coffee finca his father had established in Las Palmeras and which he had supplemented with two thousand plants donated by the SEP.[193] Second, he acted as the principal money lender in the Región Mixe. His agents forced subsistence farmers to accept high-interest loans to plant coffee trees on their lands. In 1936 he ordered the peasants of Santiago Zacatepec to cultivate at least one thousand coffee plants per adult, under the threat of imprisonment and forced works.[194] By 1950 Moises de la Peña estimated that 350 families had planted six hundred coffee trees each; over the preceding five years, the Santiago Zacatepec area had doubled coffee production.[195] Rodríguez

FIG. 4. The band of Santiago Zacatepec, Región Mixe. This was key to Luis Rodríguez's self-presentation as the defender of Mixe culture. (Courtesy of the Biblioteca Bustamante Vasconcelos)

established a mercantile monopoly in the region in conjunction with the Oaxaca City coffee entrepreneur Francisco Cue, who established the Mixe Coffee Company in 1940.[196] Peasants would deliver their bags of coffee to Rodríguez's warehouses throughout the region in lieu of payment on their loans. The cacique would then coerce local peasants to carry the coffee to Cue's agents in San Pablo Mitla. In September 1952 Rodríguez reminded the municipal president of Santa María Tlahuitoltepec that two peasants from the village had promised to carry coffee from Santiago Zacatepec to San Pablo Mitla. He threatened to prosecute the peasants for robbery if they did not deliver the merchandise as requested.[197] Third, he acted as the manager of labor for the coffee plantations of the ex-district of Choapam. As the fincas of

Choapam had been carved from the jungle, the yearly coffee harvest was undertaken by *mozos* or workers from the Sierra Mixe, press-ganged and organized by Rodríguez. In November 1953 he wrote to the municipal president of Santa María Tlahuitoltepec to demand workers for Ramón Puga y Colmenares's coffee plantation in Yaveo, Choapam.[198]

As the *cacicazgo* lacked the sophisticated system of remuneration and the clientelist network offered by the corporatist triumvirate of unions, agrarian leagues, and party apparatus, resistance was endemic, and political control was asserted though intimidation and violence. Since the establishment of the Región Mixe in 1938, the constituency had been divided between villages that followed Rodríguez and a coalition of opponents, loosely grouped under the leadership of the former cacique Daniel Martínez. In basic terms Rodríguez held sway in the municipalities around Santiago Zacatepec—including San Sebastián Totontepec, Villa de Morelos, Tamazulapam del Espíritu Santo, Santa María Tlahuitoltepec, Santiago Atitlán, and San Juan Cotzocón—while municipalities on the geographical periphery of the region followed Martínez, among them San Pedro y San Pablo Ayutla, San Juan Juquila Mixes, Asunción Cacalotepec, Santa María Alotepec, San Pedro Ocotepec, and San Juan Mazatlán.[199] Within these simple divisions there were often more complex ones, as municipal agencies often opposed the political standing of their *cabecera*, and Rodríguez often managed to convert some members of the opposition communities to his cause.

The conflict concerned the establishment of Santiago Zacatepec as the center of the ex-district. Martínez's supporters had demanded that San Pedro y San Pablo Ayutla function as the Mixe capital and after 1938 continually requested that they be returned to the administration of their former districts. The tone of the divergence was set on 1 July 1938 at the inauguration of the new district. During the celebrations Martínez attacked Santiago Zacatepec with more than a hundred armed peasants but was repelled by Rodríguez's well-equipped retainers.[200] Similarly, in San Juan Mazatlán the majority of residents led by municipal authorities refused to submit to the Santiago Zacatepec cacique and his coterie of administrative allies.[201] In response, in June 1938 Rodríguez led forty armed men to the village and demanded the payment of taxes and the transfer of municipal authority to the rural teacher, Manuel G. Luna, who had assembled support from among the municipal agencies of San Juan Mazatlán.[202]

At first, Rodríguez attempted to impose his will through persuasion. He called all the villagers to a junta, where he and the head of the local DAAI office urged them to leave the municipal authorities and unify under the banner of the Mixe race. The majority declined the offer and tried to argue with Rodríguez, "talking in dialect, showing papers," and stated that "they wished to remain under the administration of Tehuantepec as those of Santiago Zacatepec shot them." Tensions grew and the next day there was a gunfight. Rodríguez's men shot up the village, stole the crops, raped several women, and forced the supporters of the authorities to flee to Tehuantepec.[203] With the majority of the villagers in hiding, Rodríguez now succeeded in changing the municipal authorities.[204] Despite the creation of an indigenous administrative district, his modus operandi and the widespread opposition to it encouraged the continuation of armed clashes, assassination, murder, theft, arson, and rape until the Rodríguez's death in 1959.

The establishment of his *cacicazgo* on assumptions of ethnic unity warrants comparison with other *indigenista* power structures established during the Cárdenas period. In Juchitán, Heliodoro Charis balanced the repression of mestizo political groups with the establishment of schools, hospitals, and irrigation schemes designed to placate his Zapotec supporters. In contrast, although Rodríguez attempted to present himself as the paternalist leader of the Mixe race, his plans for local development were demonstrably shallow. Whereas memories of Charis in Juchitán are at worst ambiguous, memories of Rodríguez are universally negative, even in his hometown of Santiago Zacatepec: "He forced us to work so hard we never had time to eat." "It was the worst time for the Mixe people." "He made us work on his coffee plantations and never gave us anything in return."[205] Even one of the Rodríguez pistoleros complained that the cacique had kept him as a virtual prisoner for over twenty years.[206] Although he claimed on his deathbed that his only aim has been the educational improvement of the Mixes, visible improvements were few.[207] Despite the arrival of SEP and DAAI representatives in the ex-district, they were often employed in overtly political roles and did little to improve standards of education. Literacy rates of the Región Mixe were comparatively low even by the standards of Oaxaca. In 1950 the population of the Región Mixe had a literacy rate of 21.52 percent. In comparison, the neighboring district of Ixtlán was 56.10 percent literate, and overall the state of Oaxaca had a literacy rate of 36.04 percent.[208] According to SEP official reportage in 1948, the schools were a "disgrace." The teachers were "involved in the politics of the region and do little to assist the learning of the children."[209] Legal cases brought to the judicial seat of Santiago Zacatepec bear witness to the inefficacy of Rodríguez's educational effort. Only three of the 428 cases brought to the judge between 1938 and 1945 invoked the Constitution of 1917.[210]

Jan Rus and Luz Olivia Pineda have described how indigenous caciques in Chiapas utilized the rhetoric of *indigenismo* to draw ethnic groups into the corporatist party system. But Rodríguez's *cacicazgo* was not "modern," "corporatist," or "bureaucratic" and added little to state control.[211] First, although Luis Alberto Arrioja Díaz-Viruel argues that the peasant confederation established in 1939 was a key instrument of corporatist control in the Región Mixe, it was a paper organization that consisted of little more than Rodríguez and a handful of loyal teachers.[212] It controlled no ejidos, offered no credit, and established no agricultural schools. Second, the corporatist party was nonexistent. There was no mention of the PNR or the PRM in the region in any of the federal, state, or municipal archives. As late as January 1953 the inhabitants of Santa María Puxmetacan lamented that there was "no government or party in this region except for that of the Santiago Zacatepec cacique."[213] Third, the federal and state personnel who did arrive in the ex-district during the late 1930s added little to state control. As they were concentrated in Rodríguez's hometown of Santiago Zacatepec, they were forced to choose either loyalty and obedience to the local leader or opposition and possible assassination. For example, Juan Carlos Martínez has shown how Rodríguez dominated the local judicial system. Legal cases were decided on the logic of local factionalism. As a result, although the majority of cases concerned homicides or other instances of serious violence, only 10 percent were actually resolved. One judicial worker recounted the following:

> In the 1940s no one wanted to go to Santiago Zacatepec; it was very far and very dangerous. Once, one of my friends went there. He showed his papers to the secretary and asked where

he would live and receive food. The secretary replied that he had to talk to Don Luis. The new judge presented himself to the cacique, who told him no one would give him food or put him up. The judge had taken a few sardines and biscuits with him and he managed to survive on these for a few days as he sought other people to assist him. But no one would receive him. Two days later the new "judge" returned to Oaxaca to take up his job again in the main judicial administration.[214]

As Rodríguez's *cacicazgo* fits uneasily into traditional models, previous judgments of Rodríguez have varied considerably. James B. Greenberg, Salomon Nahmed, and Orlando Barahona, and Guido Münch Galindo argue that Rodríguez's educative and cultural program and the relative absence of mestizos prevented the *cacicazgo* from pursuing more exploitative political and socioeconomic practices; in contrast, Luis Arrioja Díaz-Viruel and Iñigo Laviada stress the abusive nature of the region's power structure.[215] Rodríguez's system of control was both modern and traditional, both *indigenista* and authoritarian. The Janus-faced nature of *caciquismo* allowed Rodríguez to present himself as a radical Indianist educator to the state and central governments but as an armed and brutal *mandón* to those who would not bend to his imperious will. Although he maintained a veneer of cultural munificence, ethnic unity, and administrative control, his *cacicazgo* was still ruled by traditional means. Even though Rodríguez attempted to present himself as the leader of a modern unit of Mexican governance, his appropriation of state programs appears opportunistic and merely provided a convenient smokescreen for continued—and, with the coffee boom, increased—exploitation. Internally the dominant "language of contention" continued to be force, making resistance to Rodríguez's *cacicazgo* endemic. Over the next two decades, individual villages came together to oppose the *indigenista* cacique. However, unlike in Juchitán, where opposition merged with new state organizations, in the Región Mixe the absence of similar associations led to increasingly bloody armed conflict. Rodríguez's peculiar power structure makes comparisons hard to draw, but there is evidence that Celestino Ruíz in the neighboring ex-district of Yautepec founded a similar *cacicazgo* in league with the local teachers.[216]

Conclusion

On a micro level, this chapter has delineated the sheer variety of Cardenista caciques and the opposition to them. The trajectories of capitalist incursion, strategies of resistance, and arrival of Cardenismo formed a complex matrix of ethnic and state power. In Juchitán ethnic opposition to mestizo settlement and speculation allowed the maintenance of an indigenous *cacicazgo*. But over the next three decades Heliodoro Charis would face opposition from a faction of mestizo politicians with close ties to the national party and its corporatist organizations. Luis Rodríguez forged a similar indigenous *cacicazgo* in the Región Mixe based on state programs of *indigenismo* and socialist education. But the allure of the coffee boom weakened his putative assumptions of ethnic unity and encouraged the institution of a set of deeply exploitative means of control. As a result, there was also continuous resistance to Rodríguez from other Mixe villages. In Pochutla more than eighty years of immigration and coffee capitalism had acculturated many of the region's Zapotec inhabitants, whom Francisco Ramos Ortiz utilized to cultivate local coffee plantations. Pochutla's workers eschewed traditional forms of opposition and instead relied on radical organizations managed by outsiders. Although the strategy of making links with mestizo radicals would continue, the sheer ferocity of Ramos Ortiz's campaign against "communist" influence limited any Cardenista reforms. In Juxtlahuaca another mestizo, Celestino Guzmán, used violence, intimidation, and force to attempt to take advantage of the regional coffee boom. Triqui villagers were shaken down, murdered, and removed from their lands. However, resistance also depended on a long history of deliberate isolation from outside interference. Opposition took the form of declarations of local independence and continuous indigenous infighting.

Taken together the *cacicazgos* in this typology point to the importance of the regional coffee boom to formations of political power in Oaxaca. As Alan Knight argues, coffee booms throughout Mexico during the postrevolutionary period precipitated the continuation of Porfirian forms of political domination.[217] In addition, the relative stage of the coffee economy also defined modes of ethnic resistance. In regions such as Pochutla, where coffee had been introduced decades earlier, an emerging rural proletariat turned to state organizations. In regions such as the Región Mixe or Juxtlahuaca, where strategies of ethnic resistance during the Porfiriato had limited mestizo intrusion, indigenous peasants relied on more traditional forms of revolt.

At the more macro level, I argue that in the regions of the state that lacked established economic and strategic importance, the transfer from traditional to modern caciques was at best weak and at worst nonexistent. Undoubtedly some new mestizo or indigenous caciques, such as Luis Rodríguez and Heliodoro Charis in Oaxaca, Juvencio Nochebuena in Huejutla, and the Nahua caciques of Pajapam, cemented their control through the careful manipulation of fashionable government cant, especially the cultural nodes of *indigenismo* and education.[218] What emerged then was what Matthew Butler has described as "constantly evolving, hybrid *caciquismo* containing a mixture of traditional and modern elements."[219] Yet many other caciques, including those who exploited ethnic differences within their fiefdoms—Francisco Ramos Ortiz, Agustín Bazán, Celestino Guzmán, Tiburcio Cuellar, and the strongmen of Juquila—survived the fall of López Cortés and had little time even for the rhetorical niceties of Mexican socialism. If interfering agrarian engineers, labor organizers, or members of the DAAI entered these regions they were bought off or eliminated. Here traditional practices of economic exploitation, ethnic discrimination, and political imposition continued. Power continued to rest on kinship ties, on the appointment of the various administrative, legal, and fiscal authorities of the ex-district capital, and more than anything else on armed force.

The continued existence and "enormous importance" of these liminal figures at the lower levels of the Mexican political hierarchy counters revisionist interpretations of the corporatist Mexican state that emerged in the postrevolutionary period. As Alan Knight and Jeffrey Rubin argue, in many regions the federal state was weak, and its corporatist organizations were often compromised or nonexistent.[220] As a result, the state had to insert a measure of decentralization into the system and allow the persistence of a group of autonomous local strongmen. At the most basic level, in the Región Mixe, Juchitán, Pochutla, and Juxtlahuaca, the caciques' peasant pistoleros still held the monopoly of force. If Cárdenas's gifts to the exposed plantations of Yucatán and La Laguna were the ejido, the National Bank of Ejidal Credit, and the agrarian league, his legacy to Mexico's remote countryside was the independent cacique. As Rubin claims, "while in the national ambit, mechanisms of control and potentially authoritarian mediations were developed, at the state and local levels other mechanisms were strengthened."[221] Consequently the state that emerged from this process of administrative compromise was not the pyramid of revisionist lore with its clear lines of hierarchy and command.[222] Although the Partido Revolucionario Institucional (PRI) gradually asserted control over gubernatorial elections, union bosses, and peasant confederations in some regions, the political periphery was still the preserve of these caciques and their pistol-wielding peasant posses. The description of Oaxaca's multiform *cacicazgos* does not conform to revisionist models of state formation, and it challenges recent descriptions of the state's growing cultural hegemony over rural Mexico. In Juchitán and Pochutla, peasant groups learned to speak very different "languages of stateness," but in regions historically more isolated, such as the Región Mixe or Juxtlahuaca, caciques provided a buffer to state discourses. Rodríguez's assumption of *indigenismo* and socialist education operated externally but not internally. Further, the historical formation of Triqui and Mixe identity produced a deep distrust of the state. As a result, both groups countered local boss domination without recourse to outside help. Counter-hegemonic discourses, more common to the Andean political society examined by Florencia Mallon, remained strong during the 1930s and beyond.[223]

Finally, we must ask why Cárdenas allowed the maintenance of these traditional caciques. First, there was the simple matter of practicalities. The federal state, as Alan Knight argues, had neither the personnel nor the financial capacity to reach into these regions.[224] Second, there was the matter of political stability. The contrast between Cárdenas's imposition of the gubernatorial candidate and his acceptance of *serrano* autonomy described in chapter 4 displayed his political flexibility, his pragmatism, and most important, the premium he placed on stability and avoiding conflict. It was these values rather than those of socioeconomic reform that he stressed in his speech to assembled Oaxaca dignitaries during his 1937 tour of the state. Citizens were to "take their role in communal work, helping with their intelligence and resources to develop new forms of work in harmonious collaboration." Villages and individuals were urged not to fight against one another but to cooperate. This was a "patriotic contribution to the work of national unification."[225] Cárdenas's policy toward the ruling caciques in Oaxaca's economic and geographic periphery was also motivated by this desire for unity. Maintenance of these figures clearly maintained the socioeconomic status quo and thus avoided the complete disintegration of social relations. These powerful regional strongmen also balanced the power of the governor and guarded against the emergence of another powerful state caudillo such as Francisco López Cortés. As long as the governor's dipsomania and disinterest permitted these deals between Cárdenas and the local caciques to continue, conflict was limited to the localities involved. As we shall observe, during the 1940s, more ambitious governors upset this careful equilibrium and caused a series of conflicts between these caciques and the state government.

SIX

Politics and Socioeconomic Reform, 1936–40

The *sexenio* of Lázaro Cárdenas was characterized by far-reaching social reform. In the cities Cárdenas championed the right to strike and the implementation of a strict interpretation of the 1931 Law of Work.[1] In the countryside he enforced the tenets of the Agrarian Code of 1934, widening the *ejidatario* base by permitting hacienda peons to petition for land.[2] In February 1936 he gave his support to the *agraristas'* armed defense of their territorial gains, announcing that the government should "give them the Mausers with which they made the Revolution . . . so they can defend the ejido and the school," and allowing them to join the official army reserve.[3] Finally, he greatly increased the number of ejidos donated by the government. In the period 1916 to 1934 the Mexican state had offered fewer than a million peasants more than ten million hectares of land.[4] During Cárdenas's presidency 771,636 *ejidatarios* were provided with more than seventeen million hectares.[5] At the same time social reform fed into political restructuring. He supported the creation of the Confederación Nacional Campesina and the Confederación de Trabajadores de México. Although these confederations came into conflict over which organization had the right to control Mexico's rural masses, by 1937 Cárdenas had disciplined their leaders and delineated their national roles. The following year he recreated the

PNR as the PRM and permitted members of the CNC and the CTM automatic membership of the corporatist organization.[6]

Historians have long debated the significance of Cárdenas's reforms and their interim motives and long-term political and socioeconomic effects. Revisionist historians and social scientists have argued that the achievements of Cardenismo were more apparent than real. *Agrarismo* and especially the communal projects of the Yucatán, Nueva Italia, La Laguna, and Lombardia were failures, badly led, ineffectively implemented, and poorly funded.[7] Land redistribution on a smaller scale was either usurped by the provincial petit-bourgeoisie or mitigated by the efforts of the landholding elite.[8] Moreover, *agrarismo* was not only an economic fiasco; it was also a deliberate program of restraint and co-option. Cardenismo, by retreating from the more radical reform program of the communists and Tejedistas, stabilized the countryside, protected the national bourgeoisie, and allowed the "development and strengthening" of capitalism in the country.[9] By linking land reform to membership of the national political party, Cárdenas achieved "the political debilitation and even immobilization of the organized masses" and, as a result, established the framework of the corporatist state.[10] In contrast, over the past decade historians have attempted to resurrect the reputation of the Cardenista reform movement.[11] By querying the coercive power of the state, they have concluded that *agrarismo* was an organic, radical project and not "the stepchild of political patronage and elite cultural meddling."[12] Furthermore, it entailed "a massive transfer of resources that profoundly changed the country's socio-political map."[13]

This chapter explores these opposing views of the Cardenista reform program and its political framework through an investigation of the personnel, ideology, and actions of Oaxaca's worker and peasant leagues, local examples of the practice of *agrarismo*, and an analysis of the attempted reform of the palm weaving industry. Although some of the more radical members of the Cardenista coalition resisted co-option, between 1936 and 1940 the CCM (then CNC) and the CTM were gradually commandeered by local elites and career bureaucrats. However, at the local level, this did not automatically lead to the failure of agrarian reform. Again the state project was delineated by myriad local factors including ethnic relations, elite politicking, landholding patterns, ecclesiastical power, and the health of individual crops. In Jamiltepec and Huajuapam, an alliance of CNC leaders and landowners and the insensitive misapplication of *agrarismo* did damage attempts at land redistribution. Peasants in both districts consequently refused to bow to the demands of their corporatist leaders. In Tuxtepec disputes between the CCM and the radical wing of the CTM dented the dreams of many aspirant *ejidatarios* but also provided liberty of political movement and forced many agrarian leaders into applying genuine reforms. Only in the Central Valleys did the implementation of *agrarismo* follow a more familiar pattern of limited reform and peasant compliance. Finally, Cárdenas's experiment in regulating the manufacture of palm products showed how the government machinery could operate with a degree of flexibility and vigor.

Peasant and Worker Politics at the State Level

By the end of 1935 the CCM had grown into a powerful political force in the ex-districts of Tuxtepec, Jamiltepec, and the Central Valleys. Although it was led by members of the Agrarian Department and was closely connected to the gubernatorial campaign of

Constantino Chapital, it mitigated the less democratic aspects of its political formation through the necessary tolerance of agrarian committee leaders with radical agendas, ties to their communities, and genuine peasant status. These leaders had started to challenge local oligarchies in municipal elections and were adept at organizing land redistribution in line with local practice. However, over the next four years the central and state government desire for unity and conciliation, together with the growing political influence of the CCM, which acted like a magnet to the aspirant bourgeoisie, radically altered the political formation of the peasant organization as the provincial elite gained control of the governing posts. At the same time, although some of the more radical former members of the CCM formed their own branch of the CTM, this was slowly absorbed by a more conservative wing of the same confederation.

With Cárdenas and García Toledo's victory over the corporatist organizations of former governor Francisco López Cortés and the merging of the CCM with the COC, the political atmosphere in the organization changed. The impetus for this move toward central control came from the top. In February 1936 there was a division in the ranks of the state CCM between members of the Agrarian Department, such as Carlos Belleza, Adalberto Vélez, and Daniel Muñoz Estefan, and the former leaders of López Cortés's labor organization, such as Manuel Castellanos, Gustavo R. Castro, and Jeronimo Altamirano.[14] The rupture appears to have been over the admittance to the newly merged CCM of "reactionary" former elements of the COC. Muñoz Estefan was particularly disgusted by the pardon offered to Miguel Ortiz—a large landowner, the cacique of San Lucas Ojitlán, and a virulent enemy of the CCM since 1933. In February 1936 men from the Agrarian

Department, angered by what they saw as unnecessary concessions, attacked the offices of the CCM and attempted to substitute
Castro as interim secretary-general of the organization.[15] The central and state governments backed the former labor leaders, perhaps more in hope than in expectation that administrative conciliation would bring about the pacification of warring bands in
the rural zones of the state. Belleza, Muñoz Estefan, and Vélez
were unceremoniously dismissed from the organization.[16] In a
move of rare rapidity, the federal government sent replacement
Agrarian Department agents under Arturo Calderón to the state
within weeks.[17] The move by the central government displays a
shift away from its policy of using the department's employees
as the shock troops of the agrarian reform movement. Members
of the Agrarian Department such as Belleza now had links to the
PCM and, influenced by a new ideological belligerence or the simple lack of a traditional power base, many were offering increasingly radical concessions to the peasantry and causing rifts amid
the state's governing classes.[18]

Instead the CCM was now to be staffed by regional caciques
and ambitious politicians, whose loyalty was first and foremost
to the central government but whose roots in the Oaxacan political landscape reduced their ability to act independently of the
state oligarchy. This was affirmed with the appointment of Jorge
Meixueiro, a CCM functionary and the cacique of Villa Alta, to
the leadership of the state CCM.[19] As the upper echelons of the
peasant unions swelled with members of the bureaucratic bourgeoisie, the practice of democracy suffered. On 18 August 450
campesino representatives arrived in Oaxaca City at the behest
of the PRM's peasant unification committee to form a state branch
of the CNC.[20] According to a government agent the election of the

executive committee was a farce. On entering, peasants were offered voting slips that had already been filled in with the names
of the official candidates. "Although some peasants protested,
government cheerleaders and musicians drowned out their complaints."[21] As a result, Virgilio Salmeron, an unknown bureaucrat
who had spent most of his time in Mexico City, was appointed
director of the new organization.[22] Furthermore, in line with new
government policy, the rhetoric of agrarian reform changed. The
1937 regional peasant congress had demanded the reduction of
small properties to the minimum allowed by the Agrarian Code,
but by 1938 Chapital argued that the small property "must in-
variably be respected."[23] At the state level the peasant corporatist organizations had come full circle, returning again to the tight
governmental control of the Chicolopista regime.

The gradual takeover of the state campesino organization did
not go unchallenged. Radicals left the CCM and formed the local branch of the new worker organization, the CTM. During the
late 1930s the organization still had designs on partial control of
Mexico's peasants and welcomed the additional support. At first
support for the CTM centered on the municipality of San Lucas
Ojitlán, Tuxtepec. Here, Miguel Ortiz had joined the CCM and
removed the original members, led by Daniel Muñoz Estefan,
from the organization.[24] As the CCM was gradually brought under central control, the pattern laid out in San Lucas Ojitlán became more generalized. The CTM grew as it attracted a mixture
of labor bosses, landowners, teachers, communists, disenfranchised CCM leaders, and village radicals. From 22 to 24 March
1937 the organization, now called the Federación Regional de
Trabajadores del Estado de Oaxaca (FRTEO), held its first meeting in Oaxaca City. The representatives were diverse in political

outlook and socioeconomic background, but the majority were men from Tuxtepec. They included followers of Muñoz Estefan, such as his son and daughter, but also former CCM members. These headed up a mixture of agrarian and *ejidal* committees as well as federations of banana plantation and transport workers. Outside Tuxtepec the representatives were electrical, sugar, and textile workers from the handful of industrial enterprises in Oaxaca as well as a host of school inspectors and teachers from throughout the state.[25] Many had allied themselves with the CCM in 1935 but by 1937 saw little commitment to radical change from the peasant organization.[26]

Although by August 1938 the FRTEO claimed to comprise 80 worker unions and 137 peasant organizations, it was not accepted by the state government or the national CTM.[27] Consequently, former members of López Cortés's labor organization, who were unwilling to make a pact with the radical teachers, communists, and workers of the new organization, attempted to set up a rival body. In January 1937 they contacted the national leadership of the CTM and persuaded Vicente Lombardo Toledano and Francisco Velázquez of their revolutionary credentials.[28] On 9 April 1937 one of their number, Francisco R. Lobo, was named official state representative of the CTM and claimed that the FRTEO was not recognized by the national organization as it did not correspond to the "discipline and order that is the norm for the CTM."[29] On 16 April he held a congress of worker unification in the Theatre Alcala in Oaxaca City. Lombardo Toledano and Velázquez arrived to endorse the organization, which was named the Federación Regional de Obreros y Campesinos (FROC). Another former labor leader, Porfirio Cervantes, was elected head. State and federal leaders lined up behind the new organization. The representative of Governor Chapital announced that workers should "put to one side all selfish passions," "work for the benefit of the organized worker," and join the organization.[30] Lombardo Toledano, in an interview with the state government newspaper, denounced the FRTEO and claimed it was necessary to "control all the organizations with the end that . . . they can present in the future a front of responsibility in which the obligations and rights of the class I represent are firmly guaranteed and comprehended."[31] Gradually this less radical organization took control. FRTEO members were banned from CNC and FROC meetings, and Lombardo Toledano warned both organizations of potential contamination.[32] Although divisions remained, by the end of 1939 the FROC was the official recognized CTM organization in the state.[33]

The politics of peasant and worker organizations at the state level in some ways confirms the revisionist interpretation of Cardenismo's retreating radicalism. There was extensive land redistribution, but it was paid for with the co-option and regulation, at least at the state level, of the campesino class. Although the FRTEO initially provided shelter for regional radicals, an old guard of Chicolopista caciques and Oaxaca City bureaucrats ruled the state CCM and eventually the CTM. This should come as little surprise. Even Nathaniel and Sylvia Weyl, defenders of Cárdenas's populism, admit that state and national committees of the campesino organizations consisted of "non-peasant politicians who determine[d] organizational policies in an autocratic fashion."[34] In order to understand the relations among campesinos, leaders, landowners, landholding, and *ejidal* lands, it is necessary to look at Oaxacan *agrarismo* at a more local level.

Land Reform

Official figures for the amount of ejidos donated by the federal government in Oaxaca during the Cardenista *sexenio* vary. Although S. Perelló's work estimates that there were 292 land grants, restitutions, and amplifications during the period, totaling 565,435 hectares, the Agrarian Department estimated that from 1 January 1934 to the end of 1940 there were only 262 land allocations, affecting a total of 374,735 hectares. According to both sources, the period saw a dramatic increase in land distribution in comparison with the previous presidencies. Perelló estimates that from 1917 to 1934 there were only 134 official actions, offering a total of 158,086 hectares, whereas the Agrarian Department assesses that there were 112 *ejidal* decisions, which gave peasants 128,828 hectares of land.[35] Although Anselmo Arellanes Meixueiro is probably right to choose the department's lower approximation as a more realistic evaluation of the amount of land that passed into peasant hands in the period, my own work on the *Periódico Oficial* confirms Perelló's higher assessment of the land actually pledged to the *ejidatarios*.[36] Such is the disparity in official estimates and the apparent disjunction between paper promises and practice that it is necessary to take a closer look at the reality of land reform in Oaxaca. The implementation of *agrarismo* differed throughout the state and followed distinctly local interactions of ethnic relations, elite politics, landholding patterns, church power, and the health of individual crops.

Tuxtepec

As described in chapters 1 and 2, Tuxtepec had been Oaxaca's center of commercial agriculture since the late nineteenth century. At first Mexican and foreign *finqueros* planted tobacco and various other tropical crops. But from 1909 onward, the local elite moved toward a monoculture based on the production of bananas for the national and international markets. As in Pochutla, local elites quickly recaptured the ground lost during the Revolution. As early as 1924 the local elite's magazine, *Tuxtepec Moderno*, described the scenery of the region as a patchwork of huge haciendas, broken only by the occasional municipal center.[37] Despite some union activity, the banana boom of the 1920s was maintained in the early years of the next decade. In 1933 Governor García Toledo still held that bananas were "the most important single crop in the state."[38] Local capitalists continued to buy up land in the region. For example, in late 1933 three merchants from the Central Valleys, Francisco Ramon García, José Zorrilla Barrundia, and Arturo Ruíz, formed a limited company and acquired extensive territory in the municipality of Ozumacin. A year later they acquired 823 hectares of land in the municipality of San Juan Bautista Tuxtepec. At the same time the American tropical fruit company Standard Fruit now not only monopolized the transport, purchase, and export of the bananas but also continued to buy up large fincas from local producers. In September 1935 the company acquired the fincas of Cuba, México, Bote, and Pegaso, worth fifteen thousand pesos, from the widow of Marcelino García. Despite the predominance of banana production, other entrepreneurs also sought land for other tropical crops. The Veracruz tobacco company Bolsa Brothers purchased 1,415 hectares spread over six properties in the municipalities of Santa María Jacatepec, San Juan Bautista Valle Nacional, and San Juan Bautista Tuxtepec.[39]

The prolonged period of capitalization continued to change the region's ethnic landscape. By the postrevolutionary period there were still important populations of monolingual Chinantecs in the municipalities of San Lucas Ojitlán, San Juan Bautista Tuxtepec, San Felipe Usila, and San Juan Bautista Valle Nacional and of Mazatecs in San José Independencia, San Miguel Soyaltepec, San Felipe Jalapa de Díaz, and San Pedro Ixcatlán. But as in Pochutla, fifty years of capitalist production and voluntary and forced migration had also created a mobile rural proletariat dependent on wage labor in the enormous plantations. In 1940 in the municipality of Tuxtepec, nearly 90 percent of the population spoke Spanish exclusively. In Acatlán de Pérez Figueroa, over 92 percent of the inhabitants spoke no indigenous language. By the 1930s Chinantecs, Mazatecs, Mixtecs from western Oaxaca, Zapotecs from the Sierra Juárez, and mestizos from Veracruz and central Mexico worked together in the stifling tropical heat of the banana groves.[40] Thus although there were undoubtedly divisions along ethnic lines throughout the region, these were less pronounced than in other more isolated areas of Oaxaca. As a result, Tuxtepec's peasantry failed to develop strategies of resistance built upon the individual indigenous communities or a unifying sense of ethnic identity. Instead, the region's rural proletariat sought salvation in federal and state corporatist organizations, which had thrived throughout the late 1920s and early 1930s principally owing to the region's proximity to the revolutionary hub of Veracruz and because of divisions among the ruling elite. It was the conflicts among these various groups that delineated the direction and limits of Cardenista land reform.

Since 1933 there had been divisions in Tuxtepec society between members of the FTOC and the CCM. However, in early 1936 the sides were radically redrawn when Miguel Ortiz defected to the CCM. Ortiz was the owner of four large banana plantations in San

Lucas Ojitlán and had been a leading member of the FTOC.[41] On 7 April 1936 he expelled the old CCM leaders, including the regional cacique, Muñoz Estefan, and other employees of the Agrarian Department, claiming they were communists who had shouted "death to Lázaro Cárdenas and *vivas* to Benito Zaragoza."[42] Ortiz, who had been the scourge of the CCM for over three years, now vocally defended its cause, protesting the death of Fortino Pacheco, the peasant delegate he had castrated and butchered two years before.[43] Ortiz's defection changed the constituency and tactics of the CCM. At first he relied on former FTOC communities, such as Loma de Cedro and Aguacate, which were involved in land disputes with Muñoz Estefan's elite backers.[44] Soon Ortiz started to undermine Muñoz Estefan's support network of agrarian committees and worker unions through a mixture of violence, political imposition, and measured concessions. For example, during the early 1930s the men of La Asunción, San Lucas Ojitlán, had attempted unsuccessfully to gain the lands of Spanish landowner José Casal, through their membership of the FTOC and the Law of Unused Lands.[45] Disappointed and frustrated, the inhabitants of La Asunción moved their allegiance over to the CCM in late 1935.[46] But from March to September 1936 Ortiz instigated a plan of intimidation and persuasion. His pistoleros beat up Muñoz Estefan when he went to visit his new supporters, imprisoned eight of the more recalcitrant peasants, and eventually convinced their leader to swear allegiance to his branch of the CCM.[47] Yet although violence and imposition were the norm, Ortiz also had to ensure the loyalty of the peasantry through the offer of tangible if targeted concessions. For instance, he allowed the men of La Asunción to invade the lands of Ernesto López, one of Muñoz Estefan's leading supporters.[48]

Throughout 1936 the clashes between Ortiz and Muñoz Estefan's CCM groups were focused in San Lucas Ojitlán. In 1937 Ortiz was elected federal deputy of Tuxtepec and the internecine conflict spread to neighboring municipalities. Again Ortiz employed
similar tactics of political imposition, violence, and moderate land
grants to co-opt former supporters of Muñoz Estefan. In the village of Chaparrosa, San Felipe Jalapa de Díaz, Juan Terreno had
been voted in as president of the CCM committee in January 1936.
The local cacique, Angel Villar, had created a rival white union
but was ordered by the state government to refrain from challenging that of Terreno. However, with Ortiz's defection, the state
government's attitude changed. Villar was allowed to undermine
Terreno's power base of indigenous Mazatecs by sending three
Spanish speakers who proceeded to dominate the village's agrarian committee.[49] Two years later the men of Chaparrosa's switch
of allegiance to Ortiz's CCM was rewarded by a 593-hectare grant
of land from the abandoned finca of Playa Grande.

Despite Ortiz's attempts, many agrarian and peasant organizations were unwilling to betray Muñoz Estefan, downgrade their
radical expectations, and accept the state-sponsored coup without
a fight. As Ortiz now claimed control of the CCM, they turned instead to the CTM. In May 1936 Muñoz Estefan and his followers
had formed the Federación Local de Trabajadores de la Región
Tuxtepecana (FLTRT) and claimed the support of the CTM.[50] As
federal deputy, Ortiz imposed compliant CCM supporters on the
region's municipal administrations. As a result, the FLTRT was
forced to offer its followers more radical rewards for continued loyalty. In San Juan Bautista Valle Nacional the local cacique, Mardonio D. Sánchez, had risen to power as the representative of the CCM but had offered the peasantry little in return

for their collaboration. In fact, when his camarilla moved into the municipal palace in 1938, it started to rebuild alliances with the landowners and crack down on its former supporters.[51] This led teachers in the surrounding villages to start rallying support against the local cacique by attracting disenchanted former CCM members to the CTM. The community of Santa Fe y el Mar had joined with Sánchez in 1934 to demand land from the surrounding finca, which Mateo Acevedo had rented through the employment of the Law of Unused Lands. When Sánchez came to power he quickly assured Acevedo of his support and left the peasants without their expected reward. The peasants then turned to the local teacher, Pedro Francisco Vásquez, for support. In a series of self-satisfied letters Vásquez described how he explained to them "fully and in detail . . . the rights they have to possess land in accordance with Article 27." After a series of meetings, the villagers "little by little understood their rights." Although Vásquez's role was important, it is clear that the peasants of Santa Fe y el Mar were not completely ignorant of their rights nor of the ramifications of Sánchez's betrayal. Within a month they saw the opportunity offered by the FLTRT and had switched allegiance. In March 1938 they petitioned for land again, this time under the flag of the CTM. Despite the creation of a rival agrarian committee backed by the CCM, the murder of Vásquez, and the imprisonment of many members of the CTM, they received the land and defended it from the attentions of the San Juan Bautista Valle Nacional authorities.[52]

The conflict between the CCM and the CTM was further complicated by the decline of the region's staple crop, the banana. In 1936 Chamusco disease appeared in La Esperanza finca in San Juan Bautista Tuxtepec. Although news arrived of the damage this disease had done to the banana industry of Tabasco, the authorities and growers paid little attention. But by 1938 the disease had spread throughout the plantation zones of Veracruz and Oaxaca. Some fincas had an infection rate of between 80 and 100 percent.[53] The federal government attempted to limit damage and replace the crop with sugar cane, pineapple, or tobacco, but the program was unsuccessful. Many of the banana growers left their plantations bare. Standard Fruit, which had already lost some of its properties to government expropriation, gave up its remaining fincas and concentrated on recovering ground in Jamaica and Central America.[54] Empty plantations encouraged another wave of invasion and occupation by the radical CTM organizations. In January 1938 Genaro Bravo complained that the men of Sebastopol had invaded his ravaged lands without going through the Law of Unused Lands or the Agrarian Department. The CCM-run municipal council attempted to remove the squatters, but a year later the government confirmed their right to the land.[55]

The local conflict between the CTM and the CCM for land, municipal power, and peasant loyalty clearly affected the political framework of *agrarismo* in the region. The emergence of Ortiz as leader of the CCM arrested the radicalism and nascent democracy of the organization, and some villages, such as Chaparrosa, were forced to join the peasant confederation through political imposition and violence. Yet the conflict, the weakness of village and client ties, and the encroaching environmental disaster also created space for a degree of freedom of movement for the peasant population. The type of mass regimentation of indigenous villages enacted by the labor unions in Chiapas was not possible.[56] Whole villages, such as Santa Fe y el Mar, often switched sides voluntarily. Individual peasants were also left with a choice and,

if they avoided a bullet, could weigh up the merits of the concessions tendered by either party. Isidro Muñoz of the small community of El Malotal, San Lucas Ojitlán, left the ejido when Ortiz
forced a new president on the *ejidal* committee. Despite the confiscation of his land, he applied for and received land in the neighboring CTM village of El Cantón.[57] Although the CTM tended to be
the more radical thanks to its contact with the old CCM and the
federal teachers, it did not offer the fast returns of the CCM or the
protection of the Ortiz-controlled municipal councils. José Muñoz García left the CTM-affiliated agrarian committee of Tuxtepec
to join the well-paid CCM banana workers on the finca La Esperanza.[58] As a result—even though violence and intimidation were
rife and politics was the aim of many of the confederations' leaders—because peasants could leave the organizations en masse or
as individuals, these leaders had to ensure their supporters' loyalty
with genuine benefits. According to the *Periódico Oficial*, Cárdenas signed eighty-six positive ejido land grants for the region, 56
percent more than the next closest district. In total the president
donated 82,238 hectares to the Tuxtepec peasants.[59]

Did this major redistribution of land affect the material relations in the region? Undoubtedly, many of the new ejidos were
"socially and economically disorganized." The National Bank of
Ejidal Credit often did little to defend contracts between the ejidos and the export company, the Compañía Platanera Americana.
Disease and transport delays led to the company's refusal to accept
entire shipments of bananas.[60] The need for credit to fund banana
cultivation or alternative tropical products led to the prevalence
of small credit-broking *kulaks* in the ejidos, especially where Ortiz's CCM had purged the original *ejidal* leadership.[61] There was
also growth of larger lenders based in the municipal capitals. In

San Juan Bautista Valle Nacional Alvaro Alvarez monopolized credit for the cultivation of tobacco on behalf of the company To-baco en Ramo.[62] Furthermore, Ortiz's ties to the Tuxtepec elite obstructed efficient and generous land grants, and although the division of land lessened the influence of the haciendas, they did not disappear altogether. Federal land grants concentrated on the properties of foreigners and Mexico City residents. The Tuxte-pec elite managed to save themselves by dividing up their fincas among family members.[63]

But before the Revolution Tuxtepec was Kenneth Turner's for-gotten Mexico, dominated by huge tobacco fincas, populated by debt slaves, and run by Mexican and foreign capitalists.[64] Al-though the Revolution and the agrarian reform of Veracruz had shaken the region and forced *finqueros* to raise wages and allow a degree of unionization, the basic model of exploitation had not changed. Such was the elite's devotion to stable commercial ag-riculture that landowners who had left the region to escape the violence of the 1910s were tracked down and persuaded to re-turn.[65] By 1930 a powerful state confederation monitored work-ers' rights. Suspect radicalism or demands for *ejidal* lands were dealt with ruthlessly. A decade later, the landscape of Tuxtepec had nevertheless changed completely: now dozens of ejidos, op-erated communally or individually, dominated the region. Haci-endas such as the huge Playa Grande of María de la Luz González and the Arroyo de Enmedio of Manuel González were divided into *ejidal* chunks. Companies from outside Tuxtepec, such as the Compañía Exportación Tropical, Loma y Basurto, and Stan-dard Fruit were forced to leave the area. U.S. investors who had bought up land individually or as part of the venture companies Kansas Land and American Land were forced to forsake their investments.[66] A government inspector who dismissed other efforts at social reform in Oaxaca offered warm praise for the region of Tuxtepec. Although he admitted that politics were problematic and the landowners had "done everything in their power to defend their lands," he claimed that by August 1938 there were no boss unions and no fraudulently low salaries. Many peasants had received adequate lands, and those who remained wage laborers gained a good weekly income. In all, he concluded, "The workers and campesinos have the opinion that the government is doing a beneficial job and, consequently, have followed with interest the acts of the government."[67] In many ways the socioeconomic and political ramifications of *agrarismo* in Tuxtepec that pitted CNC against CTM replicated the situation described by Heather Fowler-Salamini across the state border in San Andrés Tuxtla, Veracruz.[68]

Jamiltepec

Like Tuxtepec, Jamiltepec had been affected during the Porfiriato by a wave of rapid capitalization. Mestizo hacendados and ranchers had acquired thousands of hectares of the communal lands of Mixtec villagers for use as livestock pasture. Although the Mixtecs had rebelled against the dominant landholding class during the Revolution, mestizos under the leadership of Juan José Baños had successfully extinguished the revolt. As a result, in the postrevolutionary period the Jamiltepec elite continued to hold enormous swathes of the region's lands. Josefa Gómez del Valle still possessed the haciendas of La Natividad Vives and La Natividad in the municipality of Jamiltepec, which totaled more than twelve thousand hectares. Lewis Lamm's properties encompassed more than seventy thousand hectares of the Costa Chica.[69] Although the creation of the CCM in the early 1930s had started to channel Mixtec aspirations of land distribution, divisions within the region's elite following the death of Juan José Baños sidelined socioeconomic reform as rival camarillas sought to take advantage of federal government support.

On one side was the camarilla of the Pérez family, a group of large landowners from the municipality of Santiago Pinotepa Nacional. They had allied with the region's incipient peasant organizations in 1934 in order to ruin the properties of the Baños clan. A year later they were joined by another landowning family, led by Adelaido and Abel Ojeda, from San Juan Bautista Lo de Soto.[70] Adelaido Ojeda now supplanted the relatively radical Jesús Ramírez Vásquez as head of Jamiltepec's branch of the CCM. He was also elected to the state committee of the PNR and made local deputy for the region. His brother became agent of the public ministry and local delegate of the CCM.[71] On the other side was the Baños camarilla, consisting of the sons, nephews, and compadres of the former revolutionary leader. In order to save the family's extensive properties from imminent expropriation their leader, Felix Baños, started to "organize fake agrarian committees."[72] As each landholding faction competed to confiscate the lands of the other, their members sought to persuade government agents with escalating hypocritical complaints. Thus Enrique Galan López, who as head of the *defensa social* in 1934 had organized the murder of CCM members, now wrung his hands over the plight of the indigenous *agraristas* of San Juan Bautista Lo de Soto, oppressed by the cruel landowner (and CCM representative) Adelaido Ojeda.[73]

These political maneuvers dissolved any vestiges of class or ethnic conflict. The CCM, which had supported Mixtec peasants against the majority of landowners during the early years of Cardenismo, now became a battleground between the elite factions over political influence and the retention of their extensive landholdings. Federal agent Enrique Reyna Tello described the situation. As politics was "the only profitable occupation," all socioeconomic reform was subject to the mechanics of local factionalism. The Bañistas ran the Partido Revolucionario Unificado, allegedly adherent to the PNR. This was a mix of "landowners, *agraristas*, tailors, barbers, hoteliers and livestock owners." Opposing them was the Pérezista/Ojedista CCM faction, which consisted of teachers, peasants, artisans, landowners, and politicians. The cross-class nature of the union baffled the agrarian functionary. "It is curious that while some assassinate *agraristas*, others join with them to ask for land." But his condemnation of Ojeda's CCM was absolute: "The CCM abuses the confidence deposited in it by the peasants. They incite fights and their only interest is in controlling pueblos. They are dedicated to sacking municipal treasuries, extorting quotas from their members, demanding money from the agrarian committees for personal trips to Oaxaca and Mexico. They threaten campesinos whom they do not control, they put cantinas in the ejidos, they falsify signatures to win in the plebiscites, and their municipal presidents are caciques who dislodge the indigenous in order to allow the rich to put their livestock on the land."[74] Both sides fought for control of the municipal authorities of the region's major trading center, Santiago Pinotepa Nacional. When one faction had obtained municipal power, the other faction under the banner of the CCM encouraged surrounding hamlets to "take orders from the central government" and not the "reactionary municipal authorities."[75] At the same time both sides armed peasants and backed them to invade, steal from, and petition for the lands of the opposing faction's leaders. They also utilized border disputes and the vagaries of local landholding custom to cut across class and ethnic lines and pit villages against each other.[76]

If it was difficult to enact effective *agrarismo* in the space between two warring elites, it became practically impossible by 1939. Although the elite had split during the 1930s and allowed the peasants to invade their enemies' lands, the specter of ethnic revolt continued to haunt the coastal landowners. As a result, unlike in Tuxtepec, the divisions of the Cárdenas era did not ossify. In 1940 the Ojeda brothers came to an agreement with Felix Baños, allowing him to become local deputy in return for his support.[77] Together they now ruled the region's peasant confederation. The peasant organization, which had begun in 1933 as an expectant echo of an indigenous revolution, had now become the political base of a union of the landed elite. As a result Cárdenas's fifty-five *ejidal* land grants totaling 203,575 hectares, as listed in the *Periódico Oficial*, remained a paper fiction.[78] In 1940 the former head of the CCM, Ramírez Vásquez, wrote to the Agrarian Department demanding that the *ejidal* land grants be enacted. He explained how successive engineers from the department had been bought off in 1936 and 1938, and how the ejidos of Mártires de Tacubaya, Santiago Ixtlayutla, La Calzada, and Cerro de Chivo were still not demarcated. In the ejidos that had been officially sanctioned, the law was widely flaunted. In Caul de Ituacan the livestock of Felix Baños still grazed the *ejidatarios*' land, and in Los Positos, Juan José Baños Jr.'s recent cotton crop planted on the ejido had offered up a profit of over two thousand pesos.

Further, even when ejidos were genuinely donated, there was little change to the area's socioeconomic relations. In part this was a result of the harsh geography of the region. Much of the land handed out was dry, infertile hill soil, and the landlords still controlled the scarce water supplies, which they could dam or let flow conditional on the dependent campesinos' political pliancy. As Adolfo Rodríguez Canto argues, the "best lands were still in the hands of the few, while the Indians were still confined to the hills and the foot of the sierra."[79] Failure of land distribution also derived from the nature of Porfirian landholding. Despite the rise in large properties during the late nineteenth century, these lands did not operate like traditional haciendas.[80] Although there was some indebted wage labor on local cotton plantations, soil infertility and poor irrigation prevented the expansion of intensive agricultural landholdings. Instead most landowners ran huge pastoral haciendas. After fattening their flocks for sale, they would send huge quantities of goats and sheep up to Puebla for slaughter.[81] Few resident peasants on these latifundios were forced to work or pay rent for their land. But the hacendado claimed exclusive rights over all commercial crops within the property's boundaries.[82] As a result, the distribution of ejidos changed little. First, the livestock of the rich still trampled the crops of the poor. In 1937 the *agraristas* of Ranchería de la Muralla complained that the former landowner Manuel Vásquez grazed his sheep on their ejido, claiming the land was still his own.[83] Second, the region's continued isolation and the absence of the National Bank of Ejidal Credit meant that the *ejidatarios* still relied on the landowner's generosity for credit and the sale of their products. In 1942 the *ejidatarios* of San Juan Bautista Lo de Soto complained that the head of the *defensa rural*, Sostenes Guzmán, was taking their crops and demanding the payback of credit on behalf of the agricultural society of San Juan Cacahuatepec.[84]

However, it would be wrong to portray all the inhabitants of the ex-district of Jamiltepec as the oppressed followers of faction, passive tools of an overweening elite. The spirit of the rebellion of 1911 was not easily extinguished, and the lack of tangible rewards meant that elite control was often illusory and peasant disquiet frequently simmered below the surface.[85] In March 1936 the men of Mártires de Tacubaya set up the Frente de Campesinos de la Costa Chica de Guerrero y Oaxaca with the help of the teachers of the neighboring village of Huajintepec, Guerrero. By establishing a cross-state organization they flagged their independence from the state CCM. In their letters to the government they did not claim allegiance to the peasant organization or the CTM, and their enemies accused them of maintaining a pernicious autonomy. In reply the front claimed that it would not join the CCM, as it was a political façade. In Mártires de Tacubaya it was led by peasants who had made a pact with the rich "to better themselves economically." "Covered with the flag of *agrarismo* they have even deceived the Supreme Government."[86] This independent *agrarismo* would continue into the succeeding decades as Mixtec resistance to state control channeled this radicalism toward tax strikes and forms of social banditry.

The Central Valleys

Land reform in the rest of Oaxaca was not on the same scale as the activity in Tuxtepec or Jamiltepec, where over half of the land was given out. However, whereas in the tropical lowland areas Porfirian land tenure, ethnic strategies of resistance, and elite divisions combined to offer up complex local political responses to *agrarismo*, land redistribution in the Central Valleys followed a more predictable pattern. This was principally due to the region's proximity to the state capital, its ethnic configuration, and the fairly static system of land tenure. First, independent commercial camarillas or freewheeling caciques found it harder to avoid state interference in the flat valleys surrounding Oaxaca City. Second, although there were small groups of monolingual Zapotec and Mixtec Indians, especially in the foothills of their respective Sierras, most peasants in the Central Valleys were fairly acculturated and spoke either exclusively Spanish or Spanish and an indigenous language. In district capitals such as San Pablo y San Pedro Etla, 85 percent of the population spoke exclusively Spanish in 1940. The rest were bilingual. Even in smaller, more remote villages such as Santiago Tenango, Etla, a similar proportion spoke exclusively Spanish.[87] Although more than four hundred years of defending their pueblos against Spanish, creole, and liberal elites had produced mixed results, people were effectively trained in the rules of a game, where political interaction brought some rewards.

Third, both land use and land tenure were fairly constant. Although the Porfiriato had witnessed the construction of roads and railways linking the valleys' commercial centers to the capital, the landscape had changed little since the colonial period. The minimal market for crops produced in the region (which really extended little farther than the ring of mountains surrounding the valleys) limited agricultural expansion. Consequently the Central Valleys still consisted of small, fairly independent villages intermingled with poorly capitalized haciendas owned by a mixture of the Oaxacan and foreign elite.[88] During the late nineteenth century the Central Valleys experienced little of the rapacious land grab undergone by Tuxtepec or Jamiltepec. Lands were bought rather than stolen, low-profit haciendas changed hands each generation, and most peasants worked as sharecroppers rather than as debt peons or forced laborers. In fact, by 1910 the number of haciendas in the Central Valleys had not risen since Independence.[89] As Francie Chassen-López argues, the valleys were the only region where the model of Porfirian land tenure closely paralleled that imagined by Andrés Molina Enríquez.[90] Given the debt of Mexican agrarian reform to Molina Enríquez, it is unsurprising that land reform in the region followed a fairly regular and conventional pattern.[91]

Due the close proximity of the Central Valleys to the Carrancista base in Oaxaca City, land reform in the region started relatively early. Surrounded by hostile Soberanista forces, the state's official government was forced to acquire support by dividing up the lands of rebel or absentee landlords. Despite the complicated circumstances these first land reforms established a pattern that would reach into the Cárdenas era: slow, limited land reform, peasant loyalty, hacendado retribution, and eventual if imperfect success. The first definite possession was given to Nazareno Etla in 1917. The village was given 276 hectares of land from the San Isidro ranch of Guadalupe Baights.[92] Although the peasants complained that the lands barely covered their needs, they never defaulted on their taxes and maintained their loyalty to the local government until Carranza's death.[93] Other villages that received lands confronted more combative landlords. When the agrarian committee of El Vergel, Ejutla, petitioned for lands in 1917, the Spanish hacendados Rogelio and Celestino Gómez started a campaign of terror against the prospective *ejidatarios*. In the year of the petition hacienda administrators tortured and murdered the *agrarista* Crisóforo Nuñez and killed Manuel López, a small boy who had taken to accompanying the visiting agrarian engineers.

Eight years later the same men invaded the village, shot the men, raped the women, and stole the livestock. But whereas targeted repression in lowland regions such as Pochutla, Tuxtepec, or Jamiltepec snuffed out petitions, divided elites, or led to effective social revolt, the more acculturated peasants of the Central Valleys had greater access to state support and determinedly pursued their demands through legal channels. The Gómez brothers' murderous crusade was, for once, in vain. By 1930 the hacendados had lost half their lands. By 1940 the hacienda had almost completely disappeared.[94]

Although hundreds of Central Valley pueblos petitioned for lands during the early postrevolutionary years, during the 1920s land redistribution in the Central Valleys actually slowed down as members of the *vallistocracia* regained power within local government. Between 1920 and 1934 state governors approved fifty-seven requests for land but denied a total of twenty-nine. Most provisional negatives concerned lands in the Centro, Etla, or Ocotlán, where good irrigation made haciendas a more profitable proposition than in the drier valleys of Ejutla, Tlacolula, or Zimatlán.[95] As the CCM gained support throughout the region, the rhythm of land distribution increased once again. According to the *Periódico Oficial*, between 1935 and 1940 the federal government signed sixty-six grants and enlargements. These totaled 64,190 hectares. Previous negative decisions concerning rich haciendas such as Reyes Mantecon, Centro, were revoked. Haciendas such as El Vergel and La Compañía, Centro, which had stretched to over ten thousand hectares, were reduced to concerns of little over fifty hectares (at least according to their owners).[96] In the ex-district of Ocotlán of the twenty-five properties larger than one hundred hectares in 1938, only four were private properties, one was an agricultural society, and the other twenty were ejidos.[97] The land redistribution undeniably involved numerous problems. The complex patchwork of haciendas and villages, hemmed in by bare, infertile mountains, offered little space in which to work. As a result, *ejidal* grants often overlapped, leaving contending villages to fight over their respective spoils. The *ejidatarios* of San Miguel Tilquiapam and San Jeronimo Taviche, both located in Ocotlán, vied for the lands of the neighboring hacienda for over a decade.[98] Rushed grants often left *ejidatarios* uncomfortable and sometimes dangerous treks over the lands of bitter former hacendados or rival pueblos. The men of San Juan Lachigalla, Ejutla, had to cross the lands of San Pedro Taviche, Ocotlán, to reach their plots and often faced reprisals for allegedly trampling crops belonging to the other village.[99] Finally, there was simply not enough land to hand out to most villages. As a result peasants were forced to amend the pattern of landholding recommended by the government. In San Lorenzo Cacaotepec, Etla, the peasants had been donated 265 hectares among thirty-five heads of family. Instead of leaving other 110 families to "found another population center," as advised by the government document, they split the ejido among all the village families.[100] The tiny individual plots forced many to migrate to the growing capital city or to develop a sideline as an artisan.[101]

But despite these problems, the Cardenista land reforms in the Central Valleys worked in a way they failed to do in the rest of the state, placating land-starved peasants, ruining hacendados, and tying *ejidatarios* to state organizations. In the most basic terms, the proximity of the state capital and the clear division between village and hacienda meant that most campesinos received lands from where the agrarian laws proposed they should—the large haciendas. Conflict in the Central Valleys during the 1930s therefore followed the pattern suggested by the federal government. Prospective *ejidatarios* were not up against members of rival unions, armed groups tied to competing caciques, or small landowners little better off than themselves. Instead they confronted a more familiar alliance of landlords and clerical Catholics. This emerged for two distinct reasons, involving the Church and the larger landowners. The Central Valleys surrounded the diocesan capital. Unlike other areas of the state, the region possessed a fairly strong church organization, which had been bolstered by Social Catholicism, an influx of displaced rural priests, and a fairly virulent branch of the Liga Nacional de la Defensa de la Libertad based in Oaxaca City.[102] Although the organization had little open support in the capital, its female members, organized into the Legión Guadalupana de Santa Juana de Arco, continued to fund and supply small outbreaks of Cristero violence in the countryside around the capital.[103] In addition, landlords in the Central Valleys were not far enough away from state, federal, or military supervision to establish superficial rivals to state organizations or sophisticated terror networks of pistoleros. Consequently they were forced into collaborating with the other out-of-favor institution—the Church. Peasant complaints stand testament to this regional pact. For example, during early 1934 Cardenistas in the town of Ocotlán de Morelos complained that the municipal council permitted the existence of a private Catholic school. The same council also supported the arrest and murder of prospective *ejidatarios* by members of the landholding elite. According to the CCM, white guards attacked their confederation meetings with cries of "Viva Cristo Rey."[104] The school inspector endorsed this assessment and claimed that it stood true throughout Ocotlán. He complained that the district was divided between "those who supported the official school and those who supported the private schools established by the clergy." While the Agrarian Department and the *ejidatarios* backed the former, the landlords and local authorities sustained the latter.[105]

The configuration of conflict in the Central Valleys, which pitched *ejidatarios*, federal school teachers, and the state against landlords, priests, and clerical Catholics determined both peasant responses to socialist education and the eventual pattern of local power. In the main peasants supported the state education project, demanding, building, and sustaining local schools. In Ocotlán de Morelos the agrarian committee sent a series of vituperative complaints against the local priest's interference in state education, and *ejidatarios'* children regularly attended the local school. Furthermore, parents and children started to participate in the state's secular ceremonies. On 24 March 1935 parents, teachers, and children organized a theatrical celebration of Juárez's birth. The program included a play called *Los campesinos* and a talk titled "La escuela como centro educativo moral." After the event the local peasants voted in the local education committee and sang the "Himno socialista regional."[106] Similarly, peasants in San Fernando de Matamoros, Zimatlán, petitioned for a school in the early 1930s. In 1937 the state established an indigenous boarding school. Although most parents supported the school and sent their children, local peasant representatives claimed that "Cristeros," backed by the local landlord, tried to attack the population.[107] But despite the hostility of a clerical minority, campesinos continued to back the institution and the state's cultural project. The official newspaper claimed that the schools of Zimatlán, including the boarding institution, organized many of the dances for the celebration of the Guelaguetza in Oaxaca City in 1937. The festival was so popular "among all the social classes" that the parents even organized their own event, with their own "typical regional dress," on a hill above Zimatlán. The schools led the march up the hill and there were exhibitions of shooting, volleyball, and callisthenics.[108]

As local *ejidatarios* gradually accepted the state's land grants and its educative project, they also gained a degree of democratic control over regional politics. Municipal elections, even in the district capitals, were dominated by the agrarian sector of the official party. For example, in 1938 the popular sector of Ocotlán complained that the *agrarista* municipal president and the local police had imposed a slate consisting entirely of representatives from the agrarian sector. Furthermore, the municipal committee of the PRM refused to accept candidates from the popular sector. On 1 January 1939, the popular and agrarian sectors established their respective councils in separate buildings. However, despite myriad complaints from the town's commercial elite, the agrarian council was declared victorious and troops removed its opponents the following day.[109] This agrarian control of local politics reached into the 1940s. In late 1940 the peasant league of San Lorenzo Cacaotepec complained that the local cacique had taken over the municipal committee of the PRM and was imposing his own council irrespective of the popular agrarian vote. On 20 December the local government nullified the election. A week later it organized a plebiscite at which a member of the agrarian sector was elected president.[110]

Although land distribution brought a degree of electoral freedom to the Central Valleys, it failed to replicate that of the Sierra Juárez. Whereas *serrano* peasants negotiated their pact with federal and state governments from a position of political and even martial strength, *ejidatarios* in the Central Valleys had received their revolutionary rewards by the grace of the federal government. Without independent cross-village organizations, the peasants of the valleys had to remain loyal to the official peasant confederation as it became increasingly dominated by state bureaucrats. If they attempted any unsanctioned actions, they risked official ire. For example, when peasants from El Mogote tired of petitioning local authorities to protect them against the local Italian landlord, Domingo Tomacelli, they took the law into their own lands and stabbed him to death in broad daylight in Oaxaca City. Rather than being lost in judicial limbo or receiving a mandatory sentence, the culprits were tracked down, captured, and sentenced to death.[111]

The pattern of landholding, the level of state power, and the ethnic configuration in the Central Valleys closely paralleled that imagined by the writers of Mexico's agrarian laws. As a result, peasant responses to land reform closely mirrored state expectations. Peasants petitioned for the return of communal lands, were offered grants, formed ejidos, confronted a cabal of reactionary landowners and clerical Catholics, and in many ways won. By 1940 the Central Valleys were a patchwork of small ejidos. Few remaining landholdings exceeded fifty hectares, and peasant slates started to dominate local elections. As state rhetoric closely approximated agrarian reality, the campesinos of the Central Valleys remained fairly loyal to the state party long after Cárdenas's reforms had ceased to offer genuine socioeconomic or political improvements. Here, if anywhere in Oaxaca, peasants started to speak the "language of the state," sending their children to school, couching demands in supplicant letters to the local representative of the CNC, and voting for the official party. As such, the Central Valleys closely mirrored other regions of central Mexico, such as Tecamachalco in Puebla or Zitácuaro in Michoacán, where the local composition of haciendas, villages, ethnic groups, landed elites, state bureaucrats, and Catholic groups persuaded most peasants to throw their lot in with the state peasant and educative organizations in return for limited land reform and agrarian sector control of municipal councils.[112]

Huajuapam

In the ex-district of Huajuapam land reform was not as simple as that of the Central Valleys, where the line between villager and hacendado was clearly drawn and acted as a good approximation of the government's appreciation of the countryside's geography. In Huajuapam *agrarismo* was delineated by the atypical nature of local landholding and the strong relationship between the region's indigenous Mixtecs and the Catholic Church. The effects of the nineteenth-century redistribution of lands in the Mixteca have elicited a bewildering array of opinions. Some stress the retention of indigenous communal land, others note its division into small properties, and a few still emphasize the acquisition of lands by large landowners.[113] The debate rests partly on a misunderstanding of the actual nature of landholding among the Mixtecs and partly on stereotyping of indigenous attitudes to land. In the first place, many communal lands were privatized during the Reform era, but few were sold on to large landowners and most remained fairly equally divided among Mixtec villagers.[114] As Alan Knight argues, "where the change from communal property to private did not open the doors of speculation, hoarding and the latifundio, it could attract demands and interests, in some regions at least."[115] Second, although some Spanish families did take advantage of the privatizations to amass large latifundios, these remained exceptional.[116] Third, the Reform era threw up a novel form of landownership—the agricultural society. This was a localized institution, built on the extinct holdings of indigenous caciques who in the eighteenth century rented land to Mixtec farmers for pasture. As the increasingly acculturated caciques moved to the cities of San Juan Bautista Huajuapam de León, Puebla, or Tehuacán, their tenants became involved in legal disputes to usurp these lands. By the mid–nineteenth century many frustrated caciques had sold up the holdings to the Mixtec farmers. In turn, the purchasers transformed these lands into agricultural societies in order to protect them from the privatization of communal lands. By 1910 many villages in Huajuapam had purchased lands that they had formerly rented as agricultural societies, among them the communities of San Pablo and San Pedro Tequixtepec, Mariscala de Iturbide, San Andrés Dinicuiti, Santiago Chazumba, Santiago Huajolotitlán, San Jeronimo Silacayoapilla, Santiago Chilixtlahuaca, Santos Reyes Yucuna, San José Ayuquila, San Juan Bautista Suchitepec, San Juan Huaxtepec, Asunción Cuyotepeji, and San Pedro Atoyac.[117]

Agricultural societies, or *condueñazgos*, have traditionally been viewed as legal fictions created to maintain communal land ownership during the years of Reform and the Porfiriato.[118] Land owned by the society could only be sold on to another society member. Land surrounding the private plots used for livestock grazing and timber was still effectively communal.[119] However, in other ways the societies offered a distinctly liberal conception of land as private property, as something proudly acquired by money rather than inherently owned by the community, as something that could be sold and resold inside certain parameters.[120] In 1882 the council of Asunción Cuyotepeji defended the agricultural society's lands against invasions by the men of Santa María Camotlán. The defense was couched in the language of liberalism, explaining that the lands had been "bought by the locals" from the Villagómez *cacicazgo* in 1864 and demanding that at the very least, Santa María Camotlán should have its own properties divided because of the laws against civil bodies owning land.[121] Although the indigenous ranchers of Huajuapam were in many ways liberal landowners, they also brokered a favorable agreement with local representatives of the Catholic Church. In many areas of Oaxaca during the late nineteenth and early twentieth centuries, ecclesiastical authorities had intimidated, ignored, demeaned, or fled their indigenous parishioners.[122] But in Huajuapam priests and Mixtec Indians formed a strong alliance based on mutual interest and syncretic religious practice. On the one hand, priests helped indigenous villages purchase land as agricultural societies by brokering deals and lending money. The societies often took over former *cofradía* lands, with which they then paid the priest.[123] On the other hand, the creation in 1903 of the small diocese of Huajuapam de León, covering most of the Mixteca Baja, encouraged the cultural confluence of elite and popular forms of Catholicism. Under the mestizo bishop Rafael Amador y Hernández, local men were trained in the newly established seminary in the tenets of Social Catholicism and the regional variant of the Mixtec language. They were encouraged to establish lay charity organizations, laud indigenous religiosity, support local cults, and protect their parishioners from liberal land speculators. The union of ecclesiastic authorities and indigenous ranchers reacted strongly to the postrevolutionary state's program of anticlericalism. There were armed Cristero rebellions in Huajua-pam in 1926 and 1932 and a sustained campaign against the so-cialist school took place from 1934 onward.[124]

As a result, when Cardenista *agrarismo* reached Huajuapam, it faced a landscape that could not be explained by the stark so-cioeconomic Manichaeism encapsulated in the model topogra-phy of the Agrarian Code. Moreover, official anticlericalism had opened up divisions between the central state and the pious Mix-tec ranchers, who now reframed their liberal era purchases as pri-vate properties to be defended by the Church. Unlike in the Cen-tral Valleys, Jamiltepec, or Tuxtepec, land reform thus had little or no popular support. Instead, backing for *agrarismo* rested on a minority of ambitious politicians such as Vicente Pacheco Ramírez, who saw *agrarismo* as a means to gain power within the governing camarilla of Huajuapam merchants and landown-ers. At the same time the camarilla, led by Rodolfo Solana Car-rion and José Peral Martínez, viewed land reform as a potential threat to be avoided at best and at worst redirected. Camarilla members therefore offered Pacheco Ramírez limited support in return for the safeguarding of their haciendas. Consequently in most of the region the project was a disaster, motivated by polit-ical ambition, distorted by political strongmen, and the cause of bitter division. Acting out of a commitment to political advance-ment rather than socioeconomic reform, Pacheco Ramírez obeyed the dictates of the ruling camarilla, avoided their lands, and in-stead exploited divisions over the region's agricultural societies. The federal agrarian machinery ignored the complexities of local landholding and pushed through the requests. In San Juan Bau-tista Suchitepec, the land grant took 2,000 hectares from the so-ciety and gave it directly to another group of villagers, effectively splitting the community in half.[125] In Mariscala the *ejidal* grant of 3,266 hectares included over 1,900 hectares from the local society and thus avoided the expropriation of Peral Martínez's hacienda, Victoria.[126]

The landholding and political regime that emerged in the Mixteca was thus different from that of other areas of Oaxaca. Unlike in Tuxtepec or the Central Valleys, the land reform movement did not redistribute land to any great extent. In 1938 there were still twenty properties of more than one hundred hectares in the ex-district of Huajuapam.[127] However, nor did the local elite effectively crush the project of land redistribution, as happened in Pochutla or Jamiltepec. A pact between *agrarista* politicians and the Huajuapam ruling camarilla allowed the persistence of the program as long as it affected the populous agricultural societies rather than the large properties of the elite. Consequently, although there was a CNC presence in the region, it was controlled by politicians, subject to the surviving hacendados, and opposed by the Mixtec ranchers of the agricultural societies, who felt that their parents' perspicacity during the liberal era was being punished.

During the 1930s this bitterness over land loss combined with the devout Catholicism of the region. In August 1938 the leader of the ejido of San Juan Bautista Suchitepec complained that the priest, José Velasco Amador, had allied with the owners of the annexed agricultural society to deny the prospective *ejidatarios* their lands.[128] This early association foreshadowed more organized opposition to the state in years to come as the clergy, agricultural society members, and the Partido Acción Nacional (PAN) allied in municipal, regional, and federal elections.[129] By the 1950s the state was forced to permit Panista councils or impose loyal slates by armed force.[130] This confluence of circumstances in Huajuapam was rare, but it was not unique. There were agricultural societies likewise disguising *cofradía* lands in the districts of Silacayoapam and Coixtlahuaca.[131] Although the state avoided such heavy-handed land redistribution in these areas, it still incurred the anger of devout indigenous Mixtec and Chocho communities who had struggled to buy their lands during the nineteenth century.[132] Outside Oaxaca the limited research on both religion and Porfirian land tenure prohibits direct comparison.[133] However, one might imagine that where agricultural societies, or *condueñazgos*, remained into the twentieth century (as in the Huesteca of Hidalgo or San Luis Potosí) or where the church established new, small, dynamic dioceses (Huejutla or Zamora), similar resistance emerged.[134]

Palm Production in the Mixteca

If *agrarismo* was often unsuccessful as it failed to adapt to local circumstances, the government project in the palm-producing area of the Mixteca cannot be accused of the same inflexibility. Although the system of palm cooperatives eventually failed, the arrangement imposed during the Cardenista regime was designed specifically to deal with the problems arising from the region's system of land tenure and an economy based on one product. The ex-districts of Coixtlahuaca, Teposcolula, Tlaxiaco, and eastern Huajuapam, which together form the Mixteca Alta, are the least fertile areas of Oaxaca. Although Huajuapam and Tlaxiaco contain a few lush valleys, for the most part the area is a network of barren crags and desolate mountains. Consequently, although communal lands have been widespread and large landholdings scarce, the indigenous inhabitants of the region have always had to look beyond the cultivation of maize and beans to survive.[135]

During the colonial era they produced silk and cochineal. When competition from Peru and Guatemala made both those crops unprofitable, the Mixtecs turned toward another small household industry: palm weaving.[136] Although palm weaving was well established by the Porfiriato, most evidence for the nature and importance of the industry comes from after the Revolution. In 1923 the federal school inspector reported that palm weaving was the main source of income for over 150,000 people from Tlapa, Guerrero, Acatlán, Puebla, and the Mixteca Alta, Oaxaca. For the Mexican market the weavers made a variety of products, including mats, belts, baskets, winnowers, brushes, and ropes, but most produced palm hats for export to the United States, Panama, Costa Rica, and British Honduras. The weavers sold these to commercial agents from the major trading post of Tehuacán, Puebla. Here the agents handed over the hats to a few large merchant enterprises, where they were whitened, ironed, decorated, colored, and sent off to the foreign markets.[137]

According to government engineer Ignacio Ruíz Martínez, who during the 1930s became the state's expert on the industry, the exploitation of the palm producers by Hispanic and mestizo merchants was extremely serious. Men, women, and children as young as four were forced to work twelve to fifteen hours to produce on average three poor-quality hats a day. The commercial agent would pay just over 5 centavos per hat. After subtracting the cost of the palm, which had to be transported from Nochixtlán, the typical family had to survive on a daily income of around 40 centavos. As food had to be imported into the region and was relatively expensive, the wages failed to reach the sum needed to achieve subsistence and were "impossible to live on." As a result, those who failed to scavenge for the roots, herbs, and berries needed to supplement their diet often suffered from grave malnutrition. In contrast, the agents and merchants reaped fortunes from the palm industry. The agent made around 2 centavos per hat and up to 100 to 150 pesos per month. The merchant earned 10 centavos per finished piece. During 1937, as the Mixteca produced 42,933,060 hats, Ruíz Martínez estimated that the fifteen merchant houses received profits of over 4 million pesos.[138]

Since the Revolution the federal government had taken an interest in gross inequality of the palm industry. In 1923 President Alvaro Obregón offered money for the establishment of a cooperative for palm weavers. The society, which was formed by the Department of Public Works, had its office in Santa María Tecomavaca on the main Oaxaca-Tehuacán railway line. The idea was to buy up the hats from the producers at market price and sell them directly to the foreign buyers. However, in a move that presaged the elite's strategy in the following decades, agents, municipal authorities, and Tehuacán merchants combined to discourage the Mixtec peasants from utilizing the new society. Without sufficient government support the society quickly folded.[139] In the early 1930s the onus for the resolution of the trade's problems fell to the state government. In November 1931 Governor Francisco López Cortés opened a congress on the palm industry in San Pedro y San Pablo Teposcolula. Like many of the Chicolopista projects it was strong on rhetoric and weak on practical programs. Although a succession of worthy teachers announced that palm production was not a technique of economic survival but rather "a spontaneous expression of anthropological art, born in the first epochs of the sedentary life of the Mixtec people," López Cortés expressed "categorical reservations with respect to any concrete

plan of action," and the hastily established Permanent Commission of Palm Production failed to take hold.[140]

Despite the previous failures, in 1934 the idea for a series of
palm cooperatives designed to bypass the merchant monopoly of
Tehuacán was resurrected as part of the broader enthusiasm for
social reform initiated during Cárdenas's presidential campaign.
In early 1934 three government employees from the Mixteca, José
Trinidad Espinosa, José María Ramírez, and Leopoldo Jiménez
Córdova, founded the Comité Pro-Mixteca to resolve the economic problems of the region. In November 1934 at the behest
of the PNR candidate, who had visited the Mixteca on his electoral tour of the provinces, their request to set up palm cooperatives throughout the Mixteca was approved by the federal government. As one official argued, such was the unpopularity of the
state's anticlerical program that it was better to allow an independent group of Mixtec residents to organize the palm workers
rather than government representatives doing so. Over the next
year the members of the committee walked the length of the Mixteca and established thirty-five cooperatives with 7,789 members.
Together these formed the unaffiliated Federación de Cooperativas de Trabajadores de la Palma y sus Productos de la Región
Mixteca. At the same time, the Bank of Agricultural Credit attempted to replace the role of the Puebla merchants and bought
up a dyeing operation and a warehouse in Tehuacán. The idea
was that the new cooperatives would now sell their products to
middlemen for near market price. These agents would then hand
the hats and other palm goods to the bank, which would paint
them, store them, and export them to Mexico City or the United
States.[141]

From the start, the conflict of interest between the federation and the bank caused considerable problems. The bank was unwilling to allow the federation exclusive control of the palm workers. As a result, it proceeded to send its agents throughout the Mixteca offering the weavers immediate funds in return for the destruction of the cooperatives and the establishment of local credit societies subject to the bank. At the same time, the bank deliberately made it hard for the cooperatives to profit from use of the bank—limiting the types of hats it would purchase; refusing to dye mats, belts, or baskets; and paying the agents prices that were little greater than those paid by the merchant elite.[142] By July 1935 a local politician offered the generous opinion that "there are two entities that, although guided by the same desire to help the peasants, work in such a way as to be prejudicial to their interests."[143] The bank was aided by the governments of Oaxaca and Puebla. The Chicolopista government saw links between the federation and the CCM and had pliant municipal authorities dismantle the cooperatives. The Puebla government, although more radical than that of Oaxaca, feared the loss of taxes resulting from a state monopoly of the palm industry and taxed the federation's members at the entrance to Tehuacán.[144] By 1936 with the help of the two state governments, the bank had taken over the role of the federation but was still far from resolving the problem. First, it had only sufficient finance to purchase about a tenth of the hats produced in the region.[145] Second, it still relied on the old agents to acquire the workers' palm products. As a result, although it paid the agents one centavo per hat more than the Hispanic merchants, it did not procure enough hats to make the agents' exclusive loyalty worth their while. Thus the Mixtec peasants who did not now have the backing of a cooperative organization, sold some of their hats at the improved price to the bank. But when the agents had achieved their monthly quota, the peasants had to sell their remaining stock at the lower price.[146] As anthropologist Julio de la Fuente observed, "the bank has totally failed in the Mixtec region, and some agents have made good business out of the Indians."[147]

When Cárdenas returned to the Mixteca in March 1937, he found the project in total disarray and called on members of six government ministries to investigate the socioeconomic dependency of the Mixteca and formulate some solutions.[148] The report delivered in November of the same year suggested a dual program of reinvigorated cooperatives and crop diversification. The new cooperatives, which would also produce animal fodder and fiber and thus avoid the problem of the overproduction of palm hats, would be organized into seven confederations with their central offices in the Mixteca's ex-district capitals. Factories to finish the hats would be built in San Juan Bautista Huajuapam de León and at the railway station of Parián. Finally, the report recommended more sustained financial support for the project. Only when "sufficient money controlled the total production of the palm hats of the Mixtecas" could the peasant weavers escape the monopoly of the Tehuacán merchants.[149]

Although palm expert Ruíz Martínez took the report around a series of government conferences, it was not until members of the DAAI took up the cause that the federal government again took note.[150] Cárdenas told the Agricultural Bank to retreat from the region, and in February 1940 the National Bank of Mexico established branches of the Company of Mexican Exportation and Importation (CEIMSA) in Tehuacán and subagencies in many of the rural towns of the Mixteca.[151] These bypassed the traditional merchants' agents and bought directly from a reinvigorated cooperative structure founded by members of the DAAI. At the same time, money was distributed to the peasant producers to build small dyeing and ironing workshops so as to circumvent the factories of the Tehuacán elite.[152] The project confronted the same problems as before. Some devout peasants from the diocese of Huajuapam de León refused all government help.[153] The merchants and their representatives attempted to buy up the palm products before they arrived at the CEIMSA subagencies. The governor of Oaxaca, Vicente González Fernández, opposed the company; he not only permitted his tax collectors to demand illegal peculations but also allowed his *compadre*, the Coixtlahuaca cacique Agustín Bazán, to intimidate local peasants into giving up their hats at a third of market price. The Puebla government also supported the forces against the company. Not only had the federal palm monopoly grievously affected tax income—the new peasant workshops were ruining the workers of state cacique Maximino Avila Camacho's pet organization, the CROM.[154] Although in September 1946 the combination of state government and private business overturned CEIMSA and forced it out of business, for seven years its financial muscle had damaged the control of the Tehuacán merchants.[155] In 1950 the economist Moises de la Peña condemned the failure and pointed to the resumption of intense poverty and consequent migration in the area.[156] But during the period, palm workers' incomes rose to around 1.80 pesos a day. In late 1945 their wages reached the heady level of three pesos. As the head of CEIMSA argued, in general "the indigenous nuclei dedicated to the manufacture of articles of palm gradually improved their economic conditions of life."[157]

The successes and failures of Cárdenas's reorganization of the palm industry highlight other aspects of the era's socioeconomic reforms. Although *agrarismo* was a blunt tool, often wielded with pointless abandon in unpropitious circumstances, the Cardenista regime was not averse to more sensitive, localized reform projects. The Mixteca was not suited to land redistribution, but commercial exploitation and the resultant poverty were rife. Rather than step in with a one-size-fits-all approach to rural development, Cárdenas was astute enough during his two visits to the area to listen to expert opinions on possible solutions. Although the first experiment from 1934 to 1937 failed because of the kind of interagency rivalry and elite manipulation described by Ben Fallaw in the expropriated henequen plantations of the Yucatán, Cárdenas allowed investigation and debate of the problem before moving to improve on the previous government effort.[158] This reformed mix of cooperatives and sound financial support, buoyed by a wartime economy, actually worked, at least until late 1946.

Conclusion

How do the socioeconomic reforms enacted in Oaxaca fit into the debate over the relative radicalism and political authoritarianism of the Cardenista regime? The political formation of the CCM, CNC, and CTM during the last four years of Cárdenas's presidency reveals a general move toward the establishment of an elite hegemony over the peasant and worker organizations. As *agrarismo* gained official support, it appeared that ambitious Oaxaca politicians used it as a "convenient tool . . . to gain local supporters."[159] Throughout the state, radical leaders such as Carlos Belleza and Daniel Muñoz Estefan were expelled, their places usurped by landowners, caciques, and middle-class bureaucrats such as Miguel Ortiz and Jorge Meixueiro, who wanted to harness "the armed, electoral or organizational power of the campesinos."[160]

In their hands newly regimented peasant committees, especially in the Central Valleys, were "forcibly integrated into a national network of peasant organizations controlled by the official party" and formed the core of government support for future decades.[161] The takeover of peasant leadership by a cabal of bourgeois leaders affected not only the democracy of the organization but also the implementation of reform. In Jamiltepec and Huajuapam politicians wielded *agrarismo* as a political rather than a socioeconomic weapon. The distribution of ejidos followed patterns of political power and factional division rather than genuine inequality. Furthermore, in Jamiltepec by 1940 a reunified landowning elite was able to utilize the weakness of government agencies to block much of the proposed redistribution.

However, although by 1940 the leadership of worker and peasant organizations had been commandeered by local caciques and ambitious politicians, there is little evidence of elite intrigue or the state's clandestine embrace of market capitalism and private investment.[162] Cárdenas's agrarian policies do not seem to have been "intended . . . to preserve and stimulate the system of private farming for commercial profit."[163] The slide toward political dominance was not caused by design but rather by the ignorance and incapacity of the central government. Throughout the period the Cardenista bureaucracy was chronically understaffed, and *ejidal* committees, Agrarian Department representatives, and municipal authorities repeatedly lamented the lack of agrarian engineers.[164] At the same time, these few federal employees were causing endemic conflict in the regions in which they operated. As Ben Fallaw argues, one result was that in order to maintain unity and a modicum of control, the Cardenista state retreated from its policy of utilizing federal bureaucrats and instead "repeatedly made key concessions to regional politicos." In return, these new leaders gave up the popular politics of the Agrarian Department and "revived the kind of machine politics and cacique tactics that only a few years ago Cárdenas had denounced as Caciquismo."[165]

The increasing authoritarianism of the peasant and worker organizations was also undermined by intraelite disputes and peasant resistance. In Tuxtepec divisions between local camarillas of merchants and banana growers mapped themselves onto the national conflict between the CCM and the CTM. Although obedience was often enforced with violence, individuals and villages could change sides depending on the rewards offered by the opposing factions. In Jamiltepec the persistence of revolutionary dreams of reform and the paucity of genuine land redistribution meant that although the elite claimed dominance over the local CNC, compliance was difficult to enforce, especially over issues of taxation. In Huajuapam the existence of agricultural societies and the clumsy application of the Agrarian Code led to widespread, virulent distrust of the entire machinery of postrevolutionary Mexican governance and the emergence of radical, popular brand of Panismo. In the same way, although the elite "undermined most of the planned Cardenista reforms," it was not able to dismiss them altogether.[166] In Tuxtepec factional disputes forced peasant leaders to enforce genuine land reform, while in the Central Valleys Cardenismo built on the political *agrarismo* of the 1920s to break up the last of the region's haciendas. In the Mixteca Alta, the persistence and flexibility of the president himself eventually allowed a brief realignment of the area's oppressive mercantile regime. The ejidos and cooperatives created might not have been models of efficient modern agricultural production and were often weakened by a lack of financial and infrastructural support, but they were not "the monuments of poverty and underdevelopment" Thomas Benjamin described in Chiapas, and few *ejidatarios* wanted to "return to their status as peons."[167]

SEVEN

The Problems with Cardenista Politics and the
Rise of the Urban Social Movement, 1940–44

The few studies of the 1940s portray the era as one of increasing centralization, corporatism, stability, political control, and economic modernization.[1] The exigencies of Mexico's entry into World War II and the resulting discourse of national unity permeated all layers of the political system.[2] As a result, President Avila Camacho was able to engineer a series of party reforms, which made local and regional politicians entirely beholden to the center.[3] Although "bureaucratic institutions exist[ed] at the local, regional and state levels . . . decision making of all kinds t[ook] place in Mexico City and nearly all policy directives emanate[d] from the government offices in the capital."[4] The layers of the state government were "bypassed as the key mediating institutions by interest groups."[5] The system of corporatism was also refined and more widely applied. The CNC was bureaucratized and the CTM emasculated.[6] Furthermore, the creation of the Confederación Nacional de Organizaciones Populares in 1943 allowed the national party to normalize the increasing process of favoring the bourgeois, urban elite over the rural ruffians of the Revolution.[7] Finally, the central government asserted its control more firmly over all levels of the electoral process. In the PRM's internal elections "firmly disciplined" peasants and workers "continued to legitimate the selection of the candidates."[8] At the same time the demands of wartime put a premium on industrial and agricultural production. The redistribution of wealth, encapsulated in Cárdenas's programs of agrarian repartition and workers' rights, took a back seat to the construction of infrastructure, the modernization of old industry, and the construction of new.

This chapter examines the tensions between this revisionist cannon of presidentialism, centralization, corporatism, and electoral control and the political reality of Oaxaca. During the late 1930s President Cárdenas had attempted to avoid the problems of another Oaxacan caudillo by appointing a relatively powerless governor and balancing the authority of the state capital with a network of independent caciques. The elections for state governor in 1940 followed a similar pattern. The efforts of local strongmen to acquire the prized post were ignored and Cárdenas again appointed a relatively unknown military candidate, whose ties to the state's various regional camarillas were apparently weak. However, over the next four years Governor Vicente González Fernández upset Cárdenas's delicate political equilibrium. First, he formed a camarilla of the members of the *vallistocracia*, the CNC, and the moderate wing of the CTM. Second, he started a concerted campaign to rid Oaxaca's periphery of Cárdenas's caciques. Together these actions destabilized the political culture of the region. In Tuxtepec the war between the CTM and the CNC intensified, and in Juchitán, the Región Mixe, Miahuatlán, Juxtlahuaca, and Yautepec attacks on the local caciques by state representatives caused a wave of politically motivated assassinations. As a result, on several occasions President Avila Camacho had to intervene by denying the governor electoral impositions but also by increasing military control of the region. The urbanization of Oaxaca City, increasing importance of small merchants, growing literacy of the urban population, and revival of the Catholic

Church also ushered in a new political player: the popular cross-class social movement. Although González Fernández's political sensitivity to the city's elite meant he managed to quell the most virulent of these movements, his successors were less competent and less fortunate.

The Elections of 1940

According to the public transcript Manuel Avila Camacho's electoral victory in Oaxaca was easy. When he arrived there in June 1939 he was greeted by "thousands of campesinos, Zapotecs and Mixtecs, from the coast, from the mountains and from the region of the Valley."[9] In reality, the campaign became mired in a struggle between the state's revolutionary elite and the Huajuapam supporters of the opposition presidential candidate, Juan Andrew Almazán. These challengers saw the electoral campaign as a means to liberate their agricultural societies, municipal schools, and local churches from the attacks of the state. Throughout late 1940 and early 1941 there were multiple warnings of imminent revolts.[10] Beyond the tensions revealed during the presidential election, it was the gubernatorial election that most affected the state's political structure. During the final months of 1938 candidates for the post had begun to jostle for position. As in 1936, most were ambitious caciques supported by regionally or socially specific camarillas. Edmundo Sánchez Cano, Alfonso Francisco Ramírez, and Rafael Melgar had created careers outside the state but were supported by groups from Oaxaca City and the Mixteca. From within Oaxaca the state CNC put forward the candidacy of Jorge Meixueiro, and the dissident members of the CTM proposed Benito Zaragoza. Finally, Genaro V. Vásquez attempted to use his position as national attorney of justice to further support among contacts in the Sierra Juárez.[11] Cárdenas again ignored the pleas of the various regional elites and chose Vicente González Fernández, who, at least initially, had few ties to Oaxaca's interest groups. Although he was born in Ocotlán in the late 1880s, González Fernández, like Chapital, was a professional soldier, who had spent all his adult life outside the state. He had joined the School of Cadets in 1908 and, after a few undistinguished years of service, joined the Constitutionalist army as a captain. Over the next five years he fought Zapatistas in Morelos and Villistas in Chihuahua. After the Agua Prieta revolt he continued to rise up the ranks of the army, remaining loyal to the federal government during the De la Huerta and Escobar rebellions and operating as the zone commander in Tabasco and Puebla and finally as the chief of police in Mexico City.[12]

However, unlike Chapital, González Fernández was no political ingénue. Although his relationship with Cárdenas, forged as a member of the 1929 expeditionary force, was key to his victory in the gubernatorial elections, he was not content to rely exclusively on the support of the president. During his election campaign he began to make alliances among the regional interest groups. A pact with the *vallistocracia* came first. Although he had spent his entire career outside the state, his family had married into the Oaxacan elite. In particular, his daughter had married Jesús Torres Márquez, son of Jesús Torres Barriga, the president of the city's chamber of commerce. He built on these links by bringing Alfonso Francisco Ramírez into his campaign team and allowing the popular jurist to address the Oaxaca City and Mixtec crowds on his behalf. According to Mario Torres Márquez, he assured the capital's commercial elite of a favorable tax regime under his governance.[13] Next, he attempted to gain the exclusive support of the Oaxacan branch of the CNC. The peasant confederation had originally favored its leader, Jorge Meixueiro, as gubernatorial candidate. González Fernández promised Meixueiro significant political rewards in return for the undivided support of the CNC. Meixueiro accepted and began to force the confederation's bureaucracy to accept his new political patron's nomination.[14]

The move by González Fernández to usurp exclusive control of the CNC caused fractures between state and federal governments. In keeping with the federal strategy of balancing Oaxaca's various political forces, the national committee of the CNC attempted to limit the power of the prospective governor by denying Meixueiro's ambitions to be the CNC's official candidate for senator. Instead, the confederation's executive committee planned to maintain regional equilibrium by the appointment of the Juchitán cacique, Heliodoro Charis. Although the state CNC under Meixueiro protested its nonconformity by splitting from the national committee in February, an agreement was reached. Charis would become senator but Meixueiro would retain control of the CNC and operate as González Fernández's chief of staff.[15]

By attempting to form his own ruling camarilla González Fernández not only offended the central government and Charis; he also began to alienate other local interest groups. As in 1936, Genaro V. Vásquez had been using his position in the federal bureaucracy to raise enough support to ensure further employment in the coming sexenio.[16] But unlike Chapital, González Fernández was unwilling to share power. As a result relations between the two political aspirants became strained. González Fernández's newspaper, *Oaxaca Nuevo*, accused Vásquez of political meddling, and Meixueiro's CNC warned its members of his reactionary designs.[17] At the same time, González Fernández started to estrange the radical wing of the CTM by explicitly favoring the Valley industrialists, the La Cañada sugar planters, and the CNC and denying the nomination of the CTM candidate, Benito Zaragoza, for senator.[18] By the end of 1939 Vásquez and the disenfranchised members of the CTM—such as the San Lucas Ojitlán leader Daniel Muñoz Estefan and the head of the palm cooperatives, Leopoldo Jiménez Córdova—formed the Federación Indigenista Revolucionaria Oaxaqueña (FIRO), a pressure group designed to push for the "solution of the economic and social problems of aboriginal groups." The organization, which built its ideology on the increasingly radical *indigenismo* of certain linguists and anthropologists, attempted to usurp the role of the CNC, claiming that it would create a FIRO cell in each municipality.[19] On 20 November 1939 there were fights between the opposing sides in Oaxaca City. Less than a week later the Senate censured Vásquez's actions.[20]

Despite the warning signs proffered by his disputes with Vásquez and the CTM, González Fernández's candidacy was successful. In August 1939 the conservative wing of the CTM announced their support for González Fernández, and by October Governor Chapital had ordered the state's municipal authorities to follow suit.[21] In November federal deputies and senators met at the Roma restaurant in Mexico City to declare their backing for the military candidate.[22] The CNC voted in January 1940 to support González Fernández, and on 20 March he was elected official PRM nominee. On 4 August he was elected governor of the state. According to the official figures, the opposition candidates, Federico Cervantes and José Sánchez Juárez (Benito Juárez's grandson), received fewer than two hundred votes between them.[23] However, although González Fernández's election appeared less controversial than that of his predecessor, the process of nomination pointed to fractures in Cárdenas's political strategy. While Governor Chapital was content to depend on the president for his position and permitted local caciques and peasant and worker organizations to do the same, González Fernández wanted an independent camarilla. Although this would offer the incumbent greater control of the state's political machinery, the move would also destabilize its delicate equilibrium.

Construction of the González Fernández Camarilla

The conflicts of 1939 and 1940 continued during González Fernández's governorship as he used a fourfold strategy to strengthen his camarilla and consolidate his power base. First, he appointed family members to important posts throughout the state. Second, he extended his ties to the *vallistocracia* by safeguarding the remains of the Central Valley haciendas. Third, he assumed control of the state's peasant and worker organizations. Finally, he overlaid his political control with an intensified and more centralized program of Oaxacan cultural regionalism.

As Mark Wasserman argues, during the 1940s "personalism and nepotism continued as crucial elements in politics."[24] As soon as González Fernández became governor, he started to appoint his relatives to strategic governmental positions. Two nephews became tax collectors in Tlaxiaco and Teotitlán and a third became the treasurer of the state. One brother was imposed on the CROM unions of Salina Cruz, and another was elected the municipal president of Oaxaca City.[25] In 1943 a confidential government report claimed that nepotism was rife, and by 1944 the Mexico City newspaper *El Hombre Libre* described the governor operating a "new feudalism" whereby "family members and relatives occupy all the juicy positions in the administration."[26]

González Fernández could not depend exclusively on this network. He sought further support among the members of Oaxaca's elite by confirming the *vallistocracia*'s properties in the Central Valleys. Although these had been reduced by twenty years of agrarian reform, some were still extensive, and their proximity to the growing urban center of Oaxaca City made crops relatively profitable. However, by the late 1930s, valley *ejidatarios* threatened to overwhelm these haciendas by demanding further increases of their properties. At the same time, certificates of exemption—designed to stop the expropriation of properties smaller than fifty hectares—were difficult, costly, and time-consuming to acquire. Hence during the first three years of his governorship González Fernández bypassed the problem of exemption and solved the Valley landowners' trouble with gradual *agrarista* encroachment by provisionally denying sixty-six *ejidal* increases. Each denial listed the haciendas around the ejidos and claimed engineers had verified that they were small properties, even if the central government had yet to offer its official confirmation. Most of the properties he saved were owned by rich industrialists and merchants, such as Luis Sarmiento, Lauro Candiani Cajiga, Domingo Tomacelli, and José Baights. González Fernández nevertheless used the negative decisions to appeal to Avilacamachista ideals of agricultural productivity and small property ownership.[27]

Control of the politicized inhabitants of the state's capital was progressively more important, but González Fernández still needed links to Oaxaca's rural population. Consequently he pursued his close relationship with the state's CNC, supporting the electoral ambitions of the organization's loyal members and manipulating the more intransigent through purification campaigns and tax let-offs. Although he offered little land to the state's campesinos, he appeared to take a great interest in their welfare. He attended the CNC's annual congresses, as the "number one friend of the state's peasants," and promised to bring "the positive vindication of the Oaxacan campesinos."[28] He encouraged the further union of the peasants, organizing and sponsoring conferences of campesino unification in Tuxtepec, the Isthmus, Villa Alta, and the Región Mixe.[29] Most important, he favored compliant CNC members with the control of important municipal councils. During the Cárdenas era, Putla's sixteen thousand hectares of municipal lands had been divided into three ejidos.[30] The land grant had caused considerable friction between the predominantly Mixtec beneficiaries of the land distribution and the mestizos who had rented the lands from the council. During the 1930s elections had become increasingly bloody affairs, in which Governor Chapital seemed typically unwilling to intervene.[31] González Fernández, in contrast, firmly backed the resident *agraristas* against the mestizo ranchers, who had formed the local branch of the PRM's popular sector. In December 1942 the local deputy, Felix Baños, arrived in Putla on the orders of the governor and imposed on the municipality a council composed of *agrarista* representatives.[32] As a result, the popular sector complained to the next governor that González Fernández had always treated them with "despotism and indifference."[33]

González Fernández's policy of offering municipal political power to compliant members of the CNC effectively stratified the confederation and eased its transformation from an organization of social redistribution to one of political control. But, if deemed necessary, he also employed more negative tactics. In September 1942 he announced a campaign of ridding ejidos of nonresident members. Although he argued that this was designed as part of the national drive for greater agricultural production, it also had more local, political ends.[34] Especially in Tuxtepec, where intra-*ejidal* conflict was common, the organizations were stripped of the more disruptive members, again under the auspices of increased productivity.[35] In January 1943 Otilio Ochoa claimed he had been unfairly thrown off his *ejidal* parcel in El Yagul for opposing the CNC *ejidal* president.[36] Overall, in the municipality of Tuxtepec, 469 men were eliminated from the *ejidal* system in 1942 alone.[37] González Fernández also resurrected Francisco López Cortés's methods of peasant control, utilizing tax charges and reductions to maintain *ejidal* loyalty. Thus, three months after Avila Camacho's contentious electoral victory, the governor rewarded the fidelity of the *ejidatarios* of Huajuapam and Silacayoapam with a 40 percent reduction in taxes.[38] Alternatively, the imposition of *ejidal* taxes could be used as a punishment. The men of Magdalena Peñasco, Tlaxiaco, were suspected of supporting Almazán's presidential campaign. González Fernández denied their requests for a tax reduction, claiming to the central government that the campesinos made more than a thousand pesos a month from palm hat production but as they were "lazy and alcoholic" they quickly spent all their earnings.[39]

Although the *vallistocracia* and the CNC formed the most important elements of the ruling camarilla, González Fernández also tried, with markedly less success, to add the CTM to his governing coalition. During the elections for the governorship in 1940 the CTM had remained divided between its radical and conservative wings. With González Fernández's victory many of the radical unions that had flirted with Vásquez's FIRO organization returned to the CTM fold, but the governor did not forget their lack of support. During his tenure he used national-level indifference to the organization to further his local political vendetta.[40] On the one hand, he backed the persecution of the former CTM radicals. In Salina Cruz he allowed his brother to take control of the local branch of the CROM and to attack the rival CTM unions.[41] In Tuxtepec he ordered the disarming of CTM *ejidal* committees and the continual harassment of their members.[42] On the other hand, he sought the support of the conservative members of the CTM, led by former rural schoolteacher Melquiades Ramírez.[43] In exchange for a series of political positions, including the federal deputyship of Tuxtepec, Ramírez remained unfailingly loyal to González Fernández.[44] At the same time certain key unions, such as the electrical workers, were offered the state government's support.[45] In January 1943 González Fernández's bipartite policy came to a head. The radicals, under communist leaders Graciano Benitez and Francisco M. Ramos, left the FRTEO together with twelve other unions, including members of the railway and textile unions.[46] The governor's camarilla was left with the conservative branch of the organization.

Finally, González Fernández's camarilla of family members, Oaxaca City elite, and CNC and CTM bureaucrats was overlaid with a discourse of regional cultural difference. Traditionally, the formation of an *indigenista* identity has been linked to a federal project of Mexican nationalism. Teachers, members of the DAAI, and state officials were encouraged to "Mexicanize" the country's Indians, drawing them gradually into the ambit of modern Mexico. Yet although *indigenismo* emanated from the center and was practiced by federal emissaries, like other dominant discourses it could be appropriated selectively at other levels of the state bureaucracy for divergent aims. We saw in chapter 5 how Mixe cacique Luis Rodríguez, utilized *indigenismo* to establish hegemony over an administrative district. Similarly, in the 1940s González Fernández usurped the fashionable rhetoric and associated political theatre to boost internal and external support for his ruling camarilla. In August 1941 the governor announced that the first Gran Feria Indígena would be held in Oaxaca City from 15 to 25 December. The festival was organized by *vallistocracia* author and revolutionary Enrique Othón Díaz and was designed as an "example of social justice and the economic and cultural development of the indigenous people" as well a boost to local tourism.

Indigenous communities were to nominate representatives to display local produce and partake in competitions of agriculture, industry, indigenous sports, indigenous dances, municipal bands, and traditional clothes. According to the local press fifty thousand Indians attended the celebration, together with the governor and President Avila Camacho.[47] Although the governor was keen to tie the event to the project of national unity, as he admitted, it had distinctly local ambitions and was intended "to bring together all the sectors that make up the state."[48] It also acted to bolster his popularity in the urban center. González Fernández's allies in the chamber of commerce paid for free food and drink, and a diesel generator for the water purification plant was handed over at the inauguration ceremony.[49] As one of the governor's critics argued, the event was designed to display González Fernández's popularity to Avila Camacho: "The Feria Indígena was really a pretext for political questions. The governor's aim was to demonstrate that he was well-supported."[50] He also reinvigorated the celebration of Benito Juárez's birth, demanding that all municipalities commemorate the event.[51] Finally, he attempted to organize the state's numerous municipal bands, sending Oaxaca musician Conrado Pérez to offer artistic and organizational aid.[52] Like the major celebrations, these moves were all part of the governor's proposition "to alter the routine life of isolation and consequent backwardness" of the Oaxaca periphery, to draw people into the political and cultural ambit of the capital city and the state government.[53]

During his governorship González Fernández utilized the central government's policies of productivity, protection of small properties, and suppression of radical labor to shape his own governing camarilla composed of the *vallistocracia* and more conservative members of the CNC and CTM. As a result, his administrative staff and judicial appointments included members of the Oaxaca City elite, such as Jorge F. Iturribarría, Jorge Woolrich, Mariano Aguilar, Roberto Audiffred, and the Flores Fagoaga brothers; CNC affiliates such as Jorge Meixueiro and Virgilio Salmeron; and CTM personnel such as Melquiades Ramírez and Juan Marin Moran. With his power base secure, González Fernández now began to take on the caciques of the Cárdenas era.

González Fernández and the Cardenista Caciques

During his presidency Cárdenas had allowed the localities of Oaxaca to remain under the dominance of a handful of powerful regional caciques. As a result state and local administrations were independent of each other but individually loyal to the central state. While Chapital was governor, the system worked relatively well. Unlike López Cortés, Chapital did not acquire a network of dependent local strongmen, and during Chapital's governorship there were no major conflicts between state and local authorities. However, as governor, González Fernández was not content to depend exclusively on the favor of the elected president and limit his zone of influence to the state capital and its environs. Instead he allied with the less disruptive local leaders, and those who refused to renounce their independence he attacked with traditional tools of political imposition, armed repression, assassination, and judicial manipulation.

In his report of September 1941 Governor González Fernández laid out his plans for his political dominance of Oaxaca and, at the same time, summarized the formation of the Cardenista state with disconcerting perspicacity:

> I shall procure that personal and political influences shall not divert my own aims and I shall dedicate myself to the disappearance of the cacicazgos that have ruled the regions of the state for many years. Due to their distance from the capital and the lack of communications, they have been able to continue to exist with the support of previous governments. As a result, these governments have eluded their responsibility and by searching for a comfortable form of administration, they have washed their hands of the aspirations of these villages and instead made responsible the indispensable "cacique" who has imposed the reign of terror necessary for his security and the conservation of his role.[54]

A few months before, Jorge Meixueiro, the governor's chief of staff, had delineated the consequences of this strategy to President Avila Camacho by listing the targeted caciques: Andrés Elorza in Ejutla, Genaro Ramos in Miahuatlán, Francisco Ramos in Pochutla, Celestino Guzmán in Juxtlahuaca, Francisco Jiménez and Celestino Ruíz in Yautepec, and Adelaido Ojeda in Jamilte-pec. According to Meixueiro, González Fernández was terminating their authority in a "slow but sure manner." Two other caciques, Heliodoro Charis and Luis Rodríguez, were being handled with a more moderate approach. Meixueiro admitted that the "influ-ence of General Charis benefits some pueblos, especially the cabec-era of Juchitán," but reasoned that the geographical extent of his power was too great. Consequently the state government would attempt not to extirpate the Juchiteco strongman completely but rather to circumscribe his range. Finally, Meixueiro argued that in the Región Mixe, "the hegemony of Luis Rodríguez, which is almost absolute, is acceptable for the moment."[55] It was no co-incidence that Rodríguez, by confronting the other Mixe caci-que, Daniel Martínez, was helping further diminish the power of Meixueiro's Ixtlán rivals, Isaac Ibarra and Onofre Jiménez.[56] As a consequence, Rodríguez was one of the few regional caci-ques allowed to join the governor's camarilla and persist with-out his interference.

González Fernández's principal weapon in the crusade against Oaxaca's autonomous strongmen was the judicial police. During 1941 he ordered the formation of new police forces of fifteen to twenty-five men in the ex-districts of Jamiltepec, Juquila, Hua-juapam, Miahuatlán, Yautepec, and the Centro. According to the governor they were created because under previous governments "there did not exist sufficient public force to impose the law." Under the new judicial enforcers he envisaged a new productive, unified, and peaceful Oaxaca.[57] At least in the short term, how-ever, the judicial police were employed to confront the armed re-tainers of the local caciques. Pushy minor local politicians com-manded the forces, which made frequent violent attacks on the supporters of the resident strongmen. In Jamiltepec, González Fernández and Meixueiro were keen to eradicate the influence of the Ojeda brothers over the CNC. They allied with Ojeda's rival, Felix Baños, and together allowed Sostenes Guzmán, a landowner from the rebellious village of Mártires de Tacubaya, to vent his "satanic hate" of *agrarismo* on CNC members connected to Ojeda.[58] Most important, Guzmán acquired the scalp of Ojeda's former pistolero Cirilio Castañeda, who had led many CNC members against the Baños properties.[59] Landowners supported the crusade and often paid the members of the judicial police, but as one CNC member complained, "much blame must be put on the governor of the state who has been giving all facilities to the capitalists of the region so that they can continue developing their old, bloody action."[60] In Juxtlahuaca González Fernández also attacked the local cacique. Matters were made easier by Celestino Guzmán's murder of local dignitary Hilario Jara's son in an argument over mining rights. The governor used the outrage to arm Guzmán's rival, Josefino Feria, who hunted down and killed the scourge of the Triquis.[61]

In other regions González Fernández dispensed entirely with the legal niceties of the judicial police and instead backed the irregular armed bands. In the Región Mixe, Luis Rodríguez was supported in his persecution of the followers of Daniel Martínez. The government backed Rodríguez's demands for more teachers and his appointment as head of the ex-district's military service.[62] González Fernández also turned a blind eye to increasingly lurid tales of the brutality of Rodríguez and his pistoleros. When the cacique attacked Santiago Tutla in September 1941 and left sixteen dead, the survivors' pleas for justice were ignored.[63] When the rural teacher of Santa María Alotepec, Apolonio Sandoval, was imprisoned, had his tongue cut out, had the soles of feet removed, and was finally dismembered on Rodríguez's orders, nothing was done.[64] When Luis's uncle, Antonio Rodríguez, assailed the village of Santiago Atitlán in August 1944, assaulted women, robbed the church, and stole the municipality's musical instruments and a thousand pesos, the local judge was ordered not to intervene.[65] When Daniel Martínez was gunned down in the center of Oaxaca City and the killer, José Isabel Reyes, claimed the killing was on Rodríguez's orders, González Fernández blamed a family vendetta.[66]

Despite the governor's reliance on armed aggression, some caciques were confronted in a less violent manner. Charis was not only a senator with strong ties to members of the military and political elite; he also possessed considerable armed forces. Although after the announcement of the Second World War, this seemed a practical defensive strategy, there is evidence that even before 1942 the president had allowed Charis's men to retain their weapons. In a letter to President Avila Camacho in December 1940, Charis announced that he had one thousand men at his disposal, "in accord with the confidential talks I had with Lic. Alemán at the beginning of your political campaign."[67] Whether the armed men were part of a political deal or Oaxaca's wartime defense, González Fernández could not use his favored tactics of judicial aggression or paramilitaries. He turned instead toward political imposition and the erosion of Charis's peasant support network. In the municipal elections of December 1940 González Fernández appointed Ricardo López Gurrion president of the regional PRM and ordered him to overturn the elections of Charistas. With the support of the military zone commander he removed four *regidores* from the council of Juchitán de Zaragoza and replaced them with his own family members. These new members then elected an anti-Charis candidate, Efren Villalobos, as municipal president. López Gurrion likewise favored the anti-Charis candidates in Matias Romero, Ciudad Ixtepec, Santiago Niltepec, Santo Domingo Zanatepec, and Santiago Ixtaltepec.[68] In San Juan Guichicovi, Charista *agraristas* under Cenobio Flores claimed victory, installed themselves in the municipal palace, and were instructed by Charis to wait for the governor's imminent fall. But on 17 January 1941 they were forcibly removed by federal soldiers.[69]

At the same time as asserting his control over municipal elections, González Fernández also attempted to erode Charis's influence over the Isthmus peasants by prohibiting moves designed to benefit the cacique's followers. According to Charis, during the 1930s Lázaro Cárdenas had promised the installation of a seventy-thousand-hectare irrigation project, called the Presa de las Pilas, to the colonists of the Military Colony Alvaro Obregón and the inhabitants of Santiago Ixtaltepec, El Espinal, Juchitán de Zaragoza, Santa María Xadani, Unión Hidalgo, and Santa Rosa.[70] In 1940 Charis's men started the first step of the scheme, building a drainage channel from the military colony to Tehuantepec. Although Charis claimed that the trench took advantage of an unused gully, the residents of San Blas claimed that the colonists had simply usurped one of their channels and were funneling water away from the village lands. González Fernández took the side of San Blas and allowed the head of the village water society to take the municipal presidency and put the prospective drainage system on hold until late 1942.[71] González Fernández also prevented the invasion of the lands of ranchero livestock owners in San Pedro Tapantepec. According to one of the landowners, Charis had originally brokered a deal for some of his Juchitán followers to buy up the Guadalupe finca for forty pesos a hectare under the law of colonization. However, the Juchitecos, with Charis's consent, had simply invaded the land and refused to pay more than seven pesos a hectare. In response, González Fernández had the military zone commander expel the prospective colonists and recommended certificates of exemption for all the Tapantepec landowners.[72]

Although the federal government had appointed González Fernández governor of the state of Oaxaca, he was not expected to extend his political power much beyond the environs of the capital. Rule of the Oaxacan hinterlands was to be left to the network of caciques, with whom Cárdenas had brokered independent deals during the previous *sexenio*. But González Fernández was not content to limit his dominance to the inhabitants of Oaxaca City and a handful of regional tax collectors. Consequently during his four years in office he attempted to undermine all but a few of the Cardenista caciques. Some were politically marginalized, some were forced to leave the state, and some of the most recalcitrant were assassinated. By the end of 1944 Castañeda, Guzmán, and Martínez were dead, and Charis, Ojeda, Ramos, and Ramos Ortiz were ensconced in Mexico City.

Responses of the Caciques and Central Government

González Fernández's increasing dominance of the rural regions of Oaxaca did not go uncontested. Caciques, out-of-favor camarillas, and the central government used a variety of means to attempt to restore the balance between state governor and provincial power bases established during the Cardenista period. In Tuxtepec the radical members of the CTM continued to dispute political power with the CNC. In the Región Mixe Daniel Martínez and an array of other minor local caciques persisted in organizing violent resistance to Luis Rodríguez. In Juchitán and Mexico City Charis maintained a position of overt hostility to the Oaxaca governor, using the publicity of his position as senator and tapping into the recent strain of Juchiteco *indigenismo* to defend the area from outside interference. Finally, by 1942 President Avila Camacho was also forced to intervene in order to restore the balance between the state governor and the local caciques.

In the municipal elections of December 1942 the governor's support led to the victory of CNC throughout Tuxtepec, at the expense of the CTM. As a result the radical CTM members started to sponsor land invasions of CNC ejidos and *finqueros'* properties. In San Pedro Ixcatlán the CNC ejected the previous CTM municipal authorities in December 1942 in violent and contested elections. They then prevented CTM members from working their parcels in the neighboring ejido of Paso Nazareno. Consequently, five months later CTM members invaded Paso Nazareno and started to plant for the upcoming harvest. Eventually, with the support of the central government, they retrieved their confiscated parcels.[73] Although many radical CTM leaders attempted to oppose the CNC and González Fernández through manipulation of the Agrarian Code and the federal bureaucracy, the state government's control of the redistributive machinery led to the increasing employment of *pistolerismo*. Reports in the state archive are testament to the increase in CTM gunmen in 1943 and 1944. In August 1943 the head of the CNC branch of San Miguel Soyaltepec reported that local CTM leaders had put a bounty of two thousand pesos on his head.[74] In October 1943 CTM pistoleros and CNC *ejidatarios* confronted each other in a pitched battle in La Asunción that left three dead.[75]

However, despite the Tuxtepec CTM's efforts, the organization was constrained at the state level by its numerical limitations. Most opposition to González Fernández came not from organized workers but from the deposed caciques and their local allies. In the Región Mixe Daniel Martínez and the villages unwilling to pledge allegiance to Luis Rodríguez defended their local autonomy with guns and machetes. In Tuxtepec the tradition of radical *agrarismo* allowed angry campesino leaders to confront local powerbrokers by invading lands, taking crops, and invoking federal authority. Violence, although increasingly frequent, was a secondary weapon. But in the Región Mixe there was no custom of revolutionary economic democracy, and Rodríguez monopolized all links to the federal establishment. It seemed to many that they were "not Mexican" and lived in "a place where government did not exist."[76] As a result, beyond passive resistance such as the nonpayment of taxes and noncooperation with military service, violence was the only form of opposition.[77] At first these fighters were based in their individual villages, which they sought to defend if attacked. When Rodríguez assaulted San Juan Juquila Mixes in late 1943 with three hundred men on military service from Santiago Zacatepec, Santa María Tlahuitoltepec, Santa María Alotepec, and San Juan Osolotepec, José Ramón and other residents gunned down twenty of the cacique's men and forced them to flee.[78] By 1944 the opposition to Rodríguez's rule had become more actively hostile, and there were sporadic attacks on his local supporters. In November anti-Rodríguez forces assaulted Tamazulapam del Espíritu Santo's annual festival and the municipal palace of San Pedro Ocotepec.[79]

Although resistance to González Fernández and his camarilla of local supporters often spilled over into extralegal acts of brutality, subtler means of opposition were employed by other caciques. During the 1930s Heliodoro Charis had started to flirt with the developing ideology of Juchiteco *indigenismo*, the regionalist brand of the state discourse, forged in Mexico City by homesick students such as Andrés Henestrosa and Gabriel López Chiñas and devoted to proving the cultural and historical singularity of the Isthmus Zapotecs.[80] His links to these local intellectuals had initially been part of a broader strategy of encouraging the expansion of education in the area, but during the 1940s Charis, now likewise based in Mexico City as a senator, began to employ the emerging discourse and its political ramifications. On 4 November 1941 Charis stood up in the senate chamber and charged González Fernández with presiding over a state dictatorship that had so far ordered the murder of forty-seven campesinos. Over the next two weeks he defended and extended his charges in a series of newspaper articles. In *El Universal Gráfico* of 12 November he claimed that the governor was responsible for 175 deaths and had forced many of his fellow countrymen to flee to the mountains. During the interview he played with the Juchitecos' reputation for unruliness and martial prowess and the state's ambivalence toward this perceived element of the indigenous psyche. He insinuated that as a poacher turned gamekeeper, he was the only man capable of taming these belligerent and obstreperous Indians. In so doing, he also inadvertently defended the politics of Cardenismo, the series of deals brokered between armed local camarillas and the central state. "There is so much discontent among the indigenous Juchitecos, they are on the point of rebelling. . . . I know my *paisanos* and they are perfectly armed. At any time they could launch a revolt that could only be compared to the Yaqui rebellion. The Juchitecos are very fond of their weapons. There is not one who does not have a Mauser and cartridges in abundance."[81]

Charis's appropriation of Juchitán's history was endorsed in February 1942 by his ally, General Ruben García, in a series of articles in *El Universal* documenting nineteenth-century plans to run a canal through the Isthmus. Although the pieces were apparently innocuous, they included copious mention of the revolt of Che Gorio Melendre and were dotted with references to Juchitán's "separatist tendencies" and "rebellious spirit."[82] García's exposition of ethnic difference struck at the heart of González Fernández's project of state unification and set off a wave of sententious official historiography. The government was so sensitive to these imputations of Juchiteco autonomy that the state's official newspaper ran articles accusing Ruben García of academic apostasy. Under the headline "The Isthmus Is Not Separatist," a government journalist argued that there had never been a popular separatist movement in the Isthmus and that the region had been renowned for its love not only of the "Patria Mexicana" but also its "Patria Chica," Oaxaca. While García had portrayed Che Gorio Melendre as a democratic representative of Juchiteco sovereignty and an incarnation of indigenous independence, the state historian claimed that Melendre was the leader of a ragged, unpopular band of unpatriotic bandits.

Although CTM members and out-of-favor caciques used force and the appropriation of federal law and state discourses to confront González Fernández's camarilla, the central government was the most effective opponent of the governor's increasing domination of Oaxaca. Not only was President Avila Camacho unwilling to allow the reemergence of *caudillaje* and state autonomy; the internecine political strife caused by the governor's attempts to assert control struck at the president's concern for national unity and self-defense.[83] Yet Avila Camacho did not seek to undermine González Fernández completely; the president had reservations about Charis, who had emerged as the governor's principal opponent, and he wanted peace, not confrontation.[84] As a result, the political strategy of the central government aimed not at domination but rather at restoring a measure of equilibrium to the relationship between the state government and the peripheral caciques.

As Stephen Niblo argues, the reorganization of military forces occasioned by Mexico's participation in the Second World War was a "political windfall" for Avila Camacho as it allowed him to select rivals such as Lázaro Cárdenas and Abelardo Rodríguez as military commanders directly subject to central command.[85] It also presented the president with another more localized political benefit. On 21 September 1942 Joaquín Amaro was appointed the third regional military commander in charge of the Isthmus of Tehuantepec.[86] Amaro had been a close ally of Charis since they fought together against the Delahuertistas at the battle of Ocotlán in 1923.[87] As Isthmus military commander, he defended the Juchitán cacique and other regional strongmen from the attentions of the state governor. In September 1943 Amaro persuaded González Fernández to attempt to settle the dispute between the Mixe caciques, Rodríguez and Martínez. On 30 October all four met in Oaxaca City and drew up a plan of rapprochement. On 6 April 1944 the governor announced that San Pedro y San Pablo Ayutla would be the head of a new administrative district that included the villages of San Juan Juquila Mixes, Santa María Tepantlali, Santo Domingo Tepuxtepec, and Santiago Atitlán. At the same time, both San Pedro y San Pablo Ayutla and

San Juan Juquila Mixes would have their own tax collectors.[88] As we have seen, González Fernández and Rodríguez reneged on the agreement and had Martínez murdered, but other Amaro initiatives were more successful. In January 1943 he started the construction of the road between Miahuatlán and Puerto Angel. Avila Camacho suggested that he use the organizational talents of Genaro Ramos and Francisco Ramos Ortiz, who were "men of work, sincere and fully identified with the actual regime." At Amaro's behest González Fernández dropped the judicial charges against the two and assured the general that Ramos had "always counted in the personal estimation of the government."[89] Finally, Amaro aided Charis by assuring a power sharing arrangement in the Isthmus. The army no longer interfered in municipal elections, and in December 1942 González Fernández was unable to impose his candidates on Juchitán's municipal councils.[90]

At the same time as Avila Camacho utilized the reorganization of the military to realign the state's political scales, he also employed his national control of the PRM to maintain the equilibrium between Oaxaca's opposing factions. In June 1943 the state held pre-elections for federal deputies. At first González Fernández attempted to monopolize selection of candidates and pushed the appointment of members of his camarilla. The head of the popular sector, Alberto Ramos Sesma, was to be deputy in the Isthmus. His former private secretary, Mariano Aguilar, was to represent the popular sector in Nochixtlán. His former chief of staff, Jorge Meixueiro, was to be selected for the region of the Sierra Juárez. José Larrazabal, the prospective deputy of Ejutla, was a close relation of the governor, and other candidates, such as Demetrio Flores Fagoaga and Jorge Woolrich, were members of the *vallistocracia*. But Avila Camacho was wary of such conspicuous dominance of the lower chamber and utilized the national committee of the PRM to replace three of González Fernández's candidates. Further, in Villa Alta voters were divided, some supporting Jorge Meixueiro and others backing the former Sierra cacique Isaac M. Ibarra. Although Avila Camacho initially let Meixueiro stand as the official candidate, he was reluctant to allow the governor exclusive control of yet another area of the state. Days before the election he switched government support to Leopoldo Gatica Neri, a member of the Charis camarilla. Despite Meixueiro's apparent triumph, the PRM national committee presented Gatica Neri with the deputyship.[91]

Reestablishment of equilibrium between the presidency, the state government, and Oaxaca's caciques caused one of the most memorable events of Avila Camacho's *sexenio*, a monument to political (and mental) instability. On 18 August 1943 Jorge Meixueiro rose in the Chamber of Deputies in Mexico City to deliver a speech defending his electoral campaign. Although he admitted that trying to change the government's decision was as "futile" as "trying to melt the snow from the top of Popocatépetl with a single match," he decided to elaborate on the nature of his defeat. He explained that during his electoral campaign he had been backed by the state government and the peasant confederation. Then, just days before the election, the confederation had withdrawn its support and the federal government had imposed another candidate from outside the region on the electoral district. After twenty minutes of lamenting his unfortunate failure, he announced that he had one final argument. Taking a pistol from his belt he placed it in his mouth and "blew his brains all over the floor."[92] According to Nathan Whetton, Meixueiro's public suicide "almost brought an end to the national party" as the press, opposition groups, and even politicians from inside the PRM lamented the party's hegemonic electoral control and promoted the dead bureaucratic cacique as an apostle of *agrarismo* and an unlikely figurehead for the movement for democratic reform.[93] With the smell of cordite still in the air, Meixueiro's supporters shouted from the chamber's galleries, "Down with the political monopoly. Up with Meixueiro and up with Oaxaca."[94] The official newspaper of Oaxaca's state government called Meixueiro "an illustrious Oaxacan, a champion of democracy and a paladin of the peasants" and compared him to Emiliano Zapata.[95] In Governor González Fernández's speech to the local congress, he announced that a bust of Meixueiro would be sent to each ejido to "perpetuate his memory," and in Nazareno Etla the *ejidal* authorities named the local rural school after the deceased and invited his mother to open the institution.[96]

Although Governor González Fernández asserted control over much of the state machinery during the period 1940 to 1944 through the construction of his personal camarilla and the attacks on the remaining independent caciques, there was resistance at all levels. CTM leaders and deposed bosses leaders rearmed their followers and led a series of violent assaults on the governor's supporters. At the same time, more sophisticated caciques such as Charis appropriated the state discourse of *indigenismo* and deliberately played on the federal government's fears of indigenous insurrection. Finally, Avila Camacho opposed the centralization of power in the figure of the state governor. Although he resisted any attempt to oust González Fernández, Avila Camacho attempted (but sometimes failed) to reimpose the political equilibrium of the Cárdenas era.

Emergence of the Urban Social Movement

In addition to contending with the fallout from Cárdenas's administrative balancing act, González Fernández also confronted a new political phenomenon, the organized popular urban social movement, and a new political actor, the market woman. Accounts of prerevolutionary and revolutionary social movements abound, but there are few historical treatments of similar mobilizations in the 1940s and 1950s. Even recent accounts portray many of the mobilizations as initiated and manipulated by right-wing elites.[97] However, as the following chapters make clear, "the . . . social movements, which affected Mexico even during the heyday of the pax Priista," were not only resolutely popular but also "stand as testimony to the state's limited capacity."[98] Although this account stresses the movements' context within the dynamic process of postrevolutionary state formation, it relies on certain structural models drawn from social movement theory, particularly mobilization structures and repertoires of collective action. The following section delineates the demographic, economic, and cultural changes, which in turn threw up the three key interlinking mobilization structures in Oaxaca City during the 1940s: the *vecindades* (tenements), the markets, and Acción Católica Mexicana (ACM). These combined with a growing critical public sphere to provide space in which the government project of urban modernization was described, debated, and modified. Some aspects were accepted; others were rejected. Although González Fernández managed to counteract growing discontent over the provision of electricity, a new urban social movement based on the mobilization structures of the markets and the ACM employed new repertoires of collective action to contest his management of the city's water supplies.

To the idle observer, and few observers were more idle than Aldous Huxley, postrevolutionary urban society in Oaxaca was still deeply provincial and marked by social and ethnic division. In *Beyond the Mexique Bay* he described the *zócalo* (central plaza) as follows: "The Indians squat on the pavements to listen [to the band], their dark faces melting into the night—invisible. High-heeled, the flappers stroll giggling under the electric light. There is a rolling of eyes, a rolling of posteriors. The young men stroll in the opposite direction. In the roadway, the most correct of the correctos circulate very slowly in their automobiles—round and round and round."[99]

However, from the late 1930s onwards, the social and political landscape of Oaxaca City began to change. Between 1940 and 1950 the population of Oaxaca City rose by 60 percent to 46,632.[100] Although a higher level of infant survival contributed to the rise, urban immigration was also an important factor.[101] More than half of eighteen market vendors interviewed were born outside the city. Most came from the villages of the Central Valleys and sought economic improvement in the growing urban environment. Adela Avendano Ramírez described how she grew up in the nearby town of Ejutla de Crespo. The lack of opportunities forced her mother to move to Oaxaca City in the early 1940s and join her grandmother selling herbs in the market.[102] Eustolia Avendano was also born in Ejutla de Crespo. Her father got a contract in Oaxaca City working as builder in 1941. A year later his entire family arrived and also set up a small stall in one of the markets.[103] Other immigrants came from farther afield. María del Socorro Gonzáles Jiménez was born in Ometepec, Guerrero. In the early 1940s her mother fell in love with a man from Oaxaca City, who was working in Guerrero as an agricultural engineer.

She followed her new boyfriend back to the city but found out that he was already married. Unwilling to return to Ometepec, she used her few remaining pesos to establish a small food stall in the market.[104] As the city expanded, new immigrants and long-time inhabitants sought shelter, food, and social services. In doing so they not only formed "a new pool of residents who could place demands" but also created new social networks, which linked together individual workers, families, and kinship groups. In turn, these social networks became the key structures of the city's popular mobilizations.[105]

Most inhabitants of Oaxaca City lived in *vecindades*. These were tenement complexes of rented single apartments all facing onto a central patio. Here different families slept, cooked, washed, ate, held fiestas, formed friendships and enmities, and discussed the city's pressing political and social problems. During the 1940s the *vecindades* were located on the poorer south and west sides of the city. In contrast, the richer residents lived in the north and east where they owned private homes.[106] Although this manner of communal urban living had its roots in the colonial period, the number of *vecindades* increased markedly after the earthquake that shook Oaxaca City in 1931. According to contemporary estimates the quake damaged over two thirds of the city's properties. Many elite and middle-class families moved to other areas of the country. They sold their damaged houses to a cabal of land speculators such as Vidal García, who converted them into tenements for lower-class urban inhabitants, or Antonio Cabrera, who owned most of the Colonia de la Paz and rented out rooms in the *vecindades* there.[107] All eighteen market vendors interviewed grew up in *vecindades*, and many remember the spaces as important locations for the exchange of goods and gossip. When

María del Socorro Gonzáles Jiménez and her mother arrived in Oaxaca in the early 1940s, she explained that "very few people owned their own houses." Instead there were "very, very many *vecindades*." As Gonzáles Jiménez recollects, despite their exterior uniformity, the *vecindades* catered for different social strata. Many housed "the poor"—household servants, laborers, washerwomen—and consisted of one-bedroom apartments with communal washing and cooking areas. After establishing her market stall, her mother sought out larger *vecindades* with two or three bedrooms and private kitchens. Even the more upmarket complexes were not monuments to bourgeois isolation. Gonzáles Jiménez describes her visits to *atole* (a corn-based soft drink) sellers and washerwomen who sold their wares and services in the patios.[108] María de Jesús Ramírez Pérez described the *vecindad* at 37 Tinoco y Palacios in the west of the city. "It was enormous. There were guayaba trees in the middle of the patio which provided a large shaded area where people used to meet and talk. There were also stones on which people dried their clothes and around which they gossiped."[109]

But although the *vecindades* provided the urban population with shelter, snacks, and services, the inhabitants also relied on the city's growing markets. Commerce in Oaxaca City increased dramatically during the 1940s. The opening of the Pan American Highway in 1943 and its extension to Tehuantepec in 1948 increased commerce in general throughout the state.[110] According to Jorge Tamayo, the number of licensed commercial establishments in Oaxaca increased 1,500 percent between 1940 and 1955.[111] The shift was particularly marked in Oaxaca City. In 1940 only 7 percent of the population were involved in commercial activities. A decade later this had risen to more than 15 percent.[112]

271

Some merchants had long-established shops around the *zócalo*. Poorer inhabitants hawked their wares on foot around the city. And many established small stalls in the city's permanent markets. In the 1940s there were five principal markets: Benito Juárez Maza, La Democracia (better known as La Merced), IV Centenario (La Rayita), Sánchez Pascuas (Carmen Alto), and La Industria (San Juan de Dios). On Saturday these permanent establishments were joined by peasants from throughout the Oaxaca Valleys, who would bring their small agricultural surplus to barter and sell. While traveling in Oaxaca in the 1940s, Norman S. Hayner observed, "On that morning Oaxaca's trade area is picturesquely marked by an influx of human and animal traffic. People walk, ride burros, and, especially from the greater distances, use the buses that distinguish the new era in rural transport. Articles for sale are brought in trucks, slow-moving oxcarts, and probably to the largest extent on burros. . . . Frequently an Indian woman will ride in from the hinterland villages, sitting on her burro with the dignity of a queen."[113]

Although anthropologists since Bronislaw Malinowski and Julio de la Fuente have studied the market system of Oaxaca, they have concentrated on its economic role in integrating precapitalist and capitalist modes of production.[114] But the market was more than simply an economic hub; it was also the political center of the city, if not the state.[115] On Saturday peasants from throughout the state bartered and sold their goods, exchanged political gossip and rumor, and bought the current issue of the local newspaper, *El Momento*, or had snippets read to them by children, acquaintances, and friends.[116] During another urban movement, discussed in chapter 10, an observer gave a firsthand account of the political melee of the market and its vital importance: "The fact

FIG. 5. The Saturday market in the *zócalo* of Oaxaca City, early twentieth century. (Courtesy of the Biblioteca Bustamante Vasconcelos)

that everyone visits the market makes this commercial center the vital nerve of the politics of the state. Here is where all the indigenous people of all the regions of the state know the news and discuss what affects their interests. Any Oaxacan knows that before the governor can govern with the Congress, he must first come to an accord with the plaza or the market to use our own terms."[117] The markets, and particularly the Saturday plaza, would form another mobilization structure of popular movements in the city for the following decade. Leaders, protestors, and organizations would all emerge from the markets during the period.

Many of these leaders and protestors were female. The markets provided a rare avenue for economic betterment and political involvement for women, who formed the majority in most markets. The 1951 municipal tax records reveal that the biggest market, Benito Juárez Maza, contained 482 stalls, of which 285

273

or nearly 60 percent were run by women. In particular women dominated the selling of cooked foods, chicken, and clothes. The other markets were smaller, but women held similarly signifi-cant majorities. La Democracia had 51 stalls of which 38 were controlled by women. In Sánchez Pascuas women ran 45 of the 62 stalls.[118] The market was an arena of petty capitalism and as such a microcosm of capitalist exploitation, conflict, and rancor. But at the same time hard work, and perhaps above all fortune, could offer a degree of economic independence. A census of 225 market women taken in 1927 reveals that only 32 were married or widowed.[119] As Thomas Calvo suggests, this extraordinarily low percentage was probably caused by a fault in the census tak-ing. Nevertheless, six of the eighteen elderly market women in-terviewed had never married. Even those who did marry often managed to escape financial reliance on their spouses. María del Socorro Gonzáles Jiménez's mother married a laborer. Her supe-rior wages not only provided the children's schooling, clothes, and food but also the eventual acquisition of a new house.[120] Fur-thermore, freed from women's traditional role inside the home, these economically independent women, in daily contact with other laboring *comadres*, developed a distinct female working-class culture.[121] Porfiria García García, an elderly single woman, explained that she had never married because the other *locatar-ios* (stall holders) were her family.[122] Gonzáles Jiménez said that although she slept in the *vecindad*, she "grew up" in the markets among the other working women.[123]

While the *vecindades* and markets provided vital informal mobi-lization structures for the city's popular movements, ACM formed a more formal space for the creation of social networks. The church in Oaxaca City had always played a dominant role in the cultural sphere of the city's different social classes. Throughout the Porfiriato it had introduced a series of workers' circles and popular groups under the broad umbrella of Social Catholicism.[124] Although there was only limited Cristero violence in Oaxaca, the church remained strong, especially in Oaxaca City, where there were street demonstrations, regular clandestine church services, and a degree of support for nearby Cristero groups during the peak of persecution in the state from 1932 to 1936.[125] In the late 1930s and early 1940s the church again attempted to reach out to a wider social base, principally through the lay organization ACM. By 1938 the city's three parishes and most of its individual churches had established all four branches of the organization.

In the parish of Marquesado the priest, José Reyes, helped establish a small night school and a mutual society to aid members in case of family bereavement or illness.[126] In the church of Los Principes, sixty-four members handed out one hundred copies of the ACM magazines *Cultura* and *Onir* each week as well as forming a mutual society, catechizing children, and helping the sick.[127] Women were particularly important to the organization. Between 1937 and 1939 the diocese's female branch had set up forty catechism centers in the diocese, more than half of which were in Oaxaca City. The expansion of the ACM particularly touched the growing number of female market traders. All the markets were named after and built beside major city churches, and commerce relied on an array of religious beliefs and practices. *Locatarios* adorned their stalls with images of saints and virgins, particularly those of Our Lady of Solitude and San Martín Caballero. Priests would often come to bless newly opened stalls.[128] The ACM found fertile grounds for its organization. According to one market

FIG. 6. The expanded ambit of Acción Católica Mexicana. Austreberto Aragon is the spectacled figure in the center. (Courtesy of the Archivo General del Poder Ejecutivo del Estado de Oaxaca)

vendor, all the young female traders were in the female branch. "They taught me to read and to do my accounts."[129]

By the 1940s the ACM was offering not only spiritual but also social assistance in order to tempt the urban poor into the organization. In early 1943 the archbishop of Oaxaca assigned Padre Bulmaro Ramírez to establish a Catholic workers' center. From 13 to 15 December 1943 he held three conferences in conjunction with the ACM to explain the Catholic Church's paternalist attitude to workers' rights.[130] By 1944 the workers' center had two thousand male and five hundred female members. The center offered its associates a range of social services. For three centavos a week, an individual could acquire medical attention and medicine. For an extra seven centavos the entire family would be covered. If hospitalization was needed, members were sent to the

Charity Hospital, a Catholic institution, where patients paid according to means. When a member died, each man in the center paid fourteen centavos toward the cost of burial and a fund for the bereaved family. Besides providing basic social services, the center organized sporting events, including baseball, basketball, boxing, and football tournaments, and held weekly meetings at the church of San Agustín, where Ramírez stated the importance of cooperation among the organization's members.[131]

The city's social movements also relied on an increasingly critical literate public sphere in which journalists, political opponents, and even wandering *corridistas* (balladeers) could question and criticize government policy.[132] The role of local newspapers in postrevolutionary Mexico has generally been ignored. It is popularly assumed that they, like the newspapers of Mexico City, were censored through a mixture of intimidation and financial inducements.[133] However, the provincial press was still permitted a remarkable degree of political liberty.[134] In Oaxaca City the popular local paper was *El Momento*. The newspaper was a weekly, owned and apparently written by Oaxaca City journalist Alfredo "El Chapulin" Ramírez. Although it began in late 1936, it became increasingly important during the 1940s as it mixed investigative journalism, scurrilous political rumor, and popular campaigns. In 1940 it ran a series of articles revealing the criminal activities of the Miahuatlán cacique Genaro Ramos, which forced the governor to take legal measures against him.[135] Other pieces were more satirical. As the bodies piled up during González Fernández's campaign against provincial strongmen, the paper suggested that his government establish a school for pistoleros and hold the First Congress for Pistoleros.[136] Finally, the paper supported the social movements of the city, publishing their demands and accusing the state governors of incompetence, corruption, and falsification. The newspaper was read by all social classes. Academics at the Instituto Autónomo de Ciencias y Artes (IACA—the new name for the ICA) and leaders of the PAN, artisans, and female market traders all confessed to enjoying the weekly's political insight and wit. One market woman described it as "the defender of the pueblo."[137] The paper benefited from the high literacy of the city's population. In 1940, 53 percent of the population of Oaxaca City were literate as opposed to 32 percent in the state as a whole.[138] However, illiteracy did not preclude enjoyment, and important articles were read out to the less educated at the market, at the shoe shine stalls, in the cantinas, and in the *zócalo*.[139] Increasing literacy also promoted the emergence of other forms of political information. *Corrido* sellers such as Manuel H. Basilio from the city of Puebla would walk the roads of southern Mexico, selling *corridos* about the country's latest political problems.[140]

Into this increasingly effervescent social melee dotted with strong social networks, the federal and state governments introduced a program of rapid modernization. As Daniel Newcomer has maintained, by the 1940s modernization "came to signify the core objective of government policy." Any vestiges of Cardenista bucolic traditionalism were dismissed, and the state reinforced its ideology of progress and development, constantly evoking "an image of a futuristic 'civilized' Mexico."[141] Although the focus of the PRM's plans was the rapid industrialization of the country through import substitution, the party also promoted the necessary growth in urban infrastructure.[142] As President Avila Camacho announced in his speech to the Third Industrial Congress of 1946, the role of the government was to encourage "the construction and development of lines of communication, the intensification of the electrification of the country and the improvement of hygiene and education, all basic elements for industrialization."[143] State governors followed his lead. González Fernández's yearly reports eulogized the advantages of industry, mechanized production, efficiency, and hard work. The governor saw the development of a clean, efficient, healthy, "modern" Oaxaca City as a key part of this process of transformation. During his tenure he resolved to sort out the problems of electrification, drainage, street paving, and clean drinkable water.[144] As Christina Jiménez makes clear, Mexico's urban inhabitants were not immediately hostile to these modernization projects; rather they sought to interpret government policy according to their needs and desires.[145]

At first Oaxaca City's *vecindades*, markets, and Catholic organizations focused their attention on state policies concerning the provision of running water and electricity. During the late nineteenth century Oaxaca City had received a parlous supply of electricity from a state company. In 1906 matters improved marginally with creation of the Zorrilla Light Company by investors Federico Zorrilla Tejeda and Juan Baights.[146] There had been occasional conflicts between the company, its workers, and the state government during the two postrevolutionary decades, but by late 1940 disagreements over the quality and price of electricity reached a crescendo. One newspaper claimed that "the light service [was] terrible," that it reached only a small sector of the population, and that even then it was "not possible to read nor write during the nights, without the help of a candle next to a light bulb."[147] The company's clients formed the Liga de Resistencia de Consumidores de Luz y Fuerza Electrica and in November 1940 started a pay boycott. The company was forced to delay proposed price increases.[148] The achievements of the coalition of electricity customers clearly impressed the new governor, who saw the organization not only as a useful political ally but also as a valuable economic tool. With considerable prescience and not a little cynicism, González Fernández and twenty of the city's elite formed the Hydroelectric Company of Oaxaca in April 1942 with capital of twenty-five thousand pesos for the purpose of "administrating and generating electrical energy for public and private use."[149] Two months later the Zorrilla Company increased the monthly price of lighting a standard forty-watt bulb from 1.05 to 1.35 pesos.[150] Although the Ministry of the Economy had granted permission for the rise, the consumers again formed a league of resistance. It was now staffed by professional bureaucrats and allied to the state party's popular sector.[151] During October the state government newspaper ran supportive pieces on the league's demonstrations and demanded that the Ministry of the Economy's representative act to defuse the situation.[152] The Zorrilla Company and the ministry were unwilling to back down. At the same time, González Fernández persuaded Zorrilla's CTM-affiliated workers to push for an improved collective contract. Finally, on 9 May 1944 the workers went on strike, backed by the CTM and the popular sector.[153] For two weeks the city was plunged into darkness and its sparse industrial concerns were halted. González Fernández, who had waited to assume the mantle of the popular urban modernizer as well as to cash in on his prophetic investment, called an emergency meeting to solve the city's electrical problems.[154] On 31 May the Hydroelectric Company, fronted by Luis Sarmiento, agreed to take over Zorrilla's business, paying considerably lower than market price for the crippled enterprise.[155]

González Fernández's clever manipulation of popular demands, labor rights, and the factionalism and greed of Oaxaca City's elite allowed him to assert control of part of the state's growing urban sprawl. However, electricity was not the only issue for the capital's inhabitants. According to the monthly magazine *Oaxaca en México*, "the principal problem that afflict[ed] the City of Oaxaca [wa]s the great scarcity of drinkable water." This not only affected the refined palates of the elites but also led to periodic outbreaks of cholera and typhoid and, as a result, a high infant mortality rate. By 1941 the situation was dire. Despite some investment in piping and purification, water supply had deteriorated, prices were rising, and extortionate fines were exacted for nonpayment. In April 1941 a group of city inhabitants formed the Centro de Acción Social to pressure the government for an improvement in the water supply. They complained that Oaxaca's artisans lacked sufficient water to continue their petty industries and that the refusal of some inhabitants of Colonia Nueva to pay their fines had resulted in the Junta of Material Improvements, which ran the water supply, turning off the supply for the entire barrio. Although González Fernández attempted to resolve the situation, the supply continued to falter. Poor piping, incessant leaks, and seasonal differences in rainfall could not be corrected. Finally in November 1943 the Junta of Material Improvements had the local chamber of deputies pass a law for the installation of water meters designed to stop Oaxaca's inhabitants "leaving the tap on all day."[156]

This reinvigorated and expanded the ambit of the water campaigners. Protesters formed the Liga de Inquilinos Oaxaqueños, the Sindicato de Usarios del Agua de Ex-Marquesado, and the Liga de Resistencia de Usarios del Agua de Oaxaca (LRUAO). The leadership and membership of LRUAO came from across the class spectrum. *El Momento* repeatedly argued that while the upper and middle classes were tired of "drinking mud for four years" and paying their water bills to an undemocratic and unaccountable junta, the poor tenants of the *vecindades* complained that the six-peso monthly base rate for all households irrespective of water use penalized those who used only small amounts.[157] Poor women, many of whom worked in the expanding market sector, were notable among the organization's members. The LRUAO had subcommittees in the markets of Carmen Alto and La Merced as well as twenty sector chiefs spread throughout the city.[158] Stallholder Paula Ramírez was part of the association of tenants. Market vendors Petrona Ramírez, Mercedes Hernández, Guadalupe Colmenares, and Guadalupe Cabrera represented the LRUAO in the various markets.[159] The creation of the LRUAO marked an important development in the political relationship between the state and civil society in the urban environment. For the first time in Oaxaca City, opposition to the postrevolutionary government had extended to form a broad cross-class base of urban inhabitants. Although the governor and his supporters attempted to portray the water activists as rich, pampered reactionaries whipped up by a cabal of supporters of Sinarquismo and the PAN, the ambit of the organization incorporated a wide cross section of urban society.[160]

This broad social base, which became the model for subsequent protest and the strikes of 1947 and 1952, was organized by the head of the LRUAO, Austreberto Aragon Maldonado. Aragon was a former head of the city's Asociación de Padres de Familia, had run on the PAN slate for the municipal council, and in early 1942 had been made head of the city's male branch of the ACM. Yet despite his links to the elite, Aragon bridged the city's social divide. Although his family originally came from Ejutla de

Crespo, he was born in Oaxaca City, and like his father and grand-father, he became a knife maker. He still retained his workshop and his house on the less salubrious south side of the city, among the *vecindades*, other artisans, and market vendors. His trade put him in touch with all the social classes. He would fashion machetes for visiting peasants, knives for market vendors, and decorative swords for the country's elite. Walking around the Benito Juárez Maza market two blocks from his shop, he would listen to the complaints of the vendors and attempt to persuade them of the efficacy of his protests.[161] Beyond vocal disputes over electricity, water, and taxation, he also wrote letters to the municipal authorities on behalf of this constituency demanding safer roads, corn mills, church improvements, and better paving.[162] Although government agents and the state governor often attempted to link Aragon to Sinarquismo and the radical right, he was at pains to avoid links to extremism and claimed to speak for the people.[163] When someone accused him of prejudicing Mexico's wartime stability, he replied: "The war is not the fault of the people and they don't care what the President says. All the governors and people who call themselves revolutionaries are bandits and I have the backing of the Oaxacan people."[164] Over the next decade Aragon would become a sort of cacique of the counterhegemony, the crucial link among the elite, the church, and the general mass of the people he claimed to serve.

From April to June 1944 this cross-class coalition, forged from the mobilization structures of the *vecindades*, local markets, and ACM and led by Aragon, instigated a series of demonstrations against the "thirst-traffickers" of the state government.[165] In so doing they started to form a distinct repertoire of collective action, which would become the basis for future protests. Often they took advantage of official government festivals. On 2 April the annual commemoration of closing of the legislature, which coincided with the anniversary of Porfirio Díaz's victory at Puebla, was interrupted by women shouting abuse at the junta and the governor. According to a government agent, "a considerable number of persons of the pueblo, approximately 1,000, mostly women of the humble classes, invaded the local chamber of congress because of the bad water service and the attempt to install water meters." When the governor tried to calm them down, they replied, "We want water! We ask for justice! You are killing us with thirst!"[166]

Other demonstrations revealed that the group not only emerged from Catholic social networks but also employed religious ritual to articulate their demands. On 8 April the Easter Judas-burning celebration was directed by the water protestors. Instead of the traditional Judas, they carried an octopus through the streets squeezing a water meter. In front of the junta's building, "in a sublime gesture of protest, they burnt the 'Judas-octopus,' an image of the extortion suffered." Austreberto Aragon recounted how the police chief intervened and attempted to stop the demonstration. A firework attached to the figure exploded and hit the official on the leg. Limping back to the governor's palace, he claimed he had been knifed. As a result, the rest of the municipal police intervened, beating and arresting demonstrators.[167] But the protests continued. On 11 April between ten and twelve thousand people demonstrated outside the governor's palace. González Fernández came onto the balcony and agreed to release the prisoners and set up a commission to look into the water problem. The crowds dispersed, but by the next day rumors arose that the governor was not going to comply with his promises.[168] The organizations ordered a commercial strike. Stalls, shops, and restaurants were closed. Finally on 13 April González Fernández freed the movement's incarcerated members and ordered the local chamber of deputies to retract the order for installation of water meters.[169]

The rise of the urban social movement was new to postrevolutionary Oaxaca. Although the colonial and Independence eras had witnessed bread riots, electoral disputes, and tax protests, these new movements were better organized, were connected to a revived Catholic Church, relied on growing urban literacy, and perhaps most important, were predominantly coordinated by female market vendors. In fact, beneath the accusations of elite manipulation, one can observe the emergence of what Temma Kaplan has termed "female consciousness" in Oaxaca de Juárez in the early 1940s.[170] As the modernizing state sought to improve the city's ailing infrastructure, it reached into the traditional female sphere of the household. As a result, housewives in the *vecindades* and the growing number of female market vendors were gradually sucked into the public male arena of politics, where they tried to parley with the postrevolutionary regime over the provision of water and electricity by forming urban social movements. It was these movements and the growing power of this particular sector of society that would mark Oaxaca politics for the next decade. Although González Fernández was cunning enough to co-opt the growing discontent about lack of electricity, only at the last minute was he able to quell the anger over the shortage of water.

Conclusion

The narrative of González Fernández's governorship seems to confirm Alan Knight's statement that "the Mexican state was less powerful and less pervasive even in the years of its heyday (1940–1965) and that civil society was less docile and less amenable."[171] First, it corrects many of the assumptions of revisionist historiography and political science. During the first four years of Avila Camacho's presidency, the state was not Arnaldo Córdova's "monstrous Leviathan."[172] In Oaxaca rule was not imposed autocratically from above but rather relied on tacit deals between the center, an ostensibly toothless governor, and an array of loyal but autonomous caciques. Although Stephen Niblo argues that by the 1940s the "centralising project was nearly completed," in Oaxaca, the government was extremely decentralized.[173] Furthermore, it became more so as González Fernández developed his own camarilla and, as a result, gradually eroded his dependence on the president. Central government was also less reliant on the national party and the corporatist organizations for its political control. "Corporatist organizations only penetrated society unevenly" and *caciquismo* still "plagued" all levels of political negotiation.[174] State power, such as it was, was decentralized, a chaotic web of fragmented cross-class coalitions and geographical alliances. González Fernández and Meixueiro dominated the state CNC. Only rarely did the national committee intervene. At the same time, the governor took advantage of the "weak and divided" CTM to alienate the organization's few genuinely socialist leaders and to claim control of its ambitious conservative members.[175] Moreover, the PRM was for the most part a state organization. Although Avila Camacho could intervene on decisions over the state governor and the federal deputies, pronouncements over the elections to Oaxaca's 570 municipal councils were the preserve of the governor's stooges.

Second, not only do the conflicts of wartime Oaxaca amend

certain historical generalizations and teleological assumptions; they also point the historian toward less explored areas of post-1940s Mexican politics. The study of Oaxaca indicates the continuing importance of traditional regional caciques beyond their perceived watershed of 1940. As Jeffrey Rubin has argued, these martial figures continued to dominate the country's provinces into the second half of the twentieth century, adapting only slightly to the demands of the postrevolutionary regime.[176] They were not simply isolated anachronisms or condemned dinosaurs awaiting extinction; they were central to the governance of Mexico. Besides instilling moderate stability in their often awkward fiefdoms, they acted as counterweights to the ambitions of pushy, independent governors. Following the pattern of Oaxaca, the army was also important. Although it was no longer the freewheeling cabal of autonomous caudillos of the 1920s, it still had an important political role in the maintenance of administrative equilibrium.

If the 1940s saw the persistent importance of caciques and military generals, the decade also witnessed the creation of a new set of urban networks, cultures, and cross-class mobilizations as immigration and commercial expansion established *vecindades* and markets as spaces in which state policy could be debated and expressed. In many ways the process of urban expansion, community building, and state confrontation echoed similar events in Mexico's major industrial cities during the Porfiriato. However, whereas prerevolutionary social unrest in Veracruz, Tampico, or Mexico City was articulated through recourse to evolving discourses of dissident liberalism or socialism and class conflict, Mexico's postwar provincial instability was more likely to be conveyed through the adoption or inversion of religious imagery or ritual.[177] On the one hand, the post-Cárdenas state had claimed exclusive rights over these more radical languages. On the other hand, a resurgent Catholic Church not only provided social networks and mutual organizations outside state control—two decades of intense church-state conflict also offered an expedient idiom with which to express discontent. Thus, although some urban movements, precipitated by state modernization projects, were co-opted by the party's popular sector, many remained outside the governmental framework, as distrustful leaders from outside the political mainstream, such as Austreberto Aragon, sustained the independence of individual pressure groups. These autonomous cross-class movements were extremely hard to contain. As the modernizing state increasingly moved into the traditional female sphere of the household, greater numbers of women crossed over into the customarily male sphere of state politics, where they would remain a key constituency over subsequent decades.

EIGHT

The Rise and Fall of Edmundo Sánchez Cano, 1944–47

During the years 1946 and 1947 the governors of Chiapas, Guanajuato, Baja California Norte, Jalisco, Tamaulipas, Durango, Coahuila, and Oaxaca left office before their allotted time. At the same time the governors of Chihuahua and Sinaloa came under sustained popular pressure. Although there has been no coherent comparative study of these collective acts of protest and political bloodletting, the few monographs on the 1940s point to the operation of right-wing conspiracies, anti-Cardenista party pogroms, and a determined program of political muscle flexing by the new president.[1] In his summary of the Avila Camacho era, Alfonso Taracena asserted that the Unión Cívica of Léon was formed entirely of "individuals of recognized Sinarquista affiliation," while works on the Oaxaca coup and the Tapachula executions stress the involvement of the PAN and the merchant elite.[2] The movements against the state governors from inside the party were also held to herald a general move toward the right. Luis Medina describes how the efforts to dislodge the governors of Jalisco, Baja California Norte, and Tamaulipas were part of the Alemán government's concerted attempt to remove left-leaning governors sympathetic to former president Cárdenas.[3] Stephen Niblo's brief explanation of the "state and local crises" admits the complexity and regional peculiarity of many of these gubernatorial conflicts, but his limited analysis fails to elucidate why

"people were eager to take advantage of opportunities to em-
barrass the government."[4] The only full-length academic study
of one of the movements concentrates on the elision of elite discourse rather than popular protest.[5]

In contrast, this chapter investigates the fall of Oaxacan governor Edmundo Sánchez Cano within the context of local and
regional politics. By looking at the governance of Sánchez Cano
from the perspective of the state political structure, I attempt to
move beyond national, generalized explanations for the country's
instability. In chapter 7 I argue that the period 1940 to 1944 was
characterized by volatility, decentralized government, growing urban discontent, and unresolved tensions between the president,
the state governor, and Oaxaca's multifarious regional caciques.
Although Governor González Fernández attempted to resolve
the contradictions of the state's political structure by building his
own camarilla, asserting control over the region's provinces, and
dominating the local campesino and worker organizations, he
was less than successful. Individual strongmen, communist members of the CTM, obstreperous Catholics, President Avila Camacho, and military zone commander Joaquín Amaro all contested
the exclusive dominance of the ambitious general. During the last
half of 1944 Avila Camacho harnessed the forces of discontent
to erode the influence of the governor and attempted a return to
the system of equilibrium implanted by President Lázaro Cárdenas. Avila Camacho offered the governorship to Edmundo Sánchez Cano, an unfailingly loyal subordinate with few links to the
state's ruling classes, and he permitted Oaxaca's caciques relatively autonomous control of their individual fiefdoms. However,
the pressures of this composite governing system did not disappear. Sánchez Cano not only formed a familial camarilla; he also

sought to eliminate the influence of the state's more independent caciques. But unlike González Fernández, he was unwilling or unable to respond effectively to the demands of Oaxaca City's increasingly vocal cross-class alliance of women, Catholics, urban merchants, artisans, and politicians. With the start of a new national administration in December 1946, opposition to the governor was so strong that President Miguel Alemán removed the governor and reshaped the government of the state.

The Elections of 1944

The elections for governor in 1944 displayed a similar degree of central control and political manipulation to those of 1936 and 1940. By October 1943 candidates for the governorship had started to jostle for position. The state government's official newspaper, *Antequera*, warned presumptuous politicians of the dangers of "political futurism" and "premature political agitation," but this was ignored as an unprecedented ten aspirants lined up expectantly for the official candidacy.[6] Although some anonymous bureaucrats and career soldiers such as Adalberto Lagunas, José Pacheco Iturribarría, and Fernando Magro Soto had grasped the central government's political strategy, most candidates were again supported by specific local interest groups. Alfonso Francisco Ramírez, in his third attempt to gain the governorship, received support from the inhabitants of the Mixteca, the *vallistocracia*, and the Oaxaca-born residents of Mexico City. Another aspirant, Wilfredo C. Cruz, born in El Espinal, Juchitán, and president of the Supreme Court, counted on support from powerful Juchitán inhabitants, members of the Oaxaca City elite, and various peasant groups he had courted as senator during the Cárdenas years.

Heliodoro Charis relied on the backing of his camarilla of military colonists, Juchitán merchants, and Zapotec peasants.[7]

President Avila Camacho evaded the pleas of the assembled contenders and instead chose his close friend, Edmundo Sánchez Cano. Sánchez Cano was born into a humble family in Oaxaca City on 20 November 1894. After a brief spell in Oaxaca's Industrial Military School he applied to the Military School of Cadets in Mexico City, where he stayed until 1912. During the first years of the Revolution he operated in Sonora as a federal officer. But after three years fighting the northern radicals, he changed sides and joined the revolutionary Carrancista lines in the "Fieles de Oaxaca" division. Over the next four years he confronted Zapatistas in Puebla, Morelos, and the Federal District. During the 1920s he continued his military career in the division "Cosio Rebelo" with Vicente González Fernández. He also fought under the future governor in the unsuccessful defense of Villahermosa against the Delahuertista rebels. Following that Tabasco engagement, Sánchez Cano also served in Guerrero and Sonora and started to widen his horizons, training as a teacher for new army recruits and gaining a pilot's license as part of the Mexican Air Force.

After his first failure to gain the governorship in 1936 he started to improve his relations with the Avila Camacho family, staying at their home in Teziutlán, Puebla, until his surprise appointment as one of the military representatives to the PRM. Over the following two years Sánchez Cano became an important ally of Manuel Avila Camacho, as minister of Military Social Action of the PRM and a member of the party's Avilacamachista group. Although his newly acquired status did not aid his second attempt for the governorship in 1940, he maintained close contact with the president's family. During 1943 he stayed in Teziutlán again and used his recent training in homeopathy to aid Avila Camacho's ailing mother. Oral sources confirm that his (and his devoutly Catholic wife's) friendship with the president's family was instrumental in his appointment to the governorship.[8] The president was assured of the new governor's obedience and loyalty, and as with González Fernández and Chapital, Sánchez Cano's peripatetic military career had left little time for establishing political relations with any of Oaxaca's numerous local camarillas.

As a result, in late 1943 Avila Camacho invited González Fernández to Mexico City to discuss the party's official pre-candidature. Although the incumbent governor mentioned four viable alternatives, including Ramírez, the president insisted on Sánchez Cano. The governor returned to Oaxaca and informed his son-in-law with the hauteur of Sánchez Cano's former superior officer that "they're bringing us a disaster, the next governor is that nurse Sánchez Cano."[9] Despite the governor's disapproval, the machinery of government was utilized to establish the chosen candidate's supremacy. In early December *Antequera* included a manifesto directed to the "Oaxacan people" supporting Sánchez Cano, and the CNC declared him the official candidate of the peasant organization. In January Sánchez Cano toured all the regions of the state. By February there were "popular demonstrations" in the barrios of Oaxaca City in support of the military homeopath. In mid-February the popular sector elected Sánchez Cano as their candidate and two months later the CTM did the same. Only Cruz continued to search for support among the capital's kingmakers. However, after a meeting with Alemán, the minister of the interior, he stood down. At the beginning of June the state PRM met and declared Sánchez Cano the party's official candidate. On 6 August he was elected governor of the state.[10]

Yet the election of a new, dependable governor did not guarantee the end of González Fernández's attempts to dominate Oaxaca. Conflict between the political ambitions of Sánchez Cano and the incumbent governor mapped itself onto divisions within the local legislature. In June 1944 seven Sánchez Cano supporters clashed with four followers of González Fernández over an attempt to change the state's constitution. Eventually the majority pushed through a motion that permitted the next governor an increased term of six years. The disagreement continued into the elections for the new legislature. Although Sánchez Cano was assured the support of many of the new deputies, including relatives such as Eduardo Ramírez Mota and Jesús Barriga Rivas, other deputies were loyal to González Fernández. As the supporters of Sánchez Cano formed the majority of the existing local legislature, they dominated the commission responsible for handing out admission cards for the electoral college and refused entry to González Fernández's men. In response, on the evening of 30 August, the governor's followers took the local legislature with the support of the city police and prevented the opposition deputies from entering the institution. Finally Sánchez Cano's complaints reached the military chief, Joaquín Amaro, who demanded that the protestors leave the building. On 15 September the local legislature officially opened. Although a handful of supporters of González Fernández remained, most others had had their election overruled by the PRM's executive committee.[11]

The election of Sánchez Cano as governor of Oaxaca and the crushing of González Fernández's attempts to continue his rule through manipulation of the local congress again display the central government's preoccupation with minimizing the power of the state governor and maintaining his unquestioning fidelity. Sánchez Cano appeared to be the perfect Avilacamachista lackey, with neither the political gumption nor the reliable local support to challenge the framework of local caciques or to escape from the tutelage of the president. At the same time, the election of the PRM's candidate allowed Avila Camacho to put an end to González Fernández's aspirations for future authority.

Sánchez Cano, His Camarilla, and the State's Caciques

Sánchez Cano played the part of the devoted provincial governor and visited the president every month, but his political maneuvers in the state countered the equilibrium envisaged by his political patron, as he set up his own camarilla and alienated the state's provincial caciques.[12] Governor González Fernández had formed a camarilla composed of members of his close family and the *vallistocracia*. Although pushy provincial politicians had complained of the system's injustices, he had deflected criticism by allowing a fair cross-section of Oaxaca's ruling class to acquire work in the state's bureaucracy. Sánchez Cano was less circumspect in the creation of his camarilla. Unlike the former governor he possessed few genuine links to the Oaxaca elite. As a result, he filled the higher echelons of the state bureaucracy with members of his extended family. According to one letter of protest, his family was as extensive and confusing as "the families of the Sacred Scriptures."[13] His private secretary was his nephew Jesús Rojas Villavicencio. Another nephew, Mariano Rojas Villavicencio, was head of the state's popular sector, municipal president of Oaxaca City in 1945 and 1946, and then federal deputy. Vicente J. Villanueva, another close relative, was a federal deputy; Rogelio

Barriga Rivas was judge of Huajuapam, while other "blood relations" such as Francisco Cano García and Guillermo Sánchez became members of the PRI executive committee.[14] Although nepotism was one of the organizing principles of postrevolutionary
politics, accidents of birth and perspicacious marriages were important. Building on kinship ties to members of Oaxaca's chamber of commerce, González Fernández's favoritism had included
Oaxaca's merchant and landholding elite. Sánchez Cano's nepotism was of a more limited and hence less acceptable order, as
his low birth, poor relations, and political inexperience restricted
the ambit of his ruling group. As a result, pamphlets seethed at
Sánchez Cano for "having violated his promise of maintaining
his government free of the dishonest, disgraceful and nauseating
practice of NEPOTISM that has done so much damage to the Revolution" and for keeping local government "under strict familial
and domestic vigilance."[15]

Moreover, like González Fernández, Sánchez Cano was not
content to limit his sphere of authority to Oaxaca City and the
Central Valleys and consequently challenged some of the state's
most powerful regional caciques. His two principal targets were
Heliodoro Charis in Juchitán and Luis Rodríguez in the Región
Mixe. The appointment of Joaquín Amaro as commander of the
Isthmus military region had mitigated the effects of González
Fernández's campaign against the Juchiteco cacique, but four
years of attrition had fragmented the region's political system. In
the district capital alone there were six different parties for the
municipal council elections of December 1944.[16] Although Charis
claimed an overall majority and the backing of the central government, he was opposed by a coalition of teachers, salt workers, and peasants led by Feliciano López Felix and a coalition of

merchants, small businessmen, and disenfranchised politicians headed by Alberto Ramos Sesma. Ramos Sesma was a new breed of state bureaucrat. He was young, had not fought in the Revolution, and had gained his position through his skill at the elite sport of polo. Having caught Avila Camacho's eye at the Berlin Olympics of 1936, he was made a presidential assistant in 1941.[17] His contacts persuaded the governor to offer him control over Juchitán's political administration.[18]

In the municipal elections of December 1944 the new governor and his Isthmus ally combined to impose their candidates on the region's towns. In Juchitán de Zaragoza the election campaign resembled a meeting of all three strains of the Revolution as the populist military oligarch Charis, the teacher and union leader López Felix, and Ramos Sesma as the head of the state PRM's popular sector all claimed the support of the national party. The electoral conflict was fierce. Charis installed voting booths in his house and transported military colonists and peasants into the town from surrounding villages. In response Felix López and a thousand members of the CTM-affiliated Sindicato Unico de Trabajadores de la Industria Salinera marched through Juchitán de Zaragoza to protest the perceived electoral injustice. Ramos Sesma utilized his contacts in the state bureaucracy. The judge, whom Sánchez Cano had recently appointed, arrested CTM members and Charis supporters, while the state PRM wrote copious letters backing Ramos Sesma's candidate. The governor's campaign was successful, and in January 1945 Pedro López Yaco became the municipal president of Juchitán de Zaragoza. Elections in the other towns of Juchitán followed a similar pattern.[19] Ramos Sesma imposed candidates on the municipal councils despite the opposition of Charis's and López Felix's supporters in Santiago

Ixtaltepec, Unión Hidalgo, Santa María Xadani, San Francisco Ixhuatan, El Espinal, San Juan Guichicovi, Matias Romero, and San Dionisio del Mar.[20]

The electoral impositions of late 1944 and Sánchez Cano's attempts to impose control over the Isthmus led to repeated confrontations over the next two years. In Juchitán Charis accused the municipal authorities of ignoring the national illiteracy program, attempting to extort money from local parents, murdering local workers, and acting in a dictatorial manner. In response Sánchez Cano charged Charis with attacking the new council and paid the new commander of the military zone to disarm Charis's military colonists and maintain peace in the area.[21] The supporters of López Felix confronted the regime in a different manner. On the one hand they repeatedly claimed allegiance to the presidential candidate, Miguel Alemán, and denigrated the "pig politicians" Ramos and Charis and their supposed support for alternative appointees.[22] On the other hand, communist railway workers in Matias Romero with connections to the radical branch of Oaxaca's state CTM presented demands for lower prices, socioeconomic reform, and an end to Sánchez Cano's electoral control. In May 1945 the railway union Fraternidad, part of the CTM, went on strike in support of six dismissed engine stokers. They also called for an end to mercantile monopolies and the recognition of the electoral victory of their candidate for the municipal presidency.[23]

In the Región Mixe the governor engineered a similar process of destabilization. In June 1945 Sánchez Cano made a close ally, Francisco Eli Siguenza, Oaxaca's general attorney.[24] As the state's justice minister, Eli Siguenza often attempted to force his version of the law on the ex-district, accusing Rodríguez's accomplices of robbery, murder, and arson and demanding that village police arrest the culprits.[25] At the same time he also regularized the anti-Rodríguez forces into a series of guerrilla bands. Aimless followers of Martínez, independent villagers from San Juan Mazatlán and San Juan Juquila Mixes, and bitter victims of Santiago Zacatepec's expansion of its municipal borders joined together. These groups now dominated the hills of the Región Mixe as the soldiers of Rodríguez had previously done. In February 1945 Eli Siguenza attacked the small hamlet of La Estrella with two hundred men from Santa María Puxmetacán, who accused the new settlers of stealing their lands.[26] In April 1945 the men of San Juan Juquila Mixes and San Pedro y San Pablo Ayutla attacked Santiago Zacatepec itself, and six months later the men of Santiago Atitlán assailed the village of Santa María Tlahuitoltepec "on the bad advice of Eli Siguenza" and stole the village's maize harvest.[27] The next year, the armed men from San Juan Juquila Mixes descended on Asunción Cacalotepec, raped the women, imprisoned the men, and forced people to hand over their meager savings.[28]

Conflicts not only pitted village against village; Eli Siguenza's martial campaign also divided villages, as ambitious local politicians bypassed the traditional loyalties of the elders and assumed command of municipal councils. On 24 March 1945 gunmen murdered the authorities of Santa María Alotepec in the municipal palace and assumed control of the local government.[29] The ferocity of the campaign forced Rodríguez to leave the region and hide in Mexico City.[30] However, he "continued to direct things" from the capital.[31] In a move reminiscent of his assassination of Martínez, he had the new Santa María Alotepec municipal president killed at the celebration of Benito Juárez's birth in Guelatao in May 1945.[32] Sánchez Cano's attempt to extirpate the influence of the caciques in the Región Mixe, like his efforts to monopolize power in the Isthmus, disrupted the uneasy equilibrium between state governor and regional strongmen and led to the complete breakdown of normal political and administrative relations. Taxes were uncollectible and the law was unenforceable. In San Juan Juquila Mixes an arms dealer was selling contraband military weapons to a total of forty-seven armed followers of Eli Siguenza.[33] By the end of 1946 one government emissary reported that "all the Sierra [wa]s at war."[34] Sánchez Cano's attacks on independent caciques in the Sierra and the Isthmus were repeated throughout most of the state.[35]

As Sánchez Cano alienated many of the state's traditional leaders, he was forced to rely on his contacts with the state's peasant and worker unions. First, he appointed his nephew, Francisco Cano García, as the state PRI's agrarian representative to assert control over the CNC within the state. Genaro Ramos's CNC supporters in Miahuatlán, Francisco Jiménez's CNC members in Yautepec, and the peasants of the Central Valleys were allowed to maintain power in the municipalities.[36] However, Sánchez Cano's principal source of support was the conservative branch of the CTM. During the governorship of González Fernández the state's CTM had divided into a radical, communist wing led by Graciano Benítez and a more conservative wing under the charge of Melquiades Ramírez. In return for the loyalty of the conservative branch, Sánchez Cano offered men like Ramírez control of the administrative and municipal authorities of Tuxtepec. In the municipal elections of December 1944 the CTM assumed command of the region's councils.

Over the next two years the CTM councils and judicial authorities monopolized state generosity. As an initial gesture of goodwill

Sánchez Cano gave CTM agrarian committees in the region eight ejidos totaling more than ten thousand hectares in December 1944.[37] Four of his further ten provisional land grants also went to Tuxtepec's CTM groups.[38] The CTM also persecuted the CNC's members. In February Juan Daniel Pérez, a CNC member from San Pedro Ixcatlán, was picked up by the judicial police and taken to the prison in Tuxtepec. At first he assumed it was because he had been drunk, but it soon emerged that the CTM had accused him of murdering its members in Arroyo Zontle. He was allowed to return home only after swearing allegiance to the worker organization.[39] CNC caciques in the region, who had controlled Tuxtepec during González Fernández's governorship, resented the shift in power and accused Sánchez Cano of "being complicit with the murderers of the CTM."[40]

By siding with the conservative branch of the CTM, Sánchez Cano not only estranged members of the CNC but also distanced himself from the state's radical workers. In 1943 the leader of the Communist Party of Oaxaca, Graciano Benítez, had left the CTM with twelve unions. In December 1945 he was joined by the railway workers' union.[41] Juchitán railway workers orchestrated a campaign in Matias Romero against the steady rise in prices of staple goods. On 8 July 1946 the workers cut off electricity to the town's commerce. In response the merchants closed down their shops. Although Sánchez Cano sent a 250-watt generator to solve the electricity problem, the tensions remained.[42] Furthermore, in the Central Valleys radical members of the CTM attempted to unionize temporary peasant workers. The distillery company Nuestra Señora de Pilar had started operations in the mountains above the village of San Pedro el Alto, Zimatlán, in early 1944. In March 1944 the villagers of San Pedro el Alto had signed a contract with the company to offer their labor in return for five centavos per kilogram of resin. But by May 1945 CTM militants from Oaxaca City had met village leaders and persuaded them to back out of the collective contract. The militants argued that villagers could make more money as *ejidatarios* than the company's average daily wage of 1.50 pesos. Although Sánchez Cano ordered the municipal presidents to enforce the agreement on five separate occasions, the villagers simply refused to work in the factory and instead busied themselves on their *ejidal* plots.[43]

Avila Camacho had appointed Sánchez Cano to act as a counterweight to the state's other political interests, but the governor was not content to limit his control to the immediate environs of Oaxaca City. Instead he attempted to remove the more independent local caciques, to assume control of the state's workers and peasants, and to maintain the loyalty of his bureaucracy through the employment of close family members. However, lacking his predecessor's contacts with the *vallistocracia* and relatively deft political touch, Sánchez Cano's regime alienated a series of key groups. By late 1946 a network of caciques, CTM radicals, and disaffected CNC leaders from Tuxtepec were in open opposition to the state governor.

Oaxaca City and the Culture of Opposition

During the first months of his governorship Sánchez Cano attempted to woo the state capital's population with promises of fiscal, infrastructural, and aesthetic improvements. But within two years he had succeeded in creating a mass cross-class urban opposition. In his inauguration address of 1 December 1944 and an open letter to the state's municipal presidents the governor pledged to "protect regional industries," "suppress the 'unfair

taxes,'" and "put an end to mercantile monopolies and concessions."[44] He also assured the Oaxaca City public that he would
clean up some of the less savory activities thrown up by urban
expansion, including "drunkenness, public and clandestine pros-
titution, gambling dens and all those activities that exploit human weakness and stand in the way of the material and spiritual
development of the towns of the state."[45] Initially Sánchez Cano
attempted to uphold his promises and entrusted the task to his
nephew, Mariano Rojas Villavicencio, as municipal president of
Oaxaca City. At Rojas Villavicencio's inauguration he reiterated
his uncle's vows to stop excessive levies, improve public services,
restore "the architectural treasures of the colonial epoch," and
at the same time add "flowers to the city's gardens" and "water
to its fountains."[46] Together they set up a committee of municipal cooperation with members of Oaxaca's elite, borrowed over
five million pesos from the Bank of Public Works, published a
decree banning cantinas near places of work, started the reconstruction of the plaza, ordered the lowering of food prices, and
attempted to stop the exploitation of the city's tenants.[47] As a result, the capital's initial impressions of the governor seem to have
been favorable. *El Momento*, the critical, satirical, and often extremely scurrilous newspaper of the capital's increasingly literate
population, published a sympathetic interview with the governor
at the end of December 1944 and during the next six months issued a few complimentary articles on his work.[48] At the beginning
the city's elite was keen to assist the new governor in his plans for
urban redevelopment.[49]

However, over the next eighteen months Sánchez Cano's relations with the capital's rich and poor deteriorated rapidly as he
failed to put in order the city's electricity shortage, sanitation, tax

system, commercial monopolies, and high food prices. González Fernández had used the problems of the city's faltering electricity supply to co-opt part of the capital's growing cross-class social movements. By incorporating the Liga de Resistencia de Consumidores de Luz y Fuerza Eléctrica into the party's popular sector, staffing it with loyal bureaucrats, and aiding the organization's struggle against the electricity company, González Fernández had diffused a potential source of opposition; he had also placated the city's upper class by handing over control of electricity to an elite conglomerate led by Luis Sarmiento. Sánchez Cano's attempts to sort out the problems of the capital's lighting and power were less successful. Sarmiento's Hydroelectric Company of Oaxaca had neither the finances nor the machinery to improve the city's electricity supply. By July 1945 there were complaints that the new company was not keeping to its contracts, was not providing enough power, and was charging divergent rates for similar services.[50] In order to remedy the situation in the short term Sánchez Cano ordered the engines from the new water purification plant to be connected to the electricity plant.[51] The move was a disaster. Overuse precipitated the rapid disintegration of the machines and the end of Oaxaca City's dream of purified water.[52]

Sánchez Cano thus lost control of the energy consumers, who now sided with the more radical antigovernment groups of water consumers connected to the ACM and run by its leader, Austreberto Aragon. The alliance with the antigovernment coalition precipitated more militant action. In October 1945, after the hydroelectric company denied requests to provide twenty-four-hour service and the thirty volts of power stipulated on the original contract, the energy consumers' union called a payment boycott.[53] Although the governor promised again to buy new machinery to solve the problem, tensions increased as he struggled to acquire the financing for the purchase.[54] Finally in January 1946 the Junta of Material Improvements shut off the purification plant machines powering Oaxaca's extra energy supply, and the consumers held another boycott.[55] Sánchez Cano was forced to buy two large Rand motors to supplement power generated by Sarmiento's company, but there was little improvement.[56] In July 1946 *El Momento* published a scathing attack on the government's attempts to rectify the situation. The streets were still dark at night, Sunday service was intermittent, and the water service, which González Fernández had improved, had now returned to its previous poor level.[57]

At the same time, Austreberto Aragon and the ACM also started to militate on behalf of the city's market stallholders. Although market vendors had been key to the organization of water protests in 1944, the creation of two organizations to promote their interests amplified their political role. The roots of the original organization are difficult to discover. Aragon admitted that the group's archives had been used to fuel his new boiler sometime in the late 1950s.[58] But it appears that members of the LRUAO formed the Comité de la Defensa de Expendedores de Mercados (CDEM) sometime in 1944.[59] Women dominated the organization. They included Elena Kuri, Paula Ramírez, Petrona Ramírez, Dolores "La Diabla" Gonzáles, María "Chata la Ferrera" Henríquez, María "La China" Sánchez, Antonia "Pata Blanca" Aldeco de Sánchez, Genoveva Medina, and Inocencia Enríquez.[60] Although biographical information is scarce, it seems that religious beliefs and class as well as gender delineated the membership of the new organization. Genoveva Medina was born in Oaxaca City and was the young daughter of a successful market vendor who had already established a flourishing vegetable stall by the early 1940s.[61] Inocencia Enríquez was the daughter of a former hacienda foreman and a female stall owner. Although her family never joined the *vallistocracia*, they were members of a growing middle class. Her father owned two *vecindades* and her brothers worked as a policeman, a jeweler, and a driver. She was a deeply devout Catholic. When members of the Oaxaca Market Project interviewed her during the 1960s, she blamed the current state of the markets on the political classes' increasing ignorance of the basics of Christianity. She then pointed to a notice above her stall, which read "Anti-Christianity—NO: Anti-Communism—YES."[62]

The second organization, the Unión de Expendedores de Mercados (UEM), grew out of the CDEM. According to interviews with its founding members, many stallholders balked at taking orders from Austreberto Aragon, a man who had no financial stake in the well-being of the markets.[63] As a result, on 20 May 1944 a handful of vendors formed the UEM. The organization was to be "in charge of the economic defense of the markets." The union met every week in the nearby *vecindad* Casa Fuerte. Decisions were to be taken by majority vote, and members were to pay a weekly subscription of 0.10 pesos.[64] Again information on the UEM's membership is scarce. The organization established a female branch in late 1940s, but its founders were principally men, including Gregorio Pérez, Emiliano Bolaños, and Juan Betanzos.[65] Besides gender dividing the organizations, there is some indication that class may also have been an important factor. Pérez was illiterate, barely spoke Spanish, and still wore "sandals, cotton trousers, a cotton shirt and a palm sombrero." But other members, such as Salvador Acevedo, were clearly wealthier *locatarios*.[66] Although there were tensions between the two

FIG. 7. La Casa Fuerte, a *vecindad* in Oaxaca City and meeting place of the
UEM. (Courtesy of the Biblioteca Bustamante Vasconcelos)

organizations, at first neither accepted allegiance to a particular
political party and both voiced disquiet over the development of
the governor's fiscal system.

During the 1940s tax income in Oaxaca had increased from
2,600,684 pesos in 1940 to 4,986,748 pesos in 1946.[67] As Moises
de la Peña argues, Oaxaca had funded this increase not through
reform of the state's fiscal laws, as in other states, but through an
increase of the *alcabalas*, or taxes charged by state and municipal tax collectors on goods entering the market.[68] According to
De la Peña, these *alcabalas* accounted for more than a third of
Oaxaca's tax income, although officially they had been made illegal since the mid-nineteenth century.[69] The new governor had
promised to stop charging these levies, but the practice continued, and in October 1945 the CDEM joined forces with Aragon's
water and energy consumers and signed a letter of complaint.[70]

Again Aragon denied the organizations' connections to the PAN or Sinarquismo and simply demanded an end to the heavy fiscal tolls. Sánchez Cano tactlessly replied that the government needed money and pesos did not rain from the sky. Consequently the conflict grew increasingly bitter. *El Momento* published a series of editorials condemning the continuation of the taxes. One article jokingly asked whether the local tax collector had thought of charging the cinema, which at that time was showing a film about animals, for bringing livestock into the city. Another, on the front page, sent out an SOS to the federal government on behalf of the ailing capital.[71] Finally, in July 1946 the market stallholders sent a letter to Avila Camacho elucidating the charges. Merchants had to pay a tax on maize of 6.00 pesos per ton and another on *panela* of 16.80 pesos per ton.[72]

Aragon and Oaxaca City's market traders also protested about the continuing monopoly of commercial goods by certain wealthy merchants. Sánchez Cano had promised in his inauguration speech to end this practice, but the necessities of the state budget led the governor to continue to sell off commercial monopolies to the highest bidders.[73] According to the accusations of *El Momento*, *Oaxaca en México*, and various petitions, Ramón Montes possessed the city's monopoly of mescal; Pedro Huerta controlled eggs and chickens; Francisco Cue, coffee; and livestock was the preserve of Sánchez Cano's relation Everardo Jiménez.[74] The monopolist could fix the price of the articles at a suitably low level, and the government's tax collectors in Oaxaca City's surrounding towns of Ocotlán, Etla, Tlacolula, and Ejutla would fine small merchants who bought products directly from the producers. Huerta bought eggs from the Ocotlán farmers at seven to eight centavos each. He then sold these on at ten centavos each in the markets of Oaxaca.[75] Bread makers Armando García Pérez, Angela Gallardo, and Esperanza Chincoya were fined and threatened with prison for bypassing Huerta and attempting to buy eggs in bulk directly from Ocotlán.[76] Although the CDEM led the complaints about government monopolies, the UEM also threatened strike action if the government failed to remove merchants with low-priced goods from the main markets.[77]

By 1946 Sánchez Cano had failed to assert control over any of the city's social movements. Demands for clean water, regular electricity, and lower taxes continued and intensified. Cross-class alliances now joined together, under the tutelage of the head of the ACM, Austreberto Aragon, to oppose the state government. The consumers of electrical energy, who had been connected to the PRM's popular sector during the early 1940s, were now linked to the ACM. Furthermore, an increasingly demanding fiscal policy had driven the city's merchants and tradesmen into the arms of the antigovernment coalition. They began to overlay their accusations of fiscal mismanagement, immorality, incompetence, and bad taste with a counterhegemonic discourse of Oaxaqueñismo, which stressed the state's prerevolutionary leadership.[78] Pamphlets critical of the state government now compared Sánchez Cano's qualities with the strength, intelligence, and power of the state's nineteenth-century heroes.

A group named Por la Defensa Cívica de Oaxaca published a series of scabrous pamphlets that lauded Oaxaca's former heroes. "Children of that bronze race that offered to the Mother Country a champion of the stature of JUÁREZ, sons of this narrow Isthmus of the Republic which has formed the cradle of gentlemen like Antonio de León, Porfirio Díaz, Valerio Trujano and the brothers Flores Magón. Where are men like these now?"[79] In the magazine *Sur*, which was published by the city's intellectual elite, there were repeated articles harking back to a nineteenth and early twentieth century of good governance, fair prices, and architectural sensitivity.[80] The discourse of decline and regression was also taken up by the newspapers of the PAN and Sinarquismo.[81] On 4 January 1947 *Omega*, the official Sinarquista paper, compared the "glorious antiquity" of the state, "the prestige of its sons, Juárez, Díaz and even the decadent Vasconcelos," with today's corrupt lackeys and political pygmies.[82]

The Movement of January 1947

In two years Governor Sánchez Cano had managed to alienate some of the state's most powerful caciques, the radical branch of the CTM, Tuxtepec's CNC, the capital's elite, and its small merchants and traders. In the final two months of 1946 he plunged the state into a deeper crisis by imposing his own candidates on the most important municipal centers, increasing Oaxaca City's taxes, and seemingly threatening the independence of the state university, the IACA. Although the PAN and the new presidential administration took advantage of the governor's predicament to realign the state's administration, the movement was not simply a right-wing coup or a piece of centralized presidential planning. Rather it was a complex, non-ideological, cross-class movement with multiple aims. Members of the *vallistocracia* were pushing for greater control of the state bureaucracy, but Cardenista caciques were also militating for greater electoral autonomy, and lower-class traders of Oaxaca City and the Central Valleys were protesting for better living standards and an increase in their share of the capital's commerce.

Outside the capital Sánchez Cano caused an electoral crisis by imposing authorities on certain key municipalities in an attempt to uproot the state's major caciques. In Juchitán control of the regional branch of the PRI allowed the governor to overcome the supporters of Charis and a branch of the radical CTM and to appoint a series of loyal presidents to the municipalities of Juchitán de Zaragoza, Matias Romero, Santo Domingo Zanatepec, Santiago Niltepec, El Espinal, Ciudad Ixtepec, Unión Hidalgo, San Juan Guichicovi, Santa María Xadani, and Santa María Petapa. Throughout December 1946 Charis and the radical CTM complained of Sánchez Cano's "electoral manipulations" and "imposition of nonrevolutionary candidates."[83] Charis was particularly enraged by the imposition of Victoriano López Toledo as municipal president of Juchitán de Zaragoza. In a letter to the Ministry of the Interior on 17 December he argued that one of his military colonists had won the election with 1,714 votes, but troops had denied his victory and announced the appointment of a group of "prerevolutionary conservatives."[84] In the ex-district of Tuxtepec Sánchez Cano also circumvented the appointment of the region's traditional leaders. CNC candidates were ignored as the governor impressed conservative CTM leaders and men from outside the area on the municipalities of San José Chiltepec, Loma Bonita, San Lucas Ojitlán, San Felipe Jalapa de Díaz, San Juan Bautista Valle Nacional, and San Pedro Ixcatlán.[85] In San Juan Bautista Huajuapam de León, Sánchez Cano compounded his perceived imposition of a federal deputy in 1946 by snubbing the popular PAN candidate for municipal president. Instead, he imposed a Junta of Civil Administration led by an ally from the state of Puebla, Francisco Toscano.[86] Finally, in the administrative centers of the Central Valleys, such as Ejutla de Crespo, Etla, Zaachila, and Oaxaca City, Sánchez Cano overlooked the growing cross-class social movements demanding tax reform, electricity, water, and electoral democracy and decided on his own loyal candidates. In Zaachila he ignored the Grupo Popular de Zaachila composed of the town's workers, peasants, and small merchants and used the resident army detachment to impose an unpopular candidate.[87]

Although it was the imposition of unpopular or even unknown municipal authorities that set Oaxaca's provinces against the governor, it was his attempt to reform the state's tax system that provoked the opposition of all the social classes of Oaxaca City. The state government charged both official and "special" taxes, including the hated *alcabalas*. Decisions about the relative weighting of the official taxes had rested since 1937 with the state's chambers of commerce. Although Governor González Fernández had resolved to restructure the state's taxes and to transfer this power from the chambers of commerce to the local congress, he had retreated from such open confrontation with the capital's elite. As a result, Oaxaca had the worst fiscal position of all the Mexican states and was unable to repay any of its debts to the federal loan banks.[88] In an attempt to resuscitate the state's financial standing Sánchez Cano held a fiscal convention of the state's tax collectors in September 1946 and agreed to pass legislation to increase some of the unofficial taxes and to allow official taxes to be decided upon by the local deputies.[89] On 6 December the local legislature approved nine decrees concerning the tax system, numbering 150 to 158. Article 151 stripped the chambers of commerce of their right to decide on the state's general tax on commerce, industry, and agriculture. Article 152 ordered all owners of commercial or industrial properties, including small restaurants, to purchase metallic plaques from the state government attesting to the buildings' "Hygiene and Cleanliness." Article 153 imposed a new tax on recreational diversions and Article 154 increased taxes on agricultural products such as cotton, coffee, oranges, bananas, pineapples, and vanilla. Article 156 instructed the owners or renters of urban properties to purchase proof of tax payment from the state tax collector for between three and twenty pesos. Article 157 increased the taxes on treated water and carbonated drinks. Finally, Article 158 raised the tax on pigs from six to eight pesos per head.[90]

Sánchez Cano also angered the city's elite by making changes to the state university's constitution. If tax increases provided the movement with its mass of urban protestors, interference with the Instituto Autónomo de Ciencias y Artes supplied its eloquent, politicized leaders. Although the IACA was a public university and claimed to cater for all the state's citizens, it was essentially an elite finishing school, where Oaxaca's select few studied law, commerce, and oratory. Former IACA students dominated the state's legal bureaucracy, and other alumni, such as Eduardo Vasconcelos, Luis Cervantes, and Alfonso Francisco Ramírez, were involved in Mexico City's jurisprudence circuit.[91] Furthermore, by 1946 the university was the center of the city's PAN politicians. Luis Castañeda Guzmán, the illegitimate son of an intemperate, fanatical Catholic priest, was the director of the university and a devoted member of the new political party.[92] Other PAN members—Alfredo Castillo Gómez and José Luis Acevedo—held chairs at the IACA.[93] At the end of December the local legislature passed Article 173, which reformed the legal foundation of the university; ordered it to accommodate degrees in pharmacology, chemical biology, and mineral engineering; and enlarged the powers of its director.[94] Since the conflict over the independence of the

Universided Nacional Autónomo de México in the 1930s, there had been tensions between the IACA and Oaxaca's politicians over the institution's relationship with the state government.[95] In 1936 and again in 1941 governors had come into conflict with the university's technical board and students over the autonomy of the institution.[96] Although decree 173 seemed innocuous enough, in view of the history of government meddling and the university's connections to the PAN, the *vallistocracia* and Oaxaca's émigrés in Mexico City saw it as another example of Sánchez Cano's overbearing, autocratic governance.

By New Year 1947 Sánchez Cano had succeeded in estranging Oaxaca's urban traders, rural caciques, and the political and economic elite. Over the next three weeks, with Miguel Alemán's help, all three groups linked together to remove the governor. Before examining the composition of the cross-class alliance against Sánchez Cano, it is important to recount a narrative of the events that led to his resignation.[97] On 6 January Oaxaca's chamber of commerce met to discuss the new system of taxation and asked the governor to countermand the decrees. The following day the governor's official newspaper published a late edition denying that the new laws would lead to an increase in contributions. Nevertheless, on 8 January the chamber and other civic groups published a manifesto to the people of Oaxaca. The document claimed that the new tax structure affected all social classes and demanded a general commercial strike to start the next day. On 9 January all the shops and market stalls closed. According to one clearly frustrated journalist, "it was impossible to buy a packet of cigarettes, drink a beer or have dinner served."

The following day around twenty thousand people took to the streets of Oaxaca City to protest the tax increases. The crowd halted the governor's attempts to set up alternative food stalls before stopping at 2:30 below the balcony of the IACA. Luis Castañeda Guzmán and other members of the university addressed the assembled inhabitants, linked the issue of IACA autonomy with that of taxation, and demanded the resignation of Sánchez Cano. The scenes in the state capital were repeated on a smaller scale throughout Oaxaca. Merchants shut up shop in San Pablo Mitla, El Parian, Miahuatlán, San Juan Bautista Huajuapam de León, San Juan Bautista Cuicatlán, Ejutla de Crespo, Ocotlán de Morelos, Santa María Asunción Tlaxiaco, San Miguel Sola de Vega, Juchitán de Zaragoza, San Pedro Pochutla, Asunción Nochixtlán, Cosolapa, and Matias Romero. At the same time, the capital's newspapers reported a steady stream of Oaxacan émigrés and politicians visiting the new president in Mexico City to criticize the governor's electoral impositions, taxation program, and lack of respect for the "glorious history" of the IACA.

On 11 January Sánchez Cano was forced to act. In the morning three representatives from the Ministry of the Interior, the members of the "consultation commission" of the chamber of commerce, and the governor met in the governor's palace. The merchants demanded that Sánchez Cano call an extraordinary meeting of the local legislature to cancel the decrees and put an end to *alcabalas* and commercial monopolies. The governor agreed to all the chamber's demands and sent off a telegram to the head of the local legislature to arrange for a new session. At midday Sánchez Cano appeared on the balcony of the palace with members of the commission, explained the agreement, and asked for the demonstrators to return to their homes. In reply the crowds called the merchants traitors, shouted "Death to Sánchez Cano," and marched toward the IACA. Earlier in the day the professors, students, and employees of the institute had met to name a representative body and to demand the revocation of Article 173. Although Sánchez Cano had agreed to the institute's demands, the university's delegates were not as openly compliant at the city's leading merchants. As a result, on the afternoon of the eleventh the crowd of artisans, merchants, workers, women, and students voted in front of the IACA to sustain the protest and form the Comité Cívico Oaxaqueño (CCO). The CCO was led by university professor Alberto Vargas and included university teachers such as Ignacio Castro Mantecon and Manuel Zárate Aquino, wealthy merchants such as Jesús Torres Márquez and Leonicio Jiménez, and the domineering leader of the market stallholders, Dolores "La Diabla" Gonzáles.

The creation of the CCO prolonged the social movement and allowed the development a new range of tactics and demands. Although the Ministry of the Interior and the chamber of commerce announced that the strike was over and asked the city's merchants to reopen their premises, their pleas were ignored. Shops and stalls remained shut and there were two permanent demonstrations, outside the IACA and the governor's palace. At the IACA members of the university, the CCO, and a growing contingent of politicians from the Central Valley towns addressed the assembled crowds, warned them of the imminent danger of attack, and demanded the governor's resignation. As the crowds gained confidence, they started to take over the city. In the main plaza women set up stalls and handed out tortillas and fruit to the tired protestors. On 13 January crowds took the Public Registry of Properties, the Civil Registry, and the government's printing office. In the evening they published the first edition of *Nueva Vida*, the strike's official organ, which demanded "A New Political Life, A New Social Life.

No More Hunger. No More Slaves." During this period the cco wrote to President Alemán listing the people's demands. They now called for the end of the egg, coffee, livestock, and mescal monopolies and high taxes and for the election of new municipal authorities in San Juan Bautista Cuicatlán, Ciudad Ixtepec, San Juan Bautista Huajuapam de León, Ocotlán de Morelos, and Ejutla de Crespo. Meanwhile, in Mexico City, one of the federal deputies, Magro Soto, presented messages from Castañeda Guzmán, peasant organizations, and IACA students to the permanent commission of the national congress. In the state's provincial towns protests became more virulent. In Juchitán de Zaragoza municipal police left two demonstrators injured, and in Etla at least one protestor died after police fired on an angry mob.

Finally on 15 January the army intervened. While the cco was in Mexico City delivering a list of demands to the president, a mobilized battalion entered the state capital. Zone commander Joaquín Amaro persuaded protestors and IACA students to go back to their homes. It appeared that Governor Sánchez Cano had won. He gave the PRI national newspaper, *El Nacional*, an interview in which he claimed to have overcome the cabal of rich merchants, Sinarquistas, and PAN members who had orchestrated the movement. But President Alemán had promised the cco that if things returned to normal, he would send the minister of the interior to the state to investigate the committee's complaints. As commerce reopened and crowds dispersed, Alemán kept his promise and on the evening of 16 January Héctor Pérez Martínez arrived in Oaxaca City. The next day he met students, merchants, members of the radical CTM, resident groups, and Sánchez Cano. Although the governor promised to call the legislature in three days' time to revoke the decrees in question, Pérez Martínez demanded that he stand down. At first Sánchez Cano was hesitant, but on 18 January he presented his resignation to the legislature, which immediately appointed Eduardo Vasconcelos as the new interim governor. On the same day the governor left the city and Vasconcelos arrived to be sworn in by the permanent commission of the state congress.

The narrative of the fall of Governor Sánchez Cano reveals some of the significant aspects of the movement of January 1947, including the initial opposition of the merchant elite, the mobilization of the middle and lower classes, and the president's eventual decision. However, in order to explore the aspirations, interdependence, and relative import of the individual factions, it is necessary to examine each social and political actor in turn. It is undeniable that the *vallistocracia* was central to the resignation of the governor. The chamber of commerce, consisting of the city's foremost merchants and industrialists, had visited the merchants of León and Monterrey in late 1946 to ascertain how they had defended themselves against the "tyranny" of state government.[98] As a result the chamber precipitated the original strike against the new tax decrees. Members of the city's elite also served to prolong the crisis with their involvement in the university and the cco. The new governor, Eduardo Vasconcelos, was himself a prominent member of the *vallistocracia*, and in October 1946 he had visited the state at the request of the IACA's organization of former alumni.[99] Furthermore, the elite involvement in the movement appears to have been linked to the rise of the PAN party as an organization of urban, upper-class protest. Castañeda Guzmán was a leading PAN member and brother-in-law of the party's state leader, Manuel Aguilar y Salazar. Other members of the PAN—Alfredo Castillo, Joel Díaz, Joaquín Acevedo, José Luis Acevedo, Nicandro

Ortíz, and Fernando Ramírez de Aguilar—were all involved in the organization of all stages of the movement.[100]

Were the January protests then the exclusive work of a coherent, tightly knit community of PAN-sympathizing urban merchants, industrialists, and academics? Sánchez Cano and his supporters certainly thought so. In newspapers and letters to Mexico City they explained how "the lower classes" of the city had been "manipulated" by a thin cabal of rich, self-interested, right-wing extremists.[101] Moreover, the chamber of commerce produced alarmist, populist propaganda clearly designed to whip up support from the city's poor.[102] Yet although the movement appeared to be dominated by these elite figures, the week of intense political mobilization cannot be dismissed as mass false consciousness brought on by clever political management. The movement's trajectory indicates a more subtle appreciation of the interaction between its leaders and its popular supporters. First, on several occasions the elite failed to control the assembled crowds. After the chamber had come to an agreement with Sánchez Cano, the protestors denounced them as traitors. Further attempts by the merchant elite to reopen the markets and the city's shop were ignored.[103] As Luis Medina argues, "the leaders found that the problem of starting a movement was much easier than stopping it."[104]

Second, from 11 January onward there were increasingly radical demands against members of the elite. On 13 January members of Oaxaca's "humble class" wrote to Alemán to complain that they had been living "under the most base of slaveries" since the early 1940s.[105] Another newssheet drew links among commercial monopolies, state government corruption, high taxes, and the suffering of the poor.[106] The CCO's demands and the editorials of the movement's newspaper reflected these perceptions and now insisted on an end to commercial monopolies, unfair taxes, and "all those bad merchants" who had "enriched themselves with the sweat of the people."[107] Third, beneath the top tier of elite orators, descriptions of the movement's leaders reveal a broad cross section of the city's inhabitants. Workers including the radical railway workers of Matias Romero and the electricity workers of Oaxaca City supported the CCO.[108] Left-leaning teachers such as Manuel Zárate Aquino, Rosendo Pérez, and Policarpo T. Sánchez were also involved.[109]

Fourth, although the leaders came from the upper class, in general the repertoire of collective action of the movement was resolutely popular. The demonstrations, sit-ins, and marches reveal none of the concern with hierarchy and order that Daniel Newcomer describes in his analysis of Sinarquista mobilizations.[110] Men, women, and children screamed, shouted, and hurled abuse at everyone connected to the state bureaucracy. Sánchez Cano complained that it was impossible to impose calm on a crowd when people beat their breast and offered to take a bullet for the sake of "justice and democracy."[111] The archives are replete with ribald popular songs disclaiming the "nauseating governor with seven jobs" and his secret deals with the tax collectors and monopolists, which reveal the penumbra of received opinion about the events.[112] These songs were regularly rendered in the city's main square and in front of the IACA, operating like the political ballads of early modern England, informing the less literate of the latest scandals.[113] As well as the more traditional forms of collective action, there was the first use in Oaxaca of both the mock and real funeral procession as a political tool. On 11 January people marched though the streets with a coffin inscribed with Sánchez Cano's name to symbolize the death of his political regime.[114] Five days later, after the death of a demonstrator in Etla, crowds demanding justice paraded around the *zócalo* with the real coffin containing the body.[115]

If the January movement was on the surface an elite operation concerned with commerce and state power, underneath it seethed with popular demands and a genuine desire for popular political participation. The merger of these two strains was made possible by the unifying project of political protest, which the ACM, users of water and electricity, and the market stallholders had operated since the early 1940s. The state's project of urban modernization sucked new groups into the political sphere. As a result many of the protestors were women. According to numerous newspaper and government reports these female consumers formed the bulk of the demonstrators.[116] On 10 January the municipal committee of the PRI claimed that "locatarias from all the markets" were stirring up the rest of the city against the governor.[117] In March 1947 *El Momento* praised the "consumers of light and electricity and the women of the markets," who had "demanded democracy for Oaxaca."[118] Scrap iron merchant María "Chata la Ferrera" Henríquez, grocer María "La China" Sánchez, and Dolores "La Diabla" Gonzáles were the movement's popular leaders.[119] Undoubtedly some of the more socially conscious priests were also involved in encouraging the popular revolt. Reports from Sánchez Cano's secretary claimed that Padre Ramírez was whipping up support for the mobilization among members of the Catholic workers' center based in San Agustín Church.[120] However, the central figure in this cross-class coalition of consumers was the master knife maker Austreberto Aragon. As described in chapter 7 the ACM, led by Aragon, had become the organizational focus for opposition to the government. During the 1940s, with the aid of the popular newspaper *El Momento* and the institutional backing of the ACM, Aragon had built links with some of the markets' most influential women to form a powerful cross-class coalition to press for reform to the city's services and an end to the monopolies, taxes, and tolls that affected their trade. As a result, in early January 1947 Aragon provided the linkman for the elite members of the PAN to mobilize a large proportion of the city's population, especially the "young women of the popular class."[121] He visited his contacts in the markets, handed out pamphlets, newspapers, and newssheets, and persuaded the stallholders to join the initial movement. However, Aragon was not able simply to manipulate his constituency; he also had to represent their demands and allow their enthusiasm for the novelty of political protest. Dolores "La Diabla" Gonzáles from the CDEM and Emiliano Bolaños from the UEM were allowed to join the CCO, and despite the organization's elite composition, its protests and appeals were those of the lower and middle classes. The January movement was a mix of elite political maneuvering and popular protest, brought together by a network of merchant and artisan intermediaries connected to the consumer groups of the early 1940s.

Besides being an urban, cross-class mobilization, the episode also reflected the traditional tensions between the state governor and Oaxaca's provinces. During his governorship Sánchez Cano had attacked the leaders of Juchitán, Jamiltepec, Tuxtepec, Villa Alta, and the Región Mixe, and in the elections of 1946 he imposed candidates on many of the key municipalities of these exdistricts. These new municipal presidents, such as Victoriano López Toledo in Juchitán de Zaragoza, supported the governor in letters to the new president.[122] In contrast, the region's caciques joined the demands for the governor's resignation. Luis Rodríguez's allies in Santiago Zacatepec backed the movement.[123] In Juchitán supporters of Heliodoro Charis mobilized twelve thousand locals to demonstrate against the proposed taxes.[124] The caciques also used their contacts in the state and national capitals. Rafael Pineda León was a local deputy from Juchitán and a client of Charis. He addressed the crowds outside the IACA and canvassed his fellow deputies for support.[125]

The regional strongmen thus expanded the mobilization to encompass most of the state's major towns while also strengthening the movement in the country's capital. In Mexico City Charis gave interviews to national newspapers and discussed the imposition of municipal authorities in the Isthmus.[126] At the same time the PAN organization in Huajuapam, which had emerged during the 1940 presidential election and rested on the support of devout indigenous ranchers, also supported the movement against the governor. According to local leader Procopio Martínez Vásquez, the governor's imposition of an unpopular municipal council mobilized five thousand PAN supporters in the region. There were demonstrations in the ex-district capital, and hundreds of PAN members even took buses provided by Manuel Aguilar y Salazar to the state capital to protest.[127]

Although the January protests derived from the real grievances of those who had lost (or had never had) a political voice, the governor's fate was eventually decided by the new president, Miguel Alemán. According to Luis Medina, Sánchez Cano was one of eight governors to remain loyal to former president Cárdenas in 1945. His fall is therefore seen as part of a broader move to the right, which included the changes to Article 27 and the taming of the unions.[128] In the same way Edmundo Sánchez Cano argued that Alemán's right-wing advisors had decided on

THE RISE AND FALL OF EDMUNDO SÁNCHEZ CANO

his political destiny the day they had gained power.[129] But hindsight blurs both theories. There is no evidence that Sánchez Cano backed Cárdenas or his favorite for the presidential candidacy, Miguel Henriquez Guzmán, until after his dismissal. He was one of Avila Camacho's men and duly supported Alemán during the presidential elections. Furthermore, he cooperated with the less radical, less independent branch of the CTM, led by Fidel Velázquez. Although Alemán was instrumental in the resignation of Sánchez Cano, it was not part of a larger ideological plan for the direction of the Mexican Revolution. Rather the timing of the protests reveals the importance of "political opportunity" to the development of popular urban social movements and indicates why they are often confused with moments of elite bloodletting.[130] Many of the issues that affected the populace of Oaxaca City had been around since at least the early 1940s. The inauguration of a new president, the change in municipal authorities, and the division between the state's political and economic elites offered both space and allies for the urban protestors. Alemán's dismissal of the Oaxacan governor was an unplanned, spontaneous, and somewhat rash attempt both to appease a disenchanted urban public and to realign Oaxaca's ailing and contradictory political system.

Conclusion

Analysis of Sánchez Cano's term of office and eventual resignation offers a series of insights into the political landscape of the 1940s. By appointing an anonymous military figure as governor, the central state again attempted to weaken the power of the state administration. But Sánchez Cano, like González Fernández, was unwilling to refrain from interfering in the state's worker and peasant unions and its independent *cacicazgos*. As a result, although the imposition of the governor indicated an autocratic, centripetal, and stable system of government, underneath this layer of the administration the arrangement was decentralized, uneven, and conflictual. Corporatist organizations were subject to individual leaders, huge regions of the state were under personalist control, and although the president and the national party could affect elections for the state governor and the federal chambers, in the local political arena, as a contemporary group of politicians pointed out, ejidos and worker unions were sparse and local loyalties outweighed that to party or state. In the most prosaic terms, as one antigovernment organization put it, "the PRI d[id] not exist."[131] However, with the appointment of Vasconcelos as the new governor in January 1947, President Alemán changed Oaxaca's political system. The balance between the governor and other political and economic powers in the state, which had allowed the central government to act independently of both, disappeared. There was now a clear chain of command from the president through the state's business elite to local and municipal government.

The January 1947 movement against Sánchez Cano also reveals the nature of the resistance to the central government's revolutionary project. Although Cárdenas's presidency culminated in the closely contested and bloody elections of 1940, it is often assumed that with the more conciliatory politics of Avila Camacho, general confrontation ended. Historians have portrayed most incidents of opposition to the new government as elite, quasifascist fanaticism. There is no doubt that some of the leaders of the January 1947 politics were connected to the more extreme end of populist politics. But they did not merely impose their ideas

on compliant masses. Rather, as the revolutionary creeds of Za-
patismo or Cardenismo were appropriated and transformed at
the local level, so the ideas of the PAN were molded by cultural
intermediaries such as ACM leader Austreberto Aragon and by
Oaxaca's urban population, particularly the market women, to
suit their increasingly penurious situation. As a result the cross-
class opposition survived, constantly reformulating itself according to the dominant discourses and the pressing socioeconomic
demands. The movement of 1947 had far-reaching consequences.
The rules of the game had changed. The inhabitants of Oaxaca
City now realized that urban popular protest and its growing repertoire of collective action could be wheeled out not only to confront the problems of modernization but also to remove governors themselves.

Uncovering these incidents of popular protest throughout Mexico is an arduous task. The historian researching the 1940s is often forced to look beyond traditional sources to examine "hidden transcripts" of discontent. When examining protests that
became entangled with elite politicking, the task becomes dou-
bly difficult. Popular voices and actions often get lost as official
government sources portray the masses as manipulated by their
elite puppeteers, and opposition newspapers—especially those
of the right wing—are often at pains to depict the movements as
disciplined and ordered. Yet accounts of the movements in León,
Tapachula, and Tamaulipas all seem to indicate a broader wave
of political protest during the mid-1940s. The Unión Cívica de
León embraced rich merchants and Sinarquista and PAN elites
but also "disenfranchised peasants, workers from small industries and the middle class." Like the CCO it had a broad range of
demands, including "the superior efficiency of public services,"

"the greater satisfaction of communal needs," and more direct forms of local democracy.[132] The Partido Cívico of Tapachula included members of the PAN but was also a cross-class organization. Its demonstrations demanded greater democratic freedom and were led by young women.[133] The movement to oust the governor of Tamaulipas was aided by the desire of the national government and certain local politicians to rid the state of Portesgilistas—but it also included demands for fair municipal elections, an end to political repression, and a degree of press freedom.[134] While it is clear that elites from Oaxaca, Tamaulipas, and Tapachula attempted to link their own movements to those of León, it is possible that popular forces also saw the wave of social mobilizations as an opportunity to exact concessions from the national and local administrations.

NINE

The *Vallistocracia* Governor, 1947–50

Popular protest and elite politicking brought Eduardo Vasconcelos to power at the beginning of the presidency of Miguel Alemán Valdés. The few studies of the *sexenio* stress the growing authoritarianism of the state and eradication of its revolutionary social program. At the center of this shift were the dominant discourses of national unity and *mexicanidad*. Together these marginalized any ideological currents extraneous to those of the government's interpretation of the Revolution and, by extension, the government itself.[1] Following the international swing against extremist politics, the PCM and Fuerza Popular, the political arm of Sinarquismo, were both banned in 1949.[2] Internally the government party also underwent transformation. In 1946 its name was changed to the Partido Revolucionario Institucional. Under the rhetorical cloak of democratization, the PRI also introduced changes to its statutes in February 1950, which abolished primaries. Candidates for municipal, regional, state, and national office would now be chosen at party assemblies at the corresponding level. Although this was presented as a means to reduce the power of demagogic political caucuses and increase the options of the individual, in reality it gave greater authority to the central government in Mexico City and allowed for the top-down imposition of candidates.[3] At the same time, the peasant and worker unions were neutralized. The reform of Article 3 in December 1946 led to the resignation of the head of the CNC, Gabriel Leyva, and the election of an even more politically amenable director, Roberto Barrios.[4] Perhaps most important, Fidel Velázquez finally took full control of the CTM and *charrismo* (the practice of nominating compliant labor leaders) put an end to the independent unions.[5] In contrast, the popular sector began to assert itself as the most powerful sector of the party, claiming the most elected positions at the local level and in the lower and upper chambers.[6]

At the economic level, the retreat from Cárdenas's social policies turned from a steady march into undisciplined flight. The reform of Article 27 increased the maximum size of the small property exempt from expropriation.[7] Land grants during the *sexenio* totaled 4.2 million hectares. In comparison, Cárdenas had given out 20 million hectares and Avila Camacho 5.3 million.[8] The practice of *charrismo* limited the opportunities for strikes, wage rises, and labor reform.[9] In place of social redistribution, Alemán's government stressed the need for economic modernization through industrialization. In the countryside the newly created National Commission of Colonization and the Ministry of Hydraulic Works put a premium on large commercial agriculture projects designed to increase production. In the cities, which were growing rapidly as a result of rural migration, Alemán used the state's money and the system of import substitution to cultivate and protect the country's established and nascent industrial concerns.[10]

In many ways the situation in Oaxaca closely paralleled the shifts at the national level. As Alemán moved away from appointing revolutionary generals to the higher echelons of government, so Vasconcelos was the first nonmilitary figure to become governor since Francisco López Cortés.[11] Further, as Alemán increased the state's ties to the commercial and industrial elite, so Vasconcelos was the first member of the *vallistocracia* to hold the post since before the Revolution.[12] As governor Vasconcelos pursued policies that closely mirrored those of the president. Politically, he forsook the CNC and CTM and made the *vallistocracia* and the popular sector the most important pillars of his governing camarilla. Economically, he stressed the need for increased production, the protection of small property owners, and the modernization of agriculture. In reality this led to the suppression of radical politicians and wayward *ejidatarios* and the protection of the landed elites. However, the manner of Vasconcelos's appointment to the governorship also molded his brief tenure. In Oaxaca City Vasconcelos was forced to negotiate with the popular coalition of market vendors, artisans, and urban workers, offering improvements in taxation, water supply, electricity, paving, and schools. In the countryside Vasconcelos had to allow caciques such as Heliodoro Charis and Luis Rodríguez, who had figured in the alliance against Sánchez Cano, a degree of independence. Although there were moves toward a growing state authoritarianism in Oaxaca, the historical formation of the state's political geography countered its development in many areas.

The Vasconcelos Camarilla

Eduardo Vasconcelos's governing camarilla relied almost exclusively on members of the *vallistocracia*. Lawyers, academics, merchants, and landowners, many of whom were the sons of the Porfirian ruling class, dominated the administration. They were almost all linked by having attended the local university, the ICA. According to a government agent who visited the state in early 1949, Vasconcelos was surrounded by "members of the state's elite," who would meet daily in the Dos Equis bar of the Marques del Valle

hotel at the north of the *zócalo*. His minister of the interior, Cutberto Chagoya, was a former student of the ICA, a lawyer, and an
employee of Vasconcelos at the Supreme Court in Mexico City.
His attorney general was the Oaxaca economist Jorge Tamayo.
His state treasurer was the ICA graduate and member of the merchant elite Gustavo Alvarez.[13] Members of the *vallistocracia* also
dominated important elected positions in the state. The candidates for local deputies in August 1947 included Jorge F. Iturribarría, Alberto Vargas, Guillermo Rosas Solaegui, and Constantino Esteva.[14] The municipal council of Oaxaca City was ruled
by a junta composed of university professors such as Heliodoro
Díaz Quintas and Antonio Herrera Altamirano and then by Manuel Canseco Landeros, a doctor of medicine at the IACA and the
son of one of the city's most important merchants.[15] Vasconcelos
even imposed Mateo Solano, a Spaniard and one of the state's
leading industrialists, as an official of the council. Finally, members of this elite governing class directed the propaganda effort of
the regime. Iturribarría was director of the official newspaper, *La
Voz de Oaxaca*, and Solano wrote endless articles defending the
government for the "independent" newspaper, *El Globo*. Even
Luis Castañeda Guzmán, a prominent member of the PAN, wrote
pieces for the official paper.[16]

As the final example suggests, Vasconcelos's attachment to the
commercial, industrial, and academic elite of Oaxaca crossed ideological and party lines. According to critics his government was
"full of fanatics, Huertistas, Panistas and members of the Knights
of Columbus."[17] Iturribarría was a member of the elitist Catholic lodge; Vargas had been a Huertista and had certainly dallied
with the PAN, as had Alvarez and Solano.[18] It seems that Vasconcelos's co-option of the state's right-wing elite was acceptable to

the central government up to a point. For the most part, they were allowed to play a part in the PRI administration as long as they did not speak out in favor of any other political party. However, on at least one occasion Vasconcelos tested the limits of the central government's indulgence. It seems that in June 1947 Vasconcelos persuaded the head of the PAN, Manuel Aguilar y Salazar, that if he ran under an independent candidature, he would be allowed to become local deputy of the extremely Catholic region of the Mixteca Baja.[19] In late July 1947 Aguilar y Salazar wrote to the head of the PAN that as Vasconcelos was a "co-disciple" (presumably a reference to their joint attendance of the ICA), he would be unable to deny Aguilar y Salazar's victory.[20] Although government reports testified to the PAN's victory with more than 60 percent of the vote, pressure from the central committee of the PRI overturned the election and imposed the official party candidate in his place.[21]

Vasconcelos's attachment to the *vallistocracia* molded not only the state's political administration but also its cultural program. During the 1940s the Mexican state had retreated from the radical cultural agenda of the Cárdenas era. The discourses of national unity and *mexicanidad* softened the excesses of the cult of the Revolution and historicized the event as one step on Mexico's path to modernization rather than a roadmap for social change.[22] Radical *indigenismo*, which had celebrated Indian culture as a potential exemplar of Mexican development, was marginalized, ignored, and gradually replaced by a patronizing and folksy antiquarianism. Yet although local cultures mirrored the developments at the national level in some ways, in others they diverged. In Oaxaca the radical cults of the Revolution and *indigenismo* all but disappeared, but in their stead the *vallistocracia*'s cultural elite imposed a culture of regional peculiarity and independence based on the state's colonial heritage, the church, and Porfirio Díaz. In August 1947 Luis Castañeda Guzmán was appointed to write a weekly history section in *La Voz de Oaxaca*. As one of the leaders of the 1947 movement, whose popular support had been based in part on a revitalized popular, social Catholicism, he informed readers of the architectural and cultural marvels of the church. There were articles about the construction of the temples of La Soledad, Santo Domingo, San Agustín, San Juan de Dios, and Yanhuitlán.[23] There were also reprints of articles on the religious fiestas of Our Lady of Solitude in 1909 and Our Lady of Guadalupe in 1932. There were poems entitled "The Legend of Christ" and "The Christ of Velásquez" and hagiographies of Catholics such as Mariano Cuevas, the great historian of Mexico's church, and Carlos Gracida, the vicar of Oaxaca and founder of the Colegio del Espíritu Santo, which so many of the *vallistocracia* had attended.[24] Castañeda Guzmán also offered his opinion on the growing debate over the bones of Cuauhtémoc and Hernán Cortés, coming down firmly on the side of the Hispanic sympathizers by claiming that Cortés and not the Aztec king was the "Father of the Mexican Nation."[25]

Besides lauding the achievements of the Catholic Church, Vasconcelos's cultural program also tried to resurrect the reputation of Porfirio Díaz. In October 1947 the senator of Oaxaca, Joaquín Fagoaga, formed the Comité Nacional Pro-Repatriación to petition the senate for the return of the dictator's bones from Paris. The campaign launched a series of articles in the Oaxaca press demanding the restoration of the remains, with much praise surrounding Díaz's victory over the "invaders and imperialists" at Miahuatlán on 3 October 1866. The town itself was renamed

Miahuatlán de Porfirio Díaz on 3 October 1947. Various articles extolled Díaz's martial and patriotic virtues. In the most comprehensive piece Alfonso Francisco Ramírez argued that it was necessary to "honor the clean memory of the soldier of the country." Although he continued that it was necessary to "leave to one side the dictator," he did admit that Díaz had brought the country peace, stability, and a network of efficient railways; as a "great hero of Mexico," Díaz should not be dismissed or despised but rather spoken of in the same breath as Bolívar, Washington, Hidalgo, and Morelos. Ramírez left readers with the plaintive demand that the hero's remains "return to their maternal breast, this Mexican land that he loved so much." Díaz's functionaries were remembered not as cruel tyrants but rather as strong, cultured, and competent administrators. Alfonso Taracena argued that "because of his intellectual and ethical virtues," the last Porfirian governor in Oaxaca, Emilio Pimentel, should be judged as "the paradigm of Oaxaca governors." In many ways this conservative brand of Oaxaqueñismo emerged from the movement against Sánchez Cano, organized at least in part through church organizations. However, the establishment of a Catholic, conservative pantheon of local heroes pointed toward the marked paternalism of Vasconcelos's government.

During his four years as governor, Vasconcelos relied on members of the *vallistocracia* as members of his governing elite. Industrialists, merchants, and above all intellectuals, jurists, and academics from the local university dominated appointed and elected posts. This conservative faction, composed of men with links to the Catholic Church and the Porfiriato, defended their right to rule with the creation of a conservative culture of Oaxaqueñismo that moved away from the soft radicalism of men like Genaro V.

Vásquez and the generation of the 1920s toward an unashamed celebration of the church, the colony, and Porfirio Díaz.

Vasconcelos and the City

Although Vasconcelos governed with the open approval of the *vallistocracia*, he also had to negotiate with other interest groups in the state. During the previous five years market vendors, artisans, and urban workers had joined together to form powerful social movements. New groups including housewives and female market vendors now played important roles on the political stage. Vasconcelos attempted to co-opt these groups by offering material gains in return for political compliance. He banned *alcabalas* and monopolies; attempted to improve the city's paving, water, and electricity supplies; offered help to the city's renters; and alleviated the pressures of price rises and the devaluation of the peso. In many ways the policy was successful. At least one group of market vendors formed part of the PRI's popular sector. But the matter of democracy remained a sticking point between the governor and these popular groups. Vasconcelos was unwilling to allow the urban electorate—swelled by regulations allowing women to vote in municipal elections—free rein to appoint their representatives. Although this caused vocal displays of dissent within the city, Vasconcelos attempted to dispel the resentment through complete liberty of the press. As a result, during the late 1940s there was an explosion of regional newspapers, many of which openly criticized the governor's administration.

One of Vasconcelos's first moves as governor was to assure the loyalty of the PRI's own urban interest groups, consisting primarily of the Liga de Inquilinos. It seems that conflicts over rents in Mexico City and Veracruz during the 1920s had taught revolutionary governors the advantages of co-opting this particular faction, and the league had been one of the few urban groups to remain silent during the fall of Sánchez Cano. In June 1948 Vasconcelos cemented their fidelity by introducing a new tenants' law. According to the official newspaper, the regulations were designed to favor the "those with little resources (artisans, owners of small workshops, industrial workers, etc.) and small merchants."[26] During the 1940s tenants in Oaxaca City had repeatedly complained about the extortionate price of rents, controlled by a cabal of landlords who had bought up houses cheaply following the earthquake of 1931.[27] The new law limited the rents that the city's property owners could demand. A landlord who paid for water and electricity could charge 12 percent of the actual value of the house; one who did not pay for these services could charge only 10 percent.[28] Over the next three years the protests of tenants were dealt with efficiently and apparently justly by the state police and the judiciary. Obstreperous landlords were fined and forced to lower rents.[29] Vasconcelos also offered his support to the Liga de Inquilinos on their project to build a new "proletarian colony" in the city, appealing on behalf of the organization for funds from various local and national banks.[30]

The Liga de Inquilinos was perhaps the most compliant of Oaxaca's popular organizations. Other groups were traditionally more intransigent opponents of the state regime. Conformity required complex negotiations, efficient fiscal administration, and increased state spending. The movement to remove Sánchez Cano had concerned the level and means of taxation in the city and the connected problem of commercial monopolies. Water and electricity users and the unions of market vendors continued their campaign after the governor's departure. In February 1947

Austreberto Aragon announced that the water users and market vendors would hold a boycott of the "Gachupines that have declared themselves enemies of the pueblo" by monopolizing the sale of eggs and alcohol.[31] The official newspaper of the January 1947 strike, *La Nueva Vida*, reported the continued charging of *alcabalas* two months later.[32] By May 1947 the new government was forced to make a decision. In a report to the municipal council the state treasurer pointed out that newspapers were reporting the payment of *alcabalas* on fruit, onions, alfalfa, cheese, wood, and tomatoes entering the markets. Although they were not demanded "with the same tyranny as before," they were still exacted. As a result of Aragon's campaign, however, many people now refused to pay, and taxes had declined from eleven hundred pesos to six hundred pesos per week in the Benito Juárez Maza market.[33] Although the *alcabalas* accounted for 75 percent of the municipal taxes, the council agreed to ban the charges under Article 107 of the state's political constitution.[34] Tax collectors and agents who maintained the practice were investigated, and at least one was dismissed.[35] By the end of August 1947, weekly contributions from the Benito Juárez Maza market barely scraped two hundred pesos.[36]

Commercial monopolies were also removed. José and Pedro Huerta's monopoly on eggs was limited by the opening of new eggs stalls in major markets.[37] Moreover, during the run up to the Day of the Dead, the state governor announced a price freeze on eggs, which were necessary for the traditional light bread that accompanied the festivities.[38] Francisco Cue's monopoly of mescal was terminated as a host of other merchants entered the trade.[39] By September 1947 Vasconcelos could boast in his report to the local congress that *alcabalas* and monopolies had ended.[40] The enormous shortfall was rectified by a series of decrees designed to shift the fiscal burden from small producers and market vendors to large agricultural producers. Decree 89 in December 1948 charged twenty pesos per measure of coffee. Decree 92 charged sixty pesos per thousand pineapples. Finally, the new fiscal law of 1949 charged twelve pesos per head of livestock.[41] By January 1950 the usually critical *El Chapulin* (formerly *El Momento*) lauded the municipal fiscal regime. The councilman for the markets, Jesús Torres Márquez, had managed to collect 306,567 pesos in tax, or 86,000 pesos more than the previous year, without resort to *alcabalas* or monopolies. The newspaper called the figure "a testament to his efficiency and honesty."[42]

The other major causes of protest during the first half of the 1940s had been the provision and pricing of water and electricity. Vasconcelos moved swiftly to deal with these problems. First he appointed Guillermo Aristrain, a member of the state's elite, to the Junta of Material Improvements, with orders to "improve the supply of water to all the areas of the city."[43] Over the next four years the junta reopened a well in San Martín Mexicapam, drilled another by the River Atoyac, and cleaned up the major waterways in the city. In April 1949 Vasconcelos attempted to remove the control of the capital's water supply from the federal junta and give it back to the municipality. An improved fiscal structure allowed the governor to organize the rapid payment of the eight-hundred-thousand-peso debt and to plan restitution of municipal control by 1954. Although the electricity company was organized through a private company, Vasconcelos also drove money into the improvement of the supply. In February 1948 he invited two engineers to the city to inspect the system. As a result of their report, he invested more than forty thousand pesos in two new motors. He also forced the owner of the Hydroelectric Company of Oaxaca, Luis Sarmiento, to lower charges. Furthermore, unlike the previous governors, Vasconcelos encouraged a degree of administrative transparency in the water and electricity organizations, which was designed to offset public disquiet. After heavy rain storms in February 1948, which did not bring the expected increase in water supply, *La Voz de Oaxaca* ran an explanatory piece claiming that Aristrain had already gone to Mexico City to ask for funding for the cleaning of certain key water channels. When the lights went out on 29 May 1948, the official newspaper claimed it was due to faulty wiring done while Sánchez Cano was in power.[44] By September 1950 Vasconcelos claimed that the water problem was "about to be resolved." By then 90 percent of the city's inhabitants had access to electricity and public lighting functioned all night.[45]

As part of Vasconcelos's effort to improve the city's infrastructure he also attempted to overhaul the appalling state of paving in the capital. Complaints regarding open sewerage, broken pavements, and extortionate municipal charges for repairs had frequently accompanied other urban protests.[46] On 30 January 1947 *La Voz de Oaxaca* announced that the government would start "comprehensive work of sanitation and paving in the city" costing over 190,000 pesos. Over the following two years the newspapers were replete with information about the paving of roads around the *zócalo*, to the bourgeois neighborhoods to the north, and to the poorer *vecindades* to the south.[47] A government agent who arrived in the city in January 1949 commented on how the newly paved roads had produced a general sense of contentment in the city: people felt that "even if Vasconcelos is not doing everything, at least he is doing something."[48] The governor was quick to point out his achievements in this area. In his report of 1947 he announced that his government had improved over eight hundred meters of sewage piping. Three years later he claimed his government had paved forty-seven thousand square meters of the city.[49]

As well as tackling problems of urban taxation and infrastructure, Vasconcelos also had to deal with the effects of macroeconomic crises on the urban population. During the 1940s Mexico suffered two major economic problems: price inflation and the stagnation of real wages. Jeffrey L. Bortz estimates that between 1939 and 1950 prices in Mexico City rose by 359.9 percent. But real weekly wages in the Federal District dropped from a base of 100 in 1939 to 60.13 in the same period.[50] Although few statistics exist for Oaxaca, a similar pattern is evident, and complaints over price rises for staple products—particularly maize, beans, milk, and eggs—were frequent throughout the period and may have been another cause of the movement of January 1947.[51] In July 1948 the problem reached crisis point as Alemán's government was forced to devalue the peso. There is little research concerning the social and political impact of the devaluation, but it appears that protests by groups of every political proclivity were frequent.[52] In Oaxaca Vasconcelos attempted to maintain control by forcing his allies among the commercial elite to keep prices down. A week after the devaluation on 21 July, Vasconcelos met with Enrique Tort from the Ministry of the Economy and a group of merchants and industrialists from Oaxaca City. Joel Díaz, the head of the chamber of commerce, claimed that his members were disposed to cooperate with the federal and state governments. As a sign of collaboration, the merchants signed an accord promising to maintain prices at the level of the week before the devaluation.

They appointed a committee to watch over any infringements of the promise, including luminaries of the *vallistocracia* such as Jesús Torres Barriga, Lauro Candiani Cajiga, and Francisco Cue.[53] In a letter to Tort, Vasconcelos wrote that he had told the merchants "to keep to our agreement of 1 August." He warned them that if they did not, they risked social unrest and "the provocations of groups of a communist or anarchist tendency."[54] The *vallistocracia*, many of whom were linked to the political fate of the regime, duly complied in return for a reprieve from taxes on basic foodstuffs. On 19 August they met in the governor's palace, and the next day they published the maximum prices for the staple goods. On 21 August they established "tribunals of honor" to watch over each commercial sector. The letters in the municipal archive seem to testify to the efficacy of this piece of self-regulation. Wealthy merchants who stepped outside the regulations were duly named, shamed, and fined. But it seems that over the short term, the mercantile elite made an effort to appease the city's urban poor. There are no extant letters of complaint against the city's large merchants for continued abuse of the pricing directive. The normally critical newspapers, *El Chapulin*, *La Nueva Vida*, and *La Opinión*, are silent on the matter. Moreover, when the Huerta brothers started to increase the price of eggs in preparation for the Day of the Dead in October 1948, they were fined and told to keep their prices under the agreed limit.[55]

Many of the governor's urban policies were designed to limit the ambit of social protest, to stop the evident causes of disquiet. However, Vasconcelos wanted not only to halt the cycle of urban protest but also to co-opt these powerful social groups into the governing coalition. As a result, he also took a particular interest in improvements to the centers of urban life, the markets. In early

March 1947 the governor visited the Benito Juárez Maza market. After listening to the complaints of the vendors he promised to build a clean, efficient, and modern market with the assistance of an elected group of market vendors.[56] The following week the UEM and the CDEM appointed two men and one woman to the committee. They demanded the reconstruction of the market "that for so long has been forgotten by the municipal and state authorities" and the erection of new stalls.[57] By July 1947 the councilman for the markets, reflecting Vasconcelos's penchant for administrative transparency, offered his first report to the unions. Using the popular market names rather than their official nomenclature, he informed the vendors that he had completed the construction of five doors in the Carmen Alto market, a gutter around the roof of the Benito Juárez Maza market, a water pipe leading to La Merced market, and a new public bathroom in La Industria market. He apologized for some of the less scrupulous tax agents under his command and promised they would be reprimanded and possibly dismissed.[58] This policy of appeasement was capped by a piece of conciliatory theatre. On 15 September Vasconcelos organized a dance in the Benito Juárez Maza market and invited all the *locatarios* to attend. The following day the governor appointed the leader of the 1947 strike, Dolores "La Diabla" Gonzáles, as the representative of the Patria. She was invited to ride on the main float in the capital's celebration of Independence. Over the next three years the newspapers and government reports were replete with affirmations of the state governor's generosity toward the markets. For example, in July 1949 the new Ex-Marquesado market was opened with the governor, municipal president, and musicians of the state band in attendance. The councilman for the markets declared that "the government of Eduardo

Vasconcelos is with the men and women of the market," and for this reason "not one tax ha[d] been increased" over the past two years. The new market even included a kindergarten for children of employees, funded by the state government.[59] Similarly, when President Alemán arrived in the city in April 1950 one of his first tasks was to open the "Miguel Alemán" secondary school, right by the main market.[60] The following month the UEM thanked the council and the government for their "generosity and largesse" over the past three years.[61]

During his governorship Vasconcelos maintained a delicate equilibrium between his two main political constituencies, the *vallistocracia* and the artisans, market vendors, and urban workers who had composed the city's popular social movements. In order to preserve this balance he often demanded certain short-term sacrifices from the economic elite. Prices were kept reasonably, if not extremely, low. The fiscal burden was transferred from the urban poor and middle class to large agricultural producers. However, Vasconcelos was at best a cautious populist and at worst paternalistic patrician. Democracy was still to be the preserve of the educated elites. The governor's opinion of popular electoral democracy was made clear during the first year of his tenure. In the months before the pre-elections for the PRI candidacy for local deputy in June 1947, the water and electricity users and the CDEM had approached Austreberto Aragon and demanded that he run for the position. Although Aragon claimed he was "no politician," he eventually relented and agreed to compete.[62] His supporters met regularly by the Benito Juárez Maza market and handed out propaganda among the city's residents.[63] Vasconcelos remained unmoved and instead put forward as candidate a *vallistocracia* academic, Alberto Vargas.[64]

According to *La Tribuna*, the PRI assembly of 11 June was attended only by local bureaucrats, who had been forced to attend and vote for Vargas. The various social groups claimed that the internal elections had been a "farce" and that many of their names had been used in petitions on behalf of Vargas without their permission.[65] For the next two months they attempted to put forward Aragon as an independent candidate. On 29 June a supportive newspaper claimed they held a huge demonstration of more than ten thousand people and chanted Aragon's name.[66] In response, the same newspaper claimed, Vasconcelos's government resorted to fraud and only handed out electoral credentials to members of the PRI.[67] In a move that prefigured future attempts to employ a policy of divide and rule among market organizations, Vasconcelos offered the UEM a position on the municipal council in return for support for Vargas's candidacy. Emiliano Bolaños accepted the position, and the UEM voted to support the official candidate despite some reservations.[68] Vargas inevitably won. In the week after the election *El Chapulin* gave its opinion on the recent vote. As the January movement had overthrown "one of the clay idols of the government," people had "began to believe in the efficacy of the state's promises of democracy." During the recent elections the "people of Oaxaca genuinely believed that they were going to elect their representatives," that they were going to "be actors in the first and greatest democratic act in Oaxaca's history." Instead, it claimed, the "revolutionary hopes for democracy ha[d] been ruined."[69] The governor's fear of electoral democracy was demonstrated throughout his four years of government. Three years later he would allow the remarkably unpopular Spaniard Mateo Solano to take a place on the local council.[70]

However, if electoral democracy remained closed to the vast

majority of urban society, other avenues of political expression did appear. Following the rhetoric of the Alemán government and the manner of his own arrival in the governor's chair, Vasconcelos was forced to pay lip service to popular politics and democratic ideals.[71] In his speech of September 1947 Vasconcelos announced that the annual tradition of giving a political report was a "democratic principle" and testament to "the people's sovereignty."[72] Under the Porfirian paternalism of the *vallistocracia*, too, there lurked the vestiges of certain liberal democratic principles, in particular the liberty of the press. The official newspaper, *La Voz de Oaxaca*, and the semiofficial newspaper, *El Globo*, both lauded freedom of expression. Jorge Iturribarría wrote that the practice of "putting a black flag over all the newspapers that were outside the official camarilla" had ended.[73] Mateo Solano wrote a series of articles celebrating Oaxaca's history of political pamphleting, as long as it was "energetic, healthy and just."[74] Freedom of the press tied into Vasconcelos's drive for political transparency. The official newspaper would openly print disavowals of the state government, which the governor would answer in print. In April 1950 a columnist for *La Prensa* published a vitriolic attack on Vasconcelos, claiming he was a lazy, intemperate drunk, prone to wiling away his days listening to Wagner and ordering his pistoleros to shoot political opponents. *La Provincia*, the new incarnation of *La Voz de Oaxaca*, printed the article in full before publishing the governor's reply.[75]

The rhetoric of liberty of expression was accompanied by an explosion of newspapers published by private presses in Oaxaca. *El Momento*, the newspaper of the water, electricity, and market movements, was reincarnated as *El Chapulin* and published its first edition in March 1947. The newspaper of the January strike,

La Nueva Vida, continued. *La Opinión*, which seemed to develop connections to the Partido Popular, started to roll out editions in August 1947.[76] *La Tribuna, Donaji, Oaxaca Popular, Cuadernos de Oaxaca*, and *El Estudiante* were all published during the period.[77] These newspapers freely challenged Vasconcelos's administration, demanding that promises to end *alcabalas*, monopolies, high rents, and high prices should be fulfilled. They also reached into the countryside, offering revelations about the latest violent confrontations and criminal extortions of the government's tax collectors, judges, and agents of the public ministry.[78]

One of the most interesting aspects of this journalistic free-for-all was the emergence of articles that reflected the growing political importance of women in the city. Previous attempts to gain female readers had relied on articles about cooking, embroidery, and housekeeping. *Cuadernos de Oaxaca* ran a monthly series on professional Oaxacan women written by Ofelia Montiel de Castro.[79] An engaging column was *La Opinión*'s "Entre comadres," a satirical contribution relating the conversations of two female market vendors. Although the article had a rather patronizing comic value, it reflected poor women's growing political importance and, to an extent, their views. The two *comadres* would discuss water and electricity supplies, the continued charging of *alcabalas*, Vasconcelos's gubernatorial style, and their attachment to Austreberto Aragon.[80]

During his governorship Vasconcelos attempted to cement the loyalty of the city's market vendors, artisans, and urban workers who had brought him to office. He offered a series of material improvements in water and electricity supplies, paving and market infrastructure. He also reconfigured the tax system and removed *alcabalas* and commercial monopolies. Yet he still refused to offer these groups an active role in the electoral politics of the city, although he did allow an unprecedented degree of press liberty. Consequently, his achievements were impressive, if not entirely comprehensive. During UEM meetings in 1949 representatives of the PRI were allowed to speak.[81] By July 1950 the UEM supported the PRI candidate for the city's local deputy. Inverting their protests of previous years, they now held a march in support of the government from the *zócalo* to the IACA and then to the gubernatorial palace.[82] Nevertheless, room for independent political action still remained. First, the PRI's relationship with the urban masses depended on results. Political backing relied on economic, social, and political favors. Without these, support would quickly melt away. Second, although some members of the UEM had agreed to join the PRI, the CDEM remained outside the ambit of the national party.[83] Third, the degree of press freedom still provided space for criticism of the elite governing coalition.

Vasconcelos and the Countryside

In many ways Vasconcelos's policy outside the capital city followed the national template of the Alemán government. An emphasis on large-scale agricultural production, the end of land expropriations, and the protection of small properties allowed local landowners to recapture some of the gains made by peasants during Cardenismo. At the same time, state branches of the CNC and the CTM concentrated on disciplining their members and gradually lost political ground to the Confederación Nacional de Organizaciones Populares (CNOP). But three distinct phenomena disrupted the general narrative of conservatism, centralization, and control. First, in areas where Cárdenas's social policies had benefited the peasant and worker populations, there was a move toward alliances with more radical organizations. Second, in more remote areas where Cardenismo had been obstructed by local elites, caciques, or government weakness, indigenous resistance to state projects started to increase. Third, Vasconcelos was forced to maintain and even support caciques whose political savvy had allowed them to survive the purges of the previous governors.

Vasconcelos's speeches are replete with demands for increased agricultural production. In his first report to the local congress in September 1947 the governor announced that it was lamentable that "no local government" had "taken any efficient action to push forward the backward and disastrous state of our agriculture." He suggested studies of the agricultural possibilities of each region, colonization and irrigation projects, and the protection of landholdings of livestock on the coast. He also suggested the construction of roads from the capital to the important coffee-growing area of Pochutla and to the Tuxtepec region of commercial agriculture. At the same time he minimized the possibilities of further expropriations, arguing that in many areas there was simply not enough land to hand out.[84] His annual reports in the following years likewise stressed the need for greater agricultural production.[85] He commissioned Moises de la Peña and Jorge Tamayo to investigate means by which the state's economy could be improved.[86] Vasconcelos's close friend, Tamayo glossed over the remaining inequalities of land tenure and hailed the Alemanista triumvirate of irrigation, colonization, and road building.[87] The decisions regarding land expropriations listed in the *Periódico Oficial* reflected this agrarian policy. In 1949 the paper listed fourteen acts denying *ejidal* grants and six certificates of exemption. There were only six land grants. All of these came from foreign individuals such as Lewis Lamm, Horace Corbin, and Joseph di Giorgio, who had left Oaxaca decades before. The following year revealed a similar pattern. There were five denials of ejidos and five certificates of exemption. There were seven land grants, but again these concentrated on the lands of foreign investors.[88]

One of the political ramifications of this policy in the regions was the rise of the CNOP. Although Oaxaca's official party had contained a popular sector since 1943, it had been used only sparingly in the Central Valleys, the Isthmus, and Huajuapam—to unseat radical peasant organizations, uncooperative caciques, and Panista merchants, respectively.[89] However, in 1948 the central committee of the confederation sent a representative to Oaxaca to "reorganize the municipal committees of the CNOP." According to the official newspaper they were "in complete disarray" due to the confusion sown by certain unnamed "propagandists."[90] Over the next two months the CNOP envoy met appointed district delegates, who were ordered to found municipal organizations and distribute propaganda throughout the state.[91] By the end of the year the PRI's state committee claimed there were branches of the CNOP "in every district and almost all the municipalities."[92] Vasconcelos also sought to discipline, control, or if necessary exclude the more radical elements of the CNC and the CTM. In a speech to the CNC in March 1947, the governor urged a retreat from "pointless squabbles" and the embracing of a policy of "peace and love."[93] The same year, Vasconcelos announced to assembled worker organizations the need for "cooperation with capital" rather than the "never-ending class conflict."[94]

Reactions to the governor's policy of party management differed across the state. In Tuxtepec Vasconcelos started his campaign by imposing a compliant member of the CNOP as local deputy. Although the CNC claimed that its candidate had won the internal elections, the regional committee of the PRI declared the CNOP candidate and former Porfirian general Otilio Díaz Olguin the victor.[95] A year later when the CNC claimed victories in Tuxtepec's municipal elections, Vasconcelos nullified the elections due to "irregularities" and used military force to impose juntas of civil administration.[96] The CNOP, which had now merged with the traditional camarilla of Tuxtepec planters led by Francisco Moreno Z., was able to impose Jorge Tamayo as federal deputy.[97] The CNC, seemingly more in hope than expectation, put up as candidates Macario Gutíerrez Navaro and Carlos Belleza, but the regional committee of the PRI quickly annulled their candidacy as they were born outside the state.[98] As the popular sector imposed itself upon Tuxtepec, peasants and workers were given a stark choice: cooperation or radicalization and possible death. During the 1930s and 1940s the CTM had provided an alternative to the CNC in the region. But during Vasconcelos's governorship it was subsumed by the discipline of the national party. CTM peasant organizations were ordered to join the CNC.[99] The moderate members of the confederation, such as Genaro Yescas and Luis Roy Jr., formed the anticommunist group of the local party.[100] As a result, the CTM dropped from political scene and its candidates failed to run for the local or federal deputy positions.

The remnants of the radical CTM, led by Daniel Muñoz Estefan, formed the Federación Unica de Trabajadores del Estado de Oaxaca, part of the Confederación Unica de Trabajadores (CUT), the organization created by communist dissidents from the CTM in March 1947.[101] Although the CUT was relatively weak in the rest of the state, in Tuxtepec it remained a potential threat to the national party. In Loma Bonita, which had become the center of Mexico's flourishing pineapple industry, the CUT controlled two large unions. Over the next four years the new confederation held strikes against the *ejidal* bank, which was pressuring campesinos for repayment of their debts, and against the *finqueros* and merchants who refused to rewrite a collective contract.[102] As expected, Vasconcelos supported the conservative slate in the municipal elections. Although the CUT put up a distant relation of Miguel Alemán as candidate, the town's elite established a voting booth in the house of a rich Italian merchant "where all the rich men of the village went to vote." They then sent pistoleros to destroy the voting boxes in the surrounding villages. The elite candidate allegedly declared, "I don't need the popular vote. I have money and money buys everything."[103] The pattern was common throughout the region. The new ruling class of compliant CNC leaders and recent CNOP affiliates allowed landowners to restart their campaign against the region's peasants. Teachers, CUT organizations, and *ejidal* committees complained that pistoleros regularly attacked their lands, burning schools, bridges, and houses and shooting peasants.[104]

Similarly, the government's campaign of social conservatism, union control, and anticommunism also affected the railway workers of Matias Romero, Juchitán. At the national level the break of the Sindicato de Trabajadores Ferrocarrileros de la Republica Mexicana from the CTM had been met by co-option and force. Radical communist dissidents were removed and replaced with compliant "*charro*" leaders.[105] But resistance to state control remained. Railway workers had ruled the local council in Matias Romero since breaking free from the *cacicazgo* of Heliodoro Charis in the early 1940s. A succession of workers had laid the foundations for the new municipal palace, constructed the new school, and protested about the price rises of the past five years.[106] In 1948 Vasconcelos allied with Charis and attempted to remove the railway workers from power. In October he overturned the PRI's internal election, and two months later he invoked the rhetoric of anticommunism and imposed a council headed by the local merchant Eliseo Matus.[107] The railway workers refused the appointment and on 1 January used armed force to place their own council, composed of four railway workers, a carpenter, and a peasant, in the municipal palace. Matus was forced to run a separate government from his own residence.[108] Finally, on 25 January the head of the state PRI announced that Matias Romero had been taken over by "dangerous communists." Soldiers invaded the palace, arrested the council members, and imposed the official slate.[109]

The peasants of Tuxtepec, the workers of Matias Romero, and other groups with connections to outside radicals—for example, the plantation workers of Pochutla and the peasants of Rio Grande, Coixtlahuaca—sought refuge from the central and state governments' policies in left-wing unions that had broken off from the increasingly exclusive national organizations. In areas where state organizations had penetrated less deeply, the government's program to neutralize peasant radicalism and protect large landowners caused less organized, more traditional forms of opposition. In March 1947 the governor removed all but three of Jamiltepec's municipal councils and replaced them with members of the mestizo elite.[110] At the same time he engineered the return of military units to the region. Over the next four years, soldiers and mestizos extorted from and intimidated the indigenous population. A mixture of ethnic oppression, corruption, and the shift in the fiscal burden toward regions of commercial agriculture led tax collectors and municipal presidents to demand more money of the Mixtec peasants. In 1949 in Santa María Huazolotitlán "indigenous peasants" claimed that the municipal president had stolen the crops from the school parcel and forced the village's inhabitants to pay 4.50 pesos a month for education. They asked that the government "impose an Indian on the municipal presidency."[111] In Santiago Pinotepa Nacional the municipal president was charging thirty pesos for marriage registration and a hundred pesos for nonattendance at conscript training.[112] The soldiers often acted as the debt collectors of the local government, threatening villagers with prison or worse if they refused to pay. In Mártires de Tacubaya one of the few remaining indigenous municipal presidents complained that the soldiers stationed in the village were supporting the extortion racket of the local tax collector.[113] *Ejidatarios* also accused soldiers of burning villages, raping women, and killing anyone whom they deemed a bandit.[114]

As the CNC had been an elite organization since 1940 and the CTM had never attempted to control the region, peasant resistance in Jamiltepec lacked the organizational structure of Tuxtepec. Instead Mixtec opposition to the landowning elite was twofold. First, peasants attempted systematic tax evasion. By the late 1940s isolated refusals to pay taxes at the village level had become coordinated acts of civil disobedience as almost all the ejidos in Jamiltepec refused to pay the state taxes on the *ejidal* lands. While some excused their nonpayment with tales of natural disasters and livestock invasions (probably true), others maintained a classic discourse of moral economy. Demanding "justice," they argued that although they were "prepared to pay" an amount they believed to be "in accord with the law and the production of our lands," anything above this was extortionate. By 1948 the campesinos had started what the local tax collector called a "tax strike." "Some agrarian communities are denying their contribution in a systematic manner, sure that if they continue waiting it will all be forgiven by the Treasury of the State."[115] Second, Mixtec peasants around Mártires de Tacubaya took up social banditry against the mestizo elite under the leadership of Moises and Domingo Martínez Baños. Although the bands of peasants and former *ejidatarios* rustled cattle and stole crops, they also carried out targeted assassinations of particularly rapacious members of the local elite. During the late 1940s they murdered the municipal presidents of Santiago Llano Grande and El Maguey and livestock owner Salvador Montero.[116]

In the Triqui village of San Juan Copala, there was a similar process of repression and violent radicalization. Although the cacique of Juxtlahuaca, Celestino Guzmán, had been killed in 1941, the tensions between the state and the Triquis remained. The Triquis maintained a strategy of defensiveness to all outside incursion, and as a result state representatives continued to condemn the group as irredeemably uncivilized. Despite the employment of a single Triqui teacher, SEP reports claimed that the schools were still empty in 1946. Two years later Primitivo Pérez wrote an extensive account of the Triqui region. His "study of the psychology of the pueblo" led him to conclude that these people were "a primitive race" who refused the comforts of village living and instead preferred to inhabit hovels in the "steep mountains around." The divisions opened up by the introduction of coffee and the consequent privatization of communal property remained. Carrancista and Zapatista barrios continued the cycle of violence throughout the early 1940s.

What one government representative called the "chaotic state" of San Juan Copala forced the governor to attempt to bring the region under control. In February 1949 Vasconcelos passed an act to remove San Juan Copola's municipal status and place it under the ambit of Santiago Juxtlahuaca.[117] The move was accompanied by the usual racist rhetoric. One member of the local legislature declared that the Triquis lived "like savages in the hills, assaulting and hunting those against them." The move proved disastrous for the stability of the region as it broke down any vestiges of community loyalty. The cycle of intraethnic violence increased as closer contract with mestizos encouraged the burgeoning coffee trade and an increasing black market in guns. The Triquis turned their arms not only on one another but also on visiting representatives of their new municipal *cabecera*. In April 1950 hidden assailants shot at the local judge. A month later they took pot shots at a visiting tax inspector. The perceived lawlessness of the area precipitated increased militarization. Federal soldiers now accompanied any representatives of the state or local governments in their efforts to track down recalcitrant taxpayers or indigenous sharpshooters. Despite government repression, the Triqui fighters often escaped official prosecution, fleeing to the hills before military or state officials could capture or kill them. The situation in San Juan Copala came to a head in 1956. Triqui gunmen killed one particularly unscrupulous local army official. In response, the government used aircraft to bomb the pistoleros' barrio.[118]

The governor's attempts to increase central control and rein in peasant radicalism affected broad swathes of state's countryside. Yet the policy was far from uniform. Vasconcelos was aware of the regional importance of the caciques, who controlled areas such as Juchitán, the Región Mixe, and Miahuatlán. Consequently, in some regions the state government bypassed corporatist organizations and left power in the hands of the surviving strongmen. During the presidency of Manuel Avila Camacho, Heliodoro Charis had confronted considerable opposition from teachers, workers, and the popular sector in Juchitán. In 1946 Sánchez Cano had managed to impose municipal authorities on most of region's towns, but with Vasconcelos's support, Charis was able to reverse the steady erosion of his power. In March 1947 the governor announced reelections or the imposition of juntas of civil administration on all the region's towns.[119] With the municipal councils in place, Charis was able to impose his candidate, Enrique Jiménez, on the local deputyship.[120] Once political competition dropped away, Charis attempted to reinforce his supporters' backing. As a supreme political pragmatist, he forgot his previous demands for socialist education, which had cemented Cárdenas's support, and moved toward a more contemporary emphasis on infrastructure, irrigation, and agricultural production.

The state and national archives overflow with letters from the cacique suggesting building programs and irrigation schemes in the region. In March 1948 he asked Alemán for a hundred thousand pesos in credit for the construction of a canal linking the Estero stream to the Military Colony Alvaro Obregón.[121] Two months later he asked for seventy thousand pesos to repair Juchitán de Zaragoza's local school, education center, hospital, and X-ray machine.[122] He repeated his demands two years later for the extension of the Tehuantepec irrigation scheme to the colony and added a request for a road from the colony to the nearby village of Santa María Xadani.[123] The age of *civilismo* altered not only the substance but also the manner of cacique's requests.

Administrators were no longer harangued in rough Spanish. Instead Charis's wife began arriving at the president's residence with trays of "little delicacies" for Alemán.[124] Finally, Charis also started to build an extended network of party organizations. It appears that the growing exclusivity of the PRI system forced the cacique into moving from traditional means of control toward the party organizations he had eschewed for so long. By 1950 a government agent affirmed that Charis was the secretary-general of the Sindicato de Salineros in Juchitán as well as leader of "all the *ejidatarios* and popular sectors in the region."[125]

The state government's acceptance, even encouragement of Charis's growing organizational power presented the central government with a dilemma. By making Vasconcelos governor, Alemán had broken with the implicit policy of balancing weak state governors with local caciques and had risked the emergence of a powerful interregional alliance. In particular, with Vasconcelos's support Charis had started to interfere in the politics of the Región Mixe, Tehuantepec, Loma Bonita, and Tuxtepec as part of his campaign for the 1950 governorship.[126] Alemán had no desire to promote the creation of another state caudillo. As a result, during the elections for federal deputies in 1949, the national committee of the PRI reminded Charis of the rules of the game. Charis put forward his own candidate, Juchiteco doctor Macedonio Benitez. Opposing him was Graciano Pineda, an employee of the state railway company. Benitez won the vote of the PRI assembly without opposition on 10 April. But the PRI national committee immediately nullified the election and ordered plebiscites in Ciudad Ixtepec for the first week of May.

A government agent at that event described the arrival of busloads of Benitez's supporters "attended to by Ixtepec's municipal president" and "readily supplied with food and mescal." At 11:00 a.m. the PRI representative, Fernando Riva Palacios, counted the supporters of either side. Benitez clearly won, with five thousand supporters to Pineda's two thousand. Riva Palacios even congratulated Benitez on his victory. Two days later the national committee of the PRI nonetheless announced Pineda's triumph. Complaints flooded in from all over Juchitán. The town held two protest marches demanding the "justice and democracy" which Alemán had promised. Charis went to Mexico City, where he visited the president. It appears that he was suitably chastised. The "continuous marches" Benitez's supporters had undertaken to hold melted away.[127] The Alemán government would permit regional caciques as long as they limited their political aspirations.

In the Región Mixe Luis Rodríguez had weathered a series of difficult years under the Sánchez Cano's government. The villages that had refused to accept Santiago Zacatepec as the ex-district capital had forced the cacique from his hometown. However, days after the governor's resignation, Rodríguez returned. Over the next four years Vasconcelos openly supported the cacique's efforts to win back control of the region. In his report of 1948 Vasconcelos condemned the rebellious villagers of San Juan Juquila Mixes. He argued that "far from attending the reasons of ethnic order that the Region ha[d] put in place," they had "instead been causing difficulties." He described them as "people who do not desire the growth of their pueblos, but rather their annihilation in fratricidal wars." Circular 26 released on 27 May 1948 employed the rhetoric of *mexicanidad* and ordered the villagers of the Región Mixe to "stop their disorder and show they are worthy Mexican citizens" by accepting Santiago Zacatepec as the ex-district *cabecera*.[128] Rodríguez was given free rein to track down "bandits" from uncooperative villages. There were multiple complaints from San Juan Juquila Mixes, San Pedro y San Pablo Ayutla, and San Juan Mazatlán as Rodríguez burned houses, kidnapped merchants, stole crops, and murdered peasants.[129] Resistance, as before, took the form of armed revolt, but Rodríguez now had the advantage of a small garrison and a seemingly inexhaustible supply of arms from the local military commander.[130]

In Miahuatlán Genaro Ramos was also allowed to reestablish his *cacicazgo*. In 1947 Ramos imposed an eighty-year-old merchant, Emilio Alvarez Vasseur, as local deputy and a compliant regional chief of the CNC.[131] Over the next four years he led a band of armed *agraristas* from Miahuatlán's handful of ejidos against his political enemies. The men of San José Llano Grande complained that on 26 November 1949, Ramos arrived in the village with sixty "well-armed followers" and stole money, goats, sheep, and mescal.[132]

From 1947 to 1950 there was a sustained attempt to reformulate the government's relationship with the countryside. The governor emphasized production, infrastructure, and the protection of small, medium and even large landholders at the expense of further redistribution of land. This demanded the regimentation, co-option, centralization, and if necessary exclusion of peasant and worker groups. Many struggled on within the PRI and saw the CNOP gradually erode the electoral gains of the CNC and the CTM. Others joined new radical organizations, including the CUT and the PCM. Still others rebelled, fought off military attacks, and eventually took to the hills. However, the framework of Oaxaca's politics, and in particular the maintenance of certain powerful *cacicazgos*, limited the state governor's project. Charis, Rodríguez, and Ramos were still permitted a degree of military, administrative, and political freedom.

Conclusion

Vasconcelos's term witnessed a profound transformation in the relationships among central, state, and local governments in Oaxaca.
For the first time since the Revolution, the president attempted to
govern the state through members of the *vallistocracia*. National
and local elites bypassed conflictive issues of church-state relations, land expropriations, and workers rights, and with a shared
sense of ideological purpose they now ruled the state through a
direct chain of command. Cárdenas and Avila Camacho's policies
of political equilibrium shifted toward the political pyramid of
revisionist historiography. As a result, this new ruling camarilla
also followed the socioeconomic and political policies of the central government. Vasconcelos emphasized the need for modernization, large-scale commercial agriculture, protection of private
property, and party discipline. In many ways the period saw the
definite local implementation of the policies of economic conservatism, centralization, and authoritarianism that revisionist historians and political scientists have posited for the earlier presidency of Manuel Avila Camacho. Although Oaxaca's peasant
and worker organizations had been commanded by the state's
political elite since the late 1930s, it took another decade for this
process of political co-option to filter down to the local level.
Here, as Frans Schryer and Tomás Martínez Saldaña have argued, Alemán's presidency precipitated a civilian alliance of the
PRI and the rural bourgeoisie.[133] This decline of popular socioeconomic and political demands was only made possible by the
growing central support for the popular sector and the increasing role of the army as a political police force. The developments
in Oaxaca conform in many respects to what Luis Medina has
called "the modernization of authoritarianism," the shift from

the early postrevolutionary politics of co-option, negotiation, and inclusion toward a more rigid politics of centralization, presidentialism, and exclusion.[134]

However, this process of political control was uneven, ragged, complex, and deeply contested. In Oaxaca City Vasconcelos attempted the first sustained campaign to co-opt popular urban forces and the program was largely successful. Provision of paved streets, running water, electricity, and well-furnished markets allowed the governor to manipulate electoral demands and form PRI organizations among influential groups such as the market vendors. But resistance remained and support was conditional on the continuation of government modernization projects. Furthermore, as the next governor would discover, the growing power of independent newspapers permitted the existence of a vigilant and highly critical public sphere. In the countryside the followers of the broad catholic church of Cardenismo did not drift toward Alemán's stripped-down, new state Anglicanism without multiple schisms. In areas of developed industrial or commercial agricultural production such as Matias Romero and Tuxtepec, radical groups of former Cardenistas broke off to form independent unions. In more isolated regions such as Jamiltepec and Juxtlahuaca, recent economic booms, the political vacuum left by the death of former caciques, and growing government control were met by a wave of indigenous radicalization. Political divisions ran along ethnic lines as Mixtec and Triqui peasants contested land expropriations and political impositions with mestizo and Hispanic elites. In regions where indigenous or mestizo caciques had managed to maintain control they were allowed to continue ruling with little interference as long as they limited their ambitions to their own particular fiefdoms.

TEN

The Short Reign of Manuel Mayoral Heredia, 1950–52

The last two years of Miguel Alemán's *sexenio* witnessed the political process of exclusion reach inside the PRI itself. Alemán's changes to Article 27 of the Constitution, the authoritarian repression of the union movements, the promotion of foreign investment, and the political exclusivity of the governing camarilla persuaded a broad cross section of former revolutionaries, Cardenistas, military generals, and businessmen to support the candidacy of Miguel Henríquez Guzmán for president. At first the Henriquistas looked for accommodation within the PRI. However, it soon became clear that the president's supporters sought either Alemán's reelection or the election of his minister of the interior, Adolfo Ruíz Cortines. In late 1950 Henríquez was expelled from the PRI and in January 1951 he announced that he would run for president independently.

Over the following year Henriquistas throughout Mexico attempted to establish a rival political party, the Federación de los Partidos del Pueblo Mexicano (FPPM). In an effort to challenge the PRI, they set up confederations of peasants, workers, teachers and professionals. Henríquez sustained an electoral tour around the country in an attempt to mobilize support. The opposition rhetoric focused on the PRI's betrayal of its revolutionary principles and its erosion of democratic practices.[1] At the same time the PAN and the Partido Popular (PP) also put forward candidates for the presidency. However, despite the illusion of a multiparty election, the results were depressingly one-sided. Ruíz Cortines triumphed with 74.31 percent of the vote. The FPPM, PAN, and PP received 15.87, 7.82, and 1.98 percent respectively.[2] On election day members of the police and army murdered at least seven Henriquistas in central Mexico City.[3] Over the next few years the FPPM disintegrated until it was finally dissolved by the PRI in 1954.[4]

The few historians who have studied the presidential elections of 1952 view the failure of Henriquismo and its subsequent repression as the final dots marking the downward curve toward PRI authoritarianism. Olga Pellicer de Brody and José Luis Reyna argue that the history of the FPPM acted to reinforce the discipline of the PRI and demonstrate the vulnerability of political parties judged unruly or threatening.[5] However, in Oaxaca, local political events delineated a different narrative trajectory. If 1952 was a low point for Mexican democracy at the national level, it was the zenith of nearly a decade of popular urban social movements in Oaxaca. Despite attempts at government intimidation and repression and elite manipulation and co-option, a cross-class coalition of artisans, workers, merchants, students, and, again most important, market women forced the resignation of the state governor, Manuel Mayoral Heredia, in July 1952. Although the election of Mayoral Heredia in 1950 appeared to confirm the PRI's political hegemony in the state, over the next year the governor alienated key interest groups through top-down authoritarian economic, political, and fiscal policies. At the same time Mayoral Heredia failed to nurture the support of Oaxaca City's residents, returning to policies of press repression, fiscal exaction, and commercial monopolization, which culminated in the introduction of a new fiscal code in December 1951. Mayoral Heredia's threat to introduce the code ignited a social movement that lasted from March until July 1952 and ended in his indefinite leave from office. Although this movement has been characterized as the exclusive work of a manipulative commercial elite, it was in fact a popular, gendered affair. As in 1947 market women took advantage of a "political opening" in order to assert their political relevance and gain key concessions.

The Election of 1950

In many ways Manuel Mayoral Heredia was an archetypal Alemanista governor. He was a young modernizing civilian with few links to the state he intended to govern, whose political power emanated entirely from his close relationship with the president. Although he had been born in Oaxaca, he had left the state as a young man to pursue a career as an engineer at the National School of Engineers. Engineering work took him to Veracruz, where he became part of Alemán's governing camarilla and chief of communications in the state. Although he failed to become a federal deputy for Tuxtepec in 1943, three years later the new president rewarded his loyalty with the position of undersecretary of Communications and Public Works.[6] Despite Mayoral Heredia's minimal links to his home state, the gubernatorial elections of 1950 were the least contested since the Revolution. In late September 1949 a government agent visited Oaxaca in order to gauge opinion on the following year's elections. He reported that all the political classes supported Mayoral Heredia. Alemán had apparently indicated his preference by appointing Mayoral Heredia as his representative at the recent popular fiestas in Oaxaca City. The government agent concluded that "all the advantages" were "in favor of Mayoral Heredia."[7]

Opposition to Alemán's chosen candidate was slight. There were rumors that Manuel R. Palacios, a senator and head of the Railway Company of Mexico, would attempt to run for the position, but these soon dissipated. As usual, the gossips of the Isthmus claimed that Heliodoro Charis had his sights on the gubernatorial palace, but there is little evidence of any sustained attempt. There were also reports that Eduardo Vasconcelos favored one of his *vallistocracia* allies, such as Fernando Magro Soto, Manuel Sodi del Valle, Eduardo Bustamante, or Alfonso Pérez Garza, but again none openly spoke out.[8] The only public challenge to Mayoral Heredia came from the municipal president of Oaxaca City, Manuel Canseco Landeros. The city's newspaper *El Chapulin*, which had championed Canseco's honest fiscal administration, suggested in August 1949 that Vasconcelos might favor the appointment of his close friend.[9] Canseco's brother-in-law, Luis Macauley, was also head of the state PRI. During the last months of 1949 other politicians on the edge of the PRI, such as Roberto Ortiz Gris, put forward Canseco as a possible candidate. Ortiz Gris and other future Henriquistas distributed flyers warning voters of Mayoral Heredia's connections to unpopular former governors and announcing that Oaxaca wanted a governor who had lived in the state all his life.[10] In February 1950 Luis Macauley resigned in protest at the PRI's decision to ignore his relative's candidacy.[11]

These complaints notwithstanding, Mayoral Heredia soon established himself as the exclusive candidate of the PRI. In October 1949 he set up the Frente Democratica Oaxaqueña to campaign on his behalf. A month later he resigned from his position in the federal government. By late December the government agent reported that the only propaganda in the state was in favor of the official candidate.[12] The New Year saw Mayoral Heredia walk the familiar steps toward the PRI candidacy and the governorship. Despite the inevitability of the eventual election result, the following six months started to reveal the shape of his short and disastrous tenure. First, Mayoral Heredia's electoral tour clearly mapped out his hierarchy of concerns. He started in Mexico City, where he held a luxurious feast for Oaxaca's ex-patriot community.[13] Having cemented the support of the three branches of the state's PRI in Oaxaca City, the rest of his visit to the state consisted of brief talks with various coffee plantation owners in Miahuatlán, Pochutla, and Juquila.[14]

Second, Mayoral Heredia's electoral entourage reflected his attachment to a small camarilla of fellow Mexico City residents. When he arrived in Oaxaca City on 12 February he was accompanied by Rogelio and Enrique Melgar, Alfonso Unda Ruíz, Leopoldo Calvo Treviño, Guillermo Candiani, and Jesús Bonequi.[15] These men had little or no connection to Oaxaca, but within a year they would all be appointed to Mayoral Heredia's governing cabinet. Third, Mayoral Heredia's speeches expressed a rigorous interpretation of Alemán's doctrine of uneven economic modernization. At the meetings of the CNC, CTM, and CNOP Mayoral Heredia stated that Oaxaca needed increased agricultural production and industrialization. This would be made possible through road building, the encouragement of private investment, new fiscal legislation, and an administrative focus on particular areas of economic potential. He made special mention of the coast, which he called the "granary of Oaxaca."[16] Despite these warning signs, Mayoral Heredia was elected without incident. The senator for Oaxaca reported that the vote passed "in complete tranquility."[17] When Mayoral Heredia arrived in Oaxaca in late November 1950 the local newspaper claimed he was welcomed by over ten thousand Oaxacans chanting his name.[18]

The gubernatorial elections of 1950 seem to demonstrate the effectiveness of Alemán and Vasconcelos's policies of strengthening and disciplining the state's PRI. Internal problems were minimal and, for the most part, were kept inside the party. Outside the political elite, local PRI organizations now read official auguries with ease and acted accordingly, writing letters and petitions in favor of the chosen candidate.[19] However, hindsight offers the historian indications of future problems, including Mayoral Heredia's estrangement from Oaxaca's elite, his attachment to a small camarilla of Mexico City politicians, and his ambitious plans for prospective development.

A Year in Government

The fall of Mayoral Heredia was partly due to various social forces taking advantage of the political opportunity opened up by Mexico's presidential elections and the governor's ham-fisted treatment of public demonstrations. But over the first and only year of his government Mayoral Heredia also succeeded in alienating key rural and urban interest groups by attempting to rush through a policy of modernization and accompanying fiscal reform. In the countryside policies of privatized logging, irrigation, and colonization distanced the governor from former revolutionary peasants in the Sierra Juárez, Juchitán, Tuxtepec, and the coast. At the same time the ambitious modernization project forced Mayoral Heredia to rely on increasing fiscal exactions from the city's urban population.

Mayoral Heredia's first actions as governor were to impose his own governing camarilla. The Mexico City residents who had formed his electoral entourage now took places within the state administration. Jesús Bonequi became minister of the interior, Alfonso Unda Ruíz became state treasurer, Guillermo Candiani was made chief of staff, Leopoldo Calvo Treviño was appointed governor's private secretary, and Manuel Mayor García was made head of police.[20] Mayoral Heredia now attempted to pursue a radical project of agricultural and industrial modernization. In a series of speeches in 1950 and 1951 Mayoral Heredia stressed the "importance of increased agricultural production," "the need for mechanized agriculture," "the necessity for private investment," and the "need for greater infrastructure."[21] During his first year in government he passed a series of laws and decrees in an effort to implement this program. On 14 December 1950 the local legislature passed the annual budget for the year. Spending on roads increased from 1.38 to 2.5 million pesos, and spending on public buildings rose from 1 million to 1.4 million pesos. On the other hand, the education budget was slashed from 1.8 million to 1.28 million pesos.[22] As the figures suggest, road building, especially between areas of real or potential commercial agricultural wealth, was central to Mayoral Heredia's plans. During his electoral tour and the early months of his government he suggested the construction of five new major roads in the state.[23] On 12 July 1951 the local legislature contracted with a construction company and put out state bonds worth 12 million pesos to start work on a stretch from Santiago Pinotepa Nacional to San Juan Bautista Huajuapam de León.[24] Mayoral Heredia also sought huge loans from the central government, 1.8 million pesos for improvements to maize cultivation, 3 million pesos for fifty tractors.[25] In order to encourage industry, the local legislature introduced the Law of Industrial Development in July 1951, which

offered new industries tax subsidies for ten years and old industries similar incentives if they doubled production.[26]

Although previous state governors had consistently paid lip service to ideas of agricultural and industrial modernization, their
projects were modest, limited to a handful of wells, a few irrigation canals, a badly paved road. Mayoral Heredia's program was
both hasty and ambitious. It immediately ran into three major
problems: state administrative corruption, local rural resistance,
and fiscal incapacity. As Alan Knight argues, graft in Mexico covered a broad spectrum ranging from outright stealing through political payoffs to inclusive forms of mass co-option.[27] Governor
González Fernández's creation of the Hydroelectric Company of
Oaxaca in conjunction with members of the city's elite had forced
an unpopular capitalist out of business, offered local capitalists
a stake in the development of the city, and almost coincidentally
offered all concerned substantial financial rewards. But corruption during Mayoral Heredia's brief term was of the most offen-
sive and politically destructive type. First, as his ruling camarilla
came from outside the state, money tended to be funneled away
from the treasury to non-Oaxacan investors, thus sidestepping
local capitalists. Second, the level of corruption during the period actually led to the complete failure of the governor's projected developments.

Corrupt officials did not simply skim percentages from the investments in the state's modernization but committed wholesale
larceny. For example, during 1951 certain members of Mayoral
Heredia's clique, probably led by the state treasurer, Alfonso Unda
Ruíz, sold the contract and bonds for the construction of the
Pinotepa-Huajuapam road to the same man, an Italian investor
and crook called Silvio Oriani. Two years later not one stone of

the proposed road had been laid.[28] Unda Ruíz was also accused of charging the coffee planters of Pochutla more than a hundred thousand pesos a month for the construction of the Puerto Angel–Miahuatlán road, which again failed to materialize.[29] During the popular movement of the following year, newspapers, bulletins, pamphlets, and letters abounded with lurid tales of Unda Ruíz's supposed wealth. *El Imparcial* claimed that he had recently bought a house in Mexico City worth one hundred thousand pesos, three cars worth forty thousand pesos, and a truck for his pistoleros.[30] Even if the claims were exaggerated, in the minds of many the complete lack of actual material progress in Oaxaca confirmed their veracity.

Beyond encouraging massive corruption this state-level project of agricultural and industrial modernization also often forced peasants into the arms of the Henriquistas. Mayoral Heredia's promotion of the forestry industry increased tensions between logging companies and hillside villages. During the first postrevolutionary decades Oaxacan communities had maintained communal practices of forestry and logging.[31] But during the early 1950s small logging companies supported by the governor started to infringe on these communal forests. In February 1951 Mayoral Heredia wrote to President Alemán on behalf of Manuel F. García, who owned a logging company in Veracruz and wanted to extend his business into the Sierra Juárez. Mayoral Heredia argued that García would "exploit the forests in a rational manner."[32] By late 1951 members of the Unión Fraternal de Ayuntamientos de la Sierra Juárez, which had remained loyal to the previous governors in exchange for political and economic autonomy, were sending worried letters to the state governor, emphasizing their rights over communal lands.[33] Similarly in San Pedro el

Alto, the committee of communal lands, backed by former members of the PCM, contested rights over the forests above Zimatlán with a Mexico City–based company. The committee would form one of the first groups to join the Henriquistas.[34]

In Tuxtepec local resistance to the Papaloapan dam project dovetailed with discontent over the local control of peasant unions to form a series of Henriquista groups. The president announced the plan for the creation of the Alemán Reservoir in February 1947. Engineers proposed that by constructing a dam at Temascal, the government would be able to drain the Papaloapan basin, which was famously prone to flooding, develop an effective transport network, increase modern commercial agricultural production, and generate electricity.[35] As the illustration by Miguel Covarrubias demonstrates, the plan was deeply uneven. While it offered benefits of modern industry, agriculture, and transportation to the state of Veracruz, the indigenous people of Oaxaca were effectively banished from their villages to make way for the new reservoir.[36] During Mayoral Heredia's tenure engineers, representatives of the newly established Instituto Nacional Indigenista (INI), and teachers descended on the villages of San Miguel Soyaltepec, San Pedro Ixcatlán, and San José Independencia in an effort to persuade twenty thousand Mazatec inhabitants to move to alternative lands.[37]

At the same time members of the CUT, especially in the pineapple-growing region of Loma Bonita, started to form Henriquista groups.[38] By 1951 they were in contact with the Mazatec peasants of the Papaloapan basin and encouraged resistance to the government project and support for the opposition presidential candidate.[39] Municipal presidents, supported by Mayoral Heredia,

FIG. 8. "Mapping Modernity": Miguel Covarrubias's interpretation of the planned Alemán Reservoir in Tuxtepec. Note how the north-south axes have been turned upside down so that the industrial development of Veracruz is in the foreground. The indigenous people of Oaxaca appear as solitary figures in the mountainous background. (Reprinted from *Los Mazatecos y el problema indígena de la Cuenca de Papaloapan* by Alfonso Villa Rojas)

employed harsh repressive measures against the incipient political party. An investigation by the attorney of pueblos from Orizaba offered a detailed account of the problems in June 1951. He recorded interviews with more than thirty peasants from all over the region who complained that municipal authorities in San Lucas Ojitlán, San Miguel Soyaltepec, San Felipe Jalapa de Díaz, and San Juan Bautista Tuxtepec, supported by the head of the CNC, Moises López Guzmán, had removed or murdered incompliant *ejidal* committees and municipal agents, exacted extortionate fines, and threatened further violence. He warned Mayoral

Heredia that the problem was "extremely serious" and that aggrieved peasants were considering rebellion.[40]

Political impositions and modernization projects were also causing local resistance in the Isthmus. Although Heliodoro Charis's loyalty to the PRI precluded the emergence of Henriquismo in the region, tensions between the governor and the local cacique remained until Mayoral Heredia's eventual fall. The first conflict concerned the election of the local deputy in 1950. Charis supported a fellow Juchiteco, Norberto Cortés Rasgado, while Mayoral Heredia backed a close friend, Bulmaro Rueda. According to a government agent Cortés Rasgado won the pre-elections, but these were annulled "to the disgust of everyone," and Rueda was put in power.[41] Rueda proceeded to push through deeply unpopular colonization projects in San Blas and Santa Cruz Tagolaba. According to Mayoral Heredia both villages had enormous quantities of unused land, which they were unable to use through lack of sufficient resources. Rather than offer any more credit, in early 1951 the National Commission of Colonization and the National Bank of Ejidal Credit demanded that both villages divide up their communal lands into lots and hand them over for colonization. They also demanded that the villages start to pay back their remaining debts to the government bank.[42] Although Charis was now sufficiently disciplined to avoid challenging the move directly, he armed men in San Blas and sent a series of querulous letters to President Alemán.[43]

Mayoral Heredia might have survived if his administrative program had simply angered isolated peasants and a handful of loyal PRI caciques. But the costs of modernization also forced the governor into direct confrontation with Oaxaca City's diverse social groups. On 28 December 1950, *El Chapulin* listed hopes for the following gubernatorial term. It appears that Vasconcelos's tenure had diminished traditional demands for market improvements, paving, water and electricity. However, the director of the newspaper sustained calls for an end to commercial monopolies, the abolition of the remaining *alcabalas*, dismissal of the fiscal police and the end to the hated *mordida*.[44] Despite the previous governor's success in co-opting urban social forces into the ambit of the PRI, loyalty still depended on results. As Mayoral Heredia's term passed, it became clear that money for his ambitious projects would come from the city's market vendors. In December 1950 his cousin was elected municipal president of Oaxaca City, and the representative of the UEM was removed from the official PRI slate.[45] During the year there were increasing complaints to the state treasurer concerning his chief of fiscal agents, Guillermo Pigneon. According to *La Tribuna del Sur* and *El Chapulin*, Pigneon had started to charge *alcabalas* on all products entering the markets. Resistance was met by threats, intimidation, and violence.[46] In December 1951 the UEM wrote to the municipal authorities to protest the excessive taxes. They argued that because the market "fulfilled the necessities of the consumer," they did not believe it just "to charge the quota demanded by the authorities."[47] At the same time, Mayoral Heredia reintroduced the commercial monopoly on eggs. In the months before the Day of the Dead, the Huerta brothers again began to charge up to seventy centavos per egg.[48] The measure of urban disquiet was felt in October 1951, when the CNOP met to discuss the nomination of Ruíz Cortines as presidential candidate. The UEM, which had been co-opted briefly by Vasconcelos, now failed to "applaud the machinery of government" but instead complained about local taxes and the lack of party democracy.[49] By February 1952 the

UEM and the CDEM once again allied with the electricity and water protestors. Together they complained about the change of the
council official for the markets.[50]

Mayoral Heredia's fiscal policy also confronted an increasingly
politicized and critical public sphere exemplified by *El Chapulin*'s
general political questionnaire published in April 1951. The survey asked Oaxacan residents to reply to questions such as "Which
governor has done the most for the state?" and "Which governor
has been most honest?" The replies, which unfortunately do not
remain, were posted all over the markets and commercial stores.[51]
Throughout 1951 local newspapers condemned the actions of
the new state governor. Although *La Tribuna del Sur* claimed no
political affiliation, it was quick to censure examples of government corruption and incompetence, exposing the new egg monopoly and a series of municipal scandals.[52] *El Pueblo* was run by
Luciano Muñoz Polo, the son of Tuxtepec union organizer Daniel Muñoz Estefan. The paper openly supported the FPPM campaign and kept Oaxacans in touch with federal and state corruption and the repression of Henriquistas.[53] However, the new
newspapers were unable to compete with *El Chapulin* for political muckraking and witty broadsides. It published open letters to
Mayoral Heredia, Unda Ruíz, and President Alemán protesting
rising prices, unfair taxes, and corrupt officials. *El Chapulin* also
published letters from political opponents from throughout the
state, weekly articles mocking the democratic credentials of the
PRI, and comic songs disparaging the effects of the Revolution.[54]
The level of abuse reached a crescendo during the months leading up to the popular movement in March 1952. Mayoral Heredia responded in an autocratic and repressive manner. He invited
the director of *El Chapulin* to his house, insisted taxes were not

rising, and threatened him with death.[55] A month later he sent two pistoleros to murder Muñoz Polo. The journalist managed to escape only because of his wife's warning shouts.[56] The governor's heavy-handed tactics were in vain; newspapers reported the events and sarcastically pointed to "the new democratic government of Mayoral Heredia" and "his respect for freedom of the press."[57]

Mayoral Heredia's first year in government thus alienated peasants, caciques, and key urban groups. In the countryside his program of modernization increased political disputes in Tuxtepec and opened up divisions in areas such as Juchitán and the Sierra Juárez, which Vasconcelos had left alone. In the city the governor undermined his predecessor's policy of negotiation and co-option by overtaxing small merchants and attempting to repress Oaxaca's only real source of democratic debate, the local newspapers.

The Movement against Mayoral Heredia

The popular movement to topple Mayoral Heredia lasted four months from March to July 1952. In many ways the movement resembled the strike of January 1947. It started with the governor's promulgation of a new tax code. Once more elite and popular demands elided and a cross-class urban coalition emerged. Again government sources attempted to portray the movement as an attempted coup d'état by a manipulative political elite. But there were three principal differences. First, excluded caciques such as Luis Rodríguez and Heliodoro Charis no longer harried the governor from the localities but instead obediently waited on the central government's response. Second, the 1952 protests saw greater participation of the student body both in Oaxaca and throughout Mexico. Third, and perhaps most important, the extended duration of the protests revealed greater tensions within the cross-class coalition than five years earlier. Reading between the lines, the historian can discern a more detailed "hidden transcript" of popular politicking, protest, and mobilization that both government and opposition newspapers attempted to suppress.

On 20 December 1951 *El Chapulin* reported that the state government's budget for the forthcoming year was over 17 million pesos, a rise of nearly 6.5 million pesos from 1951. The newspaper demanded to know how the government planned to raise the extra revenue.[58] Six days later the local legislature responded by passing decree 86, which introduced a new fiscal code.[59] According to government sources, the code was merely aimed at regulating and modernizing the state's chaotic fiscal system. Yet close analysis of the code's 210 articles indicates that the new structure increased taxes on staple goods and the products of commercial agriculture. Some changes affected the capital's poor. Article 205 imposed a sales tax of 7–10 percent on eggs, 4 percent on maize, and 3 percent on livestock. Not only were the charges excessive; they also indicated that the government was going to maintain commercial monopolies on these goods in order to exact the tax. Article 137 doubled the tax on urban properties and introduced a heavy charge on new construction, leading to fears throughout the urban population of rent increases. Other changes penalized the poor and the state's commercial elite. Article 139 increased taxes on the production of maize and beans but also on sesame seeds, coffee, pineapples, and tobacco. Infractions of the new tax law were treated with uncommon severity. Citizens were unable to query or complain about the set tax values of urban or agrarian properties. Tax debts were set not from the date the shortfall was discovered but from the date the money was owed. Furthermore, tax debts were charged at an interest rate of 20 percent per month. As one financial expert from Mexico City commented, the fiscal code was "badly applied to the needs of the government and the economic conditions of the state." Furthermore, it was "very hard to comply with without incurring omissions and infractions that would be harshly punished."[60]

Although the fiscal code was not implemented immediately, during the first three months of the year rumors about the code intensified, fueled by *El Chapulin*'s alarmist editorials and Mayoral Heredia's refusal to make the new law public. Local newspapers now claimed that the owners of dogs and radios would be charged a hundred pesos per year.[61] Eventually the head of the local chamber of commerce announced a series of meetings between five hundred of Oaxaca's merchants and the governor and financial experts from Mexico City, to be held from 20 to 22 March.[62] On the morning of 21 March the merchant elite went to meet Mayoral Heredia, again demanding that the law be stopped. The governor gave in and announced that the code would not be implemented without substantial changes. He announced his decision from the balcony of the government palace and then left the city to celebrate the birthday of Benito Juárez. This promise of further discussion was not sufficient to placate a large section of the city's population. In the afternoon of 21 March students, market vendors, artisans, and workers met in the *zócalo*. Although there are diverse accounts of what happened next, it appears that the crowd entered the cathedral, rang the bells, and called together the town to march on the governor's residence. As the masses approached, soldiers guarding the governor, who had by then returned from the celebrations, opened fire. At least two of the protesters, Enrique Velasco and Arnulfo Aquino Ruíz, died immediately, and eighteen others were injured. Despite the local legislature's abrogation of the law the following day, the demonstrators' deaths prolonged the movement and the commercial strike. On 22 March the protestors met in the *zócalo* again, where they placed coffins containing the two corpses outside the governor's palace. The crowd then moved toward the IACA, where they asked the students and professors for help. By the evening they had formed the Comité Cívico Oaxaqueño (CCO).

During the following week support for the CCO and condemnation of Mayoral Heredia's strong-arm tactics increased both inside and outside the state. Moreover, the governor managed to enhance tensions on 24 March by bringing in truckloads of *ejidatarios* led by the cacique of Miahuatlán, Genaro Ramos, to "keep the peace" in the city. (These men were named *cuerudos* because of their leather coats). On 25 March the armed peasants replied to a shower of stones from the IACA by shooting up the building and beating up demonstrators. At first the central government threw its support behind Mayoral Heredia. The official newspapers and those sympathetic to the PRI accused the demonstrators of links to communism and the FPPM. On 26 March Minister of the Interior Ernesto P. Uruchurtu declared that "in a regime of law, it cannot be allowed that petitions directed to the authorities are accompanied by acts of violence or tumultuous demonstrations." He reminded the protestors that the fiscal code had been countermanded and advised them to complain through the proper channels.

After a meeting on 27 March the CCO sent a delegation to Mexico City to discuss the affair with Uruchurtu. Meanwhile, Mayoral Heredia agreed to dismiss his treasurer, Unda Ruíz, his private secretary, Calvo Treviño, and his chief of staff, Candiani.

The dismissals did little to calm public rancor. Finally, after four days of uncertainty, the delegation returned with an agreement from Uruchurtu. The minister ordered Mayoral Heredia to send home the *cuerudos*, avoid any reprisals, and offer guarantees to the demonstrators. When the shops, stalls, and schools were re-opened and everything had "returned to normality," the government promised to send an investigative team to assess the CCO's accusations. Over the next week it became clear that the central government expected the protestors to wait until after the presidential elections for any final decision on Mayoral Heredia's position. The CCO representatives visited Mexico City again on 22 April but were told that they had to wait until 6 July. The government delegation, the minister of defense, and envoys from the Supreme Court came and went. On 22 April the Supreme Court refused to involve itself in what it classed as an exclusively political matter.

Oaxaca descended into a nervous stalemate, which lasted from April to the end of June. The central government refused to do anything until after the presidential elections. Miguel Henríquez Guzmán failed to visit Oaxaca in order to avoid further inflaming the situation. Mayoral Heredia's pistoleros continued to exact revenge on urban protestors and incompliant rural authorities. Within the movement tensions arose over the direction of the protests. While members of the PAN and rich merchants stressed the need for "tranquility and order," student groups, local newspapers, and market vendors continually reminded the CCO of the need to dismiss the governor. Three days before the elections, the minister of the interior of Oaxaca, Jesús Bonequi, met with the members of the market associations to attempt to dissuade them from continuing the movement after 6 July. The CDEM, the UEM, and more than three thousand supporters bluntly refused. The local newspapers started to whip up enthusiasm for a return to the mobilizations of March. On 7 July the markets, the IACA, and the local normal school closed their doors.

Although Mayoral Heredia again laid the blame on a "handful of communist agitators," pressure on the governor increased. The local newspaper called for his immediate dismissal and the provision of the death penalty for his pistoleros. A delegation from the CCO visited Mexico City to discuss the matter with Uruchurtu and Alemán. Finally, on 24 July Mayoral Heredia requested a leave of absence from the governorship for four months for reasons of health. As news filtered back to Oaxaca, the members of the CCO organized a celebratory march through the city of "all the city's social groups." Meanwhile the local deputies fled to Mexico City to consult the central government over the appointment of the next governor. On 31 July the local legislature passed Mayoral Heredia's request for leave and the next day they appointed his recently installed police chief, Manuel Cabrera Carrasquedo, as interim governor. Although Cabrera Carrasquedo was a political nobody, it seems he was accepted by the masses because of his reluctance to enact reprisals during the preceding months.

The few works on the 1952 movement depict it as a conflict between different elite groups.[63] In the most coherent academic description of the governor's dismissal, Felipe Martínez López argues that the PAN and the local chamber of commerce, which represented the *vallistocracia*, were challenging the political hegemony of Mayoral Heredia and his new bureaucratic elite. Many contemporary accounts support this theory of overarching elite control. Already by 25 March, the government newspaper *Atbisos* claimed that "industrial and commercial leaders" were behind the rebellion.[64] In mid-April, the government newspaper *El Imagen* argued that the leaders of the movement—including Joaquin Acevedo, Luis Castañeda Guzmán, Austreberto Aragon, and the principal students—were all members of the PAN and were protesting for "political reasons only."[65] Chiapas's PRI newspaper, *El Informador*, also claimed that the movement was backed by the PAN's candidates for local deputies, Acevedo, Castañeda Guzmán, and Alfredo Castillo.[66] PRI loyalists likewise laid blame for the movement on the PAN. Benjamin Bolaños Jiménez, the leader of the popular sector in Tlaxiaco, claimed that Acevedo and Castañeda Guzmán, both "fanatical Panistas" and "exploiters of the pueblo," were directing the movement.[67] Even the Communist Party claimed that the PAN and "rich merchants" had taken over the movement by April 1952. Their bulletin warned the people of Oaxaca that the right-wing party was only supporting a return to normality in order to negotiate with the PRI in the future.[68]

There is no doubt that Oaxaca's commercial and academic elite, many of whom were members of the PAN, were involved in the movement. Government agents covering the movement listed forty-four leaders and their political affiliations. Thirteen were members of the PAN.[69] The CCO included the head of the chamber of commerce, Fernando Ramírez de Aguilar, and the important Panistas Acevedo and Ignacio Castro Mantecon.[70] The chamber of commerce was represented at major movement meetings by its vice president, Fortunato Harp.[71] In Mexico City a group of elite Oaxacan ex-patriots led by doctors, academics, and lawyers formed the Comité por la Defensa del Pueblo de Oaxaca.[72] During the three months of political turmoil members of the elite also clearly controlled the movement at key points. University professors dissuaded the people from holding a rally in the Plaza de la Danza on 29 March.[73] Acevedo and other members of the elite led the first CCO delegation to meet the minister of the interior. When he returned to Oaxaca with Uruchurtu's promises on 2 April, he attempted to persuade students and market vendors that they should lift the strike. Despite substantial resistance to the government's offer, Acevedo succeeded in swaying the assembled crowd by reminding them that "a return to normality" five years earlier had led to the dismissal of Sánchez Cano. Castro Manteco and Castañeda Guzmán then addressed the masses outside the IACA, invoking their trust "in God, in the Patria, in History, and in the Regime of Alemán."[74] During April, the *vallistocracia* also started to publish a newspaper, *Noticias del Dia*, which supported the movement but chided the protestors to remain calm.[75] After the CCO delegation returned on 23 April from Mexico City with no fresh promises from the minister of the interior, they managed to appease popular demands for the revival of the strike.[76]

Government accusations of elite political complicity were not limited to the commercial elite and the PAN. Throughout the duration of the movement Mayoral Heredia and his collaborators also claimed that the strike was inspired by the "subversive work" of Henriquistas and communists. In the days following the two deaths Mayoral Heredia and a phalanx of local deputies declared that the opposition party had initiated the strike and the attack on the governor's home for political reasons. They asserted that on 13 March two trucks had arrived in the city driven by men dressed as soldiers, who had gone around the markets handing out "subversive notes" claiming that the new fiscal code would hurt the poor. Over the next week local Henriquista agitators continued to stir up the market vendors. On 19 March the Oaxaca government's official newspaper, *Nuevo Diario*, warned its readers of a potential Henriquista coup. Although the details became hazier, Mayoral Heredia claimed that the two trucks returned on 21 March, handed out guns to the demonstrators, and instigated the attack on his residence. The governor named local Henriquista leaders Jesús Torres Márquez and Rafael Angel Pérez, and PCM leader Graciano Benitez, as the primary agitators. However, he suggested that the movement's puppet masters were former governors Vicente González Fernández and Edmundo Sánchez Cano, who had both sided with the opposition candidate.[77] Over the next three months the government's supporters frequently raised the specter of a Henriquista coup. On 1 April the governor issued a bulletin in Oaxaca warning its inhabitants not to be persuaded by "Henriquistas and communists" to continue the movement.[78] The head of the state's CNC, Moises López Guzmán, also informed peasant groups in the state that the conflict was instigated by a handful of Henriquistas and communists.[79] As the strike resumed in July, accusations of subversive political involvement again resurfaced.[80]

There is substantial evidence that Henriquistas were involved in the movement from the start. González Fernández had served under Henríquez Guzmán during the De la Huerta revolt in Villahermosa, Tabasco.[81] During 1951 he attempted to build a support network for the opposition candidate in the state. He was helped by his relative Jesús Torres Márquez, who had recently finished a remarkably popular spell as treasurer of the municipal council and who agreed to run for senate for the FPPM. While Torres Márquez organized support for the movement in Oaxaca City, the other FPPM senatorial candidate, Roberto Ortiz Gris, organized rallies in Mexico City against the state governor.[82] The government agents' list of forty-four troublemakers included twelve members of the Henriquista party.[83] These included Luciano Muñoz Polo, who ran the rabidly pro-strike newspaper *El Pueblo*. Henríquez backed the movement in speeches to supporters in Ciudad Ixtepec, San Cristobal de las Casas, and Tapachula.[84] There is substantial correlation between a list of Henriquista groups in the state and a list of all the groups who wrote telegrams in support of the movement.[85]

Two less partisan descriptions of the strike also indicate Henriquista involvement. On 28 March the Buro de Investigación Política, which appears to have been a think tank with links to the federal government, wrote a report on events in Oaxaca City.[86] The account claimed that as governor, González Fernández had not only listened to the market vendors during the electricity and water disputes but had also opened up a government pawn shop, which had effectively freed the vendors from taking high interest loans from the commercial elite. Consequently, González Fernández was "the idol of the market vendors" and had successfully formed dozens of committees in the city, which were now working to overthrow the governor.[87] A note from a government agent in Oaxaca confirms this view. The agent claimed to have found notes signed by González Fernández warning vendors of the fiscal code in early March.[88]

However, beneath the accusations and counteraccusations of elite involvement, it is possible to uncover a hidden transcript of popular mobilization by examining the trajectory of the movement and the participation of other political actors. It seems that Panistas and Henriquistas were not so much pulling strings as riding waves of mass discontent. Outside Oaxaca the recent disciplining of the CNC and the local caciques appears to have prevented the kind of mass support that the movement against Sánchez Cano engendered. Despite his disagreement with Mayoral Heredia, Heliodoro Charis maintained a guarded silence. In his single letter to Alemán during the period, he voiced backing for neither side but rather offered the president armed men from his military colony if needed.[89] The council of Juchitán de Zaragoza also avoided clear partisanship and merely asked that the problem be "sorted out peacefully."[90] Moreover, when Henríquez visited the region in May 1952, Charista thugs brutally beat two of his entourage.[91] The Región Mixe under its cacique, Luis Rodríguez, remained remarkably quiet during the entire movement. Genaro Ramos and Tiburcio Cuellar, the caciques of Miahuatlán and Teotitlán respectively, even supported the governor with armed retainers and a few politically motivated assassinations.[92]

But Mayoral Heredia's policies had managed to alienate popular groups in other regions. The municipal authorities of the Sierra Juárez rightly feared that the sale of logging rights endangered the political autonomy they had enjoyed since the presidency of Lázaro Cárdenas. On 28 May the confederation of villages met and decided to support the movement against the governor.[93] The municipal authorities of Santa Catarina Lachatao, Santa María Yavesia, San Juan Chicomezuchitl, and San Miguel Amatlán all complained about recent attempts to impose authorities and start private logging on communal lands.[94] When Mayoral Heredia asked for troops from Ixtlán to march down to the city in support of his governorship, the *serranos* angrily refused.[95] Elsewhere opposition to the governor sprang from hostility to certain caciques. Miahuatlán was one of the first towns to establish an independent civic committee, which condemned Ramos's armed *cuerudos*. Letters from local villages described how Ramos had bribed, forced, or deceived the men into following him to Oaxaca.[96] The civic committee of Tehuantepec also conflated demands for the governor's dismissal with attacks on the hegemony of Heliodoro Charis.[97] Finally, in Huajuapam the traditional hostility of the region's fervent Catholics toward both state and national governments and the consequent support for the PAN in the upcoming elections dovetailed easily with backing for the movement.[98]

Although rural groups took advantage of the political crisis to forward their own protests, it was Oaxaca's urban population that provided the movement's underlying momentum. The mobilization structure of the market again played an important part. Once more the female market vendors formed the majority of demonstrators. Although they allied with elite groups, they resisted co-option and drove the movement forward at key moments. The Buro de Investigación Política located the epicenter of the movement in the huge Saturday market, which is described as a political barometer of state opinion: "When the market approves all is well, when it reproves, nothing can be done. The market of the city of Oaxaca represents the public opinion of all the state. This explains the reason why the actual conflict has been generated in the plaza and the vendors and small merchants have been those lifting their voices in opposition and in protest. It is the market of Oaxaca that is the true and authentic congress of the state."[99] Isolated descriptions of the movement by outraged members of the elite, the tabloid press, and some sympathetic newspapers support this view.

On 1 February the government had met the members of the two market organizations, the CDEM and the UEM, in the Casa Fuerte, a block from the Benito Juárez Maza market. Despite official protestations, "poor men and women" stood up to berate the governor's representatives for attempting to implement the fiscal code.[100] On 20 March the governor's fiscal advisors met the market vendors again. As reported by the Buro de Investigación Política: "A small merchant then got up. He wore sandals and cotton trousers, carried a palm mat, and his fringe fell over his face. He said that the pueblo was tired and didn't want to pay another centavo. He asked the officials why the government wanted more money and ended by saying that the pueblo didn't have to maintain bandits, murderers and pistoleros. This was followed by a standing ovation. The group of five hundred vendors then started to shout abuse at the governor, his family members and the federal government. The officials felt threatened and were forced to leave."[101]

The next day Austreberto Aragon and the vendors María "La China" Sánchez and María "Chata la Ferrera" Henríquez visited the markets of Benito Juárez Maza, La Merced, La Industria, and Carmen Alto to round up supporters to dispute the implementation of the fiscal code. The vendors met in the zócalo, rang the bells of the cathedral, and marched on the governor's palace. After they were repelled by soldiers' bullets, they started "an orgy of destruction."[102] Although the riot may have seemed random to frightened members of the elite, the angry crowds were unerringly specific. They smashed the windows of the government palace and the office of Nuevo Diario and then burned tax records in the office of the local tax collector. They then vented their fury on the car of Jimmy Hamilton, the gringo owner of the local Chevrolet garage. Finally, they hurled stones at another member of the elite, Juan M. López.[103]

Over the next week the original demonstrators allied with members of the mercantile and academic elite to form the cco. There is evidence that this was a deliberate move in order to give their movement a degree of political legitimacy. Before the formation of the CCO, two students, Carlos Jiménez Ruíz and Agustín Márquez, had made the trip to Mexico City on their own as representatives of the movement. Only after they had returned, "disillusioned as not one member of the government received them," did the group organize a broader political front.[104] Salvador Acevedo and María "La China" Sánchez represented the market unions on the civic committee. Further, despite its predominantly elite composition, the CCO was continually pushed into more radical positions by the popular forces.[105] The divisions between the popular movement and the city's elite can first be observed in events a few days after the riots. After the abrogation of the fiscal code on 22 March, many of the city's rich merchants wanted to call off the strike and reopen their shops. On 23 March *El Excelsior* claimed that Oaxaca's merchants wanted to "reopen commerce but were frightened of reprisals from the multitude."[106] The following day former commercial monopolists Pedro Huerta and Francisco Cue met with Mayoral Heredia in an attempt to attempt to reach a solution.[107] Again it appears that the fear of retaliation forced them to stop. Pedro Huerta ran an advertisement in *La Tribuna del Sur* denying that he was a Spaniard and assuring the people he would keep his shop shut.[108] These tensions reappeared at the CCO meeting on 2 April when Acevedo urged the strikers to "return to normality" in order to remove the governor. "La China" Sánchez took the microphone from Acevedo and exclaimed that it was not the committee that should resolve these types of problems but the pueblo. She asked where the government guarantees were when the *cuerudos* beat women and children. She said she knew that rich merchants sought to come to an agreement with Mayoral Heredia, and she threatened to set up a new civic committee "of the pueblo." The students managed to assuage La China's ire only by promising to keep the university closed as long as the governor remained in power.[109]

During the long period of stalemate from April to July, market vendors continued to resist the compromise solution that many of the rich merchants clearly favored. When tax collectors returned to the markets on 3 April the vendors "ran them out of the market shouting that they would not pay taxes as they did not want the governor."[110] It seems that despite the advice of the CCO and some of the students, the men and women of the markets continued to refuse to pay taxes throughout the remainder of the conflict.[111] The UEM and the CDEM also published a series of manifestos during this period, which reminded the pueblo that the stalemate was merely an intermission in the ongoing "conflict caused by hunger for bread and thirst for justice."[112] In early June the alliance between the two organizations was formalized. "La China" Sánchez persuaded members of the CDEM to join the UEM. She defended the move by arguing that the only way to depose the governor was to remain unified. Former members of the CDEM, such as La China, Genoveva Medina, and Austreberto Aragon's son Hermenegildo, all formed part of the executive committee of the new organization, which retained the name Unión de Expendedores de Mercados or UEM. Moreover, the new organization, like the CDEM, swore to remain independent of any political party.[113]

The unified market vendors now reinvigorated the movement in early July. On 3 July the state minister of the interior and the new chief of police met three thousand members of the expanded UEM and affiliated organizations at their base in the Casa Fuerte. They again attempted to persuade the assembled crowd to renounce the struggle. The meeting opened with cries of death to the governor. Market vendor Manuel Segura then rose and talked about Article 29 of the Constitution, which gave citizens the right to elect governors. He extrapolated from this that citizens also had the right to dismiss governors if they no longer represented the interests of the people. The secretary of the UEM, Micaela Cruz, then stood up and described the murder of her son on 21 March. She claimed that various pistoleros had secreted his body in an unmarked grave. Another female market vendor added her voice to the proceedings and said that the government had been enacting reprisals on the population for the last three months. As the meeting descended into abusive attacks on the governor's representatives, they were forced to leave. The UEM then decided to continue the movement irrespective of the CCO's position.[114]

The repertoire of collective action the protestors displayed was also resolutely popular and reflected previous state conflicts. The dead protestors' bodies were paraded around the *zócalo* and laid to rest outside the governor's palace as they had been in 1947. Marches were often uncontrollable and rowdy demonstrations of popular discontent. Despite the CCO's lofty and eloquent declarations, the discourse of the movement was generally encapsulated in popular song. *La Tribuna del Sur*, *El Pueblo*, and *El Chapulin* published an array of *corridos* and *canciones* concerning the strike. Some were solemn attempts to commemorate the pueblo's fallen martyrs. The "Corrido de Mayoral Heredia" published in March 1952 began:

21 March 1952
On this day
Three patriots died
Through the bullets of a traitor

> Manuel Mayoral Heredia
> For your crime you will pay
> This comedy is over
> And they are going to judge you.[115]

Others were heavily satirical. "Corrido de los cuerudos," which was published on 2 April, included the verses

> If your mother-in-law insults you
> In very crude terms
> Don't get annoyed my brother
> Send her to the Cuerudos

> If you commit a crime
> Against a person that you hate
> Don't think for a moment
> Lay the blame on Henríquez.[116]

Both types were read and sung at demonstrations in Oaxaca City and in Mexico City, where they updated sympathetic students on recent events.[117]

Further, although printed sources attempted to capture and control the movement's general narrative, rumor provided an interlinking source of information and empowered the protestors to resist or subvert dominant discourses.[118] During the movement rumors of government brutality circulated freely, discouraging submission, delineating popular action and often emerging onto the printed page. Government agents and the Buro de Investigación Política both allude to the importance of rumor among "the popular classes."[119] *La Prensa* reported that the city was "plagued with rumors. Each moment news [wa]s reported that could not be confirmed."[120] In particular, market vendors who remember the movement focus on tales of government repression. Porfiria Juárez García claimed that she heard tales of "deaths, very many deaths," including stories of young men dragged off the street into unmarked trucks and never heard of again.[121] Although local newspapers openly wondered whether the stories were "true or simply supposition," some were printed. On 29 March *El Pueblo* revealed that some inhabitants had found the bodies of two executed young men on the Cerro del Fortin above the city.[122] *La Tribuna del Sur* reported "rumors" that various cyclists who traveled the city handing out and posting urgent CCO bulletins had been kidnapped, tortured, and killed by the military forces stationed there.[123] Rumor not only hardened resolve; it also promoted direct action. When rumors arose that the CNC meeting scheduled for 20 April was going ahead, market vendors went onto the streets to complain.[124] Rumors of the *cuerudos'* return seemed to instigate the eventual union of the two market organizations in June.[125]

The trajectory of the vendors' involvement demonstrates the leading role they played in prolonging the conflict, resisting a compromise solution and forcing elites into more radical political positions; it also suggests the different ways in which the city's lower classes viewed the conflict. Many women saw the conflict as a means to assert their rights as citizens and voters. Since the early 1940s women had taken a leading role in Oaxaca City's urban social movements through their involvement in the water and electricity protests, the CDEM, the UEM, and the 1947 strike. The 1952 movement was no different. Market vendors "La China" Sánchez and "Chata la Ferrera" Henríquez set up the first demonstration on 21 March. When the military moved into Oaxaca City on 25 March, La China led a group of female market vendors to confront the soldiers and ask them to refrain from hurting members of the pueblo.[126] As the narrative recounts, female voices often drove the movement at key junctures. La China's speech on 2 April might not have led to the continuation of the strike, but it caused the IACA to close. Similarly, the women's speeches on 3 July persuaded the crowd in the Casa Fuerte to continue the fight. Other less visible women also clearly played a major role in the movement. Genoveva Medina, who would become the leader of the UEM and Oaxaca's first female deputy, was involved with discussions with the CCO.[127] The methods of protest were also gendered. The market strike removed women from their traditional role of food producers for the whole city. Instead, they grouped inside the Casa Fuerte and the house of Austreberto Aragon and handed out prepared food only to fellow protestors.[128]

This feminization of the popular movement is best expressed in a contemporary article Patricia Leal Cienfugos wrote, which suggests how some women viewed the movement. The article addressed "Oaxacan Women" and began by lamenting women's long period of political oppression. "For a long time, you have supported the yoke of slavery on your backs." Now, however Oaxaca's women were "defending [their] dignity and [their] rights." One of these rights was what she described as democracy or "the right to choose elected representatives." She contrasted with Mayoral Heredia's barbarity the women "who believ[ed] in democracy and dignity" and who had shown that they were "worthy of protesting with dignified men."[129] Leal Cienfugos's article explains in part why the movement continued beyond the abrogation of the fiscal code. Having started as a tax protest and morphed into resistance to state repression, the movement was prolonged not only by general disquiet at the state's fiscal

system but also by demonstrators' obvious enthusiasm for the act
of political mobilization. Lower-class protestors, and especially
women, seemed to relish the opportunity for what Leal Cienfugos called democracy.

Finally, many protestors viewed the movement as religious as
well as political, a sign of God's favor and, perhaps more important, that of Our Lady of Solitude. The social movements of the
1940s had emerged from church associations such as ACM and
were directed by its leader, Austreberto Aragon. Father Bulmaro
Ramírez was also alleged to have organized some of the market
groups during the 1947 strike. In 1952 clear allegiances with the
church hierarchy were less apparent. Although Aragon led the initial
demonstration, he was forced into hiding in Mexico City by Mayoral Heredia's pistoleros.[130] According to opposition newspapers
Father Bulmaro was related to the governor and opposed his dismissal.[131] However, protestors still analyzed the movement in religious terms. The Buro de Investigación Política claimed that
the people's original anger at the governor had partly spiritual
motivations. In early 1952 Mayoral Heredia's son, Alfonso, had
tumbled out of a local bar and drunkenly shot up the cathedral's
clock. Word of the incident spread through the city and the surrounding countryside until most people believed that he had rid-
den into the cathedral on horseback and fired at the icon of the
Virgin of Guadalupe.[132] Furthermore during the strike, legends of
divine intervention surfaced. María de Jesús Ramírez Pérez, who
worked in the market as a young girl, remembered: "Every time
the soldiers tried to make holes for their munitions on the Cerro
del Fortin, lightning would strike. Eventually, Our Lady of Solitude appeared among the soldiers in their tanks and asked them

not to hurt the people as they were her children. She said that she was the queen of Oaxaca, Our Lady of Solitude."[133]

Sofia Jiménez Torres recounts a similar story. During late March some of the soldiers stationed in the capital saw an old woman dressed in black walk toward the pavilion in the *zócalo*. The soldiers followed her, and as they approached they heard a whisper asking that they leave the city. But they could not find the spectral figure and returned to the barracks believing that they had been warned by Our Lady of Solitude.[134] The UEM acknowledged the virgin's apparent support for the movement: when Mayoral Heredia left the state, the UEM's first bulletin announced prayers of thanks to Our Lady of Solitude in her local shrine.[135] Opposition newspapers also tapped into the religious discourse surrounding the movement in some of their articles. During the Easter week celebrations, *El Pueblo* ran two articles comparing the passion play with the events in Oaxaca. It portrayed the people of the city as the martyred Jesus and the various politicians surrounding the governor as Judases, "men without scruples who will do anything for 30 pieces of silver."[136]

The effort to remove Mayoral Heredia was neither a Panista coup nor a Henriquista rebellion. It was a cross-class social movement, driven on by the city's market vendors. Although cracks appeared at times in the pluralist alliance, demonstrations, tax strikes, and multiple mobilizations throughout Oaxaca and Mexico eventually led to the governor's resignation. In 1947 Austreberto Aragon had welded diverse forces together into a cogent coalition. Five years later, the movement began in a similar way. However after 21 March, Aragon spent the remainder of the campaign in hiding in Mexico City. Instead the students of the IACA took up the role of intermediaries among the various social groups. There has been no general study of student political activism in the 1940s and 1950s. In fact, it can appear that between the Cristero revolt and the Cuban Revolution, students remained politically acquiescent. However, the 1952 movement in Oaxaca reveals a dynamic, militant, and well-connected base of politicized students, who were willing to link their protests to broader demands for social justice. The reasons remain opaque. At one end of the ideological spectrum, the Communist Party had started to infiltrate the major universities.[137] At the other end, Acción Católica Mexicana had been historically powerful on Mexico's campuses since the 1920s. In Oaxaca one might speculate that Aragon's role of Social Catholic cacique had been usurped by his own students in the organization's youth branch. In contrast, some students perhaps saw mass student mobilization as a means to gain leverage within the PRI, a political party that had began to rely on university-educated bureaucrats.

Whatever the reasons, students clearly formed the bridge between the elite members of the CCO and the disgruntled poor. The government's list of protestors included six students.[138] Two IACA students, Carlos Jiménez Ruíz and Armando Gutíerrez, were members of the CCO, and members of the local student confederation met with the CCO on a regular basis.[139] Students had marched with the market vendors on 21 March. At the CCO meeting on 2 April students papered over the cracks within the movement by agreeing to shut down the IACA on a permanent basis until Mayoral Heredia resigned.[140] Although the elite displayed marked reluctance to return to the strike after 6 July, members of the local university wrote multiple pamphlets reminding Oaxaca of the governor's crimes.[141]

The city's students also managed to broaden the struggle through

connections to universities in other states. In late March Jiménez
Ruíz and Gutíerrez visited university campuses in Mexico City to
ask for support.[142] In return, representatives of the Federación de
Estudiantes Unidos (FEU) attended meetings of the cco.[143] Students
in Puebla, Michoacán, Jalisco, Monterrey, Sonora, and the Federal
District all wrote telegrams on behalf of the cco.[144] In Mexico City
various student organization arranged strikes through late March
and early April. On 3 April *El Excelsior* announced that seventy
thousand students were on strike, including those of the national
university, the Polytechnic, eighteen rural normal schools, twelve
urban normal schools, the University of Guanajuato's Faculty
of Law, and various prep schools in Tampico, Saltillo, Chiapas,
Yucatán, San Luis Potosí, and Puebla.[145] Although government
agents were able to buy off some of the striking students, the sav-
age beating of FEU leaders on 14 April reignited problems.[146] The
organization held a massive demonstration through the streets of
Mexico City protesting the beatings and the continuing state of
unrest in Oaxaca. They ended the march by burying a coffin inscribed with the word *pistolerismo*.[147]

Conclusion

The 1952 movement in Oaxaca offers multiple insights into postwar Mexico's political culture. Although national accounts of Henriquismo emphasize the movement's connections to Cardenismo
and the ramifications of its eventual demise, the presidential elections in Oaxaca delineated a different political trajectory. Divisions within the elite offered the popular classes in Oaxaca a
political opportunity to demonstrate their dissatisfaction at postrevolutionary political and socioeconomic policy. Although dissident elites from the PAN and the FPPM took advantage of the

general dissatisfaction, market vendors, artisans, and urban workers not only formed the majority of protestors but also impelled the movement at key moments. Female market vendors and students were particularly prominent members of the cross-class coalition. Women especially seem to have viewed the demonstrations as a valuable space in which to assert their political and "democratic" rights. The mobilization demonstrates the full expression of the local women's "female consciousness." As the state became increasingly involved in what was perceived as the female sphere and touched matters of household economy, women became gradually more politicized. By 1952 they were no longer pushing for reforms from behind figures such as Austreberto Aragon or groups such as the CDEM and LRUAO but were forming their own organizations, taking to the streets, and in many ways attempting to dictate state politics. In addition, the movement suggests that the ideal of female citizenship, which Jocelyn Olcott describes for the Cárdenas era, filtered down to less militant groups during the following decade and was reinvigorated by Ruíz Cortines's promise to offer women full suffrage in 1951. Although Olcott argues that the presidential candidate's declaration was a form of state patronage, it was also a means to draw women away from increasing informal and "conservative" political mobilizations and into the formal regimentation of the party.[148]

Students' motivations are less clear, but the early 1950s witnessed their increasing political involvement throughout Mexico. At least at the provincial level, the 1950s were clearly not what Jesús Silva Herzog has described as the "Paz Cuasi Octaviana" in Mexico's universities.[149] Students, like market women, often formed the vanguard of social movements in state capitals. In 1951 student groups in Yucatán played a central role in the removal of the state governor, José González Beytia.[150] In Puebla the university was the "nodal point for . . . revolts against the [Avilacamachista] *cacicazgo*" during the 1940s and 1950s.[151] David E. Lorey has suggested that student activism in Mexico emerged in periods when there was a large disparity between GDP rises and employment opportunities for professionals. He argues that at the national level this discrepancy peaked during the years leading up to the tumultuous student movements of the late 1960s.[152] However, it might be suggested that at the provincial level, these discrepancies, whether perceived or real, were a constant source of tension between state governments and students at provincial universities during the 1950s. Ambitious students in search of valuable bureaucratic posts were often more sensitive to the imposition of governing camarillas from outside the traditional ruling class as they often eschewed the employment of young, talented, local graduates.

The movement also reveals aspects of the process of state formation. On the one hand, the relative quiescence or even well-regimented obedience of the state's rural caciques and peasant groups suggests that the process of increasing party control had succeeded in many areas. Only *serrano* villages defending local political autonomy, a handful of anticacique movements, and a smattering of Henriquista groups openly supported the protests. On the other hand, the scale, vigor, and duration of Oaxaca City's popular movement imply that the process of urban regimentation was far from over. The issue of taxation remained particularly problematic. Plans for massive modernization projects demanded increased taxation, and without tangible incentives, tax collection in cities was extremely difficult. An article in *El Excelsior* on 4 April 1952 claimed that eighteen states had recently brought in new tax systems, to general popular opprobrium. It argued for more gradual tax increases accompanied by visible displays of urban modernization.[153] Paul Gillingham argues that Governor Baltasar Leyva Mancilla in Guerrero encountered serious opposition to his tax reforms in the mid-1940s. In contrast, Adolfo Ruíz Cortines in Veracruz managed to avoid popular resistance by actually reducing state taxes.[154] It appears that the social pact of the 1950s, which traded heightened obedience and the payment of increased taxes for law, order, and modern development, was yet to be established. Despite attempts by Eduardo Vasconcelos, the state, which had traded stability for strength in the countryside, had yet to negotiate a functioning agreement with the urban poor.

Conclusion

During the three decades following the Revolution, the Mexican government imposed an increasing degree of control on the country's population. In Oaxaca this political process of state formation was complex, tortuous, and extremely disjointed. Although successive presidents appeared to direct the state's reforms, the indigenous peasants, urban merchants, mestizo agricultural workers, regional caciques, obstreperous governors, and intransigent elites also ignored, bypassed, appropriated, modified, and opposed federal programs according to a series of local political, socioeconomic, and cultural histories. However, though the multiplicity of postrevolutionary experience can appear chaotic and incoherent, as Fernando Coronil argues, "fragmentation, ambiguity, and disjunctions are features of complex systems."[1] Patterns did emerge, and during the 1930s and 1940s this continual course of political flux not only fashioned contradictory and wavering narratives of state control but also formed an emerging map of regional acquiescence, resistance, adaptation, and reform.

During the Maximato, Plutarco Elías Calles allowed Francisco López Cortés to dominate the government machinery of Oaxaca with little federal intrusion. Although López Cortés never attempted to test the limits of his relationship with the Jefe Máximo, by creating regional worker and peasant organizations and a state party and monopolizing the regulation of local caciques, he formed an effective barrier against potential future interference. As a result it took almost three years for the radical project of President Cárdenas to lever the Chicolopista regime from power. After removing López Cortés from his role as regional caudillo, the president ensured that the state government did not fall into the hands of another aspiring strongman or any of the competing local camarillas. Central government now asserted control of the election of the state governor. For the next decade the presidents appointed former military men with little or no connection to the state's political and economic elites. However, this process of administrative centralization did not lead to a broader course of governmental control. The federal bureaucracy, the peasant organizations, the unions, and the party made some advances in the Central Valleys and Tuxtepec, but most of the state remained dominated by individual caciques. These local leaders controlled the administrative machinery of the ex-districts and formed a useful balance to the ambitions of the state governor. Although they prevented the emergence of another regional caudillo and consequent instability at the heart of state government, at the midlevel of political interaction, in the *cabeceras* of the ex-districts, conflict was rife. Aggressive state governors such as Vicente González Fernández and Edmundo Sánchez Cano confronted independent local caciques such as Heliodoro Charis, Luis Rodríguez, and Genaro Ramos in elections and in armed clashes.

This main narrative of divide and rule offers some corrections to traditional appreciations of the presidencies of Lázaro Cárdenas and Manuel Avila Camacho and the historical formation of the Mexican state. Most important, it reveals how the political conflicts of the 1930s brought about a dual process of centralization and decentralization. As Alan Knight argues, the state appeared to expand, but this was an "optical illusion." While "the organs of the central government appear[ed] to grow, they [we]re in fact cannibalised by local elites and interests."[2] In fact, in areas of low federal influence the one necessitated the other. As President Cárdenas removed independent regional caudillos from the state governorships and replaced them with more compliant, marginal figures, he undoubtedly ushered in a process of increased state centralization. Similarly, at least at first, the progress of state ministries such as the Agrarian Department, the SEP, and the DAAI drew Oaxaca's peasant population toward the central government. Yet at the same time, as the federal state was weak and its corporatist organizations were often compromised or nonexistent, the president also had to insert a measure of decentralization into the system and allow the persistence of a group of independent local caciques. As Jeffrey Rubin argues, "the presence of the state and the implementation of those rules are far less complete, in terms of geography, as well as domains of social life, than the model of the all-encompassing or corporatist state asserts."[3] If the state that emerged from this process of administrative compromise resembled a pyramid, it was not the modern incarnation of Teotihuacán, with its clean lines and monumental poise. Rather it resembled Tikal or Palenque, an immense edifice shot threw with shafts and passages and in ostensible danger of being sucked back into the jungle from which it was hacked.

Outside the principal narrative I have suggested correctives to the both revisionist and neo-Gramscian appreciations of the postrevolutionary regime, particularly with regard to state violence. The administrative equilibrium established by President Cárdenas was by its very nature unstable. Although conflict between the president and the state governor declined as Oaxaca's governor was hemmed in by the federal government on one side and by the state's independent caciques on the other, violence became the organizing mechanism of political debate at the midlevel of government. As Alan Knight has argued, in the "hot, dense, and often dirty undergrowth of local politics . . . political violence form[ed] an ingrained part of the Mexican habitus."[4] In many areas during the 1940s local politics was still the preserve of armed gangs, pistoleros, and paid thugs. Despite the rhetoric of national unity, the veneer of an integrated war effort, and the emergence of dominant party machinery, governors and most independent caciques maintained or resisted control through force. However, certain rules of the game regarding violence emerged. Following displays of state authoritarianism in cities such as León, Tapachula, and Oaxaca City, urban violence became a political taboo. Architects of state violence eschewed open displays of repression in cities and towns. Instead politically motivated machete slashings, executions, and kidnappings were limited to rural environs.[5] Furthermore, although military spending decreased, the army was still inexorably bound to state violence. Corpulent generals and poorly paid soldiers no longer dominated the country but rather acted as the state's shock troops, stationed in key areas of economic importance or severe ethnic tensions.

The state's weakness during the Cárdenas era not only affected Oaxaca's system of governance but also produced an intricate, heterogeneous, and conflictual cartography of state formation. Although Mexico has always been characterized as diverse, the sheer panoply of different regional arrangements, framed by alternative ethnic strategies, "contradicts the relative homogeneity of political process and outcome postulated by the state-centred approach."[6] In the Sierra Juárez minimal mestizo economic interference, a history of liberalism, and local autonomy forced President Cárdenas to permit a degree of administrative and judicial independence. Federal, state, and municipal elections were decided by a new generation of politically empowered former revolutionaries and the alumni of an efficient local educational system. Although there is little research on these "post-*serrano*" areas, this model of cacique-free local autonomy might be usefully applied to regions such as the Sierra Norte of Puebla or the Sierra Madre of Chihuahua.[7] In other regions where indigenous majorities dominated, such as Juchitán and the Región Mixe, politically savvy caciques forged relatively autonomous regions of influence by appropriating government discourses of socialist education and *indigenismo*. While Charis created what I have termed an "ethno-militarist" *cacicazgo*, Rodríguez developed an *indigenista*-authoritarian arrangement. In the most isolated regions of the state, such as Pochutla, Juxtlahuaca, and Juquila, mestizo involvement in the burgeoning coffee boom led to the maintenance of traditional caciques. These men eschewed revolutionary forms of control and instead relied on violence, kinship, and repression. While Francisco Ramos was a *finquero*-plantocrat cacique, Celestino Guzmán was a commercial-ranchero strongman. The pattern of domination and resistance here most closely parallels the framework Thomas Benjamin and Stephen Lewis describe for Chiapas.[8] Yet the state of perpetual civil unrest, especially among the Triquis, suggests a greater degree of historical independence and a lesser degree of political control.

Despite the prevalence of regions with only a very basic connection to governmental machinery, state organs did start to penetrate the economically important areas of the state. This, in turn, allowed a degree of social reform. The initial radicalism of

Cardenismo faded throughout the 1930s as the maneuverings of the landowning elites and the perceived need for political stability eroded some of the links between the agrarian bureaucracy and the state's peasants. At the same time political rivalries played out according to the "logic of the [post]-revolution," gradually divided class and union concord. However, in the plantations of Tuxtepec the government broke up the region's fincas and distributed their lands to peasants and agricultural workers. Parallels might be drawn with *agrarismo* in the neighboring state of Veracruz, where elite divisions encouraged local factionalism but also precipitated an increasing rhythm of reform.[9] The Cárdenas government was able to push up the wages of Mixteca's palm workers and implement the final stages of land reform in the Central Valleys. In Jamiltepec and Huajuapam the nature of landholding and the alliance of elite interests and government bureaucracy prevented effective reform and encouraged the elaboration of various strategies of resistance. In Jamiltepec the Mixtec peasants turned to tax evasion or armed opposition. As Paul Gillingham and Armando Bartra demonstrate, a similar pattern of elite repression, state failure, and grassroots resistance emerged in Guerrero during the same period.[10] In Huajuapam the limited process of land privatization, the creation of village-based agricultural societies, and the erection of a dynamic, sensitive, inclusive diocese led devout Mixtec ranchers to refuse government policies of *agrarismo* and socialist education and turn instead toward the local church and the PAN.[11]

Despite this unstable, diverse, highly contested pattern of state formation during the 1930s and early 1940s, it is undeniable that political relationships in rural areas changed radically during the presidency of Miguel Alemán Valdés. For the first time since the

Revolution, the central government formed a direct alliance with the *vallistocracia*. Central government and elite interests dovetailed to form a powerful alliance, which sought to arrest rural radicalism. In regions of previous social reform, divisions between peasant and worker organizations subsided, and peasants were forced to choose between regimentation and exclusion. Although flexible caciques such as Rodríguez, Charis, and Ramos were able to maintain a degree of regional autonomy, their political modus operandi changed. Their loyalty now extended beyond the president to the state governor and the national party. Although elections were initially contested, central decisions now demanded obedience. In areas such as Juxtlahuaca, Juquila, and Pochutla, where recent economic booms had precluded social reform and ethnic tensions remained, military force became increasingly conterminous with central control. Even in the Sierra Juárez government modernization programs started to curtail regional and municipal autonomy. However, resistance remained. Triquis, Zapotecs, and Mixtecs refused to pay taxes or took up arms and challenged the state and its local emissaries.

The process of state formation in Oaxaca City was markedly different from that in the state's rural hinterland. Limited social reforms, mass immigration, the persistence and importance of church organizations, and existence of a literate and sharply critical public sphere molded sustained resistance to state control throughout the 1940s. Although Carlos Vélez-Ibáñez described swathes of Mexico City as free from state or municipal interference, most anthropological studies of the country's urban environments during the 1960s and 1970s depicted a high degree of political acquiescence.[12] Richard R. Fagen and William S. Tuohy emphasized the omnipotence of the PRI, the cooperation of an

amenable local press, and the co-option and compliance of variegated interest groups in Jalapa, Veracruz.[13] Wayne A. Cornelius's work on the poor in Mexico City allowed for a measure
of private disquiet and a high degree of politicization but still
stressed the "diffuse support for the political system."[14] Taking
the example of Oaxaca City, the type of state power described
by later anthropologists was an extremely recent phenomenon.
During the 1940s and 1950s organized interest groups, especially market vendors, contested the construction of a functioning social contract that exchanged very moderate tax reforms
for visible local modernization projects. When governors failed
to comply with the demands of the urban inhabitants, market
vendors, artisans, and workers sought allies in the conservative
Catholic *vallistocracia* and chose times of political opportunity to
present their protests.

Subsequent regimes were forced to submit to their petitions.
Eduardo Vasconcelos modified the tax base, moderated extreme
price rises, and offered Oaxaca's urban inhabitants a series of
tangible improvements. Manuel Cabrera Carresquedo was also
forced to comply with popular requests. In fact, oral testimony
suggests that it was only with one market leader's extremely unpopular decision to bring the union of market vendors into the
PRI in 1961, in exchange for a position in the local congress, that
the central and state government achieved any degree of control.[15]
Because of the paucity of research on other provincial centers, it
is difficult to put Oaxaca City into a national context.[16] Work on
Veracruz, Tampico, and Mexico City suggests that early twentieth-century Mexico saw two distinct waves of urban mobilization.[17] The first wave, which struck Mexico in the 1910s and
1920s, occurred in regions of rapid industrialization, particularly

those connected to the petroleum industry. In that phase the urban popular classes drew support from radical unions and sought to extract rapid concessions in exchange for revolutionary support. The second wave, which emerged in the postwar era, was concentrated in Mexico's provincial commercial centers, where the cities' lower classes exploited divisions within local elites to push for the implementation of a functioning social contract. In both cases the state was forced to offer genuine rewards in order to maintain a degree of stability.

This examination of Oaxaca City's social movements has also placed women at the center of the process of state formation.[18] During the 1940s and 1950s the city's market women successfully sought to impose their ideas of modernization, taxation, city planning, and eventually political democracy on the state administration. At first women organized themselves around issues related to their specific roles in the home. The early 1940s witnessed growing mobilizations over water, electricity, and food supplies in the city. The movements closely resemble the development of female consciousness described by Temma Kaplan. Working to restore the balance to their household or neighborhood economy, women politicized social networks to preserve life as they knew it.[19] Yet as Andrew Grant Wood argues, the act of going onto the streets to defend essentially conservative conceptions of gender roles also radicalized many of these women, who gradually "developed a newfound political perspective centred on citizens' rights and social justice."[20] By the end of the decade women were at the forefront of two important political movements to oust unpopular governors and declaimed their own role in the democratic process. As such, the narrative of Oaxaca City's social movements offers up another example of the ambiguity of women's roles in postrevolutionary Mexico. Although many appeared to be supportive of conservative antistate movements, they reframed these mobilizations as expressions of newfound political freedom.[21]

The patterns of state formation described in this book also suggest the geography of acquiescence and resistance in Oaxaca from the 1950s onward. *Ejidatarios* in Tuxtepec and the Central Valleys were trained in the rules of the game, exchanging incremental loans and land extensions for political compliance. Outside the economic core, irrigation, logging, and road-building projects, however poorly implemented, offered some benefits. In areas where poor soils limited annual harvest, peasants supplemented subsistence agriculture with poorly paid construction work. Government contracts slowly and unevenly percolated down the social hierarchy from the regional caciques. Perhaps most important, the network of communications gradually opened up new horizons and started the mass emigration of the state's inhabitants to factories and fields in Puebla, Veracruz, Mexico City, and beyond. However, resistance remained. A handful of radical peasants in Tuxtepec and the Central Valleys and the railwaymen of Matias Romero collaborated with excluded members of the elite to form new peasant and worker organizations and to defend established ejidos and workers' rights.[22] In other regions the death of powerful caciques such as Rodríguez and Charis, on whom the state had relied for regional discipline, precipitated sharp political divisions. The governing coalitions that had revolved around the local strongmen dissolved. Some members found refuge within the lumbering party machinery, which sought to cover the cracks in the regime. Others reappropriated the foundation myths of *indigenismo* and regional autonomy on which the *cacicazgos* had been built, made alliances with previously excluded groups, and formed new radical coalitions.[23] In the most isolated regions—Juquila, Pochutla, and Juxtlahuaca—the full realization of the coffee boom brought armed conflict and increasingly radical indigenous resistance to the state project.[24] In the Sierra Juárez state peculations aimed at the region's revolutionary progressives prevented open opposition to the logging industry for decades. But some disenfranchised young peasants appropriated their parents' generation's struggle for local autonomy and joined guerrilla groups during the late 1960s.[25] In Huajuapam expropriations of agricultural societies' lands and a persistent clerical Catholicism forced Mixtec peasants into the arms of the PAN.[26] For the next half century this indigenous rancher Panismo dominated regional politics, culminating in an armed PAN rebellion in 1962.[27] Finally, in Oaxaca City the state's concern to avoid movements like those of 1947 and 1952 led to favorable policies and a long period of urban acquiescence. Subsequent governors introduced gradual and often ineffective tax reforms, offered land to poor tenants, and perhaps most important, gradually co-opted the city's market women. At the same time, central and state governments were quick to plug moments of political opportunity by allying with the *vallistocracia*. Although public displays of resistance ebbed, it appears that the project was not wholly successful. The collective memory of the earlier movements, former alliances, and repertoires of collective action reemerged in the 1970s when divisions within the elite precipitated the fall of another governor, Manuel Zárate Aquino.[28]

In all, the political narrative of Oaxaca's postrevolutionary history has pointed to the dangers of utilizing an overarching model of state formation, whether pluralist, revisionist, or neo-Gramscian.

In fact the dualities, contradictions, and paradoxes of the state and its institutions were crucial to the process of state formation. Beneath the carapace of corporatist regimentation or cultural transformation, there was the perpetual rumble of violent repression, popular revolt, and counter-hegemonic discourse. In a series of articles Alan Knight has argued that the central paradox in twentieth-century Mexico was the duration of the one party state despite only partial social reform, limited military force, and a relatively static bureaucracy.[29] As Knight argues, the postrevolutionary state, like the Habsburg state before it, traded strength for stability.[30] The dialectic of acquiescence and resistance framed the maintenance of the PRI regime. At the highest level, the state excluded dissenters with discourses of nationalism, revolutionary heritage, and anticommunism. Farther down the political hierarchy a more complex mentality emerged. Workers, peasants, and new urban immigrants saw resistance—whether encapsulated in tax strikes, political non-compliance, or armed revolt—as a viable political option. The history of the past half century in Oaxaca has been one of persistent, if isolated, conflict.

However, all but the most extreme popular groups have never imagined resistance as entirely at variance with voting for the PRI candidate, marching in a mass meeting, or signing on to the local party organization. These activities were perceived as being conterminous with the individual's ultimate goal, whether it was individual survival, economic betterment, or community autonomy. By allowing this political fluidity, the state could maintain control in two distinct ways. First, this ongoing flux of political transgressions allowed a state with a limited bureaucracy and military to monitor and manage popular disquiet. Methods varied

from popular reforms to the sacking of an unpopular tax collector to targeted military strikes. Second, resistance by one group
always opened the door for professions of loyalty by another. In
the multilayered and factional world of Oaxacan politics, the discourse of political exclusion could be and was reappropriated and
utilized for specific gain by multiple groups.

Notes

Introduction

1. Manifesto of Alianza-Revolucionaria-Oaxaqueña, 24 January 1947, Ramo Gobernación, Archivo General del Poder Ejecutivo de Oaxaca (AGPEO).
2. *El Universal*, 1 April 1952.
3. Knight, "Weight of the State in Modern Mexico."
4. Dirección General de Estadistica, *Sexto censo general de población, 1940.*
5. Suárez, *Mesoamerican Indian Languages*, 18.
6. De la Peña, *Oaxaca económico*, 112.
7. Justice Attorney of Oaxaca to President Alemán, 14 January 1947, 7 Bis 2-314-1 (17)-1, Dirección General de Gobierno, Archivo General de la Nación (AGN).
8. Huxley, *Beyond the Mexique Bay*, 140.
9. De la Peña, *Oaxaca económico*, 342.
10. Absalon García to Assistant Secretary to the Governor, 3 July 1940, Ramo Gobernación, AGPEO.
11. Rubin, *Decentering the Regime*, 13.
12. Tannenbaum, *Mexico*. For a full list see Smith, "Defending 'Our Beautiful Freedom.'"
13. Tannenbaum, *Mexico*, 71.
14. For example, Brandenberg, *Making of Modern Mexico*. For a full list see Smith, "Defending 'Our Beautiful Freedom.'"
15. Tucker, *Mexican Government*, 419.
16. For example, Anguiano, *El estado y la política obrera*. For a full list see Smith, "Defending 'Our Beautiful Freedom.'"
17. Anguiano, *El estado y la política obrera*, 139.
18. Knight, "Cardenismo," 76.
19. Córdova, *La política de masas del cardenismo*, 190.
20. For example, González Casanova, *Democracy in Mexico*. For a full list see Smith, "Defending 'Our Beautiful Freedom.'"
21. For example, O'Donnell, *Bureaucratic Authoritarianism*.
22. Collier, "Popular Sector Incorporation," 77.

23. For example, Joseph and Nugent, *Everyday Forms of State Formation*. For a full list see Smith, "Defending 'Our Beautiful Freedom.'"
24. Roseberry, "Hegemony and the Language of Contention," 357.
25. Vaughan, *Cultural Politics*, 199.
26. Guardino, *Time of Liberty*, 9.
27. Becker, *Setting the Virgin on Fire*.
28. Gillingham, "Force and Consent in Mexican Provincial Politics"; Castellanos, *México armado*; Oikión Solano and García Ugarte, *Movimientos armados en México*.
29. Lomnitz, "Final Reflections," 341.
30. Knight, "Historical Continuities"; Knight, "Mexico c. 1930–1946"; Knight, "The Modern Mexican State."
31. See Jeffrey W. Rubin's *Decentering the Regime*, "Descentrando el régimen," "COCEI in Juchitán," "Decentering the Regime: Culture and Regional Politics in Mexico," and "Popular Mobilization."
32. Quoted in Hansen and Stepputat, *States of Imagination*, 16.
33. Duara, *Culture, Power, and the State*; Laitin et al., "Language and the State"; Barkey, *Bandits and Bureaucrats*.
34. Duara, *Culture, Power, and the State*; Duara, "Why Is History Antitheoretical?"
35. Barkey, *Bandits and Bureaucrats*, 237.
36. Fallaw, *Cárdenas Compromised*; Bantjes, *As If Jesus Walked*.
37. Knight, "Historical Continuities," 79.
38. Hodges and Gandy, *Mexico 1910–1982*.
39. For a full bibliography see Knight, "Mexico c. 1930–1946."
40. Jiménez, "Popular Organizing for Public Services"; Wood, *Revolution in the Street*; Rodríguez Kuri, *La experiencia olvidada*; Lear, *Workers, Neighbors, and Citizens*.
41. Knight, "Historical Continuities," 89; Rubin, "Descentrando el régimen," 160; Márquez, "Political Anachronisms."
42. Gillingham, "Maximino's Bulls."
43. Tarrow, *Power in Movement*; Tarrow, *Struggle, Politics and Reform*; Tilly and Tilly, *Class Conflict and Collective Action*.
44. In particular, scholars have concentrated on Michoacán and Yucatán, in part because of the excellent work done by the local scholars and universities and in part because of the work of prominent Anglophone scholars.

45. Chassen-López, *From Liberal to Revolutionary Oaxaca*, 7.
46. Mallon, "Indian Communities," 49, 42–43.
47. The ethnic groups are Zapotec, Mixtec, Mazateco, Mixe, Chinanteco, Chatino, Chontal, Cuicateco, Huave, Zoque, Triqui, Nahua, Chocho, Amuzgo, Popoluco, and Ixcateco. Bailon Corres, *Pueblos indios*, 26.
48. De la Fuente, *Relaciones interétnicas*.
49. De la Peña, *Oaxaca económico*, 13.
50. Mendoza Guerrero, *Monografía del distrito de Huajuapan*, 36.
51. De la Peña, *Oaxaca económico*, 7.
52. Friedrich, "A Mexican Cacicazgo," 191; see also his "Legitimacy of a Cacique"; Friedrich, *Princes of Naranja* and *Agrarian Revolt*.
53. Wolf and Hansen, "Caudillo Politics"; Wolf, "Aspects of Group Relations."
54. Pansters and Ouweneel, "Capitalist Development and Political Centralization," 17.
55. Knight, "Peasant and Caudillo in Revolutionary Mexico"; Ankerson, "Saturnino Cedillo"; Fowler-Salamini, "Revolutionary Caudillos in the 1920s"; Guerra Manzo, *Caciquismo y orden público en Michoacán*.
56. Knight and Pansters, *Caciquismo in Twentieth-Century Mexico*.
57. Friedrich, "A Mexican Cacicazgo," 195–96.
58. For example, Fallaw, *Cárdenas Compromised*, 8, 117, 146.
59. Camp, *Intellectuals and the State*, 18–19.

1. Revolution and Stasis in Oaxaca

1. Romero Frizzi and Romero, "Introducción," 23.
2. Garner, *Regional Development in Oaxaca*, 4.
3. Chassen and Martínez, "El desarrollo económico de Oaxaca," 62.
4. Chassen and Martínez, "El desarrollo económico de Oaxaca," 55–56; Chassen-López, "El boom minero."
5. Chassen and Martínez, "El desarrollo económico de Oaxaca," 57.
6. Chassen-López, *From Liberal to Revolutionary Oaxaca*, 73–75.
7. Chassen-López, "El boom minero," 112.
8. Chassen-López, "El café."
9. Turner, *Barbarous Mexico*, 68–90; Chassen-López, *From Liberal to Revolutionary Oaxaca*, 149–61.
10. Chassen and Martínez, "El desarrollo económico de Oaxaca," 65.

11. Rodríguez Canto, *Historia agricola y agraria*, 199.

12. Charles Berry argues that the Reform laws "left practically untouched the lives of most Oaxacans." Berry, *Reform in Oaxaca*, 195.

13. Esparza, "Los proyectos de los liberales en Oaxaca," 288.

14. Esparza, "La tierras de los hijos de los pueblos," 398.

15. Esparza, "Los proyectos de los liberales en Oaxaca," 289; Esparza, "Penetración capitalista en Oaxaca."

16. Chassen-López, "'Cheaper than Machines,'" 32.

17. Chassen-López, *From Liberal to Revolutionary Oaxaca*, 114.

18. Chassen-López, "'Cheaper than Machines,'" 33.

19. McNamara, "Sons of the Sierra."

20. Abardia M. and Reina, "Cien años de rebelión," 473.

21. Abardia M. and Reina, "Cien años de rebelión."

22. Abardia M. and Reina, "Cien años de rebelión," 489.

23. Abardia M. and Reina, "Cien años de rebelión," 484–92.

24. Overmyer-Velázquez, *Visions of the Emerald City*; Wright Rios, "Piety and Progress."

25. Chassen-López, *From Liberal to Revolutionary Oaxaca*, 83–87.

26. Smith, *Labyrinths of Power*, 70.

27. Knight, *The Mexican Revolution*, 1:345.

28. Chassen-López, "Los precursores de la Revolución en Oaxaca."

29. Knight, *The Mexican Revolution*, 1:346, 373–82, 339–41.

30. Ruíz Cervantes, *La Revolución en Oaxaca*, 160–61.

31. Garner, "A Provincial Response to the Mexican Revolution," 180.

32. Ruíz Cervantes, "Movimientos zapatistas en Oaxaca."

33. Knight, *The Mexican Revolution*, 1:346.

34. Knight, *The Mexican Revolution*, 2:194–95.

35. González y González, *San José*, 125.

36. Ruíz Cervantes, "Oaxaca."

37. Wasserman, "Provinces of the Revolution," 1.

38. Sánchez Silva, *Empresarios y comerciantes en Oaxaca*.

39. Ruíz Cervantes, "El movimiento de la Soberanía," 303–8.

40. Rojas, *Un gran rebelde*, 45–78.

41. *El Mercurio*, 5 December 1920.

42. *Memoria que presenta el C. Coronel Constantino Chapital*.

43. Martínez Vásquez, "El régimen de García Vigil," 323–24, 347–49.

44. Informe de gobierno del 16 de septiembre de 1922, Ramo Gobernación, AGPEO.

45. Martínez Vásquez, "El régimen de García Vigil," 343.

46. Martínez Vásquez, "El régimen de García Vigil," 318–21, 340–41.

47. Rojas, *Un gran rebelde*, 436.

48. *Evolución*, 22 June 1924, 10 July 1924; García, *La Sierra de Huautla*, 254–55.

49. Arellanes Meixueiro, "La Confederación de Partidos Socialistas," 377–78.

50. López Chiñas, "Introducción," 1–2.

51. Vásquez, *Mensaje leido al inaugurar*, 7.

52. Arellanes Meixueiro, "La Confederación de Partidos Socialistas," 383.

53. Report of agent 3, 28 August 1928, Caja 174, Investigaciones Políticas y Sociales (IPS), AGN.

54. Jean Meyer, *El conflicto religioso en Oaxaca*.

55. Muñoz Cota, *Apuntes sobre el socialismo*; Confederación de Partidos Socialistas de Oaxaca (CPSO), *Proyecto de ley de seguro obrero*.

56. Vásquez, *Plan de acción social*, 12.

57. Vásquez, *El camino de la reconstrucción*, 8–10.

58. López Chiñas, "Introducción," 1–2.

59. Francisco Morales to Governor Vásquez, 7 October 1927, Archivo de Genaro V. Vásquez (AGVV).

60. Governor Vásquez to Otilio Jiménez Madrigal, 9 October 1927, AGVV.

61. Governor Vásquez to Matias Ramos, 10 October 1927, AGVV.

62. Absalon Santiago to Governor Vásquez, 12 October 1927, AGVV.

63. Onofre Jiménez to Governor Vásquez, 18 October 1927, AGVV.

64. Report of agent 9, undated, Caja 174, IPS, AGN.

65. *El Universal*, 28 June 1928.

66. Governor Vásquez to Tiburcio Cuellar, 29 September 1928, Ramo Justicia, AGPEO.

2. The Caudillo and the State

1. Buchenau, *Plutarco Elías Calles*; Jean Meyer et al., *Historia de la Revolución*, 11:53.

2. Loyola Díaz, *La crisis Obregón-Calles*, 25–71; Jean Meyer, *La Cristiada*, 1:249–321; Lorenzo Meyer et al., *Historia de la Revolución*, 12:64–84.

3. For example, Brading, *Caudillo and Peasant.*
4. Falcón, "El surgimiento del agrarismo cardenista."
5. Arellanes Meixueiro et al., *Diccionario histórico,* 131.
6. Purnell, "Chegomista Rebellion."
7. Sánchez Silva, "Crisis política y contrarevolución," 200–201.
8. Arellanes Meixueiro et al., *Diccionario histórico,* 131; Biografía de Francisco López Cortés, 525.3/355, Fondo Presidentes, Ramo Lázaro Cárdenas del Río (LCR), AGN.
9. Lázaro Cárdenas to Plutarco Elías Calles, 1 May 1922, 206 1/9 820, Archivo de Plutarco Elías Calles (APEC); Report of agent 8, 8 December 1924, Caja 173, IPS, AGN.
10. De la Cruz, *El General Charis,* 121.
11. Rosas Solaegui, *Un hombre en el tiempo,* 124; García, *La Sierra de Huautla,* 245; Jorge Tamayo, *Oaxaca en el siglo XX,* 66.
12. Report of agent 8, 24 December 1925, Caja 173, IPS, AGN.
13. Interview by Benjamin Thomas Smith (BTS) with Juan Vásquez Colmenares, July 2006.
14. Report of agent 10, undated, Caja 174, IPS, AGN.
15. Arellanes Meixueiro, "La Confederación de Partidos Socialistas," 384–85.
16. The other candidates were Heliodoro Charis Castro, cacique of Juchitán; Isaac Ibarra, cacique of Ixtlán; Romeo Ortega, attorney general; José Maqueo Castellanos, senator for Oaxaca; and Carlos Tejeda. Report of agent 3, 9 March 1924, Caja 174, IPS, AGN.
17. Hernández Chavez, *Historia de la Revolución,* 16:33.
18. De la Cruz, *El General Charis,* 119–89; Vasconcelos, *El Proconsulado,* 254; Report, 25 March 1929, 258.23, Ramo Periodo Revolucionario, AGPEO.
19. Alvarado Mendoza, *El Portesgilismo en Tamaulipas,* 23–25.
20. Wasserman, *Persistent Oligarchs*; Maldonaldo Aranda, "Rescutiendo el centralismo político."
21. CPSO to Plutarco Elías Calles, 29 December 1931, 90.1.946, APEC.
22. Othón Díaz, *Ante el futuro de México,* 104.
23. 107.1/3, 2/3, 3/3 2279, APEC; 98.1.1929, APEC; 408.0.12, Fondo Presidentes, Ramo Obregon-Calles, AGN; *El Mercurio,* 4 August 1928; Arellanes Meixueiro, "La Confederación de Partidos Socialistas," 403.
24. Report of agent 7, 9 August 1932, Caja 174, IPS, AGN.

25. Alvarado Mendoza, *El Portesgilismo en Tamaulipas*, 57.

26. *El Mercurio*, 22 November 1931.

27. *El Mercurio*, 8 December 1931; *El Oaxaqueño*, 17 April 1934.

28. For example, Jorge Meixueiro was drafted into the organization of the Confederación Campesinas Mexicanas. 432/506, LCR, AGN. Heliodoro Charis was appointed chief of military operations in Querétaro. De la Cruz, *El General Charis*, 141.

29. *El Oaxaqueño*, 12 April 1934.

30. *El Mercurio*, 13 October 1931.

31. *El Oaxaqueño*, 7 May 1934, 17 February 1934, 3 February 1934; *Iris*, 2 September 1934; *El Mercurio*, 13 October 1931; *Himno socialista regional*; *Sabado Rojo*, 30 September 1930.

32. *El Mercurio*, 5 December 1931.

33. Martínez Vásquez, *De la milpa oaxaqueña*.

34. Benjamin, *La Revolución*; *Album conmemorativa del IV centenario*; Vargas, *Guelaguetza*; Vásquez, *Lunes del Cerro en Oaxaca*, 16–17.

35. Martínez Vásquez, *De la milpa oaxaqueña*, 9.

36. *El Mercurio*, 25 August 1931; 213.36, Ramo Periodo Revolucionario, AGPEO; *El Trabajador Organizado*, 15 January 1930; Othón Díaz, *Ante el futuro de México*, 39.

37. *Album conmemorativa del IV centenario*, 12; *Iris*, 15 October 1934.

38. Knight, "Racism, Revolution and Indigenismo."

39. Thus Vásquez wrote in his poem "Indio hermano mio": "The Indian is like a child. He cannot speak. He does not know how to read. He cannot write. He never complains." Arellanes Meixueiro, *Los trabajos y los guias*, 247.

40. Poole, "An Image of 'Our Indian.'"

41. *Album conmemorativa del IV centenario*; *El Mercurio*, 18 August 1931.

42. *El Oaxaqueño*, 1933–34; *Evolución*, May 1926; *Iris*, 2 September 1934, 9 September 1934; *Informe que rinde Francisco López Cortés*, 1931, AGPEO.

43. *El Oaxaqueño*, 1933–34; *El Mercurio*, 1929–31; Brioso y Candiani, *Album literario de Oajaca*; *El Oaxaqueño*, 13 July 1934.

44. Lomnitz, *Exits from the Labyrinth*, 221–41.

45. *El Oaxaqueño*, 5 January 1934.

46. *Controversia juridica entre la federación y el estado de Oaxaca*.

47. Othón Díaz, *Ante el futuro de México*, 116; Sección de Commercio, 1929–35, Archivo del Registro Público de Propiedades (ARPP).
48. Dirección General de Estadistica, *Quinto censo general de población de 1930*.
49. *Tuxtepec Moderno*, October 1925.
50. Karnes, *Tropical Enterprise*, 143–67.
51. 101.12, Ramo Periodo Revoluciónario, AGPEO; *El Oaxaqueño*, 20 February 1936. The fincas in Tuxtepec were San Rafael, Santa Rosa, Santa Teresa, Las Pachotas, Paso de Canoa, San Rafael, La Esmalta, Santa Elena, La Esperanza, and San Bartolo.
52. Report of inspector general del trabajo, 23 May 1927, 209.27, Ramo Periodo Revoluciónario, AGPEO.
53. Gruening, *Mexico and Its Heritage*; *Tuxtepec Moderno*, June 1924.
54. 209.27, Ramo Periodo Revolucionario, AGPEO.
55. García Hernández, *Tuxtepec ante la historia*, 103.
56. Dirección General de Estadistica, *Primer censo agricola ganadero, 1930*.
57. Arellanes Meixueiro, *Los trabajos y los guias*, 134.
58. Mateo Solana to Presidente de la Junta de Conciliación y Arbitraje, 23 June 1926, 121, Ramo Junta de Conciliación y Arbitraje, AGPEO.
59. Enrique Martínez to Governor Vásquez, 24 April 1928, 227.22, Ramo Periodo Revolucionario, AGPEO; Enrique Martínez to Governor Vásquez, 3 January 1928, 227.26, Ramo Periodo Revolucionario, AGPEO.
60. Pedro J. Parachini to Governor Vásquez, 3 December 1926, 209.27, Ramo Periodo Revoluciónario, AGPEO.
61. Sánchez Pereyra, *Historia de la educación en Oaxaca*, 78.
62. *Informe que rinde Anastasio García Toledo*. For a comparison see Buve, *El movimiento revolucionario en Tlaxcala*, 255.
63. Recaudador de Rentas de Tuxtepec to Erario del Estado, 21 August 1929, 166.18, Ramo Junta de Conciliación y Arbitraje, AGPEO.
64. Arrelanes Meixueiro, *Los trabajos y los guias*, 217.
65. Lorenzo Meyer, *Historia de la Revolución*, 13:101–14; Guadarrama, *Los sindicatos y la política*, 170–84.
66. Hipolito Ojeda to Presidente de la Junta de Conciliación y Arbitraje, 27 February 1929, 166.5, Ramo Junta de Conciliación y Arbitraje, AGPEO; *El Mercurio*, 28 March 1929.
67. Celso Cepeda to Juez de la Primera Instancia, 2 March 1929, 166.6,

Ramo Junta de Conciliación y Arbitraje, AGPEO; Porfirio Maron to Francisco López Cortés, 26 February 1929, 166.9, Ramo Junta de Conciliación y Arbitraje, AGPEO.

68. Brewster, *Militarism*, 23–34.

69. Othón Díaz, *Ante el futuro de México*, 103; Arellanes Meixueiro, "La Confederación de Partidos Socialistas"; *El Mercurio*, 27 August 1929.

70. Anastasio García Toledo to Presidente Municipal de Tuxtepec, 15 May 1929, 166.17, Ramo Junta de Conciliación y Arbitraje, AGPEO; Jorge López to Presidente de la Junta de Conciliación y Arbitraje, 10 June 1929, 166.23, Ramo Junta de Conciliación y Arbitraje, AGPEO.

71. *El Mercurio*, 13 December 1929.

72. Arellanes Meixueiro, *Los trabajos y los guias*, 227–30; *El Mercurio*, 31 January 1930; FTOC to Plutarco Elías Calles, 8 January 1930, 63 1/3 3252, APEC.

73. *El Oaxaqueño*, 10 February 1934; Elecciones Municipales, Cuicatlán, 1934, Ramo Gobernación, AGPEO; *El Oaxaqueño*, 6 November 1934, 2 February 1934.

74. Report of CLSO, 4 February 1934, 7.2, Ramo Asuntos Agrarios, AGPEO.

75. *El Trabajador Organizado*, 15 January 1930.

76. *El Mercurio*, 26 February 1930; *El Oaxaqueño*, 3 May 1934; *Primer congreso industrial de la palma*; *El Mercurio*, 17 November 1931.

77. *El Mercurio*, 18 September 1931.

78. Alberto Bautista to Secretario del Despacho, 3 February 1933, 1003.1, Ramo Asuntos Agrarios, AGPEO; Manuel Martínez to Governor Vásquez, 26 November 1927, 165.28, Ramo Junta de Conciliación y Arbitraje, AGPEO.

79. Carlos Belleza to President Rodríguez, 4 June 1933, Ramo Gobernación, AGPEO.

80. Men of San Rosendo to Presidente de la Junta de Conciliación y Arbitraje, 4 October 1930, 167.12, Ramo Junta de Conciliación y Arbitraje, AGPEO.

81. *El Oaxaqueño*, 3 January 1934; A. J. Glover to Pedro Joaquín, 2 August 1931, 167.14, Ramo Junta de Conciliación y Arbitraje, AGPEO; Collective contract of San Bartolo, 167.19, Ramo Junta de Conciliación y Arbitraje, AGPEO; Victor Ahuja to Presidente de la Junta de Conciliación y Arbitraje, 3 January 1931, 167.30, Ramo Junta de Conciliación y Arbitraje, AGPEO.

82. Labor records of San Bartolo hacienda, March 1933, 168.31, Ramo Junta de Conciliación y Arbitraje, AGPEO.

83. Reina, "El cardenismo en Oaxaca," 69.

84. Felix Ortiz to Governor García Toledo, 11 February 1934, 193.11, Ramo Junta de Conciliación y Arbitraje, AGPEO.

85. Francisco López Cortés to José Sandoval, 2 August 1932, Ramo Gobernación, AGPEO.

86. Clark, *Organized Labor in Mexico*, 164.

87. Dirección General de Estadística, *Primer censo agricola ganadero*.

88. Report of the Confederación Oaxaqueña de Campesinos, Oaxaca, 1934, 7.2, Ramo Asuntos Agrarios, AGPEO.

89. *Memoria que presenta el C. Coronel Constantino Chapital*. See, for example, *Periódico Oficial*, 6 May 1930.

90. The distribution was as follows: Central Valleys 53, Cuicatlán 2, Huajuapam 3, Miahuatlán 1, Nochixtlán 2, Putla 2.

91. Garner, *La Revolución en la provincia*, 194–98; Knight, *The Mexican Revolution*, 2:346, 357; Cassidy, "Haciendas and Pueblos."

92. Ruíz Cervantes, "Movimientos zapatistas en Oaxaca"; García Uguarte, *Génesis del porvenir*, 291.

93. 26.6, 12.1, 27.5, Ramo Asuntos Agrarios, AGPEO.

94. *Justicia!* 7.

95. *Informe de Francisco López Cortés*, 1931.

96. *El Universal*, 2 January 1932.

97. Rosas Solaegui, *Un hombre en el tiempo*, 133; Report of the CCM, 13 June 1935, 151.3/201, LCR, AGN.

98. For example, peasants complained of federal troops defending the haciendas Dolores, Etla, San Isidro Catano, and Taniche, Ejutla. Agrarian Committee of Taniche, Ejutla, to Governor Gacía Toledo, 6 November 1934, 976.23, Ramo Asuntos Agrarios, AGPEO; *El Oaxaqueño*, 8 February 1934; Arellanes Meixueiro, *Oaxaca*, 151–58.

99. Arellanes Meixueiro, *Oaxaca*, 165–66.

100. Sección Impuestos, Ramo Asuntos Agrarios, AGPEO.

101. Buve, *El movimiento revolucionario en Tlaxcala*, 510–11.

102. Men of Villa Díaz Ordaz to Erario del Estado, 30 October 1926, 117.23, Ramo Asuntos Agrarios, AGPEO; Cirilio Rodríguez to comité agraria de Villa Díaz Ordaz, 23 April 1929, Ramo Asuntos Agrarios, AGPEO.

103. Lorenzo Meyer, *Historia de la Revolución*, 13:173–87.

104. Arellanes Meixueiro, *Oaxaca*, 150. While my investigations in the *Periódico Oficial* indicate the higher figure, as Arellanes Meixueiro points out, the reality of land given out was probably closer to the lower figure.

105. Perelló, *Reparto agrario en Oaxaca*, 23–47.

106. *Memoria que presenta el C. Coronel Constantino Chapital.*

107. 1017.33, Ramo Asuntos Agrarios, AGPEO; *Periódico Oficial*, October 1937.

108. De la Cruz, *El General Charis*, 169–85.

109. Fowler-Salamini, *Agrarian Radicalism*, 115–40.

110. M. García to Padre Espinosa, 25 September 1934, Diocesano, Gobierno, Correspondencia, Archivo de la Arquidiócesis de Oaxaca (AAO).

111. *Memoria de los trabajos del primer congreso de ejidatarios*, 85.

112. Report of the COC, December 1934, 7.2, Ramo Asuntos Agrarios, AGPEO.

113. For example, Demetrio Bolaños Cacho, local deputy and festival organizer. Herrera, *Un gobierno de lengua*, 2.

114. For example, Alberto Dordelly, the head of police. *Justicia!* 8.

115. For example, Carlos Belleza, CLSO leader. Arrelanes Meixueiro, *Los trabajos y los guias*, 67.

116. If we remove the COC figures from Jamiltepec, which seem to have been invented, only 14 percent are in the other areas.

117. *Justicia!* 8.

118. Greenberg, "Caciques, Patronage, Factionalism."

119. Beals, "Ethnology of the Western Mixe," 34–37; Laviada, *Los caciques de la Sierra*, 21–26; Beals, "The Western Mixe Indians."

120. Rodríguez Canto, *Historia agrícola y agraria.*

121. Chassen-López, "Maderismo or Mixtec Empire?"

122. 4 December 1933, Diocesis, Gobernación, Autoridades Civiles, AAO.

123. Report of Maximino Avila Camacho, 27 November 1933, Ramo Gobernación 1933, AGPEO.

124. *Informe de Genaro V. Vásquez*; Caja 25, Exp 122, Archivo de Aurelio Acevedo Robles (AAAR); Arturo Miners to Plutarco Elías Calles, 26 February 1932, 167.3741, APEC.

125. Report of Maximino Avila Camacho, 27 November 1933, Ramo Gobernación 1933, AGPEO.

126. Secretaría de Gobierno to Governor Chapital, 18 August 1937, Ramo Gobernación 1937, AGPEO. His men were called *cuerudos* because they wore thick leather jackets; the word also means "thick-skinned" or "bold."

127. José Peral Martínez to Governor López Cortés, 16 April 1932, Archivo del Municipio de Huajuapam de León; *Album commemorativo*; 194.44 and 193.10, Ramo Periodo Revoluciónario, AGPEO; *El Oaxaqueño*, 30 April 1934.

128. "Informe de Prof. Miguel Leal, jefe de la misión en Chacalapa, Pochutla, Oaxaca, 1932," in Secretaría de la Educación Pública, *Las misiones culturales*.

129. *Justicia!* 8; *El Oaxaqueño*, 23 April 1934; Enrique Liekens to President Rodríguez, 3 May 1934, Ramo Gobernación 1934, AGPEO.

130. Ugualde, "Contemporary Mexico"; de la Fuente, *Yalalag*, 24. Young, "Social Setting of Migration," 248–50.

131. "Informe de José Teran Tovar jefe de la misión en Cacahuatepec, 1932," in Secretaría de la Educación Pública, *Las misiones culturales*.

132. Brewster, *Militarism*, 115.

133. Brewster, *Militarism*, 105–8.

134. Friedrich, *Princes of Naranja*.

135. Juquila Mixes, Luis Unda to SEP, 18 April 1929, Caja 9, Archivo Histórico de la Secretaría de Educación Pública (AHSEP); Ibarra, *Memorias*, 213.

136. Wolf, "Aspects of Group Relations," 1072, 1076; de la Peña, "Poder local, poder regional."

137. Brewster, *Militarism*, 136–41.

138. Beals, "The Western Mixe Indians," 48.

139. Joseph, "Fragile Revolution"; Falcón, *Revolución y caciquismo*, 198–99.

140. CCM to Secretaría de Gobierno, 19 January 1936, 2/316 (17) 4, Dirección General de Gobierno, AGN; *Periódico Oficial*, 2 October 1940; Ximénez de Sandoval Prats, *Tuxtepec "historia y anécdotas,"* 43.

141. *Justicia!* 2–3; *Periódico Oficial*, 1936–1940.

142. Secretaría de Gobierno to Governor García Toledo, 20 March 1933, 515/54, LCR, AGN.

143. Benjamin Ramírez to Governor García Toledo, 2 February 1934, 180, AHSEP; Luis H. Valladares to Governor García Toledo, 1 June 1934,

173.13, AHSEP; Daniel Vargas to Governor García Toledo, 23 June 1934, 173.13, AHSEP.

144. Boyer, "Naranja Revisited."

145. Guerra Manzo, *Caciquismo y orden público en Michoacán*; Joseph, *Revolution from Without*; Womack, *Zapata and the Mexican Revolution*; Buve, *El movimiento revolucionario en Tlaxcala*, 367–410.

146. Simpson, *The* Ejido, 440–51; Gómez, *La reforma agraria*; Lorenzo Meyer, *Historia de la Revolución*, 13:173–87; Markiewicz, *Mexican Revolution and the Limits*, 59–69.

147. Fowler-Salamini, *Agrarian Radicalism*; Ginzberg, *Lázaro Cárdenas*, 155–242.

148. Ankerson, *Agrarian Warlord*; Alvarado Mendoza, *El Portesgilismo en Tamaulipas*, chapter 4; García Uguarte, *Génesis del porvenir*.

149. Fowler-Salamini, *Agrarian Radicalism*, 25–33; Jaime Tamayo, "La primavera de un caudillo."

150. García de León, *Resistencia y utopía*; Valverde, *Apuntes para la historia de la Revolución*, 436–37.

151. Bantjes, *As If Jesus Walked*; Benjamin, *A Rich Land*; Maldonaldo Aranda, "Rescutiendo el centralismo político"; Wasserman, "Transition from Personalist to Party Rule."

152. Shulgovski, *México en la encrucijada*, 47.

153. Maldonaldo Aranda, "Rescutiendo el centralismo político," 249.

154. Voss, "Nationalizing the Revolution," 246.

155. Falcón, *Revolución y caciquismo*, 225–32; Fowler-Salamini, *Agrarian Radicalism*, 83–107.

156. Fowler-Salamini, "De-centring the 1920s," 327.

157. Maldonaldo Aranda, "Rescutiendo el centralismo político," 241.

158. García Uguarte, *Génesis del porvenir*, 180–89.

3. The Rise of Cardenismo

1. Hernández Chavez, *Historia de la Revolución*, 16:17–26, 33–40.

2. Lorenzo Meyer, *Historia de la Revolución*, 13:230–52.

3. Garrido, *El partido de la revolución institutionalizada*, 147–49.

4. González, *Historia de la Revolución*, 15:29–35.

5. Cornelius, "Nation Building," 443–44.

6. Cárdenas, *Obras, apuntes*, 1:307; Medin, *Ideología y praxis*, 67.

7. Hamilton, *Limits of State Autonomy*, 127; Brandenberg, *Making of Modern Mexico*, 80–81.

8. Hernández Chavez, *Historia de la Revolución*, 16:87–105, 54–60.

9. Carr, *Marxism and Communism*, 95–96; González Navarro, *La Confederación Nacional Campesina*, 84–85.

10. Cornelius, "Nation Building," 454.

11. Report of Carlos Belleza, 25 November 1931, 27.4, Ramo Asuntos Agrarios, AGPEO.

12. *Memoria del segundo congreso agrario del estado de Oaxaca*, 47.

13. "Informe de Professor Marciano Z. Martínez, Chalcatongo, 1932," in Secretaría de la Educación Pública, *Las misiones culturales*, 200.

14. For example, Falcón, "El surgimiento del agrarismo cardenista," 361–63.

15. Rodolfo Navarro to Plutarco Elías Calles, 19 July 1932, 44.1.3969, APEC; Alfonso Martínez Boca to Governor García Toledo, 3 January 1933, Ramo Gobernación 1933, AGPEO.

16. Fowler-Salamini, *Agrarian Radicalism*, 120; González Navarro, *La Confederación Nacional Campesina*, 137; Portes Gil, *Quince años de política mexicana*, 475–82.

17. Jesús Gonthier to Plutarco Elías Calles, 20 March 1933, 34 1050 1, APEC; Jesús Gonthier to Plutarco Elías Calles, 21 March 1933, 34 1050 1, APEC.

18. Report of agent 9, 24 January 1933, Caja 137, IPS, AGN.

19. Simon López to Governor Chapital, 8 February 1938, 102.2, Ramo Asuntos Agrarios, AGPEO; Jesús Castro to Secretario del Despacho, 2 January 1934, Ramo Gobernación 1934, AGPEO.

20. CNC to Governor García Toledo, 31 December 1933, Ramo Gobernación 1934, AGPEO.

21. Comité agraria de Monte Rosa to Governor García Toledo, 20 December 1933, Ramo Gobernación 1934, AGPEO; Secretaría de Gobierno to Governor García Toledo, 20 December 1933, Ramo Gobernación 1934, AGPEO; Mauro Méndez to Governor García Toledo, 19 December 1933, Ramo Gobernación 1934, AGPEO; Comité agraria de Maravillosa to Governor García Toledo, 13 May 1933, Ramo Gobernación 1934, AGPEO.

22. Men of San Lucas Ojitlán to President Rodríguez, 6 July 1933, 515.3/28, Fondo Presidentes, Ramo Abelardo Rodríguez (AR), AGN.

23. *Tuxtepec Moderno*, July 1928.
24. Rodolfo J. Prieto to presidente de la Junta de Conciliación y Arbitraje, 22 January 1931, 166.71, Ramo Junta de Conciliación y Arbitraje, AGPEO.
25. Daniel Muñoz Estefan to presidente de la Junta de Conciliación y Arbitraje, 8 August 1932, 167.56, Ramo Junta de Conciliación y Arbitraje, AGPEO.
26. *Memoria del segundo congreso agrario del sstado de Oaxaca.*
27. J. B. López, Juan Quintas to President Rodríguez, 24 September 1933, 515.3/28, AR, AGN; Juan Rojas to President Rodríguez, 9 September 1933, 515.3/28, AR, AGN; Miguel Ortiz to President Rodríguez, 19 September 1933, 515.3/28, AR, AGN; Alfosina Polo de Muñoz to President Rodríguez, 19 June 1933, 515.3/28, AR, AGN.
28. Miguel Salazar to President Rodríguez, 28 March 1934, 515.3/28, AR, AGN; *El Oaxaqueño*, 30 April 1934.
29. Miguel Salazar to Governor García Toledo, 28 March 1934, Ramo Gobernación 1934, AGPEO; Juan Nicolas to Governor García Toledo, 26 March 1934, Ramo Gobernación 1934, AGPEO; Juan Nicolas to President Rodríguez, 28 March 1934, 517.1/30-1, AR, AGN. The ejidos were Santa Rosa, Cafetal Segundo, El Porvenir, El Cantón, Las Pachotas, El Nanche, and San Miguel Tlanicho, all in San Lucas Ojitlán.
30. Presidente municipal de Valle Nacional to Departamento Agrario, 29 May 1935, 1003.12, Ramo Asuntos Agrarios, AGPEO; Tomás Avendano to Governor García Toledo, 5 April 1936, Ramo Gobernación, AGPEO.
31. Men of San Juan Palanta to Departamento Agrario, 22 June 1935, 95.1, Ramo Asuntos Agrarios, AGPEO.
32. Lowry, *Selected Letters*, 231.
33. Camara del Trabajo to President Cárdenas, 5 December 1934, 404.4/8, LCR, AGN. *El Oaxaqueño*, 24 December 1934, 28 June 1934.
34. The phrases come from José Revueltas's examination of the PCM's stubborn adherence to ideological certainties in the period 1933–34. Revueltas, *Los dias terrenales*; Domingo García to President Rodríguez, 7 July 1934, 518.2/24, AR, AGN.
35. Ismael Velasco to Departamento Agrario, 2 October 1934, 141.1, Ramo Asuntos Agrarios, AGPEO.
36. GCLSO to President Cárdenas, 9 December 1934, 432.2/35, LCR, AGN; San Baltasar Guelavia to Governor García Toledo, 4 June 1934,

Ramo Gobernación 1934, AGPEO; Men of San Pedro Apostol to President Rodríguez, 15 February 1934, 525.3/462, AR, AGN; CLSO to Governor García Toledo, 7 August 1934, Ramo Gobernación 1934, AGPEO.

37. Miguel Ortiz to Governor García Toledo, 23 October 1934, Ramo Gobernación 1934, AGPEO; Eustaquio Rangel to Secretario del Despacho, 3 December 1934, Ramo Gobernación 1934, AGPEO.

38. Lorenzo Méndez to President Cárdenas, 24 August 1935, 403/380, LCR, AGN; "Dotaciones de Ejidos, 1927–33," Departamento Agrario to Secretario del Despacho, 23 July 1934, Ramo Asuntos Agrarios, AGPEO.

39. Men of Santiago Astuta to Governor García Toledo, 3 January 1934, 552.14/597, AR, AGN; Men of Santiago Astuta to Governor García Toledo, 30 April 1935, 996.22, Ramo Asuntos Agrarios, AGPEO; Secretaría de Gobierno to Departamento Agrario, 16 January 1934, 552.5/355, AR, AGN.

40. *Genuina Confederación de Ligas Socialistas de Oaxaca.*

41. Drumondo, *Emiliano Zapata*; List Arzubide, *Emiliano Zapata, Exaltación*; Benjamin Smith, "Emiliano Zapata," 17–52.

42. GCLSO to President Cárdenas, 25 December 1934, 404.4/8, LCR, AGN; Maximino Avila Camacho to Pablo Quiroga, 22 December 1934, Dirección General de Archivo e Historia, Archivo Histórico de la Secretaría de la Defensa Nacional (AHSDN).

43. GCLSO to President Cárdenas, 25 December 1934, 404.4/8, LCR, AGN; *El Informador*, 30 January 1935.

44. Falcón, "El surgimiento del agrarismo cardenista," 362.

45. *El Informador*, 9 January 1935.

46. Daniel Muñoz Estefan was awarded the lowly position of typist of the Departamento Agrario in January 1935. However by July he was interim attorney of pueblos. List of employees of Departamento Agrario, January 1936, Ramo Gobernación, AGPEO; Daniel Muñoz Estefan to Departamento Agrario, 6 July 1935, 99.1, Ramo Asuntos Agrarios, AGPEO.

47. *Periódico Oficial*, 1935.

48. Carlos Belleza to Departamento Agrario, July 1935, 969.34, Ramo Asuntos Agrarios, AGPEO; Carlos Belleza to Secretario del Despacho, 13 July 1935, Ramo Gobernación, AGPEO; Carlos Belleza to procurador del pueblos, 27 July 1935, Ramo Gobernación, AGPEO.

49. Carlos Belleza to procurador de pueblos, 27 July 1935, Ramo Gobernación, AGPEO.

50. Carlos Belleza to procurador de pueblos, 27 July 1935, Ramo Gobernación, AGPEO; Daniel Muñoz Estefan to Departamento Agrario, 19 July 1935, Ramo Gobernación, AGPEO.

51. Carlos Belleza to President Cárdenas, December 1935, 1000.29, Ramo Asuntos Agrarios, AGPEO.

52. Garrido, *El partido de la revolución institutionalizada*, 183; Carlos Belleza to procurador de pueblos, 27 July 1935, Ramo Gobernación, AGPEO; *El Oaxaqueño*, 23 July 1935, 25 July 1935; *El Informador*, 2 August 1935; Report of inspector 25, 22 September 1935, Caja 137, IPS, AGN.

53. Report of Secretaría de Gobierno, 12 March 1935, Caja 35, 106, 2.311 M, Dirección General de Gobierno, AGN.

54. 170.1–175.10, Ramo Junta de Conciliación y Arbitraje, AGPEO. The haciendas were La Esmalta, Paso Canoa, Santa Teresa, Playa de Monos, Piedra Quemada, Palo Blanco, La Aurora, Santa Rosa, Las Carolinas, El Flamenco, La Unida, Toro Bravo, La Estrella, Vuelta Abajo, La Laguna, Arroyo Tlacuche, La Esperanza, San Juan del Rio, Santa Sofia, Hondura de Nanche, Sepultura, San Cristobal, La Trinidad, La Providencia, and San José Union.

55. Unión de Trabajadores Plataneros de la Esperanza to Federación Tuxtepecana de Obreros y Campesinos, 12 March 1935, 172.14, Ramo Junta de Conciliación y Arbitraje, AGPEO; Federación Tuxtepecana de Obreros y Campesinos to Juan Casanueva Balsa, 7 November 1935, 174.19, Ramo Junta de Conciliación y Arbitraje, AGPEO.

56. Ley de Tierras Ociosas, Ramo Gobernación, AGPEO.

57. *El Oaxaqueño*, 26 April 1935; Carlos Belleza to Departamento Agrario, 25 November 1935, 95.9, Ramo Asuntos Agrarios, AGPEO.

58. Aurelio Contreras to Secretario del Despacho, 2 January 1935, Ramo Gobernación, AGPEO; Secretaría de Gobierno to Governor García Toledo, 14 January 1935, Ramo Gobernación, AGPEO.

59. Secretaría de Gobierno to Governor García Toledo, 26 September 1935, 1004.27, Ramo Asuntos Agrarios, AGPEO; Carlos Belleza to Secretaría de Gobierno, 24 July 1935, 1003.18, Ramo Asuntos Agrarios, AGPEO.

60. Liga Regional Campesina Tuxtepecana to Secretario del Despacho, 7 May 1935, 1028.10, Ramo Asuntos Agrarios, AGPEO; "Jesús Gonthier" to Departamento Agrario, 1 August 1935, 98.12, CCM.

61. Report of the Cooperativa de Plataneros de Tuxtepec, 3 July 1935, 173.11, Ramo Junta de Conciliación y Arbitraje, AGPEO.

62. *El Oaxaqueño*, 8 March 1935, 11 March 1935.
63. José Casal to Departamento Agrario, 21 November 1935, 1003.29, Ramo Asuntos Agrarios, AGPEO; Erensto López to Governor García Toledo, 12 December 1935, Ramo Asuntos Agrarios, AGPEO.
64. Men of El Moral to Governor García Toledo, 11 May 1935, 98.6, Ramo Asuntos Agrarios, AGPEO.
65. José G. de la Lama and Raúl A. Basurto to Departamento Agrario, 16 August 1935, 1003.22, Ramo Asuntos Agrarios, AGPEO.
66. David Marcial to Departamento Agrario, 28 August 1935, 1003.23, Ramo Asuntos Agrarios, AGPEO; Manuel Vásquez Bravo to Departamento Agrario, 3 September 1935, Ramo Asuntos Agrarios, AGPEO.
67. Men of Santa Flora to Secretario del Despacho, 23 July 1935, Ramo Gobernación, AGPEO.
68. Felix Ortiz to Secretario del Despacho, 23 August 1935, 172.17, Ramo Junta de Conciliación y Arbitraje, AGPEO; Daniel Muñoz Estefan to Secretario del Despacho, 7 July 1935, Ramo Gobernación, AGPEO; Ernesto López to Governor García Toledo, 15 May 1935, Ramo Gobernación, AGPEO.
69. Men of La Esperanza to SEP, 25 June 1935, 180.1, AHSEP; Gustavo Jarqín to SEP, 7 June 1935, 181.30, AHSEP; Gustavo Jarquin to SEP, 11 June 1935, 181.35, AHSEP; Gustavo Jarquin to SEP, 23 December 1935, 181.35, AHSEP.
70. Gustavo Jarquin to SEP, 23 June 1935, 181.30, AHSEP.
71. Castilo Rosales to President Cárdenas, 26 January 1935, 540/36, LCR, AGN.
72. Municipal agent of Chinango to Governor, 24 August 1896, Siglo XIX, Huajuapam de León, 57.1, Ramo Gobernación, AGPEO.
73. Rosendo Reyes to Secretario del Despacho, 23 August 1935, Ramo Gobernación, AGPEO.
74. Collective contract of Sindicato de Trabajadores of El Faro, 27 May 1936, 178.17, Ramo Junta de Conciliación y Arbitraje, AGPEO.
75. *Memoria que presenta el C. Coronel Constantino Chapital.*
76. Men of Asunción to Departamento Agrario, 14 May 1935, 991.34, Ramo Asuntos Agrarios, AGPEO; Liga Socialista de Trabajadores de Campo de la Hacienda de la Labor to Departamento Agrario, 4 July 1935, 991.34, Ramo Asuntos Agrarios, AGPEO; Municipal president of Ejutla to Secretaría de Gobierno, 9 March 1935, 911.1, Ramo Asun-

tos Agrarios, AGPEO; Aurelio Gómez Crespo to Secretario del Despacho, 16 March 1935, 911.1, Ramo Asuntos Agrarios, AGPEO; Daniel Muñoz Estefan to Departamento Agrario, 30 March 1935, 969.34, Ramo Asuntos Agrarios, AGPEO; Manuel García to Departamento Agrario, 23 April 1935, 969.34, Ramo Asuntos Agrarios, AGPEO; El Informador, 29 March 1935.

77. Otilio Concha to Departamento Agrario, 20 December 1935, 1022.551, Ramo Asuntos Agrarios, AGPEO.

78. Jesús Ramírez Vásquez to CCM, August 14 1935, Ramo Gobernación 1935, AGPEO.

79. Carlos Belleza to Governor García Toledo, 14 December 1934, 1000.29, Ramo Asuntos Agrarios, AGPEO; Dotación de ejidos, 1937–43, 15 December 1935, Ramo Asuntos Agrarios, AGPEO.

80. Knight, "Mexico c. 1930–1946," 57.

81. Calles, Correspondencia personal, 347–49.

82. For example, the appointment of Ezequiel Santillan as local deputy for Villa Alta. Ramo Gobernación 1935, AGPEO; Memorandum sobre el conflicto del estado, 29 December 1935, 2.315 EL (17)-1, Dirección General de Gobierno, AGN.

83. El Universal, 2 October 1931; El Mercurio, 6 October 1931; Grand master of the Grand Lodge of Oaxaca to Plutarco Elías Calles, 18 December 1931, 63 1/3 3252, APEC; Germán Gay Baños to Plutarco Elías Calles, 29 December 1931, APEC.

84. Zarauz López, "Heliodoro Charis y la Revolución."

85. De la Cruz, El General Charis, 152–61; El Mercurio, 6 October 1929.

86. General Charis to General Amaro, 31 May 1930, 0301 Charis 5/6, Archivo Joaquín Amaro (AJA); General Charis to General Amaro, 7 June 1930, AJA; General Charis to General Amaro, 7 January 1931, 0301 Charis 6/6, AJA; General Charis to General Amaro, 21 February 1931, AJA.

87. Juez de la Primera Instancia to Governor López Cortés, 191.1, Ramo Asuntos Agrarios, AGPEO.

88. Informe de Francisco López Cortés, 1931.

89. Report of agent 9, 22 November 1932, Caja 65, IPS, AGN.

90. Enrique Liekens to President Rodríguez, 21 November 1932, 524/52, AR, AGN; Laureano Piñeda to Enrique Liekens, 18 November 1932, AR, AGN.

91. Feliciano López Felix to SEP, 24 November 1933, Caja 31, AHSEP; Enrique Liekens to SEP, 5 December 1933, AHSEP; Feliciano López Felix to SEP, 3 March 1933, AHSEP.

92. Enrique Liekens to Secretaría de Gobierno, 5 December 1933, 2.311 M, Caja 35, (17) 88, Dirección General de Gobierno, AGN; Secretaría de Gobierno to Governor García Toledo, 11 December 1933, 552.5/331, AR, AGN.

93. Secretaría de Gobierno to Governor García Toledo, 31 December 1934, Ramo Gobernación, AGPEO; C. Villalobos to Governor García Toledo, 4 May 1934, Ramo Gobernación, AGPEO; C. Villalobos to Governor García Toledo, 23 February 1934, Ramo Gobernación, AGPEO.

94. Enrique Liekens to President Rodríguez, 24 July 1934, 515.5/17-7, AR, AGN.

95. There is evidence that the alliance began in late 1932, but it is not overwhelming. Dario Pérez Jansen to Bernardo Piñeda, 27 October 1932, 524/52, AR, AGN. El Oaxaqueño, 4 January 1934; La Prensa, 6 January 1934.

96. "José Teran Tovar en Cacahuatepec," in Secretaría de la Educación Pública, Las misiones culturales, 163–71. The league was later named the Federación Regional Mixta de Campesinos y Obreros de la Costa Chica.

97. Memorandum of the secretario general de la Federacion Regional Mixta de Campesinos y Obreros de la Costa Chica, 28 October 1934, 241.21, AHSEP.

98. Espiridion Baños to Governor García Toledo, 15 May 1933, 135.7, Ramo Asuntos Agrarios, AGPEO.

99. Jesús Ramírez Vásquez to Secretario del Despacho, 14 August 1934, Ramo Gobernación 1934, AGPEO.

100. Men of El Corrizo to Secretario del Despacho, 4 May 1934, 135.4, Ramo Asuntos Agrarios, AGPEO; Camotinchán to CLA, 3 April 1934, 35.1, Ramo Asuntos Agrarios, AGPEO; Santa Cruz Flores Magón to Comisión Local Agraria, 3 October 1934, 135.11, Ramo Asuntos Agrarios, AGPEO; Jesús Ramírez Vásquez to President Rodríguez, 2 April 1934, 244.1/36, AR, AGN.

101. Felix Baños to Governor García Toledo, 19 December 1934, Ramo Gobernación 1934, AGPEO; Claudio M. Pérez to Governor García Toledo, 25 December 1934, Ramo Gobernación 1934, AGPEO; Patricio

Sanguillan to Secretario del Despacho, 8 January 1934, Ramo Gobernación 1934, AGPEO.

102. *El Oaxaqueño*, 11 January 1934, 19 January 1934.

103. Hernández Chavez, *Historia de la Revolución*, 16:33–38; Garrido, *El partido de la revolución institutionalizada*, 148–51.

104. *Propaganda del Comité Organizador Central Pro-Cárdenas, estado de Oaxaca*, Collecion Manuel Brioso y Candiani, Biblioteca Francisco Burgoa; Circular 12, Ramo Gobernación 1933, AGPEO.

105. Anastasio García Toledo to Lázaro Cárdenas, 21 December 1934, 542.1/51, LCR, AGN.

106. Secretaría de Gobierno to Governor García Toledo, 3 August 1933, 516.1/77, Dirección General de Gobierno, AGN; Secretaría de Gobierno to Governor García Toledo, 24 February 1934, AGPEO, Ramo Gobernación 1934.

107. *Justicia!*; Claudio M. Pérez to Governor García Toledo, 25 December 1934, Ramo Gobernación 1934, AGPEO.

108. Report of agent 45, 11 June 1935, Caja 137, IPS, AGN.

109. *El Oaxaqueño* (Extra), 12 June 1935.

110. *El Oaxaqueño*, 13 June 1935; Governor García Toledo to Plutarco Elías Calles, 13 June 1935, 708/119, LCR, AGN.

111. Instituto de Capacitación Política, *Historia documental*, 3:300–301.

112. *El Oaxaqueño*, 2 July 1935.

113. *El Oaxaqueño*, 4 July 1935.

114. *El Oaxaqueño*, 27 June 1935.

115. *El Informador*, 23 August 1935.

116. Report of inspector 25, 22 September 1935, IPS, AGN.

117. Memorandum caso político y administrativo del estado de Oaxaca por Rafael Márquez Toro, 7 January 1936, 2.315 EL (17)-1, Dirección General de Gobierno, AGN.

118. Damaso Cárdenas to Secretaría de Gobierno, 17 September 1935, 2.315 EL (17)-1, Dirección General de Gobierno, AGN.

119. *El Oaxaqueño*, 1 December 1935, 2 December 1935.

120. Frente Unico de Estudiantes to Secretaría de Gobierno, 30 October 1935, 2/311.G (17) 15472, Caja 285, Dirección General de Gobierno, AGN; Mariano Aguilar to Secretaría de Gobierno, 10 October 1935, Dirección General de Gobierno, AGN; Frente Unico de Estudiantes to Secretaría de Gobierno, 20 November 1935, Dirección General de Gobierno, AGN.

121. *El Universal*, 5 December 1935.

122. Memorandum caso político y administrativo del estado de Oaxaca por Rafael Márquez Toro, 2 January 1936, 2.315 EL (17)-1, Dirección General de Gobierno, AGN.

123. Memorandum sobre el conflicto del estado, 29 December 1935, 2.315 EL (17)-1, Dirección General de Gobierno, AGN.

124. Acta de notario, 28 December 1935, 2.315 EL (17)-1, Dirección General de Gobierno, AGN.

125. Memorandum caso político y administrativo del estado de Oaxaca por Rafael Márquez Toro, 2 January 1936, 2.315 EL (17)-1, Dirección General de Gobierno, AGN.

126. *El Universal*, 14 January 1936; 544.61/44, LCR, AGN; 2.315 EL (17)-1, Dirección General de Gobierno, AGN. There are numerous letters from both groups.

127. 2/316 (17) 5, Dirección General de Gobierno, AGN.

128. Knight, "Cardenismo," 106.

129. Tannenbaum, *Mexico*, 71; Weyl and Weyl, *Reconquest of Mexico*, 122–41; Shulgovski, *México en la encrucijada*, 68–90; Medin, *Ideología y praxis*, 53–62; Gilly, *La Revolución interrumpida*, 347–55.

130. Ianni, *El estado capitalista*; Krauze, *Mexico*, 456–57; Anguiano, *El estado y la política obrera del cardenismo*, 41–45.

131. Fowler-Salamini, *Agrarian Radicalism*, 114.

132. Falcón, "El surgimiento de agrarismo cardenista"; Ginzberg, "State Agrarianism"; Carr, *Marxism and Communism*, 46.

133. Buve, *El movimiento revolucionario en Tlaxcala*, 382–83.

134. Knight, "Cardenismo," 79; Bantjes, *As If Jesus Walked*, xiv.

135. *El Oaxaqueño*, 11 June 1934.

136. Hamilton, *Limits of State Autonomy*, 127–28.

137. Shulgovski, *México en la encrucijada*, 110.

138. Weyl and Weyl, *Reconquest of Mexico*, 163; Córdova, *La política de masas*, 43; Anguiano, *El estado y la política obrera*, 55.

139. Buve, *El movimiento revolucionario en Tlaxcala*, 205–7; Hernández Chavez, *Historia de la Revolución*, 16:72–74; Pansters, *Politics and Power*, 50–51; Valencia Castrejón, *Poder regional y política*, 41–64; Bantjes, *As If Jesus Walked*, 23–55; Martínez Assad, *El laboratorio de la Revolución*, 230–37; García Uguarte, *Génesis del porvenir*, 413–38.

140. Hernández Chavez, *Historia de la Revolución*, 16:63–64, 71–72, 61; Jacobs, *Ranchero Revolt*, 132–34.

141. Medin, *Ideología y praxis*, 70–71; Garrido, *El partido de la revolución institutionalizada*, 186–87.

142. Fallaw, *Cardenas Compromised*, 59–79.

143. Graciano Benitez to Secretario del Despacho, 1 August 1935, Ramo Gobernación 1935, AGPEO.

144. Ankerson, *Agrarian Warlord*.

145. Knight, "Mexico c. 1930–1946," 16.

4. The Politics of Cardenismo

1. Aguilar Camín and Meyer, *In the Shadow of the Mexican Revolution*, 67–68.

2. Fallaw, *Cárdenas Compromised*.

3. Garrido, *El partido de la revolución institutionalizada*, 253.

4. Ankerson, *Agrarian Warlord*; Falcón and García, *La semilla en el surco*.

5. Weyl and Weyl, *Reconquest of Mexico*, 66.

6. Córdova, *La política de masas del cardenismo*, 38–39, 155–56.

7. Anguiano, *El estado y la política obrera*, 139; Lajous, *Los origines del partido unico*, 184.

8. Ianni, *El estado capitalista*, 54.

9. Governor García Toledo to President Cárdenas, 24 November 1935, Ramo Gobernación 1936, AGPEO; *El Oaxaqueño*, 9 December 1935.

10. *El Oaxaqueño*, 23 April 1934; Memorandum sobre el conflicto del estado, 29 December 1935, 2.315 EL (17)-1, Dirección General de Gobierno, AGN; Rafael Márquez Toro to President Cárdenas, 2 January 1936, Dirección General de Gobierno, AGN.

11. *El Oaxaqueño*, 10 October 1935. See also Jorge Tamayo, *Oaxaca en el siglo XX*, 67.

12. Arellanes Meixueiro et al., *Diccionario histórico*, 67; X/iii.2/15-2673, Direccíon General de Archivo e Historia, AHSDN.

13. Constantino Chapital to Governor López Cortés, 25 March 1929, 258.23, Ramo Periodo Revolucionario, AGPEO.

14. Jorge Tamayo, *Oaxaca en el siglo XX*, 69.

15. Interview (BTS) with Mario Torres Márquez, January 2004; Partido Sierra Juárez to Secretaría de Gobierno, 21 March 1936, 2/311.G (17) 15472, Caja 285, Dirección General de Gobierno, AGN.

16. Alfonso Francisco Ramírez to President Cárdenas, 11 April 1936, 2/311.G (17) 15472, Caja 285, Dirección General de Gobierno, AGN; Liga de Trabajadores del Istmo to President Cárdenas, 13 April 1936, 544.2/19, LCR, AGN; Constantino Chapital to H. E. Cabrera, 8 February 1929, X/III.2/15-2673, AHSDN.

17. X/III.2/15-2673, AHSDN.

18. Ruben García, *En la comitiva*, 25; *El Oaxaqueño*, 14 March 1937; *Oaxaca Nuevo*, 30 January 1938; *Oaxaca en México* (revista), April 1937.

19. Frente Popular Oaxaqueño, *Datos para la historia de nuestro desventurado estado*, 1; *El Momento*, 26 December 1939, 3 April 1939; *Oaxaca en México* (revista), April 1937.

20. Iturribarría, *Oaxaca en la historia*, 235; García, *La Sierra de Huautla*, 89; Rosas Solaegui, *Oaxaca en tres etapas*, 45. Chapital certainly served under Almazán in Monterrey, and Almazán periodically supported Chapital's career. Juan Andrew Almazán to Subsecretario de División, 2 March 1931, X/III.2/15-2673, AHSDN.

21. Martínez Medina, "Historia de una crisis política local," 55–56.

22. Cárdenas, *Obras, apuntes*, 1:251–52.

23. *El Oaxaqueño*, 6 March 1936; Inspector to Secretaría de Gobierno, 26 July 1936, 3.311.D.F. (17) 1, Dirección General de Gobierno, AGN.

24. Francisco Ramírez, *Por los caminos de Oaxaca*, 355–57.

25. Secretario del Despacho to Secretaría de Gobierno, 1 April 1936, 2/311.G (17) 15472, Caja 285, Dirección General de Gobierno, AGN; Delfino Cruz to Secretaría de Gobierno, 29 March 1936, Dirección General de Gobierno, AGN; *La Prensa*, 4 April 1936; Comité Pro-Chapital to Secretario del Despacho, 29 March 1936, Ramo Gobernación 1936, AGPEO.

26. Benjamin Bolaños Cacho to Secretaría de Gobierno, 26 March 1936, 2/311.G (17) 15472, Caja 285, Dirección General de Gobierno, AGN; General Aurelio Merida to Secretaría de Gobierno, 25 March 1936, Dirección General de Gobierno, AGN.

27. *La Prensa*, 1 April 1936, 6 April 1936, 12 April 1936.

28. *La Prensa*, 2 April 1936, 6 April 1936; Agrupación Obrero-Campesino Oaxaqueña to Secretaría de Gobierno, 22 February 1936, 2/311.G (17) 15472, Caja 285, Dirección General de Gobierno, AGN; Eduardo Ramírez and Juan C. Vargas to Secretaría de Gobierno, 24 March 1936,

Dirección General de Gobierno, AGN; Juan C. Vargas to Secretaría de Gobierno, 8 April 1936, Dirección General de Gobierno, AGN.

29. Rosas Solaegui, *Un hombre en el tiempo*, 110; *El Oaxaqueño*, 6 March 1936; Inspector to Secretaría de Gobierno, 26 July 1936, 3.311.D.F. (17) 1, Dirección General de Gobierno, AGN.

30. *El Oaxaqueño*, 29 April 1936; Heriberto Jiménez to President Cárdenas, 7 May 1936, 544.2/19, LCR, AGN.

31. *El Oaxaqueño*, 13 November 1936, 25 August 1936; Crecensio Martínez to Secretario del Despacho, 17 August 1937, Ramo Gobernación 1937, AGPEO.

32. Miguel Ortiz to Secretario del Despacho, 23 August 1936, Ramo Gobernación 1936, AGPEO; Unión Fraternal de Ayuntamientos de la Sierra Juárez to Secretario del Despacho, 14 January 1940, Ramo Gobernación 1939, AGPEO.

33. *El Oaxaqueño*, 6 April 1936.

34. Unnamed inspector to Secretaría de Gobierno, 25 July 1936, 3.311.D.F (17) 1, Dirección General de Gobierno, AGN.

35. *El Oaxaqueño*, 25 July 1936; Governor García Toledo to President Cárdenas, 3 August 1936, 544.2/19, LCR, AGN.

36. Governor García Toledo to President Cárdenas, 16 June 1936, 542.1/1114, LCR, AGN; *El Oaxaqueño*, 19 June 1936, 12 August 1936.

37. *Oaxaca en México* (revista), 12 August 1936.

38. Inspector to Secretaría de Gobierno, 25 July 1936, 3.311.D.F (17) 1, Dirección General de Gobierno, AGN.

39. Governor García Toledo to President Cárdenas, 3 August 1936, 544.2/19, LCR, AGN; *El Oaxaqueño*, 5 August 1936.

40. *El Oaxaqueño*, 4 August 1936; *Oaxaca en México* (revista), September 1936.

41. Benito Zaragoza to President Cárdenas, 7 August 1936, 544.2/19, LCR, AGN.

42. Martínez Medina, "Historia de una crisis política local," 54.

43. *El Oaxaqueño*, 13 November 1936, 16 November 1936.

44. Mr. Gallop to Foreign Office, 3 December 1936, 371/19794, Foreign Office Archive, United Kingdom Public Records Office; *Excelsior*, 27 November 1936.

45. *El Oaxaqueño*, 21 November 1936.

46. *El Oaxaqueño*, 28 November 1936.

47. Municipal president of Ixtlán to Secretario del Despacho, 1 December 1936, Ramo Gobernación, AGPEO; Kearney, *Winds of Ixtepeji*, 42.
48. See letters in 312 (17), Caja 11 29, Dirección General de Gobierno, AGN.
49. Jorge Tamayo, *Oaxaca en el siglo XX*, 71.
50. *Oaxaca en México* (revista), 30 December 1936.
51. Dawson, *Indian and Nation*.
52. McNamara, "Sons of the Sierra."
53. Chassen and Martínez, "El desarrollo económico de Oaxaca," 64.
54. McNamara, "Sons of the Sierra."
55. Dirección General de Estadistica, *Sexto censo general de población, 1940.*
56. Recaudador de Rentas to Erario del Estado, 4 January 1938, 13.1, Ramo Asuntos Agrarios, AGPEO.
57. Pérez García, *La Sierra Juárez*, 1:269–88.
58. Francisco I. Ramírez to Secretario del Despacho, 6 October 1937, Ramo Gobernación, AGPEO.
59. Cruz Cruz, "Surgimiento de la escuela rural."
60. McNamara, "Sons of the Sierra," 340–56; Annual report of Ramón Robles, 9 December 1933, 176.2, AHSEP; Policarpo T. Sánchez to President Rodríguez, 12 October 1936, 514.1/2-84, AR, AGN.
61. Cruz Cruz, "Surgimiento de la escuela rural," 167.
62. Cruz Cruz, "Surgimiento de la escuela rural," 165.
63. Young, "Social Setting of Migration," 145.
64. Men of Yagavia to Governor Genaro V. Vásquez, 8 August 1928, Ramo Gobernación 1928, AGPEO; Onofre Jiménez to Secretario del Despacho, 21 August 1928, Ramo Gobernación 1928, AGPEO.
65. Montes García, "Las políticas indigenistas y educativas"; Annual report of Ramón Robles, 9 December 1933, 176.2, AHSEP; "Informe de Profesor Francisco Hernández y Hernández, Ixtlán, March–July 1932," in Secretaría de la Educación Pública, *Las misiones culturales*, 215; Report of Ramón Robles, 5 August 1935, 181.1, AHSEP.
66. Annual report of Ramón Robles, 9 December 1933, 176.2, AHSEP. I am aware of debate on the purpose of *mayordomias*. However, I believe in the case of the Sierra Juárez, where there was a noticeable equality of wealth distribution, it was the main root of the system. For a précis of the various arguments see Greenberg, *Santiago's Sword*, 1–22.
67. Chassen-López, "El café."

68. Recaudador de Rentas to Erario del Estado, 4 January 1938, 13.1, Ramo Asuntos Agrarios, AGPEO.

69. *El Oaxaqueño*, 26 July 1936.

70. *Avance*, 4 August 1935.

71. *El Oaxaqueño*, 31 July 1936.

72. *El Oaxaqueño*, 10 February 1937; Sociedad Cooperativa Agricola de Atepec to Departamento Agrario, 25 October 1935, 984.23, Ramo Asuntos Agrarios, AGPEO; Congreso Segundo de Sociedades Cooperativas, Ramo Gobernación 1940, AGPEO.

73. *El Oaxaqueño*, 15 January 1936. A similar committee was also set up in Talea, Villa Alta. Report of the Liga de Mejoramiento Social del Pueblo de Talea, 1931, C56 exp 6 ff 29–32, Misiones Culturales, AHSEP. For the assumption of *tequio* by the schools see Pérez García, *La Sierra Juárez*, 1:333.

74. Pérez García, *La Sierra Juárez*, 1:245–46.

75. Report of Noé Gordillo R., 10 September 1935, 181.10, AHSEP.

76. See Vaughan, *Cultural Politics*; Rockwell, "Schools of the Revolution."

77. *Oaxaca en México* (revista), January 1937.

78. Report of Noé Gordillo R., 10 January 1936, 181.10, AHSEP; Noé Gordillo R. to Governor García Toledo, 4 January 1933, Ramo Educación, AGPEO.

79. Annual report of Ramón Robles, 9 December 1933, 176.2, AHSEP.

80. Francisco E. Velasco to President Rodríguez, 6 June 1934, 524/590, AR, AGN.

81. Report of Noé Gordillo R., 10 January 1936, 181.10, AHSEP.

82. Municipal president of Ixtlán to Governor Chapital, 3 December 1936, Elecciones Muncipales 1937, Ramo Gobernación, AGPEO; Municipal president of Zoochila to Governor Chapital, 6 December 1936, Ramo Gobernación, AGPEO.

83. Recaudador de Rentas de Ixtlán to Governor Chapital, 12 January 1937, Ramo Gobernación, AGPEO.

84. Ruben García, *En la comitiva*, 25–26.

85. Ruben García, *En la comitiva*, 26; Francisco Jiménez to Secretario del Despacho, 17 March 1937, Ramo Gobernación 1937, AGPEO.

86. Interview (BTS) with Benito Torres Pérez, Ixtlán, October 2004.

87. Ruben García, *En la comitiva*, 36. How many of these projects were actually completed is open to debate. Cruz Cruz, "Surgimiento de la es-

cuela rural," 182; Constantino Chapital to Coronel Ignacio M. Beteta, 5 December 1938, X/III.2/15-2673, AHSDN.

88. Pérez García, *La Sierra Juárez*, 1:332.

89. According to one pamphlet, Chapital did not even collect tax in the region. Frente Popular Oaxaqueño, *Datos para la historia de nuestro desventurado estado*.

90. Cruz Cruz, "El surgimiento de la escuela rural," 182-83.

91. Comité de Unificación de Ayuntamientos Serranos to Governor Chapital, 21 October 1937, Ramo Gobernación 1937, AGPEO.

92. Centro de Consejo Educativo to Governor Chapital, 20 April 1938, Ramo Gobernación, AGPEO.

93. Unión Fraternal de Ayuntamientos de la Sierra Juárez to Governor González Fernández, 11 November 1941, Ramo Gobernación 1941, AGPEO.

94. Escarcega López, "El principio de la reforma agraria," 1:187; *El Oaxaqueño*, 20 September 1936.

95. *Oaxaca Nuevo*, 9 July 1939.

96. *Estatutos de la Confederación*. The song was almost certainly rewritten by Guillermo Meixueiro during the Revolution from the earlier original. Pérez García, *La Sierra Juárez*, 1:364-65.

97. The return of the civil-religious hierarchy to Ixtlán has yet to be investigated. It may have returned as early as the late 1940s as aging revolutionaries sought to cement their political position. Alternatively, it may have returned decades later as a means to maintain local autonomy.

98. Federico S. Vargas to Confederación de Pueblos de la Sierra Juárez, 16 December 1940, Elecciones Municipales, Ramo Gobernación, AGPEO; Confederación de Pueblos de la Sierra Juárez to Absalon Santiago, 3 January 1941, Ramo Gobernación, AGPEO.

99. Unión Fraternal de Ayuntamientos de la Sierra Juárez to Governor González Fernández, 14 January 1942, Elecciones Municipales, Ramo Gobernación, AGPEO; Union Fraternal de Ayuntamientos de la Sierra Juárez to Governor González Fernández, 19 January 1942, Ramo Gobernación, AGPEO.

100. Rosendo Pérez García to Governor Vasconcelos, 3 March 1947, Gobernación, AGPEO.

101. Young, "Social Setting of Migration," 245.

102. Salvador Matthews, "Suppressing Fire and Memory"; Pérez, *Diary of a Guerrilla.*
103. Pansters, "Paradoxes of Regional Power"; Bantjes, *As If Jesus Walked;* Fallaw, *Cárdenas Compromised.*
104. Martínez Assad, *El laboratorio de la Revolución;* García Uguarte, *Génesis del porvenir;* Benjamin, *A Rich Land;* Falcón and García, *La semilla en el surco.*
105. Anguiano, "Cárdenas and the Masses," 457.
106. Fallaw, *Cárdenas Compromised,* 157.
107. Brading, *Caudillo and Peasant.*

5. Cárdenas's Caciques

1. For example, Brading, *Caudillo and Peasant.*
2. Friedrich, *Princes of Naranja;* Boyer, "Naranja Revisited," 87.
3. Buve, *El movimiento revolucionario en Tlaxcala,* 378–79.
4. Anderson and Cockcroft, "Control and Cooption in Mexican Politics"; Adie, "Cooperation, Cooption and Conflict."
5. Benjamin, *A Rich Land.*
6. Knight and Pansters, *Caciquismo in Twentieth-Century Mexico.*
7. Greenberg, "Caciques, Patronage, Factionalism."
8. Tutino, "Ethnic Resistance."
9. Kaerger, *Agricultura y colonización,* 78.
10. Chassen-López, *From Liberal to Revolutionary Oaxaca,* 104.
11. Tutino, "Ethnic Resistance," 58.
12. Abardia M. and Reina, "Cien años de rebelión," 473.
13. Purnell, "Chegomista Rebellion."
14. Rubin, *Decentering the Regime,* 31.
15. Tutino, "Rebelión indigena en Tehuantepec," 99.
16. Purnell, "Chegomista Rebellion," 64.
17. Dirección General de Estadistica, *Sexto censo general de población, 1940.*
18. Francisco López Cortés to Secretaría de Gobierno, 23 May 1930, Ramo Gobernación, AGPEO.
19. Cárdenas, *Obras, apuntes,* 1:250–51.
20. De la Cruz, *El General Charis,* 60–120.
21. Francisco López Cortes to Plutarco Elías Calles, 3 July 1929, Ramo Gobernación, AGPEO.

22. De la Cruz, "El General Charis y la educación," 65.
23. Interviews (BTS) with Margarita Altamirano, September 2003, July 2006; Covarrubias, *Mexico South*, 162.
24. Zarauz López, "Heliodoro Charis y la Revolución."
25. Cárdenas, *Obras, apuntes*, 1:251.
26. General Amaro to General Charis, 15 December 1942, 0607, Poderes Legislativos y Judiciales, AJA.
27. General Charis to Director of SEP, 9 August 1935, 101.2, AHSEP.
28. Fernando Marin to President Cárdenas, 17 September 1935, 562.5/60, LCR, AGN; *Diario oficial*, 25 March 1936, 95.21, LCR, AGN.
29. *Oaxaca en México* (revista), October 1937.
30. *Oaxaca Nuevo*, 14 July 1938.
31. *Oaxaca Nuevo*, 6 November 1937; De la Cruz, "El General Charis y la educación," 70.
32. Feliciano López Felix to President Cárdenas, 2 May 1937, XI/III/1-425, AHSDN.
33. De la Cruz, "El General Charis y la educación," 68.
34. Rubin, *Decentering the Regime*, 43.
35. *El Oaxaqueño*, 15 May 1936, 26 October 1936; Secretario del Despacho to Secretaría de Gobierno, 23 May 1936, Ramo Educación 1936, AGPEO; *Emancipación*, 18 December 1936.
36. Feliciano López Felix to President Cárdenas, 1 January 1937, Ramo Gobernación, AGPEO; Sindicato de Oficios Varios, Juchitán to President Cárdenas, 20 March 1938, 534.6/310, LCR, AGN.
37. President of STERM in Juchitán to Comité Estatal de STERM, 29 May 1938, 534.6/310, LCR, AGN.
38. Fidel Cacho to President Cárdenas, 3 June 1938, 534.6/310, LCR, AGN; *Oaxaca en México* (revista), 18 November 1936; *El Oaxaqueño*, 25 February 1937.
39. Feliciano López Felix to President Cárdenas, 8 March 1937, 2.311 M (17) Caja 39, 21086, Dirección General de Gobierno, AGN.
40. *Oaxaca Nuevo*, 8 June 1938.
41. Feliciano López Felix to Presidente de la Junta de Conciliación y Arbitraje, 3 August 1937, 127.12, Ramo Junta de Conciliación y Arbitraje, AGPEO.
42. Jacinto Guerra to President Cárdenas, 3 March 1938, 2.311 M (17) Caja 40, 34185, Dirección General de Gobierno, AGN.

43. *Oaxaca Nuevo*, 21 August 1937; Feliciano López Felix to President Cárdenas, 24 February 1938, 525/209, LCR, AGN.

44. Feliciano López Felix to Secretaría de Gobierno, 10 November 1938, 2.311 M (17) Caja 40, 34185, Dirección General de Gobierno, AGN; Jacinto Guerra to President Cárdenas, 12 December 1937, 2.311 M (17) Caja 39, 28212, Dirección General de Gobierno, AGN.

45. Comité Estatal de la CTM to Governor Chapital, 21 November 1937, Elecciones Municipales 1937, Ramo Gobernación, AGPEO.

46. Comité Estatal de la CTM to Governor Chapital, 4 November 1940, Elecciones Municipales 1940, Ramo Gobernación, AGPEO.

47. *El Oaxaqueño*, 29 April 1936; *Oaxaca Nuevo*, 22 May 1938; *Oaxaca Revolucionario*, 1 June 1938.

48. Tomás Piñeda to Governor Chapital, 8 December 1937, Elecciones Municipales 1937, Ramo Gobernación, AGPEO; Francisco Enríquez to Governor Chapital, 1 January 1938, Ramo Gobernación, AGPEO.

49. Juez de la Primera Instancia de Salina Cruz to Governor Chapital, 20 April 1938, Elecciones Municipales 1937, Ramo Gobernación, AGPEO; Mario E. Vallejo to Governor Chapital, 28 December 1938, Ramo Gobernación, AGPEO.

50. Jesús Jiménez to Secretario del Despacho, 3 December 1939, Elecciones Municipales 1940, Ramo Gobernación, AGPEO.

51. Comité de Propaganda Electoral Pro-Avila Camacho to Secretario del Despacho, 4 December 1939, Elecciones Municipales 1940, Ramo Gobernación, AGPEO; Eliseo Matus to Governor Chapital, 24 December 1939, Ramo Gobernación, AGPEO; Arnulfo Rivas to Governor Chapital, 4 January 1940, Ramo Gobernación, AGPEO.

52. Dirección General de Estadistica, *Segundo censo agricola ganadero de los Estados Unidos Mexicanos, resumen*.

53. Dirección General de Estadistica, *Tercer censo agricola ganadero y ejidal, 1950*.

54. Rojas, *El café*, 48–53.

55. Chassen-Lopez, *From Liberal to Revolutionary Oaxaca*, 140.

56. Chassen-Lopez, *From Liberal to Revolutionary Oaxaca*, 118.

57. Garner, *Regional Development in Oaxaca*, 40.

58. Chassen-Lopez, *From Liberal to Revolutionary Oaxaca*, 140.

59. Garner, *Regional Development in Oaxaca*, 39.

60. Rodríguez Canto, *Historia agrícola y agraria*, 67.

61. Rojas, *El café*, 40.

62. Chassen-Lopez, *From Liberal to Revolutionary Oaxaca*, 99; Garner, *Regional Development in Oaxaca*, 32–33.

63. Garner, *Regional Development in Oaxaca*, 32.

64. Report of Manuel Esperón, May 1904, 73.17, Ramo Conflictos por Limites Siglo XIX, AGPEO.

65. Chassen-Lopez, *From Liberal to Revolutionary Oaxaca*, 452, 99.

66. Martínez Vásquez, *La Revolución en Oaxaca*.

67. Agustín Dominguez to Governor González Fernández, 14 February 1941, 992.17, Ramo Asuntos Agrarios, AGPEO.

68. Fidel Jiménez Soriano to SEP, 9 October 1941, Ramo Gobernación, AGPEO.

69. *El Mercurio*, 30 April 1921.

70. Rojas, *El café*, 45

71. Informe de Francisco López Cortés, September 1929, Ramo Gobernación, AGPEO.

72. De la Peña, *Oaxaca económico*, 476.

73. Codigo Fiscal 1931, Ramo Gobernación, AGPEO.

74. Graciano Benitez to Departamento Agrario, 23 December 1934, Ramo Gobernación, AGPEO.

75. Recaudador de Rentas to Erario del Estado, 2 January 1938, Ramo Gobernación, AGPEO.

76. Huxley, *Beyond the Mexique Bay*, 232.

77. Liga Socialista de Oficios Varios de Pochutla to President Cárdenas, 23 April 1940, 506 1/40-45, LCR, AGN.

78. Arellanes Meixueiro, "Del camarazo al cardenismo," 76.

79. Dirección General de Estadistica, *Sexto censo general de población, 1940*.

80. Comité Estatal de la CTM to Governor Chapital, 2 April 1937, Ramo Gobernación, AGPEO.

81. Juan C. Cruz to President Cárdenas, 23 April 1940, 506 1/40-45, LCR, AGN.

82. Maximino Avila Camacho to Secretaría de la Defensa Nacional, 6 February 1934, Ramo Gobernación, AGPEO.

83. Report of Daniel Muñoz Estefan, 2 August 1937, Ramo Gobernación, AGPEO.

84. Acción Social Pochutleca to Governor Chapital, 29 August 1937, Ramo

Gobernación, AGPEO; Comité Estatal de la CTM to Secretario del Despacho, 4 December 1937, Elecciones Municipales 1937, Ramo Gobernación, AGPEO.

85. Men of Santa María Huatulco to Departamento Agrario, 28 November 1938, 992.14, Ramo Asuntos Agrarios, AGPEO.

86. Eufemia Ramírez to SEP, 9 December 1938, Ramo Educación, AGPEO.

87. Manuel Pastor to Governor Chapital, 1 February 1938, Ramo Gobernación, AGPEO.

88. Roseberry, *Coffee and Capitalism.*

89. Carlos Ziga to Governor Chapital, 14 May 1938, Ramo Gobernación, AGPEO.

90. Ramírez Ramírez, "Mis experiencias en el estado de Oaxaca."

91. "Informe de Prof. Miguel Leal, jefe de la misión en Chacalapa," in Secretaría de Educación Pública, *Las misiones culturales,* 186.

92. De la Peña, *Oaxaca económico,* 507.

93. Men of Candelaria Loxicha to Governor García Toledo, 15 March 1935, Ramo Gobernación, AGPEO.

94. *Oaxaca en México* (revista), September 1938.

95. *El Oaxaqueño,* 24 June 1936.

96. Lucas González to Secretario del Despacho, 6 July 1936, 2.012.2 (17) 18163, Dirección General de Gobierno, AGN.

97. Comité Estatal de la CTM to Secretario del Despacho, 14 July 1937, Ramo Gobernación 1937, AGPEO; Frente Popular Reinvidicador to Secretaría de Gobierno, 6 July 1936, 2.012.2 (17) 18163, Dirección General de Gobierno, AGN.

98. Daniel Muñoz Estefan to Secretario del Despacho, 7 August 1937, Ramo Gobernación, AGPEO.

99. *Oaxaca Nuevo,* 9 January 1939; *El Oaxaqueño,* 1 August 1936; Manuel Fuentes Rodríguez to President Cárdenas, 25 February 1939, 534.3/1264, LCR, AGN.

100. Otilio Enríquez to Presidente de la Junta de Conciliación y Arbitraje, 2 March 1938, 19.13, Ramo Junta de Conciliación y Arbitraje, AGPEO.

101. *Oaxaca Nuevo,* 4 December 1938.

102. Porfirio Gaspar to Governor Chapital, 15 December 1936, 61.15, Ramo Asuntos Agrarios, AGPEO.

103. *Periódico Oficial,* 1934–1940.

104. Men of Santa María Tonameca to Departamento Agrario, 7 December 1936, 61.19, Ramo Asuntos Agrarios, AGPEO.

105. Juan Vega to Departamento Agrario, 3 September 1937, Ramo Gobernación, AGPEO.

106. *El Oaxaqueño*, 28 February 1937.

107. Manuel Pastor to Governor Chapital, 16 November 1937, Ramo Gobernación, AGPEO.

108. Alfonso Gabriel to Governor González Fernández, 2 December 1940, Ramo Gobernación, AGPEO.

109. Report of Carlos Bravo, 13 March 1942, 550/35-19, Fondo Presidentes, Ramo Manuel Avila Camacho, AGN.

110. *Informe que rinde C. Coronel Constantino Chapital*, 1938.

111. Dario Meixueiro to municipal president of Santa María Tonameca, 21 November 1938, 101.6, Ramo Asuntos Agrarios, AGPEO.

112. Jorge Meixueiro to Departamento Agrario, 27 December 1940, Ramo Asuntos Agrarios, AGPEO.

113. Alfonso Gabriel to Secretario del Despacho, 2 December 1940, Ramo Gobernación, AGPEO.

114. Grandin, *Last Colonial Massacre*, 129.

115. Andres Ambrosio to Secretario del Despacho, 14 February 1940, Ramo Gobernación, AGPEO.

116. Sindicato de Campesinos "Venustiano Carranza" to Governor Chapital, 18 November 1937, Ramo Gobernación, AGPEO.

117. FPLP to Governor Chapital, 13 November 1937, 2.311 M (17) Caja 39, 23303, Dirección General de Gobierno, AGN.

118. Eufemia Ramírez to SEP, 26 March 1937, Ramo Gobernación, AGPEO.

119. Jesús Loaeza Cruz to President Cárdenas, 7 June 1937, 542.2/599, LCR, AGN.

120. FPLP to Governor Chapital, 30 October 1937, 2.012.2 (17) 18163, Dirección General de Gobierno, AGN.

121. Juana C. Viuda de Loaeza to President Cárdenas, 14 October 1938, 542.2/599, LCR, AGN.

122. José Manuel Santibañez to Governor Chapital, 2 January 1938, Ramo Gobernación, AGPEO.

123. Carlos Ziga to Governor Chapital, 6 November 1937, Ramo Gobernación, AGPEO.

124. Saturnino Gilbon Camacho to Governor Chapital, 22 August 1937, Ramo Gobernación, AGPEO.

125. Daniel Muñoz Estefan to Governor Chapital, 8 September 1938, Ramo Gobernación, AGPEO.

126. Manuel Mendoza to Governor González Fernández, 2 January 1941, Elecciones Muncipales, Ramo Gobernación, AGPEO.

127. Rodríguez Canto, *Historia agricola y agraria*, 74.

128. Knight, "Caciquismo in Mexico," 32.

129. Greenberg, *Blood Ties*.

130. Clarke, *Class, Ethnicity and Community*, 121.

131. Huerta Rios, *Organización socio-política*.

132. Sala de Asuntos y Autores Oaxaqueños, vols. 40 and 71, Collección Manuel Martínez Gracida, Biblioteca Pública de Oaxaca; Abardia M. and Reina, "Cien años de rebelión."

133. Aguirre Beltrán, *Regions of Refuge*.

134. Starr, *In Indian Mexico*, 192.

135. Juan Comas, "El problema social," 51; Report of unnamed inspector, 3 May 1930, Caja C5, AHSEP.

136. Santiago Juxtlahuaca, report, 13 August 1935, Parish records, Archivo de la Diócesis de Huajuapan de León.

137. Report of Benito Trinidad, 8 July 1928, Caja C5, AHSEP.

138. Secretaría de la Educación Pública, *Las misiones culturales*, 175.

139. Parra Mora, "Poder, violencia."

140. Although anthropologist Cesar Huerta Rios has asserted that this structure emerged with the division of communal lands into private properties following coffee planting in the early twentieth century, nineteenth-century ethnographer Manuel Martínez Gracida claimed that system was observed as early as the sixteenth century. Huerta Rios, *Organización socio-política*, 235.

141. For San Juan Copala during the Revolution see Caja 17 (A) Expedientes 103 and 84, Ramo Periodo Revolucionario, AGPEO.

142. Memorandum by A. Palomera, 10 May 1938, Ramo Gobernación, AGPEO.

143. Miguel Bennets to Secretario del Despacho, 10 July 1936, Ramo Gobernación, AGPEO; Memorandum by A. Palomera, 10 May 1938, Ramo Gobernación, AGPEO.

144. Memorandum by A. Palomera, 10 May 1938, Ramo Gobernación, AGPEO.

145. Josefino Feria to Governor García Toledo, 5 November 1936, 1936–1937 Elecciones Municipales, Ramo Gobernación, AGPEO.

146. Manuel Díaz Chavez to Governor Chapital, 13 January 1939, 1939–1940 Elecciones Municipales, Ramo Gobernación, AGPEO; Memorandum by A. Palomera, 10 May 1938, Ramo Gobernación, AGPEO.

147. Santiago Morales to Governor Chapital, 23 June 1934, Ramo Gobernación, AGPEO.

148. Francisco Velasco to Governor García Toledo, 26 February 1935, 987, Ramo Asuntos Agrarios, AGPEO.

149. Men of San Juan Copola to Secretario del Despacho, 1 June 1934, Juxtlahuaca, 1934, Ramo Justicia, AGPEO.

150. Report of Benjamin Ramírez, 4 September 1933, Ramo Educación, AGPEO.

151. Dirección General de Estadistica, *Segundo censo agricola*.

152. Carlos Belleza to Governor Chapital, 28 August 1938, Ramo Gobernación 1937, AGPEO.

153. R. Ramírez Pastelin to Governor Chapital, 7 September 1938, Ramo Gobernación 1937, AGPEO.

154. Men of San Juan Copola to Secretario del Despacho, 1 June 1934, Juxtlahuaca, 1934, Ramo Justicia, AGPEO.

155. José de Jesús to Governor Chapital, 23 August 1935, Ramo Gobernación, AGPEO.

156. Juez de la Primera Instancia de Juxtlahuaca to Governor Chapital, 30 June 1938, Ramo Gobernación, AGPEO.

157. Santiago A. Merino to Governor Chapital, 30 December 1938, 1939–1940 Elecciones Municipales, Ramo Gobernación, AGPEO.

158. José Antonio to Governor Chapital, 12 January 1939, Ramo Gobernación, AGPEO.

159. Report of Maximo Hernández, 19 February 1940, Caja 426, IPS, AGN.

160. Celestino Guzmán to Governor Chapital, 28 June 1939, Ramo Gobernación, AGPEO.

161. Efrén Villegas Zapara to Governor González Fernández, 20 December 1940, Elecciones Municipales 1940, Ramo Gobernación, AGPEO.

162. José Martín to Governor González Fernández, 3 January 1941, Elecciones Municipales 1940, Ramo Gobernación, AGPEO.

163. Greenberg, *Blood Ties*, 192–97; Greenberg, "Caciques, Patronage, Factionalism," 321–34.

164. List of Mixe villages, 7 March 1938, Ramo Gobernación, AGPEO; Martínez, *Derechos indigenas en los juzgados*, 145.

165. Greenberg, "Caciques, Patronage, Factionalism," 325.

166. Garner, *Porfirio Díaz*, 43.

167. Greenberg, "Caciques, Patronage, Factionalism," 321.

168. Beals, "Ethnology of the Western Mixe," 26.

169. Greenberg, "Caciques, Patronage, Factionalism," 323.

170. Recuadador de Rentas to Erario del Estado, 7 January 1938, Ramo Gobernación, AGPEO.

171. Recaudador de Rentas de Choapam to Secretario del Despacho, 2 January 1938, Ramo Gobernación, AGPEO.

172. Chassen-López, *From Liberal to Revolutionary Oaxaca*, 104, 146.

173. Porter, *Coffee Farmers Revolt*, 78.

174. *El Informador*, 23 August 1935; GCLSO to President Cárdenas, 25 December 1934, 404.4/8, LCR, AGN.

175. Aguilar Domingo, *Santiago Zacatepec, Mixe*, 21–9; Laviada, *Los caciques de la Sierra*, 34–40; Nahmed, *Los Mixes*.

176. Report of Ramón Robles, 9 December 1933, 176.2, AHSEP; Luis Ramírez to SEP, 8 May 1935, Caja 168, 241.4, AHSEP.

177. Report of Ramón Robles, 4 October 1935, 181.1, AHSEP.

178. *El Oaxaqueño*, 30 January 1936, 5 January 1936; Laviada, *Los caciques de la Sierra*, 39; Report of Ramón Robles, 10 September 1936, 181.1, AHSEP.

179. *El Oaxaqueño*, 16 February 1936.

180. *El Oaxaqueño*, 16 February 1936, 16 October 1936, 11 September 1936, 12 September 1936.

181. Aurelio Reyes to local legislature, 20 September 1936, Archivo de la Cámara Local de Diputados (ACLD); Neponuceno Narciso to local legislature, 21 July 1936, ACLD.

182. Luis Rodríguez to Secretario del Despacho, 24 December 1936, Ramo Gobernación 1937, AGPEO.

183. Ernestino Bautista to Samuel Pérez, 22 December 1936, Ramo Gobernación 1937, AGPEO; Aquileo Santamaría to Secretario del Despacho, 23 December 1936, Ramo Gobernación 1937, AGPEO.

184. Luis Rodríguez to Governor García Toledo, 6 October 1936, Ramo Gobernación 1936, AGPEO; Aurelio Reyes to Governor García Toledo, 2 November 1936, Ramo Gobernación 1936, AGPEO.

185. Luis Rodríguez to President Cárdenas, 22 October 1936, 533.11/3, LCR, AGN.

186. *Oaxaca Nuevo*, 27 April 1937; Comisión de Diputados to local legislature, 18 May 1937, ACLD,.

187. Decreto 203, ACLD; *Informe que rinde el C. Coronel Constantino Chapital*, 1938.

188. *Oaxaca Nuevo*, 28 June 1938, 31 June 1938.

189. *Oaxaca Nuevo*, 12 July 1938.

190. Manuel Castellanos to Governor Chapital, 16 December 1936, Ramo Gobernación 1938, AGPEO.

191. Comité Organizador de la Primera Gran Convención de Unificación de Pueblos de la Raza Mixe to Governor Chapital, 12 August 1939, Ramo Gobernación 1939, AGPEO.

192. *Oaxaca Nuevo*, 13 December 1938.

193. Interview (BTS) with Eleazar Cruz Diego, August 2003; Interview (BTS) with Pedro Regalado, August 2003.

194. Münch Galindo, *Historia y cultura de los Mixes*, 66.

195. De la Peña, *Oaxaca económico*, 431.

196. Interview (BTS) with Asunción Morales, August 2003; *Oaxaca Nuevo*, 31 January 1940.

197. Luis Rodríguez to municipal president of Tlahuitoltepec, 7 September 1950, Caja 1 1900–1950, Administración, Correspondencia, Archivo del Municipio de Tlahuitoltepec (AMT).

198. Luis Rodríguez to municipal president of Tlahuitoltepec, 2 November 1953, Caja 1 1900–1950, Administración, Correspondencia, AMT.

199. Greenberg, "Caciques, Patronage, Factionalism," 356.

200. Münch Galindo, *Historia y cultura de los Mixes*, 87.

201. Felipe Luciano to Secretario del Despacho, 30 November 1938, Ramo Gobernación 1937, AGPEO; Juventino Pérez Zorilla to Governor Chapital, 28 August 1938, Ramo Gobernación 1937, AGPEO.

202. Luis Rodríguez to Governor Chapital, 2 July 1938, Ramo Gobernación 1937, AGPEO; Dionisio Cirillo to Governor Chapital, 23 June 1938, Ramo Gobernación 1937, AGPEO.

203. José Piñeda to Governor Chapital, 19 August 1938, Ramo Gobernación, AGPEO.
204. Manuel G. Luna to Governor Chapital, 3 July 1938, Ramo Gobernación, AGPEO.
205. Interview (BTS) with Eleazar Cruz Diego, August 2003; Interview (BTS) with Pedro Regalado, August 2003; Interview (BTS) with Asunción Morales, August 2003.
206. Laviada, *Los caciques de la Sierra*, 121.
207. Münch Galindo, *Historia y cultura de los Mixes*, 76.
208. Dirección General de Estadistica, *Sexto censo general de población, 1940*.
209. Luis Mendoza to Director of SEP, 24 March 1948, AHSEP.
210. Martínez, *Derechos indigenas en los juzgados*, 171.
211. Rus, "The Communidad Revolucionaria."
212. Arrioja Díaz-Viruel, "Caciquismo y estrategias de poder."
213. Men of Puxmetacan to Secretario del Despacho, 23 January 1953, Ramo Gobernación, AGPEO.
214. Martínez, *Derechos indigenas en los juzgados*, 181.
215. Greenberg, "Caciques, Patronage, Factionalism"; Nahmed, *Los Mixes*; Barahona, *Graves tensiones*; Münch Galindo, *Historia y cultura de los Mixes*; Arrioja Díaz-Viruel, "Caciquismo y estrategias de poder"; Laviada, *Los caciques de la Sierra*.
216. Municipal authorities of San Bartolo Yautepec to Governor Chapital, 2 October 1940, Yautepec, 1939, Ramo Justicia, AGPEO.
217. Knight, "Caciquismo in Mexico," 34.
218. Chevalier and Buckles, *Land without Gods*; Schryer, *Ethnicity and Class Conflict*.
219. Butler, "God's Caciques."
220. For example, Knight, "Historical Continuities"; Rubin, "Descentrando el régimen."
221. Rubin, "Decentrando el régimen," 150.
222. Pansters, "Theorizing Political Culture"; Romero, "La confirmación del caciquismo sindical en Jalisco," 293–311, 294.
223. Mallon, "Indian Communities."
224. Knight, "The Modern Mexican State."
225. *Mensaje al pueblo de Oaxaca, dirigido por el C. Presidente de la Republica, Lázaro Cárdenas.*

6. Politics and Socioeconomic Reform

1. León and Marván, *La clase obrera*, 34–99.
2. González, *Historia de la Revolución*, 15:95.
3. Sosa Elízaga, *Los códigos ocultos*, 109.
4. Escarcega López, "El principio de la reforma agraria," 1:69.
5. Silva Herzog, *El agrarismo mexicano*, 405.
6. Garrido, *El partido de la revolución institucionalizada*, 233–300.
7. Glantz, *El ejido colectivo*; Eckstein and Restrepo, *La explotación colectiva*.
8. For example, Schryer, *Rancheros of Pisaflores*.
9. For example, Falcón, "El surgimiento de agrarismo cardenista."
10. Benjamin, *A Rich Land*, 180.
11. Bantjes, *As If Jesus Walked*; Knight, "Cardenismo."
12. Boyer, "Old Loves, New Loyalties," 454.
13. Knight, "Rise and Fall of Cardenismo," 264.
14. *El Oaxaqueño*, 4 March 1936.
15. Jeronimo Altamirano to President Cárdenas, 24 February 1936, 151.3/201, LCR, AGN.
16. *El Oaxaqueño*, 5 March 1936; Gustavo Castro to Governor García Toledo, 5 March 1936, Ramo Gobernación 1936, AGPEO.
17. *El Oaxaqueño*, 10 March 1936.
18. Carlos Belleza to Graciano Sánchez, 24 August 1936, 998.26, Ramo Asuntos Agrarios, AGPEO; Departamento Agrario, *Las masas campesinas*.
19. *El Oaxaqueño*, 2 March 1937; Jorge Meixueiro to President Cárdenas, 3 March 1936, 432/506, LCR, AGN.
20. The new organization was called the Liga de Comités Agrarias y Sindicatos Campesinos del Estado de Oaxaca. *Oaxaca Nuevo*, 2 August 1938, 5 August 1938, 15 August 1938, 17 August 1938.
21. Report of agent 102, 20 August 1938, IPS, AGN.
22. *Oaxaca Nuevo*, 29 August 1938; Daniel Muñoz Estefan to Governor Chapital, 2 December 1938, Ramo Gobernación 1938, AGPEO; Men of Santa Fe to Secretario del Despacho, 6 December 1938, Ramo Gobernación 1938, AGPEO.
23. *El Oaxaqueño*, 2 March 1937; *Oaxaca Nuevo*, 17 August 1938.
24. Secretario del Despacho to Agente de Ministerio Publico de Tuxtepec, 7 April 1936, Ramo Gobernación 1937, AGPEO.

25. *Boletín del Congreso Constituyente de la Federación Regional de Trabajadores del Estado de Oaxaca*, 23 March 1937; *Boletín del Congreso Constituyente de la Federación Regional de Trabajadores del Estado de Oaxaca*, 24 March 1937.

26. For example, Graciano Benitez, head of the Comité de Sindicatos Unificados; Andrés G. Zárate, president of the workers of San Juan Cahuaca; and Gustavo Jarquin, head of the agrarian committee of Yodovada supported the CCM in 1935.

27. Report of inspector 11, 3 August 1938, Caja 5, IPS, AGN.

28. Francisco R. Lobo to Governor Chapital, 3 January 1937, Ramo Gobernación 1937, AGPEO; *El Oaxaqueño*, 8 January 1938.

29. *Oaxaca Nuevo*, 9 April 1937.

30. *Oaxaca en México* (revista), May 1937; *Oaxaca Nuevo*, 16 April 1937, 17 April 1937; *Oaxaca en México* (revista), April 1937.

31. *Oaxaca Nuevo*, 20 April 1937.

32. Daniel Muñoz Estefan to President Cárdenas, 5 August 1938, Caja 175, IPS, AGN; Vicente Lombardo Toledano to Andres Linaldi, 1 August 1938, IPS, AGN.

33. *Oaxaca Nuevo*, 20 February 1939.

34. Weyl and Weyl, *Reconquest of Mexico*, 163.

35. Perelló, *Reparto agrario en Oaxaca*, 33; Report of Departamento Agrario, 25 July 1941, Ramo Asuntos Agrarios, AGPEO.

36. Arellanes Meixueiro, *Oaxaca*, 236–47. During my research in Oaxaca, I counted all official land grants as listed in the *Periódico Oficial*, 1934–1940. Although the project gave me a rough overview, missing copies and government errors made any exact estimate impossible.

37. *Tuxtepec Moderno*, December 1924.

38. *Oaxaca Nuevo*, 3 August 1933.

39. Propeidades, Tuxtepec, 1930–40, ARPP.

40. Dirección General de Estadistica, *Sexto censo general de población, 1940*.

41. Secretario General del Sindicato de Trabajadores Plataneros de la Finca, Arroyo Culebra, 10 September 1936, 181.3, Ramo Junta de Conciliación y Arbitraje, AGPEO; Arcadio Gallegos to Jefe de la Zona Ejidal, 3 August 1937, 1004.18 27.8.1937, Ramo Asuntos Agrarios, AGPEO.

42. Secretario del Despacho to Agente de Ministerio Público de Tuxtepec, 7 April 1936, Ramo Gobernación 1937, AGPEO.

43. Miguel Ortiz to Departamento Agrario, 10 July 1936, 1003.46, Ramo Asuntos Agrarios, AGPEO.
44. Comité Agraria de Aguacate to Governor Chapital, 11 February 1938, 102.11, Ramo Asuntos Agrarios, AGPEO; Juan Nicolas to Secretaría de Gobierno, 2 October 1937, 2-012.2 (17) Caja 47, 5367, Dirección General de Gobierno, AGN.
45. Felix Ortiz to Governor García Toledo, 20 April 1933, Ramo Gobernación, AGPEO.
46. Carlos Belleza and Daniel Muñoz Estefan to Governor García Toledo, 10 August 1935, Ramo Gobernación, AGPEO.
47. Roberto González to Presidente de la Junta de Conciliación y Arbitraje, 1 October 1936, Ramo Gobernación, AGPEO; Juez de la Primera Instancia de Salina Cruz to Agente de Ministerio Público de Tuxtepec, 23 April 1936, 1003.38, Ramo Asuntos Agrarios, AGPEO; Daniel Muñoz Estefan to Governor García Toledo, 2 August 1936, Ramo Gobernación, AGPEO.
48. Ernesto López to Jefe de la Zona Ejidal, 25 June 1936, 1003.38, Ramo Asuntos Agrarios, AGPEO.
49. Juan Terreno to Governor García Toledo, 3 January 1936, 98.13, Ramo Asuntos Agrarios, AGPEO; Governor García Toledo to Antonio Pérez, 29 January 1936, Ramo Asuntos Agrarios, AGPEO; Juan Terreno to Governor García Toledo, 31 July 1936, Ramo Asuntos Agrarios, AGPEO; Antonio Pérez to Governor García Toledo, 2 August 1936, Ramo Asuntos Agrarios, AGPEO.
50. Comité Nacional de la CTM to Governor García Toledo, 3 September 1936, 180.12, Ramo Junta de Conciliación y Arbitraje, AGPEO.
51. Comité Nacional de la CTM to Governor Chapital, 23 February 1938, Ramo Gobernación, AGPEO.
52. Pedro Francisco Vásquez to SEP, 10 May 1938, Caja 38, AHSEP; Pedro Francisco Vásquez to SEP, 2 May 1938, AHSEP; Adan López to President Cárdenas, 4 January 1937, 403/530, LCR, AGN.
53. Discursos de la Cuarta Convencion Resolutiva del Problema Platanero, Tuxtepec, 23–28 July 1939, Ramo Gobernación, AGPEO.
54. Karnes, *Tropical Enterprise*, 165–66.
55. Genaro Bravo to Departamento Agrario, 18 August 1938, 9 October 1940, 100.4, Ramo Asuntos Agrarios, AGPEO.
56. Benjamin, *A Rich Land*.

57. Isidro Muñoz to Departamento Agrario, 12 April 1938, 95.5, Ramo Asuntos Agrarios, AGPEO; Men of El Cantón to Governor Chapital, 29 August 1939, Ramo Gobernación, AGPEO.

58. José Muñoz García to Governor Chapital, 3 September 1940, Ramo Gobernación, AGPEO.

59. *Periódico Oficial*, 1934–1940.

60. Informe confidencial relacionado con la situación que prevalece en algunos de los ejidos del distrito de Tuxtepec, 8 August 1938, Ramo Gobernación, AGPEO.

61. Men of Obispo to Governor Sánchez Cano, 2 October 1946, 2.311 M (17) 62, Dirección General de Gobierno, AGN.

62. *Oaxaca Nuevo*, 8 May 1941; Boege, *Desarrollo del capitalismo*, 73–111.

63. Tuxtepec, 1934–40, ARPP; Yescas Martínez, *Los desegañados de la tierra*.

64. Turner, *Barbarous Mexico*, 68–90; Chassen-López, *From Liberal to Revolutionary Oaxaca*, 155–56.

65. *Tuxtepec Moderno*, June 1923.

66. Hart, *Empire and Revolution*, 188–93; *Periódico Oficial*, 1934–1940; Tuxtepec, 1934–1940, Ramo Asuntos Agrarios, AGPEO.

67. Isaac Campos, report, 18 August 1938, IPS, AGN; Jorge Tamayo, *Oaxaca en el siglo XX*, 68.

68. Fowler-Salamini, "The Agrarian Revolution in the State of Veracruz."

69. *Periódico Oficial*, 23 October 1935, 19 January 1937.

70. Eduardo E. Clavel to President Cárdenas, 12 April 1936, 543.1/12, LCR, AGN; *El Oaxaqueño*, 23 January 1935.

71. Jesús Ramírez Vásquez to Secretario del Despacho, 2 August 1938, Ramo Gobernación, AGPEO; Efrain Pelaez to Jefe de la Zona Ejidal, 9 May 1937, 1019.17, Ramo Asuntos Agrarios, AGPEO; Gustavo Mendoza to Secretario del Despacho, 6 May 1936, 312 (17) Caja 11, 29, Dirección General de Gobierno, AGN.

72. Cirilio Castañeda to Governor Chapital, 20 February 1940, Ramo Gobernación, AGPEO.

73. Enrique Galan López to Secretario del Despacho, 6 January 1937, Ramo Gobernación, AGPEO.

74. Enrique Reyna Tello to Departamento Agrario, 23 October 1937, 1019.18, Ramo Asuntos Agrarios, AGPEO.

75. *El Oaxaqueño*, 4 April 1936, 6 April 1936; *Oaxaca en México* (revista), October 1936, June 1937; Juan Velasco to assistant sectretary to governor, 20 October 1937, Ramo Gobernación, AGPEO.

76. Men of Camotinchan to Governor Chapital, May 1937, Ramo Gobernación, AGPEO; Ramón Rojas to Governor Chapital, 6 February 1937, Ramo Gobernación, AGPEO; Comité Estatal de la CCM to Governor Chapital, 17 March 1937, Ramo Gobernación, AGPEO; Cirilio Castañeda to Secretario del Despacho, 16 February 1938, Ramo Gobernación, AGPEO.

77. Jesús Ramírez Vásquez to President Cárdenas, 12 April 1940, 506.1/40-21, LCR, AGN.

78. *Periódico Oficial*, 1934–1940.

79. Rodríguez Canto, *Historia agricola y agraria*, 261.

80. Chassen and Martínez, "El retorno al milenio Mixteco."

81. Rodríguez Canto, *Historia agricola y agraria*, 190–201; Mouat, "Los chiveros de la Mixteca Baja."

82. Aguirre Beltrán, *Cuijla*, 101–3; Pérez Aragon, *El problema agrario*.

83. Men of Rancho de Muralla to Jefe de la Zona Ejidal, 2 January 1937, Ramo Gobernación 1937, AGPEO.

84. Moises Martínez Baños to President Avila Camacho, 2 March 1942, 541/211, Fondo Presidentes, Ramo Manuel Avila Camacho, AGN; Domingo Martínez Baños to Jefe de la Zona Ejidal, 6 April 1942, Ramo Gobernación, AGPEO.

85. There was a strong memory of the 1911 revolt even in the 1950s. Gutierre Tibón, *Pinotepa Nacional, Mixtecos, Negros y Triquis*, 30–36.

86. Men of Mártires de Tacubaya to Departamento Agrario, 19 June 1937, Ramo Gobernación, AGPEO; Bruno Castro to Secretario del Despacho, 1 April 1937, Ramo Gobernación, AGPEO; Damaso Castro to Governor Chapital, 6 December 1937, Ramo Gobernación, AGPEO.

87. Dirección General de Estadistica, *Sexto censo general de población, 1940*.

88. Arellanes Meixueiro, *Oaxaca*.

89. Cassidy, "Haciendas and Pueblos."

90. Chassen et al., "Las haciendas en Oaxaca."

91. Kouri, "Interpreting the Expropriation of Indian Pueblo Lands."

92. Arellanes Meixueiro, *Oaxaca*, 129.

93. Report of Recaudador de Rentas, 6 November 1940, 929.1, Ramo Asuntos Agrarios, AGPEO.

94. Arellanes Meixueiro, "Del camarazo al cardenismo," 37.

95. *Memoria que presenta el C. Coronel Constantino Chapital.*

96. *Periódico Oficial*, 1937; Arellanes Meixueiro, *Oaxaca*, 1940.

97. Recaudador de Rentas de Ocotlán to Erario del Estado, 2 January 1938, Ramo Gobernación, AGPEO.

98. Men of San Miguel Tilquiapam to Governor Garcia Toledo, 24 April 1936, 991.46, Ramo Asuntos Agrarios, AGPEO.

99. Men of San Pedro Taviche to Governor Garcia Toledo, 19 January 1936, 991.44, Ramo Asuntos Agrarios, AGPEO.

100. Men of Mogote to Departamento Agrario, 21 July 1941, Ramo Gobernación, AGPEO.

101. Cook and Binford, *Obliging Need.*

102. Wright Rios, "Piety and Progress"; Decree 213, 11 September 1934, Ramo Asuntos Católicos, AGPEO; Valentin Díaz to Liga Nacional de la Defensa de la Libertad, 5 April 1936, Caja 25, Exp 120, AAAR.

103. Report of the Liga Nacional de la Defensa de la Libertad, 1935, Caja 25, Exp 120, AAAR; Luis A. Aguilar to Liga Nacional de la Defensa de la Libertad, 17 August 1935, Caja 25, Exp 120, AAAR.

104. *El Oaxaqueño*, 2 March 1935, 7 March 1935; M. Mayoral to Liga Nacional de la Defensa de la Libertad, 27 September 1936, Caja 25, Exp 120, AAAR.

105. Report of Efren Ramírez, 13 April 1935, 181.7, AHSEP.

106. *El Oaxaqueño*, 24 March 1935, 22 October 1934.

107. Report of Luis Ramírez, 28 September 1937, Ramo Gobernación, AGPEO.

108. *El Oaxaqueño*, 26 July 1937.

109. *El Oaxaqueño*, 11 December 1936; *Oaxaca en México* (revista), October 1936; Ezequiel Figueroa to Governor Chapital, 2 January 1939, 1936–1939, Ramo Gobernación, AGPEO.

110. Decree of Governor González Fernández, 26 December 1940, Elecciones Municipales 1940, Ramo Gobernación, AGPEO.

111. *La Voz de Oaxaca*, 24 February 1948.

112. Butler, *Popular Piety*; Vaughan, *Cultural Politics.*

113. De la Peña, *Oaxaca económico*, 36; Riedemann, *Los comerciantes de Huajuapan de León*; Pastor, *Campesinos y reformas*, 442–47.

114. List of sales of land in Huajuapam, 12.2, Ramo Asuntos Agrarios, AGPEO.

115. Knight, "El liberalismo mexicano," 80.
116. Constantino Esteva listed only six haciendas in Huajuapam. In the rest of the Mixteca Baja there were also very few—one in Silacayoapam and none in Juxtlahuaca, Teposcolula, or Coixtlahuaca. Esteva, *Nociones elementales de geografía*. The 1912 report of the *jefe político* lists twelve haciendas. Report of jefe político, Fomento 1912, 6.2, Ramo Junta de Conciliación y Arbitraje, AGPEO.
117. Huajuapam, Ramo Civil 1800–1910, Archivo Judicial de Oaxaca.
118. Escobar Ohmstede, "Los condueñazgos."
119. Monaghan, "Mixtec Caciques," 275.
120. Monaghan, "Mixtec Caciques," 275–79; John Monaghan, "El PAN y las Comunidades de la Mixteca Baja."
121. Men of Cuyotepeji to governor, 5 July 1882, 12.7, Ramo Ajudicaciones, AGPEO.
122. Wright Rios, "Piety and Progress"; Esparza, *Gillow durante el Porfiriato*.
123. Jesus Zamora to Secretario del Despacho, 8 November 1896, Siglo XIX, Huajuapam de León, 8.48, Ramo Gobernación, AGPEO.
124. Smith, "Anticlericalism and Resistance."
125. Liga Central de Comités Agrarias to Departamento Agrario, 31 October 1934, 29.9, Ramo Asuntos Agrarios, AGPEO; Men of Suchitepec to Departamento Agrario, 31 October 1934, Ramo Asuntos Agrarios, AGPEO; Men of Huaxtepec to Departamento Agrario, 10 September 1937, 30.8, Ramo Asuntos Agrarios, AGPEO; Men of Huaxtepec to Departamento Agrario, 15 December 1939, 30.8, Ramo Asuntos Agrarios, AGPEO; *Periódico Oficial*, 1934–1940.
126. Men of Mariscala to Governor Vásquez, 16 July 1925, 26.3, Ramo Asuntos Agrarios, AGPEO; Men of Mariscala to Carlos Belleza, 1 July 1936, Ramo Asuntos Agrarios, AGPEO.
127. Recaudador de Rentas de Huajuapam to Erario del Estado, 3 January 1938, Ramo Gobernación, AGPEO.
128. Julio Calderón to Comité Nacional de la CNC, 3 August 1938, Ramo Gobernación 1938, AGPEO.
129. Smith, "Party of the Priest."
130. See Elecciones Municipales, 219-3 173 (7) "52," Ramo Gobernación, AGPEO.
131. Mendoza Garcia, "Las cofradias del curato."
132. Martínez, *La lucha electoral*.

133. Brading, *Caudillo and Peasant*, 13; Vanderwood, "Religion, Official, Popular and Otherwise."

134. Aguilar Robledo, "Haciendas y condueñazgos"; Sanchez R., "Los católicos."

135. Feria Juárez, *Estado actual de la reforma agraria*, 64.

136. Ruíz Martínez, *El problema económico*, 9.

137. Ruíz Martínez, *El problema económico*, 10–18; Report of Aurelio Bueno, 14 July 1923, 152.9, Ramo Periodo Revolucionario, AGPEO.

138. Ruíz Martínez, *El problema económico*, 18–19; de la Peña, *Oaxaca económico*, 54.

139. President Obregón to Aurelio Bueno, 2 September 1923, 152.9, Ramo Periodo Revolucionario, AGPEO; Sociedad Cooperativa Limitada de Sombreros de las Mixtecas to President Obregón, 19 October 1923, Ramo Periodo Revolucionario, AGPEO; Aurelio Bueno to President Obregón, 1 January 1924, Ramo Periodo Revolucionario, AGPEO.

140. *Primer congreso industrial de la palma*; *El Mercurio*, 17 November 1931, 18 November 1931.

141. José Trinidad Espinosa to President Cárdenas, 22 October 1937, 649 523/14, LCR, AGN; Leopoldo Jiménez Cordoba to President Cárdenas, 9 November 1935, LCR, AGN; Leopoldo Jiménez Cordoba to President Cárdenas, 17 April 1935, LCR, AGN.

142. José Trinidad Espinosa to President Cárdenas, 22 October 1937, 649 523/14, LCR, AGN; Leopoldo Jiménez Cordoba to President Cárdenas, 17 April 1935, LCR, AGN.

143. Liga Nacional de Sociedades Cooperativas to President Cárdenas, 9 July 1935, 649 523/14, LCR, AGN.

144. Men of Rancho Vargas to President Cárdenas, 19 October 1935, 649 523/14, LCR, AGN; Secretaría de Gobierno to Governor García Toledo, 26 August 1935, LCR, AGN.

145. Ruíz Martínez, *El problema económico*, 20.

146. Ruíz Martínez, *El problema económico*, 25–26.

147. Malinowski and de la Fuente, *Malinowski in Mexico*, 161.

148. Ruíz Martínez, *El problema económico*, 24.

149. Informe sobre el problema de la Mixteca Oaxaqueña, 1937, Ramo Gobernación 1941, AGPEO; Ruíz Martínez, *El problema económico*, 27.

150. *Oaxaca Nuevo*, 10 January 1938; *La Voz de la Mixteca*, 6 January 1938; Sindicato Unico de Trabajadores de Enseñanza to President Cárdenas, 4 February 1938, 649 523/14, LCR, AGN.

151. Renato Sosa Herrerias to President Cárdenas, 13 February 1939, 649 523/14, LCR, AGN; Memorandum of Vicente González Fernández, 21 July 1941, 523.8/14 28, Fondo Presidentes, Ramo Manuel Avila Camacho (MAC), AGN.

152. Men of Rio Blanco to President Avila Camacho, 30 September 1944, 523.8/14 28, MAC, AGN; Comité Nacional de la CTM to President Avila Camacho, 10 May 1941, MAC, AGN.

153. Men of Ayuquililla to President Avila Camacho, 2 October 1942, Ramo Gobernación, AGPEO.

154. Comité Nacional de la CTM to President Avila Camacho, 3 March 1942, 523.8/14 28, MAC, AGN; Sindicato de Obreros, Jarcieros y Similares de Tehuacán to President Avila Camacho, 29 March 1942, MAC, AGN.

155. Men of Nativitas to President Avila Camacho, 28 October 1946, 523.8/14 28, MAC, AGN; Marciano Marin to President Avila Camacho, 28 October 1946, MAC, AGN; Comité Nacional de la CTM to President Avila Camacho, 22 July 1946, MAC, AGN.

156. De la Peña, *Oaxaca económico*, 1404–24.

157. Men of Joluxtla to Secretaría de la Economia, 26 July 1946, 523.8/14 28, MAC, AGN; Roberto López to President Avila Camacho, 29 January 1942, MAC, AGN.

158. Fallaw, *Cárdenas Compromised*.

159. Schryer, "Village Factionalism and Class Conflict," 298.

160. Buve, *El movimiento revolucionario en Tlaxcala*, 371.

161. Craig, *The First Agraristas*, 181.

162. Córdova, *La política de masas*, 119; Ianni, *El estado capitalista*, 91.

163. Cockcroft, *Mexico*, 134.

164. Knight, "Weight of the State in Modern Mexico," 218.

165. Fallaw, *Cárdenas Compromised*, 5–6.

166. Fallaw, *Cárdenas Compromised*, 6.

167. Benjamin, *A Rich Land*, 207; Knight, "Rise and Fall of Cardenismo," 264.

7. The Problems with Cardenista Politics

1. Medina, *Historia de la Revolución*, 18:5; Niblo, *Mexico in the 1940s*, xvii.

2. Medina, "Origen y circunstancia de la idea de unidad nacional"; Miller, *Red, White and Green*.

3. González Casanova, *Democracy in Mexico*, 24–33.
4. Hellman, *Mexico in Crisis*, 101.
5. Benjamin, *A Rich Land*, 201.
6. Garrido, *El partido de la revolución institutionalizada*, 314–25, 328–34; Niblo, *Mexico in the 1940s*, 98–103.
7. Hellman, *Mexico in Crisis*, 49–51.
8. Garrido, *El partido de la revolución institutionalizada*, 312.
9. *Oaxaca Nuevo*, 25 June 1939.
10. See, for example, Report of inspector 63, 10 July 1940, Caja 176, IPS, AGN.
11. Report of inspector 18, 18 October 1939, Caja 763, IPS, AGN; *El Remolino*, 7 October 1938; *Oaxaca en México* (periodico), 5 November 1939.
12. Carpeta Vicente González Fernández, Direccíon General de Archivo e Historia, AHSDN.
13. Interview (BTS) with Mario Torres Márquez, December 2003; Francisco Ramírez, *Seis discursos*, 5; Martínez Medina, "Historia de una crisis política local," 63.
14. Martínez Medina, "Historia de una crisis política local," 65; *Oaxaca en México* (revista), April 1939; Jorge Meixueiro to President Cárdenas, 27 February 1940, 2.311. G (17-60)/4, Dirección General de Gobierno, AGN.
15. Comité Ejidal de San Lucas Ojitlán to Secretaría de Gobierno, 2 March 1940, Ramo Gobernación, AGPEO; Carlos Belleza to Secretario del Despacho, 14 April 1940, Ramo Gobernación, AGPEO; Martínez Medina, "Historia de una crisis política local," 65; *Oaxaca en México* (revista), April 1939; Jorge Meixueiro to President Cárdenas, 27 February 1940, 2.311. G (17-60)/4, Dirección General de Gobierno, AGN.
16. Enrique Vargas to Secretaría de Gobierno, 28 June 1939, 2/311 (17-38)/5, Dirección General de Gobierno, AGN.
17. Comité Estatal de la CNC to CNC, 2 November 1939, Ramo Gobernación, AGPEO; *Oaxaca Nuevo*, 20 November 1939.
18. Sindicato de Trabajadores de la Industria Azucaria to Secretaría de Gobierno, 7 July 1940, 2.311 (17) 1 Caja 12, Dirección General de Gobierno, AGN; Comité Estatal Pro-Zaragoza to Secretaría de Gobierno, 14 February 1940, 2.311.G (17-60)/3, Dirección General de Gobierno, AGN;

Leopoldo Jiménez Córdova to President Cárdenas, 20 January 1940, 2.311.G (17-60)/4, Dirección General de Gobierno, AGN.

19. *Estatutos, circulares, declaración de principios.*

20. *Oaxaca Nuevo*, 21 November 1939, 25 November 1939; *Vanguardia*, 8 December 1939.

21. *Oaxaca Nuevo*, 8 August 1939; Governor Chapital to municipal presidents, 28 October 1939, 2.311.G (17-60)/4, Dirección General de Gobierno, AGN.

22. *Oaxaca Nuevo*, 6 November 1939.

23. Martínez Medina, "Historia de una crisis política local," 65; *Oaxaca Nuevo*, 21 March 1940, 5 August 1940.

24. Wasserman, "Transition from Personalist to Party Rule," 225.

25. *Oaxaca Nuevo*, 31 December 1942; *El Momento*, 23 December 1942; Alfredo Cortés Rito to Secretaría de Gobierno, 4 March 1941, 2.311 (17), Dirección General de Gobierno, AGN; *El Hombre Libre*, 21 July 1944; Juan Reyes Spindola to President Avila Camacho, 11 May 1943, 2.311.D.F. (17) 1 Caja 41, Dirección General de Gobierno, AGN.

26. *El Hombre Libre*, 21 July 1944.

27. *Periódico Oficial*, 1940–1944.

28. *Oaxaca Nuevo*, 2 June 1941, 5 June 1941.

29. *Oaxaca Nuevo*, 19 September 1942; *Informe de Vicente González Fernández*, 1941.

30. *Periódico Oficial*, 1934–1940; Filiberto González to Departamento Agrario, 26 March 1936, 993.39, Ramo Asuntos Agrarios, AGPEO; Men of San Isidro to Departamento Agrario, 4 July 1936, 993.44, Ramo Asuntos Agrarios, AGPEO.

31. Secretaría de Gobierno to municipal president of Putla, 27 February 1936, 993.38, Ramo Asuntos Agrarios, AGPEO; CCM to Governor Chapital, 22 December 1936, 993.55, Ramo Asuntos Agrarios, AGPEO; I. Montesinos López to Governor González Fernández, 22 January 1941, Ramo Gobernación, AGPEO.

32. Manuel Vásquez B. to Governor González Fernández, 16 December 1942, Elecciones Municipales, Putla, Ramo Gobernación, AGPEO.

33. Matias Alvarez to Governor Sánchez Cano, 2 June 1945, Ramo Gobernación, AGPEO.

34. *Oaxaca Nuevo*, 25 September 1942; *Oaxaca Nuevo*, 23 December 1942.

35. Governor González Fernández to Secretaría de Gobierno, 17 November 1942, Ramo Gobernción, AGPEO.

36. Otilio Ochoa to Governor González Fernández, 14 January 1943, Ramo Gobernación, AGPEO.

37. Salvador García to Departamento Agrario, March 1943, Ramo Asuntos Agrarios, AGPEO.

38. Manuel Zárate to comités ejidales de Huajuapam, March 1941, 930.10, Ramo Asuntos Agrarios, AGPEO; Manuel Zárate to San Nicolas Hidalgo, 4 June 1941, 944.18, Ramo Asuntos Agrarios, AGPEO; Governor González Fernández to San Antonio de las Masas, 7 June 1941, 944.19, Ramo Asuntos Agrarios, AGPEO.

39. Simon Cruz to CNC, 20 March 1941, Ramo Gobernación, AGPEO; Governor González Fernández to Secretaría de Gobierno, 28 March 1941, Ramo Gobernación, AGPEO.

40. Niblo, *Mexico in the 1940s*, 98–103; Durand, *La ruptura de la nación*, 47–102.

41. Governor González Fernández to Secretaría de Gobierno, 4 March 1941, Ramo Gobernación 1941, AGPEO; Secretaría de Gobierno to Governor González Fernández, 18 March 1941, Ramo Gobernación 1941, AGPEO.

42. CTM to Governor González Fernández, 18 March 1941, Ramo Gobernación, AGPEO; Jorge Meixueiro to Alejandro Manje, 19 April 1941, Ramo Gobernación 1941, AGPEO.

43. *Oaxaca en México* (periodico), 1 December 1943.

44. Melquiades Ramírez published the newspaper *La Voz del Obrero*, which supported the governor, and often spoke on the governor's behalf during the water strike. *La Voz del Obrero*, 23 April 1944; *El Momento*, 21 June 1944; *El Universal*, 22 April 1944; *Oaxaca en México* (periodico), 12 April 1944.

45. *Antequera*, 13 January 1943; *Antequera*, 22 February 1943; José Aguilar Reyes to President Avila Camacho, 11 May 1944, 432/72, MAC, AGN.

46. *Antequera*, 25 January 1943; *Antequera*, 27 January 1943; *Oaxaca en México* (periodico), 30 November 1943.

47. *Oaxaca Nuevo*, 13 August 1941; *Oaxaca Nuevo*, 19 September 1941; *Oaxaca Nuevo*, 26 November 1941; *Oaxaca en México* (periodico), 5 January 1941.

48. Governor González Fernández to President Avila Camacho, 26 August 1941, 505.1/27, MAC, AGN.

49. Isidro Candia to President Avila Camacho, 29 December 1941, 505.1/27, MAC, AGN.

50. Juan Spindola to President Avila Camacho, 21 December 1941, 543.1/19, MAC, AGN. There was a similar festival in 1944.

51. *Oaxaca Nuevo*, 12 March 1942; *Oaxaca Nuevo*, 7 March 1942.

52. *Oaxaca Nuevo*, 23 September 1942; Bandas Municipales, 1942, Ramo Gobernación, AGPEO.

53. *Oaxaca Nuevo*, 23 April 1942.

54. *Informe de Vicente González Fernández*, 1941, 5.

55. 3 February 1941, 606.3/38, MAC, AGN.

56. *Antequera*, 2 December 1943.

57. *Informe de Vicente González Fernández*, 1941, 6; *Oaxaca Nuevo*, 16 January 1942.

58. Elisa Olmedo to President Avila Camacho, 3 January 1944, 542.1/144, MAC, AGN.

59. Gregorio Castañeda to President Avila Camacho, 26 September 1941, 541/211, MAC, AGN.

60. Moises Baños to President Avila Camacho, 7 May 1941, 541/224, MAC, AGN.

61. Oscar Ruíz to Governor González Fernández, 23 August 1941, Ramo Justicia 1940, AGPEO; Ojeda Bohórquez, *Los cuerudos*.

62. Governor González Fernández to Luis Rodríguez, 23 October 1942, Ramo Justicia 1942, AGPEO.

63. Men of Santiago Tutla to Governor González Fernández, 6 October 1941, Ramo Gobernación 1941, AGPEO.

64. Subsecretaría de Gobierno to President Avila Camacho, 22 September 1945, 54.3/136, MAC, AGN; Presidente Municipal de Atitlán to Governor Vasconcelos, 3 June 1947, Ramo Gobernación 1947, AGPEO; Francisco Martínez to Governor Vasconcelos, 15 March 1947, Ramo Gobernación 1947, AGPEO; Laviada, *Los caciques de la Sierra*, 28.

65. Presidente Municipal de Atitlán to Governor Vasconcelos, 3 June 1947, Ramo Gobernación 1947, AGPEO.

66. Governor González Fernández to President Avila Camacho, 17 July 1944, 541/1042, MAC, AGN; Laviada, *Los caciques de la Sierra*, 42.

67. Heliodoro Charis to Manuel Avila Camacho, 15 December 1940, 2/311 M (17)15, Dirección General de Gobierno, AGN.

68. Socrates Castillo Carraso to Secretaría de Gobierno, 16 January 1941, 2/311 M (17)15, Dirección General de Gobierno, AGN; Heliodoro Charis to President Avila Camacho, 13 January 1941, 2/311 M (17)16, Dirección General de Gobierno, AGN; Report of Socrates Castillo Carraso, 5 January 1941, Dirección General de Gobierno, AGN; Altamirano, *Heliodoro Charis Castro*, 82–83.

69. Miguel Ortiz to Governor González Fernández, 15 January 1941, Ramo Gobernación 1941, AGPEO; Heliodoro Charis to Secretaría de Gobierno, 25 January 1941, Ramo Gobernación 1941, AGPEO.

70. Altamirano, *Heliodoro Charis Castro*, 69, 82.

71. Manuel Reyes to Governor González Fernández, 18 December 1940, 2/311 M (17)16, Dirección General de Gobierno, AGN; Antonio Gómez Velasco to Governor González Fernández, 3 March 1941, Ramo Gobernación, AGPEO; Mucio Cristobal Marin to President Avila Camacho, 17 March 1941, 522.341, MAC, AGN.

72. Roberto Garza Cabello to Jefe de la Zona Ejidal, 29 January 1941, 986.7, Ramo Asuntos Agrarios, AGPEO; Muncipal President of Tapantepec to Antonio Gómez Velasco, 4 May 1941, Ramo Asuntos Agrarios, AGPEO; César Urbieta to Secretaria de Agricultura, 4 March 1942, Ramo Asuntos Agrarios, AGPEO; Felix Piñeda to Governor González Fernández, 3 March 1942, Ramo Asuntos Agrarios, AGPEO.

73. Manuel N. García to Governor González Fernández, 4 November 1941, Ramo Gobernación, AGPEO; Raymundo Mata to Departamento Agrario, 23 June 1942, 1028.12, Ramo Asuntos Agrarios, AGPEO; Juan Pérez Mora to Departamento Agrario, 3 December 1942, Ramo Asuntos Agrarios, AGPEO.

74. Demetrio Méndez to President Avila Camacho, 25 August 1943, 542.1/897, MAC, AGN; Miguel Ortiz to Governor González Fernández, 8 December 1943, Ramo Justicia, AGPEO.

75. Men of Asunción to Governor González Fernández, 3 November 1943, Ramo Gobernación, AGPEO.

76. Catarino Juan to Governor González Fernández, 9 February 1943, Ramo Gobernación, AGPEO.

77. Presidente Municipal de Tuxtepec to Governor González Fernández, 4 December 1942, Ramo Justicia 1942, AGPEO; Cresencio Martínez to

Amando Herrera, 11 February 1943, Ramo Justicia 1942, AGPEO;
Amando Herrera to Governor González Fernández, 20 February 1943,
Ramo Justicia 1943, AGPEO.

78. Laviada, *Los caciques de la Sierra*, 59. As revenge Governor González
Fernández would blame José Ramón for the death of Daniel Martínez.

79. Luis Rodríguez to Governor González Fernández, 6 November 1944,
Ramo Gobernación, AGPEO; José Ramírez to Secretario de Despacho,
19 November 1944, Justicia, Ramo Gobernación, AGPEO.

80. Campbell, "Intelectuales Zapotecos"; Campbell, "Tradition and the
New Social Movements," 88.

81. *El Universal Grafico*, 12 November 1941.

82. *El Universal*, 24 February 1942, 25 February 1942; *Oaxaca Nuevo*,
26 February 1942, 27 February 1942, 28 February 1942.

83. Avila Camacho did allow the *caudillaje* of his own brother, Maximino.
Valencia Castrejón, *Poder regional y política*.

84. De la Cruz, *El General Charis*, 148.

85. Niblo, *Mexico in the 1940s*, 115–17.

86. Garfias Magaña, "El General Joaquín Amaro."

87. De la Cruz, *El General Charis*, 121.

88. *Antequera*, 6 April 1944; Secretaría de Gobierno to President Avila
Camacho, 22 September 1943, 54.3/136, MAC, AGN; General Amaro
to Governor González Fernández, 4 November 1943, Ramo Gobernación, AGPEO.

89. President Avila Camacho to General Amaro, 13 January 1943, 06.08,
Autoridades Locales y Estatales, AJA; Governor González Fernández to
General Amaro, 30 March 1943, Autoridades Locales y Estatales, AJA.

90. Altamirano, *Heliodoro Charis Castro*, 82–83; Elecciones Municipales,
Juchitán 1942, Ramo Gobernación, AGPEO.

91. There is voluminous material on the elections for federal deputies in
Dirección General de Gobierno, AGN: 3.311.D.F. (17) 1; 2.311.D.F.
(17) 1 Caja 41; 2.311 DL (17) 1-4 Caja 104. *Oaxaca en México* (periodico), March–August 1943.

92. *La Prensa*, 19 August 1943; *El Universal*, 19 August 1943, 20 August
1943; Whetton, *Rural Mexico*, 541–42; Arellanes, "Testimonios, suicidio en la Camara"; Meixueiro Hernández, *Jorge Meixueiro Hernández*.

93. Whetton, *Rural Mexico*, 542.

94. *La Prensa*, 19 August 1943.

95. *Antequera*, 14 November 1943.
96. *Antequera*, 5 November 1943, 2 January 1944.
97. Newcomer, *Reconciling Modernity*.
98. Knight, "State Power and Political Stability," 42.
99. Huxley, *Beyond the Mexique Bay*, 276.
100. Dirección General de Estadistica, *Septimo censo general de población, 1950*; Dirección General de Estadistica, *Sexto censo general de población, 1940*.
101. Unikel, "Urbanización y urbanismo."
102. Interview by Noemi Morales Sánchez (NMS) with Adela Avendano Ramírez, June 2006.
103. Interview (NMS) with Eustolia Avendano, June 2006.
104. Interview (NMS) with María del Socorro Gonzáles Jiménez, July 2006.
105. Jiménez, "Popular Organizing for Public Services," 501.
106. Hayner, *New Patterns in Old Mexico*, 55.
107. Contratos, Oaxaca City, 1930–40, ARPP; Interview (NMS) with Porfiria García García, June 2006.
108. Interview (NMS) with María del Socorro Gonzáles Jiménez, July 2006.
109. Interview (NMS) with María de Jesús Ramírez Pérez, July 2006.
110. Beals, "Oaxaca Market Project," 29.
111. Tamayo, *Proyectos de integración*, 72.
112. Dirección General de Estadistica, *Sexto censo general de población, 1940*; Dirección General de Estadistica, *Septimo censo general de población, 1950*.
113. Hayner, *New Patterns in Old Mexico*, 48–49.
114. Malinowski and de la Fuente, *Malinowski in Mexico*; Cook and Diskin, *Markets in Oaxaca*.
115. See Diskin, "Structure of a Peasant Market System," 65.
116. Interview (NMS) with Maria del Socorro González Jimenez, July 2006.
117. Buro de Investigación Política, 31 March 1952, Collección Mayoral Heredia, Hemeroteca Pública de Oaxaca.
118. Impuestos, 1951, Archivo Municipal de Oaxaca de Juárez (AMOJ).
119. Calvo, "Huellas e ilusiones," 31.
120. Interview (NMS) with María del Socorro Gonzáles Jiménez, July 2006.
121. Fowler-Salamini, "Gender, Work and Working-Class Women's Culture."
122. Interview (NMS) with Porfiria García García, July 2006.
123. Interview (NMS) with María del Socorro Gonzáles Jiménez, July 2006.

124. Arellanes Meixueiro, *Los trabajos y los guias*; Overmyer-Velázquez, "A New Political Religious Order"; Lear, *Workers, Neighbors, Citizens,* 93–95.
125. Meyer, *El conflicto religioso*; Juan G. Cabral to Governor García Toledo, 26 September 1934, Ramo Gobernación, AGPEO; Report of the Liga Nacional de la Defensa de la Libertad, 1935, Caja 25, Exp 120, Archivo de Aurelio Acevedo Robles.
126. José Reyes to Acción Católica Mexicana, 1938, 2.10, Junta Diocesana de Oaxaca, Archivo de Acción Católica Mexicana (AACM).
127. Albino López, 1938, 2.10, Junta Diocesana de Oaxaca, AACM.
128. Interview of EBW, 25 June 1965, Box 58, Ralph L. Beals Collection, National Anthropological Archive (NAA).
129. Interview (NMS) with María Teresa Valera Flores, July 2006.
130. Austreberto Aragon to ACM, September 1943, AACM.
131. Hayner, *New Patterns in Old Mexico,* 164–65.
132. Warner, *Letters of the Republic.*
133. Niblo, *Mexico in the 1940s,* 346–50.
134. Gillingham, "Force and Consent in Mexican Provincial Politics," 255–56.
135. *El Momento,* December 1940–January 1941.
136. *El Momento,* 23 May 1943.
137. Interview (BTS) with Leonarda Morales Osorio, December 2003; Interview (BTS) with Luis Castañeda Guzmán, July 2003; Interview (BTS) with Guillermo Aragon, December 2004; Interview (NMS) with Maria Teresa Valera Flores, June 2006.
138. Dirección General de Estadistica, *Sexto censo general de población, 1940.*
139. Edmundo Sánchez Cano to Secretaría de Gobierno, April 1946, Ramo Gobernación, AGPEO.
140. Manuel H. Basilio to Governor Vasconcelos, 21 February 1948, 2/384.2 (17) 22, Ramo Gobernación 1948, AGPEO.
141. Newcomer, *Reconciling Modernity,* 7–8; Palacios, *La pluma y el arado.*
142. Torres Ramírez, *Historia de la Revolución,* 19:33–76.
143. Avila Camacho, *Discursos,* 32.
144. *Informe de Vicente González Fernández,* 1941; *Informe de Vicente González Fernández,* 1942; *Informe de Edmundo Sánchez Cano.*
145. Jiménez, "Popular Organizing for Public Services," 502.

146. Medina Gómez, "Introducción de la luz electrica"; Chassen-López, *From Liberal to Revolutionary Oaxaca*, 75; *El Informador*, 3 April 1935; Federico Zorrilla to Plutarco Elías Calles, 9 October 1921, 124.4946 1/2, APEC.

147. *Oaxaca en México* (periodico), 1 April 1941.

148. *Oaxaca en México* (periodico), 1 November 1940; Comité Ejecutivo de la Liga de Resistencia de Consumidores de Luz y Fuerza Electrica, 7 August 1940, 523.4/458, LCR, AGN; *Oaxaca en México* (periodico), 2 February 1941.

149. Libro Primero, Comercio, Centro, 1942–45, 22 April 1942, ARPP.

150. *Oaxaca en México* (periodico), 31 July 1942; *Oaxaca Nuevo*, 12 June 1942.

151. Liga de Resistencia de Consumidores de Energia Electrica to Governor González Fernández, 13 May 1943, Diversas Peticiones, Ramo Gobernación, AGPEO; *Oaxaca Nuevo*, 17 July 1942, 26 August 1942.

152. *Oaxaca Nuevo*, 4 September 1942, 10 September 1942, 2 October 1942, 30 October 1942.

153. *Antequera*, 13 January 1943, 22 February 1943; José Aguilar Reyes to President Avila Camacho, 11 May 1944, 432/72, MAC, AGN.

154. *Antequera*, 14 May 1944.

155. *La Alerta*, 3 June 1944; *Oaxaca en México* (periodico), 31 May 1944.

156. *Oaxaca en México* (periodico), 1 April 1941, 1 June 1941, 12 April 1944.

157. *El Momento*, 20 May 1944; *Oaxaca en México* (periodico), 5 April 1944.

158. Miguel Polo to Governor González Fernández, 14 March 1944, Ramo Gobernación, AGPEO; *El Momento*, 13 December 1943, 25 January 1944; *Oaxaca en México* (periodico), 30 May 1944.

159. Interview (NMS) with Sofia Jiménez Torres, June 2006; Interview (BTS) with Leonarda Morales Osorio, December 2003; *El Momento*, 27 May 1944; Austreberto Aragon to Governor González Fernández, 17 November 1944, Ramo Gobernación, AGPEO.

160. *Antequera*, 9 April 1944; Graciano Benitez to Governor Sánchez Cano, 11 January 1945, Ramo Gobernación 1945, AGPEO; *Antequera*, 21 June 1944. Sinarquismo was a right-wing Catholic movement, which emerged in the Bajio region after the Cristero revolt.

161. Interview (BTS) with Guillermo Aragon, December 2004; González Esperón, *Crónicas diversas de artesanos oaxaqueños*, 57–71.
162. Austreberto Aragon to Luis González, 13 October 1943, AMOJ; Austreberto Aragon to Presidente Municipal Oaxaca de Juárez, 23 May 1942, AMOJ.
163. Interview with Austreberto Aragon, 8 June 1966, box 60, Ralph L. Beals Collection, NAA.
164. Report of agent Vicente Cervantes, 3 April 1944, IPS, AGN.
165. *El Momento*, 14 June 1944.
166. Report of agent Vicente Cervantes, 3 April 1944, IPS, AGN.
167. Interview with Austreberto Aragon, 8 June 1966, box 60, Ralph L. Beals Collection, NAA.
168. *Oaxaca en México* (periodico), 12 April 1944; *El Momento*, 12 April 1944.
169. *El Momento* (Extra), 13 April 1944.
170. Kaplan, "Female Consciousness and Collective Action"; Kaplan, "Redressing the Balance."
171. Knight, "State Power and Political Stability."
172. Córdova, *La política de masas*, 74.
173. Niblo, *Mexico in the 1940s*, 89. See also Medina, *Historia de la Revolucion*, 20:10.
174. Schmidt, "Making It Real Compared to What," 40; Rubin, "Decentrando el régimen."
175. Niblo, *Mexico in the 1940s*, 99.
176. Rubin, "Decentrando el régimen."
177. Lear, *Workers, Neighbors and Citizens*, 105.

8. The Rise and Fall of Edmundo Sánchez Cano

1. Medin, *El sexenio alemanista*, 50–52.
2. Taracena, *La vida en México*, 2:352–60; Martínez Medina, "Historia de una crisis política local."
3. Medina, *Historia de la Revolución*, 20:95–110.
4. Niblo, *Mexico in the 1940s*, 232–35.
5. Newcomer, *Reconciling Modernity*.
6. *Antequera*, 10 October 1943.
7. Men of Santiago Laollaga to President Avila Camacho, 19 October 1943, 2.311 (17) 6 Caja 282, Dirección General del Gobierno, AGN;

Comité Ejecutivo de Unificación Oaxaqueña to Secretaría de Gobierno, 23 August 1943, Dirección General del Gobierno, AGN; Liga Campesina de Huajolotitlán to President Avila Camacho, 17 January 1944, Dirección General del Gobierno, AGN.

8. Carpeta Edmundo Sánchez Cano, Difuntos, AHSDN; Interview (BTS) with Carlos Sánchez, October 2003; Interview (BTS) with Mario Torres Márquez, December 2003.

9. Interview (BTS) with Mario Torres Márquez, December 2003.

10. *Antequera*, 6 December 1943, 20 December 1943, 9 January 1944, 21 February 1944, 4 April 1944; Wilfredo C. Cruz to Governor González Fernández, 3 February 1944, Ramo Gobernación, AGPEO; *Antequera*, 10 June 1944, 9 August 1944.

11. *El Momento*, 14 June 1944, 1 September 1944, 29 September 1944.

12. 111/1147, MAC, AGN.

13. Manuel Ortíz, Lucas Villar, Pedro Rios, Angel Peña, and Raúl Reyes to President Avila Camacho, 10 November 1945, 543.1/19, MAC, AGN.

14. Circular, 14 June 1945, Ramo Gobernación 1945, AGPEO; *El Chapulin*, 27 March 1947; *La Voz de Oaxaca*, 9 January 1947; *Oaxaca en México* (periodico), 30 June 1946; Rodolfo Solana Carrion to Governor Sánchez Cano, 4 June 1945, Ramo Gobernación, AGPEO; *La Voz de Oaxaca*, 12 February 1946.

15. *Por la Defensa Cívica de Oaxaca*, 18 December 1945, Ramo Gobernación, AGPEO; Fidencio Hernández to Heliodoro Charis, 23 December 1946, Ramo Gobernación, AGPEO.

16. Altamirano, *Heliodoro Charis Castro*, 89–90.

17. Report of Jorge Caballero Santos, 23 March 1946, Caja 792, IPS, AGN. The Mexican team, composed of military men, won the bronze medal at the games. Márquez and Satow, *Medallistas Olimpicos mexicanos*.

18. Alberto Ramos Sesma to Governor Sánchez Cano, 4 November 1944, Ramo Gobernación 1945, AGPEO; Governor Sánchez Cano to Alberto Ramos Sesma, 5 December 1944, Ramo Gobernación 1945, AGPEO.

19. Partido Revoluciónario Sánchezcanista Regional Istmeño to Governor Sánchez Cano, 27 January 1945, Ramo Gobernación 1945, AGPEO; Sindicato Unico de Trabajadores de la Industria Salinera to Governor Sánchez Cano, 3 December 1944, Ramo Gobernación 1945, AGPEO; Norberto Rios to Governor Sánchez Cano, 5 December 1944, Ramo Gobernación 1945, AGPEO; Germán Piñeda to Governor Sánchez

Cano, 4 December 1944, Ramo Gobernación 1945, AGPEO; Jesús
Villavicencio to Heliodoro Charis, 25 December 1944, Ramo Gobernación 1945, AGPEO; Heliodoro Charis to Governor Sánchez Cano,
31 December 1944, Ramo Gobernación 1945, AGPEO; Victoriano Fuentes to Governor Sánchez Cano, 1 January 1945, Ramo Gobernación
1945, AGPEO.

20. Felix López Felix to Governor Sánchez Cano, 12 January 1945, Ramo
Gobernación 1945, AGPEO; Eduardo Rios to Governor Sánchez Cano,
5 June 1945, Ramo Gobernación 1945, AGPEO; Feliciano López Felix to
Secretaría de Gobierno, 1 January 1945, 2/311 M (17) 36, Dirección
General de Gobierno, AGN; Heliodoro Charis to Secretaría de Gobierno,
29 January 1945, Dirección General de Gobierno, AGN.

21. Armando Rodríguez Mujica to Ricardo Luna Morales, 29 June 1945,
Ramo Gobernación 1945, AGPEO; Ricardo Lunas Morales to President
Avila Camacho, 9 April 1945, 542.1/1076, Ramo Gobernación 1945,
AGPEO; Governor Sánchez Cano to President Avila Camacho, 31 Janu-
ary 1945, Ramo Gobernación 1945, AGPEO; Heliodoro Charis to Presi-
dent Avila Camacho, 20 January 1945, Ramo Gobernación 1945,
AGPEO.

22. Crispin Carrasco M. to President Avila Camacho, 23 September 1945,
Ramo Gobernación 1945, AGPEO; Feliciano López Felix to Secretario
del Despacho, 4 August 1945, Ramo Gobernación 1945, AGPEO.

23. Constantino Martínez de Escobar to President Avila Camacho, 22 May
1945, 432.2/60, MAC, AGN; Fraternidad to President Avila Camacho,
22 May 1945, MAC, AGN; José Méndez to President Avila Camacho,
17 May 1945, MAC, AGN; José Méndez to Secretario del Despacho, 23
May 1945, Ramo Gobernación 1945, AGPEO.

24. Circular, 5 June 1945, Ramo Gobernación, AGPEO.

25. Facundo S. Vargas to Luis Rodríguez, 3 August 1945, Caja 1 1900–
1950, Administración, Correspondencia, AMT; Francisco Eli Siguenza to
Facundo S. Vargas, 26 June 1945, Administración, Correspondencia,
AMT.

26. Antonio Rodríguez to José Baights, 25 October 1947, Ramo Gobernación, AGPEO; Men of La Estrella to Governor Sánchez Cano, 12 February 1945, Ramo Gobernación 1947, AGPEO; Francisco Martínez to
Governor Vasconcelos, 15 March 1947, Ramo Gobernación 1947,
AGPEO; Francisco Eli Siguenza to Governor Sánchez Cano, 14 February
1945, Ramo Gobernación, AGPEO.

27. Luis Rodríguez to Governor Vasconcelos, 30 March 1947, Ramo Gobernación, AGPEO; Facundo Vargas to Luis Rodríguez, 18 December 1945, Caja 1 1900–1950, Administración, Correspondencia, AMT.

28. Pedro Zeferino to Governor Vasconcelos, 22 December 1947, Ramo Gobernación, AGPEO.

29. Unknown person to Governor Sánchez Cano, 21 May 1945, Ramo Gobernación 1947, AGPEO.

30. Presidente Municipal de Santiago Atitlán to Governor Vasconcelos, 12 March 1947, Ramo Gobernación 1947, AGPEO.

31. Francisco Martínez to Governor Vasconcelos, 15 March 1947, Ramo Gobernación 1947, AGPEO.

32. Marcos Torres to Governor Sánchez Cano, 16 March 1945, Ramo Gobernación, AGPEO.

33. José Baights to Governor Vasconcelos, 7 May 1947, Ramo Gobernación 1947, AGPEO.

34. Secretario del Despacho to Secretaría del Gobierno, 2 August 1947, Ramo Gobernación, AGPEO.

35. Juan Mario Méndez to Governor Sánchez Cano, 2 January 1945, Elecciones, Ramo Gobernación, AGPEO; Secretario de Despacho to Francisco Ramos Ortíz, 7 January 1945, Ramo Gobernación, AGPEO.

36. Genaro Vásquez to President Avila Camacho, 12 October 1945, 521.7/152, MAC, AGN; Elecciones, Etla, 1945, Ramo Gobernación, AGPEO; Elecciones, Nejapa, 1945, Ramo Gobernación, AGPEO.

37. Periódico Oficial, January 1945.

38. Periódico Oficial, 1945–1946.

39. Juan Daniel Pérez to Departmento Agrario, 2 February 1945, 1006.21, Ramo Asuntos Agrarios, AGPEO.

40. Manuel R. Martínez to President Avila Camacho, 2 August 1946, Ramo Gobernación, AGPEO.

41. Manifesto of Alianza-Revolucionaria-Oaxaqueña, 24 January 1947, Ramo Gobernación, AGPEO.

42. Constantino Martínez de Escobar to President Avila Camacho, 22 May 1945, 432.2/60, MAC, AGN; Fraternidad to President Avila Camacho, 22 May 1945, MAC, AGN; José Méndez to President Avila Camacho, 17 May 1945, MAC, AGN; José Méndez to Secretario del Despacho, 23 May 1945, Ramo Gobernación 1945, AGPEO.

43. Andrés G. Zárate to Governor Vasconcelos, 3 May 1947, Dirección

General de Gobierno, AGN; Secretario del Despacho to municipal president of Santa María Lachixio, 29 May 1945, 1009.38, Ramo Asuntos
Agrarios, AGPEO; David Corres Innes to Fidencio Hernández, 2 August
1945, Ramo Asuntos Agrarios, AGPEO; José de la Sierra to Governor
Sánchez Cano, 16 October 1945, Ramo Asuntos Agrarios, AGPEO.

44. *El Momento*, 25 November 1945; *La Voz de Oaxaca*, 27 February
1945.

45. *La Voz de Oaxaca*, 4 February 1945; Governor Sánchez Cano to Jesús
Rojas Villavicencio, 6 February 1945, Ramo Gobernación, AGPEO.

46. *La Voz de Oaxaca*, 2 January 1945.

47. *El Momento*, 14 April 1945; *La Voz de Oaxaca*, 23 January 1945, 25
March 1945, 10 April 1945.

48. *El Momento*, 26 December 1944, 2 February 1945, 12 April 1945.

49. *La Voz de Oaxaca*, 24 April 1945; Ramo Gobernación 1945, AGPEO.
Lists of PAN members came from foundation documents found in the
Archivo del Partido Acción Nacional del Estado de Oaxaca. Interview
(BTS) with Luis Castañeda Guzmán, June 2003; Interview (BTS) with Al-
fredo Castillo, November 2003; Interview (BTS) with José Acevedo, No-
vember 2003.

50. *El Momento*, 4 July 1945.

51. *La Voz de Oaxaca*, 11 November 1945, 18 November 1945, 10 January 1946; Governor Sánchez Cano to President Avila Camacho, 10 September 1945, 110.1/2, MAC, AGN.

52. Juan de Dios Batiz to President Avila Camacho, 25 June 1946, 110.1/2,
MAC, AGN; Juan de Dios Batiz to President Avila Camacho, 7 June 1946,
MAC, AGN.

53. *Oaxaca en México* (periodico), 30 October 1945; Luis Sarmiento
to Governor Sánchez Cano, 25 October 1945, Ramo Gobernación
1945, AGPEO.

54. Governor Sánchez Cano to Juan de Dios Batiz, 7 November 1946,
Ramo Gobernación 1945, AGPEO; Governor Sánchez Cano to Junta de
Mejoras Materiales, 30 December 1945, Ramo Gobernación 1945,
AGPEO.

55. *El Momento*, 2 January 1946, 16 January 1946.

56. *La Voz de Oaxaca*, 3 March 1946; *La Voz de Oaxaca*, 18 March 1946.

57. *El Momento*, 17 July 1946, 24 July 1946.

58. Interview with Austreberto Aragon, 8 June 1966, box 60, Ralph L.
Beals Collection, NAA.

59. Interview with Rafael Ojeda, 20 June 1966, box 60, Ralph L. Beals Collection, NAA.

60. Interview with Gregorio Pérez, 17 August 1965, box 60, Ralph L. Beals Collection, NAA.

61. Impuestos, January 1941, AMOJ; Interview with Juan Medina, 13 June 1966, box 60, Ralph L. Beals Collection, NAA.

62. Genealogy of Inocencia Enríquez, box 58, Ralph L. Beals Collection, NAA.

63. Interview with Gregorio Pérez, 17 August 1965, box 60, Ralph L. Beals Collection, NAA.

64. Statutes of UEM, box 60, Ralph L. Beals Collection, NAA.

65. Interview with Gregorio Pérez, 17 August 1965, box 60, Ralph L. Beals Collection, NAA; Interview with Emiliano Bolaños, 6 August 1966, Ralph L. Beals Collection, NAA.

66. Interview with Gregorio Pérez, 17 August 1965, box 60, Ralph L. Beals Collection, NAA.

67. De la Peña, *Oaxaca económico*, 526–42.

68. De la Peña, *Veracruz económico*, 481.

69. De la Peña, *Zacatecas económico*, 491.

70. Waterbury, "The Traditional Market in a Provincial Urban Setting"; *El Momento*, 31 October 1945.

71. *El Momento*, 21 November 1945, 7 August 1946, 30 March 1946.

72. *La Nación*, 28 September 1946; *El Momento*, 17 July 1946.

73. De la Peña, *Oaxaca económico*, 550.

74. *El Momento*, 31 October 1945, 28 November 1945; *Oaxaca en México* (periodico), 15 June 1945.

75. *Oaxaca en México* (periodico), 15 June 1945, 31 June 1945.

76. *Oaxaca en México* (periodico), 30 November 1945.

77. Acts of the UEM, 1943–1952, box 60, Ralph L. Beals Collection, NAA.

78. Pansters, "Citizens with Dignity," 250; Márquez, "Political Anachronisms."

79. Ignacio García to President Avila Camacho, 18 November 1945, 543.1/19, MAC, AGN; Manuel Ortiz to President Avila Camacho, 10 November 1945, MAC, AGN; *Por la Defensa Cívica de Oaxaca*, 3 February 1946, Ramo Gobernación 1946, AGPEO; *Por la Defensa Cívica de Oaxaca*, 16 March 1946, Ramo Gobernación 1946, AGPEO.

80. *Sur, Revista Oaxaqueña*, February 1946, January 1946, March 1946.

81. *La Nación*, 28 September 1946.

82. *Omega*, 4 January 1947.

83. Report of Inspector de la Secretaría de Gobierno, 3 January 1947, 2.311 M Caja 35, Dirección General de Gobierno, AGN; Heliodoro Charis to President Avila Camacho, 2 January 1947, Dirección General de Gobierno, AGN; José de Gyves to Secretaría de Gobierno, 3 December 1946, 2.311 (17)/42, Dirección General de Gobierno, AGN.

84. Heliodoro Charis to President Avila Camacho, 17 December 1946, 2.311 M (17) 87, Dirección General de Gobierno, AGN. Jeffrey Rubin claims that López Toledo was municipal president in the period 1944–46. This was not the case. Rubin, *Decentering the Regime*, 47, 51–52.

85. Nemesio Roman Guzmán to President Avila Camacho, 2 January 1947, Ramo Gobernación 1945, AGPEO.

86. Martínez, *La lucha electoral*, 143; Librado Ortíz to Secretaría de Gobierno, 6 December 1946, 2.311 M (17) Caja 34 (73), Dirección General de Gobierno, AGN; Angel Mora to Secretaría de Gobierno, 23 December 1946, Dirección General de Gobierno, AGN; Francisco Toscano to Governor Sánchez Cano, 1 January 1947, Dirección General de Gobierno, AGN.

87. Eugelio Ramírez Montiel to Governor Sánchez Cano, 1 October 1946, Elecciones Municipales, Ramo Gobernación 1947–1948, AGPEO; Aniceto V. Martínez to Governor Sánchez Cano, 1 October 1946, Ramo Gobernación 1947–1948, AGPEO; Emilio Martínez to Secretaría del Despacho, 6 December 1946, Ramo Gobernación 1947–1948, AGPEO; Eugelio Ramírez Montiel to Governor Sánchez Cano, 18 December 1946, Ramo Gobernación 1947–1948, AGPEO.

88. Jorge Tamayo to Manuel Heredia Mayoral, 9 January 1950, Estadistica 1945–1950, Ramo Gobernación, AGPEO.

89. *Informe del C. Lic. Eduardo Vasconcelos*, 1947; *La Voz de Oaxaca*, 19 September 1946, 22 September 1946.

90. *Periódico Oficial*, 23 December 1946, 14 December 1946; *Informe del C. Lic. Eduardo Vasconcelos*, 1947; Martínez Medina, "Historia de una crisis política local," 155–62.

91. *Ex-Alumnos*, 1 March 1943.

92. Interview (BTS) with Luis Castañeda Guzmán, July 2003; Ruíz Cervantes, "Carlos Gracida," 104.

93. Interview (BTS) with Alfredo Castillo, November 2003; Interview (BTS) with José Acevedo, November 2003; *Ex-Alumnos*, 15 November 1946.

94. *El Chapulin*, 12 March 1947.

95. *Ex-Alumnos*, 1 July 1943; *Antequera*, 27 January 1943; *Oaxaca en México* (revista), 29 August 1936, 10 October 1936, 13 April 1937; Padres de familia to President Cárdenas, 26 August 1936, 556.4/97, AGN.

96. *Oaxaca Nuevo*, 2–7 September 1941.

97. The following narrative of the mobilization of January 1947 is taken from a variety of different newspapers, government documents, and newssheets: *El Chapulin*, 5–8 March 1947; *La Prensa*, 12–19 January 1947; *Novedades*, 12–19 January 1947; *La Nueva Vida*, 13–14 January 1947, 14 May 1947, 18 May 1947; *La Tribuna*, 13 January 1947, 19 January 1947; *Noticias Extra*, 19 January 1947; *La Voz de Oaxaca*, 12 January 1947; *El Huracán*, 10 January 1947; *El Tiempo*, 17 January 1947; *El Orden*, 30 January 1947; 2/314.1 (17) 1, Dirección General de Gobierno, AGN; 2.311 M Caja 35 (87), Dirección General de Gobierno, AGN; Serie 06 November 1941–March 1952, Subserie 06 Presidencia de la Republica y Secretarías del Estado, AJA.

98. *El Momento*, 10 July 1946.

99. *Ex-Alumnos*, 31 October 1946; Ramírez Bohorquez, *Perfil de Eduardo Vasconcelos*.

100. *La Prensa*, 12 January 1947; Report, 13 January 1947, 2.311 M Caja 35 (87), Dirección General de Gobierno, AGN; Jesús Villavicencio Rojas to President Alemán, 16 January 1947, Dirección General de Gobierno, AGN; *La Prensa*, 11 January 1947; Rogelio Chagoya Villafane to Secretaría del Gobierno, 11 January 1947, 7 Bis 2-314-1 (17)-1, Dirección General de Gobierno, AGN.

101. Rogelio Chagoya Villafane to Secretaría del Gobierno, 12 January 1947, 7 Bis 2-314-1 (17)-1, Dirección General de Gobierno, AGN; *La Voz de Oaxaca*, 10 January 1947; Liga de Communidades Agrarias to President Avila Camacho, 15 January 1947, 564.1/25, Fondo Presidentes, Ramo Miguel Alemán Valdés (MAV), AGN; Melquiades Ramírez to Secretaría de Gobierno, 14 January 1947, 2/314.1 (17) 1, Dirección General de Gobierno, AGN.

102. *La Tribuna*, 13 January 1947; *Manifesto al Pueblo de Oaxaca*, 8 January 1947.

103. *La Prensa*, 11 January 1947, 16 January 1947.

104. Medina, *Historia de la Revolución*, 20:107.
105. Representantes de las clases humildes to President Alemán, 13 January 1947, 2/314.1 (17) 1, Dirección General de Gobierno, AGN.
106. *Ojos Oaxaqueños*, 14 January 1947, 2/314.1 (17) 1, Dirección General de Gobierno, AGN.
107. *La Nueva Vida*, 13 January 1947, 14 January 1947.
108. Oscar Salazar to President Alemán, 11 January 1947, 564.1/25, MAV, AGN; *La Tribuna*, 13 January 1947; Sindicato de Electricistas to Secretaría de Gobierno, 15 January 1947, 2/314.1 (17) 1, Dirección General de Gobierno, AGN.
109. Report on Oaxaca, 16 January 1947, 2.311 M Caja 35 (87), Dirección General de Gobierno, AGN.
110. Newcomer, *Reconciling Modernity*, 113–42.
111. *Orden*, 30 January 1947.
112. "La caida de Sánchez Cano," 06. 08 Autoridades Locales y Estatales, AJA; "El despertar de un pueblo, abajo los tiranos," 2/314.1 (17) 1, Dirección General de Gobierno, AGN; "Nauseabundo, siete oficios!" 564.1/25, MAV, AGN.
113. Interview (BTS) with Mario Torres, January 2004; Melquiades Ramírez to President Avila Camacho, 18 January 1947, 2.311 M Caja 35 (87), Dirección General de Gobierno, AGN.
114. *La Prensa*, 12 January 1947.
115. *Orden*, 30 January 1947.
116. *La Nueva Vida*, 7 May 1947; *Orden*, 30 January 1947; Newssheet by Liga de Usarios de Agua, 8 January 1947, 564.1/25, MAV, AGN; *El Tiempo*, 17 January 1947.
117. Comité Municipal del PRI to President Alemán, 10 January 1947, Ramo Gobernación, AGPEO.
118. *El Momento*, 7 March 1947.
119. Interview (NMS) with Sofia Jiménez Torres, June 2006; Interview (NMS) with Leonarda Morales Osorio, June 2006.
120. Secretario del Despacho to President Alemán, 14 January 1947, Ramo Gobernación, AGPEO.
121. *La Prensa*, 14 January 1947.
122. Victoriano López Toledo to President Alemán, 10 January 1947, 564.1/25, MAV, AGN; Circulo Social Tuxtepecana to President Alemán, 9 January 1947, MAV, AGN; Francisco Eli Siguenza to President Alemán,

NOTES TO PAGES 323-329

13 January 1947, MAV, AGN; Victoriano López Toledo to Secretario de Gobierno, 17 January 1947, 2/314.1 (17) 1, Dirección General de Gobierno, AGN.

123. Liga Campesino de Villa Alta to President Alemán, 14 Janaury 1947, 564.1/25, MAV, AGN; Liga Feminil to President Alemán, 14 January 1947, MAV, AGN; Liga Campesina Mixe de Santiago Zacatepec to President Alemán, 13 January 1947, MAV, AGN.

124. *El Universal*, 15 January 1947.

125. Rafael Piñeda to President Alemán, 13 January 1947, MAV, AGN; Rogelio Chagoya Villafane to Secretaría de Gobierno, 11 January 1947, 7 Bis 2-314-1 (17)-1, Dirección General de Gobierno, AGN; *La Tribuna*, 13 January 1947.

126. *El Universal*, 12 January 1947.

127. Interview (BTS) with Procopio Martínez Vásquez, October 2003.

128. Medina, *Historia de la Revolución*, 20:25, 95–112.

129. Interview (BTS) with Carlos Sánchez, October 2003.

130. Pansters, *Politics and Power*, 120–22, 143–47.

131. Manifesto of Alianza-Revolucionaria-Oaxaqueña, 24 January 1947, Ramo Gobernación, AGPEO.

132. Martínez Assad, *Los sentimientos de la region*, 182–84.

133. Moncada, *Cayeron!* 186–87.

134. Moncada, *Cayeron!* 209–17.

9. The Vallistocracia Governor

1. Martínez, *El despegue constructivo de la Revolución*, 9, 16–17.
2. Torres Ramírez, "La guerra y la posguerra."
3. Gillingham, "Force and Consent in Mexican Provincial Politics," 199–201.
4. Torres Ramírez, *Historia de la Revolucion*, 21:62.
5. La Boz, *Crisis of Mexican Labor*, 85–98.
6. Smith, *Labyrinths of Power*, 265.
7. Torres Ramírez, *Historia de la Revolución*, 21:60.
8. Medin, *El sexenio alemánista*, 127.
9. Basurto, *Del avilacamachismo al alemanismo*, 165–270.
10. Smith, "Mexico since 1946," 84–93; Torres Ramírez, *Historia de la Revolución*, 21:87–116.
11. Niblo, *Mexico in the 1940s*, 168.

481

12. Tirado, "La alianza con los empresarios."

13. Report of agent E. A. C., 25 January 1949, Caja 810, IPS, AGN. The ICA changed its name to the Instituto Autónoma de Ciencias y Artes during the early 1940s. It then became the Universidad Autónoma "Benito Juárez" during the 1950s.

14. 2.311 DL (17) 1-4 Caja 104, Dirección General de Gobierno, AGN.

15. 14 February 1947, Exp Exp 45-1 f 25, AMOJ; Report of agent E. A. C., 25 January 1949, Caja 810, IPS, AGN.

16. *La Voz de Oaxaca*, 13 September 1949, 8 August 1947; *El Globo*, 2 August 1947; *La Voz de Oaxaca*, 9 August 1948.

17. Fidel López to Secretaría de Gobierno, 2 May 1947, 2.311 DL (17) 2, Dirección General de Gobierno, AGN.

18. Roberto Ortiz to Secretario del Despacho, 3 April 1935, Ramo Justicia, AGPEO; Sánchez Silva, "Crisis política y contrarrevolución," 200–201; Bishop Méndez to Manuel Cubas Solana, 23 September 1936, Archivo de la Diocesis de Huajuapam de León.

19. *El Globo*, 9 August 1947; Martínez, *La lucha electoral*, 170–72.

20. Manuel Aguilar y Salazar to Manuel Gómez Marin, 25 July 1947, Archivo Manuel Gómez Marin.

21. *El Globo*, 23 August 1947.

22. Benjamin, *La Revolución*.

23. *La Voz de Oaxaca*, 27 February 1948, 11 December 1948, 26 December 1948, 15 January 1950; *La Provincia*, 22 January 1950.

24. *La Voz de Oaxaca*, 18 April 1948, 28 March 1948, 12 December 1948, 26 December 1948, 12 June 1949, 4 December 1948.

25. *La Voz de Oaxaca*, 12 September 1948; Gillingham, "Emperor of Ixcateopan."

26. *La Voz de Oaxaca*, 4 November 1948, 1 October 1948, 2 April 1949, 8 May 1949, 5 October 1947, 7 November 1948, 28 November 1948, 3 July 1948; *Periódico Oficial*, 14 July 1948.

27. Miguel Polo to Governor González Fernández, 2 October 1943, Ramo Gobernación, AGPEO; Luis Hernández to Governor Sánchez Cano, 7 March 1945, Ramo Gobernación, AGPEO.

28. *La Voz de Oaxaca*, 2 October 1947.

29. Pedro García to Governor Vasconcelos, 3 October 1950, 2.082.4147, Ramo Gobernación 1948–52, AGPEO.

30. *El Globo*, 17 February 1948; Miguel Polo to President Alemán, 3 March 1949, 568.11 141, MAV, AGN.

31. *La Tribuna*, 2 February 1947. *Gachupine* was a derogatory term for a Spaniard.

32. *La Nueva Vida*, 7 May 1947

33. Junta de Administración Civil, Libro, 23 May 1947, AMOJ.

34. Report of Alejandro Pérez Castro, 15 May 1947, 21 7f 1947, AMOJ.

35. Alejandro Pérez Castro to Heliodoro Díaz Quintas, 23 July 1947, AMOJ.

36. Impuestos, August 1947, AMOJ.

37. *La Voz de Oaxaca*, 8 December 1947, 12 December 1947.

38. *La Voz de Oaxaca*, 22 October 1947.

39. Report of Manuel Zarate Aquino, 5 January 1948, AMOJ.

40. *Informe del C. Lic. Eduardo Vasconcelos*, 1947, 24–25.

41. *Informe del C. Lic. Eduardo Vasconcelos*, 1949, 74.

42. *El Chapulin*, 12 January 1950.

43. Eduardo Vasconcelos to Guillermo Aristrain, 4 May 1947, 2 082 67 47, Ramo Gobernación, AGPEO.

44. *La Voz de Oaxaca*, 20 June 1950, 15 April 1948, 29 April 1950, 18 February 1947; Eduardo Vasconcelos to Alejandro Pérez Castro, 30 May 1947, AMOJ; *La Voz de Oaxaca*, 7 June 1947, 25 August 1948, 27 May 1947; *La Tribuna*, 1 May 1947; *La Voz de Oaxaca*, 1 June 1948.

45. *Informe del C. Lic. Eduardo Vasconcelos*, 1950, 61–62.

46. Austreberto Aragon to Luis González, 3 February 1944, AMOJ; Miguel Polo to Governor González Fernández, 25 January 1943, Ramo Gobernación, AGPEO.

47. *La Voz de Oaxaca*, 30 Janaury 1947, 12 April 1947, 17 January 1948, 6 October 1949.

48. Report of agent E. A. C., 25 January 1949, Caja 810, IPS, AGN.

49. *Informe del C. Lic. Eduardo Vasconcelos*, 1947, 58–59; *Informe del C. Lic. Eduardo Vasconcelos*, 1950, 78.

50. Bortz, *Industrial Wages*.

51. *El Momento*, 23 January 1946, 30 January 1946; *La Voz de Oaxaca*, 30 September 1945.

52. Torres Ramírez, *Historia de la Revolución*, 21:121–23; Gillingham, "Maximino's Bulls."

53. *La Voz de Oaxaca*, 1 August 1948, 5 August 1948.

54. Eduardo Vasconcelos to Enrique Tort, 4 August 1948, 1 082 76 48, Ramo Gobernación 1948–52, AGPEO.

55. *La Voz de Oaxaca*, 20 August 1948, 21 August 1948, 28 August 1948, 3 September 1948, 20 October 1948.

56. *La Voz de Oaxaca*, 4 March 1947.

57. Juan Medino to Junta de Administración Civil, 26 February 1947, AMOJ.

58. Report of Gabino Aspiroz, 5 July 1947, exp. 22 30 f, AMOJ.

59. *La Provincia*, 12 July 1950.

60. *La Provincia*, 18 May 1950, 9 January 1950, 20 March 1950.

61. *La Provincia*, 28 May 1950.

62. *La Tribuna*, 13 April 1947.

63. *La Tribuna*, 20 April 1947.

64. *La Nueva Vida*, 7 May 1947.

65. *La Tribuna*, 12 June 1947, 15 June 1947, 29 June 1947.

66. *La Tribuna*, 30 June 1947.

67. *La Nueva Vida*, 7 August 1947.

68. Acts of UEM 1946–1953, box 60, Ralph L. Beals Collection, NAA.

69. *El Chapulin*, 8 August 1947.

70. *El Chapulin*, 4 December 1949.

71. Alemán Valdés, *Programa de gobierno*, 11; Alemán Valdés, *Un México mejor*, 324.

72. *Informe del C. Lic. Eduardo Vasconcelos*, 1947, 3.

73. *La Voz de Oaxaca*, 8 August 1948.

74. *El Globo*, 22 November 1947.

75. *La Prensa*, 31 March 1950; *La Provincia*, 6 April 1950.

76. *La Opinión*, 3 August 1947.

77. *La Tribuna*, 2 February 1947; *Donaji*, 1 December 1949; *Cuadernos de Oaxaca*, June 1950; *Oaxaca Popular*, 15 August 1950; *El Estudiante*, 19 February 1949.

78. For example, *La Tribuna*, 5 February 1947, 23 March 1947; *Oaxaca Popular*, 22 August 1950.

79. *Cuadernos de Oaxaca*, August 1950.

80. *La Opinión*, 23 February 1948, 29 February 1948, 30 May 1949.

81. *La Voz de Oaxaca*, 25 May 1949.

82. *La Provincia*, 3 July 1950.

83. *El Chapulin*, 8 August 1950.

84. *Informe del C. Lic. Eduardo Vasconcelos*, 1947, 31, 51–52.

NOTES TO PAGES 348–351

85. *Informe del C. Lic. Eduardo Vasconcelos*, 1948, 45–46; *Informe del C. Lic. Eduardo Vasconcelos*, 1949, 42–44.

86. De la Peña, *Oaxaca económico*, 5.

87. Jorge Tamayo to Eduardo Vasconcelos, 4 April 1950, Ramo Gobernación, AGPEO.

88. *Periódico Oficial*, 1948–1949.

89. Germán López L. to Secretario del Despacho, 4 December 1944, Ramo Gobernación, AGPEO; Alberto Von-Thaden Arias to Secretario del Despacho, 2 December 1944, Ramo Gobernación, AGPEO; *La Voz de Oaxaca*, 17 June 1945.

90. *La Voz de Oaxaca*, 25 March 1948, 29 April 1948. It is unclear exactly who these propagandists were, but it may refer to certain PAN organizations in Huajuapam that were pretending to be members of the CNOP in order to wrestle control from PRI-supporting *agraristas*. Jesús Guzmán to Secretario de Despacho, 18 November 1952, 219-3 173 (7) "52," Ramo Gobernación, AGPEO.

91. *La Voz de Oaxaca*, 17 June 1948.

92. *La Voz de Oaxaca*, 6 December 1948.

93. *La Nueva Vida*, 15 March 1947

94. *La Nueva Vida*, 2 May 1947.

95. CNC to President Alemán, 5 May 1947, 2.311 DL (17) 2, Dirección General de Gobierno, AGN.

96. CNC to Secretaría de Gobierno, 5 December 1948, 2 311 M (17) 36 B 126, Dirección General de Gobierno, AGN.

97. José García L. to Secretaría de Gobierno, 6 April 1949, 2 311 DF (17) 2 1948, Dirección General de Gobierno, AGN; Ximénez de Sandoval Prats, *Tuxtepec, "historia y anecdotas,"* 102.

98. Jorge Tamayo to Eduardo Vasconcelos, 9 April 1949, 3 311 DF (17) 1 1948, Dirección General de Gobierno, AGN.

99. Daniel Muñoz Estefan to Secretaría de Gobierno, 3 April 1947, Ramo Gobernación, AGPEO.

100. *La Voz de Oaxaca*, 11 August 1948.

101. *La Nueva Vida*, 21 June 1947.

102. Luis Ramírez de Arellano to President Alemán, 3 May 1948, 432 146, MAV, AGN; Heriberto Hernández to President Alemán, 23 May 1947, MAV, AGN.

103. Report of Francisco Ugualde, 7 December 1948, Caja 90, IPS, AGN;

NOTES TO PAGES 351–356

Report of Fernando González, 23 October 1948, 2 311 M (17) 36 B 117, Dirección General de Gobierno, AGN.

104. For example, Venacio Avila to Governor Vasconcelos, 2 December 1949, 2/082 (25) 2575, Ramo Gobernación 1948–52, AGPEO.

105. Loyola Díaz, *El ocaso del radicalismo revolucionario.*

106. Aurelio Silva to Secretaría de Gobierno, 5 January 1949, 2 311 M (17) 36 B 118, Dirección General de Gobierno, AGN.

107. Alejo Moctezuma to President Alemán, 26 October 1948, 2 311 M (17) 36 B 118, Dirección General de Gobierno, AGN; Report of agent 7, 6 December 1948, Caja 801, IPS, AGN.

108. *La Prensa,* 4 January 1949, 18 January 1949; *Oaxaca Popular,* 8 January 1949; *El Universal,* 11 January 1949.

109. *El Excelsior,* 26 January 1949.

110. Nabor Ojeda to Governor Vasoncelos, 23 April 1947, Ramo Gobernación, AGPEO; Nabor Ojeda to President Alemán, 7 March 1947, Caja 792, IPS, AGN.

111. Domingo Ibarra to Governor Vasconcelos, 3 April 1949, 1/082 (9)/1831, Ramo Gobernación 1948–52, AGPEO.

112. Camelio López to Governor Vasoncelos, 15 August 1948, 2/082 (9). 4663, Ramo Gobernación 1948–52, AGPEO. See also Mariano Silva to Governor Vasconcelos, 5 July 1948, 2/082 (9) 4102, and Juan Salinas Narvaez to Governor Vasconcelos, 11 May 1948, 3/082 (9) 3002.

113. Moises Martínez Baños to Governor Vasconcelos, 31 July 1949, 2/082 (9)/4005, Ramo Gobernación 1948–52, AGPEO.

114. For example, Pedro Rojas to Governor Vasconcelos, 5 August 1949, 1/082 (9) 4987, Ramo Gobernación 1948–52, AGPEO.

115. 931.29–937.4, Sección Impuestos, Ramo Asuntos Agrarios, AGPEO.

116. Report of unnamed inspector, 26 March 1948, Caja 792, IPS, AGN.

117. *Informe del C. Lic. Eduardo Vasconcelos,* 1949, 12.

118. Agustín Chavez to President Alemán, 25 January 1949, 544.5 343, MAV, AGN; Juan Apolonio to President Alemán, 26 October 1948, 542.1 281, MAV, AGN; 221/41992, MAV, AGN; Juan Camilo Ramírez, 23 November 1952, MAV, AGN; Huerta Rios, *Organización socio-política,* 65.

119. *Informe del C. Lic. Eduardo Vasconcelos,* 1947, 4–5.

120. Fidel López to Secretaría de Gobierno, 2 May 1947, 2.311 DL (17) 2, Dirección General de Gobierno, AGN.

121. Heliodoro Charis to President Alemán, 16 March 1948, 507.1 92, MAV, AGN.

122. Cutberto Chagoya to President Alemán, 15 May 1948, 609 206, MAV, AGN.

123. Heliodoro Charis to President Alemán, 4 September 1950, 710.11 142, MAV, AGN.

124. Jacienta L. de Charis to President Alemán, 18 January 1949, 557 136.2 213, MAV, AGN.

125. Agent J. R. R to Lamberto Ortega Peregrina, 7 January 1949, Caja 801, IPS, AGN; Centro Orientador Político de Chahuites to President Alemán, 13 September 1950, 252 82, MAV, AGN.

126. Mariano Escobar Barrientos to President Alemán, 13 December 1949, 151.3 434, MAV, AGN; Report of Fernando López Portillo, 5 October 1949, Caja 801, IPS, AGN.

127. Caja 801, IPS, AGN, has a host of documents relating to the case.

128. *Informe del Lic. Eduardo Vasconcelos*, 1948, 6.

129. Men of Juquila Mixe, Cacalotepec, Atitlán to President Alemán, 29 October 1947, 542.1 66, MAV, AGN; Estanislao Morales to President Alemán, 5 April 1949, 542.1 883, MAV, AGN.

130. Men of Ayutla to Governor Vasconcelos, 26 October 1949, 2.082 (29) 2061, Ramo Gobernación 1948–52, AGPEO.

131. Report of unnamed agent, 2 December 1949, 2/082 (13) / 3143, Ramo Gobernación 1948–52, AGPEO.

132. Juan Lara to Governor Vasconcelos, 26 November 1949, 2/082 (13) / 3165, Ramo Gobernación 1948–52, AGPEO.

133. Schryer, *Rancheros of Pisaflores*, 107–11; Martínez Saldana, *Política y sociedad en México*, 15, 70–71.

134. Medina, *Historia de la Revolución*, 20:93.

10. The Short Reign of Manuel Mayoral Heredia

1. Servin, *Ruptura y oposición*.

2. Aguirre and Avila, "Rebelión en el PRI," 115.

3. Martínez Assad, *Henriquismo*, 9, 58.

4. Pellicer de Brody and Reyna, *Historia de la Revolución*, 22:57–63.

5. Pellicer de Brody and Reyna, *Historia de la Revolución*, 22:60–61.

6. Governor Mayoral Heredia to Miguel Alemán, 3 September 1947, 702.11 44, MAV, AGN; Report of agent L. O. P., 10 October 1949, Caja 102, IPS, AGN.

7. Report of agent L. O. P., 29 September 1949, Caja 801, IPS, AGN.

8. Report of agent L.O.P., 5 October 1949, Caja 801, IPS, AGN.

9. *El Chapulin*, 3 December 1949.

10. Report of unnamed agent, 10 December 1949, Caja 801, IPS, AGN.

11. *La Provincia*, 11 February 1950.

12. Circular of the Frente Democratica Oaxaqueña, 18 November 1949, 2.311 DL (17) 2, Dirección General de Gobierno, AGN; Report of agent L. O. P., 29 September 1949, Caja 801, IPS, AGN; Unknown press cutting, 4 November 1949, Caja 801, IPS, AGN; Report of unnamed agent, 27 December 1949, Caja 801, IPS, AGN.

13. *La Provincia*, 2 February 1950.

14. *La Provincia*, 15 April 1950.

15. *La Provincia*, 13 February 1950.

16. *La Provincia*, 20 March 1950, 26 March 1950, 19 February 1950, 15 April 1950.

17. Senator Fagoaga to President Alemán, 7 August 1950, Caja 284, IPS, AGN.

18. *La Voz de Oaxaca*, 2 December 1950.

19. There are hundreds of petitions in Caja 284, IPS, AGN.

20. *La Provincia*, 3 January 1951.

21. *La Provincia*, 25 January 1951, 26 December 1951, 30 January 1951.

22. *La Provincia*, 15 December 1950.

23. Martínez López, "Economia y política en Oaxaca," 83.

24. *El Universal*, 25 July 1952; *Cuadernos de Sur*, 16 February 1951.

25. *La Tribuna del Sur*, 26 June 1951.

26. *La Provincia*, 6 July 1951.

27. Knight, "Corruption in Twentieth Century Mexico."

28. *El Universal*, 24 July 1952.

29. Asociación Agricola Local de Productores de Café del Sur del Estado de Oaxaca to Governor Carresquedo, 22 September 1952, 461.1 3929, MAV, AGN.

30. *El Imparcial*, 7 August 1952.

31. Salvador Matthews, "Suppressing Fire and Memory."

32. Governor Mayoral Heredia to Miguel Alemán, 22 February 1951, 003.72 15411, MAV, AGN.

33. Ayuntamiento de Ixtlán to Governor Mayoral Heredia, 6 June 1951, Ramo Gobernación, AGPEO; Unión Fraternal de Ayuntamientos de la

Sierra Juárez to Governor Mayoral Heredia, 21 September 1951, Ramo Gobernación, AGPEO.

34. Pedro Zarate to Governor Mayoral Heredia, 2 December 1952, 3.082 (28) 2338, Dirección General de Gobierno, AGN.

35. Rangel Couto, *El Papaloapan en marcha*; Attolini, *Economía de la Cuenca del Papaloapan*.

36. Secretaría de Recursos Hidraulicos, Comisión de Papaloapan, *Economía del Papaloapan*; Boege, *Los Mazatecos ante la nación*; McMahon, *Antropologia de una presa*; Ewell and Poleman, *Uxpanapa*.

37. Villa Rojas, *Los Mazatecos*, 45.

38. Manuel Flores Castro to Governor Mayoral Heredia, 11 January 1952, 318.1 18677, Dirección General de Gobierno, AGN; Luis Ramos to Governor Carresquedo, 2 September 1952, 2.082 (25) 2362, Ramo Gobernación, AGPEO.

39. Boege, *Los Mazatecos ante la nación*, 241–46.

40. Report of unnamed agent, 7 June 1951, Ramo Gobernación 1948–52, AGPEO.

41. Report of Mario Coquet, 12 August 1950, Caja 801, IPS, AGN.

42. Agustian Mustieles to President Alemán, 3 June 1951, 252 9652, MAV, AGN.

43. Camerino Vicente to President Alemán, 19 November 1951, 316.2876, MAV, AGN; Heliodoro Charis to President Alemán, 11 October 1951, MAV, AGN; Tomás Sánchez to Governor Mayoral Heredia, 12 March 1952, 2.082 (10) 695, MAV, AGN.

44. *El Chapulin*, 28 December 1950.

45. Acts, November 1950, AMOJ.

46. *La Tribuna del Sur*, 3 October 1951; *El Chapulin*, 25 October 1951; *El Chapulin*, 20 September 1951.

47. UEM to Ayuntamiento de Oaxaca de Juárez, 20 December 1951, AMOJ.

48. *El Chapulin*, 18 October 1951.

49. *El Chapulin*, 11 October 1951.

50. Acts 1952, 26 February 1952, AMOJ.

51. *El Chapulin*, 5 April 1951.

52. *La Tribuna del Sur*, 30 March 1951, 16 May 1951, 25 September 1951.

53. *El Pueblo*, 23 March 1951, 15 August 1951, 4 October 1951.

54. *El Chapulin*, 24 November 1951, 13 August 1951.

55. *El Chapulin*, 10 January 1952.

56. *El Dictamen*, 17 March 1952.
57. *El Chapulin*, 17 January 1952.
58. *El Chapulin*, 20 December 1951.
59. *El Chapulin*, 27 December 1951.
60. Jesús Aguirre Delgado to Rogerio de la Silva, 22 April 1952, 511/33344, MAV, AGN.
61. *El Universal*, 25 March 1952.
62. The following narrative of the movement comes from a series of sources including *El Universal*; *El Excelsior*; *El Chapulin*; *El Imparcial*; *La Prensa*; *Imagen*; *Atisbos*; *El Tiempo*; *La Tribuna del Sur*; *El Pueblo*; *Universal Grafico*; *La Nación*; *El Nacional*; *El Orden*; *El Informador*; 511/33344 and 252/9652, MAV, AGN.
63. Moncada, *Cayeron!*; Martínez López, "Economía y política en Oaxaca"; Martínez López, "El Movimiento Oaxaqueño de 1952."
64. *Atbisos*, 25 March 1952.
65. *El Imagen*, 15 April 1952.
66. *El Informador*, 1 June 1952.
67. Benjamin Bolaños Jiménez to President Alemán, 3 April 1952, 511/33344, MAV, AGN.
68. Bulletin of PCM, 14 April 1952, Collección Mayoral Heredia, Hemeroteca de Oaxaca.
69. Dirección General de Seguridad, 19 April 1952, 252/9652, MAV, AGN.
70. Bulletin of CCO, 2 April 1952, Collección Mayoral Heredia, Hemeroteca de Oaxaca.
71. *El Universal*, 1 April 1952.
72. Bulletin, 27 March 1952, Collección Mayoral Heredia, Hemeroteca de Oaxaca.
73. *El Excelsior*, 29 March 1952.
74. *El Imparcial*, 3 April 1952.
75. *Noticias del Dia*, 17 April 1952.
76. *El Imparcial*, 23 April 1952.
77. *El Excelsior*, 24 March 1952; *El Nacional*, 23 March 1952; *Atbisos*, 26 March 1952; *Nuevo Diario*, 20 March 1952.
78. "Al pueblo oaxaqueño" by Governor Mayoral Heredia, 1 April 1952, Collección Mayoral Heredia, Hemeroteca de Oaxaca.
79. Bulletin of CNC, 28 March 1952, Collección Mayoral Heredia, Hemeroteca de Oaxaca.

80. *El Informador*, 1 July 1952.
81. Vicente González Fernández, Difuntos, AHSDN.
82. *El Pueblo*, 20 February 1952.
83. Dirección General de Seguridad, 19 April 1952, 252/9652, MAV, AGN.
84. Bulletin of FPPM, 26 March 1952, Collección Mayoral Heredia, Hemeroteca de Oaxaca; Bulletin of FPPM, 7 June 1952, Collección Mayoral Heredia, Hemeroteca de Oaxaca.
85. Compare lists of both groups in 511/33344 and 252/9652, MAV, AGN.
86. Correspondence with Gladys McCormick, 27 September 2007.
87. Buro de Investigación Política, 31 March 1952, Collección Mayoral Heredia, Hemeroteca de Oaxaca; *Mexico Nuevo*, 12 April 1952.
88. Report of unknown agent, 25 March 1952, 252/9652, MAV, AGN.
89. Heliodoro Charis Castro to President Alemán, 1 April 1952, 511/33344, MAV, AGN.
90. Ezequiel López Vásquez to President Alemán, 24 March 1952, 511/33344, MAV, AGN.
91. *El Universal*, 8 May 1952; Samuel López González to President Alemán, 6 June 1952, Dirección General de Gobierno, AGN.
92. Report of unnamed agent, 20 June 1952, Caja 815, IPS, AGN.
93. Confederación de Pueblos de la Sierra Juárez to President Alemán, 28 March 1952, 252/9652, MAV, AGN.
94. Presidente Municipal de Lachatao et al to President Alemán, 20 March 1952, 252/9652, MAV, AGN.
95. *El Chapulin*, 30 March 1952; Francisco Miguel to President Alemán, 27 May 1952, 511/33344, MAV, AGN; *Tribuna del Sur*, 6 July 1952.
96. *El Chapulin*, 29 March 1952.
97. Comité Cívico de Tehuantepec to President Alemán, 1 April 1952, 511/33344, MAV, AGN.
98. Dirección General de Seguridad, 19 April 1952, 252/9652, MAV, AGN.
99. Buro de Investigación Política, 31 March 1952, Collección Mayoral Heredia, Hemeroteca de Oaxaca.
100. *El Imparcial*, 2 February 1952.
101. Buro de Investigación Política, 31 March 1952, Collección Mayoral Heredia, Hemeroteca de Oaxaca.
102. *El Excelsior*, 24 March 1952.
103. *El Imagen*, 15 April 1952.
104. *El Excelsior*, 27 March 1952.

105. Interview with Salvador Acevedo, 24 June 1965, Ralph L. Beals Collection, NAA.

106. *El Excelsior*, 23 March 1952.

107. *La Prensa*, 26 March 1952.

108. *La Tribuna del Sur*, 28 March 1952.

109. *La Tribuna del Sur*, 2 April 1952.

110. *La Tribuna del Sur*, 4 April 1952; *El Chapulin*, 4 April 1952.

111. *La Tribuna del Sur*, 24 April 1952.

112. Bulletin of UEM, Usarios del Agua, 26 April 1952, Collección Mayoral Heredia, Hemeroteca de Oaxaca; Bulletin of UEM, 14 June 1952, Collección Mayoral Heredia, Hemeroteca de Oaxaca.

113. *El Imparcial*, 5 June 1952, 10 June 1952.

114. *El Imparcial*, 4 July 1952.

115. "Corrido de Mayoral Heredia," Collección Mayoral Heredia, Hemeroteca de Oaxaca. Other *corridos* of the movement include "Vida," "Pasion y muerte de nuestro pobre Oaxaca," "Corrido de los cuerudos," "Corrido de los sangientos sucessos de Oaxaca," and "Corrido de la huelga."

116. *El Chapulin*, 3 April 1952.

117. *El Universal*, 2 April 1952.

118. Spivak, "Spivak and Rumor, Rhetoric and Cultural Explanation."

119. Buro de Investigación Política, 31 March 1952, Collección Mayoral Heredia, Hemeroteca de Oaxaca; *México Nuevo*, 12 April 1952.

120. *La Prensa*, 27 March 1952.

121. Interview (NMS) with Porfiria García García, July 2006.

122. *El Pueblo*, 29 March 1952.

123. *La Tribuna del Sur*, 30 March 1952.

124. *El Imparcial*, 18 April 1952.

125. *El Imparcial*, 4 June 1952.

126. Interview (NMS) with anonymous market vendor, June 2006.

127. *El Imparcial*, 2 April 1952; UEM to municipal president of Oaxaca de Juárez, 8 July 1952, AMOJ.

128. Interview (NMS) with Adela Avendano Ramírez, June 2006; *La Prensa*, 1 April.

129. *El Chapulin*, 27 March 1952.

130. Interview (BTS) with Guillermo Aragon, June 2006.

131. *El Pueblo*, 23 April 1952.

132. Buro de Investigación Política, 31 March 1952, Collección Mayoral Heredia, Hemeroteca de Oaxaca.
133. Interview (NMS) with María de Jesús Ramírez Pérez, June 2006
134. Interview (NMS) with Sofia Jiménez Torres, July 2006.
135. *El Imparcial*, 20 July 1952.
136. *El Pueblo*, 10 April 1952.
137. Carr, *Marxism and Communism*.
138. Dirección General de Seguridad, 19 April 1952, 252/9652, MAV, AGN.
139. *El Imparcial*, 1 April 1952; *El Chapulin*, 4 April 1952.
140. *La Tribuna del Sur*, 2 April 1952.
141. Bulletin of Confederación de Estudiantes, 10 July 1952, Collección Mayoral Heredia, Hemeroteca de Oaxaca; *La Tribuna del Sur*, 12 July 1952.
142. *La Prensa*, 29 March 1952.
143. *El Imparcial*, 1 April 1952.
144. See the telegrams in 511/33344, MAV, AGN.
145. *El Excelsior*, 3 April 1952.
146. *El Universal*, 16 April 1952.
147. *El Excelsior*, 17 April 1952.
148. Olcott, *Revolutionary Women*.
149. Silva Herzog, *Una historia de la Universidad*; Mabry, *The Mexican University and the State*.
150. Moncada, *Cayeron!* 204–9.
151. Pansters, *Politics and Power*, 67. See also Fagen and Tuohy, *Politics and Privilege in a Mexican City*, 60.
152. Lorey, *University System*, 176.
153. *El Excelsior*, 4 April 1952.
154. Gillingham, "Force and Consent in Mexican Provincial Politics."

Conclusion

1. Coronil, "Foreword," xi; García Canclini, *La globalización imaginada*, 48–49.
2. Knight, "State Power and Political Stability."
3. Rubin, "Decentrando el régimen," 150.
4. Knight, "Habitus and Homicide," 108–9.
5. Knight, "México bronco."
6. Rubin, *Decentering the Regime*, 253.

7. For the demise of a revolutionary *cacicazgo* in one of these regions see Brewster, *Militarism*. This creation of autonomous political zones in the 1930s followed by repression and control during the 1950s offers a historical reason for the early resistance to the PRI state in all the areas. See Guerrero, *Forestry Industry in Chihuahua*; *Democracia indígena*.

8. Lewis, *Ambivalent Revolution*; Benjamin, *A Rich Land*.

9. Fowler-Salamini, *Agrarian Radicalism*.

10. Bartra, *Guerrero bronco*; Gillingham, "Force and Consent in Mexican Provincial Politics."

11. Smith, "Party of the Priest."

12. Vélez-Ibáñez, *Rituals of Marginality*, 90.

13. Fagen and Tuohy, *Politics and Privilege in a Mexican City*.

14. Cornelius, *Politics and the Migrant Poor*.

15. *El Imparcial*, 17 October 1961; Interview with Emiliano Bolanos, 17 November 1964, box 60, Ralph L. Beals Collection, NAA.

16. Knight, "Patterns and Prescriptions," 351.

17. Wood, *Revolution in the Street*; Lear, *Workers, Neighbors, and Citizens*; Ocasio Meléndez, *Capitalism and Development*.

18. Mitchell and Schell, *Women's Revolution in Mexico*; Fernández-Aceves, "Once We Were Corn Grinders"; Fowler-Salamini, "Gender, Work and Working-Class Women's Culture"; Olcott, *Revolutionary Women*; Olcott et al., *Sex in Revolution*.

19. Kaplan, "Female Consciousness and Collective Action."

20. Wood, "'The Proletarian Women,'" 162.

21. Schell, "Of the Sublime Mission of Mothers," 101.

22. Yescas Martínez, *Los desegañados de la tierra*; Boege, *Los Mazatecos ante la nación*.

23. Rubin, *Decentering the Regime*.

24. Greenberg, *Blood Ties*; Parra Mora, "Poder, violencia"; López Barcenas, *Muertes sin fin*.

25. Salvador Matthews, "Suppressing Fire and Memory"; Pérez, *Diary of a Guerrilla*.

26. Smith, "Party of the Priest."

27. *La Prensa*, 22 November 1962, 23 November 1962.

28. Martínez Vásquez, *Movimiento popular y política en Oaxaca*.

29. Knight, "The Modern Mexican State"; Knight, "Weight of the State."

30. Knight, "State Power and Political Stability."

Bibliography

Archival Sources

Mexico City

Archivo de Acción Católica Mexicana
  Junta Diocesana de Oaxaca
Archivo de Aurelio Acevedo Robles
Archivo General de la Nación
  Dirección General de Gobierno
  Fondo Presidentes, Ramo Abelardo Rodríguez
  Fondo Presidentes, Ramo Obregón-Calles
  Fondo Presidentes, Ramo Lázaro Cárdenas del Río
  Fondo Presidentes, Ramo Manuel Avila Camacho
  Fondo Presidentes, Ramo Miguel Alemán Valdés
  Investigaciones Políticas y Sociales
Archivo Histórico de la Secretaría de Educación Pública
  Misiones Culturales
Archivo Histórico de la Secretaría de la Defensa Nacional
  Difuntos
  Direccíon General de Archivo e Historia
Archivo Joaquín Amaro
  Autoridades Locales y Estatales
  Poderes Legislativos y Judiciales
Archivo Manuel Gómez Marin
Archivos de Plutarco Elías Calles y Fernando Torreblanca
Hemeroteca Nacional, Universidad Nacional Autónoma de México

Oaxaca

Archivo de Genaro Vásquez Colmenares
Archivo de Javier Sánchez Pereyra
Archivo de la Arquidiócesis de Oaxaca
  Diocesano, Gobierno, Correspondencia
  Diocesis, Gobernación, Autoridades Civiles
Archivo de la Cámara Local de Diputados

Archivo de la Diócesis de Huajuapam de León
Archivo del Municipio de Huajuapam de León
Archivo del Municipio de Tlahuitoltepec
  Administración, Correspondencia
Archivo del Partido Acción Nacional del Estado de Oaxaca
Archivo del Registro Público de Propiedades
Archivo de Luis Castañeda Guzmán
Archivo General del Poder Ejecutivo de Oaxaca
  Ramo Ajudicaciones
  Ramo Asuntos Agrarios
  Ramo Asuntos Católicos
  Ramo Censos y Padrones
  Ramo Conflictos por Limites Siglo XIX
  Ramo Educación
  Ramo Gobernación
  Ramo Junta de Conciliación y Arbitraje
  Ramo Justicia
  Ramo Memorias Administrativas
  Ramo Periodo Revoluciónario
Archivo Judicial de Oaxaca
  Ramo Civil
Archivo Municipal de Oaxaca de Juárez
Biblioteca Bustamante Vasconcelos
Biblioteca Francisco Burgoa
  Collecion Manuel Brioso y Candiani
Biblioteca Pública de Oaxaca
  Collección Manuel Martínez Gracida
Hemeroteca de la Universidad Autónoma "Benito Juárez" de Oaxaca
Hemeroteca Pública de Oaxaca
  Collección Mayoral Heredia

United Kingdom

Foreign Office Archive, Public Records Office

United States

National Anthropological Archive
  Ralph L. Beals Collection

Secondary Sources

Abardia M., Francisco, and Leticia Reina. "Cien años de rebelión." In *Lecturas históricas del estado de Oaxaca*, vol. 3, *Siglo XIX*, edited by María de los Angeles Romero Frizzi, 435–92. Mexico, D.F.: Instituto Nacional de Antropología e Historia, 1990.

Adie, Robert F. "Cooperation, Cooption and Conflict in Mexican Peasant Organizations." *International American Economic Affairs* 24 (1970): 3–25.

Aguilar Camín, Héctor, and Lorenzo Meyer. *In the Shadow of the Mexican Revolution: Contemporary Mexican History, 1910–1989*. Austin: University of Texas Press, 1993.

Aguilar Domingo, Martín. *Santiago Zacatepec, Mixe*. Oaxaca de Juárez, Oaxaca: n.p., 1992.

Aguilar Robledo, Miguel. "Haciendas y condueñazgos en la Huasteca potosina: Notas introductorias." In *Nuevos aportes al conocimiento de la Huasteca*, edited by Antonio Escobar Ohmstede, 123–52. Mexico, D.F: Centre d'Études Mexicaines et Centraméricaines (CEMCA), 1998.

Aguirre, Teresa, and José Luis Avila. "Rebelión en el PRI." In *México: Un pueblo en la historia, nueva burguesia (1938–1957)*, edited by Enrique Semo, 103–16. Mexico, D.F.: Alianza Editorial Mexicana, 1997.

Aguirre Beltrán, Gonzalo. *Cuijla: Esbozo etnografico de un pueblo negro*. Mexico, D.F.: Fondo de Cultura Económica, 1989.

———. *Regions of Refuge*. Washington DC: Society for Applied Anthropology, 1979.

———. *Teoría y práctica de la educación indigena*. Mexico, D.F.: Universidad Veracruzana, Instituto Nacional Indigenista; Gobierno del Estado de Veracruz; Fondo de Cultura Económica, 1992.

Album conmemorativa del IV centenario de su exaltación a la categoria de ciudad. Oaxaca de Juárez, Oaxaca: n.p., 1932.

Alcayaga Sasso, Aurora Mónica. "Librado Rivera y los hermanos Rojos en el movimiento social y cultural anarquista en Villa Cecilia y Tampico, Tamaulipas, 1915–1931." PhD diss., Universidad Iberoamericana, 2006.

Alemán Valdés, Miguel. *Un México major: Pensamientos, discursos e información, 1936–1952*. Mexico, D.F.: Editorial Diana, 1988.

———. *Programa de gobierno*. Mexico, D.F.: n.p., 1945.

Altamirano, Margarita. *Heliodoro Charis Castro, recuentro de una historia*. Oaxaca de Juárez, Oaxaca: IEPPO, 2003.

Alvarado Mendoza, Arturo. "Perfil politico de Emilio Portes Gil." In *Estadistas, caciques y caudillos*, edited by Carlos Martínez Assad. Mexico, D.F.: Instituto de Investigaciones Sociales, Universidad Nacional Autónoma de México, 1988.

———. *El Portesgilismo en Tamaulipas: Estudio sobre la constitución de la autoridad pública en el México posrevolucionario*. Mexico, D.F.: Colegio de México, 1992

Anderson, Benedict. *Imagined Communities: Reflections on the Origin and Spread of Nationalism*. London: Verso, 1983.

Anderson, Bo, and J. D. Cockcroft. "Control and Cooption in Mexican Politics." *International Journal of Comparative Society* 7 (1966): 11–18.

Anguiano, Arturo. "Cárdenas and the Masses." In *The Mexico Reader*, edited by Gilbert Joseph and Timothy J. Henderson, 456–60. Durham: Duke University Press, 2002.

———. *El estado y la política obrera del cardenismo*. Mexico, D.F.: Ediciones Era, 1975.

Ankerson, Dudley. *Agrarian Warlord: Saturnino Cedillo and the Mexican Revolution in San Luis Potosí*. Dekalb: Northern Illinois University Press, 1984.

———. "Saturnino Cedillo, a Traditional Caudillo in San Luis Potosí, 1890–1938." In *Caudillo and Peasant in the Mexican Revolution*, edited by D. A. Brading, 140–68. Cambridge: Cambridge University Press, 1980.

Arellanes Meixueiro, Anselmo. "Del camarazo al cardenismo." In *Historia de la cuestión agraria mexicana, estado de Oaxaca, 1925–1986, Volumen II*, edited by Leticia Reina, 25–125. Mexico, D.F.: Juan Pablos Editor, 1988.

———. "La Confederación de Partidos Socialistas en Oaxaca." In *La Revolución en Oaxaca 1900–1930*, edited by Victor Raúl Martínez Vásquez, 374–406. Oaxaca de Juárez, Oaxaca: Instituto de Administración Pública de Oaxaca, 1985.

———. "Un general y un periodo en la vida oaxaqueña." *Cuadernos del Sur* 4, no. 11 (1997): 7–30.

———. *Movimiento popular y política en Oaxaca, 1968–1986*. Mexico, D.F.: Consejo Nacional para la Cultura y las Artes, 1990.

———. *Oaxaca: Reparto de la tierra, alcances, limitaciones y respuestas*. Oaxaca de Juárez, Oaxaca: Carteles Editores, 1999.

———. "Testimonios, suicidio en la Camara: Jorge Meixueiro." *Cuadernos del Sur* 1, no. 1 (1992): 127–41.

———. *Los trabajos y los guias: Mutualismo y sindicalismo en Oaxaca, 1870–1930*. Oaxaca de Juárez, Oaxaca: n.p., 1990.

Arellanes Meixueiro, Anselmo, et al. *Diccionario histórico de la Revolución en Oaxaca*. Oaxaca de Juárez, Oaxaca: Universidad Autónoma "Benito Juárez" de Oaxaca, 1997.

Arrioja Díaz-Viruel, Luis Alberto. "Caciquismo y estrategias de poder en la Sierra Mixe: El caso de Luis Rodríguez Jacob (1950–1959)." In *Historia, sociedad y literatura de Oaxaca: Nuevos enfoques*, edited by Carlos Sánchez Silva. Oaxaca de Juárez, Oaxaca: Universidad Autónoma "Benito Juárez" de Oaxaca, 2004.

Attolini, José. *Economía de la Cuenca del Papaloapan*. Mexico, D.F.: Instituto de Investigaciones Económicas, 1949.

Avila Camacho, Manuel. *Discursos*. Mexico, D.F.: Colegio de México, 1946.

Bailon Corres, Jaime. *Pueblos indios, élites y territorio: Sistemas de dominio regional en el sur de México, una historia política de Oaxaca*. Mexico, D.F.: Colegio de México, 1999.

Bantjes, Adrian A. *As If Jesus Walked the Earth: Cardenismo, Sonora and the Mexican Revolution*. Wilmington DE: Scholarly Resources, 1998.

Barabas, Alicia. "Rebelliones e insurrecciones indigenas en Oaxaca: La trayectoria historica de la resistencia etnia." In *Etnicidad y pluralismo cultural: La dinamica etnia en Oaxaca*, edited by Alicia Barabas and Miguel Bartolome, 213–56. Mexico, D.F.: Instituto Nacional de Antropología e Historia, 1986.

Barahona, Orlando. *Graves tensiones sociales en el distrito Mixe*. Mexico, D.F.: n.p., 1963.

Barkey, Karen. *Bandits and Bureaucrats: The Ottoman Route to State Centralization*. Ithaca: Cornell University Press, 1994.

Bartra, Armando. *Guerrero bronco: Campesinos, ciudadanos y guerrilleros en la Costa Grande*. Tepepan: Ediciones Sinfiltro, 1996.

———. *Los herederos de Zapata: Movimiento campesinos posrevolucionarios en México 1920–1980*. Mexico, D.F.: Ediciones Era, 1985.

Basurto, Jorge. *Del avilacamachismo al alemanismo (1940–1952)*. Mexico, D.F.: Siglo Veintiuno, 1984.

Beals, Ralph L. "Ethnology of the Western Mixe." *University of California Publications in American Archaeology and Ethnology* 52 (1951): 1–176.

———. "The Oaxaca Market Project." In *Markets in Oaxaca*, edited by Scott Cook and Martín Diskin, 27–44. Austin: University of Texas Press 1982.

————. "The Western Mixe Indians of Oaxaca, Mexico." *America Indigena* 2, no. 1 (1942): 45–50.

Becker, Marjorie. *Setting the Virgin on Fire: Lázaro Cárdenas, Michoacán, Peasants and the Redemption of the Mexican Revolution*. Berkeley: University of California Press, 1995.

————. "Touching La Purísima, Dancing at the Altar: The Construction of Revolutionary Hegemony in Michoacán, 1934–1940." In *Everyday Forms of State Formation: Revolution and Negotiation of Rule in Modern Mexico*, edited by Gilbert Joseph and Daniel Nugent, 247–64. Durham: Duke University Press, 1994.

Benjamin, Thomas. *La Revolución: Mexico's Great Revolution as Memory, Myth and History*. Austin: University of Texas Press, 2000.

————. *A Rich Land, A Poor People: Politics and Society in Modern Chiapas*. Albuquerque: University of New Mexico Press, 1996.

Berry, Charles. *The Reform in Oaxaca, 1856–76: A Microhistory of the Liberal Revolution*. Lincoln: University of Nebraska Press, 1981.

Boege, Eckart, ed. *Desarrollo del capitalismo y transformación de la estructura de poder en la región de Tuxtepec, Oaxaca*. Mexico, D.F.: Instituto Nacional de Antropología e Historia, 1979.

————. *Los Mazatecos ante la nación: Contradicciones de la identidad etnica en el México actual*. Mexico, D.F.: Siglo Veintiuno Editores, 1988.

Bortz, Jeffrey L. *Industrial Wages in Mexico City, 1939–1975*. New York: Garland, 1987.

Boyer, Christopher R. *Becoming Campesinos: Politics, Identity, and Agrarian Struggle in Postrevolutionary Michoacan, 1920–1935*. Stanford: Stanford University Press, 2003.

————. "Naranja Revisited: Agrarian Caciques and the Making of Campesino Identity in Postrevolutionary Michoacán." In *Caciquismo in Twentieth-Century Mexico*, edited by Alan Knight and Wil Pansters, 94–122. London: Institute for the Study of the Americas, 2005.

————. "Old Loves, New Loyalties: Agrarismo in Michoacán, 1920–1928." *Hispanic American Historical Review* 78, no. 3 (1998): 419–55.

Brading, D. A., ed. *Caudillo and Peasant in the Mexican Revolution*. Cambridge: Cambridge University Press, 1980.

————. "Manuel Gamio and Official Indigenismo in Mexico." *Bulletin of Latin American Research* 7, no. 1 (1993): 75–89.

Brandenberg, Frank. *The Making of Modern Mexico*. Englewood Cliffs NJ: Prentice Hall, 1964.

Brewster, Keith. "Caciquismo in the Sierra Norte de Puebla: The Case of Gabriel Barrios Cabrera." In *Caciquismo in Twentieth-Century Mexico*, edited by Alan Knight and Wil Pansters, 113–29. London: Institute for the Study of the Americas, 2005.

———. *Militarism, Ethnicity and Politics in the Sierra Norte de Puebla, 1917–1930*. Tucson: University of Arizona Press, 2003.

Brioso y Candiani, Manuel. *Album literario de Oaxaca*. Tehuacan: n.p., 1928.

Brown, Lyle C. "Cárdenas: Creating a Campesino Power Base for Presidential Policy." In *Essays on the Mexican Revolution: Revisionist Views of the Leaders*, edited by George Wolfskill and Douglas W. Richmond, 101–36. Austin: University of Texas Press, 1978.

Buchenau, Jürgen. *Plutarco Elías Calles and the Mexican Revolution*. Lanham MD: Rowman and Littlefield, 2006.

Butler, Matthew. "God's Caciques: Caciquismo and the Cristero Revolt in Coalcomán." In *Caciquismo in Twentieth-Century Mexico*, edited by Alan Knight and Wil Pansters, 94–112. London: Institute for the Study of the Americas, 2005.

———. *Popular Piety and Political Identity in Mexico's Cristero Rebellion: Michoacán, 1927–1929*. Oxford: Oxford University Press, 2004.

Buve, Raymond. *El movimiento revolucionario en Tlaxcala*. Tlaxcala: Universidad Autónoma de Tlaxcala, 1994.

———. "State Governors and Peasant Mobilisation in Tlaxcala." In *Caudillo and Peasant in the Mexican Revolution*, edited by D. A. Brading, 222–44. Cambridge: Cambridge University Press, 1980.

Buve, Raymond, and Romana Falcón. "Tlaxcala and San Luis Potosí under the Sonorenses (1920–1934): Regional Revolutionary Power Groups and the National State." In *Region, State and Capitalism in Mexico*, edited by Wil Pansters and Arij Ouweneel, 110–33. Amsterdam: CEDLA, 1989.

Calles, Plutarco Elías. *Correspondencia personal (1919–1945)*. Mexico, D.F.: Fondo de Cultura Económica, 1993.

Calvo, Thomas. "Huellas e ilusiones de lo real, fotografias y registros en Oaxaca, (1890–1925)." In *Imagenes de la vida cotidiana en la ciudad de Oaxaca*, 28–42. Oaxaca de Juárez, Oaxaca: Universidad Autónoma "Benito Juárez" de Oaxaca, 2005.

Camp, Roderic Ai. "Camarillas in Mexican Politics: The Case of the Salinas Cabinet." *Mexican Studies/Estudios Mexicanos* 6, no. 1 (1990): 85–107.

———. *Intellectuals and the State in Twentieth Century Mexico*. Austin: University of Texas Press, 1985.

Campbell, Howard. "Intelectuales Zapotecos: Produccion y política en Juchitán." *Cuadernos del Sur* 2, no. 3 (1993): 75–102.

———. "Tradition and the New Social Movements: The Politics of Isthmus Zapotec Culture." *Latin American Perspectives* 20, no. 3 (1993): 83–97.

———. *Zapotec Renaissance, Ethnic Politics and Cultural Revivalism in Southern Mexico*. Albuquerque: University of New Mexico Press, 1994.

Cárdenas, Lázaro. *Obras, apuntes*. Vol. 1. Mexico, D.F.: Universidad Nacional Autónoma de México, Dirección General de Publicaciones, 1973.

Carlos, Manuel L. "Peasant Leadership Hierarchies: Leadership Behavior, Power Blocs, and Conflict in Mexican Regions." In *Mexico's Regions, Comparative History and Development*, edited by Eric Van Young. San Diego: Center for U.S.-Mexican Studies, 1992.

Carr, Barry. *Marxism and Communism in Twentieth-Century Mexico*. Lincoln: University of Nebraska Press, 1992.

Cassidy, Thomas. "Haciendas and Pueblos in Nineteenth Century Oaxaca." PhD diss., University of Cambridge, 1982.

———. "Las haciendas oaxaqueñas en el siglo XIX." In *Lecturas históricos del estado de Oaxaca*, vol. 3, *Siglo XIX*, edited by María de los Angeles Romero Frizzi, 291–324. Mexico, D.F.: Instituto Nacional de Antropología e Historia, 1990.

Castellanos, Laura. *México armado, 1943–1981*. Mexico, D.F.: Ediciones Era, 2007.

Cerutti, Mario. "The Formation and Consolidation of the Regional Bourgeoisie in Northeastern Mexico (Monterrey: From Reform to Revolution)." In *Region, State and Capitalism in Mexico*, edited by Wil Pansters and Arij Ouweneel, 47–58. Amsterdam: CEDLA, 1989.

Chassen, Francie R., and Héctor G. Martínez. "El desarrollo económico de Oaxaca a finales del Porfiriato." In *Lecturas históricos del estado de Oaxaca*, vol. 4, *Siglo XIX*, edited by María de los Angeles Romero Frizzi, 47–72. Mexico, D.F.: Instituto Nacional de Antropología e Historia, 1990.

———. "El retorno al milenio Mixteco: Indigenas agraristas vs. rancheros revolucionarios en la Costa Chica de Oaxaca, Mayo, 1911." *Cuadernos del Sur* 2, no. 5 (1993): 33–66.

———. *La Revolución en Oaxaca 1900–1930, el primer gobierno*

revolucionario de Oaxaca: La gestion del Lic. Heliodoro Díaz Quintas.
Oaxaca de Juárez, Oaxaca: Instituto de Administración Pública de Oaxaca, 1985.

Chassen, Francie R., Hector Martínez Medina, and Carlos Sánchez Silva.
"Las haciendas en Oaxaca." *Guchachi'reza* 36 (1992): 13–21.

Chassen-López, Francie R. "El boom minero, el auge económico y la crisis."
In *Oaxaca: Textos de su historia*, vol. 4, edited by Margaret Dalton, 70–
116. Oaxaca: Gobierno del Estado de Oaxaca, 1990.

———. "El café: Los origenes del grano de oro en Oaxaca." *Cuadernos del
Sur* (November 1998): 25–40.

———. "'Cheaper than Machines': Women and Agriculture in Porfirian Oaxaca, 1880–1911." In *Women of the Mexican Countryside, 1850–1990*,
edited by Heather Fowler-Salamini and Mary Kay Vaughan, 27–50. Tucson: University of Arizona Press, 1994.

———. *From Liberal to Revolutionary Oaxaca: The View from the South,
Mexico 1867–1911*. University Park: Pennsylvania State University
Press, 2004.

———. "Maderismo or Mixtec Empire? Class and Ethnicity in the Mexican
Revolution, Costa Chica of Oaxaca, 1911." *Americas* 55, no. 1 (1998):
91–127.

———. "Oaxaca del Porfiriato a la Revolución, 1902–1911." PhD diss., Universidad Nacional Autónoma de México, 1986.

———. "Los precursores de la Revolución en Oaxaca." In *La Revolución en
Oaxaca, 1900–1930*, edited by Victor Raúl Martínez Vásquez, 35–87.
Oaxaca de Juárez, Oaxaca: Instituto de Administración Pública de Oaxaca, 1985.

Chevalier, Jacques M., and Daniel Buckles. *A Land without Gods: Process
Theory, Maldevelopment and the Mexican Nahuas.* London: Zed Books,
1995.

Clark, Marjorie Ruth. *Organized Labor in Mexico.* Chapel Hill: University of
North Carolina Press, 1934.

Clarke, Colin. *Class, Ethnicity and Community in Southern Mexico: Oaxaca's Peasantries.* Oxford: Oxford University Press, 2000.

Cline, Howard F. *Mexico, Revolution to Evolution, 1940–1960.* London:
Oxford University Press, 1962.

Cockcroft, James D. *Mexico: Class Formation, Capital Accumulation, and
the State.* New York: State University of New York Press, 1983.

Collier, Ruth Berins. "Popular Sector Incorporation and Political Supremacy: Regime Evolution in Brazil and Mexico." In *Brazil and Mexico: Patterns in Late Development*, edited by Sylvia Ann Hewlett and Richard W
Weinert, 57–109. Philadelphia: Institute for the Study of Human Issues,
1982.

Comas, Juan. "El problema social de los indios Triquis en Oaxaca." *America
Indigena* 2, no. 1 (1942): 51–57.

Confederación de Partidos Socialistas de Oaxaca (CPSO). *Proyecto de ley de
seguro obrero*. Oaxaca de Juárez, Oaxaca: n.p., 1927.

*Con que anhelos inicia su administración el C General de División Vicente
González Fernández*. Oaxaca de Juárez, Oaxaca: n.p., 1941.

Controversia jurídica entre la federación y el estado de Oaxaca. Oaxaca de
Juárez, Oaxaca: n.p., 1932.

Cook, Scott, and Leigh Binford. *Obliging Need: Rural Petty Industry in Mexican Capitalism*. Austin: University of Texas Press, 1990.

Cook, Scott, and Martin Diskin. *Markets in Oaxaca*. Austin: University of
Texas Press, 1975.

Córdova, Arnaldo. *La política de masas del cardenismo*. Mexico, D.F.: Ediciones Era, 1974.

Cornelius, Wayne. "Nation Building, Participation and Distribution: The Politics of Social Reform under Cárdenas." In *Crisis, Choice and Change:
Historical Studies of Political Development*, edited by Gabriel Almond,
Scott Flanegan, and Robert Mundt, 389–498. Boston MA: Little Brown,
1973.

———. *Politics and the Migrant Poor in Mexico City*. Stanford: Stanford University Press, 1976.

Cornelius, Wayne, and Ann L. Craig. *Politics in Mexico: An Introduction and
an Overview*. San Diego: Center for U.S.-Mexican Studies, University of
California, 1988.

Coronil, Fernando. "Foreword." In *Close Encounters of Empire: Writing the
Cultural History of U.S.-Latin American Relations*, edited by Gilbert M.
Joseph, Catherine C. LeGrand, and Ricardo D. Salvatore, ix–xii. Dur-
ham: Duke University Press, 1998.

Cortés A., Guadalupe. *Las derrotas obreras, 1946–1952*. Mexico, D.F.: Instituto de Investigaciones Sociales, Universidad Nacional Autónoma de
México, 1984.

Cosio Villegas, Daniel. *El estilo personal de gobernar*. Mexico, D.F.: Editorial
J. Mortiz, 1974.

Covarrubias, Miguel. *Mexico South: The Isthmus of Tehuantepec.* New York: A. A. Knopf, 1946.

Craig, Ann. *The First Agraristas: An Oral History of a Mexican Reform Movement.* Berkeley: University of California Press, 1993.

Cruz Cruz, Florencio. "Surgimiento de la escuela rural en la Sierra Juárez." In *Los maestros y la cultura nacional, sureste,* vol. 5, 155–86. Mexico, D.F.: SEP, 1987.

Dávila Alfaro, Gustavo. "Testimonios del 52." *Testimonios de Oaxaca* 8 (1984): 15–22.

Dawson, Alexander S. "From Models for the Nation to Model Citizens: Indigenismo and the 'Revindication' of the Mexican Indian, 1920–1940." *Journal of Latin American Studies* 30, no. 2 (1998): 279–308.

———. *Indian and Nation in Revolutionary Mexico.* Tucson: University of Arizona Press, 2004.

De la Cruz, Victor. "Che Gómez y la rebelion de Juchitán: 1911." In *Lecturas históricas del estado de Oaxaca, 1877–1930,* vol. 4, *Siglo XIX,* edited by María de los Angeles Romero Frizzi, 247–71. Mexico, D.F.: Instituto Nacional de Antropología e Historia, 1990.

———. "El General Charis y la educación." *Cuadernos Políticos* 1, no. 1 (1992): 61–70.

———. *El General Charis, y la pacificación del México posrevolucionario.* Mexico, D.F.: Ediciones de la Casa Chata–CIESAS, 1993.

———. "Rebeliones indigenas en el Istmo de Tehuantepec." *Cuadernos Politicos* 38, no. 4 (1983): 67–90.

De la Fuente, Julio. *Relaciones interétnicas.* Mexico, D.F.: Instituto Nacional Indigenista, 1965.

———. *Yalalag, una villa zapoteca serrana.* Mexico, D.F.: Museo Nacional de Antropología, 1949.

De la Peña, Guillermo. "Poder local, poder regional: Perspectivas socioantropológicas." In *Poder local, poder regional,* edited by Jorge Padua and Alain Vanneph, 27–56. Mexico, D.F.: Colegio de México, 1988.

De la Peña, Moises. *Oaxaca económico.* Mexico, D.F.: n.p., 1952.

———. *Veracruz económico.* Mexico, D.F.: n.p., 1946.

———. *Zacatecas económico.* Mexico, D.F.: Revista de Economía, 1948.

Democracia indígena, film. Directed by Bruce "Pacho" Lane. Rochester NY: Ethnoscope Film and Video, 1999.

Departamento Agrario. *Las masas campesinas y el Departamento Agrario.* Mexico, D.F.: n.p., 1938.

Díaz, María Elena. "The Satiric Penny Press for Workers in Mexico, 1900–1930: A Case Study in the Politicization of Popular Culture." *Journal of Latin American Studies* 22, no. 3 (1990): 497–526.

Dirección General de Estadistica. *Primer censo agricola ganadero, 1930.* Mexico, D.F.: Secretaría de la Economia Nacional, 1936.

———. *Quinto censo de población de 1930.* Mexico, D.F.: Secretaría de la Economia Nacional, 1936.

———. *Segundo censo agricola ganadero de los Estados Unidos Mexicanos, resumen.* Mexico, D.F.: Secretaría de la Economia Nacional, 1951.

———. *Septimo censo de población, 1950.* Mexico, D.F.: Secretaría de la Economia Nacional, 1956.

———. *Sexto censo general de población, 1940.* Mexico, D.F.: Secretaría de la Economia Nacional, 1946.

———. *Tercer censo agricola, ganadero y ejidal, 1950.* Mexico, D.F.: Secretaría de la Economia Nacional, 1956.

Diskin, Martin. "The Structure of a Peasant Market System in Oaxaca." In *Markets in Oaxaca,* edited by Scott Cook and Martin Diskin, 49–66. Austin: University of Texas Press, 1982.

Drumondo, Baltasar. *Emiliano Zapata.* Mexico, D.F.: Imprenta Mundial, 1934.

Duara, Prasenjit. *Culture, Power, and the State: Rural North China, 1900–1942.* Stanford: Stanford University Press, 1988.

———. "Why Is History Antitheoretical?" *Modern China* 24, no. 2 (April 1988): 105–20.

Durand, Víctor Manuel. "La decomposición política del lombardismo." In *Entre la guerra y la estabilidad política,* edited by Rafael Loyola, 163–92. Mexico, D.F.: Instituto de Investigaciones Sociales, Universidad Nacional Autónoma de México, 1990.

———. *La ruptura de la nación: Historia del movimiento obrero mexicano desde 1938 hasta 1952.* Mexico, D.F.: Instituto de Investigaciones Sociales, Universidad Nacional Autónoma de México, 1986.

Eckstein, Salomón, and Iván Restrepo. *La explotación colectiva en México: El caso de la comarca Lagunera.* Mexico, D.F.: Fondo de Cultura Económica, 1975.

Eckstein, Susan. *The Poverty of Revolution: The State and the Urban Poor in Mexico.* Princeton: Princeton University Press, 1977.

Escarcega López, Everado. "El principio de la reforma agraria." In *Historia de la cuestión agraria mexicana: El cardenismo, un parteaguas histórico en el proceso agrario 1934–1940,* vol. 1, edited by Everado Escarcega López and Saul Escobar Toledo, 39–251. Mexico, D.F.: Siglo Veintiuno Editores, 1990.

Escarcega, López Everado, and Saul Escobar Toledo, eds. *Historia de la cuestión agraria mexicana, el cardenismo: Un parteaguas histórico en el proceso agrario 1934–1940.* 2 vols. Mexico, D.F.: Siglo Veintiuno Editores, 1990.

Escobar Ohmstede, Antonio. "Los condueñazgos indígenas en las huastecas hidalguense y veracruzana: ¿Defensa del espacio comunal?" In *Indio, nación y comunidad en el México del siglo XIX,* edited by Antonio Escobar Ohmstede, 171–88. México, D.F: Centre d'Études Mexicaines et Centraméricaines (CEMCA), 1993.

Esparza, Manuel. *Gillow durante el Porfiriato y la Revolución en Oaxaca, 1887–1922.* Oaxaca de Juárez, Oaxaca: SAGEO, 1988.

———. "Penetración capitalista en Oaxaca, 1890–1920." *Cuadernos del Sur* 1, no. 1 (1992): 52–59.

———. "Los proyectos de los liberales en Oaxaca (1856–1910)." In *Historia de la cuestión agraria mexicana, estado de Oaxaca, prehispanico–1924,* edited by Leticia Reina, 269–330. Mexico, D.F.: Juan Pablos Editor, 1988.

———. "La tierras de los hijos de los pueblos: El distrito de Juchitán en el siglo XIX." In *Lecturas históricos del estado de Oaxaca,* vol. 3, *Siglo XIX,* edited by María de los Angeles Romero Frizzi, 387–433. Mexico, D.F.: Instituto Nacional de Antropología e Historia, 1990.

Estatutos, circulares, declaración de principios y plan de acción de la Federación Indigenista Revolucionaria Oaxaquena (FIRO). Mexico, D.F.: n.p., 1939.

Estatutos de la Confederación de Pueblos de los Ex-Distritos de Choapam, Mixe, Villa Alta e Ixtlán. Oaxaca de Juárez, Oaxaca: n.p., 1939.

Esteva, Cayetano. *Nociones elementales de geografía histórica del estado de Oaxaca con un reseña del movimiento revolucionario en cada distrito desde 1911 hasta 1913.* Oaxaca de Juárez, Oaxaca: n.p., 1913.

Ewell, Peter T., and Thomas T. Poleman. *Uxpanapa: Agricultural Development in the Mexican Tropics.* New York: Pergamon Press, 1980.

Fagen, Richard R., and William S. Tuohy. *Politics and Privilege in a Mexican City.* Stanford: Stanford University Press, 1972.

Falcón, Romana. *Revolución y caciquismo, San Luis Potosí, 1910–1938.* Mexico, D.F.: Colegio de México, 1984.

———. "El surgimiento del agrarismo cardenista, una revision de las tesis populista." *Historia Mexicana* 27, no. 4 (1978): 333–86.

Falcón, Romana, and Soledad García. *La semilla en el surco: Adalberto Tejeda y el radicalismo en Veracruz, 1883–1960.* Mexico, D.F.: Colegio de México, 1986.

Fallaw, Ben. "Cárdenas and the Caste War That Wasn't: State Power and Indigenismo in Post-Revolutionary Yucatán." *Americas* 53, no. 4 (1997): 234–67.

———. *Cárdenas Compromised: The Failure of Reform in Postrevolutionary Yucatán.* Durham: Duke University Press, 2001.

Feria Juárez, Salomón. *Estado actual de la reforma agraria de Oaxaca, desde el punto de vista de la estadistica.* Mexico, D.F.: n.p., 1963.

Fernández-Aceves, María Teresa. "Once We Were Corn Grinders: Women and Labor in the Tortilla Industry of Guadalajara, 1920–1940." *International Labor and Working-Class History* 63 (Spring 2003): 81–101.

Fowler Salamini, Heather. *Agrarian Radicalism in Veracruz, 1920–1938.* Lincoln: University of Nebraska Press, 1978.

———. "The Agrarian Revolution in the State of Veracruz, 1920–1940: The Role of Peasant Organizations." PhD diss., American University, 1970.

———. "De-centering the 1920s: Socialismo a la Tamaulipeca." *Mexican Studies/Estudios Mexicanos* 14, no. 2 (July 1978): 287–327.

———. "Gender, Work and Working-Class Women's Culture in the Veracruz Coffee Export Industry, 1920–1945." *International Labor and Working-Class History* 63 (Spring 2003): 102–21.

———. "Revolutionary Caudillos in the 1920s: Francisco Múgica and Adalberto Tejeda." In *Caudillo and Peasant in the Mexican Revolution,* edited by D. A. Brading, 169–92. Cambridge: Cambridge University Press, 1980.

———. "Tamaulipas, Land Reform and the State." In *Provinces of the Revolution: Essays on Regional Mexican History, 1910–1929,* edited by Thomas Benjamin and Mark Wasserman, 71–92. Albuquerque: University of New Mexico Press, 1990.

Frente Popular Oaxaqueño. *Datos para la historia de nuestro desventurado estado.* Oaxaca de Juárez, Oaxaca: n.p., 1938.

Friedrich, Paul. *Agrarian Revolt in a Mexican Village*. Chicago: University of Chicago Press, 1980.

———. "The Legitimacy of a Cacique." In *Local-Level Politics: Social and Cultural Perspectives*, edited by Marc J. Swartz, 243–69. Chicago: University of Chicago Press, 1968.

———. "A Mexican Cacicazgo." *Ethnology* 4, no. 2 (1965): 190–209.

———. *The Princes of Naranja: An Essay in Anthropological Method*. Austin: University of Texas Press, 1986.

García, J. Guadalupe. *La Sierra de Huautla en la gesta oaxaqueña: La soberanía de Oaxaca en los ideales de la Revolución*. Mexico, D.F.: n.p., 1955.

García, Ruben. *En la comitiva del Presidente Cárdenas*. Mexico, D.F.: n.p., 1937.

García Canclini, Néstor. *La globalización imaginada*. Buenos Aires: Paidós, 1999.

García de León, Antonio. *Resistencia y utopía: Memorial de agravios y crónica de revueltas y profecías acaecidas en la provincia de Chiapas durante los ultimos quinientos años de su historia*. Mexico, D.F.: Ediciones Era, 1997.

García Hernández, Tomás. *Tuxtepec ante la historia*. Mexico, D.F.: Consejo Nacional para la Cultura y las Artes, Dirección General de Culturas Populares, Unidad Regional de Tuxtepec; Club Rotario de Tuxtepec, 1989.

García Uguarte, Marta Eugenia. *Génesis del porvenir: Sociedad y política en Querétaro (1913–1940)*. Mexico, D.F.: Fondo de Cultura Económico, 1997.

———. "Santurnino Osornio: Remembranzas de un época en Queretaro." In *Estadistas, caciques y caudillos*, edited by Carlos Martínez Assad, 335–61. Mexico, D.F.: Instituto de Investigaciones Sociales, Universidad Nacional Autónoma de México, 1988.

Garfias Magaña, Luis. "El General Joaquín Amaro: El Istmo de Tehuantepec y la soberania nacional." *Boletín de Fideicomiso Archivos* 38 (2002): 1–13.

Garner, Paul. "Federalism and Caudillismo in the Mexican Revolution: The Genesis of the Oaxaca Sovereignty Movement (1915–1920)." *Journal of Latin American Studies* 17 (May 1985): 111–33.

———. *Porfirio Díaz*. Mexico, D.F.: Planeta, 2001.

———. "A Provincial Response to the Mexican Revolution, State Sovereignty, and Highland Caudillismo PhD Diss., University of Liverpool, 1983."

———. *Regional Development in Oaxaca during the Porfiriato (1876–1911)*. Liverpool: Institute of Latin American Studies, University of Liverpool, 1995.

———. *La Revolución en la provincia, soberania estatal y caudillismo serrano en Oaxaca, 1910–1920*. Mexico, D.F.: Fondo de Cultura Económico, 2003.

Garrido, Luis Javier. *El partido de la revolución institucionalizada: La formación del nuevo estado en México (1928–1945)*. Mexico, D.F.: Siglo Veintiuno Editores, 1982.

Genuina Confederación de Ligas Socialistas de Oaxaca. Oaxaca de Juárez, Oaxaca: n.p., 1934.

Gillingham, Paul. "The Emperor of Ixcateopan: Fraud, Nationalism and Memory in Modern Mexico." *Journal of Latin American Studies* 37, no. 3 (2005): 561–84.

———. "Force and Consent in Mexican Provincial Politics: Guerrero and Veracruz, 1945–1953." PhD diss., Oxford University, 2005.

———. "Maximino's Bulls, Strategies of Public Dissent in Mexico, 1940–1960." Paper presented at LASA conference, Puerto Rico, March 2006.

Gilly, Adolfo. *La Revolución interrumpida en México, 1910–1920: Una guerra campesina por la tierra y el poder*. Mexico, D.F.: Ediciones el Caballito, 1971.

Ginzberg, Eitan. *Lázaro Cárdenas, gobernador de Michoacán (1928–1932)*. Zamora: Colegio de Michoacán, 1999.

———. "State Agrarianism versus Democratic Agrarianism: Adalberto Tejeda's Experiment in Veracruz, 1928–1932." *Journal of Latin American Studies* 30, no. 2 (2001): 341–72.

Glantz, Susana. *El ejido colectivo de Nueva Italia*. Mexico, D.F.: Centro de Investigaciones Superiores, Instituto Nacional de Antropología e Historia, 1974.

Gledhill, John. *Casi Nada: A Study of Agrarian Reform in the Homeland of Cardenismo*. Albany: Institute for Mesoamerican Studies, State University of New York, 1991.

Gómez, Gildardo. "Desarrollo de las vias de comunicación en el estado: Auge ferroviario." In *Oaxaca: Textos de su historia*, vol. 4, edited by Margaret Dalton, 158–60. Oaxaca: Instituto de Investigaciones Dr. José María Luis Mora, 1990.

Gómez, Marte R. *La reforma agraria de México: Su crisis durante el período 1928–1934*. Mexico, D.F.: M. Porrúa, 1964.

González Casanova, Pablo. *Democracy in Mexico*. Translated by Danielle Salti. New York: Oxford University Press, 1970.

González Esperón, Luz María. *Crónicas diversas de artesanos oaxaqueños*. Oaxaca de Juárez, Oaxaca: Instituto Oaxaqueño de las Culturas, 1997.

González Navarro, Moisés. *La Confederación Nacional Campesina*. Mexico, D.F.: B. Costa-Amic, 1968.

González y González, Luis. *Historia de la Revolución mexicana, periodo 1934–40*. Vol. 15, *Los dias de Presidente Cárdenas*. Mexico, D.F.: El Colegio de México, 1981.

———. *San José: Mexican Village in Transition*. Translated by John Upton. Austin: University of Texas Press, 1974.

Grandin, Greg. *The Last Colonial Massacre: Latin America in the Cold War*. Chicago: University of Chicago Press, 2004.

Greenberg, James B. *Blood Ties: Life and Violence in Rural Mexico*. Tucson, University of Arizona Press, 1989.

———. "Caciques, Patronage, Factionalism and Variations among Local Forms of Capitalism." In *Citizens of the Pyramid: Essays on Mexican Political Culture*, edited by Wil G. Pansters, 309–36. Amsterdam: CEDLA, 1997.

———. *Santiago's Sword: Chatino Peasant Religion and Economics*. Berkeley, University of California Press, 1981.

Gruening, Ernest. *Mexico and Its Heritage*. New York: Century, 1928.

Guadarrama, Rocío. *Los sindicatos y la política en México: La CROM (1918–1928)*. Mexico, D.F.: Ediciones Era, 1981.

Guardino, Peter. *Time of Liberty: Popular Political Culture in Oaxaca, 1750–1850*. Durham: Duke University Press, 2005.

Guerra Manzo, Enrique. *Caciquismo y orden público en Michoacán, 1920–1940*. Mexico, D.F.: El Colegio de México, 2002.

Guerrero, María Teresa. *The Forestry Industry in Chihuahua: Social, Economic and Environmental Impacts Post-NAFTA*. Austin: Texas Center for Policy Studies, 2000.

Gutierrez, Natividad. *Nationalist Myths and Ethnic Identities: Indigenous Intellectuals and the Mexican State*. Lincoln: University of Nebraska Press, 1999.

Haber, Stephen H. *Industry and Underdevelopment: The Industrialization of Mexico, 1890–1940*. Stanford: Stanford University Press, 1989.

Habermas, Jurgen. *The Structural Transformation of the Public Sphere: An Inquiry into a Category of Bourgeois Society.* Cambridge: Cambridge University Press, 1989.

Hamilton, Nora. *The Limits of State Autonomy: Post-Revolutionary Mexico.* Princeton: Princeton University Press, 1987.

Hansen, Roger. *The Politics of Mexican Development.* Baltimore: John Hopkins University Press, 1971.

Hansen, Thomas Blom, and Finn Stepputat, eds. *States of Imagination: Ethnographic Explorations of the Postcolonial State.* Durham: Duke University Press, 2001.

Hart, John Mason. "The 1840s Southwestern Mexico Peasants' War: Conflict in a Transitional Society." In *Riot, Rebellion, and Revolution: Rural Social Conflict in Mexico,* edited by Friedrich Katz, 249–68. Princeton: Princeton University Press, 1988.

———. *Empire and Revolution: The Americans in Mexico since the Civil War.* Berkeley: University of California Press, 2002.

Hayner, Norman S. *New Patterns in Old Mexico: A Study of Town and Metropolis.* New Haven: College and University Press, 1966.

Hellman, Judith Adler. *Mexico in Crisis.* New York: Holmes and Meier Publishers, 1978.

Henderson, Peter. "Un gobernador maderista: Benito Juárez Maza y la Revolución en Oaxaca." In *Oaxaca: Textos de su historia,* vol. 4, edited by Margaret Dalton, 308–22. Oaxaca: Instituto de Investigaciones Dr. José María Luis Mora, 1990.

Henkin, David M. *City Reading: Written Words and Public Spaces in Antebellum New York.* New York: Columbia University Press, 1998.

Hernández Chavez, Alicia. *Historia de la Revolución mexicana, periodo 1934–1940.* Vol. 16, *La mecanica cardenista.* Mexico, D.F.: El Colegio de México, 1979.

Herrera, Antonio. *Un gobierno de lengua.* Oaxaca de Juárez, Oaxaca: n.p., 1933.

Himno socialista regional. Oaxaca de Juárez, Oaxaca: n.p., 1930.

Hodges, Donald, and Ross Gandy. *Mexico 1910–1982: Reform or Revolution.* London: Zed Press, 1979.

Homenaje racial. Oaxaca de Juárez, Oaxaca: n.p., 1932.

Huerta Rios, Cesar. *Organización socio-política de una minoria nacional, los Triquis de Oaxaca.* Mexico, D.F.: Instituto Nacional Indigenista, 1981.

Huxley, Aldous. *Beyond the Mexique Bay*. London: Harper and Brothers, 1934.

Ianni, Octavio. *El estado capitalista en la época de Cárdenas*. Mexico, D.F.: Ediciones Era, 1977.

Ibarra, Isaac M. *Memorias de Isaac M Ibarra, autobiografia*. Mexico, D.F.: n.p., 1975.

Informe de Edmundo Sánchez Cano. Oaxaca de Juárez, Oaxaca: n.p., 1945.

Informe de Francisco López Cortés. Oaxaca de Juárez, Oaxaca: n.p., 1930.

Informe de Francisco López Cortés. Oaxaca de Juárez, Oaxaca: n.p., 1931.

Informe de Genaro V. Vásquez. Oaxaca de Juárez, Oaxaca: n.p., 1928.

Informe del C. Lic Eduardo Vasconcelos, gobernador del estado, rendido ante la XL legislatura. Oaxaca de Juárez, Oaxaca: n.p., 1947.

Informe del C. Lic Eduardo Vasconcelos, gobernador del estado, rendido ante la XL legislatura. Oaxaca de Juárez, Oaxaca: n.p., 1948.

Informe del C. Lic Eduardo Vasconcelos, gobernador del estado, rendido ante la XLI legislatura. Oaxaca de Juárez, Oaxaca: n.p., 1949.

Informe del C. Lic Eduardo Vasconcelos, gobernador del estado, rendido ante la XLI legislatura. Oaxaca de Juárez, Oaxaca: n.p., 1950.

Informe de Vicente González Fernández. Oaxaca de Juárez, Oaxaca: n.p., 1941.

Informe de Vicente González Fernández. Oaxaca de Juárez, Oaxaca: n.p., 1942.

Informe de Vicente González Fernández. Oaxaca de Juárez, Oaxaca: n.p., 1943.

Informe que rinde Anastasio García Toledo. Oaxaca de Juárez, Oaxaca: n.p., 1933.

Informe que rinde el C. Lic. Anastasio García Toledo, gobernador del estado de Oaxaca. Oaxaca de Juárez, Oaxaca: n.p., 1934.

Informe que rinde el C. Lic. Anastasio García Toledo, gobernador del estado de Oaxaca. Oaxaca de Juárez, Oaxaca: n.p., 1935.

Informe que rinde el C. Lic. Anastasio García Toledo, gobernador del estado de Oaxaca. Oaxaca de Juárez, Oaxaca: n.p., 1936.

Informe que rinde el C. Coronel Constantino Chapital. Oaxaca de Juárez, Oaxaca: n.p., 1937.

Informe que rinde el C. Coronel Constantino Chapital. Oaxaca de Juárez, Oaxaca: n.p., 1938.

Instituto de Capacitación Política. *Historia documental del partido de la*

Revolución. Vol. 3, PNR-PRM *1934–1938.* Mexico, D.F.: Partido Revolucionario Institucional, 1981–87.

Iturribarría, Jorge F. *Oaxaca en la historia: De la epoca precolumbina a los tiempos actuales.* Mexico, D.F.: Editorial Stylo, 1955.

Jacobs, Ian. *Ranchero Revolt: The Mexican Revolution in Guerrero.* Austin: University of Texas Press, 1982.

Jiménez, Christina M. "Popular Organizing for Public Services: Residents Modernize Morelia, Mexico, 1880–1920." *Journal of Urban History* 30, no. 4 (2004): 495–518.

Joseph, G. M. "The Fragile Revolution: Cacique Politics and Revolutionary Process in Yucatán." *Latin American Research Review* 15, no. 1 (1980): 39–64.

———. *Rediscoving the Past at Mexico's Periphery: Essays on the History of Modern Yucatán.* Tuscaloosa: University of Alabama Press, 1986.

———. *Revolution from Without: Yucatán, Mexico, and the United States 1880–1924.* Cambridge: Cambridge University Press, 1982.

Joseph, G. M., and Allen Wells, eds. *Summer of Discontent, Seasons of Upheaval: Elite Politics and Rural Insurgency in Yucatán, 1876–1915.* Stanford: Stanford University Press, 1996.

Joseph, Gilbert M., and Daniel Nugent, eds. *Everyday Forms of State Formation: Revolution and Negotiation of Rule in Modern Mexico.* Durham: Duke University Press, 1994.

Justicia! Clamor del proletariado de Oaxaca. Oaxaca de Juárez, Oaxaca: n.p., 1934.

Kaerger, Karl. *Agricultura y colonización en México en 1900.* Mexico, D.F.: Universidad Autónoma Chapingo, 1986.

Kaplan, Temma. "Female Consciousness and Collective Action: The Case of Barcelona, 1910–1918." *Signs* 7, no. 3 (1982): 545–66.

———. "Redressing the Balance: Gendered Acts of Justice around the Mining Community of Rio Tinto in 1913." In *Constructing Spanish Womanhood Female Identity in Modern Spain,* edited by Victoria Lorée Enders and Pamela Beth Radcliff, 283–300. Albany: State University of New York Press, 1999.

Karnes, Thomas. *Tropical Enterprise: The Standard Fruit and Steamship Company in Latin America.* Baton Rouge: Louisiana State University Press, 1978.

Kearney, Michael. *The Winds of Ixtepeji: World View and Society in a Zapotec Town.* New York: Holt, Rinehart and Winston, 1972.

Knight, Alan. "Caciquismo in Mexico." In *Caciquismo in Twentieth-Century Mexico*, edited by Alan Knight and Wil Pansters, 1–51. London: Institute for the Study of the Americas, 2005.

———. "Cardenismo: Juggernaut or Jalopy." *Journal of Latin American Studies* 26 (February 1994): 73–107.

———. "Corruption in Twentieth Century Mexico." In *Political Corruption in Europe and Latin America*, edited by Walter Little and Eduardo Posada-Carbó, 219–36. Basingstoke, U.K.: Macmillan Press, 1996.

———. "Habitus and Homicide: Political Culture in Revolutionary Mexico." In *Citizens of the Pyramid: Essays on Mexican Political Culture*, edited by Wil G. Pansters, 107–29. Amsterdam: CEDLA, 1997.

———. "Historical Continuities in Social Movement." In *Popular Movements and Political Change in Mexico*, edited by Joe Foweraker and Ann L. Craig, 78–102. Boulder CO: L. Rienner Publishers, 1990.

———. "El liberalismo mexicano desde la Reforma hasta la Revolución (una interpretación)." *Historia Mexicana* 34, no. 1 (1985): 59–92.

———. *The Mexican Revolution*. 2 vols. Oxford: Oxford University Press, 1985.

———. "México bronco, México manso: Una reflexión sobre la cultura civica mexicana." *Política y Gobierno* 3, no. 1 (1996): 12–15.

———. "Mexico c. 1930–1946." In *The Cambridge History of Latin America*, vol. 7, edited by Leslie Bethell, 3–82. Cambridge: Cambridge University Press, 1990.

———. "Mexico c. 1930–1946." In *The Cambridge History of Latin America*, vol. 12, edited by Leslie Bethell, 671–79. Cambridge: Cambridge University Press, 1990.

———. "The Modern Mexican State: Theory and Practice." In *The Other Mirror, Grand Theory through the Lens of Latin America*, edited by Miguel Angel Centeno and Fernando López-Alves, 177–218. Princeton: Princeton University Press, 2001.

———. "Patterns and Prescriptions in Mexican Historiography." *Bulletin of Latin American Research* 25, no. 3 (2006): 340–66.

———. "Peasant and Caudillo in Revolutionary Mexico 1910–1917." In *Caudillo and Peasant in the Mexican Revolution*, edited by D. A. Brading, 17–58. Cambridge: Cambridge University Press, 1980.

———. "Popular Culture and the Revolutionary State in Mexico, 1910–1940." *Hispanic American Historical Review* 74, no. 3 (1994): 393–444.

———. "Racism, Revolution and Indigenismo: Mexico, 1910–1940." In *The*

Idea of Race in Latin America, 1870–1940, edited by Richard Graham, 71–113. Austin: University of Texas Press, 1990.

———. "The Rise and Fall of Cardenismo, c. 1930–c. 1946." In *Mexico since Independence*, edited by Leslie Bethell, 241–320. New York: Cambridge University Press, 1991.

———. "State Power and Political Stability in Mexico." In *Mexico: Dilemmas of Transition*, edited by Neil Harvey, 29–63. London: ILAS, 1993.

———. "Weapons and Arches in the Mexican Revolutionary Landscape." In *Everyday Forms of State Formation: Revolution and Negotiation of Rule in Modern Mexico*, edited by Gilbert Joseph and Daniel Nugent, 24–68. Durham: Duke University Press, 1994.

———. "The Weight of the State in Modern Mexico." In *Studies in the Formation of the Nation-State in Latin American*, edited by James Dunkerley, 212–53. London: ILAS, 2002.

Knight, Alan, and Wil Pansters, eds. *Caciquismo in Twentieth-Century Mexico*. London: Institute for the Study of the Americas, 2005.

Kouri, Emilio H. "Interpreting the Expropriation of Indian Pueblo Lands in Porfirian Mexico: The Unexamined Legacies of Andrés Molina Enríquez." *Hispanic American Historical Review* 82, no. 1 (2002): 69–117.

Krauze, Enrique. *Lázaro Cárdenas: El general misionero*. Mexico, D.F.: Fondo de Cultura Económico, 1979.

———. *Mexico: Biography of Power, a History of Modern Mexico, 1810–1996*. New York: Harper Collins, 1997.

La Boz, Dan. *The Crisis of Mexican Labor*. New York: Praeger, 1988.

Laitin, D., Roger Petersen, and John W. Slocum. "Language and the State: Russia and the Soviet Union in Comparative Perspective." In *Thinking Theoretically about Soviet Nationalities*, edited by Alexander J. Motyl. New York: Columbia University Press, 1992.

Lajous, Alejandro. *Los origines del partido unico en México*. Mexico, D.F.: Instituto de Investigaciones Históricas, 1981.

Laviada, Iñigo. *Los caciques de la Sierra*. Mexico, D.F.: Editorial Jus, 1978.

Leal, Juan Felipe. "The Mexican State 1915–1973: A Historical Perspective." In *Modern Mexico: State Economy and Social Conflict*, edited by Nora Hamilton and Timothy Harding, 21–42. Beverly Hills CA: Sage Publications, 1985.

Lear, John. *Workers, Neighbors, and Citizens: The Revolution in Mexico City*. Lincoln: University of Nebraska Press, 2001.

León, Samuel, and Ignacio Marván. *La clase obrera en la historia de México.* Vol. 10, *En el Cardenismo (1934–1940).* Mexico, D.F.: Siglo Veintiuno Editores, 1985.

Lewis, Stephen E. *The Ambivalent Revolution: Forging State and Nation in Chiapas, 1910–1945.* Albuquerque: University of New Mexico Press, 2005.

Linz, Juan J. *Totalitarian and Authoritarian Regimes.* Boulder CO: Lynne Rienner Publishers, 2000.

List Arzubide, Germán. *Emiliano Zapata, exaltación.* Puebla: n.p., 1930.

Lomnitz, Claudio. *Exits from the Labyrinth: Culture and Ideology in the Mexican National Space.* Berkeley: University of California Press, 1992.

———. "Final Reflections: What Was Mexico's Cultural Revolution?" In *The Eagle and the Virgin: National and Cultural Revolution in Mexico, 1920–1940,* edited by Mary Key Vaughan and Stephen E. Lewis, 335–50. Durham: Duke University Press, 2006.

———. "Remains of the Dead: The Bare Bones of Caudillismo." Paper presented at conference on Caudillos and Caciques, St. Antony's College, Oxford University, September 2002.

López Barcenas, Francisco. *Muertes sin fin: Cronicas de represión en la región Mixteca oaxaqueña.* Juxtlahuaca, Oaxaca: Centro de Orientación y Asesoría a Pueblos Indígenas, 2002.

López Chiñas, Gabriel. "Introducción." In *Espiritu de la música oaxaqueña,* edited by Genaro V. Vásquez, 1–16. Mexico, D.F.: n.p., 1965.

Lorey, David E. *The University System and Economic Development in Mexico since 1929.* Stanford: Stanford University Press, 1993.

Lowry, Malcolm. *Selected Letters.* London: Harmondsworth, Penguin, 1985.

Loyola Díaz, Rafael. *La crisis Obregón-Calles y el estado mexicano.* Mexico, D.F.: Siglo Veintiuno Editores, 1980.

———. *El ocaso del radicalismo revolucionario.* Mexico, D.F.: Instituto de Investigaciones Sociales, Universidad Nacional Autónoma de México, 1991.

Mabry, David J. *The Mexican University and the State: Student Conflicts 1910–1976.* College Station: Texas A&M University Press, 1982.

Maldonaldo Aranda, Salvador. "Rescutiendo el centralismo político: Elites políticas, el Gomismo y el PST en el estado de México (1923–1940)." *Relaciones* 82 (2000): 233–67.

Malinowski, Bronislaw, and Julio de la Fuente. *Malinowski in Mexico: The*

Economics of a Mexican Market System. Boston: Routledge and Kegan Paul, 1982.

Mallon, Florencia. "Indian Communities, Political Cultures, and the State in Latin America, 1780–1990." *Journal of Latin American Studies* 24, Quincentenary Supplement (1992): 35–53.

———. *Peasant and Nation: The Making of Postcolonial Mexico and Peru.* Berkeley: University of California Press, 1995.

———. "Reflections on the Ruins: Everyday Forms of State Formation in Nineteenth-Century Mexico." In *Everyday Forms of State Formation: Revolution and Negotiation of Rule in Modern Mexico*, edited by Gilbert Joseph and Daniel Nugent, 69–106. Durham: Duke University Press, 1994.

Markiewicz, Dana. *The Mexican Revolution and the Limits of Agrarian Reform 1915–1946.* Boulder CO: Lynne Rienner Publishers, 1993.

Márquez, Enrique. "Political Anachronisms." In *Electoral Patterns and Perspectives in Mexico*, edited by Arturo Alvarado Mendoza, 111–26. San Diego: Center for U.S.-Mexican Studies, 1997.

Márquez, Ramón, and Armando Satow. *Medallistas Olimpicos mexicanos.* Mexico, D.F.: Comisión Nacional de Deporte, 1990.

Martínez, Juan Carlos. *Derechos indigenas en los juzgados: Un analisis del campo judicial oaxaqueño en la region Mixe.* Mexico, D.F.: Instituto Nacional de Antropología e Historia, 2004.

Martínez, Luis de Guadalupe. *La lucha electoral del PAN en Oaxaca.* Vol. 1, *1939–1971.* Mexico, D.F.: n.p., 2002.

Martínez, María Antonia. *El despegue constructivo de la Revolución: Sociedad y política en el alemanismo.* Mexico, D.F.: Miguel Ángel Porrúa–CIESAS, 2004.

Martínez Assad, Carlos. *Henriquismo: Un piedra en el camino.* Mexico, D.F.: Martín Casillas Editores, 1982.

———. *El laboratorio de la Revolución: El Tabasco garridista.* Mexico, D.F.: Siglo Veintiuno Editores, 1979.

———. *Los sentimientos de la region: Del viejo centralismo a la nueva pluralidad.* Mexico, D.F.: Instituto Nacional de Estudios Históricos de la Revolución Mexicana, 2001.

Martínez López, Felipe. "Economia y política en Oaxaca: La crisis de 1952." BA thesis, Universidad Autónoma "Benito Juárez" de Oaxaca, 1979.

———. "El movimiento oaxaqueño de 1952." In *Sociedad y política en Oa-*

xaca 1980, 15 estudios de caso, edited by Raúl Benitez Zenteno, 271–87. Mexico, D.F.: Miguel Ángel Porrúa–CIESAS, 2004.

Martínez Medina, Héctor Gerado. "Genesis y desarrollo de Maderismo en Oaxaca (1909–1912)." In *La Revolución en Oaxaca, 1900–1930,* edited by Victor Raúl Martínez Vásquez, 88–157. Oaxaca de Juárez, Oaxaca: Instituto de Administración Pública de Oaxaca, 1985.

———. "Historia de una crisis political local: La caida del gobernador de Oaxaca, Edmundo Sánchez Cano, 1947." MA diss., Universidad Nacional Autónoma de México, 1984.

Martínez Saldana, Tomás. *Política y sociedad en México: El caso de los Altos de Jalisco.* Mexico, D.F.: Centro de Investigaciones Superiores, Instituto Nacional de Antropología e Historia, 1976.

Martínez Vásquez, Victor Raúl. *De la milpa oaxaqueña.* Oaxaca de Juárez, Oaxaca: Comunicación Social, 1990.

———. *Historia de la educación en Oaxaca (1825–1940).* Oaxaca de Juárez, Oaxaca: Instituto Estatal de Educación Pública de Oaxaca, 1995.

———. *Movimiento popular y política en Oaxaca, 1968–1986.* Mexico, D.F.: Consejo Nacional para la Cultura y las Artes, 1990.

———. "El régimen de García Vigil." In *La Revolución en Oaxaca, 1900–1930,* edited by Victor Raúl Martínez Vásquez, 309–73. Oaxaca de Juárez, Oaxaca: Instituto de Administración Pública de Oaxaca, 1985.

———, ed. *La Revolución en Oaxaca, 1900–1930,* Oaxaca de Juárez, Oaxaca: Instituto de Administración Pública de Oaxaca, 1985.

McMahon, David F. *Antropologia de una presa, los Mazatecos y el proyecto del Papaloapan.* Mexico, D.F.: Instituto Nacional Indigenista, 1973.

McNamara, Patrick J. "Felipe Garcia and the Real Heroes of Guelatao." In *The Human Tradition in Mexico,* edited by Jeffrey M. Pilcher, 75–90. Wilmington DE: Scholarly Resources, 2002.

———. "Sons of the Sierra: Memory, Patriarchy, and Rural Political Culture in Mexico, 1855–1911." PhD diss., University of Wisconsin–Madison, 2002.

Medin, Tzvi. *Ideología y praxis política de Lázaro Cárdenas.* Mexico, D.F.: Siglo Veintiuno Editores, 1972.

———. *El sexenio alemánista: Ideologia y praxis política de Miguel Alemán.* Mexico, D.F.: Ediciones Era, 1990.

Medina, Luis. *Historia de la Revolución mexicana, periodo 1940–1952.* Vol.

18, *Del cardenismo al avilacamachismo.* Mexico, D.F.: Colegio de México, 1978.

————. *Historia de la Revolución mexicana, periodo 1940–1952.* Vol. 20, *Civilismo y modernización del autoritarismo.* Mexico, D.F.: Colegio de México, 1979.

————. "Origen y circunstancia de la idea de unidad nacional." *Foro Internacional* 14, no. 3 (January–March 1974): 265–90.

Medina Gómez, Gloria. "Introducción de la luz electrica en la ciudad de Oaxaca: Modernización urbana y la Revolución mexicana." MA thesis, Instituto Nacional de Estudios Historicos sobre la Revolucion, n.d.

Meixueiro Hernández, Ernesto. *Jorge Meixueiro Hernández, martir del ideal democrático.* Oaxaca de Juárez, Oaxaca: n.p., 1999.

Memoria de los trabajos del primer congreso de ejidatarios de Oaxaca. Oaxaca de Juárez, Oaxaca: n.p., 1932.

Memoria del segundo congreso agrario del estado de Oaxaca. Oaxaca de Juárez, Oaxaca: n.p., 1933.

Memoria que presenta el C. Coronel Constantino Chapital, gobernador constitucional del estado, ante la H. XXXVIII legislatura del mismo, en cumplimiento de la fracción VII del Articulo 80 de la Constitución Política Local, 1936–1940. Oaxaca de Juárez, Oaxaca: n.p., 1940.

Mendoza Garcia, Edgar. "Las cofradias del curato de Coixtlahuaca durante el siglo XIX: Independencia económica de los pueblos." In *Personajes e instituciones del pueblo mixteco*, edited by Angel Ivan Rivera Guzmán et al., 31–55. Huajuapan de León: Universidad Tecnológica de la Mixteca, 2004.

Mendoza Guerrero, Telesforo. *Monografia del distrito de Huajuapan.* Mexico, D.F.: n.p., 1992.

Mensaje al pueblo de Oaxaca, dirigido por el C Presidente de la Republica, Lázaro Cárdenas. Oaxaca de Juárez, Oaxaca: n.p., 1937.

Meyer, Jean. *El conflicto religioso en Oaxaca (1926–1938).* Oaxaca de Juárez, Oaxaca: Universidad Autónoma "Benito Juárez" de Oaxaca, 2007.

————. *La Cristiada.* 3 vols. Mexico, D.F.: Siglo Veintiuno Editores, 1973–76.

————. "'Los Kulaki' del ejido (los anos 30)." *Relaciones* 29 (1987): 23–43.

Meyer, Jean, Enrique Krauze, and Cayetano Reyes. *Historia de la Revolución mexicana, periodo 1924–1928.* Vol. 11, *Estado y sociedad con Calles.* Mexico, D.F.: Colegio de México, 1977.

Meyer, Lorenzo. *Historia de la Revolución mexicana, periodo 1928–1934.* Vol. 13, *El conflicto social y los gobiernos del Maximato.* Mexico, D.F.: Colegio de México, 1978.

———. "Historical Roots of the Authoritarian State in Mexico." In *Authoritarianism in Mexico,* edited by José Luis Reyna and Richard S. Weinart, 3–22. Philadelphia: Institute for the Study of Human Issues, 1977.

Meyer, Lorenzo, Rafael Segovia, and Alejandra Lajous. *Historia de la Revolución mexicana, periodo 1924–1928.* Vol. 12, *Los incios de la institutionalización, la política del Maximato.* Mexico, D.F.: Colegio de México, 1978.

Miller, Michael Nelson. *Red, White and Green: The Maturing of Mexicanidad, 1940–1946.* El Paso: Texas Western Press, 1998.

Mitchell, Stephanie, and Patience Schell. *The Women's Revolution in Mexico, 1910–1953.* Lanham MD: Rowman and Littlefield, 2006.

Monaghan, John. "Mixtec Caciques in the Nineteenth and Twentieth Centuries." In *Codices, caciques y comunidades,* edited by Maarten Jansen and Luis Reyes García, 265–81. Netherlands: Asociación de Historiadores Latinoamericanistas Europeos, 1997.

———. "El PAN y las comunidades de la Mixteca Baja." Paper presented at the American Anthropological Meeting, Oaxaca de Juarez, 2002.

Moncada, Carlos. *Cayeron!* Mexico, D.F.: C. Moncada, 1979.

Monsivais, Carlos. "'Just Over That Hill': Notes on Centralism and Regional Cultures." In *Mexico's Regions: Comparative History and Development,* edited by Eric Van Young, 247–54. San Diego: Center for U.S.-Mexican Studies, 1992.

Montes García, Olga. "Las políticas indigenistas y educativas en la Sierra Juárez: 1930–1940." Paper presented at Seminar on the History of Oaxaca, Universidad Autónoma "Benito Juárez" de Oaxaca, n.d.

Mouat, Andre. "Los chiveros de la Mixteca Baja." MA thesis, Universidad Nacional Autónoma de México, 1980.

Münch Galindo, Guido. *Historia y cultura de los Mixes.* Mexico, D.F.: Instituto de Investigaciones Antropológicas, Universidad Nacional Autónoma de México, 1996.

Muñoz Cota, José. *Apuntes sobre el socialismo y la Confederacion de Partidos Socialistas del Estado de Oaxaca.* Oaxaca de Juárez, Oaxaca: n.p., 1928.

Nahmed, Salomon. *Los Mixes: Estudio social y cultural de la región del*

Zempoaltepetl y del Istmo de Tehuantepec. Mexico, D.F.: Instituto Nacional Indigenista, 1965.

Needleman, Carolyn, and Martin Needleman. "Who Rules Mexico? A Critique of Some Current Views on the Mexican Political Process." *Journal of Politics* 31, no. 4 (1969): 1011–34.

Needler, Martin. *Politics and Society in Mexico*. Albuquerque: University of New Mexico Press, 1971.

Newcomer, Daniel. *Reconciling Modernity: Urban State Formation in 1940s León, Mexico*. Lincoln: University of Nebraska Press, 2004.

Niblo, Stephen R. *Mexico in the 1940s: Modernity, Politics and Corruption*. Wilmington DE: Scholarly Resources, 1999.

Nugent, Daniel. *Spent Cartridges of the Revolution: An Anthropological History of Namiquipa, Chihuahua*. Chicago: University of Chicago Press, 1993.

Ocasio Meléndez, Marcial E. *Capitalism and Development: Tampico, Mexico, 1876–1924*. New York: P. Lang, 1998.

O'Donnell, Guillermo. *Bureaucratic Authoritarianism: Argentina, 1966–1973, in Comparative Perspective*. Translated by James McGuire in collaboration with Rae Flory. Berkeley: University of California Press, 1988.

Oikión Solano, Verónica, and Marta Eugenia García Ugarte, eds. *Movimientos armados en México, siglo XX*. Morelia: Colegio de Michoacán, 2006.

Ojeda Bohórquez, Ricardo. *Los cuerudos: Una historia de la Revolución mexicana en Oaxaca*. Mexico, D.F.: Editorial Porrúa, 2007.

Olcott, Jocelyn. *Revolutionary Women in Postrevolutionary Mexico*. Durham: Duke University Press, 2006.

Olcott, Jocelyn, Mary Kay Vaughan, and Gabriela Cano, eds. *Sex in Revolution: Gender, Politics, and Power in Modern Mexico*. Durham: Duke University Press, 2006.

O'Malley, Ilene. *The Myth of the Revolution: Hero Cults and the Institutionalization of the Mexican State, 1920–1940*. New York: Greenwood Press, 1986.

Othón Díaz, Enrique. *Ante el futuro de México (Oaxaca y el Plan Sexenal)*. Oaxaca de Juárez, Oaxaca: n.p., 1934.

Overmyer-Velázquez, Mark. "A New Political Religious Order: Church, State and Workers in Porifiran Mexico." In *Religious Culture in Modern*

Mexico, edited by Martin Austin Nesvig, 129–56. Lanham MD: Rowman and Littlefield, 2007.

———. *Visions of the Emerald City: Modernity, Tradition and the Formation of Porfirian Oaxaca, Mexico.* Durham: Duke University Press, 2006.

Padgett, Vincent. *The Mexican Political System.* Boston: Houghton Mifflin, 1966.

Palacios, Guillermo. *La pluma y el arado: Los intellectuales y la construcción sociocultural del "problema campesino" en México 1932–1934.* Mexico, D.F.: Centro de Estudios Históricos, Colegio de México, 1999.

Pansters, Wil. "Citizens with Dignity: Opposition and Government in San Luis Potosi, 1938–93." In *Dismantling the Mexican State*, edited by Rob Aitken, 244–66. New York: St. Martin's Press, 1996.

———. "Paradoxes of Regional Power in Post-Revolutionary Mexico: The Rise of Avilacamachismo in Puebla, 1935–1940." In *Region, State and Capitalism in Mexico*, edited by Wil Pansters and Arij Ouweneel, 134–57. Amsterdam: CEDLA, 1989.

———. *Politics and Power in Puebla: The Political History of a Mexican State, 1937–1987.* Amsterdam: CEDLA, 1990.

———. "Theorizing Political Culture." In *Citizens of the Pyramid: Essays on Mexican Political Culture*, edited by Wil Pansters, 1–37. Amsterdam: CEDLA, 1997.

Pansters, Wil, and Arij Ouweneel. "Capitalist Development and Political Centralization Before and After the Revolution: An Introduction." In *Region, State and Capitalism in Mexico*, edited by Wil Pansters and Arij Ouweneel, 1–25. Amsterdam: CEDLA, 1989.

Parra Mora, León Javier. "Poder, violencia y conflictos entre los Triquis de San Juan Copala (1910–1970)." MA diss., Universidad Autónoma "Benito Juárez" de Oaxaca, 1988.

Parra Mora, León Javier, and Jorge Hernández Díaz. *Violencia y cambio social en la región Triqui.* Oaxaca de Juárez, Oaxaca: Universidad Autónoma "Benito Juárez" de Oaxaca, 2001.

Partido Nacional Revoluciónario. *Domingos culturales, Diciembre 1930– Enero 1931.* Mexico, D.F.: n.p., 1930.

Pastor, Rodolfo. *Campesinos y reformas: La Mixteca, 1700–1856.* Mexico, D.F.: Colegio de México, 1987.

Pellicer de Brody, Olga, and José Luis Reyna. *Historia de la Revolución mexicana, periodo 1952–1960.* Vol. 22, *El afianzamiento de la establi-dad política.* Mexico, D.F.: Colegio de México, 1978.

Perelló, Sergio. *Reparto agrario en Oaxaca.* Oaxaca de Juárez, Oaxaca: Instituto de Investigaciones Sociológicas, Universidad Autónoma "Benito Juárez" de Oaxaca, 1989.

Pérez, Ramón "Tianguis." *Diary of a Guerrilla.* Translated by Dick J. Reavis. Houston: Arte Público Press, 1999.

Pérez Aragon, Gonzalo. "El problema agrario del pueblo de Tututepec." BA thesis, Universidad Nacional Autónoma de México, 1955.

Pérez García, Rosendo. *La Sierra Juárez.* Vol. 1. Mexico, D.F.: n.p., 1956.

Pineda, Luz Olivia. *Caciques culturales: El caso de los maestros bilingües en los Altos de Chiapas.* Puebla, México: Altres Costa-Amic, 1993.

Poole, Deborah. "An Image of 'Our Indian': Type Photographs and Racial Sentiments in Oaxaca, 1920–1940." *Hispanic American Historical Review* 84, no. 1 (2004): 37–82.

———. "Tipos 'raciales' y proyectos culturales en Oaxaca, 1920–1940." *Acervos* 16 (2000): 23–29.

Porter, Robert M. *The Coffee Farmers Revolt in Southern Mexico in the 1980s and 1990s.* Lewiston NY: Edwin Mellen Press, 2002.

Portes Gil, Emilio. *Quince años de política mexicana.* Mexico, D.F.: Ediciones Botas, 1954.

Primer congreso industrial de la palma. Oaxaca de Juárez, Oaxaca: n.p., 1931.

Propaganda del Comite Organizador Central Pro-Cárdenas, Estado de Oaxaca. Oaxaca de Juárez, Oaxaca: n.p., 1934.

Purnell, Jennie. "The Chegomista Rebellion in Juchitán, 1911–1912: Rethinking the Role of Traditional Caciques in Resisting State Power." In *Caciquismo in Twentieth-Century Mexico,* edited by Alan Knight and Wil Pansters, 51–70. London: Institute for the Study of the Americas, 2005.

———. *Popular Movements and State Formation in Revolutionary Mexico: The Agraristas and Cristeros of Michoacán.* Durham: Duke University Press, 1999.

Ramírez, Alfonso Francisco. *Por los caminos de Oaxaca.* Mexico, D.F.: n.p., 1958.

———. *Seis discursos.* Mexico, D.F.: n.p., 1939.

Ramírez, Elisa. "Charles Brasseur y su viaje al Istmo de Tehuantepec." In

Oaxaca: Textos de su historia, vol. 3, edited by Margaret Dalton, 88–96. Oaxaca: Instituto de Investigaciones Dr. José María Luis Mora, 1990.

Ramírez Bohorquez, Everardo. *Perfil de Eduardo Vasconcelos*. Oaxaca de Juárez, Oaxaca: n.p., 1970.

Ramírez Ramírez, Guillermo. "Mis experiencias en el estado de Oaxaca." In *Los maestros y la cultura nacional, sureste*, vol. 5, 187–214. Mexico, D.F.: SEP, 1987.

Ramírez Rancano, Mario. "Violencia en Tlaxcala bajo el gobierno de Adolfo Bonilla." In *Estadistas, caciques y caudillos*, edited by Carlos Martínez Assad, 313–33. Mexico, D.F.: Instituto de Investigaciones Sociales, Universidad Nacional Autónoma de México, 1988.

Rangel Couto, Hugo. *El Papaloapan en marcha*. Mexico, D.F.: Stylo, 1947.

Reina, Leticia. "El cardenismo en Oaxaca: Un proyecto social 1934–1940." *Cuadernos del Sur* 2, no. 3 (1993): 59–74.

———. "De la reformas burbonicas a las leyes de Reforma." In *Historia de la cuestión agraria mexicana, estado de Oaxaca, prehispanico–1924*, edited by Leticia Reina, 181–268. Mexico, D.F.: Juan Pablos Editor, 1988.

———. "Etnicidad y genero entre los Zapotecos del Isthmo de Tehuantepec, Mexico, 1840-1890." In *La reindianización de America, siglo XIX*, 340–58. Mexico, D.F.: Siglo Veintiuno Editores–CIESAS, 1997.

———, ed. *Historia de la cuestión agraria mexicana, estado de Oaxaca, prehispanico–1924*. Mexico, D.F.: Juan Pablos Editor, 1988.

Revueltas, José. *Los dias terrenales*. Madrid: ALLCA Siglo Venturo Editores, 1991.

Reyes Aguilar, Saúl. *Mi madre y yo: Sucesos históricos en la Mixteca*. Mexico, D.F.: n.p., 1972.

Reyna, J. L., and R. S. Weinert. *Authoritarianism in Mexico*. Philadelphia: Institute for the Study of Human Issues, 1977.

Riedemann, Cristina Steffen. *Los comerciantes de Huajuapan de León, Oaxaca, 1920–1980*. Mexico, D.F.: Plaza y Valdés Editores, 2001.

Rockwell, Elsie. "Schools of the Revolution." In *Everyday Forms of State Formation: Revolution and the Negotiation of Rule in Modern Mexico*, edited by Gil Joseph and David Nugent, 170–208. Durham: Duke University Press, 1994.

Rodríguez Canto, Adolfo. *Historia agricola y agraria de la costa oaxaqueña*. Mexico, D.F.: Universidad Autónoma Chapingo, 1996.

Rodíguez Kuri, Ariel. *La experiencia olvidada: El ayuntamiento de México, política y gobierno, 1876–1912*. Mexico, D.F.: El Colegio de México, 1996.

Rojas, Basilio. *El café: Estudio de su llegada, implantación y desarrollo en el estado de Oaxaca, Mexico*. Mexico, D.F.: n.p., 1964.

———. *Un gran rebelde: Manuel García Vigil*. Mexico, D.F.: n.p., 1965.

Romero, Laura Patricia. "La confirmación del caciquismo sindical en Jalisco: El caso de Heliodoro Hernandez Loza." In *Estadistas, caciques y caudillos*, edited by Carlos Martínez Assad, 293–311. Mexico, D.F.: Instituto de Investigaciones Sociales, Universidad Nacional Autónoma de México, 1988.

Romero Frizzi, María de los Angeles, and María Eugenia Romero. "Introducción." In *Lecturas históricas del estado de Oaxaca*, vol. 4, *1877–1930*, edited by María de los Angeles Romero Frizzi, 15–50. Mexico, D.F.: Instituto Nacional de Antropología e Historia, 1990.

Ronfeldt, David. *Atencingo: The Politics of Agrarian Struggle in a Mexican Ejido*. Stanford: Stanford University Press, 1973.

Rosas Solaegui, Guillermo. *Un hombre en el tiempo*. Mexico, D.F.: B. Costa-Amic, 1971.

———. *Oaxaca en tres etapas de la Revolución mexicana*. Mexico, D.F.: n.p., 1965.

———. *La vida de Oaxaca, en el carnet del recuerdo*. Oaxaca de Juárez, Oaxaca: Lito Offset de Oaxaca Jesús Torres Márquez, 1978.

Roseberry, William. *Coffee and Capitalism in the Venezuelan Andes*. Austin: University of Texas Press, 1983.

———. "Hegemony and the Language of Contention." In *Everyday Forms of State Formation: Revolution and Negotiation of Rule in Modern Mexico*, edited by Gilbert Joseph and Daniel Nugent, 355–66. Durham: Duke University Press, 1994.

Rubin, Jeffrey W. "COCEI in Juchitán: Grassroots Radicalism and Regional History." *Journal of Latin American Studies* 26, no. 1 (1994): 109–36.

———. "Decentering the Regime: Culture and Regional Politics in Mexico." *Latin American Research Review* 31, no. 3 (1996): 85–126.

———. *Decentering the Regime: Ethnicity, Radicalism and Democracy in Juchitán, Mexico*. Durham: Duke University Press, 1997.

———. "Decentrando el régimen: Cultura y política regional en México." *Relaciones* 96 (2003): 125–80.

———. "Popular Mobilization and the Myth of State Corporatism." In *Popular Movements and Political Change in Mexico*, edited by Joe Foweraker and Ann L. Craig, 247–67. Boulder CO: L. Rienner Publishers, 1990.

Ruíz Cervantes, Francisco José. "Carlos Gracida: Los primeros años difíciles (1914–1919)." In *A dios lo que es de dios*, edited by Carlos Martínez Assad, 99–110. Mexico, D.F.: Aguilar, 1995.

———. "El movimiento de la Soberanía en Oaxaca (1915–1920)." In *La Revolución en Oaxaca 1900–1930*, edited by Victor Raúl Martínez Vásquez, 225–308. Oaxaca de Juárez, Oaxaca: Instituto de Administración Pública de Oaxaca, 1985.

———. "Movimientos zapatistas en Oaxaca, una primera mirada, 1911–16." In *Lecturas históricas del estado de Oaxaca*, vol. 4, *1877–1930*, edited by María de los Angeles Romero Frizzi, 273–88. Mexico, D.F.: Instituto Nacional de Antropología e Historia, 1990.

———. "Oaxaca: Campesinos no revoluciónarios? Campesinos en revolución?" In *Memoria del congreso internacional sobre la Revolución mexicana*, 28–35. Mexico, D.F.: Instituto Nacional de Estudios Históricos de la Revolución Mexicana, Secretaría de Gobernación, 1991.

———. *La Revolución en Oaxaca: El movimiento de la Soberania, (1915–1920)*. Mexico, D.F.: Instituto de Investigaciones Sociales, Fondo de Cultura Económica, 1986.

Ruíz Martínez, Ignacio. *El problema económico social de los trabajadores de la palma en las Mixtecas*. Mexico, D.F.: n.p., 1939.

Rus, Jan. "The Communidad Revolucionaria Institucional: Subversion of Native Government in Chiapas, 1936–1968." In *Everyday Forms of State Formation: Revolution and the Negotiation of Rule in Modern Mexico*, edited by Gilbert M. Joseph and Daniel Nugent, 265–300. Durham: Duke University Press, 1994.

Ryan, Mary P. "Gender and Public Access: Women's Politics in Nineteenth-Century America." In *Habermas and the Public Sphere*, edited by Craig Calhoun, 259–88. Cambridge: Cambridge University Press, 1992.

Salvador Matthews, Andrew. "Suppressing Fire and Memory: Environmental Degradation and Political Restoration in the Sierra Juárez of Oaxaca, 1887–2001." *Environmental History* 8, no. 1 (2003): 77–108.

Sánchez Pereyra, Javier. *Historia de la educación en Oaxaca 1926–1936*. Oaxaca de Juárez, Oaxaca: Instituto Estatal de Educación Pública de Oaxaca, 1995.

Sanchez R., Martin. "Los católicos: Un grupo de poder en la política michoa-
cana (1910–1924)." *Relaciones* 51 (Summer 1992): 195–222.

Sánchez Silva, Carlos. "Crisis política y contrarevolución en Oaxaca (1912–
1914)." In *La Revolución en Oaxaca 1900–1930*, edited by Victor Raúl
Martínez Vásquez, 159–224. Oaxaca de Juárez, Oaxaca: Instituto de
Administración Pública de Oaxaca, 1985.

———. *Empresarios y comerciantes en Oaxaca (1919)*. Oaxaca de Juárez,
Oaxaca: Instituto de Administración Pública de Oaxaca, 1985.

———. "Estructura de las propiedades agrarias de Oaxaca a fines del
Porfiriato." In *Lecturas históricas del estado de Oaxaca*, vol. 4, *1877–
1930*, edited by María de los Angeles Romero Frizzi, 107–34. Mexico,
D.F.: Instituto Nacional de Antropología e Historia, 1990.

Schell, Patience A. "Of the Sublime Mission of Mothers of Families: The
Union of Mexican Catholic Ladies in Revolutionary Mexico." In *The
Women's Revolution in Mexico, 1910–1953*, edited by Stephanie Mitchell and Patience Schell, 99–123. Lanham MD: Rowman and Littlefield,
2006.

Schmidt, Arthur. "Making It Real Compared to What: Reconceptualising
Mexican History since 1940." In *Fragments of a Golden Age: The Politics of Culture in Mexico since 1940*, edited by Gilbert Joseph, Anne
Rubenstein, and Eric Zolov, 23–68. Durham: Duke University Press,
2001.

Schmitter, Philippe C. *Corporatism and Public Policy in Authoritarian Portu-
gal*. London: Sage Publications, 1975.

Schryer, Frans. *Ethnicity and Class Conflict in Rural Mexico*. Princeton:
Princeton University Press, 1990.

———. *The Rancheros of Pisaflores: History of a Peasant Bourgeoisie in
Twentieth Century Mexico*. Toronto: University of Toronto Press, 1981.

———. "Village Factionalism and Class Conflict in Peasant Communities."
Canadian Review of Sociology and Anthropology 12 (1975): 290–302.

Secretaría de la Educación Pública. *Las misiones culturales*. Mexico, D.F.:
n.p., 1933.

Secretaría de Recursos Hidraulicos, Comisión de Papaloapan. *Economía del
Papaloapan*. Vol. 1, *Evaluación de la inversiones y sus efectos*. Mexico,
D.F.: Secretaría de Recursos Hidraulicos, 1958.

Semo, Enrique. *Historia mexicana: Economia y lucha de clases*. Mexico, D.F.:
Ediciones Era, 1978.

Servin, Elisa. *Ruptura y oposición: El movimiento henriquista, 1945–1954*. Mexico, D.F.: Cal y Arena, 2001.

Shulgovski, Anatol. *México en la encrucijada de su historia*. Mexico, D.F.: Ediciones de Cultura Popular, 1968.

Siguenza Orozco, Salvador. *Mineria y comunidad indigena: El mineral de Natividad, Ixtlán, Oaxaca (1900–1940)*. Mexico, D.F.: Centro de Investigaciones y Estudios Superiores en Antropología Social, 1996.

Silva Herzog, Jesús. *El agrarismo mexicano y la reforma agraria: Exposición y critica*. Mexico, D.F.: Fondo de Cultura Económica, 1959.

———. *Una historia de la Universidad de México y sus problemas*. Mexico, D.F.: Siglo Veintiuno Editores, 1986.

Simpson, Eyler N. *The Ejido, Mexico's Way Out*. Chapel Hill: University of North Carolina Press, 1937.

Simpson, Lesley Byrd. *Many Mexicos*. Berkeley: University of California Press, 1952.

Skidmore, Thomas E., and Peter H. Smith. *Modern Latin America*. New York: Oxford University Press, 1985.

Smith, Benjamin. "Defending 'Our Beautiful Freedom': State Formation and Local Autonomy in Oaxaca, 1930–1940." *Mexican Studies/Estudios Mexicanos* 37, no. 1 (February 2007): 125–53.

———. "Emiliano Zapata: Contestation and Construction." M. Phil. diss., University of Cambridge, 2002.

———. "The Party of the Priest: Local Religion in Huajuapam de León." Paper presented at Conference on Faith and Impiety in Revolutionary Mexico, 1910–1940, Queens University, Belfast, 2005.

———. "Anticlericalism and Resistance: The Diocese of Huajuapam de León, 1930–1940." *Journal of Latin American Studies* 37 (August 2005): 469–505.

Smith, Peter H. *Labyrinths of Power: Political Recruitment in Twentieth-Century Mexico*. Princeton: Princeton University Press, 1979.

———. "Mexico since 1946." In *The Cambridge History of Latin America*, edited by Leslie Bethell, 83–160. Cambridge: Cambridge University Press, 1990.

Sosa Elízaga, Raquel. *Los códigos ocultos del cardenismo: Un estudio de la violencia política, el cambio social y la continuidad institucional*. Mexico, D.F.: Universidad Nacional Autónoma de México; Plaza y Valdés Editores, 1996.

Spivak, Gayatri Chakravorty. "Spivak and Rumor, Rhetoric and Cultural Explanation: A Discussion with Gayatri Chakravorty Spivak." *JAC* 10, no. 2 (1990).

Starr, Frederick. *In Indian Mexico.* Chicago: Forbes and Company, 1908.

Stephens, Lynn. *Zapata Lives! Histories and Cultural Politics in Southern Mexico.* Berkeley: University of California Press, 2002.

Stern, Steve. *The Secret History of Gender: Women, Men and Power in Late Colonial Mexico.* Chapel Hill: University of North Carolina Press, 1995.

Suárez, Jorge. *The Mesoamerican Indian Languages.* Cambridge: Cambridge University Press, 1983.

Tamayo, Jaime. "La primavera de un caudillo: José Guadalupe Zuno y la constitución del Zunismo." In *Estadistas, caciques y caudillos*, edited by Carlos Martínez Assad, 269–80. Mexico, D.F.: Instituto de Investigaciones Sociales, Universidad Nacional Autónoma de México, 1988.

Tamayo, Jorge L. *Oaxaca en el siglo XX: Apuntes históricos y análisis político.* Mexico, D.F.: n.p., 1956.

———. *Proyectos de integración vial en el estado de Oaxaca.* Mexico, D.F.: Universidad Nacional Autónoma de México, 1960.

Tannenbaum, Frank. *Mexico: The Struggle for Peace and Bread.* New York: Knopf, 1950.

Taracena, Alfonso. *La vida en México bajo Avila Camacho.* 2 vols. Mexico, D.F.: Editorial Jus, 1977.

Tarrow, Sidney. *Power in Movement: Social Movements, Collective Action and Politics.* Cambridge: Cambridge University Press, 1994.

———. *Struggle, Politics and Reform: Collective Action, Social Movements and Cycles of Protest.* Ithaca NY: Cornell University Press, 1989.

Terrones López, María Eugenia. "Istmeños y subversión en el Porfiriato, 1879–1881." In *Lecturas históricas del estado de Oaxaca*, vol. 4, 1877–1930, edited by María de los Angeles Romero Frizzi, 135–70. Mexico, D.F.: Instituto Nacional de Antropología e Historia, 1990.

Thomson, Guy P. C., with David G. LaFrance. "Agrarian Conflict in the Municipality of Cuetzalan (Sierra de Puebla): The Rise and Fall of 'Pala' Agustín Dieguilllo, 1861–1894." *Hispanic American Historical Review* 71, no. 2 (1991): 205–58.

———. "Bulwarks of Patriotic Liberalism: The National Guard, Philharmonic Corps and Patriotic Juntas in Mexico, 1847–88." *Journal of Latin American Studies* 22, no. 1 (1990): 31–68.

———. *Patriotism, Politics, and Popular Liberalism in Nineteenth-Century Mexico: Juan Francisco Lucas and the Puebla Sierra.* Wilmington DE: Scholarly Resources, 1999.

———. "Popular Aspects of Liberalism in Mexico, 1848–1888." *Bulletin of Latin American Research* 10, no. 3 (1991): 265–92.

Tibón, Gutierre. *Pinotepa nacional, Mixtecos, Negros y Triquis.* Mexico, D.F.: Universidad Nacional Autónoma de México, 1961.

Tilly, Charles. *Social Movements, 1768–2004.* Boulder CO: Paradigm Publishers, 2005.

Tilly, Louise A., and Charles A. Tilly. *Class Conflict and Collective Action.* Beverly Hills CA: Sage Publications, 1981.

Tirado, Ricardo. "La alianza con los empresarios." In *Entre la guerra y la estabilidad política: El México de los 40,* edited by Rafael Loyola, 195–221. Mexico, D.F.: Instituto de Investigaciones Sociales, Universidad Nacional Autónoma de México, 1990.

Torres Ramírez, Blanca. "La guerra y la posguerra en las relaciones de México y los E.U." In *Entre la guerra y la estabilidad política: El México de los 40,* edited by Rafael Loyola, 65–82. Mexico, D.F.: Instituto de Investigaciones Sociales, Universidad Nacional Autónoma de México, 1990.

———. *Historia de la Revolución mexicana, periodo 1940–1952.* Vol. 19, *México en la segunda guerra mundial.* Mexico, D.F.: Colegio de México, 1979.

———. *Historia de la Revolución mexicana, periodo 1940–1952.* Vol. 21, *Hacia la utopia industrial.* Mexico, D.F.: Colegio de México, 1984.

Townsend, William Cameron. *Lázaro Cárdenas, Mexican Democrat.* Ann Arbor MI: George Wahr Publishing Company, 1952.

Tucker, William P. *The Mexican Government Today.* Minneapolis: University of Minnesota Press, 1957.

Turner, J. K. *Barbarous Mexico.* Austin: University of Texas Press, 1969.

Tutino, John. "Ethnic Resistance, Juchitán in Mexican History." In *Zapotec Struggles: Histories, Politics, and Representations from Juchitán, Oaxaca,* edited by Howard Campbell, 41–62. Washington DC: Smithsonian Institution Press, 1993.

———. "Rebelión indigena en Tehuantepec." *Cuadernos Politicos* 24 (1980): 89–101.

Ugualde, Antonio. "Contemporary Mexico: From Hacienda to PRI, Political Leadership in a Zapotec Village." In *The Caciques, Oligarchical Politics and the System of Caciquismo in the Luso-Hispanic World*, edited by Robert Kern, 119–34. Albuquerque: University of New Mexico Press, 1973.

Unikel, Luis. "Urbanización y urbanismo: Situación y perspectiva." In *La sociedad mexicana: Presente y futuro*, edited by Miguel Woinczek, 254–75. Mexico, D.F.: Fondo de Cultura Económica, 1974.

Valencia Castrejón, Sergio. *Poder regional y política nacional en Mexico, el gobierno de Maximino Ávila Camacho en Puebla (1937–1941)*. Mexico, D.F.: Instituto Nacional de Estudios Históricos de la Revolución Mexicana, 1996.

Valverde, Sergio. *Apuntes para la historia de la Revolución y de la política en el estado de Morelos: Desde la muerte del gobernador Alarcón, pronunciamiento de los generales. Pablo Torres Burgos y Emiliano Zapata mártires, hasta la restauración de la reacción por Vicente Estrada Cajigal, impostor*. Mexico, D.F.: n.p., 1933.

Vanderwood, Paul. "Religion, Official, Popular and Otherwise." *Mexican Studies/Estudios Mexicanos* 16, no. 2 (2000): 411–42.

Vargas, Alberto. *Guelaguetza, costumbre racial oaxaqueña*. Oaxaca de Juárez, Oaxaca: n.p., 1935.

Vasconcelos, José. *El Proconsulado*. Mexico, D.F.: Ediciones Botas, 1946.

Vásquez, Genaro V. *El camino de la reconstrucción, la semilla esta echada: Hemos sembrado para nuestros hermanos*. Oaxaca de Juárez, Oaxaca: n.p., 1928.

———. *Carreteras, monumentos, industrias y folklore*. Oaxaca de Juárez, Oaxaca: n.p., 1928.

———. *Doctrinas y realidades en la legislación para los indios*. Mexico, D.F.: Departamento de Asuntos Indígenas, 1940.

———. *Lunes del Cerro en Oaxaca*. Mexico, D.F.: n.p., 1965.

———. *Mensaje leido al inaugurar el primer periodo de sesiones de la XII legislatura local*. Oaxaca de Juárez, Oaxaca: n.p., 1928.

———. *Para la historia del terreno*. Mexico, D.F.: n.p., 1931.

———. *Plan de acción social*. Oaxaca de Juárez, Oaxaca: n.p., 1926.

Vaughan, Mary Kay. *Cultural Politics in Revolution: Teachers, Peasants and Schools in Mexico 1930–1940*. Tucson: University of Arizona Press, 1997.

Vélez-Ibáñez, Carlos. *Rituals of Marginality: Politics, Process and Cultural*

Change in Central Urban Mexico, 1969–1974. Berkeley: University of California Press, 1983.

Vernon, Raymond. *The Dilemma of Mexico's Development.* Cambridge: Cambridge University Press, 1963.

Villa Rojas, Alfonso. *Los Mazatecos y el problema indígena de la cuenca del Papaloapan.* Mexico, D.F.: Instituto Nacional Indigenista, 1955.

Voss, Stuart F. "Nationalizing the Revolution, Culmination and Circumstance." In *Provinces of the Revolution: Essays on Regional Mexican History, 1910–1929,* edited by Thomas Benjamin and Mark Wasserman, 273–317. Albuquerque: University of New Mexico Press, 1990.

Warman, Arturo. *We Come to Object: The Peasants of Morelos and the National State.* Baltimore: John Hopkins University Press, 1980.

Warner, Michael. *The Letters of the Republic: Publication and the Public Sphere in Eighteenth Century America.* Cambridge: Cambridge University Press, 1990.

Wasserman, Mark. *Persistent Oligarchs: Elites and Politics in Chihuahua, Mexico, 1910–1940.* Durham: Duke University Press, 1993.

———. "Provinces of the Revolution: An Introduction." In *Provinces of the Revolution: Essays on Regional Mexican History, 1910–1929,* edited by Thomas Benjamin and Mark Wasserman, 1–16. Albuquerque: University of New Mexico Press, 1990.

———. "The Transition from Personalist to Party Rule: Chihuahuan Politics during the 1930s." In *The Revolutionary Process in Mexico: Essays on Political and Social Change, 1880–1940,* edited by Jaime E. Rodríguez O, 213–26. Los Angeles: UCLA Latin American Center Publications, 1990.

Waterbury, Ronald. "The Traditional Market in a Provincial Urban Setting, Oaxaca, Mexico." PhD diss., University of California, Los Angeles, 1968.

Wells, Allen. *Yucatán's Gilded Age: Haciendas, Henequen, and International Harvester, 1860–1915.* Albuquerque: University of New Mexico Press, 1985.

Wells, Allen, and Gilbert M. Joseph. "Clientelism and the Political Baptism of Yucatan's Urban Working Classes, 1876–1929." In *Citizens of the Pyramid: Essays on Mexican Political Culture,* edited by Wil G. Pansters, 66–106. Amsterdam: CEDLA, 1997.

Weyl, Nathaniel, and Sylvia Weyl. *The Reconquest of Mexico: The Years of Lázaro Cárdenas*. New York: Oxford University Press, 1939.

Whetton, Nathan L. *Rural Mexico*. Chicago: University of Chicago Press, 1948.

Williams, Raymond. "Selections from Marxism and Literature." In *Culture/Power/History: A Reader in Contemporary Social Theory*, edited by Nicholas B. Dirks, Geoff Eley, and Sherry B. Ortner, 585–609. Princeton: Princeton University Press, 1994.

Wolf, Eric. "Aspects of Group Relations in a Complex Society: Mexico." *American Anthropologist* 58 (December 1956): 1065–78.

Wolf, Eric, and Edward Hansen. "Caudillo Politics: A Structural Analysis." *Comparative Studies in Society and History* 9 (1966–67): 168–79.

Womack, John. *Zapata and the Mexican Revolution*. New York: Vintage Books, 1969.

Wood, Andrew Grant. "'The Proletarian Women Will Make the Social Revolution': Female Participation in the Veracruz Rent Strike, 1922–1927." In *The Women's Revolution in Mexico, 1910–1953*, edited by Stephanie Mitchell and Patience Schell, 151–64. Lanham MD: Rowman and Littlefield, 2006.

———. *Revolution in the Street: Women, Workers, and Urban Protest in Veracruz, 1870–1927*. Wilmington DE: Scholarly Resources, 2001.

Wright Rios, Edward. "Piety and Progress: Vision, Shrine, and Society in Oaxaca, 1887–1934." PhD diss., University of California, San Diego, 2004.

Young, C. M. "The Social Setting of Migration: Factors Affecting Migration from a Sierra Zapotec Village in Oaxaca, Mexico." PhD diss., University of London, 1976.

Ximénez de Sandoval Prats, Rafael. *Tuxtepec "historia y anecdotas."* N.p., n.d.

Yescas Martínez, Isidro. *Los desegañados de la tierra (una experiencia de lucha campesina en Tuxtepec, Oaxaca)*. Oaxaca de Juárez, Oaxaca: n.p., 1989.

Zarauz López, Héctor. "Heliodoro Charis y la Revolución en Juchitán (un proceso de rebelión e integración)." *Acervos* 2, no. 6 (1997): 19–23.

Index

Charis Castro, Heliodoro (*cont.*)
land distribution, 61; and Manuel
Mayoral Heredia, 373, 376, 386,
387; and red and green party alliance, 94, 140; and Revolution, 30
Charity Hospital, 276–77
charrismo, 329
Chassen-López, Francie R., 26, 218
Chatinos, 28, 159, 174
Chiapas: agriculture in, 73, 240; caciques in, 187, 406; and Cardenismo, 132, 136; coffee production
in, 149–51; governorship of, 289;
labor unions in, 208; and movement of 1952, 382, 398; regional
ties in, 1
Chiapas Mayans, 115
Chicolopista regime. *See* López Cortés, Francisco
Chihuahua, 46, 73, 244, 289, 406
China, 9, 11
Chinantecs, 89, 116, 204
Chincoya, Esperanza, 309
Choapam: cacique in, 63, 177; commercial agriculture in, 57, 176,
183–84; and Ixtlán autonomy,
127; Mixes in, 175; in Porfiriato,
25, 26, 41; Revolution in, 32
Chocho, 230
cigarette monopoly, 70
Ciudad Ixtepec, 93, 102, 140, 258,
311, 317, 357–58, 385
Civil Registry, 316
Clark, Marjorie, 57
clergy, 68, 71
Coahuila, 104, 289
cochineal trade, 150, 231

cocoa beans, 26
coffee monopoly, 308, 317, 338. *See
also* coffee production
coffee production: and Cardenista
caciques, 136, 138, 189–90, 406;
and ethnic tensions, 412; and *finqueros*, 19, 54; in Ixtlán, 120–21,
122; in Juchitán de Zaragoza,
139; in Juxtlahuaca, 122, 164–74,
354, 355; and Manuel Mayoral
Heredia, 377; in Pochutla, 148–
63, 190, 370; and popular urban
movements, 313; in Porfiriato,
25; in Región Mixe, 122, 175–83,
188. *See also* coffee monopoly
cofradías, 111, 227, 230
Coixtlahuaca, 163, 230, 236, 352
Colegio del Espíritu Santo, 333
Colmenares, Guadalupe, 282
Colonia de la Paz, 270
Colonia Nueva, 281
colonization, 367, 373
Comité Cívico Oaxaqueño (CCO):
and Jamiltepec land reform, 326;
and January 1947 movement,
316–20; and movement of 1952,
379, 380, 381, 383, 388–91, 393,
394, 397, 398
Comité de la Defensa de Expendedores de Mercados (CDEM):
complaints of, 307, 309; and
Eduardo Vasconcelos, 342, 343,
347; formation of, 305–7; and
January 1947 movement, 322;
and Manuel Mayoral Heredia,
375; and movement of 1952,
380–81, 387–88, 390, 393, 399;
and UEM, 306

Comité Electoral Pro-Avila Camacho, 147
Comité Nacional de Defensa Proletaria, 77
Comité Nacional Pro-Repatriación, 333
Comité por la Defensa del Pueblo de Oaxaca, 382
Comité Pro-Mixteca, 233
commerce: and Cardenista caciques, 136; and Edmundo Sánchez Cano, 301; and Eduardo Vasconcelos, 349, 351; and González Fernández camarilla, 248; in Ixtlán, 122; in Juxtlahuaca, 171; in Pochutla, 155–56, 159, 161, 163; and popular urban movements, 271–72, 310, 312–19, 321, 388–89; in Región Mixe, 183. *See also* commercial monopolies; markets; prices
commercial monopolies: and Edmundo Sánchez Cano, 298, 303, 308–9, 315–21; and Eduardo Vasconcelos, 335–37, 346; and Manuel Mayoral Heredia, 363, 374, 377
communism: and Cardenismo, 195; and CCM, 81, 90, 199; and Edmundo Sánchez Cano, 301; and Eduardo Vasconcelos, 351, 352; and Genaro Vásquez, 38; and González Fernández camarilla, 290; and labor movement, 200; and movement of 1952, 381–84, 397; in Pochutla, 157, 158, 162, 163, 190; and Tuxtepec land reform, 205

Compañía Exportación Tropical, 210
Compañía Platanera Americana, 209
Company of Mexican Exportation and Importation (CEIMSA), 235, 236
Concordia, 158
condueñazgos. See agricultural societies
Confederación Campesina Mexicana (CCM): and Baños camarilla, 97; and Cardenismo, 101, 105, 196, 237, 239; and Central Valleys land reform, 219, 221; and Constantino Chapital, 109; and end of Chicolopista regime, 97; and gubernatorial election (1936), 112; and Jamiltepec land reform, 212–16; and Jesús Gonthier, 84–85; in 1940s, 241; and palm industry, 234; rise of, 78–91; and state-level politics, 196–201; in Tuxtepec, 204–9; unification of organizations under, 77–78, 82–83
Confederación de Ligas Socialistas de Oaxaca (CLSO): and caciques, 56, 63; and Cardenismo, 75, 78, 105, 146; and CCM, 84; creation of, 54–55, 57; and LNCUG split, 80. *See also* Genuina Confederación de Ligas Socialistas de Oaxaca (GCLSO)
Confederación de Partidos Socialistas de Oaxaca (CPSO), 33, 38–40, 45–51, 48, 54

Confederación de Pueblos de la
Sierra Juárez, 127–30
Confederación de Trabajadores de
México (CTM): and Cardenismo,
107, 194, 195, 196, 237, 239;
and Cardenista caciques, 259–61,
263, 267, 286; and Edmundo
Sánchez Cano, 297, 298, 300–
302, 324; and Eduardo Vasconcelos, 330, 347, 349–51, 353,
359; and elections (1944), 293;
and elections (1950), 366; and
González Fernández camarilla,
250–51, 253, 290; and Jamiltepec land reform, 216; in Juchitán
de Zaragoza, 145–47; in 1940s,
241–43, 246; in Pochutla, 153,
157; and popular urban movements, 280, 310, 311, 317–18;
and state-level politics, 197, 199,
201; in Tuxtepec, 206–9, 211
Confederación Nacional Campesina
(CNC): and Cardenismo, 107,
194–96, 237, 239, 256, 259,
260, 286; and Central Valleys
land reform, 225; and Edmundo
Sánchez Cano, 300–302, 310; and
Eduardo Vasconcelos, 330, 347,
349–51, 353, 359; and elections
(1944), 293; and elections (1950),
366; and election statutes (1950),
329; and González Fernández
camarilla, 248–51, 253; and
Huajuapam land reform, 229; and
Manuel Mayoral Heredia, 372;
and movement of 1952, 384, 385,
393; in 1940s, 242, 243, 245–46;

in Pochutla, 160; and state-level
politics, 198–99, 201; and Tuxtepec land reform, 211
Confederación Nacional de Organizaciones Populares (CNOP), 241,
347, 349–51, 359, 366, 374
Confederación Oaxaqueña de
Campesinos (COC): and Cardenismo, 101, 105; and CCM, 78, 81,
82, 84, 85, 89–91, 197; and
Chicolopista caciques, 63, 95–96;
creation of, 61; under Lázaro
Cárdenas, 75; peasant league
under, 95
Confederación Regional de Obreros
Mexicanos (CROM), 53–55, 57,
75, 236, 247
Confederación Unica de Trabaja-
dores (CUT), 350–51, 371
Consejo Regional Mixe Pro-Cultura
y Defensa, 180
Constancia del Rosario, 167
Constitution, 16, 88, 100–101, 186,
294, 362, 391
"Constitutionalists of the South," 32
cooperatives, 159, 233–36, 240
Corbin, Horace, 349
Córdova, Arnaldo, 108, 286
Cornelius, Wayne A., 409
Coronil, Fernando, 402
corporatism: and agrarian policy,
195–97, 199; and Cardenismo,
104, 134, 140, 146–48, 191; and
CCM, 90–91; under Francisco
López Cortés, 20, 43, 46, 52, 62,
63, 71, 74–75, 97; in 1940s, 241,

Estrada Cajigal, Vicente, 73
ethnic groups: and CCM, 89; and
Central Valleys land reform, 225;
in Chiapas, 187; and Chicolopista
caciques, 65, 66, 72; in Juxtlahuaca, 164–74; in Oaxaca, 1, 3,
15–16; in Pochutla, 148–63; and
popular urban movements, 269;
role of, in state formation, 8, 11,
15–16, 19, 21, 405–6; in Tuxtepec, 204. *See also* indigenous
peoples; *specific groups*
Etla: and Cardenista caciques, 267;
and CCM, 84, 89; and Central
Valleys land reform, 217–20;
and commercial monopolies,
308; ejidos in, 35; popular urban
movements in, 311, 317, 321;
Revolution in, 31; workers' demands in, 35
Eureka, 152
ex-districts, 16–19
Ex-Marquesado market, 342

Fagen, Richard R., 408
Fagoaga, Joaquín, 333
Fallaw, Ben, 11, 104, 133, 238
Federación de Cooperativas de
Trabajadores de la Palma y sus
Productos de la Región Mixteca,
233
Federación de Estudiantes Unidos
(FEU), 398
Federación de los Partidos del
Pueblo Mexicano (FPPM), 362,
363, 375, 379, 384, 398
Federación Indigenista Revolucio-

naria Oaxaqueña (FIRO), 246,
251
Federación Local de Trabajadores de
la Región Tuxtepecana (FLTRT),
206, 207
Federación Regional de Obreros
y Campesinos (FROC), 146,
200–201
Federación Regional de Trabajadores del Estado de Oaxaca
(FRTEO), 157–58, 160, 199–201,
251
Federación Tuxtepecana de Obreros
y Campesinos (FTOC), 55, 56, 80,
86, 87, 89, 91, 204–5
Federación Unica de Trabajadores
del Estado de Oaxaca, 350
Federal District, 292, 340, 398
federal government: and administrations in Oaxaca, 3; and Cardenismo, 77, 78, 103, 105, 191, 195,
238, 259–67; and CCM, 79, 84,
85, 90, 91; and Central Valleys
land reform, 221, 224; and Constantino Chapital, 110; and CPSO,
47; and elections (1936), 113;
and elections (1940), 245; and
elections (1944), 291; and election
statutes (1950), 328; and Francisco López Cortés, 51, 70–71, 96,
97, 99, 101; and Genaro Vásquez,
37, 40; and González Fernández
camarilla, 251; and Huajuapam
land reform, 228, 229; and Ixtlán
autonomy, 116, 123, 126, 127,
131, 133; and Jamiltepec land
reform, 212, 213; in Juchitán de

168; as cacique, 136, 163–74, 190, 191, 254, 256, 406; death of, 354

Guzmán, Sostenes, 215, 256

Hacienda de Dolores, 59, 84
Hacienda de la Luz, 167
Hacienda de Los Negritos, 83
Hacienda of Concepcion, 31
haciendas: and caciques, 70; and Cardenismo, 104, 138, 139; and CCM, 90, 91; and Central Valleys land reform, 217–20, 225, 239; description of, 19; under Francisco López Cortés, 73; FTOC contracts with, 86; and González Fernández camarilla, 247, 248; and Huajuapam land reform, 226, 228–29; and Jamiltepec land reform, 211, 215; of Juan José Baños, 66; and labor unions, 54, 56; and land distribution, 58, 59; in Porfiriato, 26, 31–32, 41; and Revolution, 31, 33; and socioeconomic reform, 194; and Tuxtepec land reform, 203, 210. See also fincas
Hacienda San Nicolas, 67
Hamilton, Jimmy, 388
Harp, Fortunato, 382
Hayner, Norman S., 272
health, 122, 144, 182, 276–77, 279, 281, 312–13
hegemony: and Cardenismo, 132, 133, 192, 237; concept of, 7–9; and indigenous communities, 252;

in Maximato, 43; of mestizos, 15; planter, 152

Henestrosa, Andrés, 262

Henríquez, María "Chata la Ferrera," 305, 321, 388, 393

Henríquez Guzmán, Miguel, 324, 362, 380, 385, 386. See also Henriquistas

Henriquistas, 370, 371, 373, 375, 383–85, 396, 398, 400. See also Henríquez Guzmán, Miguel

Hermanos Pacheco, 167
Hernández, Benigno, 120
Hernández, Fidencio, 120
Hernández, Mercedes, 282
Hernández Chavez, Alicia, 45, 104
Hernández Díaz, Jorge, 168
Herrera Altamirano, Antonio, 331
Hidalgo, Juan Carlos, 144–45
Hispanics, 15, 65, 66, 138, 139, 142, 231, 234, 361
Historia de un agrarista, 179
Huajintepec, 216
Huajuapam: *agrarismo* in, 196, 238, 239; and Alfonso Francisco Ramírez, 112; cacique in, 66, 255; and Eduardo Vasconcelos, 349; education in, 39; and elections (1940), 243; and González Fernández camarilla, 250; land distribution in, 58, 225–30, 407, 412; land quality in, 79; under Manuel García Vigil, 36; palm industry in, 230; popular urban movements in, 323, 387; Rogelio Barriga Rivas in, 296

Huajuapam de León, 227, 236, 317

land distribution: and banana production, 52; under Cardenismo,
5, 78, 138–39, 151, 154, 158–60,
162, 194–96, 202, 238–40, 258–
60, 329; and CCM, 82–83, 85–87;
in Central Valleys, 216–25;
under Eduardo Vasconcelos, 330,
348–49, 351, 353, 357, 359, 361;
under Francisco López Cortés,
59–62, 72–74, 95–96; in Huajuapam, 225–30; in Ixtlán, 117–18,
120, 127; in Jamiltepec, 211–16;
in Juxtlahuaca, 164, 167, 169–71,
174; and Manuel Mayoral Heredia, 373; Mixtecs on, 41; under
Onofre Jiménez, 37; and palm
industry, 230; peasants' role in,
35; in Porfiriato, 26–28, 31–32,
158; postrevolution, 33; in Región
Mixe, 175–76; and Revolution,
31, 57–58; and state formation,
15, 19, 407, 411–12; in Tuxtepec, 202–11. *See also* agriculture;
ejidos; fincas; haciendas
La Noria, 66
La Nueva Vida, 316, 337, 341, 346
La Opinión, 341, 346
La Palma, 88
La Pe, 90
La Prensa, 345, 392
La Providencia, 150
La Provincia, 345. See also *La Voz
de Oaxaca*
La Rayita market, 272
Larrazabal, José, 265
La Sabana, 167
Las Carolinas, 70, 80–81

Las Nubes, 152
La Soledad, 81, 158, 333
Las Palmeras, 177, 182
latifundios, 225–26
La Tribuna, 344, 346
La Tribuna del Sur, 374, 375, 389,
391, 393
La Unión, 158
Laviada, Iñigo, 188
La Voz de Oaxaca, 331, 333, 339,
345
Law of Dominion and Jurisdiction
of Archaeological Monuments, 51
Law of Ejidal Patrimony, 59
Law of Industrial Development,
368–69
Law of Unused Lands, 86, 87, 90,
95, 205, 207, 208
Law of Work (1931), 194
Leal Cienfugos, Patricia, 394–95
Lear, John, 12
Legión Guadalupana de Santa Juana
de Arco, 221
Lenin, Vladimir, 38
León, 326, 327, 405
León, Luis L., 73
Lewis, Stephen, 406
Leyva, Gabriel, 329
Leyva Mancilla, Baltasar, 401
Liberal-Conservative War, 28
Liekens, Enrique, 94, 114
Liga de Campesinos y Obreros
"Juan José Baños," 96
Liga de Inquilinos Oaxaqueños, 281,
335, 336
Liga de Resistencia de Consumidores
de Luz y Fuerza Electrica, 279,
304

workers (*cont.*)

López Cortés, 46, 74, 94, 97;
under Genaro Vásquez, 38; and
González Fernández camarilla,
247, 290; in Juchitán de Zaragoza, 141; under Manuel García
Vigil, 34–35; in 1940s, 242;
and popular urban movements,
276–77, 312, 316, 320, 378,
399; postrevolutionary changes
in rights of, 33; in Región Mixe,
184; and Revolution, 1, 4, 30;
role of, in state formation, 6, 14,
402, 408, 409, 411, 413; and
state-level politics, 196–201; in
Tuxtepec, 205, 211. *See also* railway workers

World War II, 241, 257, 283,
286–87

Yalalag, 176
Yanhuitlán, 333
Yaqui, 115
Yaqui Valley, 133
Yatacu, 66
Yaterini, 34
Yautepec, 63, 175, 189, 242, 254,
255, 300
Yaveo, 184
Yerbasanta, 167
Yescas, Genaro, 350
Yocupicio Valenzuela, Román,
132
Yosotiche Canyon, 167
Yosoyuxi, 167, 171–72

Young, C. M., 119
Yucatán, 70, 104, 132, 191, 195,
398–400

Zaachila, 36, 311, 312
Zamora, 230
Zapata, Emiliano, 49, 267
Zapatistas (1910–20), 31, 58, 167,
171–72, 174, 244, 292, 326, 354
Zapatistas (1994–), 16
Zapotecs: autonomy of, 115–23,
133; and banana production,
204; and Cardenista caciques,
262; and CCM, 89; and Central
Valleys land reform, 217; and
Chicolopista caciques, 93–94; and
elections, 112–13, 243, 292; and
indigenismo, 49–50; in Juchitán de Zaragoza, 138–40, 144,
147, 186; in Pochutla, 150–51,
153–54, 156, 158, 159, 162, 189;
population of, 15; in Porfiriato,
28; and Región Mixe, 175, 176,
178; resistance of, 408
Zaragoza, Benito, 111–15, 123, 124,
131, 205, 243, 246
Zárate Aquino, Manuel, 316, 320,
412
Ziga, Carlos, Jr., 155
Ziga, María, 159
Zimatlán, 35, 83, 89, 219, 222–23,
301–2, 371
Zitácuaro, 225
Zorrilla Barrundia, José, 203
Zorrilla Light Company, 279, 280

www.ingramcontent.com/pod-product-compliance
Lightning Source LLC
Chambersburg PA
CBHW030835300326
41935CB00036B/65